D0946609

THE STRENGTH OF *Family Therapy*

SELECTED PAPERS OF

Nathan W. Ackerman

The Strength of *Family Therapy*

Selected Papers of *Nathan W. Ackerman*

Edited by

Donald Bloch, M.D.

and

Robert Simon, M.D.

Ackerman Institute for Family Therapy
New York

BRUNNER/MAZEL, *Publishers* • New York

Library of Congress Cataloging in Publication Data

Ackerman, Nathan Ward, 1908-1971
The strength of family therapy.

Bibliography: p.
1. Family psychotherapy. I. Bloch, Donald, 1922-
II. Simon, Robert, 1934- III. Title.
RC488.5.A248 616.89'15 82-4285
ISBN 0-87630-271-1 AACR2

Published by
BRUNNER/MAZEL, INC.
19 Union Square
New York, NY 10003

MANUFACTURED IN THE UNITED STATES OF AMERICA

The strength of family therapy derives from its capacity to join forces with the spontaneous healing powers of the family group.

NATHAN W. ACKERMAN

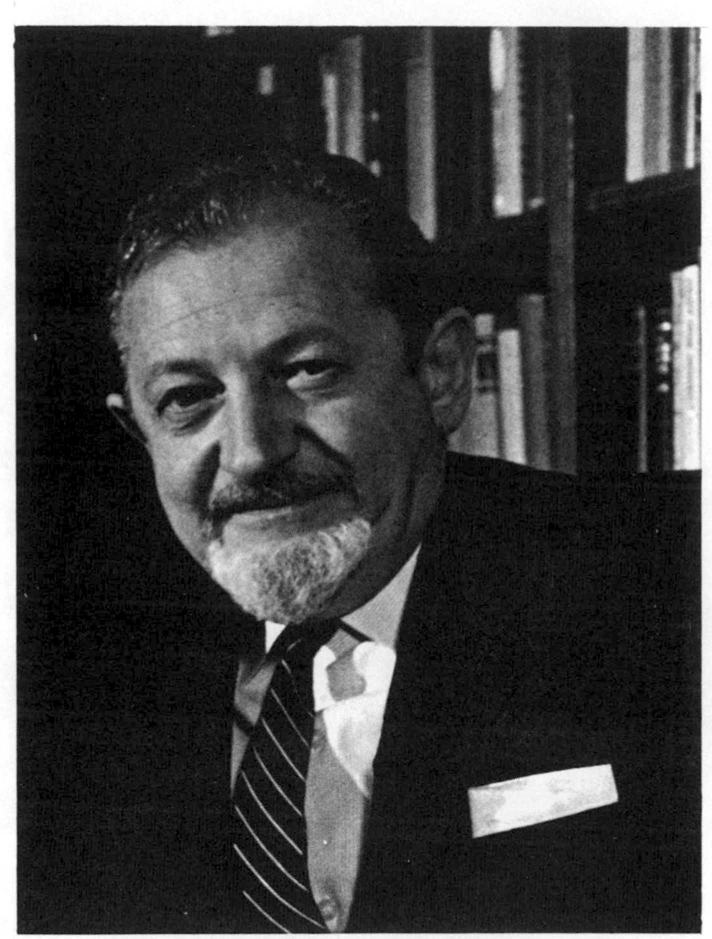

NATHAN WARD ACKERMAN
1908-1971

Nathan Ward Ackerman died on June 12, 1971.

The following note appeared in *Family Process*:

The news of Nathan Ackerman's death came this morning; thus suddenly departed the man who, with Don Jackson, co-founded this Journal. For some years he had lived with the Angel quietly waiting at his elbow; they had not agreed on the propitious moment.

Ackerman had little use for sentimentality; he would have been the first to agree he could be difficult to live with. He was occasionally prideful and sometimes unduly expansive. Often he took a devilish delight in tweaking obsessional tails.

For all of this he was a great man, in the flawed, human way all men are truly great. He could know himself, honestly and humorously; he had a sense of seriousness and mission—and would not lose sight of these or let go of them in adverse circumstances. He taught therapeutic courage and exemplified it—nor did he do so vaingloriously, but rather with the sure troubled instinct of the healer who does not flinch from the painful necessities of his work.

Black Elk, the Sioux Holy Man, speaking of the murdered chieftain Crazy Horse says, "It does not matter where his body lies, for it is grass; but where his spirit is, it will be good to be." So too with Nathan Ackerman.

Contents

PART III: *Social and Cultural Issues* 119

PART IV: *Family Theory* 149

PART V: *Family Therapy* 217

PART VI: *Marriage* 357

Introduction

The decision to undertake preparation of this volume developed in association with the tenth anniversary of Ackerman's death in the spring of 1971. Until shortly before that occasion the issue had been avoided, probably to avoid deification of the man and fixing of the "Ackerman Method." Our sense of the development of our institute, originally The Family Institute, renamed for Ackerman after his death, was that it would build on his foundations but not be unalterably cast in their mold. Indeed, looking back on this, it is evident that we had not only avoided enshrining our teacher, but had in fact on occasion neglected to convey to our students and colleagues in the field the magnitude and brilliance of his accomplishment.

Thus, it was only after almost a decade had passed that it seemed timely to review his work critically and to assess the appropriateness of publishing in one volume the papers he had written. Our original intention was to publish Ackerman's complete papers, but it quickly became apparent that this was inadvisable. Ackerman was uneven as a writer; he constructed many articles on a conceptually strong base but writing did not come easily to him and he often wrote out of a sense of obligation. Many papers were primarily polemical and often repetitious. Ackerman had no doubt as to the importance of his ideas; therefore, there was a moral imperative to disseminate them. This was much the same spirit in which he did his countless workshops, lectures and public demonstrations of family therapy.

At times the writing speaks out of exhaustion and obligation rather than the imperative of fresh ideas. Consequently, we have been stringent in our own criteria for the admission of papers to this volume; we have included only those papers that made a unique contribution when they were written—and that still do. It is gratifying to realize how many meet these requirements.

A complete bibliography can be found at the end of this volume. All of Ackerman's papers are listed chronologically; those that are reprinted here are preceded by an asterisk.

ACKNOWLEDGMENTS

The Editors wish to thank the friends and colleagues who were so helpful in the enormous task of finding and organizing Nathan Ackerman's published legacy. Chief among these was his widow, Gwen Ackerman, who responded with her characteristic generosity and enthusiasm. Not far behind her were Ackerman's chief social work colleagues, Judith Lieb and Marjorie Behrens, and his longtime secretary, Sylvia Schwamenfeld. We are indebted also to Jessie Reiss, who tracked down many of the missing papers and assembled the final bibliography.

D.B.
R.S.

Biography and Retrospective

Nathan Ackerman's arrival in America was indistinguishable from thousands of others in 1912: First had come the father, seeking employment, and in due course he sent for his wife and children. In Bessarabia they had been fairly comfortable, merchant-class people, strong on education and on musical and artistic pursuits. Three children had died within a year of each other, but the second generation-within-a-generation, two girls and three boys, survived and seemed destined to fulfill the intellectual Jewish-American dream. The two eldest, Gertrude and Isabelle, became writers, Gertrude winning a Guggenheim Fellowship. Nathan, eldest of the surviving sons (b. 1908), became a physician. Harry, the next child, was a talented artist who won a Yale scholarship in fine arts and the Prix de Rome. Bernard, the youngest, attained a Ph.D. and became a psychotherapist.

Their parents would later be remembered as models of hardworking responsibility: the father laboring all day to support them, then studying pharmacy at night so that he could open his own drugstore when Nathan was 13; the mother nurturing, supporting, darning, cooking, counseling, and doing all those wise and wonderful things which later would become Nathan's view of what all mothers should be.

Of course, the dream soured in important ways, as the American Dream or any other life-dream must inevitably do. The family drugstore had to close in 1933 owing to the father's ill health and his mounting debts. Gertrude and Bernard knew ample misfortune in their married years, and—most tragic of all—Harry suffered a mental breakdown with permanent residua before his career could be launched.

Through this shifting web of family fortune and tragedy emerged Nathan: a short, feisty, brilliant, and sometimes charming man whose "miraculous" recovery from two near-fatal illnesses left him physically with a mitral stenosis and spiritually with the conviction that he was very special, perhaps chosen. We note in addition that he was simultaneously the younger brother of sisters and the oldest brother of brothers. According to the research of Walter Toman, one would expect such a man to be adored by women and deferred to by men throughout his life. On both counts he would have scant respect for established status and authority—other than his own—and if any one trait characterizes the professional life of Nathan Ackerman, that is it. He is said to have argued his way into Columbia (past a Jewish quota), out of its medical college (past a failed pediatrics exam), and later, onto the staff of the Jewish Board of Guardians. Innumerable minor skirmishes and border wars were never chronicled but clung to the man's

---

This biography is based in part upon material compiled by Ackerman's longtime friend and colleague, Marjorie Behrens, M.S.W.

reputation like the leathery scars on an old warrior chief.

It was after Nathan's graduation from medical school that Harry had his breakdown and for the rest of his life Nathan participated actively in his brother's care. Perhaps this experience stimulated his unique sensitivity to the problems of the "well" sibling in families. However, the demands of Harry's care did not keep Nathan from pursuing what he felt would be the best psychiatric training. After a year in residency at Montefiore Hospital in New York, he trained at the Menninger Clinic and then joined the staff of Stoney Lodge Hospital in Ossining, New York, as Assistant Medical Director. He had Harry transferred to Stoney Lodge from another hospital so that he could keep an eye on him personally.

Nathan's training analyst was Clara Thompson, and he attended the New York Psychoanalytic Institute between 1937 and 1942. Early in this stage of his career he met and married Gwendolyn Hill, a nurse at Stoney Lodge, and the first of two daughters was born in 1938. His career from this time onward is outlined in the professional chronology at the end of this sketch, and the development of his thinking about families is the substance of this book.

To the psychoanalytic movement Ackerman was a pesky gadfly. He enlisted with spirit in its internecine wars as well as in its painstaking intellectual standards. They commanded his allegiance while he railed at their limitations. He was admitted to the American Psychoanalytic Association in 1943. Two years later the Second World War ended. Large numbers of physicians had been trained as military psychiatrists; returning home they stormed the beaches of the psychoanalytic training institutes, transforming them into centers of fierce competitive struggle. A key issue was whether psychoanalysis was to be limited to being a medical specialty, despite the prominence of such non-medical psychoanalytic figures as Erik Erikson and Anna Freud. Ackerman early on was with those who fought against the orthodoxy through a series of intense debates. These led ultimately to the creation of new training facilities, such as that at Columbia University led by Sandor Rado. Here Ackerman became a faculty member in 1957 and taught for the balance of his career. In 1955 he helped form the American Academy of Psychoanalysis, which became a principal alternative organization to that bastion of orthodoxy, the American Psychoanalytic Association. Nevertheless, Ackerman maintained his allegiance to some aspect of psychoanalytic thinking to the end. He was a believer in psychoanalytic theory but not a true believer.

Ackerman worked incredibly long hours, usually starting by 7 A.M. and, when the day's clinical work was finished, writing late into the night. If Gwen insisted, he ate; otherwise he might be fortified only on bourbon. It was not unusual for him to arrive home, eat while getting undressed, and fall asleep almost immediately. He had grown up, after all, in the age of *Arrowsmith*, each physician also a scholar with his faithful Leora and a supper tray next to the bed. For Ackerman it also recreated the world of his parents: the father working day and night, the mother raising the children and supervising the home with warmth, wisdom, and utter reliability. His only respite from this routine came in weekends at their country home. He dearly loved his house and land and perhaps it was fitting that he should die there in June 1971.

Although it might seem less so today, Ackerman's office was a wonder for that of an established psychoanalyst. Patients came and went at irregular intervals, some staying as little as 15 minutes, others requiring two hours or more. They congregated in the waiting room and were encouraged to get to know each other. He established an adjunctive therapy group for which the ticket of admission was simply that Ackerman was your therapist, either individually or as a family. With child and adolescent patients he used the fullest range of activity, playing ball with some in the park and sending others to do self-expressive work with artist friends of his. He was always available by telephone, to the delight of the caller and the exasperation of the patients in his office. In every way, his practice reflected what he held dear in theory: to be himself, to encounter others honestly and directly, and not to be bound by professional conventions unless they had some definite value for the problem he was trying to solve.

Like many great physicians (and older brothers), he was most at ease when he had the upper hand. He encouraged students to think for themselves but did not hesitate to walk in on a therapy session and take over. Independent thinking that challenged his beliefs was apt to cause trouble between the heretic and Ackerman. These upstarts were usually men and their challenges were not easy for Ackerman to tolerate. Even when he shared his ongoing work with them he might introduce it by saying, "This is good, isn't it?", thereby cueing what he expected the response to be. He got on better with social workers, probably because they were usually women and also held a slightly lesser professional status. The Women's Movement was gathering steam in the closing years of his life; he would have had a hard time with it if he had lived into the seventies. Most particularly, he could not accept a woman's abandonment of her traditional supporting and nurturing role, as can be seen in his comments on "maternal failure."

Throughout the papers one senses the tradition of the European-Jewish family, child-centered, headed by a paterfamilias who is closely bonded to his wife, a "woman of valor." This was the family Ackerman knew most intimately and which he intuitively took to be the way families ought to be. He knew that this model was a recent social invention and that it might be transient; yet he was captured by its clear demarcation of sex roles—for the orderly march of the generations through time and for the actualization of conjugal, parental, and filial love. His later writings, in the decade of the sixties, seemed tinged with despair as the possibility of achieving a society based on this model appeared to recede. Ackerman was an intensely moral man, quite knowing about deceit and hypocrisy, yet without cynicism. He knew that fathers strayed, mothers drank, kids peeked. He viewed these interstices of the human spirit with humor and a slightly weary acceptance. The amusement and tolerance with which he would accept, even delight in, the petit larcenies of everyday life did not compromise his vision of the just and loving family harmoniously composing the biological, psychological, and social forces that played upon it. Ackerman's commitment to this model seems to have been profound and to have consistently informed his views of deviance and the goals and methods of treatment.

Arising also out of European Jewish culture was the tradition of the physician-scientist-healer. He would jokingly refer to himself as a "rabbi," but his professional identity was most clearly defined as a physician—and he meant by that a devotion to the welfare of his patients, careful and painstaking attention to clinical detail, and, above all, the courage to do what was required by the problem at hand. Courage for the surgeon meant to carry on in the face of catastrophe, not to break technique or compromise procedures out of fear or weariness. Courage for Ackerman as a psychotherapist meant to persist in the face of another's terror, to speak plainly about the unmentionable, to be fair to the strong as well as to the weak. All of these qualities were subsumed for him under the responsibilities of the physician. The ambiguities of such a definition of his role, the possibility for condescension and noblesse oblige were dangers that at times tripped him up. But less so than one might expect. He was protected by his profound candor.

Within the Family Institute, his irritating or intimidating traits were more than balanced by his openness, his availability, and the excitement of watching him work with families. In the professional world outside, however, his readiness to fight made some enemies. (Even among those there were many who admitted that they would come to Ackerman before anyone else when their families got into trouble, and they did.)

In the early years of family therapy, such feuds could be rationalized as part of a crusade against the unbelievers, the old guard of the psychoanalytic establishment. Eventually Ackerman encountered the problem closer to home. In the 1960s he sought to organize the now-burgeoning field of family therapy into a central organization, perhaps modeled on the *Landsmanshaft* his father had organized to unite the clan that emigrated to America. The family organization had fared well; Ackerman's Family Council did not. He was accused of trying to aggrandize himself and his Institute, to personally dominate the field. He was deeply hurt, angered, baffled. These kid brothers would not yield to his wisdom and guidance. He responded by working harder, driving himself more, ignoring his health. In the end, like the old doctor in *The Last Angry Man,* he may have succumbed as much to a sense of finishing as to a coronary reality.

At one time Nathan wrote to his sister: "For people of quality, it is a never-ending struggle for the truth of life and oneself in it. . . . We all have moments of siege and do strange and frantic things for self-preservation. We get through somehow. Mostly the memories of those other moments of satisfaction, deeply experienced, linger and sustain us through bad times. . . ."

In the huge legacy of his books, papers, and films, Nathan Ackerman left his colleagues just such moments of satisfaction, ever so deeply experienced.

NATHAN ACKERMAN: PROFESSIONAL CHRONOLOGY

1929: B.A., Columbia University
1933: M.D., College of Physicians and Surgeons
1933-34: Internship, Montefiore Hospital, New York City
1934-35: Assistant Resident in Neurology, Montefiore Hospital
1935-36: Resident in Neuropsychiatry, Menninger Clinic and Sanitarium, Topeka, Kansas
1936-37: Assistant Director, Southard School, Topeka
1937-38: Assistant Medical Director, Stoney Lodge Sanitarium, Ossining, New York
1937-42: Candidate at New York Psychoanalytic Institute
1937-42: Psychiatrist, Jewish Board of Guardians, New York City
1941: Diplomate, American Board of Psychiatry and Neurology
1942-52: Chief Psychiatrist, Jewish Board of Guardians
1943: Membership, American Psychoanalytic Association
1944-45: Psychiatrist, Red Cross Rehabilitation Clinic
1945-49: Instructor in Psychiatry, Community Service Society
1946-49: Psychiatrist, Council Child Development Center
1952-53: Visiting Lecturer, University of Pittsburgh
Lecturer, Department of Child Psychiatry, University of Pennsylvania
1955: Membership, American Academy of Psychoanalysis
1957: Appointed Attending Physician in Psychiatry, Presbyterian Hospital
1957-66: Supervising Psychiatrist, Family Mental Health Clinic, Jewish Family Service
1959: Adolph Meyer Award of the Association for Improvement of Mental Health
1960: Founded The Family Institute, New York City
Founding Editor, *Family Process*
1966: Award of the Eastern Group Psychotherapy Association

At the time of his death in 1971, Nathan Ackerman was Clinical Professor of Psychiatry at Columbia University; Visiting Professor, Albert Einstein College of Medicine, Yeshiva University; Director of Professional Programs, The Family Institute. After his death, the Institute was renamed in his honor and today is the Ackerman Institute for Family Therapy.

THE STRENGTH OF
Family Therapy

SELECTED PAPERS OF
Nathan W. Ackerman

PART I

Child Therapy and Psychoanalysis

We have grouped together Ackerman's papers on child therapy and psychoanalysis in the belief that they represent one complete aspect of his professional life. Chronological order has been slightly varied to allow for a clear thematic presentation.

The first four papers concern the therapy of children. The earlier ones are traditional in style. By 1956, however, Ackerman published the plan for the Council Child Development Center, in which family therapy was regarded as a *basic necessity* in evaluation and treatment of children. How did this transition occur? Ackerman never described it as such but surely, like the origin of life, it had something to do with necessary ingredients juxtaposed and energized over time. These ingredients were his keen awareness of the parents' importance to the developing child, and his substantial post-war experience in treating groups. The gradual confluence of this Tigris and Euphrates is reflected in our bibliography for the 1950s (see p. 458). For example, the 1951 paper "Social Role and Total Personality" (which we placed in the part on *group* therapy) obviously relates also to the plan of treating families at the Child Development Center, where it came under the rubric of "therapy for the environment."

Ackerman the training analyst appears in the next two papers. "Trends in the Terminal Phase of Student Analysis" (1955) brings the social role concept to bear on the evolution of the analyst's professional identity. Ackerman's notion is that the fully analyzed candidate qualifies as such not only by having his neurosis cured, but in terms of overall congruence with his family, society, and profession.

This congruence does not exclude dissent; in the final papers Ackerman criticizes psychoanalysis as too inner-directed and unmindful of the patient's social identity. He also states bluntly his criteria for mental health: "Cure also has the meaning that the individual, freed of crippling anxieties, can now unfold his capacity to love others, for sharing with them both pleasure and responsibility, and can experience the full gamut of satisfaction in making a positive contribution to the welfare of family, friends, and community." This goes farther than *lieben und arbeiten,* and can probably be linked with the idealistic socialism that was so much a part of New York's Jewish community in the first half of this century. Whether or not one agrees that social responsibility is a tenet of mental health, at least Ackerman made public how he would judge his patients' progress. Surprisingly few in this field, some of them at least as dogmatic, have stated as openly what they felt to be good or bad in their patients' lives. But, as Ackerman characteristically remarked in the paper on countertransference, it makes no sense to ignore something when in any case it is omnipresent.

CHAPTER 1

"Accidental" Self-injury in Children

Accidental self-injury is a common event in child life, but is inadequately understood by parents, teachers and even by some medical practitioners. It is quite certain that many such accidents are pure chance occurrences. It is equally certain, however, that many injuries of this same sort, often attributed to chance or Providence, are in reality not at all due to unpredictable and uncontrollable forces in the external world, but rather are they determined mainly by certain obscure psychological factors. In other words, some forms of self-injury, although seemingly accidental, may actually be an expression of morbid psychic purpose. This thesis has been advanced with convincing clinical evidence by Freud[5 6], Abraham[7], Klein[2] and Menninger[4]. It is important that this manifestation of psychopathology be understood and receive appropriate treatment before it assumes a malignant character.

The conception of the phenomenon of accident, the proclivity of people to attribute the cause of certain events to chance, is indeed a product of civilization. Primitive man knows no accident. He considers all things that happen to him as purposefully willed and executed by the gods, the devils or his enemies, all of whom may assume the guise of inanimate objects in his immediate environment. Mythology is full of such animistic thought. Similarly, the small child does not at first accept the concept of accident, but learns it by precept from older people. Like the primitive man, his thinking is animistic. When he is hurt he blames someone or something and frequently kicks the toy with which he has hurt himself or else strikes an innocent bystander. Such events occur in the life of every child. Sooner or later an older person tells the child, perhaps repeatedly, that no one deliberately hurt him, that the injury was an accident, could not have been prevented and no one was to blame. The child, however, when he is himself injured is not prone to excuse others readily. Not until he has successfully used the word "accident" to excuse his own guilt in the injury of others does he accept the concept of accident. It affords him one means by which to deny magically his own hostility to others; it tends to allay anxiety which emerges from this source, and thus eases his contacts with other persons. The

---

Reprinted with permission from *Archives of Pediatrics*, November 1936, Vol. LIII. No. 11, 711-721.

This paper was co-authored with Leona Chidester.

following is an illustration of how a child learns, accepts and utilizes the concept of accident.

A mother is scolding one of her children for being too noisy, and is at the same time rocking another child in a chair. She tends at the moment to rock the chair somewhat too energetically and in so doing overturns it, bumping the child's head. The child cries in pain. The mother then explains contritely that it was an accident. She tells the child the bump on the head was in no way intended, and she is not really to blame. The child feels the tender bump on his forehead and is loathe to believe the mother's explanation. An hour later, the same child upsets a bowl of hot soup in the mother's lap. His excuse is: "I didn't mean to—it was an accident." The child has by now accepted the parental taboo against open expression of hostility and has learned the social inexpediency of retaliating hurt for hurt by direct means. Moreover, he has discovered the magical word "accident" which excuses everything, and provides such a convenient protective cloak for his own hostility. The child may now utilize it to veil the aggressive motive of his acts from others, and, after a time, even from himself.

"Accidental" injuries constitute an important share of the experiences of the growing child. Sometimes the hurt is to others, sometimes to the self, often to both others and the self. Because of the early taboo against interpersonal hostility, the tendency to hurt the self in lieu of others is commonly evident in small children who are engaged in temper tantrums. They kick their feet against the floor, bump their heads vigorously, pull out their own hair[1], hit, bite and scratch themselves. With older children the expression of this tendency is more subtle and more highly disguised, because of the child's increased sensitiveness to the reactions of other people. While none would consider it accidental (unintentional) that the small child repeatedly bumps his head when enraged, few people are able to accept as intentional (unconscious intention) many of the injuries that befall older children, such as cutting and mashing fingers, stubbing toes, skinning knees, burns, etc. Yet we must consider a goodly number of such injuries in a similar light. Moreover, must we not regard from a like standpoint those children whose habitual reckless abandon in play brings with it repeated "accidental" injuries? Adults are often amazed that such children should hurt themselves repeatedly and yet never seem to learn caution. Have such children no fear? Quite the contrary; they often have more fear, but also more unexpressed hatred and guilt feeling than the average child. We have seen such a boy with much conscious fear and unconscious hate of men and bigger boys injure himself repeatedly through rash play; as, for, example, leaping down a flight of stairs. We have seen a girl with similar conscious fears and unconscious hates who allowed herself to be repeatedly bruised in falling, by being pulled around on roller skates in a narrow circle. So commonly are these injuries attributed to accident that they are little understood as expressions of disturbance in personality function. The question must be asked: How do such children make these "accidental" injuries possible?

It is not sufficient to point out that certain so-called accidents, especially certain forms of self-injury, are determined by obscure psychological factors. One must see what is their purpose, and what indirect gain is afforded the individual by them, namely, their role in the economy of the personality. Let us at this point cite a quotation from Melanie Klein[2]:

> A tendency to plaintiveness in children and a habit of falling down and knocking or hurting themselves are to be regarded as expressions of various fears and feelings of guilt. Analysis of children has convinced me that such recurrent minor accidents—and sometimes more serious ones are substitutes for self-inflicted injuries of a graver kind, and may represent attempts at suicide with insufficient means. With many children, especially boys, excessive sensibility to pain is often replaced very early by an exaggerated indifference to it, but this indifference is, I have found, only an elaborate defense against and modification of anxiety.

We must, therefore, impute to so-called accidental self-injury the basic motives of hurting the self out of guilt, or symbolically hurting others out of revenge, or both. The following is an illustration of a fusion of both motives.

An adolescent boy is chauffeuring his mother on a shopping tour. As the boy is driving, he pleads insistently with his mother for permission to take the family car on a fishing trip the next day with his friends. The mother adamantly refuses to yield, telling her son he is yet too young and impetuous—*that he might have an accident*. The boy, feeling sorely thwarted, fidgets angrily in his driver's seat, and in so doing unwittingly steps heavily on the accelerator. As the car leaps ahead, the wheel slips slightly in his hands, and the car crashes into the ditch. Both his mother and he are seriously bruised and cut. Are these injuries the consequences of pure chance occurrence? No. It does not require a long stretch of the imagination to see how the son's upsurging resentment toward his mother might have made the automobile accident possible.

Sometimes self-injury serves as a means to other goals. During the World War there were many cases of accidental minor injury which protected soldiers against the necessity of fighting in the front lines. In industry, there always were many cases of self-injury, in which there was a partial motive of benefit by monetary compensation. These persons not only injured themselves, but actually seemed able to keep themselves incapacitated over a remarkably long period, during which time they continued to receive compensation. Also to be considered is the additional gain of attention and sympathy given to injured persons. These latter indirect benefits of injury, that is, avoidance of disagreeable or dangerous situations, evasion of responsibility, acquisition of monetary benefits, additional attention and sympathy, are spoken of as secondary gains. The motive of hurting others or the self is primary.

In most cases of self-injury more than a single motive or purpose is served, i.e., the injury plays a many-sided role in the economy of the personality.

The following is a case that has been carefully observed and treated for seven months, and affords many examples of so-called accidental self-injury. By means of detailed study the purposeful psychological role of these injuries is clearly indicated.

The patient is a 12-year-old girl with serious social maladjustment, educational retardation, a history of lying, sexual misdemeanors and a badly scarred left hand and arm, injured in an accident. She was brought to the Southard School for psychiatric treatment with the hope that with rehabilitation of her personality she might adjust satisfactorily in a foster home.

The patient was the second sibling by her father, but had four half-brothers and sisters, born to the mother in a previous marriage. The parents were emotionally incompatible and their home was the scene of incessant conflict. When the patient was six years old the mother, having spent what money the father had, deserted him and the two younger children.

From this time on it was difficult to trace the patient's experiences in chronological order. She lived first with one parent and then with the other. The father was always kind to her. The mother, however, beat, scolded, cursed her and discriminated sharply between her and her other children. On one occasion the mother angrily told the two youngest children she had no love for them. They ran away to join the father who was not able to provide a stable home for them and left them much to their own devices.

In 1933 she and her brother were placed in a semi-private boarding school to prevent their irresponsible, vagrant wanderings. A report from that school stated that she was bold, crude, quarrelsome and domineering. She is said to have fought a great deal, engaged in numerous immoral practices, and, though intelligent, appeared disinterested in learning. During this period she was tested several times with varying results. The I.Q. varied from 65 to 113. In August 1934, while at this school, she had a serious accident, in which her left arm and hand were severely maimed and burned. The injury resulted in extensive scarring. In the hospital she suffered intensely, but was stoical and uncomplaining.

At the time the child entered the Southard School seven months ago, physical, neurological and laboratory examinations were essentially negative. On the Stanford-Binet test she scored a mental age of 8 years and 4 months and an I.Q. of 70. On the Porteus maze test she scored a mental age of 12 years, but her drawings scored scarcely more than 6 or 7 years. She was handicapped by a meager vocabulary and a poor grasp of arithmetic. She could read little except her name. Despite her poor test scores and poor academic achievement, her social behavior revealed good judgment, alert quick thinking and her motor skill was superior.

On admission she was docile, compliant and uncommunicative. She spoke only when spoken to, and always answered in a vocal tone totally devoid of expression, "Yes, Ma'am," or "No, Ma'am." Outwardly her demeanor was as mechanical as that of a robot. Gradually she became more emotionally expressive and more aggressive, striking, correcting and domineering all the other children. All attempts to approach her in a personal, kindly way were promptly met with tears and sobs, as though she were about to be accused and punished. Crying was found to be her defense against all unpleasant situations. She was also found to be stealthy, sly and deceitful, and intensely afraid of being apprehended in misbehavior. Her insecurity and need for love were so great that she could tolerate no disapproval, but she seemed perpetually to anticipate criticism or unfair treatment. In many ways her entire behavior seemed to say: "You see, I have suffered so much already that I must not be hurt more and should be awarded special privileges." When disappointed in not having her way *she picked and pulled at the scar on her injured hand till it bled,* or whined plaintively of the times she had been taunted about it. Later it was noted that she constantly complained of having been hurt by the other children. Investigation revealed instead that she had been the aggressor. Then for a period of several months it was observed that *she suffered minor accidental injuries each and every day*. First one, then another part of her body was covered with mercurochrome, but always where it could be prominently seen. She fell down and skinned her knees, stubbed her toes, bumped her injured hand, cut her fingers, etc., several times each day, all this despite her excellent motor skill. Whenever injured in this way she directed sullen, angry looks at all those about her as though accusing them of responsibility for the injury. At first the teachers and doctors expressed sympathy. Then it was noticed that she insisted on taking many unnecessary risks, that she seemed to invite accident and then utilized her injuries as a means of securing attention. This being the case, thereafter her injuries were rewarded with a minimum of attention. Immediately she tried to compel people to notice her injuries by complaining of pain. The psychotherapist pointed out to her that she was injuring herself to get attention; that after all she did not have to hurt herself to be loved, and that pity was not what she really wanted. It became apparent that these physical injuries had the same psychological significance as her too easily hurt feelings. "You see how I'm hurt all the time. It's your fault."

Meantime she was exceedingly sadistic with the other children, hitting, taunting, frightening and domineering them. Her sadism, being more prominent, was first discussed with her in psychotherapeutic conferences. She either denied the sadistic acts altogether or exaggerated their provocation. She complained that she was discriminated against by both children and adults at the various schools and hospitals where she had been as well as in her own home. Again she attempted to protect herself from further suffering and punishment by complaining about how much she had already suffered. She seemed to feel that her past suffering should make her an exception to all rules. Later she confessed that she tormented the other children but alleged that her acts were justified because everyone was hurting her.

She had a distorted image of the world as existing in a state of constant and chaotic conflict. She seemed unable to believe human relationships could be friendly and without hate. She seemed to feel that her psychotherapeutic conferences were a matter of attack and counterattack. Whenever some pertinent material was uncovered she cried or sulked, was very angry, threatened to run away or attempted to interfere with the work the therapist was doing with other children. Only very gradually was she convinced that the purpose was to help her, not to accuse and punish her.

Slowly she began telling more and more of the experiences of her storm-tossed life. She told of the many deprivations, misunderstandings and abuses which she had suffered. She related that she had engaged in many fights and had perpetrated many cunning dishonesties in order to protect herself. She was helped to see that in her old environment fighting on every side was essential for the preservation of her welfare, whereas at the school she was loved, protected and cared for; therefore fighting was no longer necessary. The effect of this insight was not to eliminate the sadism immediately, but rather to modify it. Her physical assaults on other children became less vicious, but she grew relentless in her domineering and disparaging attitude toward them. These aggressions were camouflaged in the alibi that she wanted to help the smaller children.

In the meantime, her masochistic expressions, equally prominent, slowly gave way. Daily for several months she seemed to find new ways of hurting herself or of getting others to hurt her. Her masochism was exposed to her again as a means, primarily, of expressing resentment toward others and of provoking punishment for her own aggressions; secondarily, as a device for gaining added attention and sympathy. Following this explanation, the accidental injuries to her body happened less and less frequently, but her masochism was no more cured than was her sadism. It, too, was forced to find another but more benign means of expression. It was soon noticed that she maneuvered situations so as to get her feelings hurt. For example, she seemed exceedingly sensitive whenever her father was mentioned, no matter what was said of him. Repeatedly she talked to the other children about their fathers, indirectly inviting them to ask or remark about hers. At such times she would burst into tears and run to the adults sobbing: "They are talking about my father and I don't think it is nice of them. They want to hurt my feelings." Both her sadism and masochism had gradually assumed more benign and more socially acceptable forms.

As her fears of those in the immediate environment were disappearing, it was noticed that she complained increasingly of fears of skeletons and ghosts. Her bodily injuries had been replaced by hurt feelings, and these in turn gave way to fears of the people about her and ghosts of her dead father. She was afraid the ghost of her father would kill her. Formerly, she had been unable to speak of her father except in praise. Now she told of his severe whippings. She felt exceedingly guilty for having disobeyed her father and reproached herself for not having made sure of his forgiveness before his death. Of all the tragedies that had befallen this child, this grief seemed the greatest. She was told that her father had lived a long time, knew the ways of children and that he was not angry with her for her disobedience. Rather, he had had a long and disappointing journey through life in search for love and she was the only one who had ever cared much for him and thus she had made his life very happy.

Her dreams were concerned chiefly with two kinds of experience, fighting and sex, and were often associated with terror. One morning she related the following significant dream, the fright of which she associated with her wetting of the bed. *The wife of a certain man was unfaithful. The man returning from town discovered his wife in the sexual act with another man, so he cut off the strange man's genitals.* The injured man then ran out of the tent only to collapse and bleed to death. From this it seemed plausible that her enuresis signified both erotic and aggressive strivings. It seemed probable, too, that she used it as an indirect means of inciting punishment—punishment for bedwetting as a substitute for the real crime, her sexual phantasies. The context of the dream perhaps suggests her aggressive attitude toward men, and suggests that if she accepted vicarious forms of punishment she would then be able to ward off the most severe punishment—sexual injury and death.

Her sadism appeared to be a reaction to the frequent and violent thwartings of her early childhood, and her masochism was an inverted expression of her hostility to others, and of her need for punishment. With this explained to her, her anxiety definitely diminished and her asocial behavior seemed to abate definitely. It is still too early, nevertheless, to state the complete outcome of the case as the child is still under treatment.

However, her very excellent adjustment is indicative of remarkable therapeutic progress. This once stoical, expressionless child now has a very mobile, vivacious, expressive face that is distinctly pretty. Socially she has become one of the best adjusted children at the school. She is interested in learning etiquette, makes friends easily and has developed a natural grace and charm. Her sadism and masochism have dwindled greatly until they can scarcely be called abnormal, and have taken on a more socially acceptable form. She has become interested in learning and in five months of part time school work she has accomplished much more than many children do in two years. When asked why she had not learned before she replied: "Well, they just hurt my feelings all the time so I just put my head down on my desk and did not pay much attention." Her scores on intelligence tests have steadily risen until now her score is superior on some of the performance tests. Her I.Q. on the Stanford-Binet is about 86, but maximal development has not yet been reached since she is still handicapped by a limited vocabulary. In behavior she has made an excellent improvement. Neither by action or speech is she immodest and she is as truthful as most children. Her emotional maturity is well advanced for her age. It is significant that she has always seemed more mature in judgment and social interests than her educational achievement or intelligence test results have indicated.

In conclusion, the self-injury, as well as other expressions of her masochism, were determined by obscure (unconscious) psychological factors. The self-injury played a varied role in the psychological economy. First, only the secondary gains were apparent, i.e., the utilization of these injuries to obtain attention and sympathy. Later, it was obvious that deeper purposes were involved. She frequently injured herself as an expression of her anger toward another person; she did to herself what she wished to do to another. In addition, the self-injuries appeared to be a punishment for her sexual phantasies for which she felt overwhelmed with guilt. Her conscience would not permit her any form of sexual indulgence without coincident severe punishment. Finally, educational counselling and systematic psychotherapy prevailed against her relentless conscience, and she attained a good social adjustment. With suitable placement in a foster home, educational and vocational guidance, the rehabilitation of the personality should be expected to endure permanently.

SUMMARY

Certain forms of recurrent self-injury in children, ordinarily interpreted as accidental, are actually manifestations of a personality disturbance, which is amenable to psychiatric treatment.

BIBLIOGRAPHY

1. Bleyer, Adrien: Hair Plucking. Am. Jour. Dis. Child., 51: 336-337, Feb. 1936.
2. Klein, Melanie: The Psychoanalysis of Children, 1932, pp. 26 and 146.
3. Von Hug-Hellmuth, H.: A Study of the Mental Life of the Child. Psychoanalyt. Rev., 5: 414-415, 1918.
4. Menninger, Karl A.: Purposive Accidents as an Expression of Self-Destructive Tendencies. Internat. Jour. Psychoanalysis, 17: 6-16, Jan. 1936.
5. Freud, Sigmund: Collected Papers, 1925, Vol. III, p. 145.
6. Freud, Sigmund: Psychopathology of Everyday Life, 1914, pp. 198-209 and p. 216.
7. Abraham, Karl: Selected Papers on Psychoanalysis, 1927, pp. 58-62.

CHAPTER 2

Psychotherapy and "Giving Love"

One aspect of the psychotherapeutic process attempts to meet and satisfy a patient's need to be loved. In the field of child guidance, more especially in social agencies which undertake psychotherapy with children, such phrases as: "This child needs warmth and affection;" and, "We must give love to this child," are often heard.

In the following discussion certain limited aspects of this therapeutic problem are to be considered, with special emphasis on some misapplications of the concept of "giving love." The phrase "giving love" seems too frequently misconceived and misused. Actually, to speak of this aspect of psychotherapy as a technique is to give it a wrong connotation. Fundamentally, giving love can neither be a technique, nor a device, nor a strategy; it must be as genuine and sincere in psychotherapy as in ordinary human experience.

The importance of "giving love" to a patient has received marked emphasis in the training of psychotherapists, both in the field of psychiatry and in social work. Yet, the therapist's role of "giving love" in a psychotherapeutic experience has taken many forms; some desirable, others less so, to say the least. That a large number of patients who seek the aid of psychotherapy are able initially neither to receive, nor to give love, has been observed. For them, the psychotherapist's aim must be not so much to "give love," as to modify their characters in order to prepare them to accept love and then return it.

In my experience, what has been called the "technique of giving love" is often applied with an inaccurate conception of the pathological aspects of the patient's demand, and is often applied long before the patient is able to receive such attention as love. Frequently, this so-called giving love is transformed into something quite different; often, a jockeying of emotional roles such as will give the therapist the controlling position and the power to make the patient accept the therapist's influence. Were I to yield to the temptation to be facetious, I would call this paper, "To Give Or Not To Give Love—And How."

The comments which follow have been influenced by my personal experiences as a psycho-

Reprinted with permission from *Psychiatry: Journal of the Biology and Pathology of Interpersonal Relations*, May 1944, Vol. 7, No. 2, 129-137.

therapist but have emerged more specifically from experiences in supervising the psychotherapeutic efforts of psychiatric social workers in social agencies. In many instances, I have had the opportunity of following the worker's treatment experience from beginning to end. Where the worker's effort ended in a therapeutic failure, I have tried to find an explanation. In so doing, I have found it necessary to closely study this so-called "technique of giving love."

It was my impression that a misconception and misdirection of this technique was the basis of some of these failures; that, in its name, some of the more serious errors in psychotherapy were committed. Actually, the need to be loved is expressed in a great variety of ways, each of which must be clearly and accurately understood as it relates to the character of the individual patient, if the therapy is to succeed.

Granted, these patients need love. Granted, they have suffered privations in their childhood, more especially, that they have been denied love by their own parents. Nevertheless, certain important obstacles interfere with compensating for that original lack. Is it not true in many such instances that the therapist who tries to "make up" such an early lack of love attempts the impossible? The therapist can achieve much by his understanding of the patient and by gradual reorganization of the patient's interpersonal patterns, but he can never replace the love the patient lost in his childhood relationship with his parents.

Some patients need love but do not understand its nature, nor are they aware of their need. There are others who have a glimmering of what it might be like to be accepted and loved, but are completely barred from asking it because they have a dread of the price which they think they must pay for it. They fear being exploited or injured, and are emotionally unable to ask for gratification of their needs.

When the patient's fear of humiliation, pain or injury is stronger than the need to be loved, the price which he must pay for gratification is too high, and he ceases to ask for love. Sometimes, a patient will endure the pain without even then being free to take the pleasure of being loved. Then there are those who accept love, but feel guilty in their acceptance of it; the guilt makes them hostile or depressed. Others, unable to ask for love, are impelled to steal it or take it by other means, sometimes by force, expressing their need, not directly, but in the disguise of some form of aggression. These are merely a few of the many possible forms in which the need for love may be expressed. Unless the particular means by which the patient expresses his need is understood, the technique of giving love will be unsuccessful.

A misuse of the "technique of giving love" may develop in three ways. First, it may result from an inadequate knowledge of the normal and pathological patterns of interpersonal relations. Secondly, it may derive from the intrusion into the patient-therapist relationship of unconscious but highly rationalized and misdirected motives springing from the therapist's unconscious, which, of course, constitutes the whole problem of counter transference. Thirdly, it may eventuate from deficiencies in therapeutic skill.

Let me consider, for example, one important type of personality problem which provides a test for this technique, that is, the treatment of an aggressive behavior disorder in a child. These are disturbances in which, generally, a deficient self-control is found.

In one such instance, a social worker made the comment that a particular boy patient had been reared in an unfavorable environment in which he had been subjected to severe punishment. Therefore, she deduced, "This boy needs affection, and that is what we must give him."

Surely this boy needs affection; he needs it urgently, but the question of whether he is ready to receive it must also be asked. When this boy becomes enraged in a therapeutic interview and hits the therapist in the eye, it may be because of a desire to inflict injury; but it may also be that he wishes to knock the therapist's eye out because the therapist is blinding himself to the child's real desires. It is by no means rare that a hostile child communicates his deepest need to the therapist by whacking him first, concealing his dependence and his unsatisfied yearning for affection behind this defensively aggressive act. In this warped form, he demonstrates his need to be loved.

What happens if the therapist tries to give love at the moment the boy wants to strike out against the therapist? Is the boy aware of his need for affection? Is he in an emotional position to accept any affection? That is the question. This discussion is equally relevant to those patients in whom the aggressive urges are not "acted out" but are deflected back on the self with more or less depressive reaction. Inherent in the depressive reaction is a deep hunger for affection, for food, for security; yet, such persons are not able to accept love. Several fundamental considerations hinge on this question of how to deal with an aggressive demand for "love." In the first place, is the child really asking for love? If so, what form of love? What is the meaning of the aggression? Should it be tolerated? How should the unrestrained aggression be controlled?

To define the appropriate therapeutic attitude, one must more clearly examine the character of this type of child, who shows his wants by acts of uncontrolled aggression, and for that matter, of adults with similar traits. Let me cite a few examples.

"The hostility of others brings out the very best in me," a patient once emphatically remarked. This patient was a more effective person when he encountered hate than when he met with kindness. Only when he was attacked did his best resources come into full play. He thrived in a hostile atmosphere.

Similarly, a patient of Dr. Lander's described his ties to other people as "a bond of unfriendliness." Such people often feel helpless, lost, bewildered and anxious when their environment does not contain the threat to which they are accustomed. They are likely to feel disarmed, and without an excuse for their familiar patterns of hate, they become more fearful than ever. Their patterns of hate represent their individual form of effectiveness in life. They are not frightened by hostility because they know how to defend themselves. They do fear love, or, more accurately, what is offered to them as love. Against this, they are defenseless. This is readily illustrated by the type of patient who displays a reasonable effectiveness in her behavior, so long as her goals and activity are oriented to a pattern of opposition to domination by parent figures. Once the customary threat of domination is removed, such a patient becomes bewildered, disorganized, gropes vainly for new goals, and may even enter a panic state. In such instances, the whole concept of self is predominantly conditioned by a pattern of compulsive counteraction of expected destruction in the parent figure.

A patient of this type, at the age of 12 years, stole a warning sign which hung over some high tension wires in a railroad station. She took it home and hung it outside her door. Elaborated somewhat by her, it read, "Beware—High Voltage—If you come too close you will be electrocuted." Her purpose was to ward off the "affection" of her mother. It must be obvious that one cannot offer a friendly handshake to a high tension wire unless one shuts the current off first. So it is with these patients.

Faced with an insoluble dilemma, they can neither trust other persons enough to risk depending on or submitting to them; nor can they derive sufficient satisfaction from themselves. They try to isolate themselves emotionally, but are unsuccessful. Any approach to a close relationship constitutes a threat and a challenge to their aggressiveness. They defend themselves either by "hitting out first," or by maintaining a safe distance between themselves and others. A barrier of hostile defenses alone enables them to live in an emotionally detached state. But this can be erected only at the price of chronic unsatisfaction.

Love is a strange experience to such a person. Since he is familiar with patterns of hostility in himself and in others, he can readily defend himself against it, but the intentions of a person who appears to offer love are a mystery which he cannot easily fathom. He is apt to suspect an unfamiliar form of betrayal against which he must be on guard. He is therefore wary, pushes away the affection which is offered him; and when he anticipates aggression, tries to forestall it by taking the offensive. It is well to remember that the very person who is most starved for affection is also least able to digest it, just as one who has endured actual starvation for some time cannot immediately stomach food.

How then can the technique of "giving love" be applied to such patients? Can the therapist ignore the child's aggression? Usually he cannot, at least not for long. Such a child is not likely to make therapeutic control so simple. Can the the therapist accept the aggression? If he does, he sanctions sick behavior. Can the therapist dissolve the child's hostility by a generous offering of love? This is easier said than done. It is difficult to stop a flying fist with love.

This raises two questions. One, whether the patient is capable of receiving love, and the other, whether the therapist can give it. If the patient is normal enough to accept affection, the therapist's aim will be achieved. But unfortunately, the kind of patient under discussion has but little capacity for the reception of love.

The boy who hits first and asks questions afterwards shows that he is not familiar with affection and is suspicious of such offerings. It is delusion to believe that the therapist can ever compensate a child for the love which he has missed since early years. He can only teach him that it is not inevitably his lot to remain unloved, and that there are other ways than those he takes to gain it. Once the therapist has achieved that much, the patient will have but little more need of him, and can begin to experience love with others. The problem is not whether the therapist should give love, but when and how it is possible to make a patient ready to receive it.

The therapist's wish to "give love" must be adjusted to the particular ways in which his patient expresses his need for it. This need may show itself openly, or in some warped or hidden form. It is necessary that the therapist deal first with the particular suspicions and fears which conceal the underlying need for love.

Obviously, if such fears and suspicions represent an obstacle to the child's acceptance of love, this obstacle must be removed. This is an integral part of "giving love" to the patient. How to deal properly with the child's fears, suspicions and aggressions represents no new psychotherapeutic problem. The proper handling of such attitudes is fairly well established. Long ago, it was learned that there was no place for punishment in therapy because punishment, although it might deter aggressive acts, could never cure their cause. The therapist can tolerate them only up to the point at which lack of restraint will seriously threaten his own person or jeopardize his therapeutic control of the situation.

To tolerate aggressive acts, so far as this can be done safely, does not mean, however, either to accept them or condone them passively, much less to encourage them. To allow the expression of deep aggressive urges to relieve guilt is one thing; to license the "acting out" of these abnormally intense urges is quite different. It is wrong to encourage or morally reinforce pathological patterns of aggression, even passively, whether they are overt acts or whether they are confined to fantasy. The purpose of an attitude of tolerance toward such pathological aggression is to arrive at an understanding of its causes and eventually eliminate these.

Basically, therapeutic tolerance is a method of passive control of abnormal aggression until such time as the causes can be identified and progressively better understood by both therapist and patient. When the aggression exceeds the point at which it can be safely tolerated and becomes actually dangerous, some form of restraint becomes indispensable.

The concept of passive restraint is useful for this purpose, but it must be clearly distinguished from punishment. Such restraint may be exercised by verbal, or where necessary, by physical means. Passive restraint implies a systematic effort to impede dangerous degrees of aggression in the complete absence of any vindictive motives on the part of the therapist. The distinction between passive restraint and punishment lies in the actual motives of the therapist, not in what the therapist does, or in the child's interpretation of what he does. When necessary, the therapist may firmly and decisively thwart extreme acts of aggression by physical means, without the intention to punish.

For example, a 9-year-old boy with a compulsion neurosis, who was absorbed with phantasies of injury and death, tried to kick the therapist, and then attempted to twist his testicles. The therapist tolerated this impulse only to the extent of helping the boy acknowledge his urge to emasculate the therapist, understand why he had this wish, and relieve his guilt and fear of retaliation. He restrained the boy from carrying out the impulse. It would neither be safe for the therapist nor therapeutic for the child to permit full expression of this impulse. To do so would be unrealistic and would tremendously heighten the boy's guilt and anxiety. To even passively encourage this aggressive impulse would increase the child's anxiety, and be therapeutically undesirable.

The goal should be to remove the boy's fear of attack by the therapist, not the encouragement of the boy's attack on the therapist. Therefore, passive physical restraint of such a boy is indicated.

It is an indispensable part of an adult's responsibility to protect the child, even from itself. Such passive restraint may need to be applied consistently for a long time before the child is ready to accept affection for what it is. Should the child interpret this act of restraint as punishment, this is not to be regarded as the fault of the therapist, but rather as an expression of the child's misconception of interpersonal reality. The child cannot benefit from any affection which the therapist tries to bestow on him, until such obstacles for giving and receiving it are removed. This may sometimes be achieved within a single hour, but the effect at this early stage may be only temporary. Or, it may be achieved only after a period of many months. This depends on the dynamic interchange between the child and the therapist and the child's ability at a given time to perceive the therapist's true intentions.

It is necessary to emphasize that there are specific indications for the application of passive restraint; that it must not be confused with punishment, and that it must be applied in the proper dynamic context. This is by no means an easy task and all the therapist's talents and energy must be summoned to this end. He must be sure of his own strength and confident of his own ability to stop undue aggression. If he has this security, he need not feel either threatened or vindictive. Without such inner security, he cannot give love to the child. In self-defense he may detach himself emotionally from the child, while seeking refuge in rationalized disciplinary measures.

I turn now to certain other examples of the misuse of this concept of "giving love" due to inadequate knowledge of psychopathology and of certain phenomena of interpersonal relations.

Let me consider the first interview with a child who is shy, withdrawn and unable to make friends. He and the worker are, in the beginning, strangers; no effective rapport has yet been established. The child has no awareness that his behavior represents a deviation from normal adjustment and is not conscious of having a problem or of being regarded as ill. The worker says to the child: "I want to help you," or, "I am here to be your friend." What does such an offer of help and friendship mean to the child at a time when no real relationship has as yet been formed? In this setting preliminary to a treatment relationship, the worker makes a promise of help. Can the worker at this stage be certain of being able to fulfill this promise? Can the child understand the real meaning of such an offer of help before it understands its own needs? Furthermore, has he had any basis in his own experience for understanding what "help" or "friendship" means? In my mind, this is highly doubtful.

In the initial contact with the child, I believe that these terms of "help," "friendship" or "affection" are often but vague abstractions to the child, which necessarily bewilder and frighten him. Such an approach seems to me to be inappropriate because the offer of help or friendship or love is too formal and fails utterly to carry the intended meaning to the child. Actually, while absorbed in making such an offer, the worker may fail to see those meaningful reactions of the child which represent the early patterns of transference. An offer to give anything at this early stage, whether it be help, friendship, or love, is likely to fail of its purpose unless it is made with a clear perception of the dynamics which prevail in the relationship at that time.

Several years ago, I reviewed the record of a boy ten years of age who had been treated by a social worker for about three years. Initially, the psychiatrist made the following note: "This boy's conduct disorder constitutes a reaction to the desertion by his mother when he was 2-years-old. He has a deep need for a mother's love, and this need should be met in a therapeutic relationship with a social worker. The outlook for recovery is good." The social worker interpreted this recommendation literally and for three years tried intensively to satisfy the boy's need for a mother's love. The therapeutic result was exactly nil.

It seems to me that this failure reflects a basic fallacy in psychiatric thinking. The disorder of this boy's personality at the age of ten years represented far more than a simple deficiency in mother love. By this time, it had become a warping of his whole character.

Diagnostically, this child's pathology fits into the category of "affect hunger" or psychopathic personality. He had little capacity for emotional rapport with people. His interpersonal patterns were conditioned by the aggressive urge to blackjack people into coming across with all kinds of indulgences. He was not open to receiving love from any source. It is a mistake to assume that a child of this sort will get well if, at the age of ten years, the therapist tries to replace the love which his mother denied him in his first two years of life. This early lack of love may have contributed basically to his disturbance, but at the age of ten, "giving love" will not cure that disturbance. It is magical thinking to imagine that it would.

Personality disorders are not simple deficiency diseases. Such a conception of them is wholly unsound clinically because it ignores the significance of distortions of character which develop in the child's personality following early privations.

Still another illustration of such clinical naïveté is presented: A 17-year-old boy showed a grave maladjustment characterized by an unreasonable belligerency towards older men. The psychiatrist elucidated the paranoid quality of such belligerent reaction. The social worker, however, was anxious to satisfy the boy's need for love as revealed by his earlier history. He had suffered rejection and humiliation, particularly at the hands of his father.

"The severe trauma to which this child was subjected explains everything," was the worker's remark. "No wonder he is belligerent. I see no reason why he should not get well if we treat him kindly and try to satisfy his demand for love."

The therapeutic zeal of such a worker is commendable but his attitude is oversanguine to the extent that he overlooks the importance of the paranoid warping of the boy's character, which now is very different from what it was when his father first rebuffed his passive craving for love. At this time, the boy's underlying suspicion acts as a defensive barrier against any attention that is offered him as love.

I wish to draw attention now to those misdirected efforts at "giving love" which arise when various inappropriate motives on the part of the social worker intrude themselves into the treatment situation. Often, the therapist is not conscious of such motives. They are usually highly rationalized and exercise an important influence on the whole course of therapy but are neither understood nor adequately controlled either by the therapist or the child. Inevitably this complicates the course as well as the outcome of treatment.

Some social workers have an exaggerated need to give love to the child and attempt it prematurely. Naturally, the motive for such tendencies vary greatly, and I can speculate only on some of them here. They are to be found in feelings of insecurity on the part of the worker, doubts concerning professional adequacy, the worker's need to assert intelligence and power, a competitive drive with other therapists, a drive to compete with the child's mother, a fear of the child's hostility and rejection, a fear of losing the child as a patient, with a consequent need for ingratiation of the child. In addition, there are motives of "giving love" in order subtly to intimidate or control the child, often because of a need to receive love from the child; also, there is a tendency to identify with the needs of the child, and finally, a tendency to derive vicarious satisfaction from the child's destructive fantasies.

I might illustrate from records concerning the treatment of both child and mother, the child suffering from an obsessional neurosis and the mother suffering from an anxiety hysteria. The two neuroses were closely interwoven. The child refused to be separated from its mother in any and all circumstances.

After some preliminary meetings, the therapist became convinced she could not treat the child effectively unless she could separate her from her mother. She succeeded ostensibly in doing so by recourse to certain strategic devices and then proceeded to try to treat the child independently. Then it became clear that the forced separation had been premature, that the child sensed the coercive attitude of the therapist and responded with an intensified distrust of both the therapist and the mother.

During the first few hours of contact with the child, the worker proceeded to interest the child in play but the child soon began to sob agitatedly and insisted that she did not want to see the therapist any more.

"I don't want to come, there's no reason," she cried, "I'm not afraid any more. Why should I come?"

At first, the worker reacted to the child's efforts to deny symptoms by reiterating the fears which the child had experienced, but this was of little avail. The child persisted in denying a reason for coming. When the child began to cry with a show of great agitation, the worker was affected by the child's misery, put the child in her lap and embraced her with a show of great tenderness. At first the child seemed to respond warmly, but nevertheless, while returning the show of affection, she looked at her watch, and again wished to leave.

"I don't want to come, you haven't helped me," she exclaimed, sobbing.

"I don't want to let a friend like you leave, especially when you suffer," the worker explained with recourse to a different tactic. "I like you and I would be sad if you did not come to see me any more. You do have fears and need my help." When this in turn failed to persuade the child, she said, "Perhaps I shall have to make you come at least once more. For your own sake, we may have to force you."

The child continued to come, both in obedience to the worker's command and in response to a bribe from the mother. Thereafter, there was no more sobbing, but the treatment bogged down. The child ceased to exhibit any spontaneous activity in play or in the more direct aspects of the relationship with the worker. She ceased to bring any new or meaningful material to the treatment experience and the entire relationship entered a static and sterile phase characterized by the child's stereotyped, obsessive preoccupation with a single game. No further progress was made.

My impression was that the therapist used the technique of "giving love" to allay her fears of therapeutic failure, to appease her own guilt feeling, to shut off the stream of the child's hostility and to try to bind the child to her, lest it leave treatment. When these efforts failed, the therapist resorted to open compulsion. Here the worker's effort to intimidate the child was not even thinly disguised. The eventual result was stagnation of the therapeutic process. I have observed on a number of occasions such unconscious exploitation of "the technique of giving love," used for the purpose of restraining the mounting aggressiveness of the child. This is purely and simply a method of unconscious intimidation.

In the next illustration, a worker attempts prematurely through hasty reassurances to convince a boy that she will not hurt him. The worker arrived late for the treatment hour, and assured the boy that he would not suffer because of this. The boy denied that she had deprived or hurt him in any way by being late. He began to play with finger paint, and quickly showed evidences of anxiety.

"Oh, I forgot," said he, "I'm supposed to know that I don't have to be afraid of you—that you're different from my mother."

Following this, he proceeded immediately to recite experiences which clearly exposed his feeling that the worker was fully as dangerous to him as his mother. In obedience to the implied wish of the worker the boy makes a conciliatory effort to deny his fear of her. This gesture is a transparent failure, however.

A phenomenon closely related to this is one in which the therapist's effort to give love is not for the purpose of really meeting the child's needs, but rather to make the child give love to the therapist. Here the therapist's own unconscious need to be loved comes into play. The unconscious plays a trick on the therapist, the roles are reversed and the therapist becomes the patient, with the child playing the role of the therapist.

This raises the question of unconscious identifications on the part of the therapist with the child which reflect themselves in many interesting ways. An outstanding example of this is one in which the therapist unconsciously places a selective emphasis on the child's destructive fantasies. This occurs sometimes because some therapists "get a kick out of" the child's destructiveness, identifying with the child's hostile drives and experiencing a vicarious pleasure in their expression. Again, they may identify themselves over-strongly with the injury sustained by the child at the hands of his mother. They are then stimulated to give exaggerated love to the child, unwarranted because it is out of harmony with the actual relationship to the child at that stage of therapy. Such love is not so much love of the child as it is an unconscious reproach leveled against the child's mother.

The therapist tries too soon to give love to the child, in order to quickly convince the child of the sharp difference between the maternal attitude of the therapist on the one hand, and that of the mother, on the other hand. This is a wish to prove prematurely that the mother is a bad person and the therapist is a good person. Sometimes the therapist more openly gives love in order to win the child's favor and allegiance away from the mother and hurt the real mother.

Such instances of unconscious overidentification with the child, or unconscious competition with the child's mother, bring about other undesirable influences affecting the course of the therapeutic experience. The therapist unconsciously gives love to the child to reward her for a more emphatic rebellion against the mother.

Sometimes it is the wish directly or indirectly to "show up" the inadequacies of the real mother and to assert by contrast the adequacies of the therapist. In so doing, the therapist sometimes becomes unduly absorbed in this unconscious battle with the mother, instead of using her capacities and energies in the more direct treatment of the child.

Still another form of rationalization of the technique of giving love is the premature use of interpretation, which often has most undesirable effects. Interpretation is used sometimes to attack the patient's defenses before the relationship between child and therapist is sufficiently developed to permit the replacement of such defenses by more constructive patterns of behavior. As a consequence of this premature stripping of necessary defenses, the child may abandon the treatment entirely. Equally evident is the opposite tendency to delay or avoid logical interpretations because of an inappropriate fear of hurting the patient's feelings. Here, the therapist's need to keep the child's favor impedes therapeutic progress.

I have reserved the question of whether the therapist can give love for the last. Some have much love to give, others have less; no two therapists have the same amount of love to give, and certainly no one has an infinite capacity for it. Yet, one might ask how many therapists are aware of their personal limitations in this respect. I have often seen social workers proceed blithely on the assumption that their capacities in this respect are really boundless. They seem to imply the promise that they can continue to shower the child with affection indefinitely and unconditionally. This is a promise which should not be made and most often cannot be fulfilled. The child's own behavior may make it impossible, or the therapist's own limitations in giving love may defeat such a purpose.

I have observed the most conspicious examples of this type of illusory fantasy of a boundless love where the child's demands for love were exaggerated and often really insatiable. This type of uncritical behavior on the part of some social workers is really another example of a delusion of omnipotence. This impressed me so deeply that I have often called it "the delusion of the boundless breast."

Laboring under such a delusion, what can a therapist achieve? What happens if he tries to give love beyond the limits of his capacity?

In the first place, an exaggerated demand for love on the part of some children is not actually a demand for genuine affection. Instead, it may be a testing of the therapist's attitude, a testing of the power of the child over the therapist, an expression of his need for domination, a concealed reproach, a placation, or a disarming of the therapist. Basically, this is a denial of hostility rather than an asking for love; if the therapist, therefore, in response to such motives, tries to give love, there will ensue an inevitable failure of understanding between him and the child, with a consequent confusion of the relationship.

In the second place, if the therapist exceeds his capacity for giving love, he is in danger of depleting himself or having his love for the child sour. The real danger is not the mere provocation of a hostile attitude in the therapist, but rather his unawareness of it. Actually, what a therapist gives when he exceeds the capacity for giving love is not love. The giving often becomes a ritual behind which a variety of far less wholesome attitudes and motives lie concealed. There may, for example, be fear of the child's demand and aggressions, a need to appease, a need to control the child, concealed sadism and other unconscious motivation. To the extent to which this happens, the effectiveness of the therapy will inevitably suffer.

In some measure the so-called technique of giving love has become an unfortunate *cliché*. The first objective of therapy is the growth of understanding between the child and therapist. In one sense, this is simply an expansion of self-understanding. The aim is to bring the patient finally to a point where he is ready to receive love as love. In relation to child therapy, the therapist may give as abundantly as he pleases, provided that giving is genuine and does not exceed his capacity. When eventually a child is able to ask for love, he is also near to being able to give it and as near to being cured. The therapist's task of preparing the child for love is reaching its end; the child has not much more need of the therapist, and may then turn to real relationships.

There was once a famous German comedy entitled, *Muss Die Kuh Milch Gaben?* It is well to remember that the human breast also has its limits.

CHAPTER 3

Failures in the Psychotherapy of Children

Success and failure in psychotherapy are alternative aspects of a single experience. Different therapeutic concepts of aim and method, when applied to the key elements of a child's emotional disturbance, will determine one or the other result.

Psychotherapy with children, as with adults, strives for the achievement of two basic aims.

1. The elimination of emotional disabilities, expressed in anxiety and specific symptoms;
2. The promotion of positive growth and maturation of personality, and, with this, effective social adaptation.

These two aims are interrelated to the extent that, as pathologic symptoms are resolved, the normal patterns of growth and adaptation tend to reassert themselves; that is, with the removal of psychic obstacles, the full potentialities for healthy maturation are released.

In this connection, it is necessary to remember the so-called "normal adaptation" is in itself merely a working hypothesis, which each individual therapist evolves somewhat differently, and is therefore colored to some extent by the vicissitudes of individual experience. Obviously, this does not provide a uniform criterion for "normal" behavior.

Our purpose here will be not simply to illustrate failures in the therapy of children, but rather to provide a conceptual orientation to the many possible pitfalls in this field; we will endeavor to draw a dynamic frame within which the varied and contrasting types of failure can be traced.

In undertaking this task, one serious obstacle immediately confronts us, the problem of finding a communicable language. The ever-present semantic problem dogs the field of dynamic psychiatry at each step in its progress.

Currently, in the child field, consensually validated definitions of such phenomena as social reality, treatment method, and "cure" are lacking. So much ambiguity surrounds the use of these concepts that clear communication between professional persons working with children becomes difficult to achieve. We hope, however, to make ourselves reasonably understood, without tackling the whole issue of semantics.

Reprinted from *Failures in Psychiatric Treatment*, P. Hoch (Ed.) 1948, 85-102.

This paper was co-authored with Peter B. Neubauer.

Nevertheless, it is necessary to offer at least a working definition of failure of therapy in order to provide a basis for further discussion. In our judgment, failure is signified by the persistence of symptoms, by a lack of change or insufficient change, in the child's effective adaptation to self and to the outer real world.

In considering the issue of cure or failure, we are accustomed to focus first on specific psychiatric disabilities. In child therapy we deal primarily with an organism in growth. It is especially characteristic of the fluid, shifting organization of the child's personality that symptoms come and go, or that one symptom disappears in growth, and is replaced by another. It is imperative with children to take a larger view of the concept of cure, and to evaluate at each point the total functioning of the child's personality. This implies careful study of the child's assimilation and mastery of reality, his image of self, his control of inner impulses and outgoing aggression, his guilt and punishment tendencies, his expression and modification of affect in interpersonal relations, his capacities for genuine human attachment, and his characteristic defensive ways of dealing with anxiety, whatever its specific origin. Each part of the child's behavior must be seen in its proper dynamic relation to the whole.

This task is by no means easy, but any effort arbitrarily to simplify it for the convenience of the therapist is doomed to failure; it will boomerang against both the patient and therapist. The fundamental complexity of the problem must be recognized and respected. In psychotherapy, nothing is gained by such attempts at simplification as tend to separate the behavior problem from its true dynamic content.

This has a special relevancy for the field of child therapy. The child organism is distinct from the adult. The personality of the child is incomplete; it is in the formative state. Patterns of behavior are fluid, changing and unstable. With each succession, from one stage of growth to the next, there is a shift in the dominant personality configurations. In the beginning the child is separated from the mother physically only. Gradually it becomes separated from the maternal environment, psychologically as well as socially. Up to a certain age, the child's enforced dependence on his environment, his inability to control it, or to remove himself at will from it, makes him and the environment an indivisible dynamic unit. Only later does the child become a clearly differentiated psychological entity. The principles of therapy must therefore harmonize with this concept; the therapeutic technic must first approach the child-environment relationship as a unit. Failure to do so may produce failure in treatment.

There is, too, the additional consideration that the child's immaturity precludes a consciousness of emotional illness as such; he has no insight comparable to the adult, and can assume at best only limited, if any, responsibility for illness. Failure to realize this may also produce failure in therapy.

For the many reasons bearing on the differences between child and adult, clinical syndromes in children tend to be fluid, impure; symptoms are often multiple, of mixed character, and represent pathologic offshoots at different stages of development. The distinctions between the child and adult organisms necessarily change the context of treatment for the child.

Most difficult is the task of achieving an accurate measure of change in the function of personality. Psychic processes, intrinsically, are relatively intangible phenomena. We have not yet discovered objective yardsticks for such measurement. In fact, the most accurate method of appraising change in psychic functioning has a subjective rather than objective basis. We refer here to the two-person psychotherapeutic situation in which the therapist participates subjectively in the child's emotional experience, even while observing and treating it. He perceives subtle changes in the child's emotional behavior by a close, disciplined awareness of changes in his own reciprocal emotions. If adequately exploited, such a method of observation can yield the most penetrating understanding of the child's behavior. Social scientists call this method "participant observation." Improvement, or the failure of improvement, can be accurately discerned by this means, particularly when such observation is supplemented and checked by additional information gained from other sources.

Theoretically, the treatment of children ought to offer greater possibilities of success than in the case of adults. In actuality, however, the treatment of children is less standardized than the therapy of adults, and is pursued with less confidence. Statistical reports of therapeutic results are few; failures often remain unadmitted. It is our impression that under conditions of present-day practice failures in the therapy of children are actually more common than in the treatment of adults. In one sense, this is an unexpected paradox, because the treatment of children basically should offer greater hope, and should open the path to the development of effective technics of prevention. Yet, in another sense, the large incidence of failures in the therapy of children is understandable for a variety of reasons: Scientific knowledge of child psychopathology is a recent development, the treatment of children presents greater complexity, is more difficult to execute skillfully, imposes a greater emotional strain on the therapist, and, last but not least, there is but limited power on the part of the therapist to effect the necessary changes in the family life in which the child functions and grows.

For purposes of organized presentation, we shall orient our expanded discussion of the bases of failure in the psychotherapy of children to the following issues:—(1) Environment (mainly, the family); (2) Age level (growth, maturation of personality); (3) Nature of disturbance (diagnostic evaluation, aim of therapy, choice of treatment); (4) Role of therapist (knowledge, skill, "countertransference"); (5) Setting of therapy (clinic, social agency, school, private practice).

THE RELATIONSHIP OF ENVIRONMENT TO TREATMENT

The child's total environment, of course, consists of a myriad of factors which we cannot hope to encompass within the confines of this paper. Of great importance are the dominant cultural patterns which mould and shape the character of family life. They affect the child's development significantly but only indirectly through the patterns of influence which other family members exercise on the child. From this point on, we shall arbitrarily restrict our consideration of the child's environment to family.

The family is a consanguinal unit, the members of which are bound together by emotional, social and economic ties. From the mental health point of view, the family must be studied and understood as a dynamic unity. The multiple interacting relationship patterns between various members, as well as the personality structure of each, must be clearly visualized.

Severe social pathology in the family as a whole is one of the first causes of failure. Deprivation in the economic sphere, illness, separation of the parents, divorce, or permanently broken families are frequent handicaps to success in child therapy. Even when this does not happen, chronic hostile tension between parents represents a continuous menace to the successful therapy of the child. The limited powers of the therapist to modify the total emotional atmosphere of family life, and the pathology of the parental relationship in particular, represent an ever-present threat of failure in the therapy of the child.

The dynamic balance of family life rests first with the interpersonal pattern which characterizes the parental relationship. Any pathology in this relationship will be instantaneously reflected in a disturbance of the child-parent pattern. The slightest lack in the love relationship, or a minor distortion in the sexual adaptation between the parents, casts an immediate shadow over the child's emotional development. The common expressions of this disturbance are either that the parent punishes the child in lieu of the other parent, or depends excessively on the love of the child in an effort to compensate for the lack in the parental relationship. This imposes an unwarranted emotional burden on the child, which precipitates pathologic behavior.

Conventional child guidance procedure tends to condense treatment of the child's environment to therapy of the mother. The fundamental closeness of child to mother is a recognized factor. Nevertheless, this is one example of oversimplification which sometimes leads to failure in treatment. If the therapy of the environment is to be child-oriented, the primary need is an intimate knowledge of the relationship between the parents, and the relationship of each parent to the child. The father's personality, as well as the mother's must be understood, and the emotional interaction between these two persons must be dealt with. Often, the father must receive treatment as well as the mother, if adequate results are to be achieved. It is necessary, of course, to recognize the practical obstacles which often stand in the way of such a program.

Nevertheless, the relevant issues must be clearly seen, if success in therapy is to be assured. Where the tenderness of the mother is deficient, it is not to be forgotten that the child often turns away from the mother to the father for the needed mothering.

While the emphasis on the child-mother relationship should not be an exclusive one, its fundamental role is self evident. From early infancy the child is part of the mother, and is separated from her only in a physical sense. In the first years, a disturbance in the child is merely a reaction to maternal attitudes. Later, the disturbed reaction patterns of the child become incorporated, and represent established intrapsychic personality patterns. Even after the fixation of established personality patterns takes place in the child, his vital dependence on the mother continues for many years. The dynamic situation at this later stage requires direct therapy of the child as well as treatment of the mother. Treatment of the mother alone, however, will relieve significant conflicts in the child, even though certain pathologic patterns have become established. Therapy for both mother and child is preferable, of course.

One conceptual issue which influences success or failure in therapy is the extent to which the therapy of the mother is oriented primarily to the pattern of disturbance in the mother-child relationship or is oriented to the pre-existing independent pathology in the mother's personality, which antedates her role in the child's life. While there is logically an overlap between the mother's original pathology and her currently disturbed attitude to the child, the therapy will be differently oriented in two alternative ways: either the therapist points his interest *first* to the disturbance in the maternal role with the child, or focuses primarily on the independent, original pathology in the mother's personality, regardless of the dynamic part the maternal attitude now plays in the child's life. This is a matter of choice of emphasis which must be carefully weighed in each case. In some instances, the experience of the birth and continued life of a particular child bears a specific causal relation to the disturbed attitude of the mother. Here the child occupies a central place in the mother's disturbance. In other cases, the child occupies a peripheral and relatively nonspecific role in the mother's disturbance. Here, the mother's pathology is deep seated and involves the child only incidentally. The therapy of the mother must be oriented accordingly.

The manner in which the mother subjectively distorts the facts of the child's disturbance, when presenting her request for treatment, provides significant clues. Too often, the child is the helpless pawn in the mother's conflict with the father. She may seek to exploit the child as a means of reproaching her husband. The mother may ask for help for the child when in reality she wants it for herself. The child is then brought for treatment for reasons other than the child's own need.

Illustrative Cases

Case 1

A mother came for the treatment of her five year old son because he was unmanageable and extremely jealous of his younger sister who was two and a half. The father was a lawyer and did not know of her plan for treatment. The following history was elicited:

There were just the two children in the family. The mother felt that the younger, the girl, was normal, outgoing and affectionate, while the boy always had been difficult to control. The disagreement between the parents as to how the children should be raised brought other difficulties. The mother complained that the father himself was a child and competed with the children instead of training and helping them. The father felt that the boy was like all boys and that there was nothing wrong. He felt that the girl was like the mother, slow and without charm. In bringing the boy for treatment without the knowledge of the father, who was against it, the mother sought to prove that the father was in the wrong. When she was told that the boy was in need of therapy she went home proudly to reveal her action and to tell her husband that she had been right, that the child should be treated. The father maintained his opposition and the child never did enter treatment. The very manner in which the mother handled the whole situation not only revealed her need to condemn her husband, but was instrumental in preventing the needed treatment.

In most cases, since the mother is usually the one who brings the child, it is possible to achieve earlier and easier access to her problem than to that of the father. Therefore, one may easily overlook the pathology in the father.

In other cases the mother is unable to separate her identity from that of the child. Some mothers exploit their concern over their child as a means of defense against their own personal disturbance; whereas others, competing with their own child, tend to obliterate entirely from consciousness the existence of the child, and focus with complete egocentricity on their own emotional need.

Case 2

Isa is eight and a half years old. She was brought by her mother because she was unmanageable, did not want to go to school and was enuretic. She was born out of wedlock. The mother gave a history of a depressive reaction during which time she would cling excessively to the child. The child felt frightened without the mother, particularly in the dark or during rainstorms. Her play fantasies revealed that she harbored strong death wishes against her mother. Early in treatment she established a strong transference to the therapist. The mother soon began to produce difficulties for the child's treatment. She became depressed and told the therapist that she was unable to bring the child for treatment. When a volunteer worker agreed to fetch Isa and bring her to the clinic the mother managed to leave the apartment with the child before the worker arrived. The mother finally confessed her fear that Isa did not love her any more, and subsequently discontinued treatment for the child. The therapist in charge of the case had been aware since the beginning of treatment that the mother herself was in need of therapy. She was therefore seen at a clinic where she had gone previously during her episodes of depression. In spite of this help she was unable to accept the improvement in Isa, and almost completely interrupted her own treatment.

The dynamic role which the child plays in the mother's pathology needs to be clearly defined. In our experience, it appears wise, initially at least, to orient the therapeutic experience with the mother to the emotional meaning the child has for her. In this sense the therapy of the mother is auxiliary and child-oriented, in keeping with the primary aim of curing the child.

In those cases where child and mother are independently treated by separate therapists, failure sometimes results from unsatisfactory integration of the two parallel treatment experiences.

Another frequent occurrence is that as a child improves in response to therapy, the parent becomes noticeably worse. One need not seek far for the explanation. Since mother and child form a psychic unit, any change in the child's behavior mobilizes more anxiety in the mother and forces a shift in her usual defense pattern. As a means of combating this anxiety, the parent sometimes tends to sabotage the child's treatment.

Case 3

A woman, aged 29, came for treatment. For several years she had suffered many fears; fears of being alone, traveling alone, choking sensations, and other phobias. In addition she gave a history that her older child, age five years, suffered from similar fears, had become overdependent on the mother and had developed a school phobia. For technical reasons, treatment was sought for the mother only. The younger child, a boy, was two and a half. During the mother's first pregnancy her father became seriously ill. After she gave birth she had an obsessive preoccupation with the thought that she had to choose between giving up her father or her child. She felt one of these would have to die. She decided in favor of her child. After her father's death, she developed her phobias and also homicidal fantasies concerning members of her family. During treatment her death wishes against the child became conscious. Subsequently, her phobia cleared up, and at the same time she reported that the child's phobias had also disappeared. The child had adopted fears which her mother was attempting to keep repressed. When the mother improved, the child improved also.

Failures in the therapy of children are frequently the consequence of failure properly to orient the treatment of the mother to the child's problems, failure of adequate correlation of the simultaneous treatment of child and mother, failure to anticipate mother's resistance and aggressive interference when the child begins to get better.

In passing, it is desirable to mention the importance of working therapeutically with mother surrogates. In certain sections of middle-class society the maternal function is in actuality a shared responsibility. The cultural pattern is such that the maternal responsibility is not assumed exclusively by the real mother, but is shared with or delegated to auxiliary mother persons, the grandparent, the aunt, the governess, maid or teacher.

In many instances, the shift of responsibility is determined by an emotional retreat from the maternal role, due to anxiety, immaturity, or forced by an actual illness in the mother. In any case, the therapist should be alert to the manner in which maternal functions are rejected or divided, and, if possible, work for the cooperation of these auxiliary mother persons. The daily security, the feeding and sleeping experiences of the child are subtly influenced by such factors. Occasionally, when the mother, for psychiatric or realistic reasons, is utterly deficient in executing the maternal responsibility, the therapist must cast about for the possibility of introducing a more adequate maternal personality into the child's daily life. If this is not possible and the social pathology is irretrievably bad, placement of the child with a foster family or therapeutic boarding school becomes a relevant consideration.

AGE LEVEL

The term "age level" is used here, not in the literal sense of age in years, but rather in terms of stages of maturation within which definite structures of personality and social adaptation prevail.

For purposes of clarity, let us define "growth" as biologically determined and as occurring relatively independently of environmental influence. Let us use the term "development" as denoting the influence of experience. The term "maturation" may then be used to represent both the effects of biologic growth and social experience on the progressive differentiation of personality structure.

It is necessary to consider first the arbitrary expectations in growth and behavior that are imposed on a child in relation to chronologic age. There are great individual variations. There are often discrepancies in relative growth in the form of contrasts between capacity for verbal, intellectual expression, and capacity for motor expression. Such standards of growth as we have are not fixed. In actuality, a child may function in some areas at a higher or lower level and still be within normal range. One must consider of first importance, however, any gross discrepancies that may exist between chronologic age and growth level. The failure to understand these discrepancies is most clearly demonstrated in the educational field.

The next logical issue is the correlation between stages of growth and specific disabilities.

Finally, one must measure discrepancies between growth level and maturation level. Total personality immaturity out of harmony with growth level is a serious sign, apart from the existence of specific symptoms. Evidences of fixation and regression of development must be clearly appraised.

In the process of maturation, the stages can be loosely delineated in terms of the following: (1) dependence, (2) sexual-social differentiation, and (3) establishment of personal identity.

The acquisition of a conviction of success and mastery reflects itself in a variety of behavior patterns at each of these differentiated levels.

Up to the age of one and a half or two years, the infant is not much of a social being. The satisfaction of primitive biologic needs in a setting of complete dependence represents the main issues of existence. Habit and conduct disorders leaning toward the establishment of pathologic character traits are the chief deviations. Educational and disciplinary influences begin then to play an increasing role in the child's early life, and the child's impulse patterns become modified by social factors, particularly through the child's need for affection and approval.

Instead of prescribing for the mother a detailed schedule of feeding, sleeping and training, which too often fails, it would be more helpful to investigate minutely the mother's inability to provide an acceptable training for the child. This is particularly important, for, as we have already mentioned, in early infancy the direct treatment of the child by the therapist is often not necessary. At this stage any existing pathology in the child can frequently be treated through the mother, although in selected cases even at this age direct therapy of the child is sometimes most effective.

Between two and five years, functions of conscience become gradually incorporated into the child's growing personality. During this transitional phase, neurotic traits represent the main pathologic offshoot. Finally, when the child enters the oedipal phase of differentiation, certain specific types of psychoneurosis emerge.

At later stages of maturation, when the child becomes more independent biologically and socially, has an internal conscience and a separate identity, direct therapy of the child becomes most profitable. At this stage transitional phobic behavior often appears. It is then incumbent upon the therapist to decide whether the disturbance is temporary, its extent, and whether it is still within the range of the normal development, or whether the behavior signifies a pathologic state which requires treatment. The early diagnosis of emotional conflicts in children is not only important for the relief of fear and for the facilitation of the task of current adaptation, but also is most essential for preventing distortions of later personality development.

The latency period brings a strengthening of conscience and social adaptation and, with it, a suppression of the early infantile sexual and aggressive impulses. The child becomes absorbed in social and intellectual achievement in extrafamilial activities. While the early latency period is considered by many therapists as the most promising one for treatment, the pre-adolescent child in the period of advanced latency is relatively difficult to treat.

Throughout, spontaneous changes in the child's behavior due to maturation itself should not be interpreted mistakenly as improvement due to psychotherapy. Sometimes the apparent disappearance of a phobia does not mean cure, but rather spells the emergence of a new symptom structure, due to the rechannelization of anxiety.

In the observation of the child during this more mature period, it is most important to keep in mind the fact that a phobia or a destructive behavior pattern often leads the parents and the child to seek psychiatric help, while other patterns such as overorderliness, and submissiveness are often accepted and even praised by parents and teachers in spite of the fact that they may signify deep-seated distortion of personality. The following case illustrates the point.

Illustrative Case 4

A twelve year old boy was brought for consultation because of his constant provocative behavior toward his parents and his younger sister, and his often expressed wish to be sent away from home.

The history showed that when he was three and a half years he had had many fears: he had been afraid of the dark, and of animals hiding under his bed; he also had become a stammerer. Later, at four and a half, a physician was consulted who prescribed sedatives and assured the parents that the boy would outgrow his difficulties. By the time he was six, most of the symptoms had disappeared, and the child began to be preoccupied with science. The parents were pleased. When there was no interference on their parts, and he was allowed to follow his new interests, the relationships within the family were harmonious. His interests included biology, and cosmic phenomena. The parents and teachers encouraged him. Later he added dissection to his field of endeavor and won several prizes in school for this. When he reached eleven, he became more irritable, was inclined to stay at home alone, developed shyness, and when he was asked to join a group would refuse, especially if it meant being in the presence of girls. He withdrew completely from any outdoor activity, stayed by himself all the time except when he was at school. When approached by any member of the family, he would flare up and react violently. He was obviously unhappy and often expressed it in his wish to leave his home and parents, and go to a boarding school.

Here we can see that the phobic reaction subsided and that in its place an abnormal obsessive preoccupation with science developed, which helped him to control his fears. The parents, teacher and physician had surmised mistakenly that he had successfully overcome his disturbance, until later in puberty when the difficulties were reactivated.

As pointed out in the foregoing case, puberty often reactivates earlier conflicts which are related significantly to sexual differentiation and the establishment of personal identity. Failure of treatment at this period occurs because these manifestations are considered a disturbance endemic to puberty rather than a re-expression of a conflict which had been latent until this time. Another reason for failure is the lack of a specific technic of treatment which takes into account the unique structure of the child's personality at that age level.

NATURE OF THE DISTURBANCE, AIM OF THERAPY AND CHOICE OF TREATMENT

It is impossible to do more than touch on some aspects of the problem of failure as related to specific disabilities, the formulation of treatment aim and choice of treatment method. Frequent causes of failure are inaccuracies of clinical diagnosis, the failure to appraise total personality function, the lack of clear-cut therapeutic aim, and improper choice of treatment. We shall briefly mention the following pathologic entities: (1) schizophrenia; (2) psychopathic personality; (3) primary behavior disorder; (4) psychoneurosis. We shall omit consideration of emotional disturbances secondary to organic pathology.

Schizophrenia in Childhood

We do not need to enter here the controversy as to the validity of the diagnosis of "schizophrenia in childhood." We believe the evidence for the existence of such conditions is affirmative.

Failure in therapy stems from three major sources: (1) the lack of understanding of the cause of the disease; (2) the lack of specific therapy; (3) the insufficiency of skill in recognizing the condition in its early manifestations.

Up to the present time a specific psychotherapeutic approach is still to be found; the treatment technic with children is not even comparable with the therapy of schizophrenia in adult life. Yet, enough knowledge is available to make it clear that the general management of the problem must be quite different from that of other disabilities. Failure in the treatment of this condition derives both from insufficient knowledge and the misapplication of treatment technics. The aim should be to prevent the withdrawal from interpersonal reality, and to minimize the child's dependence on autistic fantasy for pleasure.

These children seem to need actual continuous contact with an ever-loving mother or mother-substitute in order to keep in contact with reality. Treatment, therefore, should attempt to establish and preserve such a relationship; in such conditions, the original pattern of child-mother dependence must be perpetuated for years. The treatment of choice is such "individual" therapy. Controlled play therapy or group therapy does not seem to be effective, except as adjuvants.

Very often the mothers of schizophrenic children are either schizophrenic themselves or otherwise are unable to offer such a continuous accepting attitude to the child. Too often the therapist fails because he tries to understand the child's disability purely on the basis of the mother's rejection instead of giving full recognition to the difficulties these mothers encounter due to the child's basic pathology. Frequently, too, these children are kept in a rejecting environment, and valuable time is lost, while the mother makes a futile struggle to understand the difficulties exclusively through a search of her emotional relationship to the child.

Illustrative Case 5

A mother came for treatment of her nine year old son. She impressed the physician immediately as a severely disturbed person, and soon revealed that she had intense fears lest she might lose control of herself and become mentally ill. In the course of study, it was found that she had suffered from a disturbance during adolescence, which probably had represented a psychotic episode. She described her child as being different from other children. "He does not like to play with children; he is interested in astrology and cosmic rays instead. In school, he does not live up to his intelligence capacity; he daydreams; he is not interested in listening to the teachers." When the school had complained about his behavior about one and one-half years previously, he had been examined by a psychiatrist, who believed that he suffered from an anxiety neurosis. Treatment appropriate to this incorrect diagnosis had been suggested. The mother was seen on a regular schedule. She felt she was the one cause of her son's trouble, which increased the tension between them. When the child was seen, he was found to be tall, slender, and he showed poor motor coordination. He heard voices and had numerous somatic delusions. His preoccupation with fantasy replaced most of real experiences. The diagnosis of schizophrenia was clear. Placement of the child was recommended, since the mother was too ill mentally to play the necessary part in the boy's treatment.

Psychopathic Personality

Here, again, failure in treatment is largely based on lack of understanding of the cause of the underlying disturbance as well as the absence of a specific treatment technic. We do not restrict this diagnosis to cases with only constitutional disturbance, but include those which are the product of environmental pathology. Obviously, it is of extreme importance to diagnose this picture as early as possible, but this purpose is often foiled because differential diagnostic criteria are not sharply enough formulated to enable an early diagnosis.

In early childhood the symptom picture is sometimes indistinguishable from the manifestations of severe primary behavior disorders. The salient dynamic characteristics of this condition are a defect of rapport, a limited capacity for identification, a disturbance of the affective evaluation of social qualities, an inadequate moral reaction, a defective perception of reality; additional characteristics are egocentricity, impulsivity and omnipotent power drives. These qualities lead to antisocial and delinquent behavior.

The treatment should aim at providing the child with an environment which will allow and promote identification with adults. For such children, a plan of "total treatment" is necessary. This implies a therapeutic control of the social reality in which the child grows.

Most often, the pathology of the family is severe, and an early transfer to a "treatment home" is important. Here, the therapeutic effort is often endangered because the children do not stay long enough to promote firm identification with parent-surrogates. Too often, the duration of such institutional experience is determined by the penal code rather than by therapeutic principles. Frequently, delinquent children are sent back into the home or institution which contributed to the cause of disturbance. The creation of special treatment "homes" for these children, or cottages organized around a parental unit, should certainly be considered. Most institutions do not provide for such possibilities. Foster parents are changed too rapidly. Present day institutions which function inadequately not only fail to correct psychopathic character traits but may even fixate or make such conditions worse. The reports of successful individual therapy are very rare. Even with the best of treatment, the eventual outcome remains uncertain.

Primary Behavior Disorder

Behavior disorders differ in structure in relation to age level, maturation level, and the quality of the environment. Such disorders represent conflict between the child and his environment. They begin as reactions to rejection and frustration by the parents. At the reactive level, they are readily modifiable. When they persist over a period of years, however, the pattern of clash with the persons in the environment becomes firmly established and eventuates in specific forms of disordered character. The hostility reactions constitute a fixed aspect of the social maladaptation. This is a disturbance in which the child's personality has not matured to the point of having the capacity to love.

In the early stages, treatment of the mother alone is often a sufficient measure for resolving the child's disorder. At times a change in environment may be indicated, at least for part of the day. Emotional re-education in a therapeutic nursery or group therapy may produce the desired therapeutic change.

In the more difficult cases, individual psychotherapy may be indicated. In this relationship the child tests out the parent-surrogate by expressing his feeling of rejection, loss of love, his hate, and fear of retaliation. The essential narcissism of these children, their defensive hostility, and their incapacity for a genuine love attachment presents the greatest challenge to the therapist. Infinite patience is required. The struggle is finally won if the child gives up his destructive attitude and is willing to comply in order to win the affection and approval of the therapist. It is his task to make such a step in motivation possible. He has to provide in his relationship to the child an experience which will be devoid of the quality of danger which the real parent represented to the child.

Psychoneurosis

This condition implies the presence of specific psychopathologic symptoms related to chronic, unresolved unconscious conflicts. Always there is disturbance in the child's emotional relationship with the parents. Such a condition implies, in contrast to the primary behavior disorder, maturation of the child's personality to a point where the child has some capacity for love of other persons.

This condition requires direct psychotherapy of the child as well as of the parent. Failures in psychotherapy here are again due to inadequate diagnosis, failure of efforts to change the child's environment, or modify parental attitudes, and, finally, insufficient skill in therapeutic technic.

The success or failure of the treatment will in addition depend on the type of defense pattern which characterizes the particular form of the neurosis. Children who suffer from acute anxiety symptoms are more eager to come for treatment. They and their parents are aware of the disability and cooperate more readily with the therapist. The treatment is usually more successful. It is different with obsessive-compulsive disorders, which characteristically minimize consciousness of conflict and anxiety. Often, in these conditions awareness of suffering is insufficient, and the pathology either remains unrecognized by the parent, or fails to provide incentive for treatment. The same is true, often, of hypochondriacal syndromes, which are rationalized as concern over real illness. In general, therapeutic access is less possible for those children whose anxiety is concealed behind defense patterns which receive social sanction, such as passive, submissive attitudes, cleanliness, etc. Reports from group therapists suggest that the children with such character problems profit by group therapy.

EVALUATIONS OF THE TOTAL FUNCTIONS OF PERSONALITY

We have already underlined the importance of the concept of "total diagnosis." Quite apart from the detection of specific psychiatric disabilities, it is necessary to evaluate the total functions of personality in a specific social setting. The progress of the patient in therapy has to be measured by periodic reappraisals. One contributing cause for failure in therapy is the carelessness and incompleteness of such appraisals. This is especially pertinent in follow-up studies of the results of therapy. The total performance of the child must be measured in the more significant test situations: the home and family, the school, the neighborhood, the therapeutic situation. The following criteria can be used for this purpose.

1. *Attitude toward Self*
   - egocentricity (self absorption, emotional isolation, egotism)
   - concept of self (adequate or inadequate; self esteem, high or low; self-debasement or aggrandizement)
   - body image (weak or strong; intact or defective; motor coordination good or poor)
   - sexual identity (masculine or feminine)
   - discrepancy between aspiration and achievement.
2. *Self-Control*
   - impulsiveness
   - conscious inhibition
   - unconscious inhibition (repression)
   - guilt tendency (balance between destructive and self-destructive tendencies, depression)
3. *Organization of Affects*
   - spontaneity
   - richness and depth
   - flexibility
   - appropriateness
   - range of emotional interest; capacity for rapport
4. *Adaptation to Reality*
   - assimilation
   - mastery, special skills
   - denial
   - distortion
5. *Attitude toward Other Persons*
   - capacity for relationship (none, partial, total)
6. *Characteristic Defenses against Anxiety*
   - sublimation
   - avoidance
   - opposition
   - denial
   - constriction
   - rationalization
   - reaction formation
   - repression
   - projection
   - introjection

7. *Specific Psychiatric Symptoms*

The use of such general criteria enables one to appraise changes in function and to mark out discrepancies between growth and maturation levels. It is also helpful in distinguishing spontaneous changes due to growth from those maturational changes which are actually produced by psychotherapy.

ROLE OF THE THERAPIST

From the foregoing discussion it must be clear that the role of the child therapist is quite distinct from that of the adult therapist. The child therapist must assume greater responsibility and participate more actively in the child's emotional experience. In part, he must be a real parent person; he must give actual security, and offer direct gratification to the child's needs. He must allow release of infantile aggression, though within definitely prescribed limits. He conducts the relationship between child and therapist largely on a nonverbal level; emotional drives are "acted out," dramatized in play. He has an educational as well as therapeutic role. He does not deal with a "transference neurosis" as in adult psychoanalysis. He interprets the child's real experience with other significant persons, as well as with himself. Above all, the therapist must have the art of using his own personality in the service of releasing the child's conflicts and fear. In this connection it is imperative that the therapist be without any disturbing conflict of his own. Because of a child's natural keenness in perceiving the true intentions of the adult towards him, emotional blind spots and countertransference difficulties in the therapist will seriously endanger the therapy.

The most dramatic failures in child therapy occur in this context. The therapist may overidentify with the child. This often represents the original subjective motivation for becoming a child therapist. In so doing, he may show an inordinate hostility to the child's mother. He may have a need to blame and scold her. Such child therapists have sometimes been called facetiously, "mother killers." Such attitudes are reprehensible and may easily cause failure of the child's therapy. If the therapist attacks the mother, he may lose the child as a patient; the mother, feeling menaced and guilty, may displace her aggression from therapist to child, or she may otherwise encourage the child's resistance to therapy. As trite as it may seem, it is necessary to re-emphasize one point: for the child's therapy to succeed, the mother must receive the same acceptance and emotional support as the child; otherwise, she is apt to be jealous of the child, and resist the treatment.

In another direction, the therapist, by overidentifying with the child, may derive a vicarious pleasure from the child's destructiveness. This will interfere with treatment, too. The therapist may unconsciously compete with the child, as does the mother. The effect of this, too, would be harmful. He may overidentify with the parent's distress, and turn hostile to the child; or he may too strongly need the approval of the parents, and try in inappropriate ways to control the child's aggression. At the opposite pole, he may be too masochistic, allowing the child to dominate the situation or make an attack on the therapist's person, and so fail to introduce the necessary realistic restraints. Any unconscious assumption of omnipotent attitudes on the therapist's part, whether in terms of capacity to give or to control, will also threaten the success of the therapy.

To insure against failure the therapist must have full knowledge of the child's environment as well as of the child. He must have working contact, therefore, with the parents, school, and other aspects of the child's daily reality.

Naturally, the systematic professional training and the individual skill of the therapist are of the utmost importance. Rigorous training in the psychodynamics of child development and psychopathology is indispensable. Without entering the broad problems involving the training of child therapists, we might emphasize in passing the necessity for more comprehensive teaching of child psychiatry as part of the general curriculum for training of psychiatrists and psychoanalysts.

The question arises also as to whether in this field sufficient study is made of the extrapsychic factors, the social and cultural factors influencing family life.

But, child therapy is an art as well as a science, and in the final analysis, it is the individual endowment which makes a good or bad therapist.

THE SETTING FOR CHILD THERAPY

Up to the present, in our opinion, too little consideration has been given to the question of the setting in which child therapy is done. The criteria which determine therapeutic aim and method for children's problems are multiple and complex. All facets of the problem need to be carefully evaluated, even if the therapist sees fit deliberately to set up a limited goal and restrict his efforts to one part of the problem. Ideally, at least, the setting should provide for the therapy both of the environment and the child, with facilities for a controlled environmental experience, for individual and group treatment, in accordance with individual need. This, in our sense, is provision for "total treatment." Child analysis, by itself, is not enough. We believe that the treatment of parents, oriented to the child's disturbance, should be adequately provided in the same setting. Such treatment can be superficial or deep, in accordance with need. It may be individual, or group therapy, or both. This means a treatment center for children. At the preschool level, a therapeutic nursery is vital to the task. In such a nursery, the mother can profit through the educational influence of the nursery teachers. Mothers need a feeling of belonging as much as the children. A treatment center can answer this need. To a lesser extent, similar considerations hold for treatment of fathers.

At the school age level, the organization and program of a treatment center would necessarily be somewhat different but the same basic principles apply. An extended aim of such centers should be the constructive modification of the pattern of family life as a whole in the interest of preventing mental ill health in growing children.

Obviously, such centers providing a plan of "total treatment" offer rich opportunities for research and training of personnel in this most basic section of psychiatry.

In summary, let us repeat that failure of child therapy is determined by misunderstanding or misapplication of some aspects of the following component factors: clinical psychopathology, total personality function, social pathology, the individual therapy, the setting of therapy.

CHAPTER 4

Psychoanalytic Principles in a Mental Health Clinic for the Preschool Child and His Family

A mental health clinic for the preschool child and his family would, at first glance, appear to be the ideal setting for putting into actual practice some basic principles in psychoanalysis. The very nature of the undertaking provides a powerful lure—the possibility of evolving effective techniques for the prevention of mental illness. This is the daydream which excites the imagination of mental hygiene practitioners the world over. Translations of such a phantasy into reality might, at first blush, appear to be feasible; and with bold, creative strokes of planning, it might even appear easy, as deceptively easy perhaps as that age-old dream of transforming common metals into gold in the bathtub. But although, in the long view, the obstacles to such an achievement may not prove insuperable, in the present stage of knowledge of human conflict and suffering they are certainly of mountainous proportions.

Reprinted with permission from *Psychiatry: Journal for the Study of Interpersonal Processes*, February 1956, Vol. 19, No. 1, 63-64, 68-76.

The psychoanalytic principles of childhood causation of mental and emotional illness, the plasticity of the young child's personality, and the potential which a clinic setting could offer for early detection and early treatment of illnesses—all these suggest the importance of such a venture. But among the major problems as yet unsolved are the implementation of psychoanalytic concepts in a broad mental health program dealing with child-parent relations and family life as a whole, and the merging of psychodynamic insights with the principles of social science and child education.

There is little precedent for such grandiose enterprises. Previous undertakings in this direction have been few in number and modest in their goals, and have represented piecemeal efforts rather than a comprehensive plan. There is some background of early attempts to employ psychoanalytic principles in programs of nursery education in Vienna; there is the pioneering work of Anna Freud and Dorothy Burlingham at the Hampstead Nurseries in London; and there is the development of the Children's Center in Boston. From this work has come some progress in the fields of child guidance, child psychotherapy, and analytically oriented pedagogy. In the main, however, the attempt to implement the insights of psychoanalysis systematically in a community mental health clinic for the preschool child and his family is a new kind of venture, an exploratory thrust into the virgin territory of what might be termed preventive psychoanalysis.

The establishment of the Council Child Development Center in New York City in 1946 represented an experimental venture of this sort. The difficulties experienced in planning the Center were many. No ready-made model for the design of a mental health clinic for the preschool child and his family was available. Nor was there a model for an integrated mental health approach to the family as a group. Finally, there was little precedent for the application of psychoanalytic concepts to the specific tasks of such a clinic, and for this aspect of the undertaking, those responsible for designing the clinic[1] had to start almost *de novo*. Was this a fool's errand we had embarked upon, a mission to be shunned by wiser folk? Perhaps. Yet, now and again, it is the fool who stumbles upon some useful discovery.

I shall discuss here the Center's experiences in attempting to integrate psychoanalytic thought into its program. In so doing, I shall allude to some of its trials and tribulations, its complex problems—many still unsolved—and its inevitable discouragements, but also to some indications of positive progress toward its goal. In the main, this paper proposes to raise problems, rather than give answers.

(In the next portion of the paper, Ackerman reviews the establishment of the C.C.D.C. as a community clinic designed to address the developmental problems of children from both a psychoanalytic [that is, individual-oriented] and family [environment-oriented] viewpoint. The elements in the program are educational [daily nursery school] and therapeutic. In the latter category are consultations within the nursery and a full range of individual and group psychoanalytic services for parents and children. Family therapy is mentioned here under the concept of "therapy for the environment"; in the early 1950s Ackerman was just beginning to realize the indissolubility of child and family as a clinical entity.)

From Freud himself, we inherited something of a paradox. Freud recognized the dependence of a child's emotional and social development on the care, affection, and discipline of his parents. Yet he placed his observations in a theoretical frame of biological causation. He described the unfolding of the child's behavior, not in terms of family influence, but in terms of phylogenesis. In this context, all the vicissitudes of a child's adaptation had to be squeezed into the mold of instinctual expression, mainly determined by heredity. What, then, is the role of the child's environment, the family? Though recognizing environmental influences, Freud provided virtually no place for them in his libido theory. He tended to stereotype the roles of parents and could not then visualize the cultural patterns which shape conflict in parental attitudes, family interaction, and childrearing.

At the Center, where the psychoanalysts faced the task of relating child to parent, parent to family, family to community, were we to begin with the child and move from there to the family group and community, or start with the family group and move from there back to the child? Should we, like Freud, stress the biologically determined evolution of instincts in the child, or should we focus on the problems of social adaptation? Should we place the primary emphasis on the inner or the outer life of the child, the "individuality" of the child or the interactional patterns within the family? How could we integrate individual and group dynamics? In effect, in confronting the problem of child, parent, family, and community, the choice was really one of direction—whether to move mainly from inside outwards, from the child to the environment, or from outside inwards, from the environment to the child.

In facing these problems, if we thought alike, unity of conceptualization among the staff might facilitate our task. If we thought differently, a richer interaction of experience and opinion might be achieved. A price tag was attached to each of these preferences. In actuality, this dilemma turned out to be more hypothetical than

[1]The author, then Chief Psychiatrist of the Jewish Board of Guardians; Herschel Alt, Director of the Jewish Board of Guardians; and Fredrika Neumann, Case Consultant of the Jewish Board of Guardians.

real. While there are analytic schools which carry the flag for major differences of theory, there are few individual analysts who think precisely alike on these basic questions. Each analyst weighs the evidence in his own way, integrates his personal experience and training in a unique manner, and orients himself to the issues of psychoanalytic theory accordingly. I, for one, as the Director of the Center during its early years, preferred to preserve the growth potential inherent in an interchange of different concepts, and was willing to face some jeopardy to the unity of staff thinking. I merely hoped that we might avoid psychoanalysts with closed minds; but even in this, we were not altogether successful. We must face it: psychoanalysts are not yet agreed as to the basic determinants of personality development, not to speak of the subtler nuances of behavior theory. Crucial to the whole unanswered problem is the relation of the dynamics of the individual to the dynamics of group behavior.

As was to be expected, staff discussions produced diverse convictions on the proper place of psychoanalytic concepts in the various phases and levels of the clinic program. Before very long, it became clear that each analyst on the staff was riding a particular hobbyhorse. Each had his own area of preferred interest and special competence, and each demanded a place in the sun. The "pure child analyst" vigorously asserted her special sphere, the work with those children who were receiving intensive psychotherapy, the equivalent of child analysis. The more classically minded analysts "listened with the third ear," paid special attention to the patient's phantasy life, his unconscious conflicts, and the technical details of psychoanalytic process, but tended to neglect the realities of the patient's day-to-day life situation. Another analyst asserted a special interest in the integration of the insights of child analysis with the proven principles of nursery education. Another emphasized the need for prolonged analytically oriented therapy of the parents. Still another reiterated over and over the importance of studying the emerging ego patterns of the child and relating these to the group dynamics of the family.

Throughout these discussions there was the tendency to assign prejudicial priority to this, that, or the other phase of psychoanalytic theory, to this, that, or the other phase of the Center's mental health program. Thus there was a problem as to which of these positions was right, if any. And beyond all this, there was the problem of making room for the data of the social sciences, of somehow finding a means for integrating the biological and social factors in causation. To achieve this, the analysts needed to be welded into a cooperating group, able to communicate with each other and capable of integrating their contribution with that of the social scientists. This was no easy path. We traversed it with considerable hardship, but with some eventual success.

Various constructive forces were at play: scientific curiosity, empathy with child and family, the fascination of preventive health work, the desire to prove the worth of this project in the eyes of the community. But also at play were the vested interests of some analysts, their competitiveness, their egocentric preoccupation with highly specialized phases of the problem, their inadequate conception of the interaction of individual and group, their omnipotent-mindedness, their urge to treat phenomena they had not yet clearly defined. A certain inertia was apparent; some of the analysts were so specialized, so concentrated on partial phenomena of personality, that they tended to resist the expansion of view so vital to a broadly conceived mental health program for young children and their families.

In retrospect it is apparent that none of us knew exactly where to begin. Should we focus first on the individual or on the group? On the pathology of individual members of the family or on the pathology of family relationships? Actually, this misstates the problem. The question is not so much where to begin, but rather how best to integrate the several interrelated levels of an essentially unified program—how best to fuse knowledge of intra-and extra-personality processes, real and unreal experience, conscious and unconscious conflict. Clearly, what is needed here is an integration of the social and psychological determinants of behavior.

Looking back on the first phase of this clinic experiment, it is clear that there was a continuous struggle between those members of the professional staff who placed the prior emphasis on the interactional phenomena of the family and those who were primarily concerned with their specialized interest in the mechanisms of intrapsychic pathology. Here the issue is plain. Psychoanalysts, or at least too many of them, continue to be plagued by a needless and wrong kind of question: Are the basic determinants of behavior biological or social? Once and for all, the ghost should be buried. The dilemma is a false one. From the beginning, all behavior is biosocial.

But we had to make a start somewhere—child, mother, or family as a whole. Because we were better equipped with knowledge and techniques for dealing with individual personality than with interpersonal relations in family life, we gravitated first to the sphere of greater familiarity, the individual approach to family members. And because this was a child development center, we started with the personality of the child and moved from there to the mother, to the parental relationship, and to the family as a whole.[2] My discussion will therefore be organized in this way.

PSYCHOTHERAPY OF THE CHILD

There was general agreement that the psychotherapy of the child could not be conceived of as standing alone, that it should be continuously correlated with procedures dealing with child-mother interaction, with psychotherapy of the parents, and with procedures aimed at study and treatment of the family as a group, both social and psychological. Individual psychotherapy for the child was not prescribed immediately but only after a variably extended period of exploration and evaluation of the entire family group and direct observation of child and parent in the nursery. Direct psychotherapy of the child was prescribed only when there was clear evidence that pathological conflict had already become internalized within the child's personality. Where the pathology was severe, the child received three therapeutic sessions per week; where less severe, one or two sessions per week. Therapy was conducted both by analysts and by analytically trained social workers. In either case it was supervised by experienced teaching analysts.

Was it legitimate to call our individual psychotherapy of the child "child analysis"? In one sense this might be answered in the affirmative for those children who were receiving intensive psychotherapy three times per week under analytic supervision. This procedure covered roughly one-third of our child population. But the question whether this is child analysis is in the final view one of definition. There is as yet no clear consensus as to what constitutes child analysis. I have yet to see a definition of child analysis, or an attempt to distinguish child psychoanalysis from psychoanalytically oriented child psychotherapy, which does not contain arbitrary elements.

The following statement from the *Bulletin of the American Psychoanalytic Association* will illustrate my point:

> . . . the core of analytic treatment of a child consists of
>
> 1. the systematic investigation of
>   a. unconscious, or as yet unverbalized pathogenic association between certain facts, phantasies and affects.
>   b. defense mechanisms developed or made rigid in the attempt to deal with the association.
> 2. the systematic selective communication to the child of the results of such investigation.
> 3. the systematic follow-up which investigates secondary phantasies, affects and defenses resulting from treatment.

This is to continue till the child's ego mastery has become more adequate for his age and can be expected not only to weather the next maturational crisis but also to exploit its potentialities.[3]

By contrast, the *Bulletin* states:

> Psychoanalytically oriented psychotherapy, although it utilizes the unconscious productions of children, is essentially a manipulative and focus type of therapy aimed at the solution of immediate conflict. It attacks a specific problem. No deep systematic in-

[2]With present knowledge, it is logical to argue for an emphasis in the opposite direction—namely, to begin with the family as a unit and move from there to evaluation of the child.

[3]Conclusions reached at the Washington meeting and accepted by the Committee for Psychoanalysis in Childhood and Adolescence, as stated in the *Bull. Amer. Psychoanal. Assn.* (1949) 5:34.

vestigation of the unconscious phantasies is undertaken. Interpretation is confined to the preconscious productions. Re-education plays a large part in the treatment situation as well as the active use of the environment to provide acceptable outlets for the sublimation of the instinctual forces.

Only in psychoanalysis is there genetic investigation and interpretation of unconscious phantasies together with analysis of the ego defenses.[4]

Just how valid is this differentiation? In treatment which is oriented to the needs of the child, rather than to a predetermined concept of technique, can one separate the past from the present, can one concentrate on ontogenesis without consideration of current conflict? Is not the main concern those elements of past experience which continue to be expressed in present behavior, although no longer adaptively appropriate? Furthermore, is it possible to psychoanalyze a child without recourse to educational influence?

Finally, appended to this definition of child analysis, there is the casual statement, "Contact with parents is necessary so that the child can preserve the treatment gains." This is a most revealing statement. Its connotations must inevitably dispel any illusion that removal of pathological units in the child's personality through analysis will automatically result in healthy personality growth. The outcome depends heavily on what is done concomitantly to mitigate the pathogenic factors in the child's environment.

I cannot avoid the conviction that this distinction between child psychoanalysis and child psychotherapy represents a prejudiced evaluation, that the sharp dissociation of the two methods as here defined is artificial, and, further, that the definition of the process of child analysis begs the question of the child's interaction and essential unity with his personal environment. As I see it, the final qualifying statement—that contact with parents is necessary to preserve treatment gains—invalidates the alleged distinctions.

To be sure, there are differences in techniques. There are partial devices suited for access to surface conflict in the child's psyche and other techniques suited for access to deep conflicts. But the utilization of the one or the other or both should be determined primarily by the nature of the child's psychic needs as of a given time; the selection of treatment technique should not be based on a therapist's narcissistic preoccupation with his own area of technical competence. What the child needs, rather than what a therapist has learned to do technically, should dictate the technique applied.

At the Child Development Center there should be no concern with the label attached to the therapeutic work with children. It seems idle and pointless quibbling to argue, Is this or is this not child analysis? It is enough to say that the psychotherapy of children at the Center is psychoanalytically founded, that it uses psychoanalytic principles of investigation of child development. In this sense the therapy of children having sessions three times a week is no more psychoanalytic than the therapy of those having one session a week. The issue need not be, Do we or do we not conform religiously to this or that arbitrary definition of child analysis? It is, rather, Are we using the fruits of Freud's pioneer studies to discover more facts about the psychodynamics of child development? Can we join useful techniques of study and treatment of children with study and treatment of parents and families toward building a theoretical frame for a mental health program aimed at prevention?

This is the objective which the Center sets for its work. To pursue this objective, it is necessary to come to grips with the question: What parts of psychoanalytic theory are useful as stepping stones for the acquisition of new knowledge; what parts fail to find validation in our studies and need to be modified as a basis for further investigative work?

PARENTAL THERAPY

By and large the therapy of the child proved to be a less complex task than the therapy of the parents or the attempts to modify the group dynamics of family relationships. It is one thing to determine the emotional needs of a child. It is quite another to make over a set of parents so that they can meet these needs. This is decidedly the more arduous task. Therapy of the parents of a disturbed child has never been adequately conceptualized by psychoanalysis.

[4]This definition was added by Dr. Lydia G. Dawes of the Boston Regional Committee.

By definition, this is the therapy of an adult person in a special family role, that of parent. Is there a therapy for a parental role, as distinct from the total therapy of a person who happens also to be a parent? To what extent is it possible to establish a preferential focus on those operations of personality expressed in the execution of the parental responsibilities—to concentrate on the specific conflicts intrinsic to this family role? To what extent must the sphere of therapeutic concern extend to the total functions of personality, to overlapping conflicts in the marital role, to conflicts in relations with grandparents, and the like?

These are difficult questions, mostly unanswered as yet. Nevertheless, the problems posed by therapy of a parent are not identical with that posed by the therapy of a whole person. In the therapy of a person fulfilling a family role, recognition must be given to the basic interdependence and reciprocity of family roles. This is the case whether the economy of personality is such that major conflict and anxiety are linked to the role of parent or mainly associated with the sexual or marital role. The dynamic and therapeutic implications are, of course, quite different where major conflict is tied to extra-familial occupational roles. Clinically, in this respect, one finds all kinds of permutations and combinations. This is a phase of the broader problem of conflict-ridden and conflict-free areas of personality functioning; it is also a phase of the problem of the dynamic relations of family role and personality structure.

In principle, the Center is prepared to involve all parents of disturbed children in an appropriate form of psychotherapy. Some, on a selected basis, receive group therapy as a supplement to individual therapy. However, there are tremendous variations in the readiness of parents for a therapeutic experience. Some come with an avid hunger for it. Others, while in need of it, are by no means emotionally prepared for it. In these cases, contact is initiated on a guidance and educational basis, and individual psychotherapy is deferred until the parent is judged ready. Usually, parents have therapeutic sessions once or twice a week; occasionally, in critical situations, three times a week.

Clearly, by procedural standards, this is not psychoanalytic therapy; the therapy is conducted in face-to-face relations; there is no couch technique; the appointments are less frequent. The therapy is primarily oriented to the child's needs and to the parents' role as parents, not to the total functioning of personality. Nevertheless, by dynamic standards, it may be valid to speak of this as psychoanalytically oriented therapy. The question is, Where does one draw the line between treating disturbances in parental role and treating total personality? Can the behavior exhibited in the parental role be artificially separated from that shown in other roles? Can the parental role be dissociated from the marital role, from the role as companion, from the work role? No, but in a special therapy of this sort, the therapist can establish certain priorities. And the priorities he establishes must vary from one case to the next. A high degree of individualization and flexibility of technique is called for when one uses psychoanalytic concepts in a specialized psychotherapeutic task. In some instances, disturbances in the parental role are specifically related to the dynamics of rejection of parenthood. In others, they are nonspecific and are secondary elaborations of primary conflict in another area—marital conflict, specific sexual anxieties, or conflict arising out of tension in a work role. These questions as to where the primary conflict lies are responsible for special problems in the psychotherapy of a parent.

One parent discusses, to the exclusion of all else, her relations with her child. She utilizes her problems with the child as an obsessional defense against the disclosure of sexual failure with her husband. Another quickly forgets the child and talks of nothing but her dissatisfaction with her husband. Some mothers tend to balk and resist therapeutic influence, insisting that it is the father who should be in therapy, that it is his attitude that needs to be changed. Such complaints are not always merely projections of guilt; often there is a valid core in them. These are some samples of the difficulties encountered in the attempt to give psychotherapy to parents.

It must be apparent that some of the Center's most complex problems emerge from its orientation to interaction patterns in the family and emotional functioning in a particular family role. Basically, certain differences result from the fact that the analyst is oriented to the particular patient, while a mental health clinic is oriented to the child-parent unit, to male and female parental roles, and to the group dynamics of family life.

Early in its career the Center undertook an experimental trial of group psychotherapy for parents. In the child guidance field generally, there has been a considerable lag in the therapeutic contact with the fathers of disturbed children. We attempted to counteract this by providing individual psychotherapy for some fathers, where the need was critical; but this covered only a small fraction of our paternal population.

We attempted group therapy with several conditions in mind: our professional resources could not provide individual psychotherapy for each mother and each father; we wished to test certain hypotheses with regard to the usefulness of group therapy when used alone and when used as a supplement to individual therapy; also, we wished to test certain hypotheses as to the possibility of access to interpersonal disturbances through group therapy. We conducted a group for mothers, a group for fathers, and also planned a group for selected marital couples. These experiments do not yet permit the full reporting of results.

A number of our parents expressed in a variety of ways their need for a more direct therapeutic approach to disturbances of the parental relationship. Some mothers felt that they could carry out their maternal functions more effectively if the fathers gave them a better quality of emotional support; also, they accused the fathers of failing to assert their paternal authority. Some fathers, in turn, complained that the child and mother receive special attention but the father feels like the forgotten man. He does not like being left out in the cold. In group therapy with couples we hoped to test out possibilities of therapy of interpersonal disturbances between husband and wife.

One point worthy of emphasis was the parents' own enthusiasm for group psychotherapy. Some showed intense interest and expressed unequivocal conviction as to its value. Group psychotherapy was applied to parents on a selective basis. There were instances where it seemed contraindicated. Some forms of psychotic personalities did not do well in a parents' group because of the depth of their suspiciousness and their tendency to distort interpersonal events. Psychopathic personalities were excluded, as were also those types of neurotics in whom the tendency to act out was too strong.

The psychodynamics of group psychotherapy are not well understood. Partly for this reason, it is widely misconceived and is suspected by some as being "wild" therapy. This criticism is not valid, in my opinion, when group therapy is carried out by qualified and responsible therapists. The mechanisms by which a group exerts its therapeutic influence are not identical with the mechanisms of individual psychotherapy. The psychological effects are exercised at a different level of personality integration. From my own experience with group psychotherapy over a period of 15 years, I have drawn some tentative conclusions, elsewhere reported,[5] as to the different levels of influence represented by psychoanalytic therapy on the one hand and group therapy on the other.

APPRAISAL OF THE FAMILY LIFE

From what has been said, it is apparent that in a mental health clinic of this type, the psychoanalytically oriented treatment of the preschool child and family members must be pursued logically in the context of a careful psychosocial appraisal of the family as a group. The young child cannot be treated in a social vacuum, but only in intimate relation to the environment on which he is basically dependent. The therapeutic approach to the person must be related to the dynamics of family role. In order to implement this principle, we have made systematic studies of family patterns through home visits[6] and through careful observation of family interaction within the Center itself.

[5]See the following, by Nathan W. Ackerman: "Psychoanalysis and Group Psychotherapy," *Group Psychotherapy* (1950) 3:204-215. "Some Structural Problems in the Relations of Psychoanalysis and Group Psychotherapy," *Internat. J. Group Psychotherapy* (1954) 4:131-145. "Dynamic Patterns in Group Psychotherapy," *Psychiatry* (1944) 7:341-348. "Interview Group Psychotherapy with Psychoneurotic Adults," in *The Practice of Group Therapy*, edited by Samuel Slavson; New York, Internat. Universities Press, 1947; pp. 135-155. "Group Psychotherapy with a Mixed Group of Adolescents," *Internat. J. Group Psychotherapy* (1955) 5:249-260.

[6]Marjorie L. Behrens and Nathan W. Ackerman, "The Home Visit as an Aid in Family Diagnosis and Therapy," *Social Casework* (1956) 37:11-19.

A word of explanation in passing regarding the techniques of psychosocial study of the family: our experience has shown beyond question the indispensability of direct observation of the family life *in situ*. Through systematic home visits it is possible to observe directly such crucial and revealing factors as the dominant mood within the home, the eating, sleeping, and toilet habits, play behavior, interior decoration and physical planning, and so on. All this casts significant light on the operations of personality in the context of family relationships. Certain pertinent facts were illuminated by home study in a way never possible in an office interview.

Also, in the same direction, we have undertaken a type of family diagnosis which attempts to integrate systematically the social and psychosocial data relevant to a given family and relate these to the emerging emotional disturbances of the young child. Within this frame, psychotherapy for individual family members is apt to be more rewarding. Our work with family diagnosis is reported elsewhere in a series of papers.[7]

INTEGRATION OF THERAPEUTIC INFLUENCE

The tasks of integrating the several levels of therapeutic influence have been the most difficult. The effects of individual psychotherapy have first to be integrated with the educational and guidance program, both for child and parent. For the child, this means specifically the integration of psychotherapy with parental care and nursery education; for the parent, it means the integration of psychotherapy with the daily experience at home with the family group. Then, overlapping these, there is the task of integrating all levels of psychotherapeutic influence aimed at correcting disturbances in interpersonal relations. This last consideration clearly involves integrating the effects of individual and group psychotherapy of parents and integrating the effects of these varied levels of psychotherapy with social therapy for the family as a group.

The results of clinical investigation have led to one inescapable conclusion: if psychoanalysts are to discover new knowledge concerning the psychodynamics of child development, they cannot rely so heavily as in the past on data derived from retrospective memory of childhood of adults in analysis but must make a concentrated approach through the direct observation of the child as an emerging biosocial organism, adapting to an expanding sphere of social relations. Nor can they rely so heavily on the process of child analysis as traditionally practiced; child analysis cannot be conducted in a social vacuum, but in a setting which permits adjunctive study of the child's total environment and the processes of his interaction with the significant adults in that environment.

At this stage in the development of psychoanalytic theory there is no easy answer to the questions posed in this report. In the sphere of child development, infant-mother relations, and relations of child with family and wider society, only a small part of psychoanalytic theory has really been put to the test. It is exceedingly difficult in this sphere to state definitively what psychoanalysts really know and don't know, what has really been validated and what remains very much in the realm of doubt. It is a curious historic paradox that while Freud himself was profoundly skeptical if not pessimistic concerning the scientific validity of some of this theoretical constructs, recognizing their provisional nature, many of his disciples fail to emulate his scientific humility. Freud's pioneering explorations have opened up vast reaches of the mind, but he did leave later psychoanalysts with the heritage of a tremendous gap in conceptualization, the task of framing biological disposition in terms of social interaction. He discovered much about the inner life of the individual psyche, but he did not encompass as well the family group and the structure of society. This would be too much to expect of one man. It is fitting to quote the judgment of an outstanding social scientist of our day, George Murdock: "Without detracting in the slightest from Freud's extraor-

[7]The publications pertaining to family diagnosis are the following: Nathan W. Ackerman and Marjorie L. Behrens, "Child and Family Psychopathy; Problems of Correlation," in *Psychopathology of Childhood*, edited by Paul H. Hoch and Joseph Zubin; New York, Grune & Stratton, 1955; pp. 177-196. Ackerman and Raymond Sobel, "Family Diagnosis; An Approach to the Pre-School Child," *Amer. J. Orthopsychiatry* (1950) 20:744-753. Ackerman and Behrens, "A Study of Family Diagnosis," *Amer. J. Orthopsychiatry* (1956) 26:66-78. Ackerman, "Disturbances of Mothering and Criteria for Treatment," *Amer. J. Orthopsychiatry*, April 1956.

dinary insight into individual psychology, or from his revolutionary contributions in this field, we must admit that his ventures into cultural theory are little short of fantastic."[8]

Any effort to apply psychoanalytic concepts to the problem of personality development of children, to family relations, and to larger issues of community mental health must therefore take a broader view of the psychoanalytic contribution than the purely Freudian view. It must consider the limits of fruitfulness of the concept of individual personality; it must take into account the relativity of this entity. It must fully recognize the interdependence of individual and group. It must approach the unsolved problems of ego development and organization through systematic study of processes of social interaction. It cannot afford the luxury of an exclusive preoccupation with the investigation of the unconscious.

For those who wish it, this investigation is a legitimate specialty. But for those who are oriented to a broader objective—namely, understanding the whole process of child development in relation to the tasks of social adaptation — unconscious phenomena must be viewed in the light of conscious experience and in the context of social structure and organization; that is, the unconscious must be defined in the context of the reality of social relations. In other words, the internal psychic life of man can never be separated from his external relations with the environment; the individual, the family, and the community constitute a phenomenological unit. Throughout the history of psychoanalysis this dualism has persisted between concentration on the inner phenomena of the psyche and on the external adaptive relations of man with his environment.

Nowhere in psychoanalysis is this problem more pertinent than in the sphere of child analysis. Effective application of psychoanalytic insights to the social field is hampered by the lag in relating biological disposition to the processes of social participation and thereby illuminating more fully the ego-integrative functions of personality. A further difficulty is the lack of criteria for evaluating the mental health status of groups, the family, and the community.

The lack of definitive knowledge of ego development in children must be recognized as a profound handicap to the understanding of child development. Obviously, the infant cannot be conceived of purely as an individual, and ego growth must be defined not only in terms of the infant-mother unit, but also in terms of the infant-family unit. The prolonged dependence of infant on mother makes it impossible to regard the psyche of the infant as separate from a sustaining human environment. The way in which the mother carries out the maternal functions is influenced by the mother-father relationship, the group structure of the family as a whole, and the dominant social patterns which condition child-rearing.

The failure to conceptualize adequately the extent to which therapists can approach a disturbed child as a separate individual or as an organism biopsychically bound to its environment has hampered progress. It is not an accident that a satisfactory definition of child analysis has been so extremely difficult, if not impossible, to formulate. Attempts at such definitions tend almost always to be arbitrary.

Is it not illogical to attempt to define a technique of therapeutic intervention before achieving a sufficiently precise definition of the phenomenon one is trying to change with therapy? In other words, until one can define with some exactness the personality of the child and its social adaptation, one cannot give exactness to a definition of a therapeutic method designed to influence child personality and child growth. This is putting the cart before the horse. It is time to reverse this conceptual error.

A parting word would seem to be in order with regard to the current status of the Child Development Center, which I have characterized as an experiment in community mental health. It continues its clinical services to its community in New York City, and continues its struggle to discover some useful principles in the study and treatment of the young child. It focuses a strong interest on teaching and research. At present it is engaged in projects on anxiety and aggression in children and on integrative and disintegrative trends in family life. But the really big question is this: Can the Center succeed in its avowed purpose of opening up new paths to the prevention of mental illness?

---

[8]George Peter Murdock, *Social Structure;* New York, MacMillan, 1949; p. xvii.

In this particular respect, can it achieve something new and different? Or will it settle down to a respectable middle age and become just another treatment center? This is a question that only the future can answer.

(The C.C.D.C. has dropped Council from its title but otherwise continues to flourish, under the direction of Dr. Peter Neubauer, as a division of the Jewish Board of Family and Children's Services.)

CHAPTER 5

Selected Problems in Supervised Analysis

In approaching the subject of supervised analysis, it might be interesting to note that all aspects of psychoanalysis have been and must continue to be matters of controversy. The fundamental structure of a science of psychodynamics has been established, but beyond that, there is little that is fixed and immutable in this field, and much that is creatively changing. Theories of personality organization, personality development, and interpersonal relations, concepts of social maturation and mental health, principles of therapy, and the relation of psychoanalytic thought to other disciplines—all these are in a state of flux. Of special importance today is the increasing trend toward the integration of training in psychiatry with training in basic psychodynamics and toward the process of mutual fertilization between psychoanalysis and the social sciences.

At the very outset it seems appropriate to recognize candidly that attitudes toward supervised analysis—as well as toward psychoanalytic training in general—are highly charged with feeling. If useful conclusions are to be reached regarding supervised analysis, it can only be through some understanding of the personal involvement of the teacher as well as of the student. Throughout the history of the psychoanalytic movement, the policy of having the student conduct his first analysis under an experienced analytic practitioner has been the very kernel of the psychoanalytic training program. This has been the case regardless of the many points of disagreement in the philosophy of psychoanalytic education. The principle of learning through an apprenticeship experience is therefore axiomatic. The objective purpose is that the student, under properly safeguarded conditions, will learn by doing—that he will come to understand, step by step, the process of analysis and will move through the entire course of his patient's analysis to the point of successful termination. In so doing, he will be helped by his supervisor to understand the pathology of his patient's personality, the mechanisms of patient-analyst interaction, the role of the unconscious in both patient and analyst, and so on. Finally, he will be instructed in the principles of therapeutic technique.

Reprinted with permission from *Psychiatry: Journal for the Study of Interpersonal Processes*, August 1953, Vol. 16, No. 3, 283-290.

Important as it is for the supervisor to sensitize the student to the infinite expressions of the unconscious, his real responsibility is to cultivate and nourish the student's capacity to observe and to think—to be imaginative, creative, and yet scientifically sound. The difficulties which emerge in the student's apprentice relationship stem in part from unresolved conflicts in psychoanalytic theory. While the supervisor may try to protect the student from conceptual confusion, he must not try to conceal these theoretical conflicts from the student or try to get him to accept uncritically some fixed ideological system. An important part of every student's education should be that he acquire a critical appreciation of these unresolved controversies.

The dynamics of the student-supervisor relationship merit some thought. What are the emotional orientations of the student and the teacher to this relationship? Do they like or dislike each other for realistic reasons, or for irrational ones? What are the goals, aspirations, and expectations of each one? Is the relationship one of mutual satisfaction or mutual frustration? Certainly, this is a two-way relationship in which the teacher learns as well as teaches. In the very process of teaching, he shapes his own development as much as he does the student's. Just as in a patient-analyst relationship one must know the part played by both patient and analyst, so, too, in the interpersonal exchange of student and supervisor one must not only know what the student does but also the specific contribution of the teacher.

This emphasis on the teacher's role is important since there are real problems involving the teacher's grasp of his subject, his gift for teaching, his ability to communicate, and so on. It is conceivable that a supervisor may impose on a student his private prejudices, may project onto him his own countertransference difficulties, or may inject into his relations with the student his own unsolved personal problems. He may intrude into his conduct an ill-defined urge to subordinate the student—to castrate him, if you will—or he may have a need to show up the deficiencies of a rival teacher. Mere seniority offers no immunity against the vagaries of the unconscious, and in this respect a teacher may occasionally be as vulnerable as the student.

The dynamics of this interpersonal situation of supervisor and student cannot be viewed in a vacuum. The movement in this relationship — the specific give-and-take between student and supervisor—is qualified not only by the personalities and capacities of the two persons involved, but by certain other meaningful connections as well: the student's experience with his personal analyst, his status in the analytic school, his relations with fellow students and with patients, his personal strivings, his orientation to his profession and his community, and so on. Similar factors influence the role of the teaching analyst, though of course in a different context. Infiltrating all of this is the effect of the theoretical orientation of the particular analytic training institute itself, its ideology, its special educational policies, and the auspices under which its training is conducted.

This broader matrix for the student-supervisor relationship requires mention because only too often, in my opinion, the problems of a student in supervision are blithely dismissed with a characterization that is rather too narrow and oversimplified. Such arbitrary characterizations, even when partly true, are incomplete and can be misleading. For example, we hear again and again that the problems of analyses conducted by students are essentially those of countertransference or that the processes of supervision of such analysis for the student. These may be penetrating generalizations, but when they are unqualified and removed from their proper context, it is difficult to appraise their meaning or to see them in correct relation to other pertinent facts.

Some of the emotional trends observed in a student are the result of the frequent coincidence in time of his relationships with his personal analyst, his supervisor, and his analytic patient. As one student aptly put it, he is caught in a triple play. It is only to be expected that the student will tend to identify his supervising analyst with his personal analyst. The influence of the one may complement that of the other, or the two influences may clash. The student may be tempted to pit the authority of one against the other, or he may displace emotions belonging to one onto the other. A variety of trends may occur here; some of these may be strengthened somewhat by the actual responsibility the supervising analyst has for checking the judgment of the personal analyst as to unanalyzed residual pathology in the student, his immaturity, or his unreadiness for therapeutic analysis of patients.

At the other pole is the student's tendency to identify with his patient, which may conflict with his need to identify with his personal analyst or supervising analyst. Depending on the processes going on in his personal analysis, a student may overidentify with his patient's pathology and rebel against the influence of his analyst and supervisor; or he may react defensively against his empathy with the patient and consequently be irrationally overaggressive with the patient; or he may lack empathy with the patient, overidentify with his personal or supervising analyst, and, as a result, uncritically imitate the strategy and tactics of his seniors. This last tendency may reach an extreme point where the student simply parrots his teacher. These are crucial problems which underscore the importance of the supervisor's accurate perceptions of the subtly shifting expressions of the unconscious in the patient, in the student (who is in the dual role of patient and therapist), and sometimes in the supervisor himself. The issue is not so much one of preventing the intrusion of the student's personal emotions, but rather one of being continually alert to their nature and source, and of properly discriminating and controlling them.

Admittedly, a central responsibility of the supervising analyst is to sensitize his student to the multitudinous masks of the unconscious, but a successful therapeutic result requires much more than this. Equally vital is the stress on the student's understanding of the dynamics of emotional control, on integration of behavior, on social interaction, and on growth of personality. Certainly, a true perspective on the unconscious can be achieved only in the context of knowledge of the role of the ego and the phenomena of adaptation. Of therapeutic significance is the student's understanding of the differences between conscious and unconscious conflict, real and unreal motivation, and control of emotion versus loss of control.

One basic consideration, which has a significant effect upon the outcome of a student-supervisor relationship, is the process of mutual selection: How does a particular student select a particular supervisor, and vice versa? This particular selection is of course influenced by the prior selections that have been made by student and analyst, and by student and training institute. It is important to bear in mind that each of these selections is made by both parties, and I shall consider both the student's selection of a supervisor, and the supervisor's selection of students. Situational as well as personal factors enter into these selections, but I shall emphasize here only the personal factors.

It is axiomatic that a student learns more and better when he and his supervisor like and respect each other. The spontaneous pairing off of students and supervisors tends to be mutually profitable, but this type of flexibility becomes less easy to preserve as the number of students in an institute increases and training becomes more formalized. The student's choice may be influenced by his personal analysis, or by the known theoretical slant of a particular supervisor. He may admire what a certain teacher stands for, his ideas, clinical skill, ways of teaching, and so on. In this setting, a student will usually absorb avidly everything that comes his way. Yet most students are mature enough to seek out a varied supervisory diet in the interests of a rounded education. One contributing factor to the process of selection should be borne in mind: in his personal analysis, the student often feels like a child. When he is declared ready to do analytic work with patients, he is admitted to the estate of a grown man. This shift in the image of self influences the student's processes of identification with his personal analyst and his supervisor, and thus shapes his attitudes toward the learning experience.

Now and then, a student may be drawn to a particular teacher for irrational reasons which escape his own awareness. Such situations bear careful watching. I make it a regular practice to inquire into a student's motivation in seeking me as his supervisor. One student may be neurotically attracted to an authority figure he strongly but ambivalently fears. Another student may be burdened with an unconscious need to destroy the symbol of his teacher's authority: he may attempt neurotically to show up his instructor, and consequent guilt may interfere with the learning process; he may be belligerent, or ingratiating and submissive; he may provoke his own humiliation in class or cause his own failure in his school career, and not infrequently, such self-destructive aggression is displaced from the personal analyst to the supervisor. Or, a student may choose an instructor whom he irrationally idealizes and wishes to emulate—one whose qualities he lacks and envies. In some instances, a student may choose a particular instructor because of a strong homosexual attraction—where the instructor represents a kind of father figure with whom the student wants closeness; such a relationship may be gratifying to the student but may arouse so much anxiety in him that the learning process is seriously impaired. One such student confessed in analysis that he was so completely wrapped up in the study of his supervisor's handsome head that he simply heard nothing that was said of the patient. Still others, personally insecure and excessively fearful of exposure and criticism by the faculty, select a supervisory figure who symbolizes a protective parent. The student's emotional expectation is that this parent figure will aggressively protect him from attack by other faculty members. One encounters also in some students the need to be the fair-haired boy of the school or the outspoken favorite of a powerful faculty figure.

Interesting conflicts may be observed, too, in the choice of male or female supervisors. This is especially clear where a student fears aggressive women and nurtures sadistic sexual phantasies toward a female instructor. Analogous conflicts emerge in relation to the symbolization of the Jewishness and non-Jewishness of instructors, with the expression of corresponding preferences. Not to be ignored, finally, is the motivation of students in selecting a supervisor who has a reputation of generousness in referring private patients.[1]

Now, let us look at the other side of the relationship, the factors influencing the supervisor's choice of students. Here, too, subjective as well as objective elements play a part. First comes the instructor's appraisal of the worth of the student. Each instructor has his special prejudices as to the student qualities that make the best analyst. Each has his personal image of the ideal student. Faculty discussions may reveal a consensus on some necessary attributes, but beyond this there is considerable discrepancy in the judgments and values of individual instructors. There is naturally some inclination to prefer the more rewarding students, the brighter, more gifted, more perceptive of the candidates. On a more individual basis, a spontaneous empathic bond not shared by the others, may spring up between a given student and a given instructor.

Instructors, however, are impelled by their logical responsibilities to work with the less-gifted students just as earnestly, and sometimes more so. Occasionally, an extraordinary effort with a backward student brings in the end an extraordinary result. One large difficulty appears with those students who simply do not feel close enough to their patients. It is important to distinguish here between the student who by temperament has a basic deficiency of empathy and psychological perceptiveness, and the student who is only temporarily blocked by anxiety. Some students who are emotionally blocked for a while, show eventually a rapid and dramatic improvement in their conduct of control analyses.

The subjective reactions of supervisors to students are infinitely varied. Some are reserved, some authoritarian, others democratic and comradely. For myself, I must confess a willingness to indulge myself emotionally in the student session, in a way that I cannot do with clinical patients. I feel free to like some students better than others, to put more of myself into the teaching of some than others; and I am more open and direct. For me, the greater emotional freedom with students provides an avenue for personal catharsis, a significant antidote to the necessary constraint with clinical patients. But it works both ways. By my own behavior, I encourage the students to let loose with their feelings, with every assurance that what they express will be treated as privileged communication. This is particularly useful in relation to their gripes concerning any aspect of their training.

I now want to consider the specific role of the pathology of the student's personality. There is still only limited agreement as to types of pathology which preclude the possibility of training in psychoanalysis. In a general way, psychoses, psychopathic personality, perversions, alcoholism, and those other forms of character disorder which result in a lack of integrity are broadly conceived as irreconcilable with psychoanalytic

[1]A consideration of the various resistances and emotional blocks to learning which can arise in a student-supervisor relationship is beyond the scope of this paper. Suffice it to say here that these resistances and blocks are often akin to disturbances in feeding deriving from ambivalent attitudes, and they are critically influenced by the processes of student-supervisor interaction described above.

training. Beyond this, standards get fuzzy. There is little systematic conviction regarding the varied forms of schizoid character and little consensus on the forms of neurosis commensurate or noncommensurate with such training. In general, those neuroses which are conceived of as not too deep-seated and as therapeutically reversible are not excluded. However, there can often be no certainty except with a trial period of personal analysis. Similarly, one often cannot be sure that there is no danger of intrusion of a student's pathology into his clinical work unless he has a trial period of supervised analysis. Some students are likable in spite of their pathology, and occasionally because of it. These are intangibles of character and temperament, but they nevertheless play a significant part in the student's relations with his instructor, and therefore affect his learning experience—how much he learns, what he learns, and how he learns it.

Now and then, a student appears to be disliked, nelgected, or otherwise penalized because he happens to be just "too normal." But this occurs not really because he is normal and healthy, but rather because his emotional responses are apt to be banal, conventional, untuned to human suffering, and unperceptive of the unconscious. This is a common form of instructor prejudice, although, wishing to be fair, he will usually try deliberately to compensate for it.

The part played by the student's emotional pathology in his conduct of the analysis of his patient is of course central to the whole problem. The student's irrational acting-out of his unconscious needs is an ever-present danger. There is naturally a large propensity in this direction in the sicker students, although this varies tremendously with character structure. It should be borne in mind, however, that this risk is by no means confined to the group of sicker students. The so-called healthy ones act out, too. In fact, the hazard for the patient may actually be greater with the so-called healthy student because he is often less vigilant against his deeper impulses and is rather more apt to make them appear plausible. He may therefore be in greater danger of losing effective therapeutic control.

Other common sources of a student's countertransference disturbances are lack of confidence, fear of the patient's disapproval, fear of losing the patient, a misplaced need for the patient's love, and, of course, irrational aggressive urges that are not consciously understood. One must watch particularly for signs of aggression displaced onto the patient from the personal analyst or the supervising analyst. To feel an occasional antagonism to one's patient is no crime, provided it is brought into consciousness, understood, and controlled.

When the student submerges his own individuality and overidentifies with his personal analyst or his supervisor, he may act out with his patient his projected image of the omnipotent and omniscient analyst. Or, in a rebellious spirit, he may act out his feeling of competition with the senior analyst. If he assumes the garb of his teachers and, as if in caricature, mimics their therapeutic conduct, the patient in all likelihood will penetrate this disguise and expose the student. In infinite combinations, the student may get his emotions inappropriately involved in the conduct of his patient's analysis, and the resulting burden of anxiety will jeopardize his therapeutic control.

The following series of personal supervisory experiences with students illustrates some of the countertransference problems that have come to my attention.

Student A, while gifted, was compulsive, rigid, dogmatic, rather detached emotionally, and needed some loosening of these character patterns to do his best work clinically. He had difficulty managing an excess of aggressive feeling with his patient. For a time he would keep it repressed or struggle consciously to suppress a break-through of this feeling. Sooner or later these efforts would fail, and he would abruptly become very aggressive with the patient. When the supervisor called this to his attention, he said little at first, seeming on the surface to accept the criticism. Nevertheless, his shooting attacks on the patient continued unabated. Inevitably the supervisor was compelled to repeat his warning several times. When he did so, the student exploded. He acted as if he knew better than the supervisor what was best for his patient. The supervisor permitted a discharge of the student's tantrum and quietly instructed him to discuss the matter with his personal analyst. This did the trick. The hostility had been displaced from the student's personal analysis into the analysis of his patient and from there into the supervisory relationship. Later, the student apologized and expressed gratitude for the uncovering of this personal problem.

Student B, another bright student also detached emotionally, loved to analogize his patient's psyche with a machine. Ordinary persuasion made not the slightest dent in this attitude. He simply refused to separate himself from this, to him, very appealing simile. It required the most patient and adroit handling of the student to weaken this mechanized approach to a human being. The final result was imperfect. This student continued to show some deficiency of his capacity for empathy. Though keen and competent, he simply could not empathize enough with his patient.

Student C had been reared in a highly prudish, strict, rural family; he was passive, inhibited, and rather obsessive. He seemed repeatedly to bog down in his analysis of an aggressive female patient. At a certain point, the relationship between the patient and himself became completely static. The patient sensed that the student feared the slightest forward movement on her part, and the analytic material demonstrated that he acted in such a way as to stop the earliest signs of her initiative, although he talked as though this were not the case. As soon as the patient would begin to confess her sexual urges, the student would become anxious and cease to be receptive. When she was silent, he chided her for her resistance. The timing of his interpretive comments was wrong, and so precisely wrong as to suggest unconscious purposefulness. The student finally admitted his fear that this patient would make overt sexual advances. Frank discussion and further work in his personal analysis resolved the problem satisfactorily.

Student D, in treating a beautiful young woman of the theatre suffering from a severe character neurosis, interpreted her conflicts purely in terms of libido. His therapeutic behavior reflected a stubborn resistance to seeing and dealing appropriately with her cruelty to men. This student was intelligent and mature, but rather alone in the world. He had an ingratiating, compulsive character. His own aggressiveness was well disguised and compensated for. He had a conspicuous need to prove himself to everyone, was oversensitive to criticism, and strongly craved the acceptance of this woman patient, whom he feared to lose. Extensive discussions brought the real problem to light and enabled the student to proceed effectively with the analysis.

Student E, an intellectual narcissist, displayed particular affinity for searching out the smartest, subtlest, most precious symbolic expressions of the patient's unconscious. He was so enamored of the esthetic delicacy of unconscious symbols as to neglect in effect the more basic conflict trends. He had a special need to demonstrate his omniscience and his athletic prowess with the language of the unconscious. He was an outstanding student, but in character he was on the arrogant, argumentative, smart-alecky side. With continued guidance, he achieved better control of his narcissism, curbed his temptation to exhibit his precious familiarity with the unconscious, and reached a better balance in the execution of his analytic role.

Student F, sincere, devoted, and obsessional, plodded along laboriously with his analytic work. He was unable to be spontaneous; he delayed his interpretations overlong and then injected them into the proceedings in inappropriate places. In a typically obsessional way, he separated thought from affect. As a result, effective communication with the patient deteriorated and the therapeutic result was poor. Supervisory efforts in this instance were not rewarding.

Student G, another obsessional student, displayed several related difficulties. He controlled the patient too strongly and tended without knowing it to push the patient in the direction he thought the patient should go. In a reciprocal manner, he allowed the patient to push him back. He choked off the patient's spontaneity and initiative by structuring for her in advance the meaning of her emotional experiences. Because of his obsessional preoccupation with details, he lost sight of the woods for the trees. This problem he shared with his patient. As a result, he frequently got shunted off the main path of the analysis.

Student H expressed his personal anxiety in his clinical work by accelerating the pace of the analysis to a point where he raced along at an amazing speed, with the patient making a distressed, submissive, panicky effort to keep up with him. This was a foreign student in this country for a limited period of training. He was in a compulsive rush to complete his requirements and return to his native land. The fact that his mother had suffered a heart attack increased his desire to hurry.

Student J had a habit of anticipating her supervisor's words and taking them right out of his mouth, before he had hardly had a chance to utter them. This was an ambivalent haste to agree ingratiatingly with him, and even while in the very act of agreeing, to usurp his position of control. The trouble was the student was so avid to steal the words out of his mouth before they got said, that she often took the wrong words. It is hard to say who was the more embarrassed, the student or supervisor. In the end, it turned out well.

Student K got into difficulty because of neurotic competitiveness, envy, and acquisitiveness. He made trouble for his patient by asserting a claim for a higher fee at the very moment that the patient began to experience some success in living. The patient became depressed and the student failed to see why. In his excessive preoccupation with fee, the student was not aware of the bad timing of his demand and of the patient's readiness to feel that he was robbing her of her success, in fact penalizing her for it.

These are more or less random examples of the emotional difficulties of students in supervised analysis. Several patterns are outstanding: fear of failure, a need to appease the patient, fear of loss of the patient and a consequent loss of face for the student, fear of the supervisor's criticism and a too strong preoccupation with his authority, the intrusion of the student's own unsolved needs, and the encroachment of the student's own aggression in a displaced, inappropriate form. The concomitant relationships of student and patient, student and analyst, and student and supervisor multiply the complexity of these reactions.

This raises again the question of how far it makes sense to consider the supervised analysis in effect a second personal analysis for the student. There is an important core of truth in this characterization. Yet this very truth brings a temptation to carry the idea too far. The supervising analyst is continually responsible for appraising the emotional well-being of his student; it is his duty to spot those trouble zones which reflect inadequate understanding of self, unsolved pathology, lack of readiness for supervised clinical work or the risk of acting-out in clinical work with patients. The supervisor is, in effect, a control not only for the student but for the personal analyst as well. The supervisor may discuss these problems with the student and suggest he take them up with his personal analyst. Occasionally, it may be advantageous for the supervisor to consult with the student's analyst, but with the student's consent.

On the other hand, the supervisory situation would become unreal, confusing, and detrimental to the student were the supervising analyst to invade the role of the personal analyst. The function of the personal analyst is to remove pathology; the function of the supervisor is primarily that of the educator, to promote the student's maturity in his professional field. At certain points, the roles of therapist and educator overlap but it is important to preserve a clear distinction between these separate functions. Occasionally a supervisor takes an extreme position in vigorously exposing the student's troubled unconscious, and in so doing jeopardizes both the student's personal analysis and the student's analysis of his patient. If the supervisor exceeds his proper function in checking and balancing the student's use of his emotional self in the therapeutic role, there is a real hazard for the student in that the supervisor may become distracted from his primary duty of guiding the analysis of the patient. The clinical pathology of the patient should never become a matter of incidental interest. At the other pole, a supervising analyst may be overprotective of a student and avoid confronting him with the evidence of his inappropriate therapeutic behavior. The supervising analyst may justify this with the notion that such problems are strictly the business of the student's personal analyst, whereas his role should be a more supportive one. Sometimes this is mistaken kindness. The problematic behavior of the student needs to be faced.

Many analytic teachers hold the conviction that the student is too heavily burdened emotionally in having to bear concomitantly the problems which derive from personal analysis, analysis of a clinical patient, and the relationship with the supervisor. Since the possibilities of disturbance are so abundant, and the disturbance may carry over from one relationship to another, it is argued that the personal analysis should be completed before permission is given for supervised analytic work. Some schools actually require completion of personal analysis even earlier, in advance of matriculation for analytic training. Perhaps in many instances, completion of personal analysis prior to undertaking clinical work is necessary, but in principle I am opposed to generalizing this rule. I am not convinced of its universal wisdom. There are, in my opinion, important positive values to be preserved in the arrangement in which there is an overlap in time between personal analysis and supervised analysis. Certain emotional conflicts would simply not come to light or fail to be activated and would thus be lost to the student's personal analysis if this were completed before the student began supervised analysis. In a similar sense, any residual pathology which the supervising analyst uncovered would remain out of reach if the student could not bring this back to his personal analysis. There is therefore some merit in the partly concomitant arrangement of personal analysis and supervised clinical work.

The problems of supervised analysis are varied, complex, and often multiply determined. To conceive them in oversimplified terms is not helpful; it tends to distort their meaning in that it removes certain partial processes from their true interpersonal context. It is rather more accurate to try to view the phenomena of supervised analysis within the broad frame of several overlapping interpersonal relationships: student and personal analyst, student and supervising analyst, student and patient. In all these, the teacher's role should be scrutinized as carefully as the student's.

CHAPTER 6

Trends in the Terminal Phase of Student Analysis

To end or not to end a student analysis? That is the question! When is a student analysis finished? The answer comes hard. The intricacies of student analysis comprise all of the difficulties of ordinary clinical analysis plus those which are unique to the student's position. The discernment of a suitable set of criteria for the termination of the usual clinical analysis is itself no easy accomplishment; it offers a challenge of considerable magnitude. Since the therapeutic emphasis in our age has shifted from symptom analysis to character analysis, the complexities of this challenge are multiplied. Among students, disorders of character take on a special significance. The unique features of student analysis and the necessity of harmonizing the goals of student analysis with the over-all objectives of psychoanalytic training create a whole set of problems of a new order. Thus far, universal standards for the termination of student analysis have not been formulated.

Putting aside formal or quantitative standards, it is safe to assume in our time that each training analyst evolves his own relatively unique criteria for the completion of student analysis. This proposition is easily documented in the spontaneous comments of students reacting to the striking contrasts in judgment of different training analysts in the same institute as they discharge their students from analysis. From one point of view, this high degree of individualization is inevitable. In each such analysis, four variables are involved: the individual training analyst, the individual student, the quality of the relationship which develops between them, and the characteristics of the particular training institute under whose auspices the student analysis is conducted. To the extent that analysis is a healing art which rests partly on the analyst's unique use of himself in the curative role and on the student's participation as a willing patient, there must always be something distinct about each such analytic experience. To a corresponding degree, therefore, judgments as to the appropriate point of ending must vary. Inevitably the interaction of the goals and values of the analyst, and those of the student, must play a potent part in the final decision as to termination within the general frame of the standards which prevail at a given training institute.

Reprinted with permission of the Editor, *The American Journal of Psychoanalysis*, 1955, Vol. XV, No. 2, 107-114.

Despite these individual variations, however, training analysts continue to seek a consensus with regard to a set of criteria which are generally germane to the question of completion of student analysis. To the extent that psychoanalysis aspires to the standard of scientific method and objectivity of judgment, agreement in principle among training analysts and institutes as to the necessary conditions for successful conclusion of student analysis is an ideal toward which we should strive.

To start with, any decision as to termination must rest on a clear perception of the original purposes and goals of analytic therapy within the frame of professional training, and a thoughtful appraisal of the extent to which these have been achieved. Analysis of students has always a twofold orientation: therapeutic and educational. In its educational aspect, there is the axiomatic principle that criteria for termination must overlap with the criteria which initially decided the student's suitability for matriculation in a psychoanalytic training institute, and with the criteria employed in periodic reevaluation of the student's progress during the course of training. From the beginning and at every succeeding phase of the student's training, we are concerned with the student's fitness as a human being, the breadth of his professional equipment, his perceptive understanding, particularly of deeper and hidden motivation, and his specific capacities for integrating his personality into the role of psychoanalytic therapist and investigator. All this we must judge in the context of progressive change in the mental health of the student and his powers of psychological observation as induced first by the experience of personal analysis, and later by supervised analysis. In this sense, the weighing of the issues of termination of personal analysis constitutes a check on those judgments which were drawn at the point of acceptance of the student for training, and may also constitute a check on certain subsequent evaluations of the student's progress. But the checking process operates in two directions: the periodic evaluations and final examination of the student at the point of graduation serve also as a check on the validity of the judgment drawn at the point of termination of personal analysis.

Since analysis in essence is an experience shared between two persons and moves toward a point where student and analyst achieve equality and mutual respect, it is the responsibility of both student and analyst to agree regarding the wisdom of termination. This ought not to be an arbitrary unilateral decision on the part either of student or analyst.

Termination of analysis, however, means merely the discontinuance of formal therapeutic sessions. It is axiomatic that self-analysis in one form or another must continue. This is so for several reasons: the responsibility for understanding and integrating one's own unconscious urges can have no point of termination for a person undertaking a career in psychoanalysis. Formal analysis, regardless of its length, cannot be expected to resolve for all time conflicts involving personal, and often unconscious factors. Formal analysis offers no guarantee of favorable vicissitudes in life, nor can it provide a permanent immunity against emotional illness.

If we regard personality and environment as representing a dynamic continuum, and agree there is no absolute homeostasis of individual personality, it is self-evident that the struggle for successful adaptation and continued personal growth must be a continuous one. Any critical disturbance in the unstable equilibrium of person and environment may again induce pathogenic conflict.

The issue therefore is: What are some effective guideposts for the termination of formal analysis? The primary criterion is, of course, therapeutic cure, and the widening of the horizons of awareness of self and others. But, how to test the adequacy and relevancy of cure in this special situation? It seems to me that the question of cure, and its realistic test in these circumstances, may be posed in the following categories:

1. The mental health status of the student's personality.
2. The understanding of the processes of emotional interaction between student and analyst, with special emphasis on the perception of unconscious forces, transference and resistance.
3. The group adaptation of the student.
4. The interdependence of the student's experience in analytic therapy and his other training experience.
5. The progressive shift in the student's image

of himself, his surrounding world and the corresponding changes in value orientation.

The first and second categories refer specifically to the cure of the student's pathology and the education of the student's awareness of hidden motivation. The remaining categories represent different levels of reality testing of the adequacy and relevancy of this therapeutic change.

The therapeutic cure of the student's pathology needs to be checked at several levels: the alleviation of specific mental symptoms, the extent and depth of character change, the understanding and strengthening of self, and the student's capacity for continued growth as a person.

There is considerable agreement among analysts that the task of resolving specific disabling symptoms presents the least difficulty for the therapist. Far more resistant is the challenge of inducing the desired modifications of character. The task of melting down the defensiveness of the patient, loosening rigidities and egocentric fixations, resolving exploitive and manipulative attitudes, releasing spontaneity, clarifying the self-image, enhancing the capacity for empathic identification with others, nourishing healthier values and freeing dormant capacities for love and creativity, is by far the harder job. Here one often confronts in a frozen state pathological defenses which rest on the original childhood perception of parent authority. Of particular importance are those rigid defense structures which reflect subtly concealed components of regressive adaptation. I refer here to residual dependence patterns, exploitive, coercive attitudes toward parent figures, omnipotence attitudes, childhood conscience patterns, denial of guilt and paranoid projection of responsibility. Frequently the stubborn clinging to these pathological and regressive defense structures derives from a deeply rooted damage to self-esteem. Until this problem of a crippled sense of self is brought fully into the open and alleviated, the student is compelled to cling to these rigid defenses, in order to forestall further exposure of the already wounded and vulnerable self.

In approaching these character problems, it is important to realize that the student's strivings for professional success are part of his security system, and the urge to protect this system impels him all the more strongly to resist change in his defense patterns. As familiar examples of this, we may cite the student's need of recognition, reassurance, support, his rivalry with other students in the quest for faculty approval, and status in accredited psychoanalytic organizations.

The security-mindedness of the student is often expressed initially in his resistance to being analyzed. It is amazing how many students enter analysis as part of their professional training and yet deny to consciousness that they either need or want to be analyzed. Coming to analysis becomes a ritual in which they go through all the motions of the couch, unconsciously hoping they will remain immune and untouched. Often in a curious, contradictory way students enter training with great conscious admiration of analytic therapy, yet preserving unconsciously the secret belief that analysis is a kind of hocus-pocus which may induce dramatic effects but actually cures nothing. The training analyst is challenged to reach and resolve this secret core of resistance in which the student preserves the conviction that the therapeutic powers of analysis are nil. Such forms of resistance occur not only early in analysis but often persist doggedly.

The relevance of this for the problem of termination is that often at the tail end of analysis, this resistance gains new life and rises to a climactic pitch. The fantasy associated with it is that the student by some subterfuge will be able "to grab the ball and run"—i.e., grab the professional prerogatives and escape untouched and unharmed. The driving motive is to steal from the analyst the symbols of parental power and flee the coop before the analyst can retaliate.

Assuming a reasonable measure of success in the dissolution of regressive forms of defense, and repair of damage to self-esteem, one needs to see to what extent the self-identity of the student has been cleared of confusion and strengthened, the consistency and dependability of this new image of self, and the extent to which the student is now ready to fulfill that self in productive and satisfying activity. Having achieved a firmer, more integrated image of self, can he now act maturely and realistically? Can he now make effective use of an appropriate set of personal standards, unburdened by irrational childhood guilts, regressive searching for the absolute security of the womb, or the security of infantile omnipotence? Can he subordinate the negatively toned goals of prestige, power, aggrandizement and material acquisition to more appropriate adult goals of personal and professional fulfillment? Experience has clearly shown that distorted, regressive motives of greed, envy and the desire for quick success and wealth impair the student's capacity for personal and scientific growth.

The fate of analysis hinges on the processes of emotional communication. Such communication can be good or bad, efficient, distorted or even absent. The primary condition for movement in the analytic relationship is the gradual heightening of the quality of emotional communication. Effective progress toward therapeutic resolution of the student's pathology is the product of and mirrored by a steady advance in the understanding by both participants of the dynamics of the analytic relationship. While affective communication is a subtle process, there are available significant indices of change in the quality of this process. Such indices can be discerned in the interplay of affectivity, motor response, and verbal utterance. Significant information is conveyed from student to analyst through mood behavior, body response, motor actions, and words. Clues to important unconscious communications are derived particularly from sub-verbal levels of behavior. It is the dynamic balance between these several levels of communication which supplies the relevant signs of improvement in the quality of affective communication. Are verbal utterances used to hide or reveal significant affects? Are the verbal statements integrated with or isolated from the student's affective experiences? Does the student use the instrument of speech to preserve alienation from his deeper emotions, or to integrate awareness of them? Another criterion is the extent to which the posture, spontaneous body movements and action patterns are in harmony with or dissociated from the patient's affectivity. Where there is significant incongruity between these several levels of behavior, it is inevitably an index to the disproportionate pressure of anxiety and the prevalence of repressive and other pathological defense behavior. To a corresponding degree, the quality of affective communication may be impaired—i.e., communication between the student and his deeper emotional experience, and communication between student and analyst. As the student nears the point of termination, ideally his verbal utterances, body movement, action patterns, affectivity, perception of dreams and other unconscious mental experience, should be approaching a harmonious whole.

In a parallel way, one can discern the degree to which the investment of the student's self in the therapeutic relationship is partial, segmented or relatively total. The effect of anxiety and pathological defense is to commit only a segment of the emotional self to the relationship. When the quality of emotional communication has reached its optimal pitch, the student commits himself wholly to the relationship, and in accordance with this, verbal utterances, body behavior and affective expression represent an integrated unity. This is simply another way of saying that the student is successfully integrating hitherto unconscious forces into his expanding awareness. When this happens the ego-integrative trend is reflected in the increasing clarity with which the student patient perceives the meaning of his dreams. In essence, the student is succeeding in the process of pulling previously dissociated components of himself into one piece. To put it most simply, he is pulling himself together. This can eventuate only when the student is finally able to trust the analyst as a helping person, instead of perceiving him as an authority figure by whom he may be injured as he has been by others in the past. A full trust of the analyst comes late and with a show of great stubbornness. When full trust finally emerges, the analyst's sincerity and helpful intentions have already been tested in innumerable ways; the analysis may be said then to be really beginning and also approaching its end.

The termination of formal analysis requires a working through of various levels of transference and counter-tranference. In so far as these are functional expressions of an interpersonal relationship, they should be conceived as the reciprocal elements of a single dynamic unit. In other words, the unsuited emotional expectations the student projects toward the analyst must be worked out side by side with any unreal emotional expectations the analyst may project toward the student. Time and again, students will say, "Whatever I say or do, I'm licked. You've got me coming and going. No matter how I behave, it turns out to be wrong." The implications of this for the student's neurotic past and also the implications of the analyst's expectations of the student need fully to be worked through. Part of what is involved here is the illusion that the analyst's rejection of the sick parts of the student's self constitutes a rejection of the student's whole self. This is inevitably the case when the student's sense of self is extensively identified with his pathological modes of adaptation. The student needs to be reminded here of his capacity to energize healthier, though dormant modes of adaptation.

Two interrelated aspects of transference need to be commented upon here: the student's perception of that phase in his relationship with the analyst, in which he occupies the position of child to parent, in which the distribution of power is unequal, and the student feels helpless and unable to defend himself; also in this position the relations of child to parent are perceived as oppositional rather than complementary, that is, the analyst is a potential enemy; he may turn treacherously against the student rather than be his friend and helper.

It takes a long time to work out the various permutations and combinations of this one basic theme. Gradually, the sense of unfairness in the disparity of power distribution and the perception of the analyst as a treacherous enemy weakens. As this happens, the student feels more equal, less like a child, and challenges the authority of the analyst increasingly. In the course of this process, the student becomes ever more frank in his criticisms of the analyst, alluding more and more to his observations of the real behavior of the analyst. At this stage, I have found it useful to have the student sit up and continue the therapeutic relationship in a face-to-face experience. I have been impressed that this is an especially valuable technique in the terminal phase of analysis. In my opinion, it facilitates the essential task of enabling the student to see the analyst as he really is, to bring his true opinion of the analyst's personality and limitations into the open, and thus avoid leaving unresolved residuals of hostility, guilt and dependence in the student. If one follows this procedure in the last phases of analysis, one discovers that subsequent social and professional contacts of student and analyst are much more comfortable. The clue to the pragmatic value of this terminal technique came from the spontaneous urge of students to work out residuals of transference conflict in a more equal and more real interpersonal relationship.

For similar reasons, I am inclined to suggest to a student in the terminal phase, a tailing off of the analysis to once-a-week sessions, and after that intermittent single sessions to work through whatever unfinished business remains of transference and counter-transference.

As is generally known, resistance patterns are especially subtle and stubborn in the terminal phase of analysis. The analyst must be on the alert to spot them, since they act as foci around which tendencies to regression converge. These take a multitude of forms, but the more significant centers of resistance are apt to follow patterns similar to older forms, and if the analyst has been vigilant in the detection of these, he will not fail to recognize new crystallizations of resistance, intensified by conflicts related to severance of the analytic relationship.

For example, one student with a brilliant intellect, but with deep-seated pathology, revealed his terminal resistance indirectly in an extensively rationalized plan for his future professional career. In this immensely plausible undertaking there was a subtly concealed unconscious motive for escaping the environments of all previously familiar father figures, and barricading himself with his wife in a suburban community where he might slip back with impunity into certain regressive play patterns, an as-if level of reality, where his compensatory self-sufficiency and omnipotence might reassert itself. This same student had earlier disclosed similar patterns of resistance. In the working through of this fantasy, he rediscovered the fears of the first phase of analysis: an underlying panic related to his basic submissiveness, his fear of castration and his fear of being destroyed through provocation of the analyst's retaliatory rage. In the early phase of his analysis, he withdrew from his wife emotionally and sexually, thereby creating domestic conflicts and blaming these on the analyst. Then he talked a blue streak, but really avoided a significant emotional contact with the analyst. Secretly he refused to admit he was really in analysis until the impact of critical transference change forced itself into his consciousness. At each turning point in the analysis which signified forward movement he balked and tended to "act out." At the point where he was given permission to initiate supervised work in analysis, he brought about a minor car accident. After that he tried his damnedest to flunk the examination of the American Board of Psychiatry.

Finally, he demonstrated in his behavior that he could tolerate emotional intimacy in his relations with everyone excepting his analyst. This student's need to preserve the barrier of emotional isolation from his analyst was the core of his resistance. Letting down this barrier symbolized surrender to a lethal paternal invasion. At all costs, even self-destruction, this had to be prevented.

Other resistances took the form of residual projections of the student's need to outwit the analyst, and triumph over his authority by a final magic destruction of him. Through subservience, he sought to lull the analyst, put him off guard, and then grab the required professional privilege for analytical practice, before he was caught in his secret crime.

There is endless diversity in the resistance patterns of students. The special complications of their position as patients, their professional and social contacts with training analysts and other analytic faculty add subtlety to their disguises of resistance. This demands the utmost in alertness and perspicacity of training analysts.

Another level at which the progress of analysis and appropriateness of termination can be tested is through the group adaptation achieved by the student. Significant insights into the adaptational success of the student may be found in the quality of his family relationships, marital, child-parent, etc. Similarly, significant information may be elicited regarding the quality of his extra-familial relationships, with friends, peers, and especially his fellow students. The judgments drawn of an analysand by his fellow students are of inestimable value in appraising his mental health and the progress of his analysis. The judgments of degrees of change in the student's personality by fellow students and their opinions as to his nearness to completion of analysis prove often to be remarkably accurate. At another level, the quality of relationships the student achieves with persons outside the professional field are also informative. But the surest test of all is the consensus among his fellow students. In these various ways, the effective mental health of the student may be appraised in terms of everyday interpersonal performance.

An indispensable consideration which must always be taken into account is the suitability of the timing of termination in relation to other phases of the student's training experience. This may be measured in several ways. The analyst's own judgment may be checked against the more objective opinions of other teachers who appraise the level of his work in seminars, and in supervised clinical work. Because of the different interpersonal setting, instructors may be enabled to observe and evaluate the adequacy of the student's emotional functioning in ways that are not easily possible for the analyst. Particularly valuable are the observations of the supervising analysts. Residual pathology and defects in the optimal use of self in the therapeutic role can be readily discerned under the conditions of supervised work. Not uncommon are those instances where residual pathology and countertransference disturbances are detected by a supervising analyst after formal personal analysis has ceased. Often, in such cases, the student is asked to resume personal analysis.

Perhaps the acid test of a student's readiness to leave analysis is the way in which he fits his image of himself to his image of the world, molds his personal and professional goals, resolves the confusion of his value conflicts, and sets himself a decisive path in life. Assuming that the student has come to terms with his inner needs, his intrapsychic conflicts, and has succeeded in bringing his previously alienated parts into a balanced unity, he now faces the delicate task of bringing into harmony his newly integrated image of self with his image of the world in which he seeks to contribute. Now, student and analyst together must check the answers to several questions: How intact is the student's sense of self, how strong, how clear? Has he achieved a healthy equilibrium for the various parts of himself? How adequate is the student's perception of the reality of himself and the world about him? How appropriately does he fit the one with the other? What is the effect of all this on his groping for goals and values? With what effectiveness can the student apply himself to his professional responsibilities? On the analytic stage is lived out dramatically the student's struggle to find what he seeks in family life, and at the same time to integrate his personal and family needs with his professional strivings. In both spheres, the student seeks the optimal level of self-expression. Throughout the course of analysis, changes in sense of self have been paralleled by changes in the perception of the surrounding world. Now, as the analysis approaches its end, the student is challenged to precipitate a set of personal and professional values appropriate to his identity and the nature of the real world of which he is a part.

The relative success or failure of this effort can be effectively measured by scrutinizing the dynamic integration of the student's personality into each of the several significant roles which he must fulfill in life. Specifically, a student integrates his personality into his family roles, as husband (wife), father (mother), and/or son (daughter); he integrates his personality into his role as student in an analytic institute; he fits his personality into another role as researcher or private practitioner. If his personality has shaped itself into a harmonious healthy whole, and he has evolved a consistent set of values and goals, one finds little evidence of clash in the student's adaptation to the requirements of these several roles. There is a minimum of stress and strain in the reconciliation and integration of these several social roles. He can demonstrate in each a fairly even degree of successful performance. If there are residuals of pathology and failure to build a consistent and clear image of self, there will be inaccurate and distorted perceptions of the surrounding environment. Together with this, there will be evidences of excessive stress in the task of reconciling the requirements of the several significant roles the student must play in life. In fact, the student may experience critical conflict and pain with some degree of failure in reconciling his family role with his professional role, or reconciling his role as student with his aims in private psychiatric practice.

There are ways of examining the dynamic relations of individual personality and role behavior which may be useful to a training analyst. It is possible to appraise degrees of success and failure of adaptation in each of several roles, also success or failure in the harmonization of multiple roles. The relations of personality and role behavior may be illuminated through the use of the following criteria: What is the student's image of the interpersonal requirements of a given social role? What image of self is projected in this role? What specific personal needs are mobilized in this role? What anxieties and conflicts are activated? How does the student control the emotional interchange between himself and the significant others who occupy the reciprocal social role? What are his techniques of mastery, his defenses against anxiety? What degree of gratification results or what degree of frustration and failure? By comparing the integrations of the student's personality into each of his several significant roles it becomes possible to shed light on the fit or clash of these roles, and the corresponding tension and impairment of adaptation. A tracing of disturbances of this sort will quickly illuminate areas of residual personal pathology, and conflicts of aims and values, which need to be resolved before the student and analyst call "quits."

At this critical stage the attitudes and value orientation of the training analyst play a potent role in the resolution of the student's own struggle to crystallize a suitable value position. The training analyst is obligated to be explicitly clear as to his own conception of mental health, healthy values for the individual, for members of the profession, and for society. Unless he is explicitly clear as to his own value position, there is great danger that he will unwittingly and prejudicially influence the student's value orientation and significant life choices. How much of himself does the student give to his family, to his professional pursuits, to his personal pleasures? What are his capacities and bents? Would he best fulfill himself in the practice of analytic therapy, in teaching, in research? Can he carve out a significant career in a medical school or in some branch of applied psychoanalysis in the community? Is he motivated to achieve a modicum of the world's goods, to assure himself creature comforts, or has he caught the scientific bug, and is he willing to give up other satisfactions for the joys of scientific discovery? The student needs to set up for himself clear guideposts by which to pilot his way through his personal and professional life. Nothing is so discouraging as the sight of a young analyst wobbling from pillar to post, confused, uncertain, wafted by the winds, opportunistic, undirected. Analytic practice is no sinecure. It is not for him who seeks the easy life.

Finally, some comment is in order with regard to the confusion between long and thorough training analyses. In some quarters, the stress on thoroughness takes the form of encouraging student analyses of unusual length or dictating the frequency of sessions per week. The length of a student analysis or the frequency of sessions is in no sense a guarantee of its thoroughness. The quality of dealing with transference and counter-transference, the quality of the interpersonal communication is what really counts, not its sheer duration in time. We must be as fully alert to the dangers of over-long analyses, as to the dangers of defective analyses. We must be vigilant against those forms of prolonged training analyses which exhaust and ennervate both student and analyst, sometimes paradoxically weakening the potential strength and independence of the student, rather than fostering their development. Needless to say, at the other pole, there lurks all the dangers of an incomplete and abortive analysis. I wonder, too, sometimes if training analysts give more than lip-service to the principle that students often achieve their greatest growth in the post-analytic phase rather than in the throes of the process itself.

Finally, if we recognize the doubtfulness of anything approaching permanent immunity against emotional illness, would it not be in order to place stronger emphasis on Freud's own suggestion of future reanalysis, at a point when the student is more mature, more experienced and faces a new set of life problems?

The ultimate criterion, and this cannot possibly be over-stressed, is the student's ability to live the full cup of life, to be emotionally free to confront life, not only with security and confidence, and without the constrictions of neurotic fear, but to realize his full potential as a person, to be creative in the fullest sense of the word, in his profession, in his family life and the community at large.

CHAPTER 7

Goals in Therapy

The single, all-encompassing goal of psychotherapy is cure. But, what is a cure in psychotherapy? In confronting this challenge, we must be concerned with several questions: the multiple meanings of the term "cure"; the relations of cure to our changing conception of emotional illness; partial cure, complete cure, the quality of cure; the proof of cure, the relations of cure to the specific illness and person being treated; and finally, the relations of cure to the nature of the curing process itself—the dynamics of the psychotherapeutic relationship.

At the present stage, it is safe to assume that standards for cure, the relations of cure to illness and to the curing process, are by no means uniform. In these respects, there are in our day wide divergences of orientation between the various schools of psychotherapy, and among individual therapists themselves. In one sense, it ought to come as no surprise that each therapist evolves a relatively personal set of criteria for the goals of therapy and the signs of cure. From one point of view, this perhaps will always be the case; from another, it reflects a present state of affairs which is by no means ideal. In so far as psychotherapy is a healing art, which expresses the therapist's unique use of his personal talents in the curative role, there must always be striking variations from one therapist to the next in the practice of this art, and in the corresponding judgments of the attainment of cure. Going one step further, the therapist's creativity as an artist will achieve a varying expression in accordance with the unique interpersonal stimuli by which he is confronted in his relation with each of his patients. In consequence, the form of his art, and the convictions of cure will be somewhat different for the same therapist with each of a series of patients. In other words, the final portrait must always be molded both by the particular patient who sits as a model and the gifts of the particular artist. Psychotherapy as the practice of an art is highly personal, cannot and perhaps should not be reduced to a stereotype.

However, that component of psychotherapy which is the healing art cannot by itself go very far, with those rare exceptions of miracles wrought by geniuses, unless it is solidly buttressed by a foundation of scientific knowledge of personality, psychopathology, interpersonal relations, and the dynamics of therapeutic process. In principle, the psychotherapist labors under a critical handicap unless his talent rests on a secure feeling of scientific training, experience and wisdom. Since a scientific rationale for the practice of psychotherapy is sorely needed, we

Reprinted with permission of the Editor, *The American Journal of Psychoanalysis*, 1956, Vol. XVI, No. 1, 9-14.

must continuously try to objectify the issues which are pertinent to the establishment of goals of therapy, and definitions of cure and the curing process.

The fate of any psychotherapeutic undertaking is influenced by at least four factors: the character of the patient, the character of the therapist, the unique features of emotional communication between them, and the impingement of environmental forces on both persons and what goes on between them.

Today, of necessity, any discussion of these issues must be incomplete, since our understanding of cure and the curing process reflects the same lag as currently prevails in our changing conception of mental and emotional illness and its causation. The definitions of goals of therapy, cure and methods of therapy must inevitably mirror these changing conceptions.

The mentally ill person has at various times in history been thought to be a demon, a witch, a sacred prophet, a person cursed with a hereditary taint or an organic defect of the brain and nervous system; more recently, as a person disabled by a functional disorder of individual personality, or a distortion in interpersonal adaptation.

Against this background, present hypotheses concerning cure and the curing process must be conceived as tentative and provisional. With this in mind, we shall consider here the multiple meanings of cure, the manifestations of cure, the relations of cure to current conceptions of mental illness and mental health, and finally, the relations of means to ends—namely, the correspondence of cure to the curing process itself.

The term "cure" implies first the therapeutic removal of symptoms, those specific signs of disordered functioning which characterize a particular illness. For some therapists, this constitutes the sole meaning of cure; it is conceived as a significant result, sufficient unto itself. Perhaps for certain forms of mental illness, this outcome is good enough. For many therapists, however, and for a great variety of disturbances of mental health, this first meaning of cure is too limiting. The concept of cure carries other meanings—among them, the strengthening of the personality so that the patient may not again fall ill. In this context, it is expected that the process of cure will provide some degree of immunization against a further invasion of illness. Still another meaning of cure is contained in the notion that the personality of the patient must have undergone a basic change, which signifies not only increased adaptive strength and a capacity for resistance to illness, but, in a positive sense, that the individual is now able to realize his potential, to capitalize on his personal resources, so as to feel free, happy, to satisfy personal needs and be an efficient, productive person. Finally, cure also has the meaning that the individual, freed of cripping anxieties, can now unfold his capacity to love others, for sharing with them both pleasure and responsibility, and can experience the full gamut of satisfaction in making a positive contribution to the welfare of family, friends, and community.

In this broader scheme, the goals of therapy and the connotations of cure constitute a hierarchy of meanings, which may be applied with flexibility and discrimination to a wide assortment of illnesses and psychotherapeutic undertakings. In some, it may make sense to rest content with a lesser cure; in others it is fitting and right that we aspire to a more complete and superior quality of cure.

Then comes the question, how do we know? What in any given case constitutes the proof of cure? The challenge here is to build a set of criteria by which we may appropriately test the adequacy of cure in these several hierarchical meanings. The first criterion is the easiest, namely, the evidence for the disappearance of structured psychopathological symptoms. This is certainly basic to cure, and the least equivocal criterion. However, as soon as we move from here to the question of evidence of the strengthening of personality and immunization against recurrent illness, we enter upon less sure ground; the standards grow hazy and differences among therapists mount. Some speak vaguely of the signs of "ego-strengthening," and increased "maturity" and stability. Others erect more stringent and specific criteria which pertain to favorable directions of change in anxiety response, ways of coping with conflict, control of emotion and impulse, defense operations, affectivity, self-esteem, interpersonal relations and reality perception. Finally, if we inspect those criteria which demonstrate increased capacity for self-fulfillment, and healthier interpersonal relations, we discover almost as much diversity among therapists as there are therapists themselves.

Some of the reasons for this are clear. As we move away from the traditionally narrow concern with the individual and internal economy of personality to interpersonal adaptation, and the relations of individual to society, our scientific knowledge becomes progressively less precise, and we enter into that no-man's land which is the border area of the relation of values to mental health. As soon as we think of cure not merely as the absence of mental disease, but in positive terms of healthy emotional living within the self and in human relations, there is no escape from the confrontation of values. Values have to do with the search for meaning in life. Meaning is not to be found in the isolated individual; for one who walls himself off from other humans, life becomes more and more empty; meaning is lost. The meaning of life can be discovered only in the alignment of one's conception of self with the significant relations with others. Values are derivatives of social relations, and serve as guideposts for social action. They reflect basic life attitudes, ideals and motivations upon which we base our actions toward desired goals. They provide points of reference for the individual's orientation to his place and role in his family and wider community. They are functions of the interaction of self-image, the image of others and the perception of reality. Values, and the direction and quality of the corresponding social actions, are symptomatic of healthy or unhealthy mental functioning. To quote Burgum: "In this sense, it is impossible to define mental health apart from considerations of appropriate action toward common good. Common good may be between parent and child, husband and wife, friend and neighbor, workers on a job, members of a community."*

Assuming such premises are valid, it follows, then, that the goals erected for psychotherapy and the appraisal of evidence of cure would be directly affected by the interaction of the respective value orientations of patient and therapist. To make the issue concrete, would a therapist consider a patient cured if his values remained oriented to a goal of self-realization at the expense of others? Would the patient be cured if his self-esteem remained tied to a form of competitiveness and ruthless aggression which threatened injury or destruction to other persons? To be secure, is it inevitable that one individual sit on another's head, or would it be healthier if they stood shoulder to shoulder on the same bench? When therapists encourage patients in self-assertiveness, it behooves them to consider the interpersonal matrix in which this is expressed. When the "strengthening" of self-assertion is translated into annihilation of another person, the therapist had better take heed. To encourage this is to cripple the patient's self-esteem. To build oneself up by tearing another down brings shame, mortification and a crippling of capacity for effective action. This is no strengthening of the ego. The therapist's goal is not to unharness such destructiveness, but to modify the image of self and others, and related values, so they may learn for the first time the satisfaction of self-expression in consonance with the good of others, rather than in opposition.

When a patient asserts a claim on the therapist for unconditional acceptance and love, this usually reflects a need to deny inner guilt concerning destructive motivation. Here the patient behaves as if he demanded an uncritical tolerance of the bad in himself as well as the good. It is the therapist's task here to win the allegiance of the healthier and more reasoning parts of the patient's mind in the struggle to modify the sick and destructive parts. The patient needs to discover that the therapist may understand and accept him as a human being while rejecting the sick part of him, his destructiveness and the related distortions of value attitudes. Where a manipulative patient treats people as things, it is not in the interest of the cure that the therapist be accepting of this value. At a certain stage of therapy the clash of values between patient and therapist becomes the stage for the working through of residual components of pathology. This need not mean in any sense that the therapist engages in a mission of morally converting the patient to the therapist's value position. It does mean that the patient is required to examine critically the implications of value conflicts within himself, and between himself and the therapist, if he is to get well.

Inevitably, a therapist must concern himself

---

*M. Burgum—"Values and Some Technical Problems of Psychotherapy," presented at the 1955 meeting of the American Orthopsychiatric Association.

with the problems of joining value and action, action and consequence. His aim should be to heal the split in the patient's perception of reality by rejoining these pathologically dissociated facets of experience.

Present notions of health and illness are in flux. We tend less to view illness exclusively as a distortion contained within one individual. We lean more toward a view of mental illness as a consequence of the internalization within the individual of pathological social processes. We think of mental illness more broadly as being reflected at three phenomenological levels: the distortions within the one individual, the pathology of interpersonal relations, and the unhealthy patterns of social interaction which prevail in the group itself.

Inevitably, this extended view of illness is paralleled by significant changes in the principles of psychotherapy and in the criteria of cure. There is discernible today an increasing need among therapists to consider cure not merely in terms of bringing about the "return of the repressed," or expanding awareness of intrapsychic conflict, but in dissolving distortions of self-identity and corresponding distortions of interpersonal relations. The sharp increase in preoccupation with ego-psychology and group dynamics bears testimony to this. There is increasing concern both with child and adult patients in exploring the emerging relations between the inner concept of self and the concept of personal environment. More and more we see the need for relating disturbances of the mental health of the family group and the surrounding community with emotional disturbance inside the individual. This constitutes a shift of emphasis from an exclusive preoccupation with the internal economy of personality to a broader probing of the relations of individual personality with processes of emotional integration of the individual into the group, and the mental health of the group itself. The growing investigations of problems of interpersonal communication all move in the same direction: that mental health needs to be evaluated on the continuum of individual, family, social structure and culture. When we view the issues of restoration of mental health in this broader conceptual frame, the role of values becomes less ambiguous. Cure becomes an experience in which the assertion of individual needs, whether for security, self-esteem, power or sexual fulfillment, complements the needs of significant other persons, rather than that one person achieves satisfaction at the cost of another. The achievement of a healthy image of self involves, then, a correct perception of the image of others, their needs, a respect for the dignity, integrity and worth of others, a growing capacity for equality in human relations, as against an orientation to power and exploitive relations between human beings. As we learn more about the relation of values to mental health, we may find a way in psychotherapy to diminish the tensions of interpersonal adaptation, particularly in those spheres where the individual must integrate himself into multiple roles, the requirements of which seem to clash, as for example in the case of the woman who must harmonize the role requirements of wife, mother and career.

Now, let us attempt to relate the goals of therapy with cure and the curative process itself. If we accept the premise that a logical relationship exists between ends and means, then the means of cure—the psychotherapeutic relationship and communication process—must correspond to the goal of therapy. If the goal of therapy is cure in its several meanings, then the therapist must himself be properly cured. It is the ethical obligation of a therapist to do everything conceivable to get cured, stay cured, and continue to grow as a person. To paraphrase Erich Fromm, the only tool a psychotherapist has is himself, and as a surgeon cares for his knife, so must a therapist keep himself clean and sharp. Only as he fulfills this responsibility can he achieve his goal with his patient. The therapist, through his own being, must provide the proof to his patient that mental health is no mirage, that it can be achieved. The patient uses his therapist as a model, a test for his faith in psychotherapy. Does mental health really exist? Do people really love? Is it possible, after all, to reconcile one person's strivings for satisfaction with the needs of others, or is it inevitable that in asserting oneself, one hurts another? When a patient seeks an answer to these questions, he takes a close look at this therapist. The therapist personifies in himself the ideal of mental health as reflected in his behavior as an individual, and as a living representation of healthy patterns of human relations. In this sense, through his attitudes, goals, values, and interpersonal relations, he epitomizes a standard of a healthy social reality. Through the emotional interaction of patient and therapist, it becomes possible to correct the patient's distorted image of self and also his view of social reality.

Another significant criterion for progressive change toward cure, therefore, is the patient's increasing understanding of his relationship with his therapist. Step by step, as the twists of transference are worked through and a more appropriate image of self and therapist emerges, we may feel increasing confidence in the cure.

Mistrust of psychotherapy cannot be dissociated from mistrust of the therapist and mistrust of the self. Mistrust in the patient expresses itself in avoidance of a close relationship, in the defensive preservation of a certain detachment from the therapist. Emotional alienation from the therapist is usually paralleled by the patient's alienation from his own emotions. This tends to express itself in specific patterns of resistance, self-protective behavior which reflects a fear of exposure to hurt and apprehension of exploitation or betrayal by the therapist. In this context, the patient reveals a lack of faith in the possibility of therapeutic change.

The patient enters therapy yet cherishes the secret belief that therapy is some magic hoax that doesn't really change anyone. Here we come flush against a glaring and irrational paradox. The patient sets out to relieve his suffering and change himself, but clings privately to the conviction that the powers of psychotherapy are nil.

The relevance of this for the goal of therapy and criteria of cure is that at a point nearing termination these deeper suspicions and resistances often become critically intensified. This may at this stage of therapy attain to climactic strength, and unless the therapist is vigilant, such trends may nullify the results of therapy. In this connection, the patient will often harbor the secret plan of mollifying the therapist and escaping from the relationship untouched. He may treasure the fantasy of outwitting the therapist, so that he may stay exactly as he was.

Regardless of critical waves of suspicion and resistance, effective and secure progress toward cure must be mirrored in a tangible forward movement in the patient-therapist relationship, expressed in several ways: diminution of evidences of emotional alienation, increased intimacy, heightening of the quality of emotional communication, increased sincerity and spontaneity, progressive clarification of the image of self and image of the therapist.

Assuming some measure of success in the lessening of anxiety, the resolution of pathogenic conflicts, the removal of symptoms, the melting of regressive defenses and repair of damaged self-esteem, the therapist must keep a close watch for tell-tale signs of growing trust and intimacy, and an increasing sense of equality between patient and therapist. The greater openness, spontaneity and honesty of the patient takes the place of the prior mistrust, fear of exposure and hurt at the hands of the therapist.

As the patient enters this stage, there is progressively less discrepancy between the patient's verbal utterances and his affective behavior. Words are used not to hide but to reveal. Verbal statements, body movement, action patterns and affectivity begin to reflect something approaching a harmonious whole. Whenever there is a significant incongruity between the several levels of behavior, this is invariably an index to the disproportionate pressure of anxiety, and the prevalence of pathological defense behavior. Under such conditions, effective emotional communication is interfered with. As trust in the therapist increases and emotional communication improves, the patient pulls previously dissociated components of his psyche into one piece; he is, in effect, pulling himself together. In a parallel trend, instead of investing himself in the therapeutic relationship in a partial, segmented and compromised way, he commits himself more totally to the relationship. In accordance with this, verbal utterances, body behavior and affective expression merge perceptibly into a unity. At the same time, he is better able to assimilate evidences of unconscious tendencies, particularly as revealed in dreams.

All these trends converge to a point of optimal trust and acceptance of the therapist as a helping person, a friend rather than enemy, a supporter rather than a punitive authority. A full trust of the therapist comes late and with a show of great stubbornness. When genuine trust emerges, the therapist's sincerity and benign purposes have already been tested in innumerable ways. The therapy may then be said to be really beginning and also approaching its end.

In the course of this process, the patient's

inner face and the face he presents to the outer world tend to merge and at the same time, he reaches a clearer and more accurate perception of surrounding realities.

These critical shifts in the interpersonal experience of patient and therapist are increasingly reflected in the patient's performance in real life, in work, in personal relations with family, friends and community.

Since by its very nature, psychotherapy is a shared experience, any decision as to the goal of therapy and the proof of cure must take into account the patient's strivings as well as the therapist's standards. Such judgments, as well as the timing of termination of therapy, should not be arbitrary or unilateral decisions on the part of the therapist, but should rather reflect a consensus of patient and therapist as to cure.

The ultimate test is, of course, the objective one: the patient's performance in life itself, the alleviation of his suffering and dread, his confidence and courage in facing life, his capacity to grow, to live fully, to love and share with others the great adventure of the only life he knows.

CHAPTER 8

Transference and Counter-transference

Transference is a vivid and inspiring idea. Yet, somewhere in the sharing and cultivation of it, we become muddled. In the very exertion of tracing its endlessly subtle nuances in human relations, the process of clarification bogs down. Beginning with Freud's basic formulations, this subject has occasioned ceaseless debate. Despite this, there persists till now an element of ineluctable mystery. The complexities of transference mount geometrically as we try to define its relations with reality, maturation and social learning. The element of mystery extends beyond transference; it encompasses the entire system of psychoanalytic theory and practice.

On occasion, a writer vividly absorbed in communicating a vivid idea discovers that the flow of his expression suddenly slows down and threatens to break off altogether. The right words simply do not come, his writing turns awkward and labored. His thought processes become confused and blocked. He experiences a mounting distress. When this happens, the writer wise in his ways calls a halt. He takes time out to clear away the cobwebs. He casts aside what he has written, and starts all over again.

I propose, therefore, to take a fresh look at the idea of transference. I shall endeavor to reexamine transference and counter-transference from a particular point of view, namely, in relation to the shift from a conceptual model of psychoanalysis as representing essentially a one-person phenomenon, non-social, though influenced by an external agent, to a conceptual model of psychoanalysis as a two-person, social phenomenon.

Freud's term, transference, derives its specific definition within the theoretical scheme which he devised for psychoanalytic therapy as a whole. The evolution of Freudian thought is complex and reveals a special feature which should be explicitly stated. In conceptualizing transference, resistance, change and cure, Freud tried valiantly but did not always keep faith with his own reference frame. In the course of his determined mining of the unconscious, he sometimes expressed contradictory opinions; in asides he violated his conceptual model. Although this is sometimes confusing, in the long view it is all to the good. Freud's contradictory asides are a

Reprinted with permission from *Psychoanalysis and the Psychoanalytic Review*, Fall 1959, Vol. 46, No. 3, 17-28.

measure of his integrity. It is by close study of these very contradictions that we may find a few more answers.

In erecting a comparison of a one- and two-person theoretical model of analysis, I must draw broad, schematic generalizations and omit some of Freud's own qualifications. In the Freudian frame, the goal of cure is to remove amnesias, to undo repressions, to make the unconscious conscious. "Where the id was, there must ego be." Psychoanalysis endeavors "to take something away, a pathogenic idea." "It does not seek to introduce something or add anything new."* Transference represents the perceptual experience of the present in terms of the past. Transference is positive or negative. The favorable components of transference are undisturbed. The negative transference and the erotically-tinged transference expectations are analyzed. Resistance derives from negative transference. "Cure is a re-education in the overcoming of internal resistance." But Freud also said, "it remains a mystery why transference provides the strongest resistance to cure."

The analyst is anonymous. He is a mirror. He hides his face. He reflects "only what is shown to him."† As a blank screen, he receives the imprint of the patient's projected phantasies but withholds the usual social cues. He does not fulfill the part of a real person. The patient behind the couch is literally in the dark concerning the real qualities of the analyst. The Freudian model, therefore, does not provide the architecture for a true social experience.

The analyst energizes the patient's explorations of his inner past life. Conflict with the analyst is reinterpreted in terms of conflict with the older parts of self, linked to childhood conditionings with mother, father, sibling, etc. The primary focus is on disturbed and conflicted orientation to past experience. Intrinsic to the process is the temporary subordination of reality. Transference achieves not only a position of prominence, but one of dominance over existing realities. Ultimately there comes the task of working through by way of interpretation and reality testing. The analyst personifies objective reality. But the check with this representation of reality is delayed. There are unsolved problems in the reality testing phase of the analyst's role. For the patient, there is not one reality, but many realities. The analyst's function does not clearly reflect these realities. Often the analyst lacks definitive information concerning significant aspects of the prevailing realities, or he is deficient in his capacity for translating them to the patient. Insofar as the analyst has no face, no identity, and shows no emotion, I repeat, this is not a true social experience.

The classical analytic process favors a reliving of the symbiotic component of conflict in the original child-parent unit. It reactivates the craving for magic omnipotence. It propels into the foreground the autistic, magic core of the psyche. As defined, this process lends access to the egocentric, symbiotic nucleus of intrapsychic pathology which contains the distorted percepts of the joined infant-parent image and the own body. The analyst does not intrude his personality and emotions. Such emotions are conceived as a contamination, an impurity injected into the patient's expressions of primary process. Here, in Freud's view, the primitive, irrational expressions of the patient's unconscious may dangerously contaminate the analyst's mind.

The patient projects his irrational, conflict-ridden emotions, phantasies, and magic expectations, i.e., primary process; the analyst injects the modifying, organizing, and disciplining effects of secondary process. As the patient brings into awareness his unconscious, the analyst contributes insight, reason, reality and conscious control. Between them they make up the functions of one mind.

Now what happens the moment we conceptually join transference to counter-transference? Just as soon as we view these as reciprocal processes, the heads and tails of a single phenomenological entity, we have, in effect, executed a shift from a theoretical model of analysis as a one-person to a two-person phenomenon. Once we admit counter-transference into the conceptual framework, we are compelled to envisage the interaction of two minds, two whole persons. This is now a dyadic relationship, involving a circular interchange of emotion. We must then be concerned for each of these persons with the balance between real and unreal, healthy, appropriate emotions, and pathological, inappro-

*FREUD, S.: On Psychotherapy (1904). *Collected Papers*, Vol. I, p. 254.

†———: Recommendations for Physicians on the Psychoanalytic Method of Treatment. *Ibid*, Vol. II, p. 331.

priate ones. The shift to a two-person interaction model now provides the potential for a true social interaction and requires the redefinition of all the part processes. Each part must be interrelated with every other, and with the whole. Transference is then conceived as a failure of social learning and must immediately be tested against the backdrop of reality and the potentials for new social learning. In order to achieve internal consistency in such a framework, we require an expanded foundation for the dynamics of personality, namely, a biopsycho-social model. Intrapsychic events must be matched against the corresponding interpersonal ones; the unconscious must be paralleled by a definition of the conscious organization of experience and the related modes of social adaptation. The unreal must be matched against the real. The essential continuity of past, present, and future must be respected; a person's behavior may be molded by his view of the future as well as by his view of the past. The theoretical and clinical implications of this shift in conceptualization are enormous. Transference, counter-transference, free association, resistance, working through, interpretation, reality testing and new learning—all become interrelated parts of a unified process.

Freud characterized counter-transference as the influence of the patient on the analyst's unconscious. The analyst receives and interprets these messages from his own unconscious. But he must exclude them from the analytic process; they are an impurity, a contamination. In recent years the literature reveals an increasing concern with the problems and uses of counter-transference. Clara Thompson highlighted the significance of the analyst as a real person. Benedek asserted the view that the therapeutic personality is the most important agent in the whole therapeutic process. Tower hypothesized a regular and inevitable emergence of a counter-transference neurosis in the analyst. Weigert, Fromm-Reichmann, Tauber, Gitelson, Heiman, Orr and many others have made specific contributions (see bibliography).

In the light of present-day knowledge, could we not say: the real issue is not whether the analyst has or shows emotions, but rather, which emotions are right and which wrong for the healing of the given patient. And exactly here, emerges the critical importance of the subverbal components of communication. In my opinion, true healing does not take place unless the understanding of emotion goes both ways, not only that the analyst understands the patient's emotions, but also that the patient understands the analyst's emotions. The analyst must sift out his own emotions and inject those selected emotions which the patient requires to experience in order to become well. Freud stated that analysis takes something away, a pathogenic idea; it does not add anything new. As I see it, were this literally correct, there could be no reality testing and no new social learning. Since transference is a failure of social learning, to accomplish its resolution, the analyst must inject something new, namely the right emotions to neutralize the patient's wrong ones.

The history of psychoanalytic thought reveals this as a huge area of controversy, and a problem not yet solved. It is the battleground of an impassioned war. It is the unsettled controversy as to the proper balance of affect and reason in the therapeutic process. It brings up the contentious historical issues argued between Freud and Ferenczi. It stirs up the whole argument concerning the role of insight and the limitations of insight. It activates the many discrepant views concerning the dynamics of change during analysis; the aims, goals, patient-therapist interaction and indices of cure.

Surely, the crux of the matter rests on the testing of the conflicted affects against a rational definition of interpersonal reality. Surely, the injection of reason, insight, and conscious control is indispensable, but true change and true learning comes only with feeling and doing, the actual experiencing of the clash between affect and reason in social action and reaction.

Is there danger in the analyst's use of his own sense of self, and in the injection into the process of various selected emotions? Certainly there is. But nothing ventured, nothing gained. And there is certainly no magic erasure of danger in the principle that the analyst shows no face, no identity, and no emotions. This, in my opinion, is an understandable caution on the analyst's part, but also a questionable one. Such caution may lead to stasis. Certainly analysis holds danger both for the patient and the analyst. Life itself holds danger, but also the thrill and adventure of expanding experience and new growth. Nothing in life stands still; it is never safe. We must take a calculated risk, but must know clearly what we are doing.

As I see it, the withholding of emotion on the analyst's part, the hiding of the analyst's real self, is no answer to the dangers of emotional contamination. These dangers are there, both ways. To play it too safe, however, is to sterilize the potential of analysis as a therapeutic instrument. The sheer avoidance of emotional engagement with the patient may protect a cautious and frightened analyst, but it will not heal anyone. Is it not so that some analysts are overprotective of a patient's anxieties? This may, in fact, be not a genuine protection of the patient against psychic pain, but rather a cautious protection of the analyst's own anxieties from exposure to the public eye. In such instances, the analyst is hiding himself. He is giving himself immunity against possible criticism rather than assuring the welfare and growth of his patient.

It is my conviction that people can tolerate emotional upset and psychic pain much more readily than we generally suppose. Basically, a patient's need for his emotions to be deeply understood is a far more potent force than his fear of personal exposure and psychic pain. In other words, if the patient is given his choice between exposing his psychic wounds and the opportunity to be deeply understood, he will decisively choose to be understood and take his chances with the pain. On the other side of the fence, if the analyst hides his emotions, the patient will surely find him out, and will indict him as being insincere and self-protective. Therefore, as I see it, there is only one choice for the analyst, and that is to face squarely the possible dangers of emotional contagion in a close relationship, but using to the best of knowledge the right emotions and taking maximal advantage of the potential for inducing change and new learning.

Closely related to this question is the issue of the criteria one uses for the judgment of change in a patient's behavior. Some analysts have stressed the use of dreams as the index of change, others have emphasized insight, still others a diminution of anxiety. It seems to me, however, that no one of these indices is adequate by itself. What we seek is total change, certainly not mere intellectual insight which fails to be translated into life action. The only dependable evidence for change is a shift toward integration of previously dissociated elements of the personality, a change best expressed as the ability to pull oneself together into one piece. This is reflected in a growing harmony in the expression of words, feeling, body movement and integration of self into social roles. Ultimately, this moves toward the creation of a new identity and a changed value orientation.

The problem of evaluation of change during analysis confronts us with a basic problem: how shall we judge the question of decision making and action in real life? The dangers of irrational decisions and actions during analysis are self-evident. The awareness of this underscores the principle of postponement of critical life decisions until the completion of analysis. But decision making is the essence of life; it means action. Action is the core of aliveness. Without decision and action, there is no movement. There can be no life. There arises then, for analysis a crucial value judgment: the distinction between action that is appropriate, rational action, and "acting out"—inappropriate, dangerous action. Then, there is—to coin a phrase—"acting in." "Acting in" may be viewed as those forms of "acting out" in the analytic relationship which are untested against reality. This may sometimes be fully as dangerous as "acting out" in real life. Freud himself distinguished between the mild, relatively harmless forms of "acting out" and the dangerous ones. Often, there is only a hairline difference between appropriate action and "acting out." It is my conviction that the issue in analytic therapy is not at all to discourage action, but only to promote progressively more appropriate action toward the solution of conflict and opening up of new avenues of personal and social development. Analysis ought to be a means toward a better way of life, not a substitute for living.

In a basic sense, all action in all places represents a varying balance of appropriate and inappropriate, rational and irrational experience. In this view, some forms of "acting in," i.e., "acting out" in analysis, provide the opportunity for solution of conflict and for the promotion of new learning and new maturation. By a similar token, however, some, and I emphasize some, forms of "acting out" in real life may also provide avenues of solution of conflict and new growth, depending upon the character and involvement of the persons who are partners in the "acting out." There can be no "acting out" without the complicity of a partner. It seems to me there is a bias here, to the effect that "acting in" which is "acting out" in the analytic relationship is a desirable experience, while "acting out" in real life is an undesirable and dangerous experience. I don't think we can so arbitrarily entrench this distinction. We must more carefully differentiate benign and malignant forms of such action. This is ultimately a problem of the emotional complementarity of the patient's personality and the analyst's personality; also, the complementarity of the patient's personality and the personalities of other significant individuals with whom the patient is emotionally engaged in a close way.

In this context, I raise a question. Why do we prize the irrationality of transference neurosis? Why do we enhance the value of "acting in" and so arbitrarily indict "acting out" in other relationships? I sometimes wonder. The patient is supposed to be as normal as possible in real life while reserving his neurosis for analysis. Is the analyst's role the opposite? Is he expected to be normal in analysis and reserve his neurosis for real life outside? With respect to the solution of conflict and new learning, varying combinations of real and unreal present a certain danger, but they may also afford the opportunity in action for solution of conflict, learning, and further maturation.

The weakest aspect of the Freudian conceptual model seems to be the crucial question of reality testing and new social learning. Therefore, the validity of psychoanalysis as a treatment method rests squarely on the issue of the analyst's use of his sense of self and his own emotions to maximize the potentials of reality testing and new learning. The limits of this paper do not permit me to consider this subject exhaustively. At some future date, I will consider in detail how the analyst's use of his sense of self and his emotions may foster in the patient a change at all levels of personality functioning, resolution of conflict, change in verbal expression, body behavior, emotional communication, integration of personality into social roles, and the creation of a new personal identity oriented to healthy values. In the final analysis, we cannot effectively drain the pus of a pathogenic cavity without, at the same time, enhancing to the fullest extent, those favorable life conditions which fortify immunity, promote greater strength and fuller living.

If we would truly venerate Freud's memory, we must come to grips with the limitations of his theoretical system and struggle valiantly to resolve the ambiguity and contradictoriness of some of his ideas. With respect to psychoanalytic technique, he made conflicting statements. On the one hand, he said that the analyst must remain anonymous. On the other hand, he said that the analyst must be father confessor, teacher, as well as elucidator. He must be a mentor to the patient. He stressed psychoanalysis of the elements of the mind and decried the task of synthesis. Whether we like it or not, we must search out in these very contradictions a clearer and more complete answer.

Freud said, "I cannot recommend to my colleagues emphatically enough, to take as a model the surgeon who pushes aside all his own feelings, including that of human sympathy and concentrate his mind on one single purpose, that of performing the operation as skillfully as possible" and: "the physician should be impenetrable to the patient and like a mirror, reflect nothing but what is shown to him." It is against this background that Freud feared that counter-transference might "spoil the mirror." But he also said that the sympathy and truthfulness of the analyst is indispensable to cure. In a different vein he remarked, "I must expressly state that this technique has proved to be the only method suited to my personality. I do not venture to deny that a physician quite differently constituted might feel impelled to adopt a different attitude to the patient and to the task before him." Still another time he said, "the task will arise to adapt our technique to new conditions. The application of our therapy to numbers will compel us to alloy the pure gold of analysis plentifully with the copper of direct suggestion."*

Let us return here to our original statement. Somewhere in the process of clarifying transference, we have bogged down. The main reason now seems clear. We have attempted to clarify transference somewhat in isolation from related part processes: counter-transference, the con-

*FREUD, S.: Recommendations for Physicians on the Psychoanalytic Method of Treatment (1912). *Collected Papers*, Vol. II.

trol of conflict, reality testing, decision making and action, and new social learning. The effective elucidation of transference can come only as we conceive these processes as interrelated parts of a unitary phenomenon, adaptation and growth of the individual within a significant close group.

The root of transference is interaction of individual and family. But transference is inextricably connected to control of conflict, reality testing and new social learning. The source of all this, too, is emotional conditioning in family relationships. But what did Freud do about direct observation of family interaction? He avoided it. Freud's need to isolate the patient from his family runs parallel with his need to isolate the patient from his analyst, and to isolate the inside of the mind from the outside. His remarks concerning family and relatives of the patient are curious, indeed. "The most urgent warning I have to express is against any attempt to engage the confidence or support of parents and relatives. . . The interference of relatives in psychoanalytical treatment is a very great danger, a danger one does not know how to meet . . . One cannot influence them to hold aloof from the whole affair". . . . "As for treatment of relatives, I must confess myself utterly at a loss and I have altogether little faith in entering any individual treatment of them" . . . "the psychoanalyst who is asked to undertake treatment of a wife or child of a friend, must be prepared for it to cost him his friendship, no matter what the outcome of the treatment."† In a recent paper Burchard says: "There is indeed irony in the fact that Freud, who successfully put to rout the combined forces of Victorian morality and conservative medicine, had to admit defeat at the hands of his patients' relatives."* Ironic, yes, but inevitable! Was this not an expression of Freud's disillusionment about family, his pessimism about friendship and love? This part of Freudian tradition has exerted a noxious effect on the value attitudes of some members of the analytic profession. To exemplify, I paraphrase the remark of a leading training analyst at a panel on problems of termination of student analysis. "At the close of a student analysis, student and analyst part company. When they do, it is the greatest blessing if geographically, they become permanently separated and they never again meet face to face." This is a sad commentary on the humanity of the analytic profession. It is, in my opinion, both unreal or wrong.

To a varying extent, psychoanalytic ideology has fostered a schism between individual and social, unconscious and conscious, pain and pleasure, phantasy and reality. The confusions of conceptualization have somehow complicated our understanding of the relations of mind and body, past and present, individual and group. The solution of the core problem of homeostasis has also been complicated by this tendency to schism.

In my recently published book, *The Psychodynamics of Family Life*†, I said as follows:

> The more literal and dogmatic interpretation of the Freudian theoretical system falls short of providing a uniform framework for tracing a pattern of transition from the family of childhood to the family of adulthood. It discloses with remarkable brilliance how man perceives and falsifies his image of family, but does not disclose with equal clarity how man assimilates and uses the more correctly perceived experiences, the realities of family life. The Freudian image of love as a positive, healthy source of family relations is incomplete. So too, is the view of the impact between old and new experience. Therefore, the psychodynamics of learning, the forward moving, creative phase of development remains only vaguely outlined. Freud perceived the individual and culture as being set against one another. He conceptually opposed parent and child, somewhat in the way in which he opposed reality and pleasure, and culture and personal freedom. He saw vividly the oppositional aspect but not the joining of these relations. It is not in fact the merging of these contrasting, complementary forces that is essential to learning and creativity. To this extent, Freudian theory is incomplete. It does not give us a positive, healthy image of family relations; it does not elucidate learning and creative, expansive development.

In our time, we must confront squarely the incompleteness of present-day knowledge of personality dynamics and mental illness. We must appreciate fully the sheer fact that the

†FREUD, S.: Further Recommendations on the Technique of Psychoanalysis (1913). *Ibid*.

*BURCHARD, E.M.L.: The Evolution of Psychoanalytic Tasks and Goals. *Psychiatry*, Vol. 21, No. 4, 1958.

†New York: Basic Books, Inc., 1958.

forms of mental illness are themselves changing. The human relations patterns of our day are in an agitated state. The inter-relations of individual and group are in acute flux. The integrative defects of society are imposed upon individual and family. This results in a profound shift in sense of self, personal identity, and in the patterns of control of conflict. More and more, conflict is lived out in human relations, rather than stably contained within the self. The fate of conflict is determined more by partial experiences of psychic union with other persons than by isolated intrapsychic devices of ego control. "Mind is inside, it is outside, it is everywhere all the time." The effect of culture change is to shift the stage of pathogenic conflict from inside the mind to the outside. Conflict is now dramatized more prominently in the zone of the person and environment, rather than exclusively within the person. In other words, as life changes, so does the nature and definition of illness and health change. We must, therefore, strive to fit psychoanalytic therapeutic process to the patterns of human experience of our time.

The only decent way to honor Freud's genius is to sift out the invalid parts of his writings from those insights which have immortal meaning. We can do this today, by giving full respect to the newer, conceptual developments, the adaptational view of personality, the collaboration between psychoanalysis and social science, and communication theory. We must give thought to the psychological effects of the world crisis, the revolutionary transformation of human relations patterns and the changed forms of illness and health. We must consider the special role of family in a time of crisis, and the influence of a shifting balance of power between individual and group. We must examine the relation of values to mental health. We must help the patient not only to free himself of symptoms and suffering, but to create a new sense of personal identity which gives him a meaningful and creative bond with family and society.

REFERENCES

1. BALINT, A. and M.: On Transference and Counter-transference. *International Journal of Psychoanalysis*, Vol. 20, 1939.
2. BENEDEK, T.: Dynamics of the Counter-transference. *Bulletin of the Menninger Clinic*, Vol. 17, 1953.
3. BERMAN, L.: Counter-transferences and Attitudes of the Analyst in the Therapeutic Process. *Psychiatry*, Vol. 12, 1949.
4. COHEN, M.B.: Counter-transference and Anxiety. *Psychiatry*, Vol. 15, 1952.
5. DEFOREST, L.: The Therapeutic Technique of Sandor Ferenczi. *International Journal of Psychoanalysis*, Vol. 23, 1942.
6. FENICHEL, O.: Problems of Psychoanalytic Technique. *Psychoanalytic Quarterly*, 1949.
7. FREUD, S.: Analysis Terminable and Interminable. *International Journal of Psychoanalysis*, Vol. 18, 1937.
8. GITELSON, M.: The Emotional Position of the Analyst in the Psychoanalytic Situation. *International Journal of Psychoanalysis*, Vol. 33, 1952.
9. HEIMAN, P.: On Counter-transference. *International Journal of Psychoanalysis*, Vol. 31, 1950.
10. JACKSON, D.: Counter-transference and Psychotherapy. In *Progress in Psychotherapy*. Edited by F. Fromm-Reichmann and J. L. Moreno. New York: Grune & Stratton, 1956.
11. LITTLE, M.: Counter-transference and the Patient's Response to It. *International Journal of Psychoanalysis*, Vol. 32, 1951.
12. LOW, B.: The Psychological Compensations of the Analysis. *International Journal of Psychoanalysis*, Vol. 2, 1954.
13. ORR, D.W.: Transference and Counter-transference. *Journal of the American Psychoanalytic Association*, Vol. 2, 1954.
14. REICH, A.: On Counter-transference. *International Journal of Psychoanalysis*, Vol. 32, 1951.
15. STERN, A.: On the Counter-transference in Psychoanalysis. *International Journal of Psychoanalysis*, Vol. 11, 1934.
16. TAUBER, E.: Exploring the Therapeutic Use of Counter-transference. *Psychiatry*, 1954.
17. THOMPSON, C.: The Role of the Analyst's Personality in Therapy. *American Journal of Psychotherapy*, Vol. 10.
18. ———: Ferenczi's Contribution to Psychoanalysis. *Psychiatry*, Vol. 7, 1944.
19. TOWER, L.: The Counter-transference. Address to the Chicago meeting, International Psychoanalytic Society, Spring 1955.
20. WEIGERT, E.: The Importance of Flexibility in Psychoanalytic Technique. *Journal of the American Psychoanalytic Association*, Vol. 2, 1954.
21. WINNICOTT, D.W.: Hate in the Counter-transference. *International Journal of Psychoanalysis*, Vol. 30, 1949.
22. WHEELIS, A.: The Place of Action in Personality Change. *Psychiatry*, Vol. 13, 1950.

PART II

Group Therapy

Ackerman's work in group therapy is largely unknown today, eclipsed as it is by his major contributions in family therapy. Yet he published 11 papers on group work between 1943 and 1961.

These papers repeatedly emphasize the contrasts between classical psychoanalysis and the then-novel techniques of group therapy. Ackerman's view of that contrast is best summarized in the 1950 paper, "Psychoanalysis and Group Therapy," an obvious forerunner of his 1962 publication, "Psychoanalysis and Family Therapy: The Implications of Difference." In both instances, psychoanalysis provided the norm; therapies deviating from this norm had to be explained and justified. In the psychiatric world of the forties and fifties this was no trivial matter. If the "pure gold of psychoanalysis" was to be alloyed by unorthodox techniques and views, the only hope of retaining high professional status was to make deferential and scholarly comparisons with the accepted standard. Ackerman's struggle with this issue never ended and his speculative imagination was frequently at odds with the requirements for scholarly orthodoxy.

Like most of his output, the papers offer theoretical speculations based on a core of clinical experience. Scholarly integration of other people's theories, never an Ackerman strong point, is less in evidence, though there are passing references to Freud, Harry Stack Sullivan, and Kurt Lewin. Throughout, Ackerman struggles with the idea of personality as field-related: one side turned towards the inner man as understood by Freud, the other towards the social group. Ackerman avoids the easy reductionism of defining group experience in psychoanalytic terms or psychoanalysis, on the other hand, as merely a "two person group." Instead, he tolerates the tension of different epistemologies and attempts to organize them in a non-competitive though hierarchical way. His diagrammatic scheme for this in "Social Role and Total Personality" (1951) looks forward to the impact of General System Theory upon psychiatry a decade later.

The final paper in this part, "Symptom, Defense, and Growth in Group Process" (1961) is particularly interesting because at the time of its publication Ackerman was already heavily committed to family therapy. In fact, *The Psychodynamics of Family Life* had been in print for three years. It is therefore not surprising that, after his usual bow to psychoanalysis, Ackerman presents the family group as a special form of the therapy group:

> At any given point in time the individual has an image of his personal identity and his family identity, with both continuously influenced by the images which outside persons hold of these same identities. The identity of the family pair or group refers to elements of joined psychic identity . . . represented in layers of joined experience and enacted in the complementary role behaviors of these joined persons. The processes of identification in family relationships are balanced against processes of individuation. In this way, elements of sameness and difference among the personalities of family members are held in a certain balance.

(No wonder Ackerman and Bowen joked about being brothers!)

Allusions to group therapy would appear from time to time in his writing, but this paper was Ackerman's farewell to the subject. His remaining ten years were devoted almost exclusively to the family.

CHAPTER 9

Some Theoretical Aspects of Group Psychotherapy

A theoretical discussion of group psychotherapy, at the present stage of development, is a hazardous undertaking. I assume this risk with the utmost humility. While it is true that fools will go where wise men fear to tread, it is likewise true that, were there no fools, there would also be no wise men. Therefore, with chastened spirit, and with full awareness of the relative dearth of controlled clinical and empirical data in this field, I shall attempt a short discussion of some theoretical principles. In doing so, I shall lean heavily on my own clinical experience with this form of therapy, which involved group treatment of veterans at the Red Cross and group treatment of disturbed adolescents in my private practice. This background inevitably implies some wide gaps of factual knowledge, and perhaps some personal prejudices as well.

It should be understood unequivocally, at the outset, that there are numerous and diverse forms of group psychotherapy. There are all types and levels of group psychotherapy, just as is the case with individual psychotherapy. The quality and patterns of emotional contact between patient and therapist vary accordingly. Such contact may be predominantly on the supportive level, release level, or insight level, or any admixture of these. It is only logical that there should be these different levels of treatment since the therapeutic aim, the role of the therapist, and the actual treatment techniques must be specifically accommodated to the special needs of distinct personality types, the problems arising out of the patient's social situation, and also to the particular environment in which the therapy is conducted.

The specific level of therapy and the treatment techniques applied in a given case reflect the therapist's aim, which may be: 1) to improve the adaptation to a specific social situation; or 2) to relieve certain forms of acute emotional distress with a view to restoring the pre-existing personality balance; or, 3) to produce a basic change in personality organization; or, 4) any combination of these. Such aims determine the proportionate degrees in which support, release, reality testing and insight are emphasized in the therapeutic experience.

In accordance with these differences, the

Reprinted with permission from *Group Psychotherapy: A Symposium*, J. Moreno (Ed.), 1945, 355-362. Copyright 1945 by Heldref Publications, Washington, D.C.

group may be small or large. It may be homogenous or heterogenous. It may be composed of similar personality types presenting a common psychological problem, or may be composed to some extent of contrasting personality types. The dynamic equilibrium of the group can be controlled by mingling timid and aggressive types of patients, or on occasion by including a special stimulus in the form of a particular personality type playing a special emotional role in the group. Still another variable factor is the social setting in which therapy is conducted. Depending on whether it is conducted in a hospital, in an out-patient situation, in a military environment, in a civilian community, or in a prison, the therapeutic experience carries a different meaning to the patient.

All these variables result in differences in treatment method. The existence of these differences renders the task of extracting some useful general principles more difficult. I have neither the space nor the qualifications for assaying the significance of all these variables, but I do wish to emphasize the validity of differences in method based on these variables.

In any case, when group therapy is indicated, we have to ask the further question, what special form of group treatment is appropriate, both in relation to the unique needs of the patient, and the unique features of the total life situation surrounding the patient.

Group therapy is, first of all, a special kind of social experience. It may be exploited for purposes of social re-education of attitudes and emotional drives, in which case, mainly, the conscious organization of behavior is modified. Or, on the other hand, it may go deeper, stimulate release of unconscious urges and emotions and catalyze new insight into the meaning of these deeper experiences. In this case it is a treatment in depth simulating in quality some of the processes involved in psychoanalysis. In this connection there has been some confusion in the literature as regards the terms "group work" and "group therapy." Some writers have claimed identity between these terms and some have claimed a basic distinction. For purposes of clearer orientation, I believe it is useful to restrict the term "group work" to processes of social re-education, and reserve the term "group psychotherapy" for depth treatment involving a systematic approach to the total personality, involving access to unconscious mechanisms, and bearing the potentialities for basic reorganization of personality.

Bearing in mind these numerous differences in aim and method, I should like to indicate briefly the features which characterized my method of group treatment of veterans. These veterans represented a mixed group diagnostically. Included in the group were men with social maladaptation, character disorders (neurotic characters and schizoid personalities), psychoneuroses, and psychosomatic disorders. The group was restricted to from four to eight patients. This limitation was imposed in order to insure adequate emotional contact and continuity in the inter-personal relationships, both patient-patient and patient-therapist relationships. In the main there was sufficient similarity in the conflict patterns present in the individual patients to insure a dynamic basis for the development of empathy and identification. To this extent there was homogeneity in the group. Beyond this point, however, there were numerous individual differences in personality, which I considered desirable because it provided an inexhaustible reservoir of challenging stimuli to the social reactions of the members. I should add one point: the emotional equilibrium of the group was balanced by including some timid, and some aggressive personalities.

My therapeutic aims were concretely the following:

1) To provide a continuous flow of emotional support through the group relationships.
2) To activate emotional release in the area of specific anxiety-ridden conflicts; in particular, to encourage the release of pent-up aggression. This meant utilizing group psychological influences for the selective reinforcement of some emotional trends and the dilution of others.
3) To reduce guilt and anxiety.
4) To provide opportunity for the testing of various forms of social reality as personified by individual members of the group, the therapist, or the group as a whole.
5) To provide opportunity for the modification of the concept of self in the direction of increased self-esteem, and recognition of constructive capacities. This in turn tends to increase the acceptance of other persons and

tolerance for frustrating experience.

6) To foster the development of insight arising from an actual living out of emotional drives in the context of the multiple inter-personal relationships within the group. The technique of interpretation was employed only when the expression of specific emotional trends was sufficiently solidified.

I wish here to underline one significant point, namely, that the unique dynamic characteristics of group living impose specific modifying effects on all partial therapeutic processes, such as we know them in individual psychotherapy. The processes of emotional support, release, expression of unconscious tendencies, reality testing, resolution of guilt reactions, and finally, the acquisition of new insight operate somewhat differently in a group.

I introduced the veterans to this new experience by a brief statement outlining the aim and the method of this form of treatment. Essentially this was as follows: all the men had been soldiers but they were now experiencing difficulties in restoring their place in their families, communities, jobs, and in their social life, often in their love life. All of them were experiencing some emotional suffering. Our purpose in coming together was to freely discuss their problems, their confusions and anxieties, and, to attempt through mutual help to bring about some improvement. The patients were asked to be completely candid, and to express their difficulties spontaneously.

They responded by unburdening their personal problems, frustrations, and fears. They released their pent-up feelings, often acting them out with a high degree of freedom. They expressed dramatically their wishes and their hostilities. Their conflicts became more sharply defined; the related guilt feelings and anxieties were clarified. They used the group experience as a sounding board for testing the real meaning of their impulses, and the validity of their particular concepts of social reality.

The activity of the group was patterned motivationally by the patients' perceptions of the purpose of the group experience. The therapist personified this purpose, which was to solve human problems, and lessen emotional suffering. Certain dominant attitudes emerged which conditioned the "group atmosphere." This was characterized by a feeling of belonging, a wish to receive and give emotional support, a tolerance of differences, a tolerance of weakness, of conflicting emotions, and a mutual striving for better adaptation.

The group became something akin to a men's club or fraternity. The relationship of patient to therapist catalyzed patterns of conflict reminiscent of son-father relationship. In this connection, varying reactions to the symbol of authority were activated. The members of the group felt each other as brothers. Corresponding patterns of loyalty and competition emerged.

Of tremendous importance to these men was the security of belonging. Because of their dependent tendencies, the need to be accepted by the group was quite prominent. This was especially conspicuous when the men had no close family ties and felt emotionally and socially isolated. They sought a dependable social reality which all too frequently in their real lives was lacking. Because of this lack, their social values were often confused. The more aggressive personalities in the group activated the more timid ones. The passive, submissive patients attached themselves to the stronger ones. The weakness of some patients invited sharp attack by the more sadistic ones, or led to veiled flirtations of the homosexual type. The retiring patients envied the more exhibitionistic types, and sought vicariously to live out their experiences through others. This dynamic interplay provided an effective basis for therapeutic exploitation.

In this process of spontaneous group discussion, inadequate or stereotyped explanations of motivation were challenged. Gradually the layers of evasion, defense, and rationalization were removed piecemeal so as to expose the real nature of the reaction. This permitted a clearer view of the underlying emotional trends and related anxiety patterns. Patients often interpreted to each other the real meaning of their behavior. Sometimes this reflected a genuine wish to help the other person; sometimes it represented merely a sadistic attack, by way of showing up another man's weakness in order to avoid the necessity of exposing one's own.

It is imperative that such attempts at mutual therapy be controlled and directed by the therapist in order to achieve the best results. In the role of therapist, I participated actively in these discussions. I felt the necessity for stimulating empathy between patients, and also for controlling aggressions in order to preserve the essential unity of the group. This might be called the stabilizing function of the therapist. I played a role in catalyzing the release of repressed feeling and channellizing this release toward a more accurate understanding of the patient's emotional drives. I employed the technique of interpretation only when the emotional trends had become clearly crystallized.

In this particular form of group treatment, I gradually evolved a few tentative hypotheses, which I am ready to modify with wider experience. These are as follows: group psychotherapy neither substitutes for, nor competes with, individual psychotherapy. It is an independent method having certain unique dynamic characteristics of its own, and serves special purposes. The interpersonal relationships in the group are more realistic than is the case in individual psychotherapy. The group experience offers direct gratification of certain emotional needs. Group dynamics are more specifically adapted to "externalized" patterns of emotional conflict, namely, those conflicts in which the struggle is mainly between the person and his environment, rather than between two opposing forces within the psyche. The group experience heightens the expression of emotional drives which can be experienced in common with others. It fosters a living out of emotional experiences and tends to release tension on a motor level. For adult patients with serious intrapsychic distortion, it is either contra-indicated or represents, at best, a partial therapy.

Having come to group psychotherapy through my experience in psychoanalysis, I have been impressed with certain basic differences in the two methods. In this brief report I can only suggest the direction in which these important differences lie. Dynamic trends emerge in the group situation which either are not present in a two-person relationship, or at least not in an identical form. Emotional interplay between two persons, such as in psychoanalysis, provides the potentiality for a social relationship, but it requires a group of three or more persons to provide a foundation for an organized social order with dominant aims, ideas, values, and patterns of interpersonal experience. Of necessity, this fact influences in specific ways the application of psychotherapeutic principles to a group setting.

In psychoanalytic therapy the patient relives his inner struggle between his pleasure drives and his anxieties. In this struggle the analyst gives the patient emotional support, and wittingly or otherwise, takes the side of the patient's unconscious drives in order to facilitate their release. Simultaneously, he endeavors to relieve the pressure of conscience and the inhibiting effect of reality. In this process, it is part of the analyst's role to personify reality, both in the context of the patient-therapist relationship and in the context of the wider outer world as well. Since the patient is unsure of his own standards, he seeks to rely on the presumably more valid reality standards of the analyst. But this special role of the analyst in personifying reality does not always work satisfactorily. In the analytic situation there is no actual social reality against which a patient may measure the impact of his impulses. It is in this respect that group psychotherapy offers a special advantage.

In the group situation, the therapist deals with the same three levels of psychic functioning as in analysis, namely, unconscious drives, conscience reactions, and reality, but the balance of these forces is different from what it is in individual psychotherapy. In the group setting, the impact with concrete forms of social reality is immediate. The patient's accommodation to social reality can be shifted or modified but can never be avoided entirely. In psychoanalytic therapy, in contrast, contact with social reality can sometimes be temporarily subordinated or minimized. In a group situation, adaptation to social reality is a constantly changing phenomenon. The immediate social reality is a fluid one, because it is variously personified by one patient or another, the group as a whole, or by the therapist.

Moral reactions and guilt patterns vary tremendously in the group setting. The less rigid types of guilt reactions can be considerably modified through group psychological influences.

Access to unconscious forces is a variable phenomenon in the group situation. At times, it is possible to effectively modify unconscious mechanisms; at other times, contact with such unconscious forces is difficult to sustain, and therefore, difficult to work with systematically.

In this respect, individual psychoanalytic therapy has a definite advantage since it is a means for systematic modification of unconscious behavior.

SUMMARY AND CONCLUSIONS

Group Treatment can be conceived both as social re-education and as a special form of psychotherapy. It is a special variety of real social experience, which can be exploited to correct social (reactive) disturbances, personality disorders of some types, and also, in a positive sense, promote personality growth. The interpersonal relations in the group approximate experiences in ordinary social life. The therapist is a more real person than in the individual therapy situation. The group provides emotional support for its members. In this setting social reality is a fluid entity, personified at various times by individual members, the therapist, or the group as a whole. Group dynamics offer opportunity for free impact between repressed emotional drives and varied forms of social reality, through which the patients may test the nature of these realities and achieve better understanding of their impulses. Guilt reactions of the less fixed types can be effectively modified. Access to unconscious mechanisms is more variable and less predictable than in individual therapy. At times, therapeutic contact with unconscious forces is effective, at other times, difficult to sustain, and in such instances, the therapeutic results are less reliable.

The form of group treatment I have described offers a useful approach to some types of social maladaptation and emotional disturbances of recent origin. It is also a valuable means, within limits, of modifying socially inefficient defense patterns, and for the analysis of maladapted character traits, for example, a chronic tendency toward failure, a drive for perfection, and a tendency to emotional isolation. Such group dynamics are better adapted to "externalized" patterns of conflict. In addition, group influences can be used to encourage sublimation and reaction formations of a socially useful type.

To summarize, Group Therapy is an independent method; it neither competes with, nor substitutes for individual therapy. It is a more real experience than individual therapy. It is less bound to the irrationalities of the unconscious and is weighted on the side of allegiance to social reality. It is only a partial therapy for the more serious personality disorders. Its powers are sharply limited with personality disorders having deep unconscious roots. Its greatest effectiveness lies in the area of reintegration of ego patterns with consequent improvement in the level of social functioning. For some disturbances of personality it may be usefully combined with individual therapy.

CHAPTER 10

Interview Group Psychotherapy with Psychoneurotic Adults

It is axiomatic that any form of psychotherapy for the neuroses must accommodate itself specifically to the unique imbalance of emotional forces that characterize the neurotic state involved. The corrective techniques must be systematically pointed to the conflict patterns which must be resolved to make way for a healthier adaptation. The only specific therapy for the neuroses so far widely recognized is psychoanalysis. If one attempts to apply group treatment to the neuroses, one is obliged to demonstrate tangibly how this method can benefit them. Some efforts in this direction have been made by Paul Schilder, Louis Wender and Alexander Wolf.[1]

Since the term, psychoneurosis, is used in a variety of ways, it is perhaps best at the outset that the term, as it is used here, be defined. It has been often said that a psychosis constitutes a denial of outer reality, and a neurosis represents a denial of inner reality while allegiance to outer reality is preserved. This is a striking description of neurosis, but it is not entirely accurate. It is not possible to deny inner reality without to some extent distorting external reality as well. The reality sense in neurotic persons is always impaired to some degree. The focal symptoms of a neurosis are anxiety and inhibition resulting from conflict. The anxiety is sometimes diffuse, but more often manifested in

Reprinted with permission from *The Practice of Group Therapy*, S.R. Slavson (Ed.), 1947, 135-155. Copyright 1947 by International Universities Press, New York.

[1]Alexander Wolf has made effective use of group psychotherapy for the neuroses in private practice; an account of his experiences came to me through private communication.

Paul Schilder: The Analysis of Ideology as a Psychotherapeutic Method, especially in Group Treatment, *Amer. J. Psych*. November, 1936; *Psychotherapy*, New York, W. W. Norton and Co. Inc. 1938, pp. 157-159, 197-255; Results and Problems of Group Psychotherapy in Severe Neuroses, *Mental Hygiene*, January, 1939; Introductory Remarks on Groups, *J. Soc. Psychol*. August, 1940; Social Organization and Psychotherapy, *Amer. J. Orthopsych*. October, 1940.

Louis Wender: Dynamics of Group Psychotherapy and Its Application, *J. Nerv. Ment. Dis*. July, 1936; Group Psychotherapy; A Study of Its Application, *Psychiat. Quart*. October, 1940.

specific symptoms. The central characteristic of a neurosis is the presence of an unresolved conflict between prohibited underlying tendencies (erotic or destructive) and conscience. The presence of excessive guilt feelings and fear of punishment impair the sense of pleasure and cause chronic insecurity. The buried impulses are displaced, disguised, and find vicarious release in symptomatic behavior. There is a self-protective effort to wall off the disturbance within the area of symptom behavior, somewhat in the same way as pus is walled off in an abscess. The symptom usually incorporates within its structure: (1) a symbolic representation of a buried urge, (2) the need for punishment, (3) the ego reaction to the conflict, and (4) a varying amount of secondary emotional exploitation of the neurotic suffering.

Besides this, certain other changes take place in the personality. The emotional capacity for close, satisfying human ties is impaired. Neurotic persons cannot commit themselves fully to personal relationships, since they fear they must pay too high a price in suffering or renunciation. In consequence, the whole process of social maturation is retarded. In addition there is a weakening of aggressive powers, a lack of confidence, a fear of failure, a defective ability to deal with new situations, and a discrepancy between aspirations and actual achievement. Thus, such individuals always show some degree of deficiency in the total adaptive functions in addition to the disability that results from specific symptom formation.

The therapeutic aims in employing the group method with the neuroses are the following:

1) To provide emotional support through group relationships.
2) To activate emotional release in the area of specific anxiety-ridden conflicts; in particular, to encourage the release of pent-up aggression. This process entails the utilization of group psychological influences for the selective re-enforcement of some emotional trends and involves the suppression or dilution of others.
3) To reduce guilt and anxiety, especially through the universalization of common forms of conflict.
4) To provide opportunity for the testing of various forms of social reality as personified in individual members of the group or in the group as a whole.
5) To provide opportunity for the modification of the concept of the self in the direction of increased self-esteem and recognition of constructive capacities. This in turn tends to increase the acceptance of other persons and tolerance for frustrating experience.
6) To foster the development of insight arising from an actual living out of emotional drives in the context of the multiple relationships within the group. Interpretation is employed only when the expression of specific emotional trends has been sufficiently solidified.

In order to demonstrate in a concrete manner the effects of the group experience on neurotic conditions, a condensed summary of six sequential therapeutic sessions will be presented. It must be kept in mind that a completely convincing record of the therapeutic process in a group can be presented only through the medium of talking moving pictures, which would record all the subtlety of varying facial expressions, vocal inflections, gestures, and other physical movements. It is obvious that a purely verbal description inevitably loses some of the most significant nuances of the psychological phenomena in group treatment.

For the purpose of demonstrating the proceedings and of illustrating group interactions and their value, the experience of one neurotic patient will be highlighted in this chapter.

John was thirty-four years of age. His illness had begun some ten years ago following the death of his father by suicide. This shocking episode precipitated a deep change in the patient's whole personality: he brooded over his father's suicide and felt depressed for three years. He had a feeling of emptiness in his stomach, was morose, irritable, and worried. He had developed numerous symptoms among which were insomnia, and fear of crowds, of dirt, and of heights. He engaged in chronic self-reproach and had a compulsion to re-check everything he did. He suffered also from somatic disturbances such as generalized weakness, dizziness, palpitations and diarrhea.

Before the time of his father's suicide, John had led what he considered a normal existence. He had not been nervous. He and his father had been close companions and the father had been very indulgent with John who, in turn, was extremely dependent upon his father and leaned upon him for all decisions. He had felt much closer to his father than to his mother or sister. His father had been quite wealthy, but shortly before his death had suffered financial reverses. The family was thus impoverished and the patient was forced to assume the role of provider. Before this time, he described his state as follows: "I didn't have a care in the world, I got everything I needed from my father."

SESSION I. John reproached another member of the group for having absented himself without informing the physician. This was a characteristic gesture of respect for authority. He began by saying: "Group therapy helps you realize that there are others who have the same problems, and it makes you feel less alone." He then described his symptoms and his sufferings. The therapist asked him why he had to constantly check up on himself. John answered this question by telling of a terrific rage he had had against his sister. He said: "I lost my head and smashed a coffee cup. She took a muffin I wanted for breakfast. I worry a lot. I'm not sure of myself. I can't concentrate. I can't sleep. After an attack of Vincent's Angina[2] five years ago, I thought I was going to die. I thought I caught it from a girl. It was a murderous kiss."

At this point he veered off to the question of his job. He had held it seven years and intended to keep it because his boss was tolerant of his peculiar behavior. Whenever he felt anxious, he jumped up and left the office. He felt there were not many bosses who would allow that. Other members chimed in, advising John to keep his job because it was a "cinch." John remarked that at one time he had hoped to make a million dollars a year, but he now knew that his hope was fantastic. Although he had a college degree, he was now resigned to starting at the bottom of the ladder as a shipping clerk. He had always tried to do things perfectly, for his own satisfaction. He vigorously told Bill, another group member, that you have to be willing to start at the bottom and not start with any high-flown ambitions. He preached to Bill that his trouble was that he did not want to work at all. Bill replied: "I don't want a job, I want a future."

The therapist commented that Bill had the habit apparently to begin doing something but actually stalled in order to make someone else do it for him. He was not interested in work as such, but really wanted an insurance policy for the future; he wanted someone to take care of him. Further discussion revealed that Bill had no regular earnings but depended on his wife's salary. John remarked, with a sharp show of envy: "I wish I had a wife to support me." Bill described how he defeated his own purposes, how he had lost all hope and had completely resigned himself to failure. He said: "My father used to tell me the best thing for me would be to be shoved back where I came from and be made all over again."

The therapist pointed a remark at John, who seemed to prefer talking of Bill's failures rather than of his own. The therapist said, among other things: "This is a case of the lame and the halt leading the blind. You, too, feel you're a failure." As in reaction to this, John was stimulated to confess more of his personal difficulties, his checking up on himself constantly and his having to keep his feelings locked within himself. He was unmarried and, since his father's death, had lived with his mother, for whose support he was responsible. He said: "For this reason I can't marry, except if the girl has a good job." He described his relationship with his father. He was tremendously shocked and dazed by his father's suicide. He said: "It was not like father and son. We were like two pals." He had never fully recovered from the shock of his father's death. His father had been indulgent, but had taught him the necessity for work. His mother had been shocked, too. She had developed hyperthyroidism, high blood pressure, and later had to have an operation. Both John and his mother had been ill since his father's death. He had many of his mother's symptoms.

He was usually depressed in the morning, often upset by bad dreams. He related one of these: "I fell in a trap and wanted to run, but my feet were glued. I felt paralyzed and woke up in a cold sweat." He had had this dream repeatedly in childhood. The therapist remarked: "The danger seemed right on top of you." To which John replied, "Yes," and added that in this mood he was irritable and did not

[2]Vincent's Angina is a diphtheroid angina.

want people anywhere near him.

In the latter part of this session, another member took the center of the stage and discussed a dream in which he walked about dressed as a woman. Further discussion linked this dream with this man's habitual provocative and exhibitionistic behavior. John was stimulated by this recital: he teased and accused the man of being conceited and showy. At this point all members of the group had become dramatically excited and tried hard to show each other up. This was clearly a contagious defensive response, indicative of repressed "homosexual anxiety" (fear of attack) in all of them.

In a characteristic manner John was ingratiating in his initial contact with a man in authority. He chastised another member of the group for being disrespectful of the of the psychiatrist's authority. He attempted also to disarm the psychiatrist of any possible hostility to himself by elaborating on the subject of his physical suffering. This signified at once his self-punishment and his wish for protection. At this point the therapist tried to penetrate the disguise of the patient's hostilities by challenging him on his need to constantly check on himself. John gave a clear answer to this challenge, namely, that he needed to check up on himself in order to control his suppressed rage. He gave an instance of this violent rage against his sister. He then quickly shifted from this to relating an experience of infectious illness, seemingly the result of his having kissed a girl. Here the punishment was obviously linked with the theme of sexual transgression and, significantly enough, connected associatively with an assault upon his sister. Immediately after this he reverted to the problem of his relationship with older men. He evidently became extremely dependent upon employers who took care of him and forgave him his "peculiarity," which actually represented his concealed rage.

In the sharp interaction with other members, John saw in bold relief some of his own tendencies, namely his extreme dependence, his wish to be cared for, and his resentment of exertion. His envy of another man, who was supported by his wife, was unmistakable. He saw also that his guilt feeling did not allow such self-indulgence. He therefore preached to other members against yielding to such temptations. At this point the therapist actively interpreted to the patient his preaching role. He induced him to confess his feeling of failure, his fear of marriage because of his own wish for the dependent, protected position. John described how his father had indulged him, how he felt guilty about it, how he and his mother were shocked in a similar way by his father's suicide, both having the same physical symptoms and neither having recovered. He then reported a dream in which he was trapped in a position of danger, was paralyzed, and unable to escape. One might conjecture that this dream reflected his fear of being caught and punished by his father. This account stimulated another member to present a dream of himself as a woman; a sequence of events that stimulated in John and in other members of the group an anxious feeling of being exposed to attack. They responded to this anxiety with excitement and a defensive urge to attack each other. John's guilt and his feeling of being exposed to bodily injury were deliberately not linked by interpretation in this session.

Session II. In this hour John described other symptoms: fatigue, upset stomach, sweating, pounding in his chest, numbness, pain in his arm. He made a suggestion to the group that the doctor not be called a psychiatrist; he resented the use of the term "psychiatrist." In his mind the use of the term "psychiatrist" was like "syphilis." He could talk much more easily if he could regard the doctor simply "as one of the boys." He associated the word "psychiatrist" with bars. It made him feel locked up. He resented the emphasis on the difference between the doctor and himself. He resented social barriers.

Another member disagreed, insisting that there was an actual difference and, if one recognized the doctor as a superior person, a more important person, one could get more out of him. The therapist interpreted this to John as a desire to feel closer, even equal; and as a feeling of being menaced by conceiving of the doctor as in a superior, authoritative position, whereas the other member welcomed his feeling of inferiority in order to get more out of the doctor. The therapist suggested that if, on the other hand, John had felt superior to the doctor, it would actually make him feel guilty and fearful.

John went on to say that he checked up on everything he did to make sure he did not do wrong. He amplified his fear of failure. "I go through what I call a thousand deaths a day through fear. I get exhausted. I sweat, my heart pounds, my pulse races. I feel I am dying and I get terribly irritated. I am afraid of the boss. I try to be perfect because I am afraid he is going to bawl me out. I am afraid that I might leave the gas jet on, so I check up on myself. This fear makes me urinate frequently. I get thirsty. My tongue gets dry and I drink a lot and have to urinate more. I get tongue-tied with the boss. I am afraid I might say the wrong thing. I have the impulse to curse. I feel guilty all the time."

The therapist remarked that because of his guilt feeling John had to pay in suffering for his hostile feeling to the boss. John confirmed this comment with a story. At fifteen years of age he had caught his elbow in a door. He had experienced severe pain but had returned again and again to put his elbow back in the door. He felt drawn to do it repeatedly; he wanted to see how much pain he could take. He was afraid of heights, yet he felt drawn to them. John went on to say that at the age of nineteen or twenty, he had a tonsillectomy and the anesthesia had not taken. He had a feeling of choking. In dreams he felt trapped and choked. He was fascinated by situations in which he experienced pain or in which he suffered in other ways. The therapist remarked that he seemed to enjoy the attention he got when he displayed all of his sufferings. Perhaps he felt that the therapist would be kinder to him than the boss was because he suffered so much, and also, by evincing so much punishment of himself, he would avoid punishment by the therapist.

Once again the patient had started out with an effort to disarm the therapist of hostility to himself by complaining of his suffering. Immediately afterward he proceeded to try to strip the psychiatrist of his professional authority, seeking to make his own position safer by making the psychiatrist "one of the boys." He explained this by confessing his fear of the psychiatrist and his feeling that the difference between them made him feel locked up. This was reminiscent of the dream he had reported in the previous session in which he had been trapped and paralyzed and unable to protect himself against anticipated assault. John interacted with other members who felt differently about this issue and not menaced by the psychiatrist's position. The therapist took occasion here to bring into focus John's guilt as the basis of his fear of the psychiatrist. John proceeded to validate this interpretation by confessing his conviction that he always did the wrong thing, by which he meant that he had to struggle constantly to control violent feelings against his superiors. In consequence he had an intense fear of retaliation; his anxiety became translated into somatic manifestations and fears of death.

The therapist made a clear-cut interpretation at this point to the effect that his physical suffering was his way of paying for his aggressive feeling against the boss. John affirmed this by giving an example of an actual experience, wherein he had inflicted pain upon himself. He linked this trend associatively with experiences of surgical operations, which had evoked in him the fear of being killed. The therapist made a further interpretation that if John punished himself by his physical suffering he hoped that the boss would then be kind rather than hostile and injurious.

SESSION III. Other members of the group held the center of the stage and, for a time, John was pushed into the background. He injected himself into the discussions, attempting to interpret the meaning of other members' problems. For example, he disagreed with one man by saying that it was no solution to run away from one's problems, to escape to a farm because one disliked people. He interpreted the desire of another man to evade responsibility for his wife. At the same time, he admitted to difficulties of his own. He said he felt better but still suffered from sweating, diarrhea, and rapid pulse. If anyone made a mistake at work, he said, he got angry and grumbled. Often he simply left the office and ate something. No matter who made the mistake, he felt responsible for it. He had thoughts of falling from a high place and killing himself, but usually stopped such thoughts at the point where he was falling out of the window. He did everything fast: talked fast, ate fast, walked fast; in fact, he raced with himself. He was not able to calm down or relax.

The patient again indulged in some preaching

to other members of the group. He held that escaping one's problems was no solution. Here he seemed to identify his own tendency to evade responsibility, and glided once more from this to a preoccupation with his own suffering which represented self-blame and self-punishment.

SESSION IV. In this session John reminded another member that he should respect the doctor and avoid offending him. A third member talked about his depression, his feelings of tension when with people, and his urge to scream when in a crowd. John said he had a similar impulse to flee from crowds. The therapist interpreted this as his fear of losing control over his violent impulses against people. John again talked of his inability to assert himself with the boss, his feeling of paralysis when in the presence of any authority, his intense fear of disapproval, his compulsion to be obedient and ingratiating. He felt completely under his employer's control. He was afraid for his own life. Getting the boss' approval was much more important than getting a raise. However, it was John himself who insisted on being perfect. He criticized himself constantly and felt guilty all the time. He was afraid that if anything went wrong he would be blamed. The therapist remarked that perhaps he felt guilty about many small things in order to hide his real crime. John responded by recalling a childhood memory: at five years of age he had taken some money out of his father's penny bank. (His father had symbolized an inexhaustible source of money.) Thereupon, his father had given him the worst licking of his life. He never stole after that. He had learned his lesson well.

John said he did not understand why, but he was always building up a fantastic story in order to get a girl to feel sorry for him. At this moment he was staring at the therapist's secretary who was a good-looking woman. John wanted to be sure that a girl would not rebuff him, but he did not really want the girl. Another member advised him to be more aggressive. John went on to say that he felt obligated to the boss because he had helped him to take care of his debts. He was always afraid to ask the boss for anything. At the same time, inside himself, he wished he could "show the boss up." "The whole thing is a fight, a continuous battle within myself."

Other members described their own emotional conflicts. One told of his fear of being caught in situations from which he might not be able to escape. Another told of how he could help others build up their lives but could not help himself. John said of this last man that he built himself up and knocked himself down repeatedly, that he got panicky in the middle of doing something, that he puffed himself up too big, got scared by what he had done, and retreated from the situation.

Again the patient started out with his usual ingratiation through reproaching another member for a disrespectful attitude toward the therapist. John then experienced together with another member the fear of losing control over his suppressed rage. He linked this with his feeling of paralysis and with his compulsive obedience. The therapist interpreted John's readiness to blame himself and to confess small offenses as a device for hiding the real basis for his guilt. John responded by recalling a childhood memory in which his father beat him severely for having stolen money. John then shifted his interest to the therapist's secretary, as though unconsciously desirous of stealing this woman's attentions from the therapist. He did so, however, in a way that would inevitably end in the defeat of his wish. Another member sensed that he had not really intended to succeed in his competitive effort and advised John to be more aggressive. John then discussed his ambivalent feeling toward his boss which involved dependence, on the one hand, and resentment of obedience on the other. Various members of the group indicated how they trapped and defeated themselves, a tendency that John also displayed. John saw his own self-defeatist tendencies reflected in the personalities of the other members and, in particular, his tendency to retreat when he became fearful of his own aggressiveness.

In this session for the first time John's aggressiveness was expressed in the form of competition with the therapist for a woman's favor.

SESSION V. A new member joined the group who was in the same line of business as John's father had been. The new patient said he did millinery designing, but was starving to death. He said all the men and women in his family were millinery designers. There was some discussion of competition with women which was described as "tough." The discussion turned to the suicide of John's father. Then men questioned him concerning it. John's father had been very wealthy but had lost heavily on the stock market, and had then begun to draw heavily on his $250,000 insurance. On the day he had committed suicide, he had taken a bottle of whisky with him. John feared whisky. It always made him depressed and reminded him of his father's suicide. He did not blame the liquor, but thought it had helped. He got pleasure out of talking of morbid things; he wanted to get them off his chest. When the policeman stood at the door of his house to inform him of his father's death, John inwardly knew that his father had committed suicide even before the policeman opened his mouth to speak.

Another member hinted that John wanted his father to die in order to collect the insurance. The others laughed. John quickly perceived the implied accusation, but said his father and he had been pals and his father had been very indulgent, even to the extent of taking him to a speakeasy and letting him take out one of his own models. One member of the group pointed out to John that even though he had felt convinced his father would kill himself he had done nothing to stop him. John said he had thought of keeping a close watch on his father, but actually had not done so.

His father had felt very guilty for having withdrawn the insurance money to the detriment of the family; he had even cried. John had fantasied that his father would jump under a train. Another man interjected the remark: "So you could get the insurance money?" The member who had accused John of wanting his father to die, confessed that his one big ambition was to have money. John said that he had had many fantasies of his father's death before it actually happened, explaining this as a pleasure in having morbid thoughts, for he had experienced pleasure in the thought of his father's dying. By way of further explanation he said he was extremely worried. He did not have the confidence that he could take his father's place and support his mother. Another member said that he would much rather hold on to his father than have the insurance money, because his father might recoup his losses and make another fortune: a father might actually be worth more alive than dead.

This session made dramatically clear the patient's death wish for his father and his consequent guilt. Another member of the group accused John of having wanted his father to die so that he might collect the insurance money. John at first made a weak attempt to deny the truth of this accusation, but seemed to accept it by confessing his pleasure in having had morbid thoughts of his father's death before it had actually taken place. John expressed his ambivalence about his father's death in his feeling of inability to fit into his father's shoes and assume responsibility for the support of his mother. In this session it was noteworthy that the group members themselves carried the momentum of the therapeutic activity. They channeled the direction of release and did their own interpreting. There was little active intervention by the therapist.

Session VI. In this session John again receded into the background as the problems of other members became the center of attention. John was strongly annoyed because another member absorbed the attention not only of the therapist but of the whole group, and he reacted by tormenting this other member. They argued, and then, to some extent, analyzed the content of their argument. John was annoyed because this member tried to impress people by his showiness, whereas he himself tried to impress people by his humility. While he was teasing him, John said: "I would probably play with him and then kill him, but after that I would miss him." He confessed to irritation because this fellow simply did not want to work for a living. There was some discussion of the obvious envy reaction involved and of the connotations of John's fantasy of killing this member of the group and afterwards missing his company. Some parallelisms were drawn between this ambivalent attitude and John's feeling toward his father.

Here again the patient dramatized his envy of another man who seemed less guilty about his dependent tendencies and was able to indulge himself more than John's own conscience would allow him to do. Toward this man John displayed the same ambivalent emotions that he had shown in regard to his father.

In reviewing this case we find that the salient

symptoms of this patient were anxiety, hysterical conversions, obsessive-compulsive traits, and psychosomatic disorders. He had fears of bodily injury and of death. Both his sexual and his aggressive drives were inhibited; he showed psychic impotence, and he was conscious of being a weak man. He had desires for a woman but tended to disown them because of his guilt and fear. His heterosexual urges were concealed behind defensive cruelty and a fear of damaging any woman he might possess. He degraded women and at the same time competed with them. He showed a tendency to regress from oedipal conflicts to earlier levels of psychosexual adaptation. Toward men he had a passive homosexual attitude, but displayed a violent ambivalence, alternating attitudes of flirtatiousness, submissiveness and ingratiation with attitudes of violent hostility. He carried on an incessant struggle to control his destructive, assaultive impulses. The death wish against his father was a central phenomenon. He had excessive guilt feelings and a need to suffer, as well as a need to inflict pain on others. His suffering was exploited secondarily for exhibitionistic purposes.

It is necessary to discern just how this neurotic behavior was received in the group and dealt with by the group method.

The patient attached himself strongly to the group and attended all sessions faithfully. To be accepted by the group was an important experience for him; the group represented a family. Of special significance was his need for a close bond with men. He used the therapist and the group as continuous sources of kindness and emotional support. He established a strong transference on a dependent basis; but his aggressiveness easily revealed itself behind his passivity. He erected an image of the therapist as a strong father, and of other members as weak fathers. Toward the therapist he was mainly submissive, ingratiating, and careful to avoid offense; toward the other members he was at times flirtatious or fawning, at other times provocative or sadistically overbearing; still at other times silently contemptuous. At first, not daring to challenge the paternal authority of the therapist, he displaced the hostile aspect of his ambivalence on to other members, evidently because he conceived them as weaker than the therapist, and so was less afraid of retaliation from them. In this way he hoped magically to preserve the strong father's support and approval. Later he became more openly aggressive against the therapist, and his murderous destructiveness was only thinly veiled. He also identified the other members with himself, attacking and disparaging them instead of attacking himself. He exposed their weaknesses and failures instead of his own. This provided a rich therapeutic opportunity to penetrate to and strip the patient of his defenses and rationalizations. These appeared as resistance to revealing the real unconscious source of his anxieties hidden behind a compulsive camouflage of aggression and an effort to deny sexual desire, particularly in the context of the therapist's relationship with his attractive secretary.

It was evident that group interaction exposed the significant neurotic conflicts of the patient. The patients activated in each other release of repressed feelings surrounding their central conflicts. The therapist exploited group pressures to guide the direction of release and, when emotional trends became ripe, he engaged in active interpretation. In this connection it should be noted that often spontaneous interpretations offered by other members rendered unnecessary such activity by the therapist.

On the cathartic level the experience promoted a release of pent-up feelings. This occurred in the group interaction through which the discharge of emotion was not simply on the verbal, but rather on the more primitive action-level. The most notable illustrations of the patient's neurotic "acting out" were his flirtations with other members, his tendency to humiliate them, and the dramatization of his death wish against another member, identified with his father.

The emergence of anxiety was plainly visible in connection with the dramatization of his conflict patterns. The central conflict, and the one which generated the greatest anxiety, was his need to possess a love object completely, to force gratification of his passive wishes for love, protection, childish indulgence, and then to destroy that person. As these conflicts were expressed and the corresponding defenses and rationalizations removed piecemeal, the anxiety and guilt appeared and could be relieved. In this phase of the process it was not the therapist exclusively but all the members of the group who interpreted the real basis of his fears. Insight, therefore, was acquired by this patient in a context of an actual social experience. There was a significant impact between unconscious drives and interpersonal reality, as personified by the therapist, some other members, and the group as a whole. Certain irrationalities were clearly exposed in the interpersonal contacts within the group. It was possible to direct the group experience so as to utilize this situation for continuously correcting the patient's distorted perceptions of the attitudes and motives of others toward him. It should be added, for purposes of caution, that the maximum therapeutic effect is achieved only after the significant problems are "worked through" repeatedly in many sessions.

The manner in which neurotic disturbances can be favorably influenced by a group experience was demonstrated in these six sessions. John shared anxiety-laden experiences with other patients of the group. He saw in them, as in a mirror, the reflection of his own neurotic trends. He saw anxiety reactions to suppressed rage, to fear of losing control, to feelings of inadequacy and failure as a man, to fears of bodily injury sustained through the assault of a punishing parent figure. In the relationships within the group, both with other members and with the therapist, he lived out his dependent patterns and his resentment of obedience. He expressed his aggressive feelings against persons in authority more and more openly. The sources of his guilt were laid bare by interpretation. He exposed to the group and to the therapist his worst side, and found it tolerated and understood. As a result, he derived emotional support and increased strength as a person. Through releasing his aggressive feelings without evoking the kind of rebuff and punishment that the fixed emotional patterns of the past had led him to anticipate, he felt more accepted and more powerful. This provided a background in which his image of himself could gradually become constructively modified. As his guilt and his feeling of unworthiness diminished, he could restore his sense of self-esteem and lessen his feeling of having been irreparably injured.

The group situation is one in which interpersonal patterns are actually "lived out," not merely verbalized; this is highly significant since it is commonly known that release on a motor level is far more effective therapeutically than the more superficial verbal release. It should be borne in mind, however, that the degree of "acting out" is continuously controlled by the directing influence of the therapist, and thus can be prevented from jeopardizing the unity of the group and the therapeutic goal.

In the group situation a tangible social reality is always present. The patient's contact with it is immediate and inescapable. The therapeutic process moves back and forth between this social reality and the patient's inner emotional life. This supplies a basis for a continuous impact of the patient's images of interpersonal relations upon their actual nature as perceived and interpreted in the group interactions. It would seem to be a form of psychotherapy operating both "from inside outward" and "from outside inward," contrasting somewhat with traditional psychoanalytic therapy, which is mainly a therapy operating "from inside outward."

In the analytic situation the neurotic patient is insecure. He is unable to pursue pleasure or success without anxiety. He fears the irrational and destructive elements in his impulse life. He vacillates: at one time he may side with his impulses and fight his conscience, at another time he may ally with his conscience against his impulses. In any case, he can release these impulses only in the context of some form of interpersonal reality, but he is confused concerning the validity of his social reactions, and in his personal values and concepts of reality. Fundamentally, he is confused in his image of himself, and is therefore never clear as to his exact role with other persons. Consequently, he gropes blindly in an effort to test the suitability of his reactions. Unsure of his own standards, he seeks to rely on the presumably more valid, safer reality standards of the analyst. He seeks to organize his impulses and in particular his hostilities in relation to the analyst's concepts of reality. In essence, this is a process in which the patient temporarily borrows the analyst's ego orientation to bolster his own security. On the other hand, the analyst is loathe to interfere with the patient's spontaneous effort to resolve his conflict. He, therefore, maintains a relatively neutral position and tries to avoid, as far as possible, imposing his own reality standards. But all the while it is a part of the analyst's role to personify reality for the patient, not only in the context of the therapeutic relationship but in that of the whole outer world as well.

The analyst is a symbol of reality, but actually there is no tangible social reality (group pattern) in the analytic relationship. This produces something of a dilemma. In actual practice it is most difficult to carry out satisfactorily the analyst's role as the representative of social reality. This is at once the most complex and yet most responsible aspect of his function which is rendered even more delicate by the realization that there is an ineradicable subjective component in every person's definition of reality. In this sense, concepts of reality, interpersonal values, patterns of integration of primitive drives and, finally, concepts of a co-ordinated self, tend to remain in an unresolved state in analysis for a long time.

Thus, in psychoanalysis we have a type of experience in which the inhibiting effects of reality and conscience are deliberately and specifically minimized in order to free the expression of repressed urges; that is, the analyst plays a role that causes the menacing aspects of reality and moral restraint to recede so that the patient may feel safer in the realization of unexpressed needs. Yet there remains the paradox of the analyst's having continuously to represent social reality. In the larger sense this is predominantly a therapy "from inside outward."

Group psychotherapy functions somewhat differently: it seems to operate in both directions. In contrast to the analytic situation, a tangible social reality is always present in a group in the form of dominant aims, ideas, values, and interpersonal patterns. The patient's contact with this tangible social reality is immediate and inescapable, and the therapeutic process moves back and forth between this social reality and the emotional life of each individual patient.

From these considerations a significant speculation arises. It is common knowledge that even those patients who have had a successful analysis seem to experience some amount of confusion and often a considerable lag in effective social readjustment in the immediate post-analytic period. This is entirely logical, since the patient uses this period to re-orient his ego-patterns to his newly achieved insights. Often, however, such patients experience a real distress in their efforts to translate the analytic understanding into new and more constructive forms of social experience. One is tempted to wonder in this connection if group psychotherapy would not be a valuable supplement to psychoanalytic treatment as a bridge between the newly structured insights and the establishment of new forms of interpersonal relationships.

The group situation allows a greater degree of "acting out" of neurotic tendencies. In analysis, the temptation to "act out" neurotic tendencies is ordinarily considered a menace. The patient escapes awareness of anxiety through the discharge of tensions that result from an "acting out" of neurotic drives. The aim in analysis, therefore, is to suppress the "acting out" and to deal with the patient's subjective awareness of anxiety. The opportunity to actually live out neurotic tendencies in the group situation, if carefully controlled, proves to some extent to be an advantage.

While it is true that this "acting out" may conceal latent anxiety, it is nevertheless also true that the "living out" of neurotic tendencies in the context of the multiple interpersonal patterns of the group, provides an opportunity for a detailed analysis of character traits as, for example, a chronic tendency to failure, a drive for perfection, or a tendency for emotional isolation. The inappropriateness and inefficiency of such maladaptive patterns can be strikingly demonstrated in a group. Sometimes when a patient feels the full impact of the irrationality of his behavior within the actual social situation of the group, intense anxiety is stimulated which, in turn, can be therapeutically exploited. Another point worthy of emphasis is that the "acting out" level of experience provides for a significant emotional release on a predominantly motor level, which is advantageous. In general, the therapist must play a more active role in the group than in the psychoanalytic situation.

Group psychotherapy, operating on an interpersonal level different from that in psychoanalysis, yet gains much from applying psychoanalytic insight to the dynamics of group living. On the whole, group therapy is a more real experience than is individual therapy. It is less bound to the irrationalities of the unconscious and is weighted on the side of social reality. Its greatest effectiveness seems to be in the area of re-integration of ego-adaptive patterns with resulting improvement of social functioning.

CHAPTER 11

Psychoanalysis and Group Psychotherapy

At the present time, the effort to shed light on the dynamics of group psychotherapy, through the application of psychoanalytic concepts, is fraught with complications. It is a task indispensable to progress, nevertheless, and in the end promises a substantial reward. The serious interest of psychoanalysts in group psychotherapy is distinctly on the increase. A number of them, myself included, have been groping toward a better understanding of the relevance of psychoanalytic principles for the dynamics of group treatment.

With the wide gaps of knowledge which prevail in this field, there is great room for prejudice in the approach of individual analysts to the issues of group therapy. My present views, highly tentative as they are, may reflect some amount of personal prejudice. For this reason, it may be useful to offer the background on which I have developed these views:

1) A primary orientation as a psychoanalytically-trained psychiatrist.
2) Experience in the application of group psychotherapy to school-age children, adolescents and adults.
3) Acquaintance with the literature on group psychotherapy.
4) A personal incentive towards the study of processes of social interaction, expressed in membership in two committees: The Committee on Social Issues of the American Psychoanalytic Association and the GAP Committee on Social Issues.

One episode out of the past will illustrate the particular slant with which I approached the problem of group psychotherapy. At a luncheon meeting of the American Orthopsychiatric Association, at which the plan for the American Group Therapy Association was launched, I timidly suggested that a study of the processes of Group Therapy might provide a natural setting for the acquisition of sorely needed knowledge in a new science, social psychopathology. My remark was not then received with favor, but I still cling to that same prejudice. I believe careful study of the processes of group psychotherapy may yet give real substance to the now-emerging science of social psychopathology.

Reprinted with permission from *Group Psychotherapy, Journal of Sociopsychopathology and Sociatry*, August-December 1950, Vol. III, Nos. 2 and 3, 204-215. Copyright 1950 by Heldref Publications, Washington, D.C.

I should like, first, to point concretely to some of the difficulties involved in applying psychoanalytic thinking to the problems of group treatment. Immediately, three types of phenomena and three kinds of knowledge are involved:

1) The psychodynamics of group behavior, including both the processes of group formation and the processes of group change.
2) The dynamic processes of emotional integration of an individual into a group.
3) The internal organization of individual personality.

In all three areas, we are handicapped by an insufficiency of knowledge, but the lack of knowledge is conspicuously great in categories 1 and 2; i.e., in the processes of integration of an individual into a group, and in the dynamics of group formation and group change. In addition, there is the difficulty of correlating the intrapsychic functions of personality with those adaptive operations of personality which are involved in the integration of an individual into a group. Partly because of these handicaps, we are not yet able to set up an adequate conceptual frame for applying psychoanalytic principles to the processes of group treatment.

At the very outset, we are confronted by a thorny semantic problem. Conventional psychoanalytic terms and definitions have not yet achieved a satisfactory level of scientific clarity and precision. The term "psychoanalysis" itself has come to mean many different things. The more important usages of this term offer at least four distinct meanings:

1) A theory of personality.
2) A therapeutic technique.
3) A method of investigating the unconscious life of man.
4) A special point of view toward human nature and toward the problems of living.

In addition, each of these connotations of psychoanalysis has been continuously changing through a process of evolution, especially the psychoanalytic theory of personality, and the psychoanalytic concepts of therapy.

It is now almost axiomatic that psychoanalysis, as a device for systematic exploration of unconscious mental life, does not by itself guarantee therapeutic change. In exceptional circumstances, it may even constitute a crucial danger to the therapeutic objective. Mental health is not achieved in a simple way: it is not achieved merely by increased awareness or release of unconscious urges. It means not only the elimination of specific disabilities of personality, but also the positive fulfillment of the potentialities of the individual in the context of prevailing patterns of social relations. It is reached through the establishment of an optimal balance between the individual's orientation to his deeper strivings and his orientation to the real requirements of his relations to other persons and to the group as a whole.

This immediately sets up a distinction between psychoanalysis as a means of study of the unconscious and as a therapy. This consideration has direct relevance for both the goals and processes of group psychotherapy.

Psychoanalysis, as a theory of personality, has added a wealth of insight into the nature of man's inner conflicts, but has not yet reached the status of a scientifically unified theory. As a biological psychology, psychoanalysis has done much to correct the deficiencies of the older academic theories of personality. Yet, this very advantage has introduced certain complications. Psychoanalysis stresses the individual's deeper relationship to himself and those operations of personality which are oriented to the task of gratifying basic biological needs. It emphasizes unconscious motivation, the individuality and the egocentricity of man, and the primary importance of the individual's relation to body function. It gives rise, however, to a definite complication; namely, the difficulty of integrating the concept of man as an individual and man as a social being.

From the first, Freud admitted the importance of the social determinants of behavior, with special reference to the conditioning influences of family life, but a measure of ambiguity has always characterized Freud's formulations of the interrelationship of the biological and social determinants of behavior. This is rather clearly reflected in Freud's own statement concerning individual and social psychology:

> A contrast between individual psychology and social or group psychology, which at first glance might seem to be full of significance, loses a great deal of its sharpness when it is examined more closely. It is true that

individual psychology is concerned with the individual man, and explores that paths by which he seeks to find satisfaction for his instincts, but only rarely and under exceptional circumstances is individual psychology in a position to disregard the relations of this individual to others. In the individual mental life, someone else is invariably involved, as a model, as an object, as an opponent, and so from the very first, individual psychology is at the same time social psychology as well.[1]

Here we have an illustration of Freud's brilliantly penetrating wisdom, and yet, at the same time, a fair sample of his tendency to somewhat beg the question as regards the precise relationship between the biological and the social determinants of behavior. While making his bow to the "social man," he tends to show a preferential interest in the "individual man." He sought to explain the social role of man and woman in terms of biologically-determined instincts and the related unconscious drives; the social function of man was represented as a projection onto the social scene of his unconscious strivings and fantasies. The broader patterns of culture were similarly interpreted.

While sharply illuminating the role of family life in shaping the child's personality, he tended, nevertheless, to stereotype the roles of mother and father, failed adequately to take into account the cultural patterning of these roles, isolated the dynamics of family life from surrounding social institutions and subordinated the feminine half of humanity. He failed to see the way in which child-rearing concepts were influenced by cultural as well as the developmental factors of neurosis.

But what has all this to do with group psychotherapy? Mainly this: in order to illuminate effectively the dynamics of group therapy, the conceptual frame for a theory of personality must be expanded in a way that satisfies two necessary conditions:

1) The operations of personality must be conceived in terms of a bio-social unit. The biological and social determinants of behavior cannot be dissociated. Out of the interaction between the organism and environment, a new unit of behavior emerges which is bio-social. The adaptive functions of personality must be so viewed as to take into account the continuous interplay between those processes that reflect the individual's relation to his inner (biological) being, and those which reflect his orientation to social participation. It is necessary, furthermore, to find criteria for the dynamic relations between the adaptive expressions of personality in group action and the relatively more fixed internal structure of personality, as conditioned by developmental influences. In other words, man has an identity that is, at once, both individual and social.
2) The functions of personality must be defined within the context of a broader theory of social organization and social relations. The adaptive behavior of the individual must be viewed in relation to the characteristics of the group to which he belongs. Differences between individual and group behavior must be understood. The behavior of a group has certain unique characteristics of its own, and the adaptive processes of personality, both normal and pathological, need to be viewed within this wider frame.

Until we satisfy these requirements in the basic concepts of personality structure and function, it will be difficult to usefully transpose psychoanalytic principles to a group treatment setting.

In a group setting, the therapist cannot directly observe, nor does he have access to, the total potentialities of individual personality; instead, the therapist establishes emotional contact with the shifting adaptive phases of the personality in action, which are expressed through the role of the person in that social situation. The role of the individual in the group represents a particular form of integration of his emotional tendencies in a specific situation. The adaptive expressions of the person are limited and shaped in two ways: by the relatively fixed organization of the individual personality, and by the requirements of a given situation, as this individual interprets them.

It must be emphasized, therefore, that the immediate therapeutic influence in a group is exercised not through what is called "total personality," but rather through those particular forms of emotional expression, through which

[1]Sigmund Freud's "Group Psychology and the Analysis of the Ego."

the patient displays his personality in the group—namely, through his role in the group. The continuity of group therapeutic experience is such, however, as to induce in the person a series of changes in adaptive role and, through these changes, the therapist may gradually achieve access to a variety of layers of the personality.

Thus, social interaction can be understood only if we broaden our conception of personality so as to consider the continuous interplay between the individual's relation to his biological make-up and the individual's orientation to social participation. Each individual has layers of emotional reactivity which are relatively fixed, and others which are more pliable. Each individual is capable, within the limits set by his fixed intra-psychic structure, of modifying his adaptive form in diverse social situations; he can change his "social role." The identity of each individual holds both individual and social components. In a shift from one social situation to another, the dynamic equilibrium between the individual and social components of personal identity undergoes change.

In a recent paper, "Social Role and Total Personality,"[2] I endeavored to illuminate the relationship between the social functions of personality and individual personality. I suggested that the adaptive forms or roles of personality in different groups might be appraised by the application of the following criteria: the group-conditioned aim of the individual, his quality of apperception of surrounding interpersonal realities, the concept of self projected into the role (including personal values, ideals, standards, etc.), his techniques for control of the group environment, his pattern of conflict, the quality of anxiety engendered by this role, and the defenses mobilized against it.

It seems to me that some attempt to define the adaptive functions of the personality can be made in these terms, and this adaptive role can then be correlated with our knowledge of the fixed intra-psychic structure of this individual. In order to establish such correlation, more exact knowledge of ego functions is needed.

When we turn to a consideration of the relation of psychoanalytic therapeutic technique to the techniques of group treatment, it becomes imperative to contrast the different psycho-social potentialities of the two therapeutic situations. The two-person psychoanalytic relationship provides a unique experience in which the earlier patterns of child-parent relations are relived and their destructive elements removed. Group psychotherapy, involving three or more persons, however, has its dynamic base in the fact that the child's character is influenced not only by the mother, but all the interacting relationships within the family group, especially the relationship between the parents. These multiple interpersonal patterns, each affecting the other, also contribute to the distortion of personality.

The psychoanalytic method applies to a pair of persons, but the techniques are pointed almost exclusively to the experience of only one of these persons—the patient. In considerable part, the analytic relationship does not constitute a true social experience; it provides no model for society. It is a process of working-through of the patient's internal conflict with self, with the analyst acting as catalyzer of this process. External conflict with the analyst becomes translated back into terms of the patient's internal conflict with self. A further aspect of analytic therapy involves a degree of temporary shedding of the patient's inhibiting ego, of his rational control, a denuding of the social layers of the patient's identity, so as to accentuate the patient's awareness of inner conflicted emotion and biologically-conditioned urges. Thus, the importance of outer reality, and reality as personified by the analyst, is temporarily diminished. Such an experience heightens the patient's deeper communication with his private self and his unconscious, but at some cost in terms of temporary subordination of social communication. As access to the deeper self is achieved, the reality elements of the patient's ego, and the reality of the analyst are reasserted, and play their part in re-integration of the patient's emotional life. In this sense, analysis is predominantly a therapy which moves from "inside outward."

The group situation is different. Interpersonal processes emerge in a group which either are not present in a two-person relationship, or at least not in an identical form. Contact between two persons provides the potentiality for a social relationship, but does not provide the founda-

[2]Presented before this paper was written, but not published until the following year—Editors.

tions of a society. Only a group of 3 or more persons makes possible an organized social unit, with a set of dominant aims, ideas, emotions, values and patterns of social relations. Here we have multiple interpersonal patterns, interacting continuously with each other. Some of these relationship patterns may be in harmony; others in conflict. They vie with each other for a position of dominant influence. The way in which the group forms, integrates, changes and is affected by leadership, determines the channels along which emotion is released or restrained. Thus, in a group, a tangible social reality is always present. The therapeutic process moves back and forth between this social reality and the patient's inner emotional life. Here we have a basis for continuous impact between the patient's image of interpersonal relations and their actual nature, as perceived and interpreted in the group interaction.

In order to try to see the extent to which therapeutic mechanisms operate similarly or differently in the group and individual settings, it is useful to outline the partial processes of psychotherapy, in general:

1) The development of an emotional relationship with a dynamic "give and take" between patient and therapist.
2) Through this relationship, provision of emotional support for the patient.
3) Reality testing; modification of concept of self, and patterns of relation to others in the direction of more realistic perception.
4) Release of pent-up emotion.
5) Expression of conflict, both conscious and unconscious.
6) Change in patterns of resistance and defense against anxiety.
7) Diminution of guilt and anxiety.
8) Growth of new insight, and emergence of new and healthier patterns of adaptation.

All of these processes overlap, influence each other, and together they provide the dynamic basis for therapeutic change. A number of questions arise.

Is therapeutic change in the group and individual settings dependent on the same or a different set of processes? Are there some processes which are specific and unique for one or the other form of psychotherapy? Do some particular processes play a more important role in one form of treatment than in the other? Or, if the basic processes are in essence similar, are the separate elements of therapy integrated and balanced differently in the two situations? On these questions, I offer my present views humbly, tentatively, with keen awareness of the handicap of limited knowledge.

First, I would tend to doubt that the group therapy situation involves any unique processes. I do believe, however, that the different psychosocial potentialities of the group necessarily modify the pattern of the balance between the partial processes of therapy, intensifying some, lessening or inhibiting others. The therapeutic processes in a group tend to operate on an interpersonal level, rather different from that which prevails in psychoanalysis. The nature of group experience is such as seems to place a first emphasis on conflict with the environment, rather than with the self. In the group, conflict tends to be externalized, projected into the social scene. Through such projections are reflected the patterns of inner conflict with self. Externalization of conflict encourages some measure of "acting out" in the group relations. Expression of feeling in a group, therefore, is more than verbal, it extends to the sphere of social action, and fosters a higher degree of motor discharge of tension. In individual psychoanalysis, the primary emphasis is in the opposite direction; namely, on conflict with self, and, in harmony with this, the tendency to "act out" is discouraged. Through the conflict with self, one gets, in turn, the mirror reflections of conflict with the environment.

But there are other differences as well. The pattern of intensive exclusive dependence on one person is not so readily possible in a group as in psychoanalysis. Relationships in a group tend to be more influenced by reality. The irrationalities of transference are held in check. The multiple interpersonal relationships provide opportunity for displacement, division and dilution of transference emotion. Magical expectations and omnipotence strivings are restricted.

In the group, the function of providing emotional support for the patient is divided. The therapist is not the sole source of security and gratification of emotional needs. The group, as a whole, shares this responsibility.

In the group, discharge of pent-up emotion takes place on a selective basis. Emotion which can be experienced in common with others is reinforced. Other types of emotion may be inhibited.

Free association, in the analytic sense, occurs on a more limited scale, if at all. In its stead, we have the spontaneous emotional interactions between members and with the therapist.

In the interaction between the person and the group environment, there is a two-way selective process. The individual takes out of the group what he needs. The group takes from each individual what its processes require. The individual combines his force with those tendencies in the group which will strengthen the effectiveness of his chosen role. Also, he may submit to being used by other in the interest of their self-assertion. This two-way selective process plays a part in the assertion of certain types of control, in releasing basic drives, and in dealing with conflict, guilt and anxiety.

In the group setting, the therapist does not have immediate or direct access to the unconscious of the patient. In this respect, the analytic situation enjoys greater favor; here the access to unconscious conflict is more direct, and more systematic. In the group, conscious conflict is the first to appear. The working-through of such conflict and its reduction to concrete terms will often bring to light significant clues as to the nature of deeper conflict. Frequently, the manner in which conflict is externalized and "acted out" in group interaction, offers hints as to the content of unconscious conflict.

Some further comment may be in order here in relation to the therapeutic connotations of a patient's tendency to "act out" his impulses. In the analytic situation, "acting out" is conceived as harmful, and is systematically discouraged. In a group setting, the urge to express conflict through "acting out" is, to some degree, natural. Group psychotherapy is intrinsically an "acting out," rather than a "thinking out," type of experience. Here, a patient deals with conflict by projecting it into a relationship; he lives it out with the other person. In this manner, inner conflict is translated into outer conflict with another person. It is this "acting out" in relationships which enhances the motor discharge of emotional tension. In this setting, the therapist can work with the irrational elements of conflict not in the form of fantasy but rather in those forms which are projected onto the social scene. The group therapist may then translate this back into the context of the patient's inner conflicts. Because of the selective nature of the group process, however, some kinds of unconscious conflict may remain totally inaccessible.

Patterns of resistance and defense against anxiety are dramatically transparent in the proceedings of a group. Resistance should not be regarded as pathological behavior; it can be defined as the natural mechanism of self-protection when a patient fears harm through exposure of himself in a close relationship. Anxiety, the defenses against anxiety, and patterns of resistance are a functional unit. By tracing out the resistance paths, and the types of defenses employed, one sees the way in which a patient attempts to escape his anxiety and conflict. By pursuing closely these paths of escape, one is led, step by step, to the actual content of the conflict.

Individual patterns of guilt can be modified to a variable extent by group treatment . . . some forms temporarily, others more permanently. The more superficial types of guilt are easily reached and relieved, especially if they represent a shared form of guilt. The technique of universalization is a device for mitigation of guilt through reassurance, but may not alleviate it at its source. A lasting relief of guilt in the more rigid, automatized types of reaction is more difficult in a group. In general, however, the impact between the impulse tendencies of the individual and the fluid standards and moral reactions of the group, does offer a substantial basis for diminishing guilt feeling. Here, the standards of individual conscience, immature and inappropriate as they often are, are checked against the more balanced and realistic standards of the group.

The group situation provides a wide range of possibilities for the testing of reality. In this setting, social reality is not a fixed entity. Each member of the group, and each pattern of relationship, personifies a given form of interpretation of social reality. In this sense, social reality is fluid, relative, and is represented by multiple interacting concepts, rather than by a single fixed interpretation. As the group evolves, however, there is increasing unity and stability in these interpretations of reality. On this background, the patient tests out his fear of dangers from the real world, and his fear of his own impulses. In this setting, the clash between his impulses and the standards of this fluid form of social reality offers a chance to expand his emotional orientation to his own nature and the nature of society. Such increased understanding may develop with or without therapeutic interpretation. Patients often spontaneously offer their own interpretations. Sometimes these are uncanny in their accuracy, sometimes utterly inappropriate because of the patient's egocentricity and projections. It is the therapist's task to guide these emotional cross currents toward correct understanding. He may use the technique of interpretation sparingly, and only when the emotional trends have become sufficiently ripened. Here we have a broad opportunity for growth of insight, modification of social standards, and values and the development of healthier patterns of social adaptation. Of particular importance in a group is a growth of confidence in dealing with people, and a basic increase in self-esteem.

SOME DIFFERENCES BETWEEN THE PSYCHOANALYTIC TWO-PERSON SITUATION AND THE GROUP THERAPEUTIC SITUATION

Psychoanalysis	Group Therapy
1) Two persons.	Three or more persons.
2) Couch technique.	Face-to-face contact.
3) Temporary subordination of reality.	Reality continuously asserted by group through reality takes fluid form.
Analyst reasserts reality according to patient's need.	Patient's impact with reality is immediate.
Analyst is observer; suppresses his own personality.	Group therapist is more real person, participant as well as observer.
Relationship is not social, except in later stages.	Group provides genuine social experience.
Social standards not imposed.	Group standards emerge, but remain flexible.
4) Exclusive dependence on therapist. Emergence of irrational attitudes and expectations.	Dependent need is divided, not exclusively pointed to therapist.
Magic omnipotent fantasy prominent. Irrational motivation may rise to dominant position.	Irrational attitudes and expectations appear, but checked by group pressures.
	Magic ominipotent fantasy is controlled.
	Irrational motivation not permitted dominant position.
5) Direct gratification of emotional need not given.	Group offers some direct gratification of emotional need.
6) Communication largely verbal; Communication less real.	Communication less verbal; greater expression in social action and reaction.
Patient communicates deeply with self; also with therapist.	Higher degree of social communication.
Patient feels alone.	Patient belongs to group, shares emotional experience, feels less alone.
7) "Acting out" suppressed; little motor discharge of tension.	Higher degree of "acting out," and motor discharge of tension.
8) Access to unconscious conflict more systematic; greater continuity in "working through."	Access to unconscious conflict less systematic; lesser degree of continuity in "working through."
Emphasis on inner conflict with self; conflict with self mirrors conflict with environment.	Conflict is projected, externalized.
	Conflict with environment mirrors inner conflict.

	Psychoanalysis	Group Therapy
	Modification of specific internal disorders of personality more effective.	Modification of specific internal disorder of personality less effective.
9)	Patterns of resistance and defense more uniform and specific.	Patterns of resistance and defense more variable.
10)	Relief of guilt and anxiety more specific.	Relief of guilt and anxiety less specific.
11)	Dynamic movement to large extent from "inside outwards."	Dynamic movement to large extent from "outside inwards."
12)	Emotional change and insight more immediately related to intra-psychic conflict.	Emotional change and insight more immediately related to extra-psychic conflict.
	Method more suitable for specific psychiatric symptoms; predominantly a therapy for disturbance in basic drives.	Method more suitable for change in character traits; predominantly an ego therapy.

CHAPTER 12

"Social Role" and Total Personality

The elucidation of social process requires definition of the individual's relation to society. Social forces, abstracted from the behavior of people, have no meaning. Just as personality cannot exist in a social vacuum, so social forces cannot operate in a human vacuum. They are mediated through that phase of personality which achieves expression in group relations. In the interaction between the individual and society, three levels of phenomena are involved: the structure of the environment, interpersonal relations, and the inner psychic life of the individual. While descriptively these may appear as relatively differentiated entities, they are, of course, facets of a larger unit, personality-environment. They overlap; they are mutually interdependent, and between them there is a process of continuous interchange.

Any attempt to study social phenomena must make use of a definition of personality which emphasizes its orientation to social participation. The functions of personality are oriented in two directions: toward the internal processes of the organism, and toward the social environment. Each direction of orientation is influenced by the order. There is continuous interplay between the relations of personality with the self, and relations with outside persons. In this paper, for purposes of discussion, there is a selective focus on the external orientation of personality.

As a bridge between the processes of intrapsychic life and those of social participation, it may be useful to employ the concept of "social role." Sociologists employ this term with two distinct meanings: either as the role of the person in any given social situation, or as the characteristic role of the individual in society, as determined by his social-class position. From the psychodynamic standpoint, I shall use the term differently, namely, as representing the adaptational unit of personality in action.

"Social role" is here conceived of as synonymous with the operations of the "social self" in the context of a given life situation. The "social self," as contrasted with the individual's orientation to inner self, emphasizes those functions of personality which are externally oriented. In the jargon of everyday life, a distinction is often drawn between the "inner self" and the "outer self." The "outer self" changes with social con-

Reprinted with permission from *The American Journal of Orthopsychiatry*, January 1951, Vol XXI, No. 1, 1-17.

ditions, the "inner self" presumably stays much the same. Under some conditions, the "inner self" is realized, or even enhanced in the expressions of the "outer self." Or, the "inner self" may be submerged or denied in the social, conforming representations of personality. Sometimes the "outer self" is seen as a social front, a facade behind which is concealed the true, or real, self. When the environment goes counter to the needs of the "inner self," the "outer self" provides the protective coloring required for safe adaptation. The "inner self" represents the private, inner core of the being, the phase of the self which least yields to social exigency; it is the essence of individuality.

Under some social conditions, the "inner" and "outer" selves achieve a fine blend. Under other conditions, they may clash, at times so critically as to shake the personality to its very roots.

The problem before us is the exploration of the relations between "social self" ("social role") and "total self" (total personality). The fields of anthropology, sociology and social psychology approach the problem of "social role" each with a unique set of methods and techniques. From the psychodynamic point of view, the problem may be approached in still another way.

The purpose of this paper is threefold:

1) To discern useful sociopsychological criteria for a dynamic concept of "social role."
2) To discuss the relations between "social role" and total personality.
3) To offer some reflections on the application of the psychoanalytic method to the further study of this problem.

DYNAMICS OF "SOCIAL ROLE"

"Social role" ("social self") is that integrational aspect of the total personality which is expressed in social action. The behavior forms expressed in this role are determined by a variety of factors: the propensities of the individual personality, the processes of group participation and identification, and temporal-situational factors.

The concept of "social role" implies the capacity of the personality, in varying measure, to make fluid changes in form in accordance with the adaptational requirements of the individual's position in society. The ego orientation of this action phase of the personality presupposes a set of goals and values commensurate with the individual's position in a given group. It involves a particular quality of apperception of reality (interpreted in the context of interpersonal relations), the implementation of specific techniques of control of environment, the assertion of a particular image of self, specific defenses against anxiety, and, within the context of a given "social role," the effort to find solutions to personal conflict and to achieve gratification of inner needs.

It is recognized that a given personality type may be capable of assuming a variety of "social roles." On the other hand, sociologists indicate that the same social function may be filled, at a given time, by different personality types. It is this latter point that has impelled some sociologists to the belief that, in the analysis of social phenomena, the individual personality structure may be relatively unimportant. Perhaps within the frame of sociological criteria and methods, this is a plausible concept. From the psychodynamic point of view, it is unacceptable. While, at a given moment in time, different or contrasting personality types may appear to fill the same "social role," its social and personal consequences will always vary with the characteristics of the individual personality playing the "role"; the outcome will be influenced by a time factor, and the individual motivation entering that "role," both conscious and unconscious. In contrasting personality types, the specific pattern of ego-integrative behavior and the motivational content projected into the same "social role" will always be somewhat different; therefore, the "role" is not likely to be executed in the same way.

There are numerous vicissitudes in the relations between "social role" and individual personality which tend to strengthen the point that distinct personality types do not execute the same role in the same way, and with the same end results; for example, the effects of anxiety on "social role," the possible range and variability of "social roles" which can be assumed by a given individual, the rigidity, the stability of the "role," and its central or peripheral significance in relation to the individual's inner emotional life. More will be said of this later.

I would like now to illustrate, by diagram, the

manner in which individual personality may mold its integrational form to suit several distinct "social roles," each appropriate to participation in, or identification with, a distinct group. (See Diagram 1.)

In the configuration of each of these distinct roles, the emotional integration of the person in action reflects a unique ego balance and a distinct combination of the significant facets of behavior which go to make up the "social role"; that is, the apperception of patterns of interpersonal relations, the compliance with or protest against social pressure, the assertion or subordination of self, the effort to solve personal conflict, and the selection of particular defenses against anxiety.

In such adaptational integrations of personality, the quantity of anxiety affects the outcome of the "role"; the individual may find it easier to seek out solutions to conflict in one role, more difficult in others; the weaknesses or defects of the personality may produce exaggerated consequences in one role, and in another the same consequences may be minimized or even coun-

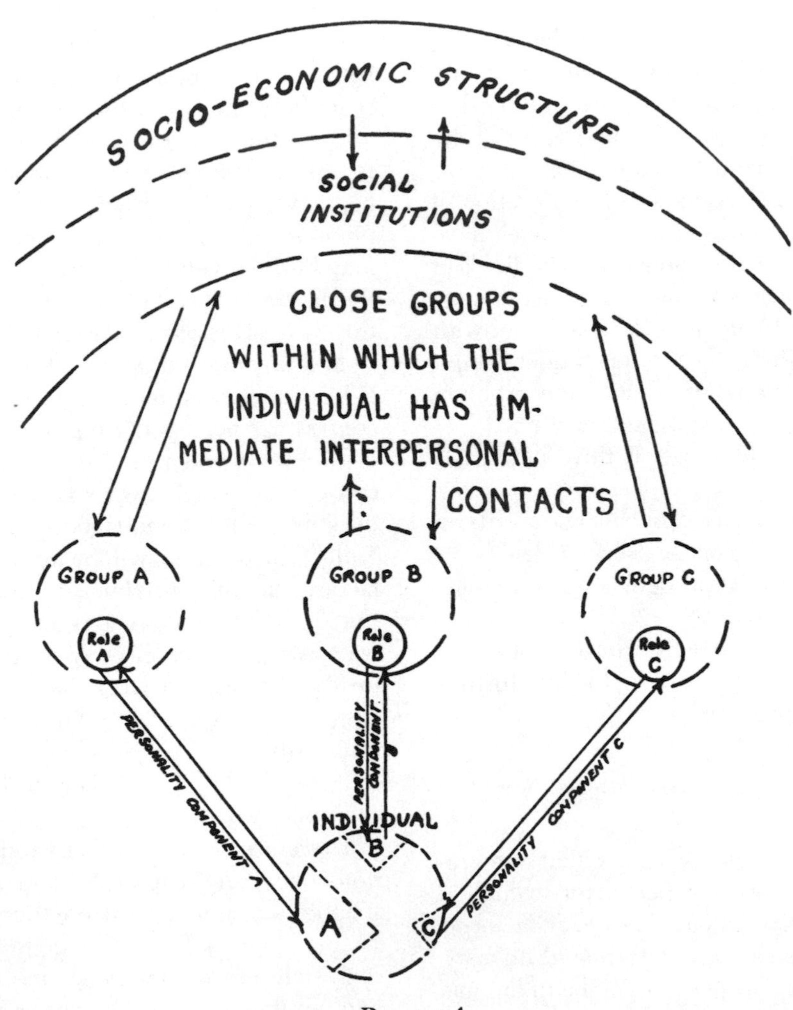

DIAGRAM 1

Role A corresponds to personality component A. The integration of the personality into the role in Group A involves a large segment of the individual self, including the projection of basic drives and related conflicts.

Role B corresponds to personality component B. The integration of the personality into the role in Group B involves a smaller segment of the individual self, reflecting repression of basic drives.

Role C corresponds to personality component C. The integration of the personality into the role in Group C involves a minimal segment of the individual self, including repression and conscious suppression of drives.

teracted; the particular configurations of defense employed will be significantly different in the separate roles. Finally, the assertion of special skills in dealing with selected elements of reality would be more successful in one role than in another.

To restate briefly, the "social role" or "social self" is that time-conditioned adaptive integration of personality in group action which is the product of interaction of all the forces in the field, those derived from the environment and those derived from the potentialities of "total personality." It seems as if out of the compound of the orienting-coordinating functions of the personality and the surrounding group forces, there is crystallized a specific pattern of action which is reflected in the form of a particular "social role."

INDIVIDUAL SELF AND "SOCIAL SELF"

Society is the nutritional medium in which the identity of a person gradually emerges. The substance of each society structures the content of that identity. As the individual matures, he achieves an identity which is at once both individual and social. These two aspects of personal identity are not clearly separable. The individual component of personal identity is represented in the more durable, less modifiable aspects of character structure. It reflects the organized, consistent behavior tendencies of the individual, those specific integrations of behavior which have been conditioned by the interaction of biological disposition and early family conditioning. It is the core of the personality, the more personal, private, relatively fixed aspect of self.

Yet, in a strict sense, the genetic process of individuation is never complete. A child never completely separates its psyche from that of the parental figure, and in a parallel sense, the adult's identity is always being influenced through the accretion of new layers of social influence. In the processes of maturation, the achievement of individuality and independence is a matter of degree; only a state of relative biosocial independence is ever attained, whether in the context of the child's need of mother, or the adult's need of society.

The social identity of a person epitomizes the continued interdependence of individual and society. The social component of a person's identity is represented in the more peripheral (later acquired) aspects of personality, in the less durable, more modifiable layers of character. It is less personal, less private, less fixed.

It is these relatively more external layers of character which permit the greater degree of penetration by social forces. The social identity of a person, therefore, is more malleable, more tentative, influenced by time and processes of group belongingness.

In a given time and social situation, certain components of the "total self" are mobilized into action, while other components are temporarily subordinated. With a change in time and group situation, a shift of emotional integration occurs, with a corresponding shift of "social role," i.e., other components of the self are moved into a dominant position in preparation for a particular type of social participation.

This is the essence of the process of social adaptation. In this process, the individual may react to social pressure with compliance, protest or withdrawal. There is also a fourth possibility; if the social pressures are overwhelming and exceed the individual's resources for plastic adaptation, the organism may respond by disintegrating its old form and structuring a new form which now shows distinct properties of its own. This is what seems to happen in the psychotic forms of integration, in some forms of war neurosis, and in psychosomatic disorders.

Such principles apply to each stage of personality development: first, within the family group, after that, school, community, and, finally, in the relations of the adult with wider society. In each stage of personality maturation, the delicate balance between the individual and social aspects of self varies, thus imparting specific characteristics to social behavior at each stage.

THE PRINCIPLE OF "COMPLEMENTARITY"

In this interaction, all too frequently and one-sidedly, emphasis is placed on the state of opposition between individual and society. Just as often, however, the two sets of forces may act in the same direction, and reinforce each other. One is tempted to apply here Robert Oppenheimer's principle of "complementarity," derived from the field of physics. Under certain conditions, the forces of society and the individual may be antithetical; under changed conditions, these same forces may mutually complement one another. The relations between individual and society may, in some senses, be analogized to those between child and mother. The emotional tendencies of child and mother may, at times, be mutually complementary, at other times, mutually opposed. The child incorporates selected parts of the mother which may strengthen or weaken its own evolving self. Similar principles pertain to the relations between the individual and society.

PERSONALITY AND SOCIETY

As background for these concepts, it may be useful to review certain pertinent principles concerning the relations between individual personality and society.

Personality and society cannot be considered apart. Human behavior is shaped both by the organization of the internal forces of personality, and the external forces of society. Just as the biologist recognizes that the broader unit of study for the life process is not the single organism, but rather the colony, so, in an analogous sense, human behavior must be scrutinized in the context of the processes of group life and the individual's part in the group. Psychoanalysts and sociologists both recognize the need for a broader conceptual frame within which to define and measure the operations of personality. Psychoanalysts require a theory of social organization. Sociologists require a theory of personality. In fact, a scientific theory of personality is hardly possible, except in the context of a broader theory of social organization. Only in a restricted and special sense is personality a closed system. While individual personality reflects a measure of unity and intactness, there is a continuous interchange between personality and society. Personality, in all its functions, preserves some measure of plasticity, though this plasticity is greater for some functions and less for others.

The surface of the personality may be likened to a semipermeable membrane; it permits a limited penetration in both directions—from outside inwards, and from inside outwards. The evidences of this penetrability are most clearly seen in childhood and adolescence. Presumably, interpenetration between society and personality is more fluid in childhood than in adulthood, but certainly does not cease with the achievement of maturity.

The internal forces of personality remain stable only so long as the individual is able to shift his relation to the environment, according to need. Such adaptive change may involve either a shift of inner equilibrium or the effort to change the environment and thus avoid the need for changing the internal balance of personality.

In the interaction between society and personality, two processes take place: the environment exercises a selective effect on the individual, and, in turn, the individual selects from the environment, both consciously and unconsciously, those elements which he wishes to influence and to be influenced by.

The social environment shapes the path along which the individual may successfully adapt to his surroundings.[1] It reinforces some individual drives, subordinates others. It determines the form and range of opportunities which are available for the individual, opportunities for security, gratification of basic needs, self-expression, as well as fulfillment of the larger aims for the self. It also defines the kinds of dangers which the individual must face and fight against. It sanctions some channels for the release of emotion, and imposes prohibitions against others; thus, it controls the flow and inhibition of emotion.

At each age level, and at each distinct level of personality organization, the environment requires of the individual distinct types of social function. The so-called "silent compulsions" of society press upon the individual, who then has the choice of complying or resisting. The molding effects of the environment on character structure vary with the distinctive features of each society. The dominant patterns of social organization influence both the form and content

[1]Some aspects of the dynamic relations of Personality and Society are discussed in an article by Heinz Hartmann, "Psychoanalysis and Sociology," in *Psychoanalysis Today*, edited by Sandor Lorand, Internat. Univ. Press, New York, 1944. These concepts are also discussed in a report, "The Social Responsibility of Psychiatry," published by the Group for the Advancement of Psychiatry (Committee on Social Issues).

of individual behavior. More concretely, the environment influences the frequency, intensity and content of mental illness; in some circumstances, it can affect the form of certain psychiatric disorders as well, though the latter is less common. Society, therefore, exerts not merely a surface effect but, potentially, affects the depths of personality as well.

Viewing the phenomenon from the opposite side, the personality seeks out, selectively, an environment which is congenial to the expression of specific individual needs. To some limited extent, the individual has the power to change or shape his environment, or to set up priorities for interaction with some elements of the surrounding reality, while rejecting contact with others. The individual chooses those forms of interaction which are favorable to the desired direction of self-expression. More specifically, this involves the interrelation between selected elements of the environment and the pursuit of particular ego aims, pleasure goals, relief of guilt, reinforcement of favorable defenses, and solutions of inner conflict.

Or, the individual may seek out an environment favorable to the need for an irrational "acting out" of unconscious urges; that is, he seeks opportunity for the projection of elements of inner conflict onto the social scene.

It is also common knowledge that certain individuals are capable of integrating their personalities in a given form, only as they derive support for such integration from the environment. In this sense, certain forms of personality balance are parasitic. The intactness and stability of the self in such instances are conditional on the support of the environment. At times such forms of adaptation appear in the guise of automatic obedience to the environmental pattern. This principle is clinically important insofar as the adaptational success or failure of certain "roles" rests with such parasitic personality reactions. One sees it exemplified not only in certain symbiotic two-person relationships, but also in the intense clinging quality of the attachment of certain individuals to groups.

The relations between personality and environment may also assume an opposite expression; that is, the personality, in striving to integrate a certain "social role," achieves it only in the context of continuous opposition to the environment.

Finally, in situations involving severe or persistent conflict between personality and environment, the environment may prove to be the stronger force and, in consequence, there may be any degree of damage to the intactness of individual personality, and failure in effectuating a given "social role."

POSITIVE AND NEGATIVE FUNCTIONS OF "SOCIAL ROLE"

In the processes of adaptation, the "social role" of the individual may serve either a positive or negative psychological function. In mature, well-integrated personalities, the "social role" can represent the strength of the individual expressed positively in participant group action. Here, there is no conflict between the individual and social components of self. They mutually reinforce each other.

In less fortunate personalities, handicapped by specific emotional disabilities and generalized immaturity, the individual and social aspects of self may be in conflict. The effort of integrating a particular "social role" may exact an excessive price in terms of anxiety and conflict within the individual self; or, conflict within the individual may damage or actually prevent effective execution of a given "social role." Such discord between individual and social aspects of self is common in a variety of psychopathological states.

In group participation, the identity of the individual is either strengthened or weakened. In a positive sense, an individual may assert his strength through group participation; on the other hand, the weaker the person's sense of individual identity, the greater the need for support of the sense of self from the group. The deeper the anxiety about self, the more intense is the dependence on group belongingness. In this sense, "social role" signifies a compensatory, defensive and negative function.

"SOCIAL ROLE" AND CAUSATION OF "NEUROTIC BEHAVIOR"

For years, the etiology of psychoneurotic behavior has been the subject of controversial discussion, some investigators stressing the role of conflict in buried past experience, others stressing conflict in current experience. It seems to me that this controversy not only lacks validity, but that it has been kept alive by inadequate understanding of the interaction of social environment with personality.

The concept of the phenomenology of "social role" may illuminate this aspect of the problem. It offers a dynamic link between society and the individual, and also provides a theoretical frame for the relations between genetically fixed patterns of individual personality and the more modifiable and later-acquired aspects of character. It seems to me that this hypothesis provides the possibility for reconciling past and present components of the etiology of neurosis.

All components of causation of present neurotic behavior must, by definition, be part of the present dynamics of the situation. Such factors must be current, either as functioning elements of the personality, or as elements of the surrounding situation. That part of the past which is relevant to present causation is the "live past," not the "dead past"; that is, that part of past experience which has been incorporated into the motivational patterns of the evolving self and represents now a live part of the current character structure. As such, it has contributed to the shaping of the individual component of personality, through which it influences the potentialities of adaptive behavior and the possible variety of "social roles." Current factors in the environment influence the social levels of personality integration and may, under some circumstances, penetrate down through the social layers of character to affect the deeper aspects of personality as well.

THE PHENOMENOLOGY OF "SOCIAL ROLE" IN CLINICAL PRACTICE

Certain remarks may here be made as to the relations between "social role" and total personality, as observed in clinical practice. In the practice of psychoanalysis one often has occasion to appraise the emotional capacity of an adult for playing the roles, in various groups, of child, boy or girl, or man or woman: for example, female patients, married, having children, capable of fulfilling the role of wife but unable to assume the role of mother—or vice versa; married male patients, assuming the role of boy but unable to accept the "social role" of a man; other patients who are adequate or outstanding in their professional role, but utterly incompetent in their family role—or, again, the exact opposite. Or, one sees successful execution of a role as social leader and inadequacy in marital relations. Certain individuals are able to achieve close relations with one or two people, but are unable to play an effective "role" in groups. They simply do not make contact with groups. To contrast with this, many social leaders in this culture, who are outstanding in their success in manipulating groups, have a shockingly defective relationship with individuals. One discerns here certain selective emotional processes, making possible reasonably successful adaptation in one "role" and failure in another. The relative success or failure of adaptation in a given "social role" is the result of coincidence or conflict between character disposition and social environment. It should be clear then that even in the case of an emotionally handicapped personality, it is possible for the consequences of the handicap to be intensified in one "social role" and minimized, or even counteracted, in another. It is known, for example, that in some instances psychopathic personalities and neurotics achieved a much more successful adaptation in military life than in civil life.

One may suppose that, in a given individual, certain sets of "social roles" abet and strengthen each other, while others are antithetical. For example, the "roles" of businessman and Rotarian may be congenial, whereas the "roles" of soldier and independent entrepreneur may be antithetical.

Still another approach to the question of the relation between "social role" and total personality is through the examination of the social functioning of distinct personality types, "normal" and psychopathological. In the "normal" person, one assumes the capacity to effect flexibly a variety of "social roles," in accordance with adaptational requirements. In our culture, some forms of social integration of personality are more stable and constant than others. Of relevance here is Kardiner's concept of the relation of "basic personality" to culture.

The capacity of a given individual for expressing himself in a variety of "social roles" is dramatically exemplified in the personality of the actor, who changes his outer coat like a chameleon, to accommodate to the requirements of a given part.

The acting personality and the hysterical personality have certain features in common: the flair for the dramatic, the romantic leaning, the exhibitionism, the heavy reliance on wish-fulfilling fantasy. The hysteric is noted for his capacity for dissociating the separate components of a multiple identity. Hysterical personalities display an "all or none" tendency in their adaptive processes. When they are obedient to external reality, they tend to deny or suppress the inner reality—the needs inherent in their fantasy life. When dominated by their fantasy life, they tend to ignore or blunt external reality. They seem unable to harmonize the two levels of reality—inner and outer. Such shifts of internal psychic balance as these are implicated in the psychic task of integrating different "social roles." Thus, the hysteric's dual selves, or dual "social roles," reflect a favoring by the ego of one or the other type of social identity, depending on the stimuli derived from contrasting group environments.

Hitler has been described as hysterical and paranoid. Is it not conceivable that world history was influenced by an extraordinary "complementarity" between the prewar social environment of Germany, the emotional state of the German masses, and Hitler's mental state? The German group psychological situation was receptive to a hysterical leader. The hysterical and paranoid "social role" of the leader was not only sanctioned, but perhaps significantly buttressed by the mood of the masses.

In the obsessional personality, something different occurs. Here, the structure of the personality is such that the strongest characteristic is obedience to social compulsion, and renunciation of sexual and aggressive needs. The obsessional is more rigid; the shift of "social role" from one group to another occurs within a more limited range. There is usually no major deviation from the prevailing ego orientation, which reflects a profound tendency toward submission to social command, and denial of basic drives. Accordingly, there are only minor shifts of "social role," the form of which is influenced by the characteristic mechanism of symbolic substitution. The ego goal of seeking security through obedience to social compulsion and renunciation of basic drives persists. In fact, this loss of spontaneity and emotional plasticity is the chief reason for the subjective distress of the obsessional in meeting the requirements of varied social situations. The rigid conformity trends of the obsessional impart a quality of insincerity to his "social role."

By contrast, the schizophrenic has contemptuously cast off ordinary conventions. In fact, for some this is often the most "appealing" feature of the schizophrenic. In respect to fluidity of social behavior and diversity of "social roles," the schizophrenic comes closer to the hysteric than to the obsessional. Rapid shifts of "social role," influenced by group stimuli, are often seen in some forms of schizophrenia. At one pole, one sees an identification of the ego with deep bodily surgings, unintegrated with the influence of social contacts. And, in contrasting group situations, there is an identification of the ego with the presumed constraints and hostile, menacing aspects of the surrounding environment, activating the urge to deny the reality of bodily needs altogether. In either case, the schizophrenic experiences great difficulty in effectuating a consistent "social role." The schizophrenic is, characteristically, apprehensive of loss or destruction of self. If he identifies his ego with his bodily experiences, he tends to renounce social participation for fear of his own destructive powers or of being injured through the exposure of his body to attack. This is one kind of destruction of self. On the other hand, if the schizophrenic denies the reality of the body and identifies his ego with the restrictive, hostile elements of his environment, he again renounces social participation because of his intense hostility toward other persons, whom he blames for the required sacrifice of the vital pleasure of body existence. This is again a kind of destruction of self. The schizophrenic's preoccupation with the threat of being destroyed through closeness with other persons induces withdrawal and resistance to social participation.

From a somewhat different angle, one often sees schizophrenics who automatically assume the mannerisms of the persons by whom they are surrounded. This is a phase of their uncontrolled obedience to social pressure. Or, they may show a bizarre pattern of negativistic opposition to those same influences. In any case, in some schizophrenic individuals, one does see remarkable shifts in adaptive behavior, with lightning transitions in "social role," stimulated by the patient's awareness of the hostile or sympathetic influence of the group environment.

Looking at the problem still another way, I have been impressed with the close association between the emergence of certain psychosomatic disorders and the adaptive breakdown of a characteristic "social role"; or, perhaps more accurately, the psychosomatic disequilibrium is associated with unresolved conflict between the emotional content of antithetical "social roles." The hypertensive personality seems able neither to stabilize a role of dependence on and submission to the environment, nor to establish a role of successful aggressive mastery of the environment. The two roles are incongruous and cannot be reconciled. Patients who break down with peptic ulcer can neither assume a "role" of passive oral dependence on environment, nor achieve the opposed "role" of superior strength and self-sufficiency. The person who breaks down with an acute skin disorder has suffered a deep injury to his pride. He can neither accept the implications of this blow to his narcissistic vanity, nor can he restore the preinjured successful "social role." Instead, he fumes with indignation and bursting fury. He gets red in the face and blows hot and cold.

"Social role" has earlier been likened to a semipermeable membrane. In somatic terms, the skin represents such a membrane; it is the partition between person and environment. In one sense, changes in skin are surface phenomena, relatively peripheral reactions. Yet, through the skin and the surface membranes of the orifices of the body are mediated all the vital processes of exchange between the organism and environment. In this sense, changes in skin function may have critical importance for the deepest biological functions of the organism. An apt analogy for this theme is the phenomenon of huge skin burns; if large areas of skin are injured, the entire vital processes of the organism are in jeopardy, the very life of the individual is at stake. In an analogous sense, one wonders if an environmental threat to the efficacy of certain "social roles" does not endanger the integrity of the entire psyche.

ANXIETY AND "SOCIAL ROLE"

The effect of anxiety on the dynamics of "social role" may show itself in two opposite ways; it may induce increasing instability and a tendency to rapid change of "roles"; or it may induce increasing rigidity. In either case, adaptive efficiency is impaired.

The quantity of anxiety generated is influenced by the degree of harmony or conflict between individual identity and social identity. The individual's inner concept of self may coincide with the aspect of self projected into a particular "social role," or may clash with it. The personality performance in a given "social role" will always be affected by the relative harmony or conflict between the social expression of self and the inner evaluation of self, both conscious and unconscious, and also by the corresponding intensity of anxiety. There is the related question of the degree of psychic distance between the individual and social selves; in terms of emotional content, the "social role" may be relatively peripheral or close to the individual self. Such relations will determine the degree to which an individual's identification with a given group is genuine or false, spontaneous and healthy, or forced and anxiety-ridden.

These issues need to be weighed in the light of a special trend in our culture, namely, the unusual degree of strain and anxiety which accompanies the effort of social adaptation. With this is associated a widespread tendency toward loneliness. Hostile, competitive feelings are overstimulated, and the need for defenses against and escape from these emotions is very great. One of the outstanding characteristics of our society is the individual's emotional isolation and lack of security in group living. The need for group belongingness is profound, but the thwarting of this need is extensive. This seems to be one of the manifestations in our society of the competitive patterns of group organization and exaggerated intergroup tensions, but is also partly an expression of a particular kind of evolution of individual personality in our cultural group, from childhood on.

Still a further aspect of the whole problem of the relations of individual personality to "social role" pertains to the dominant emotion which is implicated in the individual's identification with the group. Such identification, as Fritz Redl has pointed out, may be mediated through the dominant emotions of love or fear or hate. It is an unfortunate fact that all too frequently, in our society, an individual is integrated into a group through emotional needs relating to fear and hate, rather than love. The patterns of prejudice against minorities, fear, mistrust, and belligerence toward other nations, involve this characteristic trend. This is a separate chapter in itself, however, and cannot be dilated on here.

The above discussion of "social role" is by no means exhaustive. Many additional considerations must be omitted for lack of space.

I should like, at this point, to attempt a spatial formulation of dynamic criteria for the phenomenon of "social role." Approaching human behavior according to Kurt Lewin's field concepts, that is, that society is the total space in which personality manifestations are to be appraised, a hierarchical scheme of the relevant phenomenological levels may be represented as follows. (See Diagram 2.)

This diagram attempts to depict the manner in which the phenomenon of "social role" is influenced—from without by group organization, and from within by the factors deriving from individual personality. It represents the relative unity of personality in its position of interchange with the environment; it depicts the phenomenon of "social role" or "social self" as intermediate between the dynamics of intrapersonal life and the dynamics of group behavior. The particular configuration of a given "role" derives its clue from the goals and values which orient the individual's part in the group. Goals have to do with utility (security), pleasure and self-fulfillment. Values represent a function of the individual's relations to society; they provide directives for social action. Values are oriented both toward self and one's relations to other persons. The dual orientation of values involves, on the one hand, a particular quality of apperceptive response to the culture-conditioned patterns of interpersonal relations, and a personal attitude toward one's individual strivings.

Abram Kardiner states that: "Values describe

(a) A pattern of interpersonal relations; e.g., honesty
(b) Achievement; e.g., heroism, enterprise
(c) Goals; e.g., success, salvation

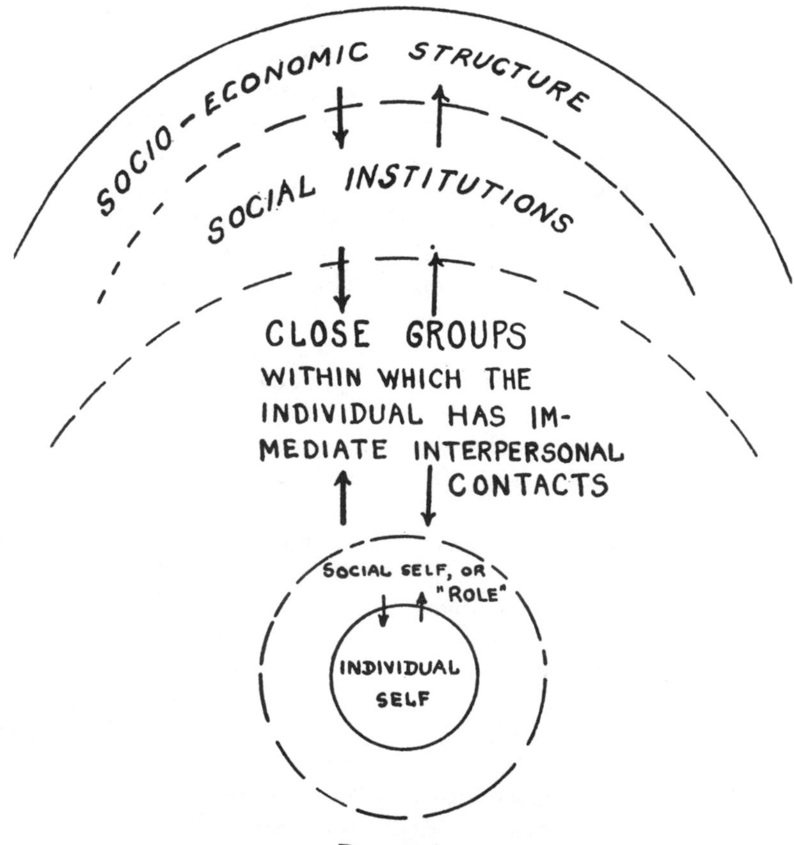

DIAGRAM 2

(d) Types of approved gratification; e.g., esthetic gratification, efficiency, orderliness
(e) Ideals; e.g., responsibility, virtue, strength."

It is clear, then, that multiple factors, deriving partly from the group organization, and partly from the individual structure of personality, determine both the value orientation and corresponding configuration of "social role." The more pertinent of these are the quality of apperception of culturally dominant patterns of interpersonal relations, the patterns of compliance with, or protest against social compulsion, social goals, the self-assertive trends or the trends toward subordination of individual aspects of self, the projection of inner conflicts into the "social role" and the configuration of defenses against anxiety.

PSYCHOANALYTIC METHOD AND THE STUDY OF "SOCIAL ROLE"

Having offered this conceptual frame for "social role," and having attempted to discern some of the criteria by which "social role" might be defined, it would now seem logical to consider some of the methods of study of "social role." In those professional disciplines which deal with human behavior, there is, currently, relatively little agreement concerning the proper methodological approach to the problem of "social role." Sociologists have one set of criteria and procedures; social psychoanalysts offer still another technique. There is no consensus even among psychoanalysts as to how suitable the psychoanalytic method of investigation is for the study of "social role."

In a symposium on "Methodological Problems in the Study of Social Phenomena," held at the annual meeting of the American Psychoanalytic Association in 1948, some analysts were of the conviction that psychoanalytic study of individuals might provide considerable insight into the phenomenon of "social role," whereas others were doubtful and tended to reject the study of social phenomena as not belonging to the sphere of the psychoanalyst's everyday work with individual persons; others suggested that psychoanalytic technique might perhaps be useful, but might be applied by psychoanalytically trained social scientists. It is self-evident that this range of views is a direct expression of the fact that the phenomena of "social role" lie intermediate between the spheres of sociology and psychology. It is the professional "no-man's land."

The psychoanalytic method applies to a pair of persons, but the techniques are pointed to the experience of only one of these persons—the patient. This situation does not provide a natural setting for the study of social behavior. Nevertheless, my conviction is that, utilized in a special way, the psychoanalytic method can offer important data on the dynamics of "social role," even though such data cannot be complete. Psychoanalytic technique cannot give us direct observations of social phenomena, but it can offer a careful study of subjective responses to participation in social phenomena.

I should like to review briefly some aspects of psychoanalytic technique as they pertain to this question. At first glance, it would appear that the phenomena of "social role" fall mainly into the category of ego dynamics. Ego functions are obviously central to the problems of social adaptation, but, in a broader sense, the vicissitudes of social role involve potentially all the functions of personality.

There has been a long lag in the systematic exploration of ego behavior by psychoanalytic means, influenced historically by Freud's preference for primary concentration on the id. But, as is well known, both Freud and his daughter have repeatedly expressed their respect for the importance of the study of ego phenomena, and some of their later writings reflect this conviction.

There are some aspects of psychoanalytic therapeutic technique that have an immediate bearing on the question of its application in the study of ego behavior. The traditional therapeutic technique has tended to emphasize a temporary shedding of the patient's ego, of his reason, a denuding by the patient of the social layers of his identity, in order to promote access to the unconscious and biologically conditioned drives. Of course, this technique, selective as it is, has brought an incalculable reward in insight into intrapsychic mechanisms of behavior. One wonders, however, at what cost, in terms of failure to understand the social functions of personality, has this emphasis on "shedding of the ego" been preserved.

The analytic relationship, in the usual sense, does not offer a true social experience. The analyst is not a person to the patient, but is more definitely an illusory image which changes from time to time as the patient projects his fantasies onto the person of the analyst. If the traditional psychoanalytic method is, in this sense, not a genuine social experience, how then is it possible to utilize psychoanalytic method for the study of "social role"?

In the first place, analysts vary among themselves as to how real, as human beings, they are to the patient. The degree to which the analysis offers a social relationship varies correspondingly. Also, analysts differ as to the relative emphasis they now place in therapy on ego mechanisms. In recent years, a larger stress has been placed upon the importance of character analysis, of systematic working through, step by step, of the character defenses. By such means, access is gradually achieved to the deeper layers of emotional life by working with each level of ego integration in turn, rather than by encouraging the patient in the analysis to artificially and temporarily denude himself of his ego covering. An increasing number of analysts are interested in obtaining, at the same time, an accurate picture of the social realities by which the patient is surrounded, and more factual information regarding the nature of the patient's participation in group life. It appears that his increased emphasis on an exact knowledge of social reality, on systematic analysis of character defenses, and on knowledge of the patient's emotional function in groups, has run parallel with a recognition that the more traditional therapeutic technique too often fails to be therapeutic. In other words, the increased emphasis on therapeutic incentive for a genuine cure has produced increased respect for the importance of understanding ego mechanisms, group participation, and character adaptation to environment. With such an emphasis in psychoanalytic investigation, it would appear to me that tangible gains toward the understanding of the relations of individual personality and "social role" could be made through psychoanalytic study. This would be especially fruitful if such studies could be pursued with the active partnership of social scientists.

One might, of course, raise the question as to whether the phenomena of "social role" and its relations to individual personality could perhaps be more profitably investigated in a setting which provides a more natural social experience; that is, in a group setting such as is provided by group therapy or group psychoanalysis. In previous publications, I have suggested that group psychotherapy offers a more natural access to the vicissitudes of ego function and to the problems of character adaptation. The therapeutic process in a group setting is mediated through the dynamics of the "social role" rather than through access to "total personality." Access to the deeper conflicts of the individual can be achieved only by a working through of the dynamics of the "social role." The whole question of the use of psychoanalytic method for the study of social behavior, and the further exposition of the relations of personality and society, merits careful investigation.

CHAPTER 13

Group Psychotherapy with a Mixed Group of Adolescents

The most striking aspect, by far, in the behavior of adolescents in group therapy is their yearning to complete their incomplete selves. They simply do not feel whole, and from this feeling arises a painful tension. Very transparent, indeed, is their effort to extract selectively from their group experience that which they lack, so that they may win approval, and in their own eyes more closely approximate their ideal image of themselves. This striving holds for male and female alike though on a different plane, and toward different goals. Such behavior is clearly a phase of the adolescents' extensive preoccupation with self in an era of development in which they must all too rapidly accommodate both to the critical growth changes occurring within themselves, and to the rigorous requirements which society imposes upon youths about to take their place in the community as adult men and women. During this phase, one observes their extraordinary sensitiveness to other persons' judgments of their worth, their constant concern with proving adequacy, their profound sense of vulnerability to criticism and attack from without. They are caught between the twin horns of conformity and defiance. It is small wonder that they show such trigger-edge irritability.

In this crucial period of maturation, these young people display tender skins, but nowhere does one see their rawness, sensitiveness, and need to prove themselves more vividly than in the relations between the sexes. The drama of male and female, each coming into their own, is intense. The awareness of each other is acute. Each stands poised, hyperalert and vigilant, prepared to react with lightning rapidity to the other's slightest move. The feeling of incompleteness and the need of each other is strong, but being immature, and lacking the sure movements of the more experienced adults, they approach each other in gingerly fashion, each waiting for the other to make the first move,

---

Reprinted with permission from the *International Journal of Group Psychotherapy*, July 1955, Vol. V, No. 3, 249-260.

each seeking to feel out the ill-defined dangers of proximity, and ready at a moment's notice to leap to their own defense, or retreat. They need each other, but fear and mistrust each other. The craving to complete themselves in the other is clear, but the fear of betrayal, and the fear of losing oneself in the other are equally intense. The elemental urge for union is tempered by the fear of injury through domination. They yearn to uncover themselves but do not dare. The unnamed dangers loom large, so they run for cover. The desire to exhibit themselves turns into a fear of exposure, and exaggerated hiding. Because of insecurity, confusion, fright, and the frantic flight to self-defense, the basic urge of the one sex toward the other turns into a battle of the sexes on a grand scale. The ambivalence is conspicuous and dramatic. The struggle of the sexes becomes waged in a domination-submission frame. In this struggle, all too frequently, safety is sought in protective alliances with members of the same sex. The drama is fierce, dangerous, deadly serious, but thrilling.

This description gives some of the emotional coloring of interaction between the sexes in an adolescent therapy group. Feelings are not merely verbally expressed; they are intensely lived out in the permissive atmosphere of a therapy group of this sort. Obviously, the experience is not without some risk, but with understanding, caution, and appropriate channeling of expression, the risk can be reduced to a minimum.

Two related dynamic trends stand out sharply: the adolescent's reactions to shifting images of self, propelled from within by the physiological processes of maturation, and from without by the demands of the outside world. On the one hand, they must accommodate to the pressures of sexual need, to changes in physique and appearance; on the other hand, they must accommodate to what others expect of them. In this last respect, they are influenced in two ways: by their beliefs as to what the opposite sex wants of them, and what members of the same sex, particularly those whom they admire and wish to emulate, expect of them. The adolescent personality is squeezed between these several conflicting pressures. This is the pivot around which much of the therapeutic interaction in the group proceeds. On this stage of conflict are reflected the confusions and anxieties relating to sexual identity, the feelings of inferiority associated with awareness of physical difference, the compensating aggressive reactions to anxiety. On this stage, too, emerge responses of guilt and shame, guilt deriving particularly from conflicted sexual temptation and aggressive impulses, and shame deriving from exhibitionistic urges, preoccupation with shortcomings and failure to live up to the idealized image of self. In this connection, the dread of ridicule and humiliation is often intense.

Again and again, conflict with parental authority intrudes on the scene, literally loaded with the ambivalent emotions of unresolved dependence, the urge to demonstrate self-sufficiency, and the apprehension of one or another form of castration. It is not true, however, that the stage of adolescent conflict represents purely the reactivation of unresolved oedipal conflict. What one observes actually is a reactivation of all significant previous levels of conflict, oedipal and preoedipal as well. Clearly dramatized here are the deep formative influences of the "oral" and "anal" levels of personality on the later emerging genital conflicts. Equally transparent are the patterns of defense mobilized against guilt and anxiety deriving from these conflicts.

The therapeutic group provides a social testing ground for the distorted, inappropriate perceptions of self, and relations with others, deriving from all the stages of maturation. On this testing ground, the adolescent has the opportunity gradually to put his confusion to one side, and achieve some dependable, stable clarity in his personal identity.

For some ten years, I have observed the reactions of adolescents of both sexes in weekly group-therapeutic sessions. Originally, each of these patients was clinically known to me. All of them entered individual psychotherapy, some with myself, others with other therapists to whom these patients were referred. The weekly group experience was conceived as a supplement to individual therapy, not as an independent therapy on its own. The role of group therapist was mainly assumed by myself, though the therapists treating other members of the group individually were regularly present. They were themselves active participants, shared with me the responsibility of conducting the proceedings, and in my absence, took over fully the role of group therapist. In this sense, the other therapists in the group were closely identified with me, and served as auxiliary therapists. Usually, there were three, sometimes four therapists present, both male and female. Not infrequently, too, we had some "visiting firemen," psychiatrists and caseworkers who wished to observe the proceedings. At such times, the patients learned to accept them into the group freely and with a minimum of anxiety. As a whole, the group evolved a rather free, mobile, fluid character, of which this casual attitude toward visiting professionals was but one feature.

For the patients, attendance was voluntary. Fees covered a broad range, and were often waived. The emotional connotations of fees for professional service did not play a prominent role. The personal atmosphere was informal, intimate; the business aspect of the relationship was reduced to a minimum. Though attendance was purely voluntary, with some few exceptions, the patients came with great regularity. No pressure was applied with regard to occasional absences, no demands for explanation were made, no stimulus for self-justification was offered. Attendance was accepted at face value as an indicator of the presence of incentive, and the wish to participate. When absences occurred, they usually turned out to have been unavoidable, and often the patient spontaneously expressed regret at having missed the pleasure of the session. The group was inconstant in size and composition. In numbers, it varied from five to six to as many as eighteen. The optimum size for effective participation seemed to be roughly eight to ten. The age range was also wide, from sixteen to twenty-three, with occasional exceptions reaching up to twenty-seven years. Also, a special influence was injected into the experience when now and then a married person entered the group, or a member changed status from single to married. When this happened, the group was fluid enough to welcome the participation of the spouse. From time to time, old patients left, new ones were added. Not infrequently, group members invited personal friends to visit once or twice, and were usually freely accepted into the group. The exceptions to this usually occurred when the visitor was arrogant or held himself defensively aloof; this generally stirred up resentment.

Diagnostically, all categories of personality and types of emotional disturbance were included excepting frank psychoses. In the case of neurotic characters with a strong propensity for "acting out," particularly the exhibitionistic personalities, there seemed ordinarily to be no special problem. The group patterns spontaneously imposed restraint on these characters, and seemed to exercise a salutary effect. If the grandiose and exhibitionistic tendencies were intense and strongly pathological and the group after a time proved not to be too congenial, such persons usually left of their own accord. Apart from clinical diagnosis, the main criteria for admission were confused attitudes concerning social and sexual adaptation and the individual therapist's judgment that the patient was emotionally ready for, and would profit from, group experience. This judgment was usually mutually agreed upon by patient and therapist, after a variable length of preparation in individual therapy. I emphasize here that improvement in individual therapy was conceived in part as preparation for group experience, because many of these adolescents were seriously ill at the time of initial examination. In making this comment, I am aware that for some categories of disturbance, the opposite principle may hold, namely, that group therapy can be considered as an emotional preparation for individual therapy.

Of immediate interest are the varied types of response patients displayed when the therapist discussed with them, in individual sessions, the possibility of entering the group. They were distinctly of two types, fear and recoil, or an instantaneous burst of enthusiasm, a "raring to go" attitude. The first type of reaction was by far the more common, the latter relatively infrequent. In the first response, one observed initially fright, dread of exposure, attack, and ridicule. The patients seemed dominated by their anticipatory fantasies of the aggressive dangers lurking in such an exposed experience. Obviously, the intensity of this initial reaction derives from projection of their own aggressive impulses. They reacted at first with a strong urge to retreat. In anxiety-ridden personalities, this is easy to understand if we remember that the individual therapeutic relationship provides a safe haven, that the patient is offered immunity against retaliation by the therapist. In the group, there is no such immunity, no guarantee of protection from aggression. The situation is an exposed one. The patient must take his chances.

Generally, after a period of time and continued discussion of the opportunities in group interaction, the initial apprehension and urge to retreat subside, and anticipatory fantasies of pleasure become stronger. Spontaneously, the patient's inner urge to seek out gratifications of personal need in the group asserts itself and soon the patient expresses willingness to try the group, though often with a sense of insecurity and with continued reservations.

At the other pole are those rarer individuals who burst with delight at the anticipation of group experience, who indulge pleasant fantasies of a grand and glorious landing in the group, creating a "wow" of an impression, smearing the landscape, so to speak, with their superiority, sophistication and irresistible attraction. These are the adolescents with a strong push to impress others with their superior attributes, with their sexual finesse, and triumphs. These are the aggressive, impulsive exhibitionists, who hide their anxiety behind their competitive aggressive drive. I have found, though, barring the extreme types, the psychopathic or near psychotic, that the group is a useful instrumentality for taming these bold ones.

Between these two extremes, the acutely frightened adolescent, and the grandiose exhibitionist, one finds every intermediate type. Most usually, the reaction to the suggestion of group therapy is a strangely ambivalent one; the effect is to whet the appetite for direct gratification of personal need in the group, while at the same time, the excitement of temptation is sobered by the stirring of anxiety connected with anticipatory fantasies of exposure, betrayal and humiliation. One possible contributing factor to this reaction may derive from certain components of transference; the patient extends from the individual therapist to the group his repressed hope of getting direct gratification of sexual need, his guilt, fear of punishment, and urge to retreat. In certain instances, the mere suggestion of group therapy energizes in the individual therapeutic experience a working through a specific problems hitherto undisclosed. For example, certain specific fantasies of punishment for sexual transgression may remain mainly repressed for a time in individual therapy, due to the special kind of protection the individual therapist provides his patient. In the group, this artificial immunity is removed. In this sense, the very anticipation of group therapy holds some potential for enhancing the value of individual sessions. The transfer of influence from the one therapeutic situation to the other moves in both directions, however; the proceedings in the individual sessions often give concrete substance to the problems the patient struggles to solve in the group; the effect of group experience activates useful work in the individual sessions. In my judgment, an arrangement for concomitant individual and group therapy is of specific value in that it holds this rich potential of mutual fertilization of the proceedings in the two therapeutic situations.

I should like now to convey something of the concrete quality of the behavior of these adolescents in a group session. Typically, at the outset, there are some rapid, casual banterings as people get seated, and the seating arrangement is of great emotional significance. Who sits next to whom and why? Sometimes, there is a dramatic parting of the sexes, in that all the males seat themselves together, on one side, and all the females on the other. This is a specific sign of sexual tension. It means awareness that someone is "making a play" for someone else; the someone else plays "hard to get" and there is suspense in the air as to whether the gamble will win. At other times, there is conspicuous recognition that a particular boy seats himself next to a particular girl and this excites admiration, envy, competitive maneuvering, and barbed jokes. A rival tries to steal the play. All the excitement becomes suppressed, however, just as soon as the therapist takes his place and indicates readiness for the session to begin. There is typically a hushed silence, a silence that speaks eloquently of the air laden with the tension of suspense. The question is, who will make the first move to expose himself, or will the therapist "pick on someone"? Facial expressions either light up or suddenly go blank; the members peer penetratingly at one another. Occasionally, a particular adolescent stares at the ceiling conspicuously or averts his gaze. This last is an indicator of his urge to reveal himself. He wants to be the center, he wants to be looked at; yet he is afraid. The struggle is between the urge to show oneself, and the fear of getting "out on a limb." The danger of hurtful consequences of exposure seems ever present. Now and then, the struggle as to who will make the first move becomes crystallized in the battle between the sexes. The mutual suspicion of the two sexes is striking. The boys shove the girls into the open, the girls shove the boys. They tease each other. The males are particularly sensitive about their adequacy, imagining that every girl wants an athletic hero, a superman. The girls make flip remarks about the boys' masculinity, thus covering their own anxiety about femaleness. Each wants the other to uncover, each wants to see and be seen, but fears being hurt in the process. The issue is: which urge will prove the stronger, to "undress," figuratively speaking, or keep safe behind one's coverings?

Sooner or later, the tension cracks, someone opens up. The initial suspense subsides, and the group gets down to work. The discussion gathers its own momentum. The problems these patients toss into the hopper of group interaction center on several main subject matters: personal fears and incapacities, conflict with parental authority, conflict concerning sex, aggressive competition, and attitudes toward future plans. Whatever the subject matter, the members of the group are "all ears," listening with rapt attention, envious of the person holding the center of the stage, but constrained by a sense of fair play, and inhibiting the urge to usurp the speaker's position lest they be accused of wanting to "hog the show"; though, with true ambivalence, if offered "the floor," they will often demur. Despite these rivalrous feelings, a high level of camaraderie evolves which insures a fair "sharing of the cheese." When the picture is added up, there is little "hogging"; the group morale is of high quality; everyone has a chance.

In a typical instance, the adolescent hides his anxieties by couching his problem initially in circumstantial or social terms, playing down and obscuring the specific psychological content of the problem. The influence of the therapist, and the group members follow his example, is to challenge the patient's incentive for a more sincere, more honest and deeper level of revelation of the personal and psychological core of his problems. The first task, then, is to strip away the protective garb and achieve a clear, straightforward definition of the problem, articulated and revealed in personal terms. At this juncture some members of the group may immediately be tempted to exploit one patient's personal exposure for purposes of attack. The greater the personal anxiety, the greather the temptation to seize this channel for the release of hostility. Should this happen, however, the therapist and the morale of the group act as restraining influences. Frequently, the opposite occurs; the patient engaged in personal revelation instead of being subjected to attack is pleasantly surprised and rewarded by a show of support and encouragement, often from unexpected quarters in the group. This emotional support is of great moment in facilitating increasing candor of expression. In any case, the problem is batted back and forth in the group. Other members are stimulated to disclose similar problems, and bit by bit, the emotional content of the problem becomes more precisely and nudely revealed.

The therapist's contribution can be defined in several facets. Words as words are anathema. It is not "talk, talk and more talk," since conversation can and is used so deftly to hide rather than reveal, but rather the effort to reach behind words to the genuine affect which is being experienced.

I am reminded here of the famous reflection on the nature of conversation by Nietzsche. He related how two people, on meeting each other for the first time as complete strangers, have an instantaneous impression of each other, before each has had opportunity to utter a word. As soon as conversation is initiated, the initial impressions the one person has of the other becomes progressively modified. Each thinks the very first impression must have been completely wrong. Nietzsche says that the first impression was exactly right and the subsequent ones wrong, and that the conversation which ensued served merely the purpose of deceiving the listener.

It is somewhat in this spirit that an effort is made in the group to reach behind mere talk to genuine feelings. The technique for accomplishing this is to be intensely attentive to nonverbal patterns of behavior, facial expressions, body posturings, quick shifts in the motor behavior of patients as they react to the stimuli of group interaction processes. At the same time, the therapist with calculated intention ignores and sidesteps the kind of talk which is mere talk. The therapist's spirit in reaching out for genuine emotional communication is contagious, affects the attitudes of group members, and the push for more honest self-revelation is accelerated.

The therapist's emphasis on the theme, "the body talks," carries over to the group; not only the therapist but patients as well search out the nonverbal emotional communications concealed in the spontaneous posturings of patients. The therapist does this sometimes by interpreting an obvious expressional attitude in a given adolescent, or by arousing the curiosity of the entire group as to its meaning. For example, an eighteen-year-old boy is greeted in the conventional manner. Asked how he is, the quick reply is "fine." But his face is like a wet blanket, frozen, hang-dog. This is immediately challenged. Or another boy, the same age, is talking, but isn't saying anything. His words are mumbled, they run into one another, as if he were rolling potatoes inside his mouth. Someone calls out challengingly, "tight ass, don't you want to give us anything?"

Four-letter words are used freely and casually, not to show off or defy social conventions, but rather because intense affects are often associatively tied to them; by comparison, the more polite, conventional terms seem feeble, because the significant emotions have been stripped away from them. When on occasion an adolescent uses four-letter words with the obvious motive of exhibiting his sophistication or in order to shock other members, he is quickly told off. Gradually, the members of the group become conditioned to a code which promotes frank self-revelation, minus rationalizations, alibis, and other self-protective dressing. Tolerance for this can and is learned. The anxiety connected with exposure progressively lessens.

Of particular importance in the group atmosphere is the shedding of conventional social hypocrisies. Adolescents detest polite dishonesties, and are genuinely grateful for a group experience in which they can shrug off the unpleasant burdens of conventionally sanctioned patterns of deception in social relations. It is a comfort for these adolescents to be relieved of the silent compulsion toward "good manners," and conformity with other aspects of hypocritical morality which prevails in adult society. It is of significant cathartic value, and it adds something to their strength and dignity to be accepted for their real selves, rather than for their conformity. The group develops a morality of its own, in many respects a superior one. The members begin to feel the group as their own creation, built uniquely for their own needs. They feel understood, and they accommodate to their increasing recognition that the group is special, that it has standards distinct from those of the wider community, that elemental honesty in human relations in the group pays off, and that the group serves its function of lessening anxiety, and sharpening the clarity of their image of themselves as young males and females.

Once the ice is cracked in terms of dissolving initial inhibitions of the group participants, the process rapidly warms up and begins to move thick and fast. There is an ebb and flow of tension, a rapid shift in the level of participation, and in the level of excitation of the group. Sometimes, there is a quick rush of the aggressive members to "undress" the more retiring ones, thus hiding their own anxieties. Some of the boys, as well as the girls, though anxious, like being "undressed." Passive, shy, coy, they seem to say with their bodies, "come and get me." The spontaneous interaction between passive and active members is heated and intense. Either mechanism, passivity or aggressiveness, may be exploited for self-protection.

A characteristic worthy of mention is the remarkable tolerance of individual idiosyncrasies shown by group members. There is much joking, teasing, bantering, flirting, a great deal of "laughing with," and almost no "laughing at." All too tangible is the evidence of empathy with the underlying fear and suffering of other members. If one member seems wounded, another rises quickly to his defense. In this way, they parentify each other. Sometimes, the group may sense an unusually strong fear of the therapist on the part of a particular member. The group responds by "ganging up" on the therapist. They offer each other protection against unwarranted incursion by parental authority. On the other hand, in other circumstances, they will turn to the therapist for refuge against the attacks of others. These trends reflect, in my opinion, the tendency of the members to identify with each other, with the group aims and with the therapist.

There is a further value to the therapist's effort to bring nonverbal aspects of patient behavior into the open. An alert awareness to the motor reactions of patients, facial and bodily posturings, provides concrete clues to particular sexual conflicts, anxieties, feelings of inferiority and shame connected with certain physical features of the patient's personality. The deliberate intention here is to exploit these clues for a ventilation of specific disturbances in self-image, so profoundly shaped both by the physiological processes of maturation and social experience. A female participant yawns at the very moment when a male points a personal, sexual comment her way. The escape motive in the yawn is interpreted. Another female is silently angry because she feels neglected; the attention of a boy she likes is moving toward another girl. She has a blank facial expression, but is agitatedly tearing a piece of paper in her hand. The therapist arouses the group's curiosity concerning this act. A girl repeatedly brings flame to her cigarette lighter and promptly blows it out. She is intensely castrative toward boys. The implications of her gestures are discussed.

Such episodes as these provide quick leads to disturbed inner images of self, and the associated conflicts. The urges connected with these conflicts, sexual, aggressive, or the effort to compensate feelings of guilt, shame and inferiority, are freely ventilated. In the course of this experience, there is opportunity to expand awareness of discrepancies between the way the adolescent sees himself, and the way others in the group see him, also opportunity to understand better the discrepancies between one image of self and another, as they shift over time. This is reality testing.

The interaction processes of the group lend themselves effectively to the purpose of pointing out the distortions in the patient's interpretation of both self and the group reality. It is this phenomenon which has impelled me to attempt a formulation of the dynamic relations of individual personality to group role. Access to personality in the group is partial, not total. The level of access achieved is the dynamic content of the patient's role adaptation in the group, to the self-image projected into the group at a particular time and under particular interpersonal circumstances. Role phenomena are conditioned by temporal and situational factors as well as by the propensities of the individual personality. As these temporal and situational factors change, so does the patient's role adaptation. It is therefore possible through group interaction processes to achieve therapeutic access to a series of integrative levels of personality functioning depending on the vicissitudes of role adaptation.

I have tentatively formulated the following criteria for examining the dynamic correlation of individual personality and role: the aim or goal of the individual, his perception of surrounding reality in terms of the prevailing interpersonal processes, the image of self projected into the group role, the techniques of emotional control of the interaction with the group, the pattern of pursuit of gratification of personal need, the related conflicts with special reference to discrepancies between conscious and unconscious components, and the defense patterns mobilized against anxiety. With knowledge of the attributes of individual personality, and the use of such criteria, it is possible to define the dynamics of role function. The implementation of such concepts may be helpful in the effort to trace the specific mechanisms of group-therapeutic influence.

Thus far my comments have been mainly descriptive. Now, some additional comments concerning dynamics. I take as my starting point for a discernment of what is unique in group therapy the processes of social participation. Starting here, it is possible to move back and trace the interrelation of the events of social participation with the intrapsychic structure of the individual, and also to move in the opposite direction, tracing the interrelations of social participation with the group entity as a social system. I believe this is a logical approach, since the phenomena of social participation are intermediate between the individual and the social system. In order to understand the dynamics of group therapy, it is necessary to take the components of the therapeutic process basic to all forms of psychotherapy, and discern their pattern of operation in the social situation which is structured in a therapeutic group. I conceive the common denominators of all forms of psychotherapy to be mainly the following: the establishment of an emotional relationship between patient and therapist, with a continuous process of interchange between them, the emotional support the patient derives from this relationship, the release of pent-up feeling, and conflicted urges, the processes of reality testing, which bring a diminution of anxiety and guilt, and create conditions favorable to a progressive modification toward reality of the patients' interpretation of experience.

All these partial processes, overlapping and interacting, point their merged effects toward a more correct perception of self and relations with others, and thus make possible, a more realistic and healthier adaptation. Now, let us agree on a few terms relevant to these processes. Transference is the projection into the experience of interaction with the other person of a set of unreal expectations. Resistance is self-protection against those forms of exposure of self which seem to threaten injury. Defense is the counteraction of anxiety generated within.

If we translate these partial phenomena into the context of an adolescent therapy group, what do we see? The therapist is the recognized leader. He personifies the therapeutic objectives of the group and organizes the processes of group interaction toward the realization of these objectives. But he is a participant as well as an observer; he has face-to-face relations with his patients. He is a real person, he must reveal himself along with his patients. He is less of an omnipotent figure. At the same time, he shares the therapeutic functions with the other members of the group. Patients occupy the dual and alternating roles of patient and therapist. As a result of this special feature, patients in the group react to images of other persons which represent a fusion of elements of the identity of other patients and the therapist. The function of support is shared by group members and therapist. Emotional release is energized by the process of multiple interacting relationships. The clash of real and unreal images takes place on the broad stage of these multiple relationships. Transference emotions are not projected exclusively on the therapist, but are divided between patients and thereapist. Sometimes, the components of transference are dissociated, certain components moving to the therapist, others moving toward other patients. Patterns of resistance and defense are shaped, not only by the intrapsychic make-up of the individual, but by the perceptions of support and threatened exposure the patient builds of the group proceedings. The vicissitudes of conflict, guilt and anxiety will vary accordingly. It is easy to see that the special social structuring of the group, as contrasted with psychoanalytic individual therapy, commands an altered view of the role of the partial processes of therapy.

The psychotherapist must modify his techniques accordingly. To carry out his role effectively it is incumbent upon him to have disciplined knowledge at three levels: the group as a social system, with a specific social structuring of its own; the processes of emotional integration of an individual into the group, which involves the dynamic relations of personality and group role; and the intrapsychic mechanisms of individual personality.

CHAPTER 14

Symptom, Defense and Growth in Group Process

(Despite its promising title, this paper adds little to what Ackerman had already said on these topics, particularly in "Social Role and Total Personality" (1951). What is novel about this paper is the passage at the very end which links the therapy group to the family group. By this time in his career Ackerman was already deep into the study and treatment of families and to the best of our knowledge had lost his former interest in group psychotherapy as a personal endeavor. The following excerpt, while rambling and inconclusive, at least connects for us these two important phases of his career.)

The aim of this paper is a fresh look, in the light of certain, more recent conceptual trends, at the concepts of symptom, defense, and growth, particularly as observed within the experiential setting of the therapeutic group.

A therapy group and a family group are, in some basic respects, distinct; psychodynamically, however, there are some striking similarities. It may be useful, therefore, to draw a partial analogy between the processes of role adaptation and role change in the two group situations. Let us then consider the possible relevance of a theory of the interrelationships of the individual and his family group. For this purpose, I have devised a group of core concepts which attempt an operational formulation of the psychodynamics of family process: the who, what, and how of family life and the corresponding functional patterns of family relationships.

One phase of this conceptual scheme deals with identity and differentiation in the ongoing relationships of individual and family; the other phase deals with stabilization of behavior influenced both from within the individual family members and among them. The concept, identity, represents the image of self and a corresponding set of strivings, expectations, and values. Identity refers to direction and content of striving. Stability, on the other hand, refers to organization and expression of behavior in action. It involves the continuity of identity in time; the control of conflict; the capacity to change, learn, and achieve further development—in effect, the quality of adaptability and complementarity in new role relationships. The

Reprinted with permission from the *International Journal of Group Psychotherapy*, April 1961, Vol. XI, No. 2, 131, 140-142.

continuity of identity in time contrasts with the capacity to change, learn, and achieve further development. The balance between the two is influenced by the vicissitudes of control of conflict.

The questions, who, what, and how, and the corresponding formulations of identity and stability can be applied not only to the psychic functioning of an individual but also to the joined experience of the family pair or family group. A joined pair of persons or a group may be conceived as possessing a unique identity, just as does the individual. Psychic identity changes as it evolves through time. It answers the question: who am I? or, who are we? in the context of a given life situation. At any given point in time the individual has an image of his personal identity and his family identity, with both continuously influenced by the images which outside persons hold of these same identities. The identity of the family pair or group refers to elements of joined psychic identity. This is a segment of shared identity, represented in layers of joined experience and enacted in the complementary role behaviors of these joined persons. The processes of identification in family relationships are balanced against processes of individuation. In this way, elements of sameness and difference among the personalities of family members are held in a certain balance.

Psychological identity and stability behavior must be considered together. Stability, in its first phase, epitomizes the capacity to protect the continuity and integrity of identity despite changing life conditions. It ensures the intactness and wholeness of personal behavior in the face of new experience. This is the conservative phase of stability. The other phase of stability must provide for accommodation to new experience, learning, and further development. It represents the potential for change and growth. Effective adaptation requires a favorable balance between the protection of sameness and continuity and the need to accommodate to change. It requires preservation of the old, coupled with receptivity to the new, a mixture of conservatism and readiness to "live dangerously." As mentioned, the balance between preservation of the old and receptivity to the new is profoundly influenced by the manner in which conflict is controlled. The control of conflict is a special dimension relevant to the relationships of individual and family. The failure to find effective solutions leads to adaptive breakdown and illness. The search for solutions to conflict, the choice of defense, and the extent to which defense is compensated or decompensated are functions both of the individual and the ongoing interrelationships of individual and family. In this sense, it is of particular importance to discern the interplay between individual defense against anxiety and family group defense. It is important to trace an individual's effort to achieve complementarity in family role relationships that provides need satisfaction, avenues of solution of conflict, support for a favored self-image, and the buttressing of crucial forms of defense against anxiety. Complementarity may be further differentiated as positive or negative.

Positive complementarity is that form which promotes emotional growth of the relationship and of the interacting individuals. Negative complementarity is more static; it signifies mainly a buttressing of defense against pathogenic anxiety but does not provide the potential for further emotional growth. In this sense, complementarity mainly neutralizes the destructive effects of anxiety and barricades family relationships and vulnerable members against trends toward disorganization. Patterns of family conflict may potently affect the outcome of individual conflicts internalized at earlier periods in the individual's development.

This is theory, and theorizing about human behavior in our time, however exciting it may be, is fraught with a special hazard. This derives from the unique turbulence of human relations patterns, the result of the revolutionary sociocultural change that characterizes our age.

Today the power centers in society are shifting. The sharp trends toward centralization of power, toward tighter organization and rigidification of social relations alter the balance of power between the individual and the group. They curb personal freedom and personal privacy. A core consequence of this whole trend is the revolutionary transformation of family life. The goals of society and family life are unclear. Between the two, there is little congruency. This imposes an extraordinary hardship on the individual. He must struggle ceaselessly to achieve a workable harmony of his view of self and his view of the world.

This special feature creates for the behavioral

sciences a peculiarly unstable climate for the further development of the theories of behavior and of psychotherapy. As people change, so do our concepts about human development and human relations; consequently, our theories of mental illness, mental health, and the principles of diagnosis and therapy are in a high state of flux. Thus, the behavior scientists and psychotherapists are presently confronted with a huge challenge. On the one hand, the fluidity of contemporary society magnifies the risk of theorizing about personality and social relations; on the other hand, it opens up entirely new vistas for creative exploration in these very fields. Especially in group psychotherapy and family psychotherapy, it is important to be explicitly aware of an unprecedented opportunity for creative experimentation, for the discovery, perhaps, of an utterly new synthesis of ideas. It is exactly in this loose, fluid, shifting climate of human relations patterns that psychotherapists are impelled to confront the challenge of the relations of identity, values, and psychotherapeutic goals, to seek new levels of social, as well as emotional, health. Dramatic, indeed, is the supporting evidence in this direction that comes from spontaneous developments in therapy groups. I have in mind here the creative potential of value conflicts which emerge in such groups, leading to the formation of a new and distinct subcultural pattern, accompanied by progressive substitution of healthy values in place of the old sick ones. Insofar as this is a significant, spontaneous development in the more traditional, artificially composed therapy groups, it is fascinating to speculate on its potential promise in the more recent emergence of a therapeutic method with a naturally formed group, the human family.

PART III

Social and Cultural Issues

The three papers published here appeared immediately after the Second World War. The first two grew out of a group effort by psychiatrists and psychoanalysts to study and understand the madness that had gripped the world during the years of fascism and virulent anti-Semitism in Europe and in the United States. Ackerman had been excused from military service because of his cardiac disease. As a Jew, an intellectual and a physician, the immediate sense of horror at the devastations of war and the gradually revealed details of the death camps was dealt with, at least partially, by action to study, perhaps even to comprehend, the personal roots of these phenomena. These papers report on those attempts.

The third paper, "Mental Hygiene and Social Work," seems historically important to us. It relates the development of family therapy to the failure of two prior reformist social movements: social work, the effort to improve the human condition by changing circumstances, and mental hygiene, the effort to improve it by changing intrapsychic organization. Ackerman is explicit that family therapy attempts to succeed where they had failed; it is to look in both directions, inwardly at intrapsychic organization and outwardly to the social system of which the sufferer is a part.

It is not too difficult to guess that Ackerman hoped to have the best of both worlds, to turn inward to mental life and outward to social life, and thereby reconcile the moral conflict that is entailed in choosing between these. These perspectives informed his professional life, made inevitable his interest in anti-semitism and scapegoating, and influenced the eventual development of family therapy.

CHAPTER 15

Anti-Semitic Motivation in a Psychopathic Personality: A Case Study

(The first section of the paper, here omitted, gives an overview of anti-Semitism as a social and historical phenomenon. Ackerman wishes to add to this body of knowledge by understanding individual psychopathology as a contributing factor.)

One approach to anti-Semitism is to consider it as a form of social pathology; the other approach is to conceive of it as an expression of psychopathology in certain personality types. These two approaches are complementary, not mutually exclusive. Anti-Semitism is primarily a socio-psychological phenomenon. It does occur in relatively normal persons. In many instances, however, it is clearly the expression of personality distortion. The dynamic significance of anti-Semitism in mentally abnormal persons may shed some light on the special emotional values it may have for relatively normal persons, in whom anti-Semitism is induced by propaganda and socioeconomic pressure.

In accordance with this hypothesis, I am now collecting analytic observations on a number of such personalities. In this report I seek to describe the life history and psychoanalytic reactions of one abnormal personality, which demonstrate in clear terms the motivational configuration of this man's anti-Semitic drives.

The patient is a man of 51 years, who has been under analytic treatment for a long time. In anticipation of the history, I shall give first the essential aspects of this man's antagonism toward Jews. These anti-Semitic feelings were violent, at times murderously so, but did not emerge in their full fury until the latter part of his analysis. I reserve for later consideration the transference implications of these hostilities.

(This is not the best organized paper. In the section omitted here, Ackerman details some

Reprinted with permission from *The Psychoanalytic Review*, January 1947, Vol. 34, No. 1, 77, 79-91, 92-95, 98-99.

anti-Semitic and fascistic statements of the patient's, though these will be presented in greater detail later on. Our impression is that he was fascinated as well as repelled by the melodramatic intensity of his patient's hatred.)

He was impelled to seek treatment by severe anxieties which were exacerbated during a period of chaos in his marital life. He was referred to me by this third wife immediately after their honeymoon, during which he drove recklessly and one night, half in jest, choked her. The patient had divorced his first two wives and had been prohibited by a previous psychiatrist from remarrying his first wife.

In appearance, the patient is short, squat, obese, but quick and alert, agile in movement. He has a large head, which sits on a short neck and broad body. He is tense, loquacious, restless; some part of his body is constantly on the move. His hands continuously rove; he behaves as though he didn't know quite where to put his hands or what to do with them, as though he were embarrassed by his sense of responsibility for their acts. He is ingratiating in a smiling, anxious, defensive way.

In character, he is passive, dependent, submissive, but has outbursts of provocative aggressiveness. He is teasing and challenging in the manner of inviting a duel of wits. He is sadistic with excessive politeness. He is compliant, easily led, but is mistrustful, suspicious and guarded. He is spiteful, delights in passive sabotage of authority, avoids taking the dominant position but is prone to enjoy secretly playing the role of "power behind the throne." He tends to develop quick and enthusiastic devotions followed by suspiciousness and an intense urge for revenge.

This patient suffered from numerous emotional disabilities. He had syphilophobia. At times he had a fear of blindness and a compulsion to stick a pen knife into his eyes. He suffered a compulsion to eat dog feces. His sexual habits were affected by his attitude toward feces and dirt. He sometimes performed inadequately the usual cleansing following defecation and tried to have sex relations at times when he and the woman were covered with sweat. He had compulsive phantasies of murder, and had convictions that he would die an early and violent death. He showed passing depressive moods, and intermittent paranoid reactions with intense anxiety, verging on panic. He had conscious homosexual preoccupations. He suffered episodes of somatic disturbance based on his acute anxieties. He had breathing disturbances; gastric disorders with diarrhea; frequent urination; itching of the skin; outcroppings of warts; a huge number of unnecessary operations on his nose (120), mostly to remove polyps; and one episode of unexplained hemoptysis. The clinical diagnosis was schizoid psychopathic personality with superimposed psychoneurotic disorders.

BIRTH AND EARLY LIFE

The patient was born in a small town in Saxony, Germany. He has been told often that to have been born there is a ridiculous thing. He imagined that he might have been an illegitimate child. His mother left some family papers locked in a desk which were supposed to solve the mystery of his birth, but the patient was enjoined not to open these documents until after her death. He opened them during the period of his psychoanalytic treatment and thus was able finally to get the truth regarding his origin. For the first year, the marriage was a common-law relationship. The father did not legalize the marriage until after the patient was conceived.

The patient's mother was German derived from an old family of country gentlemen and merchants. A part of her ancestry, several hundred years back, came from a protected French town, inhabited mainly by Jews. There was some possibility of there being some Jewish blood on her side of the family. The patient said, "There was little Teutonic blood, if any, in our family. In appearance, all are Alpine types, typical Slavs. My mother was small, with jet black hair, green eyes, and tawny complexion, typical French." Though poor, she was aristocratic in manner and bearing. She did not care for small children, was aloof and undemonstrative. She often compared him unfavorably with other boys, in particular, Jewish boys.

The paternal side of the family was American of Anglo-Irish ancestry. His paternal grandfather was executive of a large business having international connections. The patient's father was a man of polished, charming, somwhat feminine manners, but an irresponsible ne'er-do-well who drank heavily. He teetered on the fringe of a career of chronic criminality. He engaged in delinquencies, among them notably fraud and blackmail. He had a business mission in Europe, in which he failed under dishonorable circumstances. He was disowned and disinherited by the grandfather, who lived in constant fear that the father would attempt to hurt him bodily or extort money.

The patient was stirred by much doubt and suspicion concerning the basis of his birth and the legality of his American citizenship. Since he was the son of an American citizen, automatically he should have become a citizen himself, but this would clearly be the case only if he were the offspring of a legitimate marriage. The problem was further complicated by questions concerning his father's legal domicile and later by his father's threat to deny paternity. He said, "There are no laws concerning questions of citizenship in a case like mine. My whole feeling as a child was of not belonging."

Soon after the patient's birth, the family moved to France. When the patient became ill, he was given over to the care of his maternal grandmother, with whom he lived to the age of 3 years. After that he returned to the care of his parents. In retrospect he felt that his grandmother was the only one who gave him any consistent affection.

As a child, he was strictly guarded and disciplined. The family lived a frugal life, and subsisted on plain foods. Up to the age of 6 years, the patient would drink milk only from a bottle. He was full of fears. During these early years, he slept in his parents' room in a cot with high sides and later, when his father was away, in a room with his grandmother. He witnessed frequent scenes of quarrels between his parents and also saw intercourse. He was terrified by both. He imagined his father was killing his mother. These episodes took place late at night and in the dark. The patient developed a fear of the dark.

Sometimes, if his father was in a favorable mood, he drew pictures for the patient who prized them highly. Between the ages of 3 and 5 years, he was severely frightened by his father. On one occasion his father held him out of a high window. He has feared heights since. Another time, his father brought home a mechanical bug and ran it toward the patient, who was terrified by the clicking noise of the wings, as they rose and fell with each forward movement. Once his father tied his hands with a hose and the patient ran screaming to his mother. His father laughed at him. This was the father's method of toughening the boy. During this period he developed a dread of horses. Of these experiences he says, "I was brought up on fear." He was frequently ridiculed by both parents for being a baby and a coward.

Following the collapse of his business the father went to America, abandoning the patient and his mother. As a boy of six, he was somewhat relieved but felt he and his mother had been left to starve. After that they hardly ever discussed his father. From this time until he was 14 he lived with his mother and grandmother who took work into the home. His mother insisted that he be quiet and leave her undisturbed. At the dinner table she read a book and did not permit the patient to talk.

His mother was secretive about her private life and would not permit the patient to have access to her bedroom. Although she was prudish about sexual matters, she had several men friends, two of whom were probably her lovers. The patient had phantasies to the effect that one of them might have been his real father. He was jealous of his mother's lovers.

His childhood was lonely and he was absorbed in his own unhappiness. He had almost no friends. He spent his time reading and playing with tin soldiers. His only ambition was to become a soldier.

He masturbated excessively with phantasies of violent revenge, torture in a closed chamber, and other persons being masturbated against their will. He engaged in sex play with one girl, mainly ticking one another's anus. He did not observe that she had no penis. His mother warned him against masturbation and in particular against going with strange men. The danger of being kidnapped loomed large in his mind, which may have been connected in phantasy with the figures of his father and grandmother.

During his childhood, he was frequently ill, and had a number of operations for polyps. Several of his physicians were Jewish, one of whom he called "Nathan the Wise," because he had a vast store of knowledge and was unusually kind. However, he recalls certain hostilities such as biting the surgeon's finger, who removed his adenoids, and kicking another physician in the stomach.

In school he had difficulty in learning. He feared failure. He felt intimidated by the militaristic discipline of his teachers, and handicapped because of his own lack of status; he was neither the son of a military man nor the son of a civil service employee. In his class there were both Jews and non-Jews; in this setting he was exposed to considerable anti-Semitic feeling. He felt unable to compete and hated the Jewish boys.

His mother was consistently friendly to Jews. She had Jewish friends, a group of Zionist students whom she helped to collect money for Palestine. She tended toward socialism, once held "wild communist ideas" and later adopted a violently anti-Nazi attitude. The patient resented all this. His mother reproached him for his anti-Semitic expressions, sharply reminding him that he might possibly have some Jewish ancestors.

At 13 years of age, he had an intense friendship with a Jewish boy, with whom he engaged in some mutual masturbation.

While the patient had some real experiences with Jews in his childhood, he had no real contact with Negroes until he came to the United States at the age of 14, except through his fictional readings. He was especially amused by one story about a Malay head hunter, who cut off the head of an enemy warrior, had the victim's teeth inserted into the mouth of a tobacco box, so that each time he shut the box he was, in effect, slapping the face of the enemy warrior. He was strongly impressed by accounts of initiation ceremonies in Africa, particularly the tales of pain and torture, but did not specifically recall the details of circumcision. At 8 years of age, his grandmother told him about an old Samoan in Berlin who had joked about buying him and carrying him off to Samoa. While this story amused his grandmother, it frightened the patient.

Between the ages of 8 and 14 the grandfather made several unsuccessful efforts to induce his mother to place the patient in his care. This is significant in view of his mother's warnings against going with strange men and the boy's fear of kidnapping. At 14, however, when his mother placed the grandfather's offer before the boy himself, somewhat to her surprise, he greeted it enthusiastically. He was conscious of spiting his mother in accepting the grandfather's offer; nevertheless, when his mother failed to protest his leaving, he interpreted her attitude as a rejection of him.

After that, on periodic visits to his mother in Germany, he found her quarrelsome and irritable. She was critical both of him and his grandfather. At the same time, he was erotically stimulated by her habit of walking about in his presence in her underwear. He says, "We were too much alike and had too great an attraction for each other. She didn't like me as a child, but I became the sort of man she secretly admired. . . . Only once did she express admiration for me, but it made me anxious and irritable."

The patient had a difficult time adjusting to his new life in America. The grandfather was aggressive, courageous, a self-made man, who was by now elderly and lonely. His second son, after whom the patient was named, had died. He placed considerable stress on constitution, law, and conscience, and by his distrust obviously feared that the patient might take the same criminal path as his father. His attitude was a mixture of harshness and sentimentality. If crossed, he could be an implacable enemy. He was extremely possessive and dominated the patient's life at every turn, but also promised security.

Both the patient and his grandfather lived in constant fear that his father might attempt to injure them in some way, or at least extort money. When the patient was 15, his grandfather attempted to get the father's consent to a legal adoption. He refused to permit legal adoption unless he were paid off with a huge some of money and threatened to disown his son in order to reinforce his prior claim on the inheritance. In order to prevent the father's access to his wealth, the grandfather gave the patient large gifts of stock and money. However, he was haunted by the spectre of want in his old age, and insisted that the patient agree to return his money if he ever needed it.

The patient reacted to his grandfather with mixed emotions: affection mingled with fear. He was submissive, while secretly resenting his servitude.

He felt as if he were married to his grandfather, watching over his affairs, nursing him when he was ill and standing guard to prevent predatory women from capturing him in marriage, thus depriving him of his inheritance. While outwardly submissive, he felt inwardly that he was actually the "power behind the throne."

As the years went by, he became more conscious of his own feminine nature and also of his grandfather's physical attraction to him. His grandfather, proud of his prowess with women once insulted the patient by telling him he had "an arse like a woman." The patient once imagined that his grandfather had made sexual advances to his mother, but secretly nursed the belief that his grandfather was impotent. Periodically, his hostile feeling toward his grandfather became so violent that he felt compelled to leave for a time. He had frequent phantasies of murdering his grandfather. In later years, he could hardly wait for his death, which occurred when the patient was 34 years of age.

The patient was educated in preparatory school and college. He was regarded as an eccentric, had no real friends, except for one strong attachment to a scholarly professor interested in Buddhist philosophy. He read 18th century history voraciously, but, as he himself put it, his knowledge was of no practical use to anyone, not even to himself. He strongly disliked current history.

During his adolescent years, he had some overt homosexual experiences. He was consistently the aggressor, refusing the passive role in "buggery," fellatio and engaged in some mutual masturbation. His own masturbatory activities were excessive, with violent sadistic phantasies. Although dreading discovery of his homosexual activities, he openly invited detection.

After leaving college, he had a 2 year experience in government service. He liked the work; he ingratiated himself with his superiors by his clownish attitudes. He bitterly resented his grandfather's interference with this career. Following this, he entered his grandfather's business, but disliked it so strongly that after his grandfather's death he retired permanently. When he received his inheritance, a considerable fortune, at his grandfather's death, he went on a spree, traveling widely and spending money lavishly. In later years, he settled down to a more measured existence, but continued to live on income.

A series of relations with men followed a consistent pattern, usually with older teachers, doctors, or lawyers, to whom he became strongly attached in a dependent way. In some instances the management of his finances was controlled by these men. Often there was a woman involved so that the relationship took on a triangular pattern. Sometimes she was the intermediary between the patient and the other man. One of these men became his wife's lover. Another defrauded him of a large sum of money.

In the patient's life there were three wives and unnumbered promiscuous women, many of them prostitutes. His grandfather encouraged his relations with prostitutes, but disapproved of any serious interest in a woman. In his early 20s the patient fell in love with one woman, and, although bitterly resentful, gave her up when his grandfather refused to help him win her consent to marriage. Some years later he married a woman who had been devoted to the grandfather and was like a sister to the patient. He did not consider that he would be expected to have sexual relations with her. His grandfather approved of this marriage since it would assure him of the continued devotion not only of the patient, but of his wife as well. There was no essential change in the patient's life situation. The patient and his wife continued to care for his grandfather until the time of his death, but the marriage did not last much after it, for they began to lead separate lives, regardless of their two children.

With his wife's open encouragement, he launched on a wild, undisciplined, promiscuous life, consorting frequently with prostitutes. He had a fear of syphilis; nevertheless, he not only courted venereal disease, but got himself involved with prostitutes in such a way as might provoke attacks from their male protectors. On one occasion he insulted a white woman who had rebuffed him, by going to bed with a Negress and then flaunting this in the white woman's face. He was particularly friendly and solicitous toward Negro maids. They worshipped him.

After some years of this kind of living he divorced his first wife when he was 45 years of age, and married a conspicuously homosexual woman who drank heavily. The patient was magnetized by her personality, but soon after marriage hated her violently because she refused to have sexual relations with him. During the honeymoon trip, he was tempted to shove her off of a cliff. She treated him in a most humiliating way, but the patient took these insults for more than a year. Finally he divorced her, but was left in an intensely disturbed emotional state.

He began psychoanalytic treatment with me following his honeymoon with his third wife, and after a year of psychotherapy with a previous psychiatrist. He seemed to suspect his wife of secretly resisting his urge to return to the care of the previous psychiatrist. He was, therefore, hostile to her and one night, half-jocularly, choked her. At the time of referral to me, his previous psychiatrist was out of town. In the first visit, he complained of anxiety, depression and insomnia. He resented bitterly having been told that his treatment was complete, and had concluded that his former psychiatrist simply wanted to be rid of him. He felt he had been exploited.

During the first interview he displayed an intense, compulsive urge to take the analytic couch immediately. This was not permitted, since his emotional tie to his previous physician was strong, and the relationship had in no way been resolved. I called this to his attention and he readily agreed to write to the other psychiatrist, expressing his need for immediate help and his wish to begin treatment with me.

In the meantime, he discussed more fully his ambivalent emotions toward this man, his suspicions and his inner rage at having been virtually deserted. He spoke of the painful lessons he had learned from betrayals by his father, grandfather, and other men to whom he had attached himself in the past. At the end of the hour, he was immensely grateful, seemed relieved symptomatically and was zealous in his desire to return.

This is the background on which his analytic treatment was begun. The previous psychiatrist was a Jew, as am I, but the patient made no mention of this. The issue of his anti-Semitism did not emerge conspicuously until the latter part of his analysis.

The first step in his treatment was a clarification of the previous transference. The patient was confused about this experience, had placed great hopes in it, was disappointed, and agitated, but had not resolved his feelings nor been able to draw any realistic conclusions as to its meaning. It became clear that the patient had assumed as unreal attitude toward the past relationship. He did not regard it merely as a treatment experience, but rather as a real son-father relationship. The former psychiatrist was an older man, a person of dignified, impressive carriage. According to the patient, he had assumed an active role, giving him direct advice and in general guiding him in the management of his life. The patient developed an intense submissive attachment to him. He tried in every conceivable way to please this psychiatrist, imagined himself the "white-haired boy," and even had phantasies that the psychiatrist needed his devotion and love because his own sons had disappointed him. He had a wish for full, life-long protection, cherished the fantastic notion that he was blissfully safe so long as he lived within the sheltering embrace of this man. A mood of jittery elation accompanied this feeling of false security.

While his dominant attitude had been one of excessive compliance there was a distinct undercurrent of fear, suspicion and hostility which was never adequately expressed in the previous relationship. Periodically he felt trapped and was aware of a driving need to escape. He feared domination and had conscious phantasies of homosexual seduction. His infatuation with the employee who worked for his doctor and his impulsive marriage to her finally made possible his escape. When his wife referred him to me, she was, in his mind, rescuing him from the danger of homosexual seduction.

During this discussion, the obviously unreal expectations that the patient had projected into this relationship were clarified. He expressed more freely his suspicion and hostility toward the previous physician and felt correspondingly relieved. He did not, at this time, show any direct hostility to me. All the while, he continued to display his driving desire to lie down on the couch and resume analytic therapy. When the previous treatment experience had been sufficiently ventilated so that the patient could make a reasonably fresh beginning, he was permitted to take the couch.

The essential dynamic trends revealed in the first two years were as follows: Beginning with his birth, the patient was confused concerning his origin and identity. He felt basically rejected by his mother and could not safely identify with either parent. His feeling of unworthiness was later intensified by his suspicion of being an illegitimate child, by the hostility between his parents and by his father's abandonment of him. The pain of his mother's rejection was somewhat diluted by the compensatory affection which he received from his grandmother. He was displaced in his mother's favor by rivals, some of whom were Jewish boys; he therefore hated them, but loved them too. His most intense friendship, which included a sexual intimacy, was with a Jewish boy.

He believed his parents hated each other and feared that his father would do violence to his mother. He associated violence with sexual intimacy, but believed that his mother, in spite of the threat of violence, was seuxally drawn to his father. In his mind, therefore, sexual activity, while dangerous, was an important and secret source of pleasure. He attempted to barricade himself against the dangers of seeing his parents quarreling or having intercourse. This effort, namely, not to see, is probably the source of his later visual symptoms, his fear of blindness, and his compulsion to put a knife into his eye.

Although he felt his mother was inaccessible to him, or perhaps because of it, he developed a strong incestuous interest in her. This was intensified by the fact that his father later left the home. He guarded himself against this temptation by repelling his mother through a show of irritability. He developed a need to degrade her, and also a compensatory need to aggrandize her. This was connected with his phantasies of her illicit sexual activity. He was jealous of his father and of his mother's lovers. These trends aroused considerable guilt and anxiety.

His secret wish to be the "power behind the throne" reflected his need to usurp his father's place and was later seen in his effort to compete with and destroy his grandfather. His neurotic need to undergo repeated surgical operations and similarly, to surrender his money to others revealed his tendency to make bodily or material sacrifices in order to appease his guilt.

Because of his close living with his mother and grandmother, he became strongly identified with the female side of the family. His attitude toward his mother turned towards hate and he tried unsuccessfully to renounce her. Having been rejected by his mother, he projected his passive strivings toward his father, which on some occasions were gratified, but in the main were met with a cruel and menacing rebuff.

These experiences stimulated in the patient a violent struggle. To some extent he identified himself with his father, especially in relation to his concealed sadistic drives, but he strove desperately to rid himself of any kinship with his father. In fact this conflict is probably the unconscious basis for his pathological love of feces, and simultaneous feeling of persecution by dirt. In the patient's unconscious, the father-image seemed linked with feces and with the black man, the Negro, who figured prominently in his dreams.

He tried to defend himself against his passive cravings for his father with paranoid hostility. He tended to compete with his mother for his father's affection, and later, for the favor of her lovers. He felt humiliated and castrated by his father and, when his father was most cruel, he sought his mother's protection. The fact that his father had left him and his mother "to starve" aroused a violent ambivalent attitude toward him and contributed to his fear of persecution.

His life-long impotence and neurotic inability to use his hands were associated with masturbatory anxieties, which arose out of his intense sadistic impulses toward both his parents, but the most violent impulses were directed toward his father.

In real life, he failed to be productive in any sense. Of special importance was his identification with his father in respect to his impotent, sadistic attitude toward his mother and his antisocial criminal tendencies. His unresolved relationship with his father led to a repetitive pattern of homosexual attachment to older men. He showed a deep ambivalence in these relationships. With bad fathers, he sought and obtained castrative experiences, especially in surgical operations. It seems probable that he sought and obtained good fathers in the form of Jewish physicians.

Throughout his life, he was dogged by the original triangular pattern involving himself, a woman, and another man. In these relationships, he exploited the woman as bait for the other man; as a means of gaining supreme power over him and thus binding him. He had phantasies of blackmailing the other man to force more indulgence out of him. He described this, in short, as a means of "grabbing him by the balls." Basically, his motive was to preserve his passive gratification, and forestall a repetition of his father's original abandonment of him.

The outstanding transference reactions took the form of a repetitious cycle of attitudes: ingratiation and exaggerated submissiveness; then evidences of anxiety, fear of attack and a tendency towards self-injury mounting to a suicidal peak. Sometimes this self-destructiveness was associated with transitory somatic disturbances; episodes of inflammation of the eye following rubbing; gastric distress such as belching and diarrhea, distension; respiratory distress, such as coughing, shortness of breath; nasal polyps; itching; and crops of warts.

Following the initial ingratiation and submission, there were outbursts of defiance, usually violent rebellious hostility, in turn followed by attitudes of penitence, propitiation, a willingness to make sacrifices and be castrated.

In this cycle of attitudes, overt homosexual phantasies intruded themselves usually after outbursts of destructive defiance. For example, after a flare of anti-Semitic hostility, he would come to analytic hours with his fly open and then express phantasies of fellatio. The seductive motive was obvious as was his intention to intimidate the analyst with his penis. Generally, he tried to put the analyst in the passive, receiving role, thus avoiding the vulnerable, passive position for himself.

In this set of attitudes, the role of the woman had special meaning. His phantasies were that the analyst preferred his wife to him, did not want him to have his wife, and would take her from him; secondly, he wished to offer his wife to the analyst as a gift. This gift was meant to insure him the analyst's loyalty and would give him the power completely to control the analyst. On the other hand, periodically, he suffered panic at the thought of being separated from the analyst because this would leave him alone with his wife; under these circumstances he feared the breaking through of his own violent, sadistic urges toward her. Beneath all this struggle could be discerned a deep nostalgic yearning for his mother and his homeland. Competition with the analyst on a more forthright man-to-man basis came only late in his analysis.

Considerable projection marked the expression of all these attitudes. For example, he frequently accused the analyst of belittling and insulting him. He suspected it was the analyst's intention to gain complete domination over him, to steal his wife, to rob him of his money, to destroy his security, to attack him sexually. All these fears, suspicions, and hostilities impelled the patient, from time to time, to nullify completely any real closeness between the patient and the therapist. He felt the need to preserve a barrier of isolation and to keep control of the analytic situation. As a means of doing this, he relied on the phantasy of the magic inviolability of the patient's position on the couch. So long as he lay there and did nothing, the analyst in turn could not attack him. In this phantasy, both he and the analyst were rendered impotent. He attempted also to control the relationship by means of propitiation and sacrifice, by buying off the analyst, by a willingness to renounce competition, accept inferiority and castration. In addition, he attempted, periodically, to reassure himself of his own safety by the phantasy of intimidating the analyst through the threat of bodily injury. This was usually expressed in the form of his assuming more openly a threatening role similar to his father's as a criminal, a murderer, whose violence the analyst must fear. He had invented a symbol called "Bitibus," a little animal which he brought out from hiding as the occasion required. On his command, "Bitibus" would protect him by ferociously attacking the analyst. At various times "Bitibus" was symbolized in his penis, in his loose, explosive stool, in his spitting and coughing, in his nasal polyps, in his warts. "Bitibus" seemed to represent his identification with his criminal sadistic father, and also his own peculiar brand of destructive sexual potency. His attack also took another form, that of spying on the analyst's mail, hoping thereby to discover some private activity of the analyst which he could use for purposes of intimidation or blackmail.

After about two years of analysis, there was considerable improvement. The original symptoms of which he had complained had been relieved, in particular, his syphilophobia and his compulsion to eat dog feces. The most conspicuous improvement was reflected in a general lessening of tension, and a better adaptation to his everyday life situation. His homosexual fears diminished, his sexual and social relations with his wife had become much better.

(Ten sample dreams follow but there is no

comment on their place in the therapy or on Ackerman's interpretations.)

After two years of analysis, the patient first broached the question of terminating treatment. Symptomatically, he seemed relatively free; he was happier and his married life was going well. However, there was one important piece of evidence that clearly indicated his treatment was incomplete: whenever he was separated from the analyst for any period of time, that is, weekends and vacations, he generally reacted with some transitory anxiety and mild depression. This obviously had to do with his unresolved attitude toward the analyst. This was essentially the emotional problem which prevailed at the time he interrupted his treatment with the previous psychiatrist. Just so long as he could preserve his dependent tie to the father-figure, his sadistic impulses could be kept under control. As soon as the threat of severing this tie entered the picture, he had immediate anxiety.

At this point, the patient began to express more clearly the barrier to further progress. He asserted that the analysis could go no further because there was a difference between himself and the analyst, an irreconcilable difference. The best thing to do was to agree to disagree. He constructed in phantasy a series of standards that were supposed to be the therapist's criteria of a cure. He protested these standards and began to formulate his own, which reflected the irreconcilable differences between himself and the analyst.

The patient's conception of the analyst's standards for a cure were as follows: The patient must want to work for a living. He must be a liberal or a "pink." He must become like the analyst and believe in love and in friendship. He must believe in freedom. He must believe in justice and fairness. He must accept Jews and be sympathetic with Negroes. He must not worship money and be greedy for prestige or power. He must not be too possessive. He must not be authoritative or pretentious. He must discount money as a source of security. He must believe in the possibility of a better world.

The patient then asserted his conviction that analysts advocate such humanitarian ideals and social values because most analysts are Jews. In other words, these are Jewish criteria for the analytic cure of a patient.

In opposition to these standards, the patient asserted his own. In the first place, he is a non-Jew. He is too old to change; it is too late to begin a new life. He doesn't want to make peace with the world but only with his own needs for pleasure. He's a hedonist. He doesn't want to work for a living. He doesn't want to be a drudge or a slave. Money is important and he means always to have enough to live without working. He is conservative and means to protect his capital against liberals and communists. He is intellectual, derives pleasure from what he reads or learns, but his knowledge is of no interest to anyone else. He has nothing to give to this world. He has no faith in love or friendliness. He does not believe in freedom or justice. He is not an admirer of Lincoln. He feels strongly that this is no loving world; it is absurd to think that it ever could be. He has no interest in humanity. He hates reformers. He believes money is the only real security. With it he buys service and devotion. It is his sole source of power. Without it, he'd be impotent. He likes his Negro servants but he refuses to have any social contact with Negroes. They are inferior and should stay in their place. He wants a home, a wife, a sex life and books, but he has no interest in current affairs. He lives behind a wall and intends to continue living that way. He feels safe only insofar as he preserves his isolation.

His assertion of his differences with the analyst was coupled with the conviction that the analyst intended to force him to surrender his own values in favor of the analyst's values. The patient's defiance represented, in a sense, a challenge to a duel, a provocation which was intended to incite the analyst to attack him, to force conversion by a rape, to force him to give up his suspicions, his hostilities, and finally to compel him to love the analyst and adopt his values. He seemed unable to tolerate disagreement between himself and the analyst. While, ostensibly, he expected the analyst to force him into an attitude of submission, his aggressiveness at this point represented the first vigorous assertion of his competitive drives, which were obviously tinged by his homosexual feeling. This was the launching of a campaign to force the analyst to surrender to him.

The rest of the analysis dealt in large part with these competitive aggressions and the patient's effort to maintain this unbridgeable barrier between himself and the analyst, thus forestalling any real closeness in the relationship. In so doing, he continued his ambivalent attitude. Periodically, he sought to sever the relationship and escape, while at other times he strove to preserve his dependent relationship and minimize the dangerous degrees of competitiveness. He made the analytic experience a compulsion in which the analyst represented his externalized conscience, by which he was bound but at the same time protected. So long as he submitted to the restraining power of the analyst, he was safe from dangers inherent in an uncontrolled outbreak of his underlying criminal impulses. On this background, the intermittent recurrences of anxiety, depression and transitory somatic disturbances had the effect of tying him to his analysis and preventing a premature and destructive escape.

In this setting of competitive struggle, the violence of his anti-Semitic feelings emerged in full force. This brand of antagonism soon came to symbolize his irreconcilable differences with the analyst. For a time, all the issues of transference became condensed into the one problem of his hate for the Jew. In the beginning he expressed these feelings in a peculiarly dramatic way. He hissed his anti-Semitic poison rather than simply expressing it in an ordinary manner. It was as if his anxiety impelled him to suck his breath back into his lungs as he spoke, thus imparting to his voice the hissing sound of a snake. This paradoxical breathing caused him to cough, spit, get red in the face and show considerable bodily agitation. His behavior had all the appearance of a seizure; he literally spit out his anti-Semitic violence. In so doing, he achieved an expanding consciousness of the utter ruthlessness and cruelty of his underlying hostility. I shall quote directly from some of his statements.

"You hope for some good out of this world. You look forward to a better world. You believe in social reform. You are a better person than I am in ethical standards. You are gullible because you believe the world can change. You are equally gullible if you believe you can make me change. The idea of loving people is mystical. I hate communists because they would liquidate me. I am their enemy. They would kill me. I'd kill all the Jews and communists before they attacked me. I would not hesitate to use violence. This is an utterly hard world and we must be ruthless, not soft-believing damn fools. I am primitive and I hate Jews, Roosevelt, communists, and alcoholics. My father was an alcoholic."

(For several pages the patient's vituperations are recorded verbatim. Some of these statements also reflect his grudging attachment to Ackerman: "Affection destroys my defense.")

From the foregoing quotations, it is plain that being cured for this patient meant being judeified, being converted to the analyst's religion. It meant being circumcised and being forced to swallow the analyst's system of ethical and social values. Symbolically, this meant swallowing the analyst's penis, against his will, and was probably associated with a phantasy of impregnation through the oral route.

The anti-Semitic violence died a natural death with further analysis of the transference implications of these attitudes. The patient's comment on this was that his urge to hate the Jew died of inanition. "The itch gradually subsided, and I ceased to scratch."

(In a lengthy conclusion, Ackerman summarizes the foregoing material.)

CHAPTER 16

The Dynamic Basis of Anti-Semitic Attitudes

Anti-Semitism, currently a grave problem, is a sociopsychological phenomenon. It is a form of intergroup behavior, which increases in intensity at times of social crisis; it expresses itself in stereotyped accusations which seem to be part of a cultural tradition; it produces social consequences of a dangerously destructive nature. Cultural traditions, however, and social forces do not exist as mere abstractions; they have existence only in so far as they express themselves dynamically in the behavior of people. In the last analysis, a completely meaningful conception of social forces can be achieved only in terms of—or at least with close reference to—specific patterns of interpersonal behavior. But in the case of anti-Semitism especially, even those whose preferred frame of reference is primarily sociological might be disposed to turn to dynamic psychiatry for insight. It is not merely the irrational content of anti-Semitic accusations, but fully as much the self-defeating aspects of anti-Semitic behavior, which invites psychiatric clarification. Such behavior is rationalized as a means of self-preservation; yet, it ultimately brings harm both to the individual anti-Semite and to the society which nourishes such hostility. The analogy to neurotic self-destructive mechanisms is striking, and must attract attention to the relevance of a dynamic investigation of the phenomenon.

The psychiatric approach to the problem of anti-Semitism raises several fundamental questions. Why, under the same socioeconomic conditions, do some persons develop anti-Semitic attitudes while others do not? What is the role of the anti-Semitic hostility pattern in the current emotional life of an individual? What is its specific dynamic relation to unconscious needs? What genetic factors predispose a person toward anti-Semitic behavior?

We have explored the dynamic basis of anti-Semitic attitudes in a number of persons who are undergoing, or have already experienced, psychoanalytic therapy. The material was collected from twenty-five accredited psychoanalysts. We prepared a comprehensive schedule of all relevant aspects of a case history. After an analyst had presented a case study, the information was supplemented in intensive inter-

---

Reprinted with permission from *The Psychoanalytic Quarterly*, 1948, Vol. XVII, 240-260.

This paper was co-authored with Marie Jahoda.

views, which generally followed the subject matter outlined in our research schedule. Some analysts contributed more than one case study. In the use of clinical material, every precaution was taken to preserve strict anonymity.

These patients had sought psychoanalysis for a variety of complaints and symptoms. Since the analyst was primarily oriented to the therapeutic problem, the characteristics of anti-Semitic behavior were observed only incidentally. The patients had varying degrees of awareness of their anti-Semitic feelings, but they did not regard those feelings as a "symptom," and they were not aware that these particular feelings were scrutinized in any special way. So far as could be determined, the patient's consciousness was, therefore, not unduly aroused in this connection.

This preliminary paper is based on the data contained in twenty-seven case studies: sixteen men and eleven women. In age, the patients range from twenty-two to fifty-one years. Five cases of Jewish anti-Semitism are included; in addition, one was half-Jewish, and one had been converted to Protestantism during his teens; there were four Catholics, and the remainder were Protestants. So far as we could determine, the psychodynamic patterns underlying the anti-Semitic reactions were essentially similar in Jewish and non-Jewish anti-Semites. The majority of the patients had been brought up in middle or upper class families; however, seven derived from a working class background. As to their social mobility, fourteen had maintained the parental level; nine had moved upward, and four downward. Fifteen patients were unmarried; of the eleven married patients, three were married a second, and one a third, time.

A fair sampling of the accusation heaped on "the Jews" by these patients is the following. The Jews are dirty; they stink; they are vulgar, low class, debased, deformed, ugly, greedy, overaggressive, overbearing, noisy, and excitable. They exploit people and push them around. Yet, often, they are said to be intelligent, shrewd, ambitious, industrious, successful. They are social climbers. They are arrogant. They are superior, know too much, and are too ethical. They are either oversexed or impotent. Socially, they are cohesive, powerful, wealthy, control Wall Street and the government. They are also dirty communists, internationally minded and unpatriotic.

We find evidence in our case studies for suggesting two distinct, though interacting, levels of dynamic correlation between anti-Semitic behavior and personality. First, there is the anti-Semite whose hostility to the Jews seems mainly the expression of social conformity to the attitude of the dominant group; this conformity, however, represents in part the patient's defense against anxiety. Second, there is the anti-Semite whose motivation for hostility to the Jews is patterned by some basic distortion in his own personality structure to which his anti-Semitism has a specific relation. Actually, all our cases represent a fusion, in varying proportion, of both levels of correlation. The first level illuminates the nature of the anti-Semitic reaction at the group psychological level of adaptation; the second, at the individual level of adaptation.

A comparison of the diagnoses of our patients leads to the first important insight gained through this study: anti-Semitism is *not* the concomitant of any single clinical category of personality. We find a considerable variety of clinical diagnoses. Because of the absence of a uniform terminology, the information in this respect is somewhat unsatisfactory. However, we find a preponderance of character disorders, a smaller number of psychoneuroses, including four cases of obsessional neurosis, one case of paranoia, and a number of less precisely defined disturbances.

On the other hand, the evidence does suggest a negative correlation with one particular reaction, namely, depression. None of our patients suffered from a genuine, deep depression. While a few were described as having "depressed" attitudes, the classical dynamics of oppressive guilt and self-blame were absent. In a few instances, the attack on the Jew seems to serve the dynamic purpose of offsetting a depressive tendency. The qualitative insight gained from the study of the cases leads us to believe that the absence of clinical depression in our material is more than an accident due to the limited number of cases. The existence of an anti-Semitic reaction presupposes a tendency to blame the outside world rather than one's self, and dynamically, such a tendency is in contradiction to the overtly self-destructive trend of a genuine depression. When the focus of hate is directed against the self, the basis for an externalization of aggression in anti-Semitism no longer exists.

While, in general, there is no correlation with the type of clinical diagnosis or specific symptom, there is a correlation between the quality of personality distortion and the quality of anti-Semitic behavior. The intensity and violence of anti-Semitic reactions will, of course, be in harmony with the degree of disturbance of a given personality. Thus, the crudest and most irrational forms of anti-Semitism have rightly been linked with psychopathic and paranoid personalities. Milder expressions of anti-Semitic attitudes occur in less sick personalities.

The common denominator underlying the anti-Semitic reaction in our cases is, thus, not a similarity of psychiatry symptoms, or total character structure, but rather the common presence of certain specific emotional dispositions. These trends are not in themselves specific for the production of anti-Semitism. They may as well be the dynamic basis for other irrational group hostilities. Undoubtedly, they can exist without anti-Semitism. But in the culture in which our patients live, anti-Semitism does not develop without these character trends. They represent, therefore, an emotional predisposition, a necessary though not sufficient cause of anti-Semitism. In a different culture these character traits may be released in some other hostility reaction.

All the patients suffered from anxiety. The nature of the anxiety, to a great extent, was diffuse, pervasive, relatively unorganized; it was not adequately channelized through specific symptom formation. Generally, the anxiety was not experienced as a conscious dread, but manifested itself indirectly in varied forms of social discomfort and disability. The patients felt vaguely insecure, lonely, unhappy, confused, had difficulty in making friends and in establishing a satisfactory sex life, lacked a sense of direction, were vague and confused about life goals, were often unable to sustain a consistent interest in relationships and activities. Because of their inner weakness and negligible insight, the outer world seemed hostile, bad, menacing, inexplicably hard. They appeared unable to relate their difficulties in life to their personal deficiencies.

Such patients tend to live under continuous apprehension of injury to their integrity as individuals. They fear being overwhelmed by powers they are too weak to withstand. They have a wish to control, but lack the necessary strength. This wish is not realized in the normal channels of constructive social action, but instead seeks irrational outlets. Socially, economically, emotionally, and sexually, these patients are plagued by an exaggerated sense of vulnerability. They do not derive strength and emotional support from their identity as persons. They have a basically damaged self-esteem which, consciously, they endeavor to deny. At the unconscious level, they accept the damage to their personal identity as irreversible, and have little hope of repairing it. The general impression is one of weakness of personality organization, disordered self-image and, with this, an exaggerated sense of vulnerability to social injury.

Vital to the understanding of the anti-Semitic reaction is a knowledge of the concept which these patients have of themselves as individuals. The image of self is confused and unstable. There is concealed inner doubt and ambivalence. As one analyst put it, his patient just did not know how to regard herself. There is a submerged feeling of inferiority, weakness, dependence, and a tendency toward compulsive submission. The weakness, immaturity, doubt, and basic passivity of the self are rarely admitted to consciousness, however, although the patient continuously suffers from their manifestations. Hence the confusion of the self-image. The disadvantageous qualities of the self are denied, and an extreme effort is made to compensate for them.

One striking manifestation of the confusion of the self-image is the tendency toward homosexuality. While there are only two instances of overt homosexuality and one of bisexual adaptation in our material, the fear of homosexual leanings plays a considerable role in many cases. Nevertheless, it would be erroneous to hypothesize a direct link between homosexuality and anti-Semitic attitudes. These are two separate products of one basic conflict, namely, the struggle against underlying passivity, which may or may not appear simultaneously. There are many other ways in which a confusion of the self-image is manifested by our patients. They react to the differences between their parents with insecurity and confusion. They react similarly to social groups which represent contrasting standards. They do not seem to know clearly who they are and where they belong. This basic uncertainty is dramatically reflected in the wavering, fickle quality of their group allegiances.

Some of the patients vacillate between feelings of superiority and inferiority; but the main trend is toward compensatory self-aggrandizement. They exploit their economic position and their pseudoidentification with dominant powerful groups for the reinforcement of such illusions. Nevertheless, even here there is an obvious contradiction between the conspicuousness of their social anxiety and their alleged mastery of the environment. Often, the confusion of these patients is manifested in blatant inconsistencies between their acutal role in life and the inner concept of self. An interesting sidelight on this confusion of the self-image is the finding that the confusion is greater among the professed liberals (ten cases) than among outright reactionaries.

The interpersonal relationships of these anti-Semitic personalities clearly reflect this deficiency. At the individual level, they have at best the capacity to achieve only a partial relationship which is continuously endangered by their overaggression against or overdependency on their partners. Repeated failures in social and personal contacts result in a subjective conviction of isolation. Often, they try desperately to overcome their loneliness by building simulacra of human ties.

At the group level, none of our patients achieve a strong identification. Overtly these patients wish to reap the rewards of social conformity, but unconsciously their fear of submission is too great and they struggle with intense feelings of destructive rebellion. It is the desire to appear like everybody else, rather than the achievement of genuine identification, which governs the striving of most of our patients. Frequently, we find them shifting from one group to another, overprotesting the strength of their temporary allegiance to this or that cause.

To persons beset by this conflict, people who are "different" and, what is more, people who seem unwilling to wish to abandon their difference, are an eternal source of irritation. The Jews who appear to the anti-Semite as different from him in many ways, and yet alike among themselves, are uncanny because apparently they have the courage to be different and yet also succeed in being identified with a group. Thus, their very existence is a constant painful reminder of the emotional deficiencies in the anti-Semite.

The reality adaptation and the affective behavior of these patients show this same weakness. Their entire relation to external objects seems impaired; their very perception of reality is vague, dull, and indefinitely formed. This drabness permeates the entire emotional life of the patients; the affective responses seem shallow, colorless, often quite constricted. The range of interests tends to be narrow. They have few significant and strong attachments to groups, persons, ideas, or even pastimes. They seem to lack definite conscious goals; more often, they seem vaguely concerned with impotent desires to restore some relationship to the world: there is no more concrete formulation of their aims than the wish "to be happy." In one sphere of their adaptation to reality, however, they seem to have the trappings of success; namely, in the pursuit of their economic activities. Only three out of our twenty-seven patients had actually suffered from serious inabilities in the work area. It is conceivable that the successful adaptation to reality in the work sphere is related to the outwardly directed orientation of their aggression.

Associated with this syndrome of pervasive anxiety, confused self-image, and partial failure at reality adaptation is another general trend: the disturbed function of conscience. In some cases, there is little evidence for the presence of genuine guilt feeling. Examples of this abound in our cases. There is the wealthy business man who cheats his newspaper dealer out of small change; the mother who neglects her child because she feels like going for a walk; the woman of forty who does not know whether to approve or disapprove of anything unless she first asks her mother, etc. The unmitigated hatred in adulthood of one or both parents is another such indication of deficient conscience.

In other cases, there is a definite guilt reaction which may be adequate in quantity, but is unreliable and fickle in quality. Some patients tend to equate the Jews with their own conscience, and oppose both. This was most clearly expressed in the case of one woman patient who had much personal contact both with Jews and with the Irish. "The Irish," she said, "want me to play and enjoy myself. The Jews want me to work, to be serious and punctual." Other patients equate the Jews with the uncontrolled release of primitive sexual and aggressive urges. They hate the Jews because they are loud, coarse, talk with their hands, and with undisguised animation. One patient, highly successful in a business career, hated the Jews for being shams and fakers who got into grand positions by unfair means. What she projected onto the Jews was exactly what her conscience blamed her for doing in her own career. She regarded herself as a fake in her extremely successful business life. The quality of fickleness of her conscience is demonstrated by the fact that she, nevertheless, continued to do what she thought one must not do. Another patient hated the Jews because they were untamed, overemotional, and ill-mannered. In such patients, an interesting question arises: is the quality of their conscience such that they must deny primitive sexual and aggressive urges per se, or do they have a secret, partial acceptance of such urges, but object violently only to an open display of them, because "it isn't polite." The evidence in many cases points to the latter conclusion. Such trends suggest an incomplete process of internalization of conscience. Psychoanalytic concepts indicate that in such persons the process of repression is defective. This is borne out by our evidence. The relative failure of repression necessitates the mobilization of other reinforcing defense reactions.

In this syndrome of anxiety, weakness, confusion, inner doubt, disordered self-image, and instability, anti-Semitism seems to play a functionally well-defined role. It is a defense against self-hate; it represents an effort to displace the self-destroying trends in the character structure outlined above. At the individual psychic level, the anti-Semitic hostility pattern can be viewed as an irrational effort to restore a crippled self, and at the group level as a device for achieving secondary emotional gain. The anti-Semite, unable to resolve or reconcile his conflicts, flees from the painful, insoluble dilemma into a preoccupation with external experience. He attempts to externalize his inner conflicts. He does this in the vain hope of forestalling progressive destruction of precious parts of his ambiguous self. Such a defensive ego response inevitably entails significant shifts in the equilibrium of unconscious forces.

The central dynamisms around which the defense patterns cluster are the renunciation of parts of the patient's personal identity, the elimination of these unwanted parts through projection, and, parallel with this, the partial substitution of a borrowed identity through introjection. When, in the effort to assuage anxiety, certain aspects of the identity are disowned, there are immediate consequences. The more intense this effort, the greater is the inevitable damage to the integrity of the self. We have here a vicious cycle in which the effort to lessen anxiety in the end only creates more anxiety. Moreover, the ever-increasing tension leads to social situations which bring harm to the individual actually, not only in fantasy. Inevitably, the end result of this vicious cycle is increased damage to the self, and decreased capacity for coping with social reality.

Having submissively renounced parts of his own indivudality, the anti-Semite feels deep resentment against anyone who does not do likewise. He demands that others conform in the same way. The demand for conformity is thus a further expression of the process of self-renunciation. Here lies the root of the previously mentioned excessive reaction to difference which characterizes our anti-Semitic patient. Every evidence of individuality in another person becomes a painful reminder of the sacrifice the prejudiced person has made in disowning parts of his self. The fear of the different is, hence, not in proportion to the extent of the objective, measurable differences; rather it grows in proportion to the implied ego threat. Thus, the difference comes to symbolize the fruitless suppression of self in the anti-Semite, the futile effort to achieve acceptance and security through compulsory obedience. It is understandable, therefore, that the prejudiced person should want to destroy the nonconformist. "If only the Jews behaved like everybody else"—this frequently heard remark, with its emphasis on conformity rather than on merits or demerits of behavior, clearly illuminates the resentment that is directed against the person who symbolizes difference.

In this connection, the fanatic fervor displayed by the anti-Semite in his effort to convert others to his own conviction becomes understandable as a compulsion to convert lest he himself be converted. He fears his own conversion as leading to passive submission to an authority figure with its symbolic threat of final destruction of self.

Closely allied with the process of renunciation of parts of the self is the mechanism of projection. Here, socially prohibited instinctive drives are displaced to external objects, thus forestalling unconscious guilt and fear of punishment from without. The content of the projection provides, therefore, a mirror of the unconscious conflicts with which the individual cannot adequately deal. Coincidentally, the patient attempts partial restitution for the disowned parts of self by way of building up a borrowed identity. The elements which are introjected and added to the partly fragmented identity are not so clearly discernible as those which have been projected. Self-renunciation and projection play a central part in molding the content of the final anti-Semitic reaction; in addition, their influence permeates the quality of all the other defenses.

At this point, we wish to discuss the operation of auxiliary defenses which, in general, are relatively crude and tend to operate in an all-or-none way. Since renunciation and projection operate as incomplete processes, these patients are forced to fall back upon conscious or preconscious denial of socially reprehensible and disadvantageous tendencies. Qualities of weakness, inferiority, passivity are all denied. But denial, too, is inefficient. One patient tried all his life to deny emotions because they produced anxiety and increased his sense of vulnerability. He accused the Jews of being overemotional. Other patients try to deny to consciousness their fear of competition and fear of failure; they accuse the Jews of being too ambitious and too pushing.

In place of subjectively admitted anxiety, these patients substitute a pattern of social aggression. They persistently seek a dominant position from which they can intimidate others rather than allow awareness of their own fear. Thus they strive continuously to substitute an active role for a passive one in interpersonal relations. Since they cannot ever escape the inherent weakness of their character, they endeavor to preserve the efficacy of their defenses by avoiding situations in which they must be aware of anxiety. In one extreme case, a patient tended to reduce contact with current society to a minimum; he despised not only himself but the entire century, and retreated into an idealization of the eighteenth century. In another case, a highly successful broker had only one wish—to withdraw; he wished to retire as soon as possible; reduce contacts with people. Many patients shun personal contacts with Jews as far as possible. One patient gave vent to his violent anti-Semitic feelings only in analysis because he dreaded the vengeance of Jews.

The tendency to avoid is closely associated with the tendency to oppose. These people are not only against the Jew; they are against themselves and everyone else. They are notoriously "against." The reliance on attitudes of both avoidance and opposition subserves the primary defense pattern of substituting aggression for anxiety. Another mechanism frequently employed by these patients is the development of compensations for intrinsic deficiencies. In denying dependence, submissiveness, and inferiority, they assert a pseudo strength, pseudo self-sufficiency and maturity, and a false superiority. Frequent in our evidence are compensations in the direction of emphasis on external appearance and class snobbery. The patients give exaggerated attention to their clothes; the women long for glamour; they are concerned with belonging to the "best society," etc. The obvious aim of these compensatory drives is to achieve power, money, privileges, and recognition.

An extension of these efforts lies in the patients' attempts to affiliate with dominant groups. Actually, some of the patients are social outcasts. All of them are lonely and isolated, even when they have a number of surface contacts. The degree of their awareness of such isolation varies. Mostly, they try to deny it, and therefore make frantic efforts to achieve compensatory attachment to groups. The weaker their capacity for real human ties, the greater this effort to achieve compensatory identification with individuals or groups. More often than not, the pretense of belonging substitutes for true group membership. In this futile attempt to achieve acceptance, they are driven to slavish imitation of habits and ideas manifested by those who represent cohesive power. In many cases, this need to conform expresses itself in the imitation of anti-Semitic patterns in the community.

Another form of defense to which these patients resort is reaction-formation. In some social situations, they are overaggressive, gathering courage from the group to which they have temporarily attached themselves. In others, when it is to their advantage to curry favor, they show marked ingratiating and submissive attitudes. Their aggressive patterns are inconsistent. They may attack the Jew if they see him as weak and defenseless. On the other hand, when seeking social gain, they have no reluctance to ingratiate themselves with Jews who seem to hold positions of power or social superiority. Here they speak of doing business with a "white Jew." This in no way influences their usual urge to castigate Jews as a group.

Other reaction formations discernible in these patients are the substitution of conscious attitudes of righteousness and martyrdom for basic cruelty. The contrasting attitudes are also seen: overt cruelty takes the place of righteousness; often, an excessive identification with the underdog occurs as a reaction to sadistic tendencies. With this is associated exaggerated reactions of pity. In some patients, a false magnanimity is substituted for an inability to love, to give to anyone. Again, one sees the assumption of exaggerated attitudes of protectiveness to cover basic hostility; as, for example, in the case of the man who controlled his hostility to his parents and authority by becoming a prison worker.

The motivation toward secondary gain in these patients asserts itself most strongly. Superimposed on the basic defenses which these patients use in an effort to repair the damage and weakness of their personalities, there is a conspicuous exploitive drive for secondary emotional gain and social advantage. They seek attention, flattery, security in dependent situations; they dramatize their hurts in order to play the martyred role, to receive compensation or pity. They exhibit themselves, put a great stress on form rather than substance, and demand all the social advantages of adhering to conventional forms. And they are not above using their anti-Semitism to steal a rival's job.

The study of these mechanisms of self-defense in any individual takes its clue from the specific content of the anti-Semitic manifestation. In the content of the projection the link between an individual's attitude toward his conflicts and his accusation against the Jews becomes most visible. While these mechanisms are probably mobilized in all forms of irrational group hostilities, the relative specificity of the anti-Semitic pattern can be discerned in the elements of Jewish symbolism selected for projection. The mechanism of projection itself implies a previous deficiency of contact with reality and then a compensatory effort to restore contact. This mechanism seems to be necessary, in some degree, for the production of anti-Semitism.

The negative stereotype of the Jew that has been developed in the Christian era is particularly suitable as a projective screen because it is highly elaborated and highly inconsistent. Culturally, the Jew is described both as successful and as low class; as capitalist and as communist; as clannish and as intruder into other people's society; as the personification of high moral and spiritual standards and as given to low, primitive drives like greed and dirt; as oversexed and as impotent; as male and as female; as strong and as weak; as magically omnipotent and omniscient, possessing uncanny demoniacal powers or as being incredibly helpless, defenseless, and, therefore, readily destroyed.

The specific selection that an individual makes out of this wealth of contrasting attributes can be understood only if this selection is discussed simultaneously with the individual anti-Semite's attitude toward his own self. Invariably, we find in our cases that what is irrationally projected onto the Jew represents specific unwelcome components of the self or components envied in others. It is important to remember here that these partial rejections of the self are the result of ambivalence and conflict, in order to understand that in the deepest layers of the personality one often finds a lingering acceptance of just these attributes. Hence the frequent discovery that the conscious rejection of the Jew is often paralleled in the unconscious by a strong positive identification with him. The ambivalence of anti-Semites toward Jews is notorious. Thus, in one case a patient witnessed, as a child, the beating of a Jewish boy and felt in watching the scene that he was like that Jewish child. From that incident emerged his ultimate violent hostility towards Jews.

The deep-seated identification with the Jew's symbolic weakness, his crippled, castrated state and his subordinated, defenseless position, is denied because of its danger to the integrity of the individual's self and to his social position; in its place there is substituted an identification with the attacker, in order to avoid being victimized and also to draw strength from the identification. Thus, the Jew, at one and the same time, stands for the weakness or the strength of the self; for conscience, which reproaches the self for its deficiencies and badness, and also for those primitive, forbidden appetites and aggressions which must be denied as the price of social acceptance.

We have described in cross section those character trends which seem relevant to the production of the final anti-Semitic reaction. We shall attempt now to delineate the genetic patterns which underlie these character trends. One qualification is necessary, however. It is especially difficult, in psychoanalytic case histories, to correlate genetic development with the social factors which may have contributed to anti-Semitic hostility. For this reason, we wish to be cautious in arriving at generalizations.

In scrutinizing the psychological atmosphere into which the potential anti-Semite is born, a striking similarity between cases prevails: we have not a single example of a permanently well-adjusted marital relationship between the parents. In about half the cases, the parental relationship, superficially viewed, is a respectable one. In its external aspects, the parental relationship conforms to conventional standards. Basically, however, there is no real warmth, affection, or sympathy between the parents. There is no essential closeness; the parents have detached attitudes. The sexual adaptation between the parents, where we have evidence, is poor.

A sharp contrast between the parents as individuals is the general rule. There are marked differences between mother and father in temperament, social values, sexual attitudes, and feelings toward the children. These differences are often emphasized by discrepancies in ethnic origin, social and religious background. Even where the parents maintain the surface appearance of a good relationship, the fundamental hostility between them is obvious. More often than not, this hostility is not expressed directly, but may be displaced against a child or is diverted into other channels. In the parental configuration, there is usually a contrast of aggressive patterns. One parent is dominant, overaggressive; the other is weak, submissive, masochistic.

The experience of rejection by one or both parents is common in our cases. Most frequently, the rejection is overt. In several cases, it is implicit in the narcissistic exploitation of the child. The effect on the child is clear: it feels unwanted, unloved, unworthy. Perhaps these effects are exaggerated because of the basically hostile relationship between the parents. In any event, there is deep damage to the self-esteem and confidence of the child. In this emotional context, there is a fixation of passive, dependent needs, and the related aggression. Both dependent wishes and aggression are repressed because of fear of the parents.

Usually, both parents are authoritarian: in most cases, discipline is severe and rigid, often enforced by brutal beatings. Indulgent attitudes toward the child are not common and certainly not consistent. Acceptance of the child is conditioned on conforming behavior. On this background, the rejected or exploited child learns early a pattern of pretense. The child assumes an overtly submissive attitude, beneath which rebellion and hostility continue to smolder. The pent-up aggression can only be released through displacement. In some cases, the aggression is clearly displaced from the parent into the sibling situation.

In several cases, the fixation of anal character traits can be traced back clearly to severe, early toilet training which was made a test of the parents' approval and affection. There are numerous other illustrations of parental coercion of the child—arbitrary imposition of certain forms of play, or forcing the child to become a musician in order to fulfil its parents' life dream. This compels the child to be as the parents demand, but does not permit the child to be itself. Thus, the first stone is laid toward the development of an identity conflict. It also reinforces a pattern of surface compliance, covering an underlying destructive rebellion; it stimulates chronic ambivalence and, with it, sado-masochistic and self-degrading tendencies. At this stage, the attitude toward toilet activities and dirt, as conditioned by the parent, colors the later sexual patterns.

Thus, the preoedipal experiences of our patients fixate a basic passivity, while the corresponding aggression is repressed. This passivity and the associated ambivalence present a strong hindrance to healthy oedipal development, reinforce castration anxiety, and provide the matrix for sexual confusion and homoerotic leaning.

The oedipal conflict into which the child enters is intense, characterized by confusion and fear, and is never fully resolved. The process of identification with the parents is seriously distorted; the incorporation of parental images into the internal conscience often remains incomplete and variously deformed. The patient's self-image, particularly his sexual identity, is confused. Ambivalence, already strongly activated by pregenital conditioning, is reinforced by the oedipal conflict.

The process of identification with the parents is further complicated by the contradiction between the surface respectability of their relationship, and the basic hostility and mutual rejection between them. The child intuitively senses this hate, and attaches to it the frequent sharp differences between the parents. The child's fear of passive submission to either parent impedes the process of identification. Often the child begins by making a partial identification with the weaker parent, who represents, if not the kinder, at least the less menacing of the two. In many instances, this is the father, the mother being the dominant parent. The identification with the weaker parent, however, reinforces the child's exposure to the destructive hate of the stronger parent, more frequently the mother. Because of this danger, and because of the great need for the protection of a strong parent, the child tends, defensively, to renounce identification with the weaker parent and to strive for an exaggerated identification with the more aggressive parent (identification with the enemy). Under such circumstances, of course, there can be at best only a partial, ambivalent identification with the stronger parent. As a result, the patient withdraws; the identification remains incomplete and distorted with both parents. This produces a lifelong indecisiveness and confusion as to sexual identity; the patient gives his wholehearted allegiance neither to father nor mother, and, correspondingly, neither to male nor female attributes.

Such distortion of the processes of identification results in an incomplete conscience development. While guilt reactions quantitatively may be intense, the internalized standards of right and wrong remain vague and unstable in quality. Moreover, punishment is perceived largely as coming from without rather than from within. This is associated with a considerable tendency to project hated qualities of self in order to provide a basis for an extensive denial of guilt.

In many cases, one sees a clear, dynamic parallel between the patient's attitude to a parent and the specific meaning of the anti-Semitism. The hatred for "the Jew" is often identical in content with the hatred for one of the parents, or identical with the hatred of one parent for the other. In the unconscious, Jewishness is sometimes equated with the image of an aggressive, domineering mother. In other cases, it may be symbolized in the father. In one instance, a young Nazi hated the Jews and his father for identical reasons: they and his father were "more successful, more clever, more sexually potent" than he. This link between the unresolved oedipal conflict and the development and content of anti-Semitic attitudes is often striking. It becomes most visible, of course, in the cases of Jewish or half-Jewish parents. One is tempted, on the basis of these observations, to speculate that conflict between male and female, between mother and father, becomes later symbolized as conflict between Jew and Gentile. There is, of course, a common dynamic factor between prejudice against Jews and against women.

Castration anxiety is exaggerated in these patients. The accidental presence of a physical defect in several patients lends the illusion of reality to the castration threat. This often leads to either a strong pro-Semitic or a strong anti-Semitic attitude. Allegedly unattractive physical characteristics of Jews, especially circumcision, reinforce the ambivalence of the reaction. Thus, the Jews are seen as the underdog, as ugly and crippled people. The anti-Semite's unconscious identification with the Jew is such a profound threat that it must be emphatically denied and a defensive identification with the attacker results. So much for the intrapsychic development of our patients.

As indicated before, our information concerning external factors conducive to anti-Semitism is far from complete. Nevertheless, some relevant questions can, at least, be raised and partially answered. The most obvious of these questions is whether any real life experiences have brought out into the open the anti-Semitic attitudes of the patients. Especially, one would like to know what role any real contact with Jews may have played in the development of such attitudes. This has obvious relevance in connection with the observed fact that some Jews masochistically invite attack.

Our material reveals that there is no clear or simple correlation between the development of anti-Semitism and actual contact with Jews. In some cases, there was apparently no contact at all until adulthood, and then the contacts were of a superficial nature (meeting Jews in stores, in business, in the subway, etc.) In other cases, the contact was of a decidedly positive nature. One patient, who was somewhat neglected by his parents in childhood, enjoyed the warm friendship of a Jewish family who gave him delicious food and all the warmth and affection for which he longed; another patient had a Jewish friend who helped him out of trouble when he was in a tough spot in his career. The quality of such contacts does influence the particular dynamic content of an individual's anti-Semitic attitudes. But it would be entirely unjustified to hypothesize a direct cause and effect link between anti-Semitism and pleasant or unpleasant contacts with Jews.

Our data showed also that there is no simple relation between the existence of anti-Semitic attitudes in the parents and in the children. In a number of cases, the patients' parents showed no sign of anti-Semitism; the parents of other patients even felt strongly pro-Semitic. Obviously, anti-Semitism is not merely passed from one generation to the next, as is sometimes assumed. The relationship between prejudiced parents and prejudiced children must be regarded as a function of the dynamic outcome of the oedipal development and the vicissitudes of identification. Thus the entire evidence we have presented in this paper leads us to believe that anti-Semitism, like all other group hostilities, presents a reflection of a conflict in the prejudiced person, and not a rational reaction to the external world.

The pattern of character weaknesses, especially confusion in personal identity, which we have found in these anti-Semitic patients, tempts one to speculate about the mass success of anti-Semitic propaganda. It appears understandable, in the light of our study, that persons with such character weaknesses manifest a peculiar susceptibility to group pressures and propaganda. They accept them as crutches which fit their needs. Propaganda against prejudice has less effect upon them, because there is little gratification in it for those whose need is to hate.

The character weaknesses that we have outlined seem to get powerful support from certain established value trends in our society. These patients seem to have assimilated into their personality structure those social patterns which constitute the symptoms of the social pathology of our times.

In a broader social frame, anti-Semitism can profitably be viewed as the result of the mutual impact of two irrational patterns: the irrational conflict of the anti-Semite, which we have described, in his unsuccessful effort to find a definite and safe place in our society; and what we may justifiably assume to be the similar irrational conflict of the Jew who also tries, and also fails, in the same effort.

CHAPTER 17

Mental Hygiene and Social Work, Today and Tomorrow

A Herculean challenge confronts mental hygiene and social work in the present world situation. Contemporary civilization is passing through a period of revolutionary change. The tremendous impact of this change on our daily lives is hardly to be denied. Old cultural forms are disintegrating under our eyes; new ones are emerging continuously. In the wake of this revolutionary transition comes a strong tide of disorganization, occasionally mounting to sheer social chaos. The effects are clearly visible in the events that shape current world history; and at a more intimate, personal level, it is easy to see the mounting confusion of the individual's place in society, and parallel with this, the instability of his standards and ideals. Amidst this disorganization can be discerned the emergence of new socio-economic forms. One wonders about the effects of these processes of social reorganization on the individual's struggle to adapt to the community. Is it possible to foresee the future potentialities of these newly emerging social patterns, and take them into account in the process of gradual reformulation of the objectives of mental hygiene and social work? If so, the significance for future community activities in these two fields would be very great indeed.

The three wars in which the United States was embroiled in the last forty years are in part a symptom of this cultural revolution. Yet, in some respects, they have themselves served to accelerate the process of social change. While war lasts, the urgent necessity for national unity and for economic and social controls perhaps holds in temporary abeyance some aspects of the trend toward social disintegration. With the termination of war, however, and with the withdrawal of these temporary measures of social control, the potent forces inherent in the cultural upheaval are set free. It is hardly possible to predict the damage that may result, should there be a failure to keep these forces in leash. For this reason, the postwar period of transition is especially dangerous.

In such times, it is extremely difficult to establish and effectively maintain clear social aims, either collectively or individually. The disorganizing trends of present-day society have profoundly affected the patterns of both individual and communal existence. Social standards and

---

Reprinted with permission from *Social Casework*, February 1955, 63-70.

ideals reflect an amazing conglomeration of confused and contradictory values. The boom times of military expansion are a mixed blessing. Inflation and deflation are twin threats. The current state of social tension exerts a pervasive effect on our struggles to adapt to our kind of world and achieve some emotional stability in our lives. Poverty, delinquency, maladjustment, and mental illness—these are the cancers of society. To combat them is a mammoth task. How can social work and mental hygiene rise to the emergency? The future patterns of social reconstruction, the forerunners of the coming civilization, are now being shaped. Can social work and mental hygiene define these new trends, and implement that knowledge effectively in the task of rehabilitation?

Social work and mental hygiene have much in common. Mental hygiene interests itself in bettering mental health in the community; social work concerns itself with improving the general welfare of the community. Obviously, these two objectives share a broad area of common interest. In the past, mental hygiene and social work have joined forces energetically in order to marshal the greatest potential strength against the common enemies—social maladjustment and mental ill-health in the community. How will they co-operate in the future?

I should like to consider here a few pertinent aspects of the development of these two movements, both as independent and as related entities. After that, I shall discuss some significant issues facing mental hygiene in the future, and draw certain implications for the practice of mental hygiene in the social work field.

Social work grew out of man's efforts to treat the ever-present social ills of poverty, delinquency, and disease. Mental hygiene began with an inspired wish not only to treat, but also to prevent, mental ill-health. Social work, in its modern era, found it could not treat social ills without a better understanding of human personality; mental hygiene found it could not properly gauge mental ill-health in individual persons without closer scrutiny of the social milieu in which this illness was bred. Therefore, they found a common meeting-ground.

The ideologies of mental hygiene and social work are products of evolution. Each was born of a real need in the community, and each has been continuously molded by certain guiding forces within the mental hygiene and social work movements themselves, and also by certain dominant influences in the surrounding social-economic environment. Especially today, with contemporary society in a high state of flux, it is well-nigh impossible for mental hygiene and social work concepts to preserve stable, fixed forms. The ideological concepts that prevail today are fluid, at times even ambiguous, and are being continuously influenced by the vicissitudes of rapid social and economic change.

AIMS OF THE MENTAL HYGIENE MOVEMENT

It is well over forty years since Clifford W. Beers published his epoch-making book, *A Mind That Found Itself*.[1] This book launched the mental hygiene movement. As this movement expanded its influence, it also expanded its meaning. In order to illustrate the significance of this, let us contrast two statements concerning the goals of mental hygiene. The first is from Beers's book:

1) To further reforms in the care and treatment of the mentally ill.
2) To disseminate, to the public, information designed to increase human tolerance for those afflicted with mental illness.
3) To promote research into the causes, motives, and treatment of mental disorders.
4) To create services directed toward the prevention of mental illness.[2]

This is an example of a relatively realistic statement of aims. Compare with this the closing paragraph of Albert Deutsch's book, *The Mentally Ill in America:*

> A world of peace and freedom, from which the twin specters of war and insecurity will be banished; a world of equal opportunity, where people will be freed from stunting inhibitions and "guilt feelings" arising from outworn prejudices and taboos; a world where children may lead healthy, happy lives and grow into useful, well-adjusted citizens; where the personality is permitted to develop naturally and freely; where the individual is given a sense of personal worth and dignity, and where his activities and

[1]Longmans, Green and Co., New York, 1908 (later editions, Doubleday, Doran and Co., New York).

[2]*Ibid.*

ambitions are integrated with the development of group life—such is the goal toward which mental hygiene must strive.[3]

This statement, by contrast, is an example of an exalted, idealized expression of mental hygiene aims: it is a poetic vision, a picturesque image of Utopia. By such broad definitions of its aims, mental hygiene for a time inspired the community and raised high hopes for the "good life." It magnified itself to the dimensions of a panacea.

In the present world-wide clash of ideas, between the concept of the authoritarian state and the free democracy, the menace of fascist barbarity continues to persist. Human suffering is widespread; starvation and disease are still with us; mental illness is sharply on the rise; the threat of unprecedented atomic destruction haunts our daily lives. In the face of such realities, the blissful state depicted in the above statement sounds like the promise of the millennium, or a message from Mars; it has the fervent glow of a new religion. Nevertheless, such diffuse and idealistic definitions of the aims and concepts of mental hygiene have not been uncommon. One has but to pause a moment to consider the distressing chaos of contemporary life to know how infinitely remote from realization such a romantic goal actually is. This in no way denies the eventual possibility of attaining the "good life." At present, however, such a possibility certainly is not very near.

It is now common knowledge that the grandiose promises and aspirations of earlier mental hygiene propaganda acted as a boomerang. There has been an inevitable reaction against the "overselling" of the movement. This inevitable disillusionment was one unfortunate product of early missionary activity in the field of mental hygiene. Despite this disillusionment, however, one fundamental point is worth reiterating: that a true mental hygiene ideology cannot possibly be oversold. What has been oversold has been not the valid essence of mental health principles, but rather some unreal premises which might better not have been advanced in the first place. But mistakes are the price of progress. The faulty part of mental hygiene ideology must be, and is being, corrected. It must be admitted, however, that the many different, and often conflicting, meanings that mental hygiene has acquired in the course of its growth have led to some measure of failure to fulfil promises and to some degree of confusion.

PREVENTIVE ASPECTS OF MENTAL HYGIENE

The mental hygiene movement has, in fact, achieved much. It has served a great and worthy purpose in emphasizing the need for intensive, individualized treatment of maladjusted personalities and for prevention of mental disorders. In the wake of the movement has come a momentous reform in the technique of treatment of mentally sick people. There is no gain-saying this fact. But what has actually been achieved thus far toward prevention on a wide social scale? Relatively little, if one would be honest. One is tempted to ask why.

There is no easy answer, but some plausible explanations may be attempted. Prevention of mental disorders presupposes a knowledge of causation; and comprehensive knowledge of the biological and sociological causes of mental illness is still lacking. Only certain limited facts are known. Theoretically, therefore, prevention can proceed only on a limited scale. This is conceivably the most important reason; but this circumstance provides no explanation for the fact that the application of mental health principles on a broad social scale has lagged considerably behind even the slow accumulation of valid knowledge concerning causes of mental disorders. Thus, there must be reasons other than limited knowledge.

Perhaps one significant factor is our kind of highly individualistic, competitive social system, the mechanics of which tend strongly to hamper the application, on a broad social scale, of techniques for the prevention of maladjustment and mental disorder.

There is another significant limiting factor, however—the element of ambiguity in mental hygiene ideology itself with respect to scientifically valid and workable concepts of mental health, mental illness, and techniques of prevention. The pattern of our social order makes more difficult a clear and pragmatic definition of the sociological aspects of these phenomena.

[3]Columbia University Press, New York, 1946, p. 496 (3rd printing).

There have been much floundering and confusion concerning the relation of the individual person to society. There has been no sound solution of the age-old dilemma: Which comes first, the citizen or the state? This uncertainly has immediate bearing on the problems of mental health. Is the individual person expected to adapt to society, or is society expected to adapt to the needs of the individual person? To build mental health, how much must the individual change? How much must society change? To raise these naive and seemingly meaningless questions is not so absurd as it may seem at first glance. The regressive, barbaric content of fascist ideology, with its degradation of the individual, its subordination of woman to the level of chattel, and its ruthless exaltation of power, affirms their relevance.

Until recent times, it seemed that the individual had to do all the adapting in his relation to society. In the height of the capitalist era, with its emphasis on individual enterprise, individual responsibility, and uncontrolled competition, it seemed as if little or nothing could be done to alter the social condition of living. The individual citizen was expected to accept society as it was, accommodate himself to it and make all the necessary concessions, but was not expected to protest, or to attempt to remake the social scene. Inevitably, this placed a large strain on the adjustment capacities of many persons. Just as the conditions of modern warfare are regarded as an abnormal environment, so should some aspects of civilian society be conceived as a pathological environment for the human personality. In this context, we begin to see more vividly the delicacy of the balance between the individual and society. There has been something of a renascence of the old truth that the state exists for the welfare of its citizens, rather than citizens existing for the welfare of the state. Our society seems rather more ready now to pattern its structure in relation to the recognized needs of its individual citizens, viewed as human beings, not as robots on a factory belt.

From another angle, present society places a premium on certain goals, values, and concepts of success which many experts on problems of mental health view as basically irrational; it is their conviction that these social patterns assault the dignity and integrity of the human personality. In this sense, they may be interpreted as pathological social values and a menace to mental health. The all too familiar examples of such perverted values are the exorbitant importance of prestige, power, money, and material possessions, the ruthlessness of prevailing standards of competitive aggression, and the corresponding exploitative trends in human relations. These standards and values are expressions of the dominant culture pattern. Should they be adjusted to, in the sense of encouraging individuals to conform? Or, recognizing their demoralizing effects on personality, should they be vigorously fought? Here are critical problems in the zone of contact and interchange between social structure and personality. Yet, as scientists, we are not adequately equipped to cope with such questions; the science of individual psychopathology is advancing rapidly, but our knowledge in the sphere of social psychopathology is woefully deficient.

In any case, for these and other reasons, elements of confusion have arisen in the ideologies of social work and mental hygiene, with the result that there are a serious lag in the effective application of mental hygiene principles to broad community problems and a critical block in the application of valid techniques of prevention of mental ill-health.

ASSIMILATION OF MENTAL HYGIENE IDEOLOGY BY SOCIAL WORK

At this point let me trace briefly the manner in which social workers in this country assimilated mental hygiene ideology, its valid principles, and its contradictory concepts as well. In its early days—roughly, the last half of the nineteenth century—social work dealt in two ways with families in which poverty, delinquency, and disease were prevalent: by meeting certain material needs and by attempting to improve social conditions. It did as much as it could in the palliation of these problems, but the results of such efforts were disappointing. Social work also lacked both the method and the necessary power for an effective program of prevention. It aspired toward eradicating these evils, and therefore attempted to ally itself with various social reform movements. Although some gross evils were corrected, many of these efforts failed, perhaps because the social workers of the time did not sufficiently understand the connections of poverty and disease with broader social phenomena. Thus, social work reached an impasse in its endeavor to treat social ills on a mass basis, and its objective seemed blocked.

At this time—in the early twenties—social work was "rescued" by the mental hygiene movement. The novel and highly promising reformist philosophy of this movement saved social work from deep disillusionment. Social work, at this point, was disowning its roots in the reform movement and was endeavoring to develop professional helping methods.[4] Through the mental hygiene movement, social work discovered the importance of understanding the roots of human behavior, and undertook to apply psychiatric knowledge to its task of ameliorating the ills of the individual person.

To quote Albert Deutsch:

> The failure to arrive at their objective through attempts to change the environment in dealing with problems of social maladjustment was an important factor in bringing about the shift of emphasis upon individual personality rather than upon environment and social forces. . . . As social work swerved from its orientation around mass social reform movements, case work rose to an increasingly prominent position in relation to general social work.[5]

Unfortunately, the term mental hygiene was often misinterpreted as a theory of human behavior instead of being understood as a movement for the advancement of mental health through better treatment and through prevention. In the ensuing period of intense emphasis on individual personality factors, social work blinded itself to a considerable extent to the important socio-economic forces contributing to the incidence of mental disorders. In recent times this phenomenon of oscillating from one extreme to its opposite has received some thoughtful consideration. The swing of the pendulum is tending now to reach a point midway between the two extremes. There is now far less tendency to emphasize the individual personality to the exclusion of social and economic factors.

These historical trends have led finally to a reaffirmation of the role of social and economic factors in the production of social maladjustment and mental illnesses. This reaffirmation is no accident. Biological factors and early family life experiences, as determinants of behavior, have each enjoyed an era of emphasis in the years just past; but the problems of social adjustment for adult persons—the insecurity in the patterns of group living as well as other current experiential factors that precipitate breakdowns in adult life—have received up to now relatively little attention. Today there is an upsurge of intense research and clinical interest in these controversial problems. The eventual products of these studies will no doubt exercise an important influence on the mental hygiene concepts and practices of social work of the future.

Germane to this issue, a challenging argument appeared some time ago in a paper by Kingsley Davis.[6] In this critical essay, Davis elucidates the distinction between mental hygiene as a social movement and mental hygiene as an applied science. He sets forth the basic premise that mental hygiene as a social movement has cultivated a body of ideological doctrine which, in its path of development, has been greatly influenced by the social institutions and ethical preconceptions that prevail in our type of culture. He alleges further that mental hygiene as a social movement has used this ethical system as a basis for giving advice concerning those forms of conduct which are conducive to mental health and personal happiness. He asserts that mental hygiene practitioners have indulged in preachment of conformity with such an ethical system in the guise of "science." In other words, the ideology of mental hygiene as a social movement, which in part represents acceptance of or submission to a particular ephemeral system of cultural values, has been presented as a science of mental health. Probably this has been one of the consequences of the sweeping progress of the movement as a reformist enterprise. To the degree to which such advocacy of conformity has occurred, it is unfortunate, because it has tended to block true progress toward prevention of mental illness.

---

[4]Mary E. Richmond, *Social Diagnosis,* Russell Sage Foundation, New York, 1917.

[5]Deutsch, *op. cit.,* pp. 319-320.

[6]Kingsley Davis, "Mental Hygiene and the Class Structure," *Psychiatry,* Vol. I, No. 1 (1938), pp. 55-65.

To quote Davis:

> Mental hygiene hides its adherence [to ethical preconceptions] behind a scientific facade. . . . The unconscious assumption of the dominant ethic [the philosophy of private initiative, personal responsibility, and the individual achievement], together with the psychologistic interpretation, has served to obscure the social determinants of mental disease, and especially the effect of invidious or emulative relationships. . . . Mental hygiene seems to be limping along on one foot, because if there *are* social determinants, these are not being discovered and utilized in prevention.[7]

THE CHALLENGE TO BOTH FIELDS

How are the fields of mental hygiene and social work facing this challenge today? How will they face it tomorrow? Social work has been only partially able to deal with those factors in the social system which predispose to poverty, disease, social maladjustment, delinquency, and mental illness. In its impotence, it has found a comforting justification in stressing help to individual persons, with the gospel of mental health showing it the way. To whatever extent social work sidesteps the issue of social pathology, and adopts that part of mental hygiene ideology which invites conformity with the dominant ethical system, the effect is not only for it to accept—but even to support actively—the status quo in our social structure. What part of the status quo merits support? What part should be fought? For social workers troubled by this dilemma and unable to find a solution, there are several avenues of escape: to blind themselves to pathological trends in the existing social environment, and seek solace in the mental hygiene approach of helping individual persons; to seek comfort in the doctrines of the more restricted and traditional aspects of psychoanalytic theory, which stresses the past over the present; or to do the opposite—to deny the valid psychoanalytic truths regarding childhood etiology and blame everything on the "social system." This last represents a pattern of wishful escapism into radical political philosophy unchecked by a factual acquaintance with the science of psychopathology. These are two extremes, each representing a serious pitfall in the path of correct orientation of the social worker. Both attitudes represent closed systems of thought, in which effective scientific analysis of the relevant facts is no longer possible. To take flight into either of these blind alleys is no solution. It is a deep confession of defeat.

What are the answers of social work to these problems today? What will they be in the world of tomorrow, with the expansion of atomic power? Will social work sidestep the issues of social pathology? Will it confess its helplessness to affect social pathology and continue to place too exclusive a stress on the "mental hygiene approach" to the individual sufferer? Is Davis' charge that mental hygiene preaches conformity to the dominant ethical system justified today?

It is not easy to answer these questions. It is difficult to generalize about mental hygiene concepts because there is so little uniformity in the practice of mental hygiene principles. It would be necessary to define more accurately the specific mental hygiene concepts under question, and also to indicate where, how, and by whom they are practiced. In the past, and in some places, no doubt, Davis' charge was justified. It is altogether clear today, however, that in more advanced expressions of professional activity, his accusation can no longer be regarded as valid. There are abundant indications that mental hygiene principles currently are undergoing a rapid evolution, and there are some concrete proofs that Davis' charge does not universally hold. Historic forces in the present social crisis have challenged us to examine with special care the pathogenic features of the present social structure, the phenomena of group tension, the roles of conflict and insecurity in current living. The "relativity theory" of the anthropologists has forced us to scrutinize critically Freud's theories of behavior. In this connection, we recognize, too, that an exclusive emphasis on the treatment of the individual sufferer is tantamount to admitting impotence in the field of prevention of mental illness.

One other consideration, relevant to Davis' charge, I believe deserves special stress. In an effectively functioning, well-organized social system, the task of adjustment requires that people conform on a selective basis to the mores of their community. In order to integrate themselves with the group, they must identify with

[7]Davis, *ibid*., pp. 62-66.

the dominant ethics of their society. Just as children identify with their parents, so do people in general integrate the dominant ethics of the social system into their everyday lives. They incorporate the system into their growth as persons and make it a functioning part of their self-structure. However, if the social system is disorganized and unstable, and provides too little security, or if values are confused, people cannot conform. The current tragedy is not, as Davis implied, that people conform to the dominant ethics; it is rather that the prevailing social conflicts and instability make it difficult to conform—or people discover simply that it doesn't pay to conform.

Dynamically, the problem is analogous to certain elemental aspects of the child-parent relationship. If the parent does not offer enough security to a child, the child neither identifies nor conforms with the ethics that the parent represents. It is much the same with the relationship of the adult to his surrounding society. Basically, adults strive to conform to the dominant ethics of the prevailing social system. They simply cannot do so, however, if there is too little security in the pattern of group living. This is conspicuously the case if the prevailing ethical system is intrinsically unstable and contradictory. When the social ideals and human values themselves are in a state of disorder, it is extremely difficult for adult persons to identify with those values or to conform effectively. This is surely the case in our contemporary social structure.

The principles of mental hygiene which prevail in the community at large are difficult to appraise. But, in the day-to-day practices of psychiatric clinics, social casework agencies, parent education organizations, and so on, these principles become tangible and concrete; they become actualized in a specific set of policies and practices. What do we see in the community mental health services of today? To what degree are mental health problems conceived purely as those of individual personality and of individual adaptation? To what degree are they attributable to pathology of group living, and pathology of the social structure? Are individuals expected to take the prevailing social conditions as they are and conform? Is social pathology being scrutinized? Are dominant community values subjected to critical examination, from the point of view of their meaning for mental health?

It is clearly evident that the newer, more flexible concepts of personality, social structure, and mental health coming out of recent research in psychiatry and social science are taking hold. Interest centers not on therapy alone, but on the constant search for principles of prevention. Increasing stress is placed on the study of child development, child-family relations, and family-community relations. The more rigorous definitions of such abstractions as personality, community, and mental health, offered by the latest scientific studies, begin to influence the patterns of marital counseling, parent education, family life education, and, finally, concepts of family diagnosis and family therapy.

A shift in orientation of clinical practice is always preceded by a shift of emphasis in the theoretical base of that practice. Since we are in the throes of social revolution, it may be important to review critically the current concepts of causation of social maladjustment and mental illness.

In recent years, we speak less of "causes" of mental illness. Rather, we try to explain behavior patterns, both normal and pathological, in terms of patterns of total development within a given social milieu. We try to define abnormal behavior in terms of a long chain of related social events impinging on the development of a person. We place emphasis on the "how" of mental illness, and are modest in explaining the "why."

According to traditional concepts, there are hereditary, physical, emotional, sexual, social, and economic "causes"; what is significant, however, is not the single "cause," but the unified pattern into which all these influences are woven, that is, the total configuration of contributing factors.

The chain of events leading to illness may not be linear; it may be circular, or a series of influences may be pyramided. In this sense, the illness is the product of the dynamic interaction of many "causes." Etiological factors may be schematized thus:

The potentialities of the child are, first, the product of his biological heritage. But the pattern of family life and wider social factors influence the expression of biologically conditioned propensities, for example, the patterning effects of social influence on the expression of intelligence, or the conditioning effects of social experience on the sympathetic nervous control of the alimentary functions. The growth of the child's personality is profoundly influenced by the family pattern, parental attitudes, and concepts of child rearing. Wider society has a tremendous effect later on adolescent and adult life.

We must preserve the enormously important truths that have come, through the impetus of psychoanalysis, from the microscopic study of the effect of family life on the growing child. But, even as we study their effects, we must not blind ourselves to the other elements in the total pattern. We cannot pretend that parents and families live in a social vacuum. The effects of social influence on biologically conditioned behavior patterns should be studied. The effects of surrounding society on the pattern of family life, particularly, should be subjected to the same intense microscopic scrutiny as was, and is now, applied to child-mother relationships. In fact, until this is done, we shall not properly understand disturbances of parental attitude and child-rearing. A renewed emphasis on the importance of social pathology seems indicated.

With the implementation of present-day insights, it is clear that the issues of mental health need to be examined in two directions—from outside, inward; and from inside, outward. Three interrelated levels of phenomena are involved: the social organization of the community, and the related interpersonal patterns; the processes of an individual's emotional integration into the group; and the history and development of individual personality. The issue, therefore, is not whether the individual should accommodate to society, or society be reshaped to fit the individual; it is clear that the two are interdependent, and that if mental health is to be advanced, there must be parallel changes in both.

PART IV

Family Theory

The papers in this section were published over the entire life span of Ackerman's professional interest in the family. The first two are of special interest because they were written while he was still a young psychiatrist in training at the Menninger Clinic. One of the editors of the volume (DAB) reviewed this paper in 1974 and made the following comments:

> In 1937 at the age of 29, Nathan Ackerman published his first article dealing with the family. It was not his first publication—there had been five others in a little over a single year dealing with various aspects of child psychiatry—accidental self-injury, the treatment of juvenile psychosis and of retarded children, among others. The 1937 paper appeared in the Bulletin of the Kansas Mental Hygiene Society; indeed it was the lead article. Its title was "The Family as a Social and Emotional Unit." It was written while Ackerman was a staff member at the Southard School, the children's division of the Menninger Clinic. The paper is short, barely five pages long; to read it now illuminates the spirit of the man, his awareness of human interrelatedness, his compassion, and, above all, his intuitive feeling for the ambiguous quality of intimate networks. The first paragraph has a grand architectural quality:
>
>> None of us live our lives utterly alone. Those who try are doomed to a miserable existence. It can fairly be said that some aspects of life experience are more individual than social and others more social than individual. Nevertheless, principally we live with others,

> and in early years almost exclusively with members of our own family.
>
> The tone is set—a theme laid down which would occupy him for the balance of his professional life. Human aloneness, human relatedness.

Ackerman was always an acute observer of children. In the 1938 paper on "Reciprocal Antagonism in Siblings" he raised the question that must have been central to his thinking about his own family . . . "why two brothers reared in an 'identical' home environment should develop into utterly divergent personalities." At this early point he was reaching for the concept of the family as context for its members where the patterns of family members were somehow reciprocally interlocked. It is in this paper that the notion of complementarity first appears, although the word as such is not used.

In 1954, the paper "Interpersonal Disturbances in the Family" was published in *Psychiatry*. This journal was the most prestigious showcase for those authors wishing to reach an audience hospitable to newer definitions of psychiatric matters, definitions from a social science perspective. Psychoanalysis was then in its heyday but already under heavy attack by such "left deviationists" as Sullivan and Horney, who proposed conceptualizing psychoanalytic therapy as an interpersonal event. Here, as elsewhere, Ackerman is careful to treat with utmost seriousness the theories of classical psychoanalysis; he had, after all, been trained as an analyst. It is hard to realize at this distance how necessary it was to build the case for a family perspective patiently and on a sound foundation. Ackerman does a workmanlike job here, noting first the failure of individual therapy to improve social relations "paradoxically." He considers, as well, the complexities of integrating the psychoanalysis or psychotherapy of several family members, problems in the treatment of couples, and difficulties in the integration of parental treatment in child guidance settings. Ackerman takes a forthright position that the decision as to individual psychotherapy should be subordinated at the very least to a psychosocial evaluation of the family group as a whole. "Within this frame of reference, the therapeutic approach to the family group per se would be primary and the psychotherapy of individual members secondary. In other words, the relation of individual psychotherapy to the therapy of the family would be the relation of the part to the whole." Here Ackerman takes a stand that almost 30 years later is not commonly accepted by the bulk of general psychiatrists, although to family systems therapists the position would seem self-evident.

In the 1956 paper, "Interlocking Pathology in Family Relationships," he turns again to consideration of the fit between patterns, leaning heavily on the concept of role as an organizing principle for understanding reciprocal patterns. "As a bridge between the internal processes of personality and those of family participation, it is useful to employ the concept of family role, i.e., those dynamic processes by which the dispositions of a given personality integrate themselves into particular family roles: child, mother, father, husband or wife. Family roles are essentially interdependent and reciprocal." Later, he says, "Of special importance is the relative congruity or incongruity for the same individual of different familial and extra-familial roles. Certain roles fit; others clash."

The "Theory of Family Dynamics," published in 1959, opens with the recounting of an anecdote. Gregory Bateson optimistically observed to Ackerman "that in not too long a time, perhaps five years, we would succeed in evolving a satisfactory theory of family." Ackerman goes on, "That gave me good cheer, but I felt that the time estimate was rather too optimistic." This paper is noteworthy for its attention to the concept "identity." Sullivan had insisted on its utility as an organizing concept in regard to intrapsychic and interpersonal processes. While Ackerman's elaboration of this concept seems somewhat muddy to us at this remove, its utility for family therapists has not been sufficiently explored to this day. In this paper, Ackerman also deals with a view of the dynamic stability of a living system that subsumes both morphostasis and morphogenesis. In Ackerman's use of the term stability protects identity both in its conservative phase and in its ability to accommodate to new experience, learning, and further development.

The two final papers in this section continue the development of Ackerman's thinking about family theory. It is interesting to see Ackerman in 1968 speaking about ecology . . . "the perspective is an ecological one; the unit of behavior to be examined is the child within the family rather than the child alone."

The last paper seems to us to be brilliant in spots but uneven. At times too much is being covered and not very thoughtfully. Quotation marks are used to substitute for having thought an issue through such as "those features of the family environment which act as 'sensitizers, pressurizers and precipitators' of disturbance in the child." But there are gems as well.

Throughout Ackerman's work, the concepts of normality, health and disease appear and reappear. In most instances they are uncritically presented as concepts whose meaning is self-evident. In this last paper he tackles the issue head on, noting that some observers say that "health in human terms is a sheer abstraction, that it does not really exist, and therefore, can have no scientific definition. . . ." He goes on to say, "However relative such a condition may be, health is a human reality. Just as there are degrees of and depths of illness so, too, are there degrees and heights of health. If so we have no alternative, no excuse for avoiding the issue." The problem of course was "all things are relative: what goes wrong makes sense only as we place it alongside the conception of what goes right in human development and adaptation." It would have been hard for Ackerman to shift to a systemic epistemology that might declare health and illness to be punctuations. Ackerman, always the physician, needed to reify them and conceptualize them as opposites.

CHAPTER 18

The Family as a Social and Emotional Unit

None of us live our lives utterly alone. Those of us who sometimes try are fated to an unhappy existence. Most of us, figuratively speaking, divide our lives. We keep some of it to ourselves; we share the greater part of it with others. While it is only too true that at times it is almost unbearably difficult to live with certain people, it is even more true, usually, that we cannot live without them. Principally, we live our lives with others; our experiences, our personal development, our adjustment to life are in the greatest measure determined by the contingencies of our interpersonal relations. In the years of childhood, particularly, our common life with others is inextricably woven with that of the family. So much is this so that the family as a unit may be considered to have a psychological and social life of its own.

The experiences of family life leave a profound and lasting impression on all of us. It is always interesting, sometimes tragic, and occasionally comically amusing to observe the effects on the family of certain events occurring without, and certain others occurring within the family circle.

In my memory is engraved the record of an incident that bears a touch of absurd melodrama, but one which likewise points to a basic truth about family psychology. I shall relate the story to you since it illustrates so well the curious, paradoxical nature of family affairs. To get the point of the story I shall have to give you a little background.

The family I have in mind was a large one with many ramifications and numerous members scattered near and far. The senior member, a man of 80 years and himself the father of nine children, made an urgent and eloquent plea for greater family unity. In deference to the "wise old man," a family lodge was established and he was unanimously elected to the president's chair. The lodge included in its membership the entire family, even the most remote relatives who lived at a far distance. It was founded with several purposes in mind: to promote family sentiment, to foster mutual devotion, and to provide concrete aid for less fortunate members. Among other good and bad things, a treasury and loan fund were instituted. An achievement of uncertain value was the purchase and cultivation of a family cemetery. At a business meet-

Reprinted from the *Bulletin of the Kansas Mental Hygiene Society*, 12:2, 1937 (reprinted as "The Unity of the Family," *Archives of Pediatrics*, January 1938, Vol. 55, 51-61).

ing of the lodge the members were at one time trying to agree on matters relating to this cemetery; for instance, how much must each member pay for the privilege of being buried there, and what was to be the "seating arrangement," so to speak, etc. After considerable haggling they finally reached an agreement on these questions. Soon they were again bickering with one another as to whether it would be most fitting for the cemetery to be bounded by a hedge, flowers or a fence. The two elder sons of the president of the lodge argued heatedly on this question. With exactly contraposed views, they grew vehement in their oratory, their anger waxed; things went from bad to worse, and they insulted one another freely. Their father, the honorary president and founder of the lodge, attempted to intercede but his words fell on deaf ears. Finally, the younger brother shouted out bitterly to the older: "I wouldn't be buried next to you if this were God's cemetery." In the epilogue of this story, the brothers never again spoke to one another, but the existence of the family lodge and cemetery was perpetuated.

It is profitable to mull a little on such a story. Think of it—a family lodge, inspired by a father's desire to strengthen the love ties between family members results in lifelong animosity between his own two sons. The love of one brother for another changes to intense hate because they cannot agree on whether the family cemetery, in which they are both to be buried six feet under, should be bounded by a hedge or a fence. The irony of it is superb.

THE FAMILY AS A SOCIAL UNIT

With this allegorical orientation to peculiar paradoxes of family life, I shall move on to a discussion of some more general considerations of family unity. The family is a designation for an institution which is older than history itself. It is a social unit that exists today in every part of the globe, and, looking back through the ages, we see it has existed in every civilization of which history gives us any knowledge at all. It is small wonder that we accept its significant part in our life as being natural. In one sense we have had thousands of years in which to get used to it, and in another sense each generation of us in turn must get used to it all over again.

In our own time, the family group seems to rest upon the ties of kinship, but is this the sole factor which binds the family? By no means!

It is a somewhat curious fact that the family did not originally signify merely the father, the mother and the children. It represented rather an entire household functioning as a unit and was composed of all those living under one roof, or submitting to the authority of one supreme head. Besides the immediate family this often included numerous relatives, servants, slaves, and even the family dog. Here the family constituted a group of people unified for the purpose of effective social regulation or management. History discloses that the constituency of the family group has always been greatly affected by the prevailing social and economic order and by the way of life in general. With each succeeding civilization, the structure and function of the family unit has undergone some important change. Parallel illustrations of this phenomenon can be drawn alike from ancient times when men roamed the land in hordes, and from family affairs in our own current era.

Not so very long ago a great hue and cry was raised against Soviet Russia because it was alleged that the changed mores threatened the sanctity, even the very existence of the family. This is, of course, ridiculous. In the first place history, and even the Bible, make it seem doubtful that the family was ever a sacred unit. Secondly, the very survival of the family depends upon its constant adaptation of new ways of life. When the people of Russia changed their way of living it was inevitable that the character of the family should change. The family has outlived and undoubtedly will continue to outlive any ephemeral economic or social order. For anyone to believe that the sanctity and even the very existence of the family is threatened in a changing social order is a baneful blunder.

THE FOUNDATIONS OF THE FAMILY

If it is not the factor of kinship alone upon which the family rests, what then are the foundations of the family? The family bonds rest on a fusion of basic factors which are variously biological, psychological, social and economic. Biologically, they rest on the common love needs of man and woman, their joint power to perpetuate their kind, and the long period of child dependence upon the parents. Psychologically and socially, the members of a family are bound by mutual interdependency for the satisfaction of their respective affectional needs. Economically, they are bound by mutual interdependency for the provision of their material needs. The unity of the family then rests on a foundation of common needs and common satisfactions, physical and psychical.

From a genetic point of view the family is a product of social evolution. It has not been the same yesterday as it is today, nor will it be the same tomorrow as today. Its structure has gradually altered with the passing of time and with social and cultural change. The fact that today the family is a much freer group in all respects than it ever has been in the past can be ascribed to particular kinds of recent social and economic transformation. The emancipation of the woman's position in the family, coming in the wake of the industrial revolution, is an excellent illustration of this. It is not true that the family is the pillar of society, but rather that society molds the form and function of the family to its greatest social effectiveness. The family then should not be considered as a static thing, "in Heaven ordained," but rather as a living, moving, changing thing. It is a flexible unit which responds delicately in its adaptations to influences acting upon it both from without and from within.

ENVIRONMENTAL EFFECTS ON THE FAMILY

What are the external influences which impinge upon the family group, and how do they affect its unity? In its external relations the family must adapt to the prevailing customs and mores and must make wide workable connections with racial, religious, national and economic factors. Usually an unfavorable, hostile or even dangerous environment will result in greater family solidarity for the purpose of common protection and common provision. Under such conditions the emotional forces of love, loyalty and duty become stronger and the exercise of parental authority is apt to be more rigid. A modification of external conditions which offers increased opportunities for securing satisfaction and pleasure outside the family will encourage more extensive social ramification, lessen the severity of parental authority and weaken the family bonds. Under such circumstances there is less need for interdependence and mutual loyalty, and the family is apt to be a more fluid, mobile unit.

From within, the family must adjust to all the vicissitudes which affect the interpersonal relations of each family member to every other. Under certain conditions the emotions of love and loyalty prevail and the family tie is strengthened; under more unfavorable conditions mutual antagonism and hatred are intensified and the unity of the family is threatened.

Just as we speak of the age of a person so might we speak of the age of a given family, which in the course of its life span passes through different stages of development. The family of one generation is born, lives and dies, but like the individual it attains a kind of immortality in its offspring. Within a single generation the configuration of the family differs in different stages. It is not the same in the prechild period, in the child period, in the period when the parents enter their prime and the children become adolescent, and finally in the period when the parents become senescent and the children mature, marry, and go their several ways. Throughout all of these stages the emotional unity of the family is continuously influenced by external circumstances and by internal affairs. Just as in the growth of the individual there are crucial turning points, so in the life of the family there are critical periods when the family bond may be strengthened or weakened.

INTERNAL ORGANIZATION OF THE FAMILY

I may now consider somewhat more minutely the internal structure of the family. By tradition of occidental culture, our present society is prevailingly patriarchal. Some would have it that our present society is neither patriarchal or matriarchal, but rather that it is both, since the social position of the woman is growing increasingly important. Nevertheless, the father is still considered the rightful head of the family. In terms of physical might he is stronger. It is his duty to protect the family against external dangers of any kind. He is expected to provide part or all of the means of sustenance—food, clothing, shelter, and luxuries, and he must give freely of his love to the mother and the children.

The role of the mother, although it has undergone considerable change in recent times, may be pithily represented as follows: she is expected to reciprocate the father's love, to bear children, give them maternal love and care, and run the household. She may or may not occupy herself in gainful employment and share with the father the responsibility of material provision for the family. It is the duty of both parents to train and educate the children.

The children in turn reciprocate the parents' love; they respect in varying degree their authority; and as they grow older they contribute to the family welfare within the limits of their capacities by virtue of their loyalty and by offering to the family some of the fruits of their own labor. The responsibilities of the various members of the family group have been outlined in too cursory and schematic a manner, but somewhat in this general way are they divided.

Within the sphere of the family are the relationships of father to mother, each parent in turn to each child, and finally each child to every other child. To suggest even the major trends of emotional life in the family requires description in many dimensions. Here it will only be possible to indicate in a very sketchy way some major phenomena.

The currents of feeling which move between family members are myriad in kind, and of all degrees of intensity. Each of these emotional currents may, under altered circumstances, provoke an antagonistic stream. The emotional tone which governs the relationship between any two persons of a family has a development peculiarly its own, but is continuously influenced in its course by the emotional relationships of all other persons in the family. This changing manifold of emotional currents and cross-currents determines the prevailing "atmosphere" in the family. It is on the background of "family atmosphere," constantly in flux and replete with every shade of emotional experience, that a child's personality and social patterns of reaction are developed. To put the matter with homely simplicity, those processes by means of which the child absorbs or rejects wholly or in part this "family atmosphere" determine his character.

FAMILY GIVE AND TAKE

The family may be fairly regarded as a kind of exchange medium; the values which are exchanged are love and material benefits of one kind or another. Within the family sphere there is a flow of these values in all directions. Generally, however, the parents are the prime givers and the children the prime receivers. To use a simple and almost platitudinous formula, the emotional attitudes and behavior of any one member of the family are determined by what he needs, how he seeks to get it, what he is willing to give in return, and what he chooses to do if he doesn't get what he needs. When a child gets "what he wants, when he wants it," he is satisfied and happy. When he doesn't, he becomes sullen, angry, or tearful and depressed. This whole process of distribution of satisfactions in the family is governed over by the authority of the parents. It rests largely with them whether the expectations of each member from every other are destined to reasonable fulfillment. Normally, and most times, this process runs along fairly evenly, and a general atmosphere of mutual love and devotion prevails. If, however, the family atmosphere is full of sudden turns and shifts and all manner of inconsistencies, deep frustration feelings result, inevitably, accompanied by resentment and hatred. The interchange of feeling between family members revolves centrally about this oscillation between love and hate.

EMOTIONAL LIFE IN THE FAMILY

In the normal course of events in family life, it is certainly the fate of all to undergo some measure of disappointment and consequently to experience some hatred, some envy and some jealousy. The experience of a measure of disappointment and hardship, the acceptance of less than complete fulfillment of one's hopes, and the development of tolerance to frustration are all essential to the process of maturation of the personality. Without these there would be insufficient spur to new experience and new achievement. However, an excess of disappointing experience and an excess of hatred is often a serious detriment to healthful development.

The emotional development of the child is vitally affected by family life and is quite complex. For purposes of brevity rather than simplicity I shall point out only several of the more significant patterns.

As has been suggested, all children experience at various times both love and hate toward their parents. The reasonably satisfied, happy child mainly loves and succeeds in properly subordinating his hate. Out of the feeling of love he identifies with his parents and tries to make himself as much like them as possible. By thus assimilating into his own being the characteristics of his parents he develops social and moral criteria by which he judges and disciplines his own conduct. The thwarted, unhappy child experiences excessive hate, rebels directly or indirectly against his parents, and avoids similarity with them. The child who hates always fears those he hates; when it is too dangerous to hate, he conceals his feeling, and shows fear only or becomes depressed. Such a child may develop an overly severe conscience out of an exaggerated fear of hurting or offending his parents and being hurt by them in turn.

The effective control of this balance between love and hate is regulated to a tremendous extent by the personalities and emotional attitudes of the parents. Already the characters of the parents are deeply engraved as a consequence of their own family conditioning. They may carry over from their own early experience the same parental attitudes that their parents in turn revealed to them, or they may consider those attitudes unsuitable and adopt others opposite to those they themselves experienced in childhood.

The manner in which the parents characteristically show their love for one another and for the children is of the utmost significance in determining the prevailing emotional atmosphere. Parents may live with one another in harmony, or they may conflict with one another on all sorts of flimsy pretexts and fill the atmosphere with bitter feeling. Hatred always threatens family disorganization. Such conflict between the parents always engenders anxiety in the child. When parents love one another the child loves both parents; when the parents hate one another, however, the child is compelled to side with one against the other. This invokes fear in the child, since he must then be prepared to lose the love and suffer the hostility of the parent whom he rejects in favor of the other.

In some instances the mother may be too self-interested to be sufficiently warm in her show of affection toward either the father or the children, or she may shower her love on the husband and fail to give ample love to her children, or vice versa. Again, quite important is the problem of sharing of authority between the parents. Whether the father assumes the traditional role of authoritative head of the family, or, being submissive, he relinquishes this responsibility largely to a more aggressive mother, is of inestimable significance for the interparent relationship and for the child-parent relationship. Naturally this circumstance greatly affects the nature of the training and discipline imposed on the child. Neither the overly dependent nor the overly strong, dominating parent exercises a healthful effect on the emotional development of the child. With regard to child discipline, the watchword should be "intelligent direction" rather than mastery, since mastery on the part of a parent always implies the presence of some hostility toward the child, which the child intuitively recognizes with resulting detriment.

PROCESSES OF EMOTIONAL DEVELOPMENT

It is perhaps fair to say that there are two central processes upon which all other aspects of emotional development hinge. The first process is that which leads gradually from a position of infantile comfort and dependence to one of adult self-direction with its attendant benefits and responsibilities. The second process is that in which an infant gradually moves from a position of primary importance in the family into a position of relatively lesser importance, culminating finally in the proper evaluation of the child's self-importance in relation to the rest of society. The one process comprises a movement from dependence to independence; the other process signifies a movement from the center to the periphery in the field of relative personal importance and involves a proper orientation of the self to the outer world. Both processes are functions of the family as a unit. For the preservation of emotional well-being and mental health it is essential that they be imperceptibly gradual.

In the beginning the child is biologically helpless and is privileged to receive complete satisfaction of his every need. With growth and development comes an increasing capacity for independent achievement of satisfactions. Naturally with this is associated a progressive expansion into the world at large. Simultaneously the growing child finds degrees of self-importance in the cultivation of outside relationships, which substitute for his original attachments in the family. In conjunction with these developments the family unity becomes less strong.

In the course of the emotional development of the child there are certain critical turning points, the management of which by the parents influences that intangible but vital thing, "family atmosphere." Moreover, the character of such parental management of critical periods may make or mar the child's future destiny. I shall mention some of these in passing. The time of weaning from the breast, the period of training to cleanliness, the birth of a new sibling, the first important separation of the child from the family, particularly from the mother, that is, going to school, illness, death of the parents, etc. Among the above considerations, the entrance of another child into the family deserves particular emphasis. At such a time the first child feels his sole supremacy challenged, a supremacy which heretofore was inalienable and entitled him to all of the parents' bounty. Now the older child is compelled to surrender to the intruder a share of the mother's love, the family food, room, bed, toys, everything. The older child is likely to feel strong rivalry with the newcomer, is prone to feel somewhat shoved out and to react with feelings of jealousy, envy and hate. Understanding parents can usually render these disturbances innocuous by sustaining their original interest in the older child while giving the new-born its necessary care.

There is still another quite significant developmental trend which must be taken into account. This is the development of the child's image of his own sexual structure and the development of differential emotional attitudes on the part of the child toward the two sexes. The evolution of these attitudes depends directly on a process of dominant identification with the parent of the same sex. Early in life both boy and girl are dependent upon and identify with the mother. At about four or five years of age the boy displays a conspicuously strong and somewhat possessive emotional interest in his mother. Simultaneously, he is prone to regard the father somewhat in the light of a rival for his mother's love. Since his father has priority rights and is bigger and stronger than he, the boy may feel some fear of his father in connection with this rivalry. The girl attaches similarly to the father and considers the mother a rival. Gradually the child develops a dominant and lasting identification with the parent of the same sex. The boy becomes more of a companion to the father and thinks of growing up into a man like the father, and the girl thinks similarly in relation to the mother.

It is not within the province of this essay to discuss these important events in detail. Suffice it to say that the enlightened parent who clearly appreciates the nature of the two central processes of child development and can effectively regulate "family atmosphere" will avoid serious pitfalls.

In this paper certain problems relating to family unity have been delineated. It has been indicated that the family is a flexible unit which responds in both its structure and function to influences acting upon it from without and events affecting it from within. Certain types of external contingencies intensify the unity of the family; others weaken the family bond or render the family a more flexible, mobile unit. Similarly, intrafamilial phenomena, particularly the changing emotional relations between various members, may either strengthen or weaken family unity. The major factors involved in these dynamic effects on the family group have been discussed.

CHAPTER 19

Reciprocal Antagonism in Siblings

In view of the fact that the emotional influences of early family life are such potent determinants of character development, the question often arises as to why two brothers reared in an "identical" home environment should develop into utterly divergent personalities. Frequently, the one brother takes his place gracefully in society, and the other meets serious difficulties in adjustment at every turn in the road. "Both in life and in fiction it has appeared that children subject to the 'same' influences have turned out differently. The Artful Dodger and Oliver Twist both lived in the same household and under the tutelage of Fagin, but the one became a sneak-thief, while the other developed into a lovely character."[1]

The answer to this seeming paradox would appear to lie in the fact that it is an illusion to believe that the emotional influences in a particular family are ever identical for any two children.

First, it is probable that a mother never really assumes exactly similar emotional attitudes toward any two children in the family, even in the case of twins.[2] To discuss here the complex reasons for the development of distinctive maternal attitudes toward different children would take us too far afield. We may, however, point to the obvious fact that between two siblings there is usually a difference in years, in appearance, sometimes in sex, and most certainly in behavior. Furthermore, a mother's psychology is such that no two children can bear for her exactly the same emotional meaning, and consequently she always treats them differently.

Secondly, there is the important factor of emotional interplay between the children themselves: the influence of one upon the other. The rivalry aspect of this relationship, and the tendency for the siblings to assume either dominance or passivity make impossible an exact identity of human environment for any two children in a given family.

The development of widely different character traits in close siblings, which is a frequent observation, is in large part due to these factors. Such character contrasts, comprising a whole series of polarities of psychic expression, are clearly reflected in the respective attitudes of the children toward the family, toward society, toward the demands of reality, and finally, in the manner in which they strive to wrest satisfactions from the world, i.e., their respective aggressive patterns. In the development of such antitheses in the personalities of siblings, we must suspect not only some differences in experience, differences in interpretation of parental attitudes, but also some reciprocal reactions and adjustments to one another.

We may be able to discuss these determining factors more concretely if we briefly examine several clinical histories.

CASE I

Problem: Two brothers, Jerry, aged four years, and Richard, aged two years eight months, were referred to the Menninger Clinic for a consideration of their maladjusted behavior. The brothers were inseparable companions and the disturbed behavior in this instance could not alone be attributed to one of the siblings, but seemed clearly to involve both. At the time of their examination they were cared for in a day nursery and were very difficult to manage. The younger sibling, Richard, was accused of being excessively demanding, aggressive and provocative. The older brother, Jerry, was described as being unusually docile and tractable, although he occasionally had spells of extreme obstinacy or had shortlived outbursts of rage directed for the most part toward his brother.

History: The family lived on social relief. The father was chronically unemployed. The mother was young, naïve, well-meaning and affectionate. During the first two years of the older boy's life she gave him abundant motherly love and care, and during this period he was an active, aggressive child. At this time, when the older child was two years of age and the younger only eight months of age, the mother was forced to be absent from the home because of employment. She felt guilty over the consequent neglect of both children, but felt it most keenly toward the eight-month-old child. She therefore tended to favor the younger child, and trained the older boy to be with the younger one constantly and to protect and indulge him in every way.

Clinical Observations: On close study the two children presented a very striking picture of opposite behavior, and yet they were extraordinarily dependent upon one another. Richard, on the one hand, was exceedingly hyperactive, prancing about the room, darting his interest hither and thither and aggressively demanding attention from everyone. He intruded himself into every group in a provocative way. Moreover, not only did he steal whatever interest was directed toward his brother, but also he avidly tore out of his brother's hands whatever he momentarily wanted. In contrast to this, the older boy was quiet, subdued and compliant, without any show of defense or retaliation. He even submitted in a mechanical way to his brother's painful physical assaults. The younger brother roughly inserted his fingers into the elder's mouth, scratched his gums or poked a finger into his brother's eye. Although these attacks were obviously painful, the older brother merely averted his head in a kind of passive remonstrance, but showed no other reaction.

Interpretative Discussion: It must be quickly apparent that these brothers presented an exact antithesis in regard to their aggressive patterns. The younger demanded everything and expressed hostile feeling openly against the older brother. The latter in turn made no overt demands whatever, and even submitted mechanically to the brother's painful attacks. Paradoxically enough, the relationship between the brothers appeared to be a complementary, interdependent one, in which, however, the younger brother enjoyed by far the more advantageous position.

Now, we are interested in finding some explanation for the development of this antithesis in their aggressive patterns. Fortunately, for such exposition, the emotional relationships in this family were relatively simple. We have only to consider here the relationship of each child to the mother and the inter-child relationship, since the father in actuality spent very little time with the children. We naturally assume that both children, at least in their infancy, were wholly dependent upon their mother for nourishment in respect to both their love needs and physical wants. We know from the history that the older child was at first moderately aggressive in his demands upon the mother. We do not know exactly what was the course of events at the birth and during the first eight months of the second child's life. It is safe to assume that the mother necessarily had to divide her attention, but we do not know if, at that time, the older child manifested evidences of jealousy of the younger, with whom he was forced to compete for the mother's favor. We do know, however, that the mother's attitude toward both children changed when the older was two years and the younger eight months, by reason of her enforced neglect of them. From then on she distinctly favored the infant child and virtually forced the older boy to surrender most of the advantages of maternal indulgence to the younger child.

Under such circumstances what was the older child to do? What attitudes could he assume, on the one hand, toward his mother, and, on the other, toward his brother? Whatever his needs were at the time, he was wholly dependent upon his mother for their satisfaction. To sustain an attitude of aggressive demand toward the mother and openly vent his resentment and jealousy of the brother would defy the mother's bidding. It would invite an immediate threat of the loss of the mother's affection and perhaps provoke physical punishment as well. Naturally, he wished to avoid the fear and anxiety attendant upon such a threat. If, on the other hand, the older boy yielded his position of advantage to the younger child, submerged his jealousy and suppressed his aggressive striving toward the mother, he would at least insure the mother's approval and get some share of her bounty.

What, then, was the consequence? The younger boy, aggressive at first, became more aggressive; the older boy, once aggressive, now became mechanically submissive out of the sheer necessity of holding that share of maternal loving care which was still reserved for him. The attacks of the younger on the older brother and the occasional explosions of retaliative wrath on the part of the older brother gave eloquent proof of the existence of a sharp sibling rivalry, lurking behind the truce dictated by the mother's authority. It is perhaps desirable to stress again the fact that the mother's favor to the one child at the expense of the other was motivated by guilt, and that the inhibition of expression in the older boy's personality carried with it suppressed hostile feeling toward both the mother and the brother.

Comment: The reconstruction of the emotional currents in this sibling situation is partly hypothetical, to be sure. However, the facts in this brief history give support to such inferential conclusions as we have drawn in attempting a genetic explanation for the antithesis in aggressive patterns in these siblings. Indirect confirmation of our conclusions came later from the fact that when the two boys were separated and placed in independently controlled environments, giving each the emotional satisfactions he needed, the younger became less aggressive and provocative, and the older surrendered his attitude of marked passivity and began to assert himself in a more vigorous, wholesome way.

Having presented the phenomenon of antagonistic aggressive patterns in sibling rivals of infant age, we proceed now to a brief discussion of an adult neurosis, bearing in mind this same issue.

CASE II

Problem: The patient was a single man of thirty-five years who had suffered from a chronic neurosis for almost the duration of his life. The outstanding symptoms were an incapacitating social awkwardness, obsessive fears and ruminations, perverse sexual impulses, and somatic complaints. It is unnecessary to detail the many complicated vicissitudes which surrounded the development of this patient's neurosis. Suffice it to say that he was an extremely inhibited personality, so much so that his inhibitions crippled every effort at social adaptation. Although his dissatisfactions with his lot in life were many, he was unable to protest them effectively; in fact, he was unable vigorously to assert himself in any way. Instead he had evolved devices for expressing his aggressive tendencies in passive and highly disguised forms, intricately hidden in the most complicated compulsive ritualistic maneuvers. Most prominent among these passive aggressions had been his chronic failure in every undertaking, whether scholastic, occupational, social, or sexual. Particularly had he failed in each and every opportunity to hold a business position which would render him economically independent of his parents' help. This last was all the more significant, since his overstrong conscience drove him to make what appeared to be Herculean, but really totally ineffective, exertions in this direction. The harder he tried the worse he failed. In consequence, at thirty-five years he was still parasitically dependent on his parents, toward whom, nevertheless, he had all of his life harbored an infinitely bitter, but unspoken resentment, because of their harsh criticisms and insufficient show of love toward him.

The personalities of the patient and his brother, seven years his junior, presented an exact antithesis. In every important life issue, the behavior and attitudes of these brothers stood in marked contrast. The patient's brother was well adjusted and was always an aggressive personality. He severed the family ties early, married happily, and was successful in business. Here again was a striking divergence in the character development of siblings, most especially reflected in their respective aggressive patterns.

How shall we attempt to account for this psychogenetically? It will be necessary to delve briefly into the historical aspects of the family relationship.

History: The parents were derived from religiously bigoted, middle-class stock. Both the mother and father were neurotic and chronically exploited their pains, aches, and minor disabilities. The home atmosphere was continuously charged with hostile feeling: the mother, father, and the patient vied with one another in a three-cornered struggle for the privilege of commanding the major share of sympathy from one another. The self-love of the parents was so great that they showed little affection for one another or for the children. The little affection they did display was extended in greater measure to the younger brother.

In early childhood the patient was a bright, promising, moderately aggressive child. Between the ages of four and six the parents proudly showed the patient off in company, but criticized him harshly in private. At this time the patient began to show a marked change in his demeanor in the direction of timidity and exaggerated fearfulness. Moreover, the early indications of the patient's superior abilities began to lose prominence. With the birth of the brother, when the patient was seven years old, the parents were quick to show their disappointment in the early promise of the older child and now focused their affection mainly on the younger brother. It was then that definite conscious feelings of unfair discrimination arose in the patient, for which the ground had already been made fertile by the parents' primary narcissistic interest in the patient's achievements rather than in himself. As the brothers grew older, strong feelings of jealousy arose between them, heightened by the parents' unfavorable comparison of the patient's failures with the brother's successes.

The parents tolerated self-assertion in the brother, but sharply rebuffed similar inclinations in the patient. In the face of this discrimination the patient could not effectively rival the brother's aggressiveness. The parents made no attempt to hide their increasing irritation with the patient's failure. The patient, however, although inwardly agonized by his bitter antagonism toward the parents, completely withheld all expression of it, since he lived in mortal fear of its violence. Sometimes he phantasied choking his parents, but more often he envisaged his own violent injury or death at the hands of another person, whose anger he had aggressively provoked. The patient's feeling of guilt toward his parents was extreme, and he sought to excuse his chronic failures to them by perpetually wailing about his somatic disturbances. The parents, in turn, raised a storm of criticism against what they considered to be the patient's malingering. For him they assumed that work would cure all ills. The patient then launched a strenuous campaign to justify his illness, to prove his physical complaints were real, and that his distress made it impossible for him to work. All of his energy was focused toward this one goal. In every realm he was a helpless, parasitically dependent personality, unable to assert himself in any socially constructive way. We must again contrast this flagrant failure of a severely inhibited personality with the easy success of a more aggressive brother.

Conclusion: With so much of an orientation to the emotional configurations in this family we are able to appreciate the salient genetic dynamisms, which encouraged the emergence of antagonistic aggressive patterns in these sibling rivals, the one of whom became severely neurotic, and the other well adjusted.

Comment: The problem of the development of contrasting personalities in siblings is a complex one, and is not readily plumbed to its depths. There are deeper mechanisms involved which cannot be discussed here.[4] The clinical histories which we have described afford a par-

TABLE 1.

Passive (Inhibited) Sibling	*Active (Aggressive) Sibling*
Social Adjustment	Social Adjustment
Neurosis or Character Disorder	Social Adjustment
Social Adjustment	Neurosis or Character Disorder
Neurosis or Character Disorder	Neurosis or Character Disorder

tial insight into the etiological factors, but the genetic origin of some types of antagonistic patterns in siblings remains obscure.

In the emergence of antagonistic aggressive patterns in sibling rivals, the possible combinations from the standpoint of mental health may be represented as in Table 1.

In this paper, we have given a clinical illustration of antagonistic patterns in siblings of infant age, where both were maladjusted; one by virtue of an undue intensification of his aggressive drives, the other by virtue of his extreme inhibition. Among adult patients, too, one often sees sibling combinations in which one is an inhibited obsessional neurotic, and the other is an overly aggressive alcohol addict. In the second illustration, the inhibited sibling became the severe neurotic; the aggressive sibling became well adjusted. This particular configuration is perhaps the most commonly encountered. Limitations in space do not permit us to illustrate the syndrome in which the moderately inhibited sibling attains a fair adjustment, and the overly aggressive sibling develops an anti-social form of character disorder. Of such cases there are many. Finally, we may probably assume that the vast majority of sibling rivals whose personalities are divergent both make a satisfactory social adjustment.

BIBLIOGRAPHY

(1) Gillin, J. L.: *Criminology and Penology*. New York, The Century Co., 1926, p. 88.

(2) Menninger, W. C.: *The Etiology of Mental Disorders in Twins*.

(3) Humm, D. G.: Mental Disorders in Siblings. *Am. J. Psychiat*. 12:239-283, September 1932.

(4) Oberndorf, C. P.: Psychoanalysis of Siblings. *Am. J. Psychiat*. 8:1007-1020, May 1929.

(5) Levy, David: Hostility Patterns in Sibling Rivalry Experiments. *Am. J. Orthopsychiat*. 6:183-257, April 1936.

CHAPTER 20

Interpersonal Disturbances in the Family: Some Unresolved Problems in Psychotherapy

If the specific tools of psychotherapy are to be extended reliably beyond the disturbed patient into various group interactions, then the logical beginning is within the smallest social unit, the family. In this paper, I am concerned with the question: Is there a possible psychotherapeutic approach to the family as a family? At present, approaches to emotional disturbances of family life are made through the concomitant psychotherapy of several family members, sometimes with an attempt to integrate the several therapies in the interest of the mental health of the family as a whole. Certainly, concomitant psychotherapy of several family members—husband and wife, mother and child, for example—often results in some degree of improvement of family relationships, but such therapy is still one of individuals and not of family relationships or of the group. The effects of such psychotherapy on the family as a unit are in the main indirect rather than direct, nonspecific rather than specific. Even if every member of a family were given individual psychotherapy, this still would not constitute a psychotherapy of the family. Thus a systematic psychotherapeutic method for the family has yet to be evolved.

The historic province of the psychiatrist has been the individual personality and not the family. Problems of the family have traditionally been the province of the social worker and occasionally of the minister or the teacher. In recent years, the social scientist has become increasingly interested in the family as a subject for intensive investigation, but most of these studies have only broad ameliorative goals and no specific planned intervention for stated disturbances within the family. In psychiatrically oriented family agencies and child guidance clinics, one finds a broader concern with the family as a whole; but in the usual psychiatric clinic, the psychiatrist's interest tends to center on the most disturbed member of the group. Only to

Reprinted with permission from *Psychiatry: Journal for the Study of Interpersonal Processes*, November 1954, Vol. 17, No. 4, 359-368.

a limited degree is his effort ordinarily extended to encompass the problems of the family.

HISTORIC TRENDS IN THE HANDLING OF FAMILY PROBLEMS

Some brief mention of the broad historical trends in the philosophy of therapy for disturbances in family relationships may serve to make more explicit the inherent problems. Over the years there has been an ebb and flow of a variety of therapeutic styles. This is to be expected, for such changing patterns of practice are a necessary expression of the natural evolution which accompanies the acquisition of new knowledge, and are also an inevitable effect of social and cultural change. But one may question the appropriateness of seizing upon new and untried methods, while casting overboard what has been laboriously learned in the past, or the wisdom of conforming slavishly and uncritically to prevailing psychotherapeutic styles. In some measure, such tendencies have hampered progress in the field.

In discussing the changes in philosophy of therapy of family relationships, I am not attempting to present a balanced historical account, but only a trace certain trends which I have observed. A quarter of a century ago, the effort to correct disturbances in family relationships took mainly the form of social therapy rather than psychotherapy, and "therapists" attempted to meet disturbances in family relationships with social devices aimed at reorientation of attitudes and activities. Social agencies in the community emphasized a variety of social techniques for therapeutic intervention in the family, such as religious, social, and occupational guidance. In this form of help, mainly the conscious aspect of emotional experience was taken into account. Partly as a result of this, the eventual disillusionment as to the efficacy of these social techniques was abrupt and complete. Then came a new wave of tremendous emphasis on individual personality. Social agencies absorbed the philosophy of mental hygiene and entered a mad dash for an orientation to psychiatry and psychoanalysis.[1]

With the increasing emphasis on the emotional problems of the individual and on unconscious motivation, the study and treatment of the family environment became less popular. In some professional circles, the social approach to disturbances in family relations was brushed aside as "superficial"—which was, on the crest of this wave, the most damning indictment which could be made of a given therapeutic technique. Psychiatric casework came into being as a specialty with superior prestige value, and professional status and recognition came only to the social worker who achieved repute as a skilled casework therapist, relationship therapist, or psychotherapist. The influence of social and economic factors on the mental health of families was minimized, and the traditional social agency function of mitigating the real threats to family welfare by such means as providing relief and employment services became regarded as routine, mechanical, and beneath the professional dignity of trained social workers. Home visits as a systematic social work technique for the study of family problems all but disappeared. Thus the external and the conscious conflicts were put to one side; the realistic situation of the family was minimized; concern with the tensions of interpersonal relations was subordinated to the primary concern with the individual psyche—with unconscious conflicts and irrational motivation; and families as families became virtually lost as objects of study.

During this phase, without doubt, a great deal was learned about people, but not without some cost. The understanding of the individual advanced somewhat out of context, in terms of the need for a parallel knowledge of the processes of social interaction. Social workers and psychiatrists seemed often to lose contact with social reality; they lacked clarity in distinguishing the real and unreal. They misapplied or used all too loosely such concepts as transference and resistance. There was a rushing concentration on the emotional life of the individual, to the extent that the social frame, within which the individual's reactions were to be judged, was lost sight of.

For the moment I am purposely overdrawing one side of the argument to make a point. Momentous advances have been made in the understanding of individual personality, but it should be obvious that the law of diminishing

[1]For a fuller consideration of this problem see Albert Deutsch, *The Mentally Ill in America;* Garden City, N. Y., Country Life Press, 1927; pp. 318-323.

returns is now beginning to make itself felt. It appears that further significant additions to the knowledge of personality may be made if we now broaden our conceptual frame so as to examine the behavior of the individual, not in isolation, but rather in the context of comprehensive evaluation of the group structure of the family. Recently a wave of fashion has, in fact, asserted itself which once again emphasizes the relations of individual personality with family and wider society.

If we aspire to the goal of reducing to scientific terms the therapeutic approach to disturbances in family relations, it is necessary to adopt a critical, discriminating attitude toward changing psychotherapeutic fashions, to avoid stereotyping treatment methods, and to carefully test out what is specific and nonspecific, central or peripheral in these procedures. Equally essential is the building of a conceptual frame for a proper integration of techniques of social therapy and psychotherapy.

EXPERIENCE WITH FAMILY PAIRS

In attempting to devise a psychotherapy of the family, it is important to look first at the present experience with the concomitant psychotherapy of several family members, usually family pairs. As I have already said, certainly the concomitant therapy of several individual members of a family often results in some degree of improvement of family relationships; but I believe that this is usually true to the extent that the therapists concerned take into consideration the disturbances of family relationships and integrate the several therapies. It is some of the unsolved problems of individual therapy for several family members which underline the need for a psychotherapeutic approach to the family as a whole.

Although psychiatrists have traditionally concerned themselves with the problems of the individual, they have long recognized that there is usually a second person in the family involved in the patient's pathology. Among psychiatrists, it is a truism that the person who accompanies a patient on his first visit to the psychiatrist's office is significantly involved in the patient's illness. A mother who accompanies a child, a husband who accompanies a wife, are obvious examples of this. Over and over again one finds such pairs of persons bound in neurotic love and neurotic competition. Pathological trends can be discerned in the interpersonal situation as well as in the individual personality make-up of each member of such a pair.[2] It is hopefully assumed that the therapeutic resolution of neurotic anxiety in one or both partners will mitigate the interpersonal disturbance. Sometimes it does; sometimes it does not; sometimes it succeeds in part only. Some of the reasons for this are clear. Neurotic anxiety, while a significant factor, is but one among many that determine the fate of a relationship. Other factors are the contingencies of external social influence, the compatibility of temperament, goals, interests, and values, the lines of identification between the two people, the reciprocity of emotional need, the quality of communication, and so on.

Furthermore, in the psychotherapeutic approach to neurotic anxiety, some therapists place the major focus on the internal economy of individual personality rather than on social relationships. While relationship experience is relived in psychotherapy, the primary point of reference tends to be the orientation to self rather than the social interaction per se. It is of course true that a person's orientation to self influences his orientation to others, and vice versa, but this is by no means a simple one-to-one correlation. The interplay of individual and group levels of experience is a complex phenomenon, the full scope of which cannot yet be clearly conceptualized. The extent to which a disturbance in a family relationship is alleviated by individual psychotherapy of one or both partners depends upon many factors: the nature of the pathology of this relationship; the secondary effects of ancillary relationships; the psychosocial condition of the family as a whole; the individual's adaptation to this; and finally the nature of the pathology and psychotherapy of each partner in the relationship, and the extent to which the therapy of one partner is effectively coordinated with the therapy of the other.

The factors which determine disturbances in family relations certainly do not derive alone from the unconscious. Of specific relevance are

[2]See N. W. Ackerman, "The Diagnosis of Neurotic Marital Interaction," *Social Case Work* (1954) 35:139-147.

the discrepancies between real and unreal attitudes, between real and unreal experience, between conscious and unconscious conflict, between the inner emotional orientation to self and the external orientation to other persons, between idealized goals and actual achievement. Success in psychotherapy for family relationships rests on the therapist's ability to place unconscious phenomena in correct context with regard to conscious experience and the prevailing interpersonal realities. In any case, whatever the vicissitudes of therapy of a neurotically involved family pair, this is not to be conceived as a therapy of the family per se.

THE FAILURE OF INDIVIDUAL THERAPY TO IMPROVE SOCIAL RELATIONSHIPS

The social product of some forms of psychoanalytic therapy reflects certain limitations of individual therapy. Paradoxically, the patient as an individual may markedly improve, and yet in some respects his social relations may remain almost as bad as they ever were. Facetiously speaking, everything in the patient is cured except his human relations. Or, in the phrase of one analyst, "On completion of analysis, the patient is wiser, but sadder and lonelier."

It is by no means rare in the treatment of a family pair that as one member of the pair gets better, the other gets worse. In child guidance work, as the child improves, not infrequently the mother paradoxically worsens. Or, as the child responds to psychotherapy, the parental conflict becomes drastically intensified. Similarly, in the treatment of marital problems, it is often the case that as one marital partner matures and becomes sexually more adequate, the other regresses; or one may respond to analytic therapy with an increased capacity for closeness, and the other may react with depression. This is impressively illustrated in those marital situations in which one partner markedly improves with therapy, but this very fact paradoxically hastens the relationship toward divorce. Apparently, in some circumstances, the increased strength or health of personality of one family member becomes a threat to another.

For example, a wife campaigns for her husband to enter psychotherapy for sexual impotence, threatening to leave him unless he is cured. The husband yields, is treated, and the symptom of impotence is quickly alleviated. The husband's therapist, pleased with his success, is shocked to discover that directly after the husband's potency was restored, his wife deserted him. This is paradoxical behavior, to be sure, but it can and does occur. Individual psychotherapy may help the individual, but under certain conditions it may fail to ameliorate the pathology of a family relationship. The tension of interpersonal conflict may remain largely unabated even though intrapsychic disturbance is measurably relieved. Somewhat in the same vein, I might quote the caustic comment of an unanalyzed wife of an analyst, who felt alienated from her husband's special sphere of interest. She quipped, "What we wives of analysts need is to form a union."

From such considerations as these, it does appear that our capacity for promoting mental health in social relationships lags behind our techniques for promoting health in the inner psychic life of the individual. One could multiply many times these examples of a dramatic, occasionally perverse shift in the delicate balance of interpersonal relations within the family, induced by therapeutic change in the behavior of a single member. The emotional equilibrium of a family group may be seriously upset by poor timing of therapeutic intervention in two directions: by precipitously plunging several family members into psychotherapy at the same time; or by delaying too long in arranging for the psychotherapy of additional family members. In some instances where the family balance was quite tender, I have advised that only one member of the family at a time enter therapy, for if the involvement of members in psychotherapy is strategically staggered over a period of time, the danger of any critical upheaval of family life is somewhat mitigated. With precise knowledge of the existing tensions in family relationships and with appropriate timing, it is possible to facilitate therapy of individual members and also favorably influence the mental health of the family as a group; at the very least it is possible to avoid disorganization of the family equilibrium.

THE INTEGRATION OF CONCOMITANT THERAPIES OF FAMILY MEMBERS

When each member of a neurotic family pair needs psychotherapy, the question arises as to whether they should be treated by the same or separate therapist. Naturally, the most efficient form of integration of the psychotherapies is that which can be achieved in the mind of a single therapist. Strong objections have been offered to such practice, however. The premise seems to be that two members of a family, interdependent but mutually distrustful and competitively destructive, would vie with each other for the therapist's favor, and that this rivalry would jeopardize therapeutic control. Therefore, the argument goes, provision for separate treatment is preferable. I think, however, that this argument overlooks the difficulty of integrating the two therapies, and the further problems which arise out of the failure to relate the psychotherapy of the neurotic pair to the total dynamics of family life. In providing for separate treatment, there should be no self-deception on the part of the therapist that the patients' suspiciousness will be disarmed by the mere fact of having separate therapists; nor should there be any self-deception that the tensions in the family relationships will take care of themselves. Definitive indications and contraindications for the treatment of a family pair by the same or separate therapists are badly needed.

When two members of a family pair are in conflict but are essentially loyal and genuinely motivated to improve the relationship, one would be wise to respect the substantial advantages of a single therapist for both persons. If basically each trusts the other, each one will in time build sufficient trust in the therapist and not be critically apprehensive of the misuse of his contacts with the other member of the pair.

It is true, on the other hand, that when two members of a family are locked in pathological conflict, with a deep layer of mutual mistrust and a strong propensity for destructive motivation, treatment by separate therapists may be preferable. I do believe, however, that such a plan is often initiated prematurely, without adequate clarification of the interpersonal level of disturbance, without sufficient emotional preparation of each partner, and without laying a foundation for effective collaboration between the two therapists at later stages. It has the effect, sometimes, of drawing the two family members apart rather than bringing them into closer relationship. Too often a pair of parents or a child and mother are plunged immediately into individual psychotherapy, before they have any chance to gain some understanding of the relationship conflict. In such cases it is useful for a single therapist to have a short series of interviews with both patients before dividing the therapy. This offers the advantage, for patients and therapist alike, of beginning the therapy by obtaining a more accurate understanding of the meaning of the relationship conflict; clearing away misconceptions and unnecessary distortions; and getting a sharper definition of the dynamic relatedness of intrapersonality pathology to the disturbance in the relationship. I believe this often enables the separate psychotherapy of each partner to get started on the right foot, and it certainly provides a better basis for later collaboration between the two therapists — provided that their selection has been based in part on their ability to collaborate. It is then a question of careful judgment and timing as to when the members of such a family pair are emotionally ready for separate psychotherapy.

But as the principle of separate treatment is usually applied at present, it is most difficult to pursue the goal of integrating the two therapies. Occasionally such collaborative effort is successfully carried out. Frequently, in my experience, it fails. Theoretically, in a great many child and family guidance centers the integration of the effects of concomitant psychotherapy of several members of a family is supposed to be achieved through the application of the principle of the professional team. Such teams are usually drawn from the professions of psychiatry, social work, and psychology. The several therapists treating members of a single family are supposed to work within the framework of the team, collaborating with the other members. In some instances, unfortunately, allegiance to this principle turns out to be lip service, rather than effective integration.

In private psychiatric practice, effective collaboration between psychiatrists treating different members of the same family is also rare. It is interesting to observe the varying attitudes taken toward collaboration in such a situation. For instance, one of the psychiatrists may profess to the other a seemingly earnest desire for collaboration but fail to carry it out. Or he may curiously shy away from the whole question of collaboration. Some psychiatrists go so far as to openly declare that collaboration is intrinsically undesirable, that it jeopardizes the exclusiveness of their relationship with the patient, that it endangers the patient's privacy—all in all, that it menaces the psychiatrist's therapeutic control. Some psychoanalysts try to avoid involvement with other family members by refusing to interview them; while certainly they cannot avoid the impact of problems in family relationships, they tend to deal with these conflicted relationships *in absentia*. Thus, rightly or wrongly, the focus of the psychotherapy of each family member becomes sharply individual. The two therapeutic experiences tend to get dissociated, as each individual therapy goes its merry way. In such a setting the intrapsychic conflicts of each person may be ameliorated, but successful readaptation to the family relationships may nonetheless fail.

A specific difficulty which arises when two members of a family are in psychotherapy with separate therapists is that of dealing effectively with events which reflect a coincidence between reality and irrational projection. It is exactly in such situations that therapists differ in their evaluations and psychotherapeutic prescriptions. A few examples may illustrate this point:

When a child in therapy denies having emotional problems and insists, "It is my parents who are upset, not me," the child may be resisting therapy, to be sure; but the implied demand. *Do something about my parents*, is certainly not without justification.

The only son of a self-centered but highly successful attorney is in therapy because he is emotionally isolated and withdrawn, and repeatedly fails in his academic work even though he has a superior intelligence. He is weak and unassertive, but passively resists his father's ambitions for him. He does not feel like a person in his own right, but rather like a piece of his father. He accuses his father of pursuing him constantly, and expresses the conviction that his father needs the psychiatrist more than he. He is partly right.

The mother of a disturbed child projects blame upon the father; the father turns it back on the mother. In effect, the mother says to her psychiatrist, *Why blame everything on me? My husband should be your patient*—an attitude which may be promptly chalked down by the psychiatrist as the mother's projection of guilt. So it is, but more often than not such an accusation carries with it an important core of truth as well.

A rather masculine woman, with a social work professional background, is married to a weak man, whom she belittles because he has "hips like a woman and suffers hysterical fits." They have an emotionally disturbed child. The woman denies personal problems, placing the main responsibility for the child's difficulty on the father's neurotic fears. She offers to collaborate with the therapist in treating her husband. This woman resists therapy for herself, to be sure, but there is a basis in fact for her insistence that her husband should receive therapy.

Should the other person concerned in each of these situations enter therapy with a different therapist, the areas of reality and the areas of irrational projection might continue to be obscure, for the two therapists might differ in their evaluations of the situation and in their prescriptions. The therapy of each patient might proceed without an opportunity for reality testing. Bela Mittelmann[3] has drawn attention to this problem in an article on the simultaneous psychoanalytic therapy of husband and wife. In the procedure he describes, husband and wife were treated by the same psychoanalyst, thus violating the traditional psychoanalytic fashion of husband and wife being treated by different analysts. Mittelmann points out the advantageous position of a single therapist for both marital partners in being able to discern accurately the irrational projections of each partner onto the other, and thus achieving a clear definition of the reality of the marital relationship. Using in each patient's therapy information derived from the therapy of the other can, of course, be done only with the full knowledge and consent of both. This is a therapeutic plan in which collaboration is truly achieved in the mind of a single therapist. Mittelmann considers the specific gain in this arrangement to be the heightened opportunity for reality testing which can be used to effective advantage in the therapy of both partners. My own clinical experiences tend to confirm this point of view, as I shall try to illustrate by the following case:

A woman teacher, who was married to a gifted musician, was acutely depressed. They had one child who was suffering badly from the mother's disturbed mental state. In interview, the wife laid the blame

[3]Bela Mittelmann, "The Concurrent Analysis of Married Couples," *Psychoanalytic Quart*. (1948) 17:182-197.

for her depression at her husband's door. She complained bitterly that her husband, who had earlier been highly successful as a musician, now failed to earn an adequate living; she said that he didn't try hard enough, that he ought to pocket his artistic vanity and go out and get any work he could, no matter what, and that he owed this to his wife and child. In discussing her husband, she sounded vindictive almost to the point of violence. She confessed to refusing her husband sex satisfaction, and had calamitous fears of the imminent break-up of her marriage. When asked if she had directly expressed these feelings to her husband, she demurred, saying "No, it would hurt him too deeply, irrevocably." I suggested that we have a three-cornered interview, consisting of this woman, her husband, and myself, the psychiatrist. She resisted at first, fearing that this might precipitate the destruction of her marriage. It did nothing of the kind; on the contrary, it cleared the air of unreal accusations and distorted projections and, if anything, saved the marriage. The actual reality of the situation was that her husband was earnestly trying to get suitable employment; that his temporary failure was no doing of his own, but was the result of a critical turn in the economy of the music industry; and that he was deeply distressed by his wife's rejection of sex relations, but did not wish to force himself upon her. In this triangular discussion, the wife was stripped of the alibi for her depression. She was attaching her hostility and guilt to the wrong person and for the wrong reasons, since the real object of her hate was her mother. She could no longer falsely project on her husband the reason for her bitterness, and she recognized her irrational urge to exploit her husband's unfortunate professional situation for the purpose of humiliating him as a man and making him crawl before her eyes. She then admitted that her real fear was loss of sexual pleasure with the approaching menopause—a fear which had been profoundly strengthened in her by an earlier traumatic family experience in which her mother had been chiefly concerned. Further therapeutic contacts both with the wife alone and with the wife and her husband together relieved the depression and the marital crisis.

CHILD GUIDANCE AND TREATMENT OF PARENTS IN TERMS OF FAMILY ROLE

In child guidance practice, the problems of treating the parents of disturbed children have not been solved. There have been many failures. We have not yet succeeded in formulating adequate criteria for the psychotherapy of parental role. In examining the causes of failure of treatment of mothers of disturbed children, several factors loom large: the complexity of the definition of mothering; the difficulty of relating the dynamics of individual personality to the mothering role; incomplete or incorrect diagnosis; vague and changing orientation to goals with resulting confusion of the therapeutic course; failure to properly integrate the treatment of child and mother; failure to understand the parental conflict and the fundamental interdependence of maternal and paternal functioning; and finally, the failure to relate the therapy of child and mother to a total psychosocial evaluation of the family as a unit.

This raises some pertinent questions: To what degree is the therapeutic goal for mothers related to maternal role and to what degree related to the mother's total personality? To what extent is the maternal role influenced by the paternal role and by the other significant relationships in the family? Should treatment of the mother in the child guidance program always be secondary to the primary goal of treatment of the child? Or should the therapy of the mother as a person be pursued beyond the point required by the needs of the child? By what criteria do we decide on a partial goal, such as achieving merely a reduction of emotional pressures and anxieties, a modification of conscious maternal attitudes, or a redirection of hostility away from the child? In contrast to this, under what conditions should we undertake the goal of basic character change in the mother?

My own observations of separate psychotherapy of child and mother[4] indicate that the extent to which the psychotherapies of child and mother are coordinated varies tremendously, and that the degree to which the therapy of the mother is child-oriented varies correspondingly. From one child-parent unit to the next, there is little consistency. Some mothers talk, in their psychotherapeutic sessions, of their child and their child only. They seem obsessed with worry over the child and with the need to control and punish the child. Accordingly, they are motivated to exploit the social worker or therapist as the agent of their punitive attitude. They use

[4]My remarks here are based to a large extent on a review which I have made of the results of the program of separate psychotherapy at the Child Guidance Institute of the Jewish Board of Guardians, as well as some of the recommendations I have made regarding this program.

their preoccupation with control of the child's behavior as a resistance to a real understanding of their maternal role and as an escape from confrontation with their personal responsibility for the child's disorder.

At the opposite pole there is a group of mothers who begin their psychotherapeutic experience with a concern with the child, but soon seem to forget the child altogether and become exclusively preoccupied with themselves. They exploit their therapeutic interviews for dealing with a variety of other personal problems, such as their marital difficulties and their own conflicts with their parents, but neglect the issues of their relatedness to the child. The child's behavior difficulties are dropped wholly in the lap of the child's therapist, with an attitude of *let the therapist worry*. Between these two extremes, there is every intermediate shade of maternal behavior. Both types of maternal attitude represent resistance to the therapy of disturbance in the maternal role. In the first instance, the mother looks accusingly at the child, but refuses to look at herself; in the second, she looks at herself but refuses to look at her child. In either case, in this program for separate treatment, effective access to the disturbance moving between child and mother is rendered more difficult. In all probability, these polar forms of resistance in mothers of disturbed children are influenced in part by the differences in orientation of different psychotherapists.

In such programs for separate treatment, the therapeutic orientation seems to move all too quickly to an exclusive preoccupation with the child as an individual and with the mother as an individual. It moves too quickly away from the level of real relationship experience to the level of unreal emotional experience and irrational unconscious conflicts. There is a conspicuous trend toward by-passing interpersonal levels of disturbance and plunging immediately into the intrapsychic conflicts of the individual patient. To be sure, the merits of separate treatment on a carefully selected individual case basis are well established. But I fail to see the logic of routine provisions for separate treatment in every family pair, nor can I make sense of the trend toward a quick by-passing of the interpersonal level of pathology in favor of too sharp and too early emphasis on structured intrapsychic conflict patterns. Therefore I think that more considered selection of cases for separate treatment, and also more careful timing of the arrangements for such therapy are needed. Certainly in some instances it is logical for a single therapist to treat both child and mother—that in fact it may be the treatment of choice—whereas in other instances the barrier of suspicion and mistrust between the respective members of the family pair may make provision for separate treatment a necessity. In some families it is appropriate for a single therapist to interview the family pair together in the beginning, to orient his early therapeutic efforts to an understanding of the interpersonal conflict and to help each member of the pair to see more clearly the coexistence of reality and projection, and then move gradually to a plan for separate treatment.

From all this, it is apparent that an appropriate frame of reference has not yet been designed, within which it is possible to integrate the therapy of an individual with the therapy of a family group. The treatment of a mother of a disturbed child is the treatment of a role, a highly specialized family function. It is not identical with the therapy of a whole woman, but rather of the personality of that woman integrated into a special social function, that of mothering. For a proper conceptual approach to this problem, it is necessary to recognize the interdependence and reciprocity of family roles, to devise criteria for accurate appraisal of the mental health functioning of family groups and dynamic formulae for interrelating individual personality and family role.

What is the challenge in terms of a therapy for the family as a group? What frame of reference must one design for such an effort? The family may be defined in diverse ways. Waller[5] describes it as a unity of interacting personalities, each with a history. This definition fails to convey the unique features of the family group: the union of male and female to produce offspring, and insure their survival. George Murdock[6] defines the family as follows: "The family is a social group characterized by common residence, economic cooperation and reproduction. It includes adults of both sexes, at least two

[5]Willard Waller and Reuben Hill, *The Family: A Dynamic Interpretation;* New York, Dryden Press, 1951; p. 6.

[6]George P. Murdock, *Social Structure;* New York, Macmillan, 1949, p. 1.

of whom maintain a socially approved sexual relationship, and one or more children, own or adopted, of the sexually cohabiting adults. The vital functions of the family are sexual, economic, reproductive and educational."

The disturbances of family life are obviously disturbances both of the individual and the group. They must therefore be studied and treated at levels which interrelate the intra- and interpersonal processes, and the processes of the group as a whole. Logically viewed, a systematic therapy of the family would encompass techniques directed at the multiple interacting relationships, both within the family, and between family and outside community, and also techniques for psychotherapy of individual family members. Within this frame of reference, the therapeutic approach to the family group per se would be primary and the psychotherapy of the individual members secondary. In other words, the relation of individual psychotherapy to the therapy of the family would be the relation of the part to the whole. It is self-evident, however, that before we could make any substantial progress toward devising a therapy of the family, we would need to evolve definitive criteria for the psychosocial disorders of family life. We would need more exact understanding as to how the emotional forces moving between persons influence the psychic balance within the individual, and vice versa—in other words, a scientific definition of the dynamic interplay between intra- and extrapersonality factors. As we aspire to specificity in family therapy, we would hope, if possible, to reduce the definition of disturbance to a single formulation of the interaction patterns of the family, which encompasses within it the dynamics of intrapersonality processes. To achieve such formulation, it seems necessary to view the functioning of individual personality in the context of the dynamics of family role.[7]

The phenomena of family life are revealed at three interrelated levels: (1) the multiple interaction patterns between family members, beginning with the central relationship of man and wife; (2) the personal development of each family member; and (3) the interaction of the family unit with the outside community. And along with, and as a part of these three levels, one may view the dynamics of family life from the viewpoint of the emotional integration into the family group of each individual member, and the specific dynamic relations of individual personality structure to family role.

An effective therapeutic approach to interpersonal disturbances of the family may be achieved through a series of logical steps as follows: (1) a psychosocial evaluation of the family group as a whole; (2) the application of appropriate techniques of social therapy; (3) a psychotherapeutic approach to significant family relationships; (4) individual psychotherapy for selected family members, oriented initially to the specific dynamic relations of family role to personality structure.

The psychosocial pattern of a given family is determined by the dynamic balance between intra- and extrafamilial processes. Tension and conflict within the family affect the external adaptation of the family to community; similarly, stress in the relations of family with community find an echo in the internal emotional processes of the family. The psychotherapeutic approach to significant family relationships and the individual psychotherapy of selected family members should be viewed in the context of the total psychosocial diagnosis of the family. This diagnostic evaluation should be made both in terms of current functioning of the family and its historical development. The therapy of interpersonal disturbances in the family is enhanced if we view the disturbed person both as an individual and as a member of an integrated family group.[8]

It is the assumption of this paper that the ultimate goals of psychiatry are the alleviation of problems in the social community. While at present the psychiatrist has no systematic tools for either the family group or the social community, it is my belief that the psychiatrist can take the first step towards the over-all goal by

[7]See N. W. Ackerman, " 'Social Role' and Total Personality," *Amer. J. Orthopsychiatry* (1951) 21:1-17.

[8]A study of family diagnosis is in process which attempts to correlate the emerging emotional disturbance of the young child with the total psychosocial structure of the family group. See the following: N. W. Ackerman and R. Sobel, "Family Diagnosis," *Amer. J. Orthopsychiatry* (1950) 20:744-752. Ackerman, "A Study of Family Diagnosis," *Amer. J. Orthopsychiatry*. Ackerman, "Child and Family Pathology: Problems of Correlation"; in *The Psycho-Pathology of Childhood* (Proc. Annual Meeting Amer. Psycho-Pathological Assn., 1954).

focusing more specifically on the mental health problems of the family, in addition to treating individual patients. The study of disturbed patients, with its emphasis on the emotional problems of the individual and on the unconscious, has yielded rich results in the last quarter of a century. But this emphasis on the individual has, to some extent, blinded psychiatry and related disciplines to the processes of social interaction. It is to this latter area, somewhat neglected by the psychiatrist, that this paper has been addressed.

CHAPTER 21

Interlocking Pathology in Family Relationships

The mental suffering and incapacitation of the individual patient, rather than the family, has usually been the main sphere of interest for the psychiatrist. Yet, the interdependence and reciprocal effects of disordered behavior among the various members of the family unit are an inescapable fact which the psychiatrist cannot ignore.

In the behavioral sciences today there are unmistakable signs of an expanding interest in the investigation of this problem. Recent developments reflect this trend: Henry Richardson's book, *Patients Have Families;* the Wellesley Mental Health Services organized by Erich Lindemann; the project on the reaction of families to crisis at the Family Guidance Center in Boston, directed by Gerald Caplan; the GAP report, *Integration and Conflict in the Family,* formulated by Florence Kluckholn and John Spiegel; *Family-oriented Diagnosis and Treatment,* by Community Research Association, Inc.; a variety of studies of the relations of delinquent behavior with family structure; Lippman's presidential address before the American Orthopsychiatric Association in 1954 pointing to the necessity of systematic investigation of the phenomena of family breakdown; and finally, my own studies of *Family Diagnosis*.

The objectives of this paper are: (1) To consider those clinical and dynamic principles which are pertinent to the study of reciprocal and interlocking patterns of pathology in family relationships. (2) To suggest some clinical procedures which are useful in evaluating these phenomena. (3) To illustrate through case studies the application of these procedures in investigating interlocking pathology in family relationships. (4) To outline tentatively a conceptual frame for correlating individual and family pathology.

CLINICAL OBSERVATIONS AND DYNAMIC PRINCIPLES

Personality is born and bred in the social matrix of the family; only in this experiential frame can the individual mature and achieve stability. The biologic and social determinants of behavior are viewed as phases of a single dynamic process,

Reprinted with permission from *Changing Concepts of Psychoanalytic Medicine*, S. Redo and G. Daniels (Eds.), 1956, 135-150.

rather than as a dichotomy. The functions of personality are oriented both toward the internal processes of the organism and toward its environment. The perceptions of inner experience mold the perceptions of interaction with the outer environment and vice versa. Personality ought not, therefore, be conceived as a self-contained, autonomous unit nor be evaluated in isolation from the group into which its functions are integrated.

The family is the primary unit of society; its functions are sexual, reproductive, social, economic and educational. The psychological life of the family is a problem in equilibrium. The stability of the family and that of its members hinges on a delicate pattern of emotional interchange. The behavior of each member is affected by every other. A shift in the emotional interaction of one pair of persons in a given family alters the interaction processes of other family pairs. In triangular relationships, one member may serve to bind or disrupt the unity of the other two. Emotional illness may integrate or disintegrate a family relationship. The emotional illness of one member may complement that of another, or may have effects which are antagonistic. Some forms of emotional illness may be shared by two or more members of a family. A crisis in the life of the family may exert pervasive and far-reaching effects on the mental health of the family and its individual members.

It is therefore necessary to view the interplay of individual behavior and family relationships in three dimensions: (1) The group dynamics of the family, (2) the dynamic processes of emotional integration of an individual member into the family group and (3) the internal organization of individual personality, and its genetic development.

In each dimension, the current determinants of behavior must be related to past determinants.

As a bridge between the internal processes of personality and those of family participation, it is useful to employ the concept of family role, that is, those dynamic processes by which the dispositions of a given personality integrate themselves into particular family roles, child, father, mother, husband or wife. Family roles are essentially interdependent and reciprocal. Behavior in a given family role is the product of the tendencies of the individual in a specific family position, influenced by the needs and behavior of the individual occupying the reciprocal family position. Each family member is required to integrate himself into multiple family roles and also into extrafamilial roles. We must, therefore, be concerned with several questions: the relative success or failure of the individual's integration into the required family roles, how each member of a family reciprocally affects every other, how one family pair overlaps with and influences another, the degree to which effective adaptation in one family role supports effective adaptation in another, or impairs it. These are the vicissitudes which produce varying degrees of stress and anxiety and dictate success or failure in adaptation to family life.

It is observed clinically that the same individual may adapt more effectively in one role than another. The requirements of a particular interpersonal situation may bring different components of personality into effective action. In one role, the deepest weakness of the personality may be evoked with serious consequences; in another role, the exposure of this weakness may be minimal. In different roles, the solutions to conflict, the anxiety experienced, the configurations of defense employed and the assertions of special reality skills will be significantly different.

Of special importance is the relative congruity or incongruity for the same individual of different familial and extrafamilial roles. Certain roles fit; others clash. In effect, successful adaptation in one role may favor adaptation in another; or the reverse, adaptation in one role may conflict or interfere with adaptation in another. The vicissitudes of the fit or lack of fit of multiple roles determine the quantity of stress in adaptation. This depends partly on the character of the individual, partly on the requirements of the interpersonal situation and the way the group structures the role.

In many senses then, the operations of personality are dependent on the social situation. When the interpersonal environment is radically altered, the adaptive responses of the individual must also change. With radical changes in the interpersonal environment, the character of the individual must ultimately change, too.

The interrelation of mental health in the individual and mental health in family relationships is a problem which becomes magnified in the highly fluid society in which we now live. The symbols of authority are shifting, unstable and difficult to predict. The individual's relations to these symbols are ill defined. It is, therefore, more difficult for the individual to clearly perceive his position in the group. Family patterns are in a state of flux. The role of male authority in the family, the status of the female, the division of labor, the relations between the sexes and patterns of childrearing are all in a state of change. Such instability favors certain defense reactions to conflict and anxiety—the tendency to externalize conflict, to "act out," to project, to substitute aggression for anxiety, to actively reshape elements of reality through magic phantasy and to retreat behind a wall of isolation. These trends have particular relevance for current problems of stress in family relationships.

The family is a central point of reference for the psychoanalytic theory of personality. The experiences of family life are conceived as shaping the development of personality and it is these very family relationships which, as transference phenomena, occupy the center of the stage in analytic therapy. Yet in psychoanalysis, systematic study of family interaction has suffered neglect. The attitude of some classical analysts has been, in effect, that the patient's phantasies and dreams are the royal road to the unconscious and that it is relatively unessential to know the realities of the social environment. In fact, in its most extreme form, this is something to the effect: that if a psychoanalyst interests himself in the social realities which surround his patient, he will "spoil his ear for the unconscious." To the contrary, I believe that a valid understanding of the unconscious is possible only when one interprets unconscious dynamics in the context of total personality organization and a clear definition of the prevailing interpersonal realities.

The usual approach of the psychoanalysts to the phenomena of family life has been indirect, rather than direct. It is still common practice for analysts to refuse to interview other family members on the premise that this would interfere with the conduct of the individual patient's analysis. This means that the analyst is solely dependent for information concerning family experience on the perceptions of the individual patient, whose view is emotionally colored. Traditionally, the analyst detects distorted perception in the patient through the processes of transference, but his evaluation of discrepancies between real and unreal is unaided by objective knowledge of family interaction. In this context, the reality testing capacity of the analyst is somewhat handicapped. While I am not ignoring the possibility of transference complications when the analyst interviews other family members, it seems to me, first, that such complications are not magically erased by the analyst's determined isolation of himself from the patient's family and secondly, that any possible complications must be weighed against the tremendous gain in the analyst's reality testing capacity, when he does make such family observations. He then would be in a position to match his perception of the patient and his family relationships not only against the patient's perception of self, the analyst and other family members, but also against the perception of the patient by other family members.

The therapy of marital disorders by psychoanalytic practitioners has sometimes failed because of inadequate evaluation. A marital relationship has unique properties of its own, over and above the individual pathology of the partners. Conflict between marital partners is not simply an expression of the intrapsychic conflicts of each partner viewed in isolation. The marital relationship tends to influence and change each partner, and this in turn influences the relationship anew. The problem is to define the symptoms of disordered functioning in the individual partners in the frame of a systematic evaluation of the interlocking pathology of the marital relationship. To illustrate the principle, we may consider the following evaluative scheme:

*Criteria for Evaluating Marital Interaction (in abbreviated form)**

1) Strivings, ideals, value orientation of each partner for the marital relationship

2) Performance of relationship

- A) Interaction of partners
  - 1) Past interaction beginning with the courtship

*Based on considerations presented in The Diagnosis of Neurotic Marital Interaction, by N. W. Ackerman, *Social Casework*, April, 1954.

2) Current interaction
a) Compatability, nonsexual (emotional, social, economic), sexual and parental
b) Conflict
c) Complementarity (mutuality of pathologic needs and defenses)
B) Interaction of partners as a couple with the external environment
3) Achievement of the relationship (measured against an ideal conception of mental health for the marital relationship, and for fulfillment of each individual partner)
4) The relation of specific components of pathologic interaction to total marital interaction
5) Patterns of compensation for the effects of pathologic interaction
6) Integration of individual personality into the marital role
7) Specific trends toward isolation, disintegration or regression in the marital relationship

If we are motivated to rehabilitate the mental health of a disturbed marital relationship, we must take into account not only the neurotic core of behavior in each partner, but also the main areas of conflict and failure of reciprocity of satisfaction, the malleable aspects of the character of the partners, the residual strength in their personalities, the positive qualities of the marital relationship and the family life and the motivation of both partners for change. All these are needed to counterbalance the neurotic tendencies.

In my own practice of psychotherapy of adults, I have found it increasingly difficult to carry therapy to the point of satisfactory completion without an integrated effort to deal with the problem of restoration of healthy family relationships. Toward this end, I have tended more and more to interview and sometimes to treat other members of the family group in addition to the primary patient. In this same frame, I have come to weigh the quality of interaction of the patient with other family members as a most significant criterion of therapeutic progress.

This problem reveals itself another way in the field of child analysis. Here we find a peculiar contradiction. Child analysts have often tended to give up the practice of child analysis while continuing to teach the technique. By contrast, the practice of child psychotherapy, combining treatment of child and parent, has increased by leaps and bounds. It is of great interest to ask, why less and less child analysis and more and more child psychotherapy? My own conjecture is that child analysis as a classical technique has isolated itself from its necessary foundations in reality, namely, the reality of group interaction processes in current family life. Any form of child therapy, if it is to be successful, must surely avoid isolation from a parallel program for dealing with the mental health problems of the family group.

It is a curious fact that an earlier report of the Committee on Psychoanalysis in Children of the American Psychoanalytic Association, after alluding to the many problems of practice in child analysis, introduces, peripherally, the comment that a few people think it would be a good idea to study the family. One wonders, what price reality in the psychoanalytic world?

I have become increasingly skeptical of traditional cliches and stereotyped formulations regarding the psychodynamic relations of child and family. Such conceptions as Oedipal conflict, seduction of the child, inconsistent discipline, overprotection, overindulgence and narcissistic exploitation of the child can in no way be adequately understood, unless the interaction processes of the family, as well as the personalities of each member, are subjected to systematic study. It has become crystal clear, for example, that such a trend as parental seduction of the child is an empty phrase unless it is explored fully in terms of the sexual maladjustment between the parents with the associated patterns of conflict and emotional alienation. Rejection has become a hackneyed word and it is often used literally to cover a real ignorance of the history of the child's sense of betrayal by the parent. Where there is a rejection, it needs to be qualified in terms of its intensity, in form of expression, its relative specificity for the given child, the role of the rejecting motive in the economy of the mother's personality, and finally, the role of the rejecting behavior in the total psychosocial economy of the family life.*

*See Disturbances of Mothering and Criteria for Treatment. *American Journal of Orthopsychiatry*, April, 1956.

CLINICAL PROCEDURES FOR EVALUATING PATHOLOGY IN FAMILY RELATIONSHIPS

To explore the patterns of interlocking pathology in family relationships and principles for understanding the integration of individual personality into family roles, appropriate methods of examination must be used. These are patterned on the premise that a specific dynamic relationship exists between the mental ill health of the family and the illness of the primary patient.

The clinical procedures suggested are: (1) Evaluative interview of the primary patient, (2) interview of significant family pairs, in which the primary patient is one partner and (3) separate interview with other significant family members, singly, in pairs or triads.

The temporal order of these interview procedures varies from family to family. The leads for arranging the sequence in one order or another are drawn from insights gained at each stage of the proceeding.

The unit of examination is a family relationship, rather than the individual patient in isolation. The functions of personality are evaluated here as they are integrated into a relationship and a particular family role. This discloses how the patient perceives other family members and also how they perceive him. These interpersonal patterns are observed in action both in the office and at home. For the observations at home, a psychoanalytically oriented social psychologist visits the family in its own familiar home setting. Where there has been an emotional crisis and the family patterns have been disorganized, a mother's helper is selected to live with the family under professional guidance. The goal is to restore stability, while making further observations of family interaction.

In the case of a child patient, the decision to interview the child first or the mother first, or child and mother, or mother and father, rests on hints as to the most intense areas of conflict and anxiety. The question is: Where does the anxiety focus most acutely, which family relationship is most critically disabled by anxiety? For example, the first hints may be gleaned in a telephone conversation. A mother will call asking, "How shall I bring the child? Shall I tell him that you're my friend, or that you're a psychiatrist?" Or, a child's father will make the first call, sometimes suggesting his greater emotional involvement or his lack of trust of the mother. The main areas of tension in the family relationships come more sharply into view after a first interview and usually provide an effective guide for decisions as to the preferred sequence of procedures.

In the case of disordered marital relationships, the marital partner who makes the first call is often motivated to enlist the psychiatrist's powers on his side in the conflict with the other. It is axiomatic that each partner perceives this conflict in a different way. The need to deny blame induces each partner to project unreal charges onto the other. This fans the flame and the barrier between the partners becomes magnified. Between the two partners, there may be a considerable difference in motivation to save the marriage.

In order to elucidate the conflicts of the relationship, it seems helpful to see both partners together, to observe directly the vis-à-vis relations, the content of conflict, the dissatisfaction, the blaming tendencies and each partner's distortion of the other through projection. As a second step, one can interview each partner alone and through a series of such examinations, ultimately evaluate the mental health of the relationship and the relation of the pathology of each partner to the disturbance of the relationship. In this manner, the patterns of family interaction are revealed as the primary patient perceives them, as other family members perceive them, as a trained observer sees them in the usual home setting and as the psychiatrist sees them in his office. Thus, personality may be evaluated not in isolation but within the psychosocial configuration of the family group; and the specific dynamic relations of personality and family role may be delineated.

To illustrate these principles we present several family studies. Due to limitations of space, no attempt is made here to present the full data on each family, but rather the manner in which the initial sequence of an exploratory interview unfolds the patterns of interlocking pathology in family relationships.

Case Histories: Family 1

An 8 year old boy is referred because of fears of body injury. He comes with his father, who is a hypochondriac receiving psychiatric therapy and is diagnosed as a pseudoneurotic schizophrenic. The psychotic weakness is well concealed, however, beneath a suave external facade; he is poised, affable, ingratiating and glib.

In interview, the father became quickly tense, anxious, cast furtive glances around the room, feared the draft and sat with his coat tightly hunched around his body. He admitted his hypochondriac fears; he wondered whether he "inherited it or got it by osmosis." Throughout the interview he was suspicious and guarded. In a thinly disguised manner, he sought proof that the psychiatrist was at the top of his profession. He felt the boy was exactly like himself and feared psychiatry might harm him. In the same breath, he admitted the boy's terror of physical hurt and of bleeding, but insisted that such fears were not abnormal and that the child would "grow out of it."

He characterized his personal relations with his wife and children as idyllic, though the early part of their marriage was disturbed. There were critical tensions with his mother and his wife's mother. He was the oldest son and felt he was "morally and financially responsible" for his mother. His wife hated his mother. She also worried about her own mother who was in a mental hospital.

Other symptoms in the boy were acute anxiety when the parents left home, bed time rituals, nightmares, stubbornness. In the interview the boy initially displayed a sad, anguished, tortured facial expression. He was at first frightened and reticent. He showed little spontaneity in his behavior. Gradually, as he assured himself of the safety of the therapeutic relationship, he became increasingly aggressive. He put very little into words but began to act out in play his phantasies of being attacked in the dark by a man with a knife. Together with this, he acted out other phantasies of burning to death a spook, though in this play he could never quite convince himself that the spook was completely annihilated. He avoided physical activity and feared even the slightest physical brush with another person, tending to react with instantaneous anxiety about some injury to his body. Later, he talked more freely of thoughts of losing his head or losing a finger, or toe. Sometimes he exhibited the confusion of behaving like a chicken with his head cut off.

During his infancy, the parents had been acutely panicked by an X-ray report on the boy showing enlargement of the heart; they were extremely overprotective of him until reassured by other doctors that his heart was normal. The parents always felt overanxious with the children. Periodically, both parents felt exhausted by the children's demands and took themselves off on vacation, leaving the children with a nurse. The boy's sleep disturbance was precipitated in this setting.

The next interview was with the boy's mother. She was more youthful than her husband, attractive, tense, compulsive, high-pitched, mildly euphoric. She indicated that her main concern was her children. She was more relaxed with her children when her husband was not present. She felt content with her way of life, admired her husband as a brilliant, "self-made" man. She said, "I know I married my father." They led an active social life in which they received much flattering attention. Her husband's high nervous tension and excessive dependence upon her was a great strain. She felt her husband was jealous of the children; she was torn between them. Though her husband's fussiness with household matters irritated her, she appeased him; sometimes, however, she felt like screaming. She confessed, too, that her husband was sexually demanding. She placated him with a pretended sexual response. She wanted therapy for her son but felt no need for therapy herself. No effort was made at this time to induce her to take therapy. The conclusion, pro tem, was to "leave well enough alone."

This family had a position of status in the upper strata of society. It consisted of the parents and three children. In their own social group, the parents showed unusual concern for their children.

Observations in the Home

The family appeared superficially to be a unit. The children and parents seemed closely bound but the cohesiveness was exaggerated, strained, and unnatural. The parents appeared joined in their anxiousness for the children, but underneath this, there were unmistakable evidences of an emotional barrier.

The father was anxiously overinvolved with

the children; he participated in their activities in a pressured, intense way, seeming at times to displease them. He wanted the children to show off, yet was scrupulously careful that each child had his share of attention. His effort seemed self-conscious and unreal. The mother was more relaxed but overconscientious and manipulative. She seemed more distant, and appeared resigned to the father's fussiness with the children. Both parents seemed to need attention from their children. The mother permitted the father's need to come first. In general, these parents seemed to be excessively child-centered.

All activities of the family were carefully planned, overorganized; there was little evidence of spontaneity. The children were strongly competitive.

Treatment and Course

Arrangements were made for psychotherapy of the boy, with provision for regular conferences with the parents to guide their daily contacts with the child. They boy responded favorably to this program.

About three months later, the maternal grandmother, withdrawn from the mental hospital by the mother against the doctor's advice, committed suicide. The mother was interviewed the same day. She appeared shocked, agitated, strangely elated with a sense of enormous relief. She was "laughing on the outside and crying on the inside." She wore an inappropriate grin, was unable to cry, said she knew it just had to happen and felt freed of a burden. Nevertheless, she was deeply troubled.

During this same period, increasing tension had built up between the husband and wife over her sexual coldness. Her husband had begun to press her to do something about it.

For several months, the mother resisted his pressures. She had the inner conviction that if she once opened up to a psychiatrist concerning her frigidity, she would explode and "all hell would break loose" in her relationship with her husband. She was true to her word; she upset the applecart. Though she had consciously intended to keep the lid on her anger, she drank too much one night and erupted uncontrollably against her husband. She launched into a violent talking jag that lasted half the night. She screamed that she hated both him and his mother. Sex relations were a pure ordeal; she'd carried on an act pretending orgasm. She never wanted to sleep with him again, etc. The shock to her husband was critical. He became depressed, cancelled all further appointments with his psychiatrist, neglected his business, saying that he no longer cared what happened. He was on the verge of collapse.

When the wife was seen, she again wore the same fixed eerie smile she had previously displayed following her mother's suicide. She confessed her outburst, but acted like a child who had been naughty. She believed she had full power to demolish her husband. Though admitting her cruelty, she felt it was a relief to explode. She grinned as she expressed the thought that her husband might leap out the window as her mother had done. She admitted her extreme irritation with her husband for his sexual demands, his fussiness, his alleged physical ailments.

Following a long cathartic confession, she called her husband at his office. For the first time her voice broke, she shed a few tears and pleaded with her husband to return to his psychiatrist.

Her husband was the man her mother had picked for her, a rational choice—a self-made man, and an outstanding member of a country club. During the courtship, she admired his superior qualities and identified him with her father. She really knew little about him. Two weeks before her marriage, she saw the other side of her husband; this was a rude shock. As the wedding approached, she became frozen with fear, complained of illness and retreated to bed. This was what her mother used to do. Though her feelings turned sharply against him, she repressed them and went through with the marriage. After that, she froze up sexually, but play-acted the part of a loving wife. She wanted children immediately to escape her conflicted feelings toward her husband. She had one child after another, kept busy with her children, home and social life and thus evaded her tension over the marital relationship. Her husband was extremely dependent upon her. She made each decision for him down to the last detail—the shoes and ties he should wear, etc. Her sense of complete power over him gave her a secret elation.

The superficial unity of this couple rests mainly on their sharing of a common social background. They had similar aspirations for social and business success. They complemented each other's dependency and power drives. To an extent they lived vicariously through their children. They were united especially in anxiety over the older boy.

The delicate emotional balance in this family was upset by several events, the shift of the focus of the parents' anxiety from their son to themselves, the wife's increasing failure to conceal her sexual disinterest and rejection of her husband and the suicide of the maternal grandmother.

The wife's compulsive denial of conflict and her magic elation decompensated. She admitted the similarity of her husband and mother and erupted into a violent rage.

When the husband was seen, he was in a state of calm desperation. His face was blanched white. He feared the worst; the togetherness of his family might literally blow up in his face. Curiously enough, in the face of this crisis, he abruptly dropped his complaints of backache, colds, etc. and had no thought of hypochondriac retreat to bed. Instead, he mobilized his strength to meet the real danger. Following the first shock and depression, he rose to the occasion and acted sensibly. He worked concentratedly with his psychiatrist. His wife entered analysis and the family crisis was brought under control. The wife now confronts the sexual problem more honestly and is working to repair the disruption of unity with her husband and children.

Family 2

The primary patient in this case was a 3 year old boy. The first interview was with his father who stated that the boy's sleep was disturbed. He is put to bed and comes out 8, 10, or 12 times, often late at night, despite the parents' efforts to soothe him to sleep. Occasionally, the father wakes in the morning only to find the boy asleep at his side. He showed anxiety when the parents left the home, excessive mouthing, finger sucking and a tendency to hold his urine when absorbed in play. He spoke of his penis as "duty water." He was hyperactive, feared flies, tended to be enamored of good-looking strange women with long black hair and asserted that only boys and men can play with dirty things, not women. He seemed to get along better with people other than his parents.

The father is an intelligent, gifted person, concerned for the child but also worried about his wife who became depressed during her second pregnancy. The second child, a girl, is now six months old. He reproached himself for his concentration on his professional work to an extent that he is able to spend little time with his wife and children. He tried unsuccessfully to get his wife to see a psychiatrist. He admitted taking her to task for her inadequacy in managing the home and children. He was irritated by her show of hostility to the boy. He and his wife have grown apart in the last year.

The wife felt too much alone since she saw little of her husband. The husband reacted to his guilt over this neglect with periods of anxious solicitousness toward his wife and children. The difficulties of the three year old son reflected an emotional problem that encompassed all the family relationships. The next step was to explore the emotional interaction between the three year old boy and the mother and the emotional interaction between the parents. Though the boy was presented as the primary patient, there was the immediate question of the recent depression of the mother. The family relationships were evaluated to determine who was the sickest member, and whether to focus first on the interaction between child and mother or the relationship between the parents. Because of the mother's fear of being pushed into therapy, it was decided to avoid any frontal attack on her individual pathology, but to concentrate first on the disturbed family relationships.

The second interview was with the mother. She was a beautiful woman, but it was a sculptured beauty, masked, immobile, stonelike. She seemed depressed, subdued, inhibited. There was little show of initiative or spontaneity. She gave a straightforward account of her boy's disturbance and her own. The third interview was with the mother and child, in a playroom. Observations were made of the boy and mother and the emotional interchange between them. The boy was bright, alert, actively curious and exploratory in play. He seemed preoccupied; he avoided looking directly at his mother or the examiner, and showed repeatedly a quick anxiety about being left alone. Yet, he seemed to keep his mother at the periphery of his activity. He evinced concern about dirt, saying, "Only boys and men play with dirty things, women mustn't." When the woman therapist escorted him to the toilet, he asked her to unbutton his fly. He then said, "You better leave now, it might frighten you." From time to time the mother became anxious about any show of destructiveness or other ill-mannered behavior on the boy's part. She reacted with an inhibited display of irritability and tried to restrain the boy verbally. Even with this irritability, her manner was emotionally heavy, logy. She told the boy, "don't do this or that," without even rising from her chair. She was emotionally distant from the child but in another sense, watched alertly his every move. In later sessions she tried more actively to control the boy. At times she hovered over him as if suffocating his moves.

It was decided to study this child-mother pair and the parental pair for a month to six weeks, and then determine further procedure, on the basis of a fuller evaluation. Up to this point, the mother had indicated through her inhibited, withdrawn attitude and her fright, her reluctance to being involved as a patient herself. When the two parents were interviewed, the boy's disturbance was related to the mother's anxiety about being abandoned by the father. This opened the way to a discussion of the increasing alienation between the parents. The father saw the light and improved his closeness with the mother. The mother was involved in the child's therapy and responded favorably. Her anxiety about taking the plunge in therapy was discussed with her. No pressure was applied to induce her immediately to enter individual therapy but she responded well to the recognition of her depression, loneliness, her living at a low ebb. She got little pleasure for herself, depending mainly on vicarious enjoyment of her children's pleasures. Her fright diminished and she became more willing to consider a program of individual therapy for herself at a later time. Her wish to concentrate first on the problems of her mothering role was respected, and arrangements were made for periodic therapeutic interviews with both parents. Individual psychotherapy for the mother will be undertaken at a later stage.

Family 3

A four and one half year old boy was referred because of numerous fears: fears of violins, sirens, swings, fog horns, etc. He is fascinated by objects that move, yet begins to fear them. He has some preoccupation with magic transformation of certain objects into other objects. He is "heavy-handed" and destructive in play. He does not distinguish real and unreal in stories. He has occasional nightmares, wakes up and moans. He showed anxieties as early as six months of age.

This boy is well built, bright, alert, fidgety and talks volubly and under pressure. He shows some facial grimaces. He was at first loath to talk of his fears. He was observed to handle his penis. When questioned, he distinguished between "shaking" and "fiddling" with his penis. "Shaking is okay, fiddling is bad." During the interview, he was playful, teasing, facetiously provocative with his mother. He gleefully belittled her with such appelations as "dog duty" and "duty head." He seemed to equate certain foods with "duty." In the presence of the doctor, the mother constrained herself with difficulty. She was impelled to reproach him for his rudeness. She has a strong urge to control him in every way. When the boy held his penis the mother endeavored to distract him by suggesting that he go to the bathroom to "tinkle" (urinate).

The mother is a big woman, intelligent in an obsessional way but rigid, childlike, naive, aggressive to the point of being overwhelming. She systematizes everything. She is continuously preoccupied with her need to control every member of her family. She is easily irritated. She uses her power somewhat indiscriminately, yet is afraid of that power. She is obese, overeats periodically, then goes on a stringent diet. She has mood swings; when depressed she is irritable and explosive and takes it out on her husband and children. She is squeamish about bugs, fears dogs and tends to bang herself against doors.

The second interview was with the boy and father. The father seemed more gentle, warmer, more receptive to the boy. Nevertheless, he tended to belittle the boy by interfering in his activities and demonstrating that he could do things better. The father carries a stiff, frozen face. Beneath his rigid control of his emotions, he tends to be panic stricken, feels exposed to criticism and attack. He attempts to neutralize his fears through submissiveness. He has a history of numerous body fears and somatic symptoms, migraine, sinus trouble, stomach disorders, gall bladder trouble, heartburn. During periods of anxiety, he urinates frequently. He is compulsive, works long hours. He fears his wife's domination, behaves like a small boy with her, is obedient. He only rarely shows open irritation. Privately he resents her strict control of him and her prohibition of his favorite hobby, fishing. He speaks as he looks, in a quiet, expressionless voice.

The third inverview was with the two parents. In this interview, the mother, an explosive, voluble person, did most of the talking. The father took a back seat except when he felt the doctor was allied with him. Only then was he bold enough to disagree with her, and he did so in a picky, cranky way. Otherwise he backed away from open battle with her. He felt intimidated and at the same time extremely dependent upon her.

This man and woman were drawn to each other by mutual need. The mother was attracted to the father's intellect, his passivity and pliableness. She sought to keep her hold on her husband by sharing his interests. She had an intense need to escape her own unhappy home. She revolted inwardly against the strict religious control of her own mother but otherwise took panicky flight.

The father felt extremely isolated, needed a dominant maternal person and a "sexual outlet." His intense fear of venereal disease inhibited him from sexual expression; marriage provided for him a safe release. Both parents felt extremely deprived, lonely and sought each other's protection. In the courtship they took long walks, away from everyone else. Immediately after marriage, they spent long periods in bed together with incessant love making. They seemed never to get enough.

The mother dominated the relationship and interpreted the father's silence as compliance. Both aspired to security, financial independence and a position of respect in a middle-class community. They craved a good home because both had been reared in impoverished circumstances. They shared a strong need for approval. They had an intense craving to accumulate money in order to ward off hunger and a hostile outer world. In their early period of marriage, they had a good relationship. They protected each other from hurt. In the beginning the mother supported both of them, while the father attended professional school. The mother treated the father as an extension of herself.

Neither parent wanted children at first. They felt they could not afford children. The mother had divided feelings. She wanted to become pregnant to counteract fears of sterility but also feared that a baby would separate her from her husband. Also the mother hoped to prove that she could be a better mother than her own mother.

More recently, the mother began thwarting her husband's sexual advances. She felt he really didn't respect her but used her as a "sexual receptacle." Yet, she worked like a slave at home to convince her husband that he had gotten a bargain when he married her. Though the hostile tension between them is high, there is basically a strong bond of loyalty.

Therapy with the child was begun, and arrangements were made to see both parents together in an effort to alleviate therapeutically the conflicts of this relationship. After that, individual therapy for each parent is planned.

To evaluate interlocking pathology in the family, we have tried to study systematically the individual's relations with his family group. Several steps are pursued:

1) The development of the central relationship of man and wife, past to present, the earlier interaction in the courtship phase, their relationship as marital partners and later as parents. Pertinent here are the value attitudes, emotional expectations, satisfactions and frustrations of the relationship; also, the specific patterns of integration, compatibility, conflict and complementarity (mutuality of pathologic need and defense). It is possible then to estimate the actual achievement of the relationship against a theoretic model of a mentally healthy marital relationship.
2) The development of the family group since

its inception, its internal organization in terms of unity, stability, satisfaction and its external adaptation with extended families, friends, organizations and the community at large.

3) The development of the individual in continual interaction with his family group at each stage of maturation.
4) The dynamic integration of individual personality into the required familial and extra-familial roles.
5) The specific child-rearing attitudes and practices, and the child's reactions.

We have selected empirically certain criteria for the appraisal of the psychosocial functioning and mental health of the family group, family pairs such as husband-wife, parent-child and degrees of success and failure of integration of personality into family role. It becomes possible then to mark out the relatively healthy and unhealthy areas of family functioning, the balance between them and the specific compensatory or restitutive trends in the family relationships. The manner in which the pathologic tendencies of one member fit with the behavior of another can be delineated. Thus, the dynamics of the individual can be defined as an integral part of family interaction. Hopefully, this is a step toward a classification of family types according to mental health and the development of a psychosocial therapy of the family group.

CHAPTER 22

Theory of Family Dynamics

At a recent meeting of the Academy of Psychoanalysis in San Francisco, Gregory Bateson made two interesting comments. He suggested that a psychoanalytic meeting devoted to the theme of family had the flavor of something unique and that it could, in fact, be history making. Later, in informal conversation, he predicted that in not too long a time, perhaps five years, we would succeed in evolving a satisfactory theory of family. That gave me good cheer, but I felt that the time estimate was rather too optimistic.

The explicit confrontation in psychiatry of the need for a family approach to mental illness parallels the recognition of specific deficiencies in the theory of personality.

In the exploration of human behavior, there is surely no end, and we hardly agree as to where to seek the beginning. Among students of personality we find two types of people. There are those who hang doggedly on a single theoretical limb, and those others who swing freely from one theoretical limb to another. The first type adheres to his single-minded faith, places a high value on consistency, but tends to be omniscient-minded and elaborates his views within a closed system of thought. He is disposed to ignore those phenomena which do not fit snugly into his preferred theory. The second type is more open and venturesome in spirit. He toys with multiple theories or tries to merge them in the effort to explain contradictory evidence. Often he is pilloried as inconsistent, unscientific, blind to the collision of irreconcilables. He may, nonetheless, make useful discoveries. In moving into uncharted territory, researchers frequently do not adhere to a single theoretical scheme. They try rather to combine several frameworks. In seeking to explain discrepant evidence, they experiment with new integrations of theory. In this way they pursue the search for what has been aptly termed the "elegant synthesis."

"Theory," says Donald Hebb,[4] "is like skating on thin ice—keep moving or drown" . . . "when theory becomes static, it becomes dogma." In theory construction, an attitude of humility and caution is certainly indicated. Yet, there is the other side of the question too—the need to take the bold leap in an utterly new direction. Theory is not an end; it is a means. It is the inspirational

Reprinted with permission from *Psychoanalysis and the Psychoanalytic Review*, Winter, 1960, Vol. 46, No. 4, 33-49. Copyright 1960 by Human Sciences Press, New York.

source of useful forms of research design. The goal, of course, is a new formulation which gives us the power of prediction.

Right now we are at the crossroads. We do not possess a unitary theory of human behavior. As Angyal[2] put it: "It is paradoxical but unfortunately true that psychiatry is the application of a basic science which does not yet exist. We have a number of sciences related to the person, but we do not have a science of the person. Human physiology, psychology and sociology deal with arbitrarily separated single aspects of the human organism."

It is the artificial limits of these branches of behavior science which compel each to search out a theory of family. What is needed is a broader conceptual frame within which it is possible to encompass the dynamics of the individual and the dynamics of the group. Social science reaches out for a theory of personality and psychiatry aspires to a theory of family. Surely there is no one branch of behavior science that can claim the family phenomenon for its very own; there can be no question of monopoly. It is not merely that psychiatry has a claim equal to every other; it is rather the sheer responsibility of psychiatry to stake this claim. It must be recognized, however, that a theory of family born out of psychiatry may be different from those born out of other sciences. The value of any theory rests in part on the specific uses for which it is intended. Since the focus of psychiatry is on mental illness and health, a theory of family born out of psychiatry is likely to have a distinct emphasis, and surely, distinct kinds of application.

In our time, intensive efforts are being made by many persons and in a range of professional settings to devise a unified theory of human behavior. In working toward a theory of family dynamics, I have naturally scanned these larger conceptual structures, in order better to check the validity of my own efforts. The theory of family which I shall here outline is clinically and empirically oriented. Scientifically speaking, it is neither so comprehensive, nor so rigorous as, for example, Miller's general systems theory.[3] It is more pragmatic. It is intended for direct application to clinical problems. In theory construction we confront a special problem. It does sometimes seem that the closer a theory approximates a mathematical ideal, the more abstract, the more comprehensive the theory, the less easy it is to apply to a concrete human situation. It does often appear that a general, universal theory must be reduced to a lower order of abstraction before we can make practical use of it in clinical problems. The universal theory conceptualizes the problem; it defines mathematical probabilities. But it does not directly apply to a concrete case. For this purpose, middle concepts are required which qualify relevant variables more sharply in time and space.

The concepts I have evolved for the dynamics of family life do not possess the mathematical beauty and perfection of the general systems theory, but I believe they may be of some worth in clinical practice. In so far as clinical work is pragmatically oriented, it is more intimately tied to values which are bound to the space and time of particular varieties of human experience. This may narrow the breadth of the theory, but *pro tem* it may be closer to the task in hand.

With these considerations in mind I shall state explicitly the how and why of my personal incentive for coping with this problem, hoping thereby that my discussion will have greater communicative value. I came to this problem with a certain range of experience in child psychiatry, psychoanalysis, and psychosomatic medicine. I was interested in the application of psychodynamic principles to the so-called "diseases of civilization," to particular social problems, such as prejudice and delinquency, and problems of family mental health. The urge to develop a dependable means of family diagnosis became strengthened by the recognition of a range of problems in clinical practice which seemed persistently to resist solution. Something seemed wrong; something important was missing in the definition of the very problems we were trying to treat.

In the field of children, there were critical deficiencies in the standards of diagnosis.[1] Between the clinical diagnosis and the therapy of children, there loomed up an extraordinary chasm. Clinical diagnosis was of small value in planning treatment. The quest for specificity in the therapy of child patients seemed seriously obstructed. A paradoxical trend emerged which subordinated the importance of the task of diagnosis and gave to therapeutic method a priority of its own. This trend contradicted a basic tenet of scientific procedure. It purported to correct what was wrong with a person without first defining precisely what was wrong. It signified the application of a single treatment technique in a way which precluded the goal of therapeutic specificity.

This was a style of clinical practice which tended conceptually to isolate child from family. The evaluation of the child and the evaluation of family were not definitively correlated. The same schism emerged in the approach to treatment. The clinical program was child-centered. The child was the primary patient; the family received secondary attention. The salient focus was on the intrapsychic disorder of the individual child, his symptoms and core conflicts. The pathological units of behavior were not systematically viewed in the frame of total personality and the related modes of social adaptation. To be sure, the maternal attitudes were examined, but child and mother were diagnosed and treated in isolation from one another. This often had the effect of drawing child and mother further apart rather than closer together. Still another difficulty emerged from the tendency conceptually to isolate mothering behavior from fathering behavior and from the totality of the family pattern. Clearly, deficiencies in mothering are not solely correlated to the intrapsychic pathology of the mother's personality but also to a range of family relationship experiences which affect the integration of personality into the mother role.

In the individual approach to the child patient, the concurrent disorders of family relationships were evaluated incompletely, intuitively, in a more or less hit or miss fashion. In the traditional guidance clinics, the child patient was assigned to the psychiatrist, the mother to a social worker. Inferentially, the treatment of the child was more important, and called for more rigorous technical skill than the treatment of the mother. The attention given to father and family as a whole was negligible. Often the psychiatric study of the child and social study of the family were divorced. Must we not question the validity of some aspects of this fashion in clinical practice? Is it really so that the disturbance of the child patient is more complex, more difficult to treat than the corresponding disturbance of mother and family? Could it be that this is a reflection of cultural bias? Why the lack of integration in the approach to the child and family? Do we take the side of the child against mother and family? Or, do we in this manner subtly sidestep our scientific ignorance in ways to diagnose disturbances of parent and family? Or is it both?

It is true, of course, that we had until now no adequate model for the assessment of illness and positive emotional health in family processes, no definitive standards for parental role behavior and child rearing. Surely among the experts there was no clear consensus. And it is this large gap in our knowledge that made us conspicuously impotent in the field of prevention of mental illness and the promotion of positive health.

In the community-at-large, the tasks of psychotherapy, prevention of illness, promotion of health and education seemed profoundly divorced. Perhaps a basic reason for this is the lag in the development of a psychodynamic science of family behavior, which would enable us to cultivate a social psychology and social psychopathology of family life.

Now the question comes: are these ideas relevant to the understanding of deviant forms of adult behavior? What happens when we turn about to examine analogous problems in the psychiatry of adults? Taking fully into account the dynamic differences between the entities of child and adult personality, one can also discern for the adult a trend toward atomization of the individual and conceptual divorce of the individual from the family group, into which his adaptive functions are integrated. The study of intrapsychic processes seemed separated from the study of the corresponding interpersonal events. Thought and feeling were not integrated in our minds with units of social action. But, the impact of revolutionary social change, new understanding of the relations of culture and mental illness, and study of new forms of character disorder impelled us to scrutinize these questions more closely. Neatly packaged symptomatic neuroses with fully contained conflicts were no longer our main daily fare. Instead, "acting out" became a conspicuous feature in all our patients. But, acting out is impossible without the complicity of a partner. Character disorders are a social as well as individual phenomenon. These disorders, though varied, feature prominently diffuse, unbound anxiety, a trend toward confusion or fragmentation of identity, disorientation in interpersonal relations, emotional alienation and loneliness. In addition to acting out, other defenses play a conspicuous part, substitution of aggression for anxiety, projection, and isolation. Repression is no longer the central defense. We were thus led to affirm once again the principle that emotion is a shared experience, that illness is a contagious phenomenon, and that within the family, multiple members may be ill and these illnesses clash, complement, or otherwise influence one another.

Therefore, the issue is not so much that the child is dependent, the adult independent. Adult personality is not autonomous. For adults, too, we must respect the interdependence of individual and family group. It is merely that this interdependence is differently expressed by child and adult, insofar as the kind and amount of temporal and spatially conditioned experience molds the maturation of the person. This is a difference in growth and social learning, but one which in no way lessens the significance of the dependence of the operations of adult personality on the social environment.

It is these considerations which impelled me to re-think the principles of psychiatric diagnosis from a particular point of view, namely, the need to evaluate the individual within a network of family relationships, in which the maladaptive forms of behavior are patterned and maintained. The building of criteria for a system of family diagnosis offers the possibility of placing the dynamics of the individual and the dynamics of the family relationships within a single theoretical frame. In presenting this background, I am surely not implying that I alone am concerned with this need. It will take many minds to devise even a crude conceptual foundation for family diagnosis. I offer this more personal background merely in the hope of being better understood.

The psychiatric approach to family focuses on its psychodynamic aspects and highlights the challenge to interrelate emotional disturbance and health in the individual with emotional disturbance and health in the family group. It endeavors to join the knowledge of the psychic functioning of the individual with the psychic functioning of salient family pairs and the family as a whole. It strives for better understanding of the shared nature of mental illness and the circular, interpenetrating effects of multiple illness within a single family group.

But, what is the family unity? The family is the organic unit of illness and health (Richardson). It is the psychic agency of society (Fromm). Individual and family are mutually dependent, and mutually penetrating. The evolving image of self and the image of a network of family relationships are reciprocal and interdependent processes. At each stage of maturation, the image of self is linked to and differentiated from the identity of parents and family in a special way. Therefore, at any specified point in time, the organization of individual personality epitomizes a corresponding family organization. In this sense, the individual is a microcosm of the larger entity, the family; the family is part of the individual, the individual is part of the family. It is to the credit of H. S. Sullivan that he called attention some years ago to the limitations of the concept, individual personality.

The perceptual intimacy of the identities of self and family is a central feature of the multiple processes which mold the adaptation of personality to social role requirements. The on-going relations of individual and family group affect processes of illness and health; they influence the course of illness, the possibility of cure and the risk of relapse. They affect attitudes of hope or despair, influence receptivity or resistance to therapy. They condition our capacity to predict changes in behavior.

For the psychiatric profession, it is relevant to ask: What are the exact limits of mental illness as an individual phenomenon? Do the characteristics of mental illness apply to the functioning of groups as well as individuals? If so, are these characteristics the same or different; if different, are they analogous? How shall we define these differences? What are the specific features of a sick family? What is a well family? As psychiatrists, must we not be concerned with a theoretical model of positive mental health, as well as a model of mental illness, both for the individual and the family group?

Up to now, psychiatric diagnosis and therapy have been mainly individual-centered. Psychiatry concerned itself with fragments or selected aspects of the family phenomenon, not with its entirety. Mental illness was mainly conceived as a constitutionally influenced, endogenous disorder of personality. Family was considered to affect the manifestations of illness, but was otherwise treated as peripheral, not of the essence. The concern of psychiatry with family was therefore partial and selective. The role of family was examined at three levels:

1) Heredity.
2) The role of family in the traumatization of the emotional life of the child, thus inducing in the emerging personality specific vulnerabilities to illness.
3) The role of the family in the traumatization of the emotional life of the adult, impairing his adaptive competence, and thus acting as a precipitant of mental illness.

The concept of a hereditary familial factor in mental illness continues to be vaguely defined. The validity and meaning of numerous statistical studies purporting to prove a specific hereditary tendency are open to question. Even Kallman's dramatic finding of an extraordinary high frequency of schizophrenia in identical twins bears reexamination insofar as this study was uncontrolled for the social factor. In any case, the hereditary factor in mental illness, even if documented, is no greater than for certain physical diseases. The whole subject of heredity requires review in the context of the newer theoretical orientation to the determinants of behavior which no longer conceptually dichotomizes organic and functional, somatic and psychic, biological and social, past and present.

The role of family experience in inflicting trauma on the emerging emotional organization of the child has been richly illuminated through psychoanalysis. The role of family in impairing the emotional balance and adaptive potential of the adult is less well understood. The family as stabilizer of the emotional health of the adult and the family as training ground for the fitting of personality to a range of social roles has been little studied, this last despite the fact that statistical studies consistently show a lesser incidence of breakdown in married people, in people with intact families, and in mothers as compared to women who bear no children. The intermediate stage, the interrelations of adolescent and family represent in psychiatry a seriously neglected area. To this extent, the conceptual formulations which make the long leap from the family of childhood to the family of the adult must be regarded as suspect in some measure.

Precisely because of the fundamental nature of the psychoanalytic contribution to behavior theory, we ought be alerted to its present-day limitations. It was Freud himself who cautioned us against separating individual psychology from social psychology. Yet, in a strange paradox, this is exactly what Freud did, and we followed closely after him. Today, the confluence of a number of new developments demand a critical rethinking of the psychoanalytic view of family: the increased understanding of the dynamics of social change, the relations of culture and personality, culture and mental illness, the newer trends in ego-psychology, in adaptational theory, in social science and the science of communication.

"Mind is inside; it is outside; it is everywhere all the time." Psychoanalytic theory has struggled right up to the present day with a perpetual dilemma, namely, the relations between inner and outer experience, the inner and outer face of personality, the relations of subject and object. Therefore, it seemed never clearly to decide: how far does personality unfold from within, how far is it influenced from without? How far does it tend to move outward and forward, and how far does it move inward and backward? The Freudian system remains incomplete in two main respects. While emphasizing the role of irrational, unconscious, conflicted motivation and the pathologically twisted perceptions of family experience, it fails thus far to provide a picture of love and emotional health as a positive force in family life. It does not illuminate with sufficient clarity the interaction and merging of old and new experience, and to this extent fails to explain the forward moving, creative phase of development. Freud conceptually opposed parent and child somewhat in the same way that he opposed reality and pleasure, and culture and personal freedom. The child was a polymorphous, perverse little animal, pleasure driven, sub-human, antisocial; the parent was anti-pleasure. Freud saw vividly the oppositional aspects of the relations of child and parent, individual and society, but not the joining. The Freudian system tended to view reality as a contamination. It dichotomized biological and social, unconscious and conscious, pleasure and pain, phantasy and reality. It emphasized the falsified, twisted images of parents and family, the inertia and pathology of emotional development, but failed to clarify the processes of social learning, the forward, creative movement of personality.

The one-sidedness and incompleteness of the Freudian theoretical system created certain difficulties in therapeutic process: the divorce of the analyst from the patient's family, the inability to check the patient's image of family against the family's image of the patient, and the corresponding circularity of relationship influence; the inability to know accurately the patient's group involvement and his multiple role adaptations; the inadequate basis for reality testing of the patient's life decisions and actions; the confusion of discriminating between realistic action and acting out; the difficulty of assessing secondary gain, the family influence on therapeutic accessibility or resistance, and on the patient's response to therapy.

Clinical experience teaches us the necessity of coordinating our picture of a sick patient with his contemporary family life. It imposes upon us the obligation of conceptualizing the contagion of family interaction processes, and their relation to a range of reciprocating emotional disturbances. It impels us to view the first family member referred to the psychiatrist not only as a distressed and disabled individual, but also as a symptomatic expression of a sick family. The primary patient is only one link in the chain of family illness. He may be the most or the least sick part of the family. Other members of the family may maintain a tolerable emotional balance by keeping the primary patient sick. Over time, the focus of disturbance may shift from one part of the family to another. The effectiveness of adaptation of the individual to multiple family roles varies; he succeeds in some, fails in others. Degrees of success or failure in the paired family roles of husband and wife, father and mother, parent and child, child and sibling bear directly on the question of staying well or getting sick. The idiosyncratic alignments of family pairs and threesomes influences profoundly the selectivity of family role adaptation. An emotional splitting of the family into factions and the emergence of opposed camps distorts adaptation to family roles and thus intensifies susceptibility to illness. These are but a few of the clinical considerations which point to the necessity of parallel evaluation of individual and family.

The family can make or break mental health. Family interaction processes exert a selective influence on the following: the paths of expression of emotion, the assertion of individual need and the search for security, pleasure and self-fulfillment; the patterning of the sense of responsibility for others; avenues of possible solution of conflict, the range of models for coping with change, the perceptions of danger, the reactions of fight or flight, the choice of defenses against anxiety, the processes of reality testing, training in the fulfillment of social roles, and the available models of success and failure in personal performance. In these various ways the family represents a powerful force in the organization of behavior. The family reinforces in its individual members those patterns of adaptation which the family group requires for its survival and development. The individual, in turn, may actively influence the vicissitudes of family process. He interacts selectively with the emotional content of his family life in the pursuit of his personal strivings, in coping with conflict, seeking solutions and defending against anxiety. The homeostasis of personality and the dynamic equilibrium of family process are thus intimately connected. The failure of a person to integrate into one or several vital family roles may be the harbinger of breakdown and mental illness.

Now I come finally to the suggestion of a tentative theoretical framework for family diagnosis. By the term, family diagnosis, I refer to a method for identifying the family as a psychological entity in and of itself, a way of assessing its psychosocial configuration and mental health functioning, a basis of classification and differential diagnosis of family types, and finally, a means of establishing the specific dynamic interrelations of individual and family behavior. The ultimate goal is a social psychology and social psychopathology of family life.

More concretely, the criteria which we seek are the following:

1) Criteria for the differential classification of family types according to their psychosocial configuration and mental health functioning;
2) Criteria for evaluating the emotional integration of individuals into their family roles; also for identifying the emotional mechanisms by which adaptation to one family role supports or conflicts with requirements of other familial or extra-familial roles;

3) Criteria (within the definition of family types) for evaluating emotional disturbances of family pairs and threesomes;
4) Criteria for the disturbances of individual members, which emphasize the dynamic interdependence of the mental health of individual and family; also, the emotional mechanisms by which the individual, in maturing, separates his image of self from his image of family, while maintaining a level of joined identity.

In such an undertaking, the dimensions of diagnostic thinking are expanded beyond the limits of the internal economy of personality to embrace three interrelated sets of processes; what goes on inside the individual; what goes on between this individual and other significant family members; and the psychosocial patterns of the family as a whole. It is therefore necessary to gather a considerable body of data dealing with multiple overlapping phenomena: the relative autonomy of the individual; his emotional integration into the family group; the fit or lack of fit for the same individual of significant familial and extra-familial roles; the extent to which the reciprocal role behavior of other family members supports or threatens the stability of the individual; the psychological identity and value orientation of the family group and its external adaptation to the community. The data so obtained should illuminate at each successive stage of development the interrelations of individual and family, thus providing both horizontal and longitudinal configurations of the relevant processes. The goal is to correlate emotional balance within the individual with balance in role adaptation and balance in the family group itself.

For these purposes, I have devised a group of core concepts which attempt an operational formulation for the dynamics of family process, the who, what and how of family life, and the corresponding functional patterns of family relationships. Within this conceptual framework, I try to establish more reliable correlations of individual and family behavior. Limitations of space compel me to offer here only a condensed statement of the theory and its related terms. The essence of the theory is represented in the schematic diagram below, a six pointed star in which one triangular set of variables is superimposed upon another.

One phase of this conceptual scheme deals with identity and differentiation in the on-going relations of individual and family; the other phase deals with the stabilization of behavior, which is influenced both from within and between family members.

The concept *identity* subsumes strivings, expectations, and values. The concept *stability* involves the continuity of identity in time, the control of conflict, the capacity to change, learn and achieve further development, in effect, the quality of adaptability and complementarity in

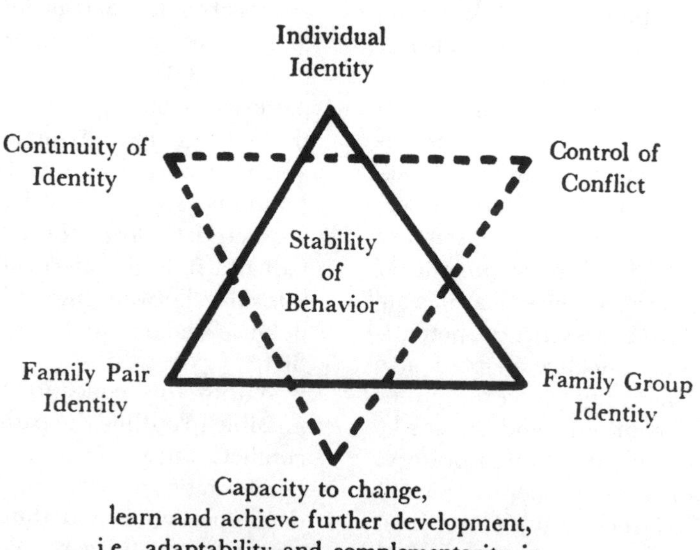

new role relationships. The concept *identity* refers to direction and content of striving, while *stability* refers to organization and expression of behavior in action. The questions, who, what and how and the corresponding formulations of identity and stability can be applied to the functioning of individual, family pair and family group. A joined pair of persons or group may be conceived as possessing a unique identity just as does the individual. Psychic identity changes as it evolves through time. It answers the question: Who am I or who are we in the context of a given life solution? It is the I and me, the we and us in a given social situation. It orients personal strivings to relations with others. At any given point in time, the individual has an image of his personal identity and his family identity; both are continuously influenced by the images which outside persons hold of these same identities. The identity of a family pair or group refers to elements of joined psychic identity. This is a segment of shared identity, represented in layers of joined experience and enacted in the reciprocal or complementary role behaviors of these jointed persons. It is this process which determines the manner in which elements of sameness and difference among the personalities of family members are held in a certain balance.

Psychological identity and stability of behavior must be considered together. I have already alluded to the component processes which mold stability, the continuity of identity, the control of conflict, the capacity to change, learn and achieve further development, i.e., adaptability and complementarity in new role relations.

Stability in its first phase epitomizes the capacity to protect the continuity and integrity of identity, under the pressure of changing life conditions. It insures the intactness and wholeness of personal behavior in the face of new experience. This is the conservative phase of stability. The other aspect of stability must provide for accommodation to new experience, learning and further development. It represents the potential for change and growth. Effective adaptation requires a favorable balance between the protection of sameness and continuity and the need to accommodate to change. It requires preservation of the old coupled with receptivity to the new, a mixture of conservatism and readiness to "live dangerously." The capacity to change and grow is a feature of family life as well as a feature of individual development.

Stabilization of behavior is influenced by the capacity to cope with conflict. The control of conflict is a special dimension relevant to the relations of individual and family. The failure to find effective solutions leads to adaptive breakdown and illness. Within the individual, pathogenic conflict and the vicissitudes of control and restitution correspond most closely to the bases for clinical psychiatric diagnosis. If we trace the fate of salient conflicts within the individual and between family members, we can trace the relations between adaptive breakdown and illness in one individual and pathogenic disturbance in the family pattern.

In this connection, it is of special importance to define the individual's capacity to achieve complementarity in family role relationships. The term "complementarity" refers to specific patterns of reciprocity in family role relations that provide need satisfaction, avenues of solution of conflict, support for a favored self-image and buttressing of crucial forms of defense against anxiety. Complementarity may be further differentiated as positive or negative.

Positive complementarity is that form which promotes emotional growth of the relationship and the interacting individuals. Negative complementarity is more static; it signifies a buttressing of defense against pathogenic anxiety, but does not additionally provide the potential of further emotional growth. In this sense complementarity mainly neutralizes the destructive effects of conflict and anxiety and barricades family relationships and vulnerable members against trends towards disorganization. Contemporary patterns of family conflict may potently affect the outcome of individual conflicts internalized at earlier periods of development. It should be remembered, too, that families as groups have characteristic forms of defense just as do individuals. It is therefore necessary to trace the interplay between individual and family group defense against the disintegrative effects of conflict.

Within this conceptual structure, it seems possible to outline the pathogenic areas of family conflict, those which push the stabilizing or homeostatic functions of the individual toward decompensation and thus aggravate the tendency toward disorganization, regression, breakdown of communication and emotional alienation;

also, at the opposite pole, to define the potential in the reciprocity of family role relations for providing paths for solution of conflict, establishing effective compensation or complementarity, fostering support of new levels of identification, thus promoting health and growth; an approximation of these opposite trends may enable us to view more clearly the balance of forces within individual and family that predispose to illness or health and positive development.

As indicated earlier, theory is not an end; it is only a means and it can never be final. The value of an evolving theory at any given stage is tested in the extent to which it fulfills the uses for which it was intended. From this point of view, one may readily ask: How good is the theory in practice? Does it meet its stated purposes? What special problems are thus far encountered in its application to clinical work? Up to now, it is possible to give only a limited and impressionistic answer to these questions. The test of worth of the theory is on the way. Its value is being appraised both in clinical practice and in specific research studies. These concepts are being applied both to disturbances in children and psychiatric problems in adults. This work is going forward at the Child Development Center and the Family Health Clinic of the Jewish Family Service of New York. It is also planned to initiate a research in concurrent family studies of young adults undergoing psychoanalytic treatment at the Psychoanalytic Clinic of Columbia University.

What can reasonably be said of this work thus far? In its application in clinical practice, the theory and its related concepts are gradually being clarified, amended, with an explicit attempt to achieve operational and communicable definition of terms. Though the general impression is one of considerable potential value, no definitive statement can yet be made. It is too early. It is unequivocally clear, however, at the level of clinical practice, that these concepts have exerted a pervasive catalytic effect on the thinking of staff members. It has immensely broadened the awareness of practitioners to the interplay of individual and family group experience. The general consensus is that it has enriched and sharpened the planning of psychotherapeutic intervention, that often it lends to therapy a greater appropriateness and potency. But all are agreed that this conceptualization must be carefully learned and practiced.

At the level of specific research, the main goal is to develop hypotheses—useful, testable hypotheses—that can be checked in more specific, partial studies. Toward this end, it is necessary in the meantime to struggle continuously for sharper definition of terms in particular, to evolve increasingly precise reliable, communicable, operational definitions, which members of the study team can use in the same way. As of now, it is admitted that there is ambiguity in the understanding of some of the terms, that there is overlapping in the connotations of others. A few concrete examples may illustrate this problem: We still have trouble with the concept, *family identity*. There is some overlap between this term and the reciprocal role relationship patterns which characterize the given family. There is still difficulty in achieving a precise statement for the joined identity of a family pair, husband and wife, or parent and child. We don't quite have the language for defining the component levels of joined and shared experience of a family pair. To illustrate further: there is some overlap between the concepts, *complementarity* and *defense against anxiety*. Perhaps these few examples will suffice to point out areas of fuzziness and incompleteness in the theory.

Still another observation in day by day implementation of these concepts is this: the characteristic features and problems of one family as compared with the next evoke in the clinician a tendency to apply selectively some parts of the theory concepts of evaluation while ignoring or leaving untested other concepts. Clinicians fit their thinking and their use of self in the participant role to the immediate pressures of particular personalities and problems. In so doing they conceptualize in a selective manner only certain parts of the family phenomenon. The net result of this is an incomplete and somewhat biased diagnosis of the family. This has two negative effects. The disturbances of a given family cannot then be evaluated within the frame of a systematic assessment of the totality of family experience, measuring components of illness against potentials for health. It also makes impossible the systematic comparison of different family types.

There is still another category of problems which must be explicitly recognized. Both the ideas and the corresponding levels of professional intervention into family processes are unfamiliar. They are unfamiliar both to patients and clinicians. Patients often experience some initial surprise and confusion in orienting themselves to the expectations implicit in this approach. They are culturally attuned to an individual approach. They are not yet perceptually conditioned to a professional contact which points explicitly to the shared and joined levels of family experience, as well as to the emotional barriers which separate the family members. Patients tend to project to the clinician an appeal for him to deal with that component of self which is separate and atomized from the family. Each demands something for the self and blurs the line of relatedness and sharing with other family members. To this extent, we are confronted with a factor of cultural conditioning in the way in which patient and clinician meet and achieve a consensus to their common work. But clinicians belong to the same culture. They, too, experience some subjective difficulty in reorienting themselves to an approach to the circular phenomena of family relationships, rather than to individuals in isolation. It is understandable, therefore, that clinicians should become aware of a mounting anxiety in the effort to integrate their personalities into the new and unfamiliar therapeutic role. They often confess the urge, in response to anxiety, to revert to the older, more familiar method, which has the effect of emotionally separating the individual from his family group. In other words, psychically speaking, both patient and clinician tend to be oriented to the privacy and separateness of the individual. It is agreed therefore that this modified use of the self in the therapeutic interaction must be learned and mastered.

In summary, then, I have offered here, as part of an ongoing study, a tentative theoretical approach to the phenomena of family life, which is exploratory in orientation, incomplete, but worthy of a real test. It requires a different perceptual orientation to emotional disturbances in family relationships on the part of both clinician and patient, but it may prove to be of some help in the struggle for mental health.

REFERENCES

1. Ackerman, N. W.: *The Psychodynamics of Family Life*. New York: Basic Books, 1958.
2. Angyal, A.: *The Foundations for a Science of Personality*, New York: Commonwealth Fund, 1941. p. 3.
3. Bateson, G.: Personal Communication, The Annual Meeting of the Academy of Psychoanalysis, San Francisco, 1958.
4. Hebb, Donald O.: *Organization of Behavior*. New York: John Wiley & Sons, N. Y. and London: Chapman & Hall, Ltd. 1957.

CHAPTER 23

Prejudicial Scapegoating and Neutralizing Forces in the Family Group

A long-time objective of family study is the development of a family typology, a classification of families according to their psychosocial organization and mental health functioning. Of special interest is the correlation of structure, function and developmental stage of the family with the emotional destiny of its individual members. This is an undertaking of huge dimensions. Present limitations of knowledge make a frontal attack on the problem in its entirety hardly feasible; we must be satisfied with a piecemeal approach. We are engaged, therefore, in a series of limited, exploratory studies, hoping to move, stage by stage, toward the ultimate goal of a systematic family classification. In so doing, we are building stepping-stones toward an integrated, conceptual framework for understanding the relations of family dynamics and health. Toward this end, we accumulate data in the following areas: (1) the harmonizing and balancing of essential family functions, epitomizing in a general way the potentials of unity, stability and growth of the family group; (2) the dominant and competing representations of family identity, goals and values: the identity associations of individual and family; (3) the characteristic alliances and splits within the family role relationships and characteristic patterns of complementarity; (4) the core conflicts of the family unit and the methods of coping: the dynamic interrelations of interpersonal and intrapersonal conflict, the interplay of family defense of the integrity and continuity of family functions, and individual defense against conflict and anxiety: the special function as defense of a change of alignments and splits within the group and the prejudicial scapegoating of one part by another; (5) the relations between selective idiosyncratic features of family structure and function and the susceptibility of its members to emotional breakdown.

For the gathering of data and insights in these several areas, we pursue a series of focused studies on one or another special aspect of family

Reprinted from the *International Journal of Social Psychiatry*, Congress Issue, 2:90, 1964, by permission of the Editor in Chief, Dr. J. Bierer, M.D., F.R.C. Psych.

development and adaptation. For these purposes, we use our library of sound moving pictures of families in treatment. We now have 120 hours of films of family treatment interviews, covering more than thirty-five different families. From such data, we hope to uncover some of the connections between family dynamics and mental health, and thereby identify criteria by which to distinguish the family types which breed a psychotic member from those others which produce neurotic members, acting-out types of character disorder, or learning failures with associated behavior deviations.

Central to the whole problem of family dynamics and health are the relations of conflict and coping within the matrix of changing patterns of interaction. The outcome of the struggle with conflict may be broadly stated in the following alternatives: (1) The conflict is correctly perceived and an early and rational solution is found. (2) The conflict is correctly perceived and is effectively contained, while a solution, not immediately available, is being sought. (3) The conflict is misperceived and distorted; it is not effectively contained, nor is it appropriately solved; it is not adequately compromised or compensated; it spills out into irrational "acting-out." (4) The control of conflict fails, resulting in progressive disorganization of family relations and impairment of family functions.

The range of mechanisms for coping with conflict and anxiety in a family may be tentatively stated as follows: (1) Enhancement of the bond of love, sharing and identification. (2) "Repeopling" of the group—the elimination of a member or the addition of a new member. (3) A change in the external environment of the family unit. (4) A change in the configuration of family role relationships brought about through a variety of devices: (*a*) shared solution of conflict and the attainment of an improved level of complementarity; (*b*) the reduction of intensity of conflict through manipulation, coercion, compromise, compensation, denial or escape; (*c*) making roles more rigid; (*d*) making roles more fluid; (*e*) a shift in alignments and splits within the group and prejudicial scapegoating of one part by another.

It is the last of these, prejudicial scapegoating, to which we now turn our attention. In the course of our clinical explorations, we have been impressed with the emergence of a special set of emotional mechanisms which we characterize as "prejudicial scapegoating and neutralizing forces in the family group." Recurrently we observe certain constellations of family interaction which we have epitomized as a pattern of interdependent roles, those of the destroyer or persecutor, the victim of the scapegoating attack, and the "family healer" or the "family doctor." We constructed a theoretical model to represent this cluster of interrelated roles. Stated in simplified terms, the destroyer or persecutor uses a special prejudice as the vehicle of his attack. Another member of the family becomes the object of this attack, the victim of scapegoating; he sustains an emotional injury which renders him susceptible to breakdown. The "family healer" or "doctor" intervenes to neutralize the destructive powers of this attack and thereby, in some measure, rescues the victim. The enactment of these reciprocal role behaviors may be overt or covert; simple or complex; sharply outlined or relatively amorphous. These processes may occur at multiple levels of family interaction. They may change as the family moves from one stage of adaptation to another, or otherwise undergoes change in its organization. We now test the theory that a specific patterning of these emotional mechanisms offers a useful diagnostic clue to the psychosocial identity and emotional health of a given family.

Close study of family interaction suggests specific kinds of prejudicial scapegoating are characteristic of a given family and become organized in an irrational way around special meanings that are attached to differences among the family members. Prejudice of this kind is of a distinct and private nature. It differs from the common stereotypes of prejudice in the wider community. Insofar as it is a recurrent and predictable manifestation of the idiosyncratic quality of family life, it provides a specific diagnostic clue to the emotional organization and functioning of a special kind of family.

From this hypothesis arise several questions. (1) What is the special role of prejudicial scapegoating in the life history of a given family? (2) How are the role functions of attacker, victim and healer organized within such a family? (3) What is the significance of these processes for the emotional health of the family and its members? (4) What is the relation between this kind of social disorder and the susceptibility to specific mental disorder?

Before amplifying these questions, we must first make clear our conception of the phenomenon of family prejudice. We distinguish here two categories of prejudice, private and public. They are different and yet interdependent. Prejudice within the private life of the family assumes a form manifestly unlike that encountered in public life, i.e. the familiar antagonisms based on differences of color, religion, ethnic origin, etc. Private intrafamilial prejudice is of another kind, so subtly different that it is often not recognized as prejudice at all, yet it is there just the same—real, abundant, intense, far-reaching in its effects. It attaches to differences, the real and unreal, among family members. Private prejudice may become displaced and translated into public forms of prejudice. Public forms of prejudice may in circular fashion aggravate the tendency to private prejudice.

In a basic sense the members of one family may be viewed as being the same kind of people. They are, in fact, related by blood. They resemble one another; they have much in common; they share the same way of life. In view of this sameness, one might expect an absence of prejudice among the insiders and the concentration of prejudice against outsiders. This is not the case, however. Among members of the same family group, there are elements of differences as well as sameness, differences in appearance, attitudes, traits, strivings and values. Depending on the idiosyncratic emotional structure of a particular family, symbolic meanings are attached to these differences which are then subjectively felt by one or another part of the family as a distinct danger. The person showing the difference is felt to be the alien, the invasive stranger who threatens the security, the needs and values of other members of the group. Sharing this sense of threat, several or most members of the family form an alliance to attack the source of the difference.

In the inner life of the family, such prejudice becomes organized around a range of differences: the battle between the sexes—male or female, or vice versa; youth against grown-ups or vice versa; brain against brawn or vice versa; money and power *vs.* a passive way of life; control *vs.* spontaneity and pleasure; a liberal *vs.* a conservative political ideology. At other levels, prejudice becomes attached to such qualities as fat or skinny, tall or short, smart or stupid, light or dark skin, smooth or hairy skin. Still other prejudices of this kind attach to such matters as habits of eating and dressing or cleanliness and orderliness.

A question may promptly be raised: Why do we call this prejudice? Are there not valid reactions to difference, legitimate likes and dislikes, preferences and aversions that may not constitute true prejudice? Certainly it is so that people who achieve sound health have a full measure of likes and dislikes, attractions and repulsions. Such attitudes become transformed into true prejudice, however, to whatever extent they become rigid, fixed or automatized and walled off from the corrective influence of the prevailing realities. Furthermore, such prejudice may be mild or intense, benign or malignant. In its benign form, such prejudice need not extend to the compulsive urge to hold the self together by breaking someone else down. In point of fact, however, the more disturbed the family becomes, the more do the members lean toward organization of malignant forms of prejudice. The significant feature is its very contagion. Some, or even all, members of the family become bound in its organization. While contagious, it is also selective in its influence. It aggravates prejudice in some members, while fortifying the immunity of others against it.

Prejudice and mental illness have something in common. Both have to do with human relations and are affected by the struggle to reconcile human differences. Both impair a person's ability to perform his tasks in life, especially that of getting along with other people. The ultimate source of both conditions is the intimate emotional exchange within the family group, which is the prime training ground for learning to get along with other people. It is exactly the striving within the family to establish one's position and to win the reward of affection and respect for one's unique quality, that affects the proneness to prejudice as well as to mental illness.

Nevertheless, in some crucial respects, the two forms of behavior are distinct. They evidence themselves in a different life context, and yet between them there is a significant dynamic connection. People moving toward an emotional breakdown frequently lean on prejudice as defense. To save themselves, to stave off the threat of their own breakdown, they are motivated to break down another member of the family. There is convincing force to such remarks as "My mother is driving me crazy" and "She'll be the death of me yet."

Our immediate concern is with these private family prejudices, both as individual defence against the fright of dangerous exposure and as family defence of the continuity of family functions. To the degree to which an individual feels incomplete, weak, exposed and vulnerable, the difference of another can become magnified, symbolically, to the dimensions of penetrating threat. In analogous fashion, to the degree to which the family as a group fails to integrate an effective identity and value orientation, or suffers a split of identity, the assertion of difference in one part of the family may be felt as a menace to the unity and continuity of the family as a whole.

To return to the questions posed earlier, when a clinician trains his eye on a troubled family, he is immediately struck by the division of the group into competing emotional alliances. Each member identifies with particular component representations of family identity, expressed in terms of what he or she wants the family to be or do. A competing faction wages its battle around the felt threat of these differences. Around these differences, there is the patterning of specific family prejudices. In the unfolding of such emotional mechanisms, we believe we can identify the three main patterns already mentioned, the role of the attacker, the victim and the healer. At a given point in time, these roles are fulfilled by particular members and with the passage of time by other members. Each of these is selected for his respective role by shared unconscious emotional processes within the group. The family destroyer punishes the member whose difference is felt as an offence and as a menace to family continuity. The member who is chosen as scapegoat suffers an emotional injury and is thus rendered vulnerable to the danger of mental breakdown. Still another family member enters the role of peace-maker, protector, healer, or if you like, family doctor, rising to the rescue of the victim of the punishing attack. To the degree to which the rescuing member holds the capacity to neutralize the destructive force of the prejudicial assault, he offers to the scapegoating victim some immunity against breakdown. At times, the member who starts out in the role of persecutor or destroyer may shift into the role of victim or healer, or vice versa. Each of these functional roles may be fulfilled at various times by members of the nuclear family or by a relative, a delegate of the extended family. Again it is to be emphasized that this is a theoretical model rather than an actuality and in the clinical observation of family life these patterns may be complex, disguised and difficult to identify.

Further developments are involved. In the unfolding of critical family conflict, a primary prejudice attaching to the conspicuous and threatening difference of one member may evoke a counter-prejudice. In this case, the emotional sequence is attack, defense and counter-attack. Thus the emergence of one pattern of scapegoating evokes the emergence of an opposite pattern of attack and scapegoating. Ultimately, reciprocal patterns of attack and scapegoating appear on the scene. The role of family healer then becomes progressively more complicated and may be fulfilled in sequence of different members of the group. In this context, one direction of scapegoating may be counterbalanced by another. The scapegoating may occur also at multiple levels and in a circular pattern. A pair of parents may scapegoat a teenager, the teenager may scapegoat a sibling. All of them together may then scapegoat a grandparent. Or the scapegoating theme may unfold in a different way. In a conflict between a pair of parents, the teenager may at one point in time enter the role of healer of the war between the parents and at a later stage turn into destroyer.

Temporarily this process may serve to bind the family closer together. At another stage it may be critically divisive in its effects. The less rational the prejudice, the more does it lead to progressive distortion of family role relationships and impairment of essential family functions. Although it may temporarily serve as a means of support for one or another partial family alliance and corresponding family identity and value orientation, at its core this process becomes progressively less rational, fragments family relationships and alienates it members.

In this concatenation of events, several other developments are possible, contingent on the emotional condition of the family. If the condition favors it, there may be a movement toward resolution of the primary prejudice and, with this, an easing of the scapegoating assault; or, if the emotional matrix so disposes, a counter-prejudice may emerge. Beyond that a range of efforts unfold, the intent of which is to neutralize and assuage the harm inflicted upon the victim of family scapegoating.

If the movement is towards the resolution of the primary prejudice, and the pressure towards splitting the family and the setting up of competing alliances is reduced, the family members reach out for an improved quality of union and love. On the other hand, if this is blocked, the primary prejudice evokes a counterprejudice and the function of family healer is stirred to action; it becomes, in fact, an urgent necessity.

But one must bear other alternatives in mind. The prejudicial attack may shift from its original object to another member of the family. One prejudice may be substituted for another. The attack may be displaced from the family scapegoat to a new target outside the family.

The vicissitudes of control of intrafamilial prejudice are the paths along which the emotional split of the family group achieves a specific pattern; one part of the family pits itself against another. Therefore, prejudice and counter-prejudice formations need to be correlated with the split of the family into warring segments, with a conflict over differences, the method of coping, and with the unconscious selection of particular family members as scapegoats and others as rescuers or healers.

If, on occasion, a member tries to avoid being sucked into the family conflict, and for his own safety seeks to remain unaligned, he achieves, at best, merely a temporary and precarious protection. Over the stretch of time, such an attempt at non-involvement is short-lived and must fail. Often such a gesture at noninvolvement is patently false; in fact, it conceals an entry into a compensatory alliance with some other part of the nuclear family or extended family, or reflects a flight for protection into alliance with a peer group. It is of the very essence of the emotional life of the family that there is no such thing as non-intervention. At the very most it is a protest, a dramatic gesture. Even so, it cannot be sustained because it disconnects the member's feeding line to the family and ultimately ends in alienation. What it really cloaks is a hidden tendency to fickleness and betrayal and the urge to find compensatory belongingness and protection elsewhere. A member of the family behaving in this way may erratically juggle his alliances from one side of the family to another. In such a setting, "acting-out" becomes not merely a unit of experience in which one member lives out the unconscious urges of another, but also the vehicle for the discharge of shared aggression as one part of the family does battle with another.

It is, therefore, of the essence to identify specific forms of family prejudice, the roles of persecutor, scapegoat and healer, the competing family alliances, the specific conflicts around which the battle rages, and the types of family group and individual defense that are mobilized to neutralize the destructive results of scapegoating.

SUMMARY OF RELEVANT HYPOTHESES

1) Disturbed families tend to break up into warring factions: (*a*) each member allies himself with one or another faction; (*b*) each faction competes for the dominant position; (*c*) each faction asserts a preferred family identity and value orientation representing a preferred set of goals, role expectations and role complementarity; (*d*) each faction attaches a specific meaning to individual difference and organizes around this specific device of prejudicial scapegoating.

2) A leader emerges in each faction: (*a*) each leader personifies the family identity and values of his faction.

3) A particular member of the family is chosen as a victim of prejudicial attack: (*a*) an idiosyncratic quality of this member becomes a symbolic representation of the perceived threat to the dominant family identity.

4) A defensive counter-attack is mobilized: (*a*) the scapegoat allies himself with another part of the family and asserts an opposed form of prejudice; (*b*) to the extent that this defensive alliance succeeds, the primary scapegoat minimizes his own injury at the expense of another. He may shift from the role of scapegoat to that of persecutor; (*c*) to the extent that this defensive alliance fails, the primary scapegoat finds himself undefended and alone; he becomes progressively more vulnerable and may suffer a breakdown; he denies that he is in the scapegoated position and pretends the victim is another

member of the group; he shifts to the role of healer; if this succeeds, he may reduce or nullify his vulnerability.

5) A member is unconsciously selected as the "healer" or "family doctor": (*a*) he provides the emotional antidote to the destructive effects of the prejudicial assault; (*b*) he may be motivated to accept this role in order to turn the attack away from himself, or he merely pretends to be the healer, while being secretly absorbed only with his own security.

6) The health-sickness continuum is influenced by the shifting balance of the effective struggle between the factions toward: (*a*) entrenchment of valid values of family identity and appropriate balancing of family functions which enhance love, loyalty, sharing, identification and growth; (*b*) entrenchment of a progressive trend towards the organization of competing prejudices, rigidifying the family organization and constricting the roles or pathologically loosening them in a way that reduces emotional nourishment for all members; (*c*) the relation of these processes to emotional health of the family group and its individual members may be examined at the following levels: (i) the preservation and enhancement of the unity of one part of the family at the expense of another—some aspects of family unity are protected and other aspects sacrificed; (ii) some essential functions are maintained and other functions are impaired or lost; (iii) in a selective manner some levels of family relationship complementarity are protected, while others are reduced, distorted or lost; (iv) some levels of coping are effective and other levels fail. This can be traced to specific patterns of interplay between family group defense and individual defense against anxiety.

These processes are reflected in a shift of equilibrium as between health-maintaining and sickness-inducing tendencies in the family with a corresponding effect on the potentials of growth for the family as a unit and for its members, and, at the opposite pole, contribute to the precipitation of mental illness in one or another member.

CHAPTER 24

The Role of the Family in the Emergence of Child Disorders

INTRODUCTION

The inclusion within this volume of a chapter on the role of family in the emergence of child disorders marks something of a turning point in the history of child psychiatry. New developments in medicine, psychiatry, and the related behavioral sciences have propelled us toward this objective; of these, two sets of influences stand out most sharply: (1) the recognition of critical deficiencies in past attempts to correlate child behavior and family environment, and (2) the rapid growth in the theory of personality. In our time we are plunged into a phase of radical reorientation to the principles of causation, diagnosis, therapy and prevention of behavior disorders. This brings us flush against the challenge to embrace the dynamics of individual and family development within a unitary theoretical framework. Are we yet ready for this complex undertaking is the question!

By tradition, the study of human adaptation and associated conditions of illness and health gravitated to one of two extremes, either to the processes of individual personality or to those of society. Accordingly, parallel advances have been made in individual psychology and in the science of society and culture. Paradoxically, however, the study of human adaptation in the intermediate area of the family unit was long delayed. This is especially striking when one realizes that the family is the critical link between the internal forces of personality and the wider forces of society and culture. Many factors contributed to this lag:

(1) The inadequate understanding of the dynamics of small groups;
(2) The long tradition of the privacy, the sanctity, the inviolability of the inner life of the

---

Reprinted with permission from *Foundations of Child Psychiatry*, E. Miller (Ed.), 1968, 509-528, 531-533.

family, which hinders systematic study of the intimate aspects of family living;

(3) The weakening of the family bond, induced by such factors as the impact of the industrial revolution, the tradition of "rugged individualism," and competitive achievement, all of which tend to atomize the family, alienate its members and foster the sentiment "each man for himself";

(4) The inertia, conservatism, and biased beliefs of the community which block critical examination of those elements in the systems of family and community that contribute to social and mental disorder, while continuing a traditional trend of quarantining and scapegoating the victims of such conditions.

Surely, looking back on the past, it cannot be said that the role of family has ever been ignored; it is rather that the emotional interplay of child and family was conceptually approached in an atomistic and one-sided way. The prevailing style of thinking tended to separate the child from his environment. The child as individual and the family as group were observed and evaluated in parallel, though separate, spheres. Formulating the relation between the two sets of observations became a matter of psychodynamic speculation, a secondary task in conceptualization. This way of thinking and doing in child psychiatry brought forth mainly unintegrated fragments of insight. Characteristically, the literature identified the deviant, inappropriate attitudes of the mother and, less regularly and more vaguely, the attitudes of the father. The conceptual orientation was mainly to the one-to-one relation of parent and child, to the parent viewed as an external influencing agent, rather than to the family as an ongoing living unit with unique, definable properties of its own. Seen in retrospect, the traditional theoretical approach was an oversimplified one. It had built-in limitations which, in effect, placed a stumbling block in the path of progress towards a unified and precise correlation of child and family behavior. To this extent a significant advance in the understanding of psychopathological states in childhood was hampered.

Psychiatry as a special phase of medicine and the healing arts has an ancient background. Modern dynamic psychiatry is something else again. Dating back roughly half a century, it is an exceedingly young science, but the psychiatry of children is even younger, covering perhaps a mere thirty years. In this short span, remarkable advances have been recorded in the understanding of the emotional development of a child in illness and in health. There is this paradox, however; the very proof of a growing maturity in this area is the increasing clarity, confidence and frankness with which we can now define the persistent gaps in knowledge, and identify the weaknesses and limitations of existing theories. At the present time, the entire field of mental health practices for children can only be described as extraordinarily fluid. This is amply attested to in the tremendous range of studies which find their way into print in child development, child psychopathology, and in the applied fields of child rearing, child education and therapy.

The impact of new perspectives can be discerned in two important ways: whereas, at an earlier stage, child psychiatry tended to follow the doctrines of adult psychiatry rather too slavishly, today the tail begins to wag the dog to a startling extent. The expanding knowledge of the psychiatry of children represents an increasing challenge, a potent catalytic force affecting the further evolution of the principles and practices of the psychiatry of adults. At another level, the changing outlines of child psychiatry, influenced by developments in the social sciences, stirs into being a new dimension in mental health, the psychopathology and psychotherapy of the family unit. Within this broader framework of the family unit, a powerful impetus emerges to understand the processes of health as well as of illness, to conceptualize the dynamic development of individual personality within the development of the family group, and to coordinate the knowledge of the psychopathology of child and adult. Inevitably, this brings a changing order to the tasks that lie ahead. It seems reasonable, therefore, to anticipate that an evolving social psychology and social psychopathology of family life will feed back and enrich both the psychiatry of children and of adults. Looking to the future, we may talk increasingly of family psychiatry and less of child psychiatry.

It is self-evident at the outset that huge gaps of knowledge continue to persist in the area of the relations of child behavior and family environment. What we offer here is mainly a point of view, a way of thinking and a method of studying the problem rather than definitive knowledge. With full awareness of the risks entailed, we undertake to schematize the issues beyond the borders of what we are yet able to document scientifically. It is in this spirit of presenting a working paper that we ask the reader's forbearance. The focus of this essay then is to try, as far as present competence allows, to transcend the limitations of past attempts of this kind by providing a more comprehensive conceptual scheme within which to define the role of family in the emergence of child disorder.

HISTORICAL BACKGROUND

A frank retrospective judgment of earlier efforts to illuminate the role of family must bring the prompt admission of critical inadequacies. Knowledge in the psychiatry of children has tended to accumulate in bits and pieces rather than in integrated wholes. The deficiency of past approaches to the role of family is sharply reflected in traditional patterns of clinical practice and teaching. Personality disorders in children were classified descriptively in terms of recurrent, identifiable symptom clusters. Symptoms were related to organic defect, physiological imbalance, or to frustrated needs and associated conflicts and fears. The conventional standards of psychiatric appraisal of the child led with disturbing frequency to inadequate or erroneous diagnosis. The single, most encompassing reason for this has been the difficulty of evaluating the role of family environment.

In psychiatric examination of a child patient, it is not possible to dissociate what is observed from the clinician who is doing the observing. Since he cannot observe everything at once, he concentrates selectively on partial phenomena, guided by his clinical hunches. What he sees depends on his selective attention, what he chooses to look at as well as what he chooses not to look at. Clearly, this is one possible source of error.

Following child guidance tradition, the labor of diagnostic assessment was divided. The psychiatrist examined the child patient. The psychologist did the testing. The social worker interviewed the mother, gathered and interpreted the social or family history. The usual procedure consisted of a sequential series of operations, clinical diagnosis of the child, history-taking, evaluation of mother, father, siblings. In the secondary task of integrating available information, another level of possible distortion arises; the emotional influence of the family on the child becomes a matter of conjecture. To be specific, when in our customary procedures we examine a child away from the parent, each parent away from the other, each of these sets of data being gathered by different persons at different times, and finally undertake the task of integrating the separate findings, the resulting interpretations of the relations of child and family can be seductively faulty. Empirical experience has shown how skewed and unreliable such conclusions can be. Failure to check the clinical examination of the child as individual against a further evaluation of the child together with parents and family, or failure to check the appraisal of a child in an office interview against the appraisal of the child in his home setting, may often lead to misleading diagnostic conclusions.

Alone with the psychiatrist, a child shows one side of his personality; in the presence of parents, a child shows a different side. It is the social structuring of the interview experience that predetermines, in large part, the selective quality of the child's reactivity. Changes in the interpersonal situation bring critical shifts in the child's response. The kind of information we obtain about a disturbed child depends upon our way of getting it. What appears in one interview situation as a serious psychoneurosis, or even as a tendency to psychosis, may later prove to be an acute transitory disturbance reactive to current family trauma. Errors may also be made in the opposite direction. A child may be diagnosed as showing normal emotional reactivity when, in fact, the psychiatric interview simply fails to mobilize the expression of the child's inner pathogenic core. Thus, the qualifying features of the examinational procedure can account for a range of errors in the initial evaluation of a disturbed child.

The difficulty of judging a child's emotional response to his family may be illustrated in another way. When a clinical history of the child is presented, certain components of the child's behavior are judged to be "reactive" to the family situation. But reactive to *what* in the family situation? As soon as one demands specificity in such judgments, it is seen that the isolation and definition of the specific pathogenic features of the family environment are no easy task. Often the distinction drawn between the reactive components of the child's behavior and other deviant responses presumed to be rooted in the child's intrapsychic organization remains loose and vague. Inner and outer, past and present determinants of behavior are thus intermingled in an unclear way.

Still another difficulty can be seen in the way in which the child's clinical record is organized. One part of this record deals with the onset of symptoms, a separate section with the child's development, another with the psychiatric examination of the child, and still another with family background. Again and again, one finds that the psychiatric examination data on the one hand and the social or family history on the other are dissociated. The two sets of observations seem to be collected and interpreted in separate contexts. It then becomes difficult to discern the relevant connections, stage by stage, between the emergence of deviant behavior in the child and the psychosocial development of the family group.

The cogency of these considerations is reinforced by empirically documented observations:

(1) The emergence of psychiatric disorder in a child is regularly preceded by family conflict. There is a demonstrable relation between conflict in the child and conflict in the family. Psychiatric disorder in a child is a functional expression of the emotional warp of the entire family; once the family disorder is internalized, the ongoing interaction of child and family affects the further destiny of the child's illness.
(2) The psychopathology of the child is a response not merely to the individual make-up of each parent, but also to a distortion in the evolving identity representations of the joined marital and parental pair. Specific disorders in the development of the marital and parental partnership are followed by a subtle process of displacement and division of these pathogenic trends among the offspring; each child absorbs and reflects, in a highly selective way, the sick qualities of each parent as individual and of the parents as a joined couple.
(3) If the child is treated and the family disorder ignored, the child again falls ill.
(4) If the child improves, other members of the family may get either better or worse.
(5) Conflict and anxiety in other family members may block the progress of the child's therapy. This is especially so if the child is the pawn of unresolved conflicts between the parents.
(6) If the family group is treated as well as the child, it becomes possible to join the goals of therapy with those of prevention of mental illness.

Other defects of traditional child guidance concepts and practices may be summed up as follows:

(1) The unsolved problems of causation of child disorder;
(2) The unsolved problems of diagnosis and classification of child disorder; the difficulties of integrating descriptive, dynamic and genetic aspects of diagnosis;
(3) The tradition of excessive conformity to the standards of adult psychiatry; the one-sided emphasis on pathology; the failure to weigh pathologic trends within the broader frame of total functioning;
(4) The failure to conceptualize the circular feed-back aspects of the relations of child and family;
(5) The lack of standards for diagnosing the whole family; the failure to assess the balance of health and sickness in child and family and to correlate diagnosis of the child with diagnosis of the family;
(6) The failure to define the interplay of multiple disturbances within the family group;
(7) The lag in conceptualizing "acting out" as a pattern of emotional complicity in family relationships;
(8) The inadequacy of our understanding "secondary emotional gain" of illness as family process;
(9) The complications of an artificial division of labor in the Child Guidance Team; the special problems of "separate treatment" of child and mother; the neglect of father; the failure to conceptualize mothering, fathering and "childing" as interdependent role functions epitomizing the psychosocial

identity of the family as a whole;

(10) The delay in integrating psychotherapy with social therapy of the family; the failure of an effective program of prevention of mental disorders in children.

The recognition of such deficiencies in the conventional theory and practice of child psychiatry should in no way be surprising. They are the inevitable difficulties of a way of working with child and family, a way of gathering information. The positive values of clinical study of the child within the usual pattern of child guidance operations have been amply demonstrated, but the limitations, weaknesses and distortions of such procedures are less understood. More often than we like to admit, the essential truths concerning stages of child development and the influence of family become twisted, when part phenomena are artificially separated from the whole for the convenience and familiarity of a particular method of study. What begins as an attempt to simplify the means of study brings in the end an aggravated complexity. We must, therefore, be consistently vigilant lest the customary procedures mislead us, give us false facts and pseudo-understanding. Drawn into a blind alley, we may be led to incorrect conclusions, faulty hypotheses, and a kind of theory-building that impedes rather than facilitates the discovery of the truths of child development. If we want to understand the relations of child and family we must engage in direct observation of these very relations; we must study child and family together. This offers a built-in corrective for a range of possible errors in clinical judgment that derives from psychiatric examination of a child which is pursued apart from the family.

PROBLEMS OF THEORETICAL ORIENTATION

Psychodynamic investigation of the interrelations of child behavior and familiy experience have been given tremendous impetus through the discoveries of psychoanalysis. Psychoanalysis pointed a beacon light to the basic needs of the child, the stages of emotional development, the integration of psyche and soma and the role of unconscious conflict. It placed in bold relief the psychic bond of child and mother, the child's fear of abandonment and loss of love, his struggle with parental authority and fear of punishment, and the balance between need satisfaction and need frustration.

Freudian formulation of the psycho-sexual stages of child development, however valuable in its own right, failed to provide a satisfactory framework. A critical difficulty resulted from the tendency to dissociate the biological and the social determinants of behavior. When a psychoanalyst alluded to a certain psycho-sexual level, oral, anal or genital, this carried a dual connotation: (a) a specific level of instinctual organization, (b) an implied level of ego development or total personality organization related to the dominant levels of instinctual drive. This is ambiguous and confusing. Missing in this framework are the identity connections of child and family, the relations of ego and superego with family interaction and the interplay of the child's defenses against anxiety with the family group defenses of its integrity, stability and growth.

In psychoanalytically derived formulations, selective patterns of interaction were suggested between the child's unconscious needs and particular elements of parental behavior, or between the overt actions of the child and unconscious wishes of the parent. Clearly such correlations are partial in nature. They hypothesize a relation between a piece of the child and a piece of the parent. This piece of the child is not defined in proper relation to the whole child, nor is the whole child seen in accurate perspective with regard to the whole parent, nor to the full breadth of the relation between the parents, nor to the psychosocial configuration of the family as a whole. Parental behavior is defined intuitively in a spotty, incomplete way, often selectively and with prejudice. Frequently neglected, furthermore, are the inevitable processes of change across time in parents and family.

Clinical interest was usually focused on the relation of specific types of reaction in the child with specific parental attitudes, neglect, rejection, harsh or inconsistent discipline, over-indulgence, overprotection; also, the connection of specific body responses in the child to specific anxieties in the parent. Some correlations were established with regard to the child's reactions to rivals for parental love and to parental punishment. Finally, conflict in the child was related to conflict between child and parent, and between the parents. Today, one must be increasingly sceptical of familiar cliches and stereotyped formulations concerning the child's response to parental rejection, seduction, oedipal involvement, narcissistic exploitation, etc. No one of these "noxious" features of the environment can be understood except in the context of a systematic examination of the dynamic processes of the family as a whole.

It is true that psychoanalytic ideology assigned an important place to family as the shaper and maker of the child's personality, but its theoretical structure has thus far dealt mainly with isolated parts of the family, not with the family as a living unit.

Psychoanalytic theory contains a profound riddle concerning the relations of individual development and family belongingness as they evolve through time. How far is the child's personality individual? How far is it familial and social? How far does the child's personality unfold autonomously from within, how far is it influenced from without? How far does it move outward and forward, how far does it move inward and backward? This is the riddle of the inner and outer face of personality, the mystery of the relations of subject and object, the I and me. In psychoanalytic theory we cannot be clear how far they are joined and how far they are separate. Psychoanalysis reveals with uncanny clarity how the child falsifies his image of family, but not how a child assimilates his correctly perceived experience of the realities of family interaction. Psychoanalysis does not adequately illuminate the merging of old and new experience. It does not show how a child learns and grows, nor does it show the forward-moving, creative expansion of personality. It focuses one-sidedly on pathology, insufficiently on health.

From another standpoint the child was viewed as a polymorphous perverse little animal, a pleasure-bent anarchist; the parent as antipleasure. The parent and child were enemies locked in battle, each exacting sacrifice of the other, or at best achieving an uneasy truce. Is sacrifice the core of parent-child relations? Is it so that what the child gains, the parent loses, that what the child loses, the parent gains? Is love in family relations impoverishing or enriching? What is mainly revealed here is the competitive, oppositional aspect, not the joining of child with parent and family. Psychoanalysis tended to dissociate the inner mental processes from the forces of the environment. It viewed social force and reality as a contaminating influence. It dichotomized the biological and the social, conscious and unconscious, pleasure and pain, reality and fantasy. Psychoanalytic theory moved from inside outward and tended, until now, to neglect the circular feedback aspects of the relations of child and parent.

Hindsight is, of course, easier than foresight. We can now recognize that psychoanalysis, with its extraordinary insights, has given rise to new problems. It is clear now that we must mark out the discrepancies between unconscious and conscious striving, illuminate the influence of specific components of pathogenic motivation within the frame of total personality organization, and finally, relate the child's psychosocial response at each stage of development to a definition of the structure and function of the family as a living unit. The processes are multiple, complex, overlapping, difficult to control and interpret.

A question may be raised about our readiness to quantify data in clinical research. How and what to measure must follow hypothesis finding and testing. The traditional method of the physical sciences which distinguishes dependent and independent variables and preserves the constancy of one variable while observing the effect of altering another, is at present hardly applicable to the problem of the relations of child and family. Nor can the principle of rigid controls in experimental design be implemented. A further handicap is the inability to replicate in any exact fashion a particular, though transitory, configuration of family relationships. For these reasons and more, this field of inquiry does not yet readily lend itself to devices of precise measurement. Again and again, psychiatry in general, and the psychiatry of children in particular, have been critically assailed as being pseudo-science. Continuing pressure has been exerted for "exact" research, for a rigorous test of assumed knowledge by scientific method. But what is a true scientific approach to the relations of child and family? Ought we not here to discriminate between science and scientism? Unfortunately, much of what passes as "scientific" in child psychiatry is merely scientistic. We must separate the wheat from the chaff. Are we yet ready to quantify data in the area of child and family psychiatry? Surely there is room for critical doubt on this issue. What exactly shall we try to measure and how shall we do it? Only after we have thought through, talked through, and fought through the complex questions involved, only after we have achieved a coherent, consistent conceptual framework, can we begin to consider the challenge of measurement and verification. We need initially to be crystal clear as to what it is we are looking at, before we can turn reasonably to the task of precise validation. Otherwise, we are in constant danger of measuring wrong events, insignificant events, or even of perverting our definitions of the problem to make them conveniently fit familiar and readily available means of measurement. We are faced today with a plethora of statistical studies that, at the least, are without essential value and, at the worst, are misleading. They may actually derail and delay the development of valid knowledge. Clearly, the discovery of new and relevant ideas is our first responsibility.

Still another set of difficult problems derives from the necessity of integrating the knowledge and methods of multiple disciplines. By the very nature of the problem, it demands the contributions of all branches of behavioral science. There is a prime need to integrate psychodynamics and social science, but how shall we provide for this contingency? The special complications of inter-disciplinary collaboration are extensively discussed in the literature. For the study of the clinical aspects of human relations problems, experience shows that one needs a special kind of social scientist. For this need, one searches everywhere but, unfortunately, only with rare success. Too often one is inclined to agree with the frequently expressed sentiment that the best kind of interdisciplinary collaboration is that which can be crowded inside one man's head.

THE CHALLENGE

We are faced with twin tasks, each related to and dependent upon the other: the design of a more satisfactory theoretical framework for the emotional relations of child and family, and the creation of new methods of clinical, social and experimental study by which to test and amend this theory. For this purpose, the older, more familiar methods will not work; we need very much to discover new methods suited to the specific nature of this problem. A clinically oriented exploratory interview with the whole family seems to provide one such approach. Such an interview may be conducted in an office or within the home. It affords us new kinds of information about the emotional relations of child and family. The observations thus gathered and the related hypotheses can be applied to a range of special studies. The data of family interaction can be examined from many points of view, using different points of reference, depending upon one's special interest. For instance, one can pursue a differential study of the characteristics of family interaction which are conducive to psychosis or to neurosis. One can examine the features of family structure and function which predispose to shared patterns of acting out, delinquency, drug addiction, etc. One can examine adolescent problems as a symptom of family disorder. One can examine the way in which the character traits, the anxieties and defenses of the two parents are parcelled out among the offspring. One can examine the relations of verbal and non-verbal communication in family interaction. Interpretation of family process and change can be checked against strategically timed interviews with selected parts of the family, individuals or family pairs. One can compare and contrast a variety of family types belonging to the same sub-culture. One can do cross-cultural studies of different family types. One can objectify the findings in these various approaches by the use of sound tape, moving pictures, TV, multiple observers, etc.

CONCEPTUAL FRAMEWORK

The basic need is for an expanded conceptual framework within which to examine the interrelations of child and family. In this larger perspective, the child is seen as part of the family, the family as part of the child. Without the family, the child is incomplete; without the child, the family is incomplete. The child takes from the family what it needs for its growth and development. The family, in turn, takes from the child what it needs for its growth and development. Each projects on to the other unwanted qualities. The relations between the two are interdependent and interpenetrating. The exchange of affect and influence is a circular one;

it moves both ways, from family to child and child to family. Any change in the behavior of family brings a change in the behavior of the child and vice versa. As the family evolves across time, the child must respond accordingly; as the child's personality emerges, so also must the family react. The correlation of child and family behavior is differently determined for each stage of evolution of the family group, for each stage of the emergence of the child's personality. The circularity of adaptation at any one stage is, of course, influenced by the quality of adaptation that prevailed in the antecedent stage. The perspective is an ecological one; the unit of behavior to be examined is the child within the family rather than the child alone. The family environment is of the essence of the child's emerging pattern of adaptation; child and family are indivisible. This point of view gives full recognition to the need to interrelate mind, body and social behavior. It integrates representations of the inside and outside of the child's mind. It evaluates within a unitary theoretical scheme conflict within and between the minds of family members. It defines the effects of genetic and constitutional factors within the matrix of the ongoing mutual adaptation of child and family group. It gives explicit recognition to the principle that social and cultural factors play a preeminent part in the progressive organization of the child's personality. This, in essence, is the psychiatry of the child within the broader matrix of a social psychiatry of the family.

The significance of this shift in orientation is profound. It dictates a movement away from the traditional, exclusive absorption with the individual manifestations of mental illness to an expanded concern for the relevant processes of social interaction. It relates social health and mental health, social disorder and mental disorder. It impels us to define the unit of pathogenic response within the larger framework of total adaptation, to weigh sickness-inducing forces against those that maintain health. For these purposes, obviously, an explicit conception of health, however elusive, becomes indispensable. The emergence of this perspective is historically reflected in the step-by-step movement away from a primary concern with symptoms to conflicts and related ways of coping, to character structure, to the total functioning of personality, to the relations of personality to social role adaptation, and finally to the dynamics of family and culture patterns. It interprets child-rearing behavior and mothering attitudes, not exclusively as a function of the woman's personality, but beyond that also as an idiosyncratic expression of the character and quality of the family as a whole. Mothering is influenced by fathering, fathering by mothering, both in turn affected by the circular interchange of parents with child, child with siblings, younger and older generations, and by the interplay further between the nuclear family and kin. The influences of social class and culture pattern become internalized in the characters of the parents and in the patterning of the family. It is in this sense that the child-rearing needs to be viewed as a shared responsibility.

Within this framework we are obliged to assess psychopathological deviation in a relation to a normative standard of the emotional development of the child. We need to understand better what is a healthy child, a healthy mother and father, a healthy family, a healthy community and culture. Admittedly the achievement of such standards is a tall order, a most difficult and complex undertaking. Some investigators shy away from the enormity of the task; they say that health is so extraordinarily relative as to defy description. Others go even further; they assert the position that health in human terms is a sheer abstraction, that it does not really exist and, therefore, we can have no scientific definition of health. However relative such a condition may be, health is a human reality. Just as there are degrees and depths of illness so, too, are there degrees and heights of health. If so, we have no alternative, no excuse for avoiding the issue. Unless we make a significant advance along this path of formulating normative standards of development and health, there will always be some question as to how far we can really be clear and confident concerning the validity of our presumed standards of pathogenic development and illness. All things are relative: what goes wrong makes sense only as we place it alongside of a conception of what goes right in human development and adaptation.

The family "makes or breaks" personality. The family has the power to enhance or impair the mental health of the individual. Interactional processes in the family exercise a selective control of emotional expression, supporting some channels for the release of feeling and restricting others. The family strengthens some individual drives, weakens others. It satisfies or thwarts personal needs. It structures the opportunity for security, pleasure and self-realization. It patterns the lines of identification, thus molding the emergence of the individual's image of self. It defines the dangers the individual must face in life. It lends specific form to conflict and may or may not provide an experimental setting favorable to solution. The group life of the family may intensify or lessen anxiety. It exerts a potent influence towards success or failure of particular defense operations. Finally, it may strengthen or weaken the reality testing power of the individual. In turn, the individual gives preference to those features of family experience which are friendly towards and supportive of his personal strivings. He interacts selectively with those aspects of family life which further his personal aims, values, pleasure goals, relief of guilt, forms of defenses and solutions of conflict.

Family roles, then, are interdependent and interpenetrating. Behavior in a family role is influenced from three sources; individual personality, reciprocity of family roles, and the psychosocial structure of the family as a whole. In triangular relationships one member may bind or disrupt the unity of the other two. Emotional illness may serve to integrate or disintegrate family relationships, the illness of one member complementing that of another or having antagonistic effects. The course of illness may be slowed or hastened by the quality of family relationships. Some forms of illness may be shared by two or more members.

The challenge is to interrelate the growth processes of childhood with the developmental processes of the child's emotional integration into his family group and social community. It is the interaction and merging of the biological and social forces, stage by stage, that molds the characteristics of child personality.

In the purview of history, the family approach to personality disorders in childhood is propelled into being by several converging forces: (1) the revolutionary transformation of the family pattern, induced by social change; (2) the recognition of principle of contagion of emotional disturbance, and the intimate relation between social and mental disorder; (3) the greater appreciation of the limitations of conventional procedures of diagnosis, treatment and prevention that are restricted to the individual child; (4) specific new developments in the behavioral sciences which include a range of studies in ego psychology, small group dynamics, social psychology, anthropology and communication; (5) the changed role of the psychotherapist in the modern community.

Such developments, rapidly unfolding on the contemporary scene, bring a rising pressure for a method of study of the family group as a behavior system.

The family approach enables us to undertake a critical review of existing concepts of causation of personality disorders in children. It leads to more precise criteria for evaluating disturbances of the central roles of mothering and fathering, for the assessment of marital and parental conflict, the effect of child on parent and the functioning of the family as a whole. It makes possible the understanding of the pathology of the individual members in the context of the life of the group. It illuminates the balance between the integrative and disintegrative forces of family life. It makes possible a parallel assessment of sickness-inducing and health-maintaining forces. It suggests some conceptual paths along which we may correct known deficiencies in child and family guidance practices and in psychotherapy. It provides a scheme for integrating social therapy and psychotherapy in family services. Of focal importance is the clarification of those specific components of marital and parental functioning that are conducive to pathological child development.

CHILD—FAMILY DIAGNOSIS

The task of achieving a more precise correlation of child and family requires the following:

(1) Criteria for the psychosocial structure and mental health functioning of the family group;
(2) Elucidation of the stages of development of the family;
(3) A classification of family types according to their mental health functioning;
(4) A theory of child personality specifying the stages of development in terms of biosocial integration with the family group;
(5) A system of evaluating deviant units of child

behavior within the context of total personality organization and adaptation to family roles;

(6) A classification of psychiatric disorders in children that can be joined with the principles of family diagnosis.

The psychosocial structure and functions of the family group may be evaluated horizontally and longitudinally. In the horizontal or cross-sectional view, we may examine the family from the following points of reference:

(1) The fulfillment, harmonization and balancing of the family functions;
(2) The typical family role relationships and patterns of complementarity;
(3) The conflicts and coping; the alignments and splits within the group; the interplay between family defense and individual defense;
(4) The identity, stability, value orientation and growth of the family;
(5) The discrepancy between the family's actual performance and a model of healthy family functioning.

On a more differentiated level, we may evaluate marital and parental adaptation, the fit of marital and parental roles, the parents as individuals, the fit of parent with child, child with parent.

In the longitudinal view, we may examine the family at sequential stages of development and adaptation:

(1) The stage of courtship;
(2) Early marriage;
(3) The expansion of family with the advent of the first child;
(4) The family with multiple children;
(5) The family in maturity;
(6) The dissolution of the old family and the creation of new ones.

We may assess the family's capacity to fulfill, harmonize and balance its multiple functions according to the following items: (1) survival and security, (2) affection, (3) the balance between dependency and autonomous development, (4) social and sexual training, (5) growth and creative development.

We may ask: which of these are selectively safeguarded? Which others are neglected or distorted? Which are sacrificed so as to protect which others? In other words, what is the priority that the family assigns to them and what is the pattern of failure to achieve balanced functioning?

As a next step, we draw judgment on the typical family role relationships and patterns of family role complementarity. In the reciprocal role adaptations of husband-wife, father-mother, parent-child, child-sibling, we examine the question of emotional complementarity with the use of five criteria: (1) support of self-esteem, (2) need satisfaction, (3) co-operation in the search for solution of conflict, (4) support of needed defenses against anxiety, (5) support of growth and creative development.

We discern at what specific levels emotional complementarity is preserved, at what others levels it is sacrificed. We draw a further judgment: in the emotional involvement of triangular relationships such as mother, father and child, does the need and anxiety of one member of the threesome invade and impair the emotional complementarity of the other two?

We classify role complementarity in three broad categories: (1) lacking, (2) partial, (3) complete.

We say there is a lack of complementarity or a negative complementarity when there is a critical reduction at all levels. We say complementarity is partial when it exists on some levels and is absent on others. For example, a satisfactory quality of complementarity in the items of need satisfaction and support of defenses against anxiety, but a relative lack of complementarity in support of self-esteem, co-operation in the quest for solution of conflict and support of growth and creative development. Partial complementarity may contribute to the control of anxiety; it may offset possible breakdown in one of the partners and yet limit growth both of the relationship and of each partner as an individual. We say that complementarity is high or relatively complete where there is emotional complementation in substantial measure on all five items.

The next stage of family diagnosis is the identification of the main patterns of conflict and coping. Conflict and coping are seen as twin aspects of a single process. We define the main conflicts of the family only in the context of a parallel statement concerning the ways of coping with conflict. Conflict within the family emerges out of a struggle between one part of the family and another about what the family is and ought to be, how the family serves or fails to serve the needs of its members, what the members do, ought to do or fail to do for family. Family conflicts revolve mainly around issues of need satisfaction, love expectation, struggle for control or support of a needed or preferred self-image. In the course of such struggle the family group may divide into competing factions. A conflict of identity, values and strivings brings a split in the family which mobilizes one segment against the other. Such splits may be horizontal, vertical or diagonal. They may set male against female, mother and son against father and daughter, younger generation against older. The opposed factions may be equal or severely unequal in power and position. It may be two against two or three against one. It is rarely "all for one and one for all." The breakup of the family into warring factions distorts the execution and balance of family functions. Family splits of this kind are often organized as a cluster of interrelated roles, that of attacker or punisher, victim of attack, the scapegoat, and the family healer.†

We refer to coping with family conflict as family defense. This has as its purpose the protection of the integrity and continuity of family functions.

We identify family defenses tentatively as follows:

(1) Enhancement of the bond of love, sharing, co-operation and identification.
(2) Selective shifts in family role complementarity in one or more of the above mentioned criteria.
(3) Rigidification or loosening of the family roles.
(4) Reduction of the intensity of the conflict by means of manipulation, coercion, bribery, compromise, denial or escape.
(5) Shifts in the configuration of alignments and splits within the family group and prejudicial scapegoating of one part of the family by another.
(6) Repeopling of the family, that is, elimination of one member or addition of another.
(7) A significant change of environment.

We endeavor to mark out the interplay between the main family defenses of the integrity and continuity of family functions and individual defenses against anxiety.

We come now to the question of family identity. Family identity is what the family stands for. It pertains to a dominant identity, a representation composed of shared goals, values and striving. Family identity is not and cannot be a fixed or pure thing; it represents a fluid, continuously evolving image of the family as a living, changing unit. It is crystallized out of an ongoing clash of multiple, competing, and co-operating partial identity representations. It is molded by the manner in which each member struggles to reconcile his personal identity and values with the shifting representations of family identity across time. It refers in a special way to the direction and content of striving. It answers the question, Who are we as a family at a given time and place and in a defined life situation?

The concept of family stability refers to the continuity of family identity across time, the control of conflict and the capacity to change, learn and achieve further development. It is reflected in the quality of adaptability and growth of family role relationships.

Family identity and stability must be considered together. Stability epitomizes the family's capacity to protect the continuity and integrity of the family's identity under the pressure of changing life conditions. It insures the intactness of family adaptation in the face of new experience. This is the conservative phase of stability. The other aspect must provide for the capacity to adapt flexibly to new experience, to learn and to achieve further development. It represents the potential for change and growth. Effective adaptation or homeostasis requires a favorable balance between the protection of sameness and continuity and the need to accommodate to change. It requires the preservation of the old coupled with receptivity to the new, a mixture of conservatism and readiness to live dangerously.

Within this theoretical framework it seems possible to outline the pathogenic areas of family conflict, those which push the homeostatic func-

†Ackerman, Nathan W. Prejudicial Scapegoating and Neutralizing Forces in the Family Group, with Special Reference to the Role of "Family Healer." *Int. J. Soc. Psychiat.* Congress Issue, 1964.

tion toward decompensation, aggravating the tendency to disorganization, regression, breakdown of communication and emotional alienation; at the opposite pole, we may define the potential in the complementarity of family role relationships for providing new paths of solution to conflict, establishing effective compensation or compromise, fostering new levels of identification and individuation, and thereby promoting health and growth. Thus we may more clearly view the balance of forces within the family, those that predispose to breakdown and illness and those that protect health and fulfillment.

The diagnosis of the marital partnership is a part of family diagnosis. To be considered are: the capacity for love, mutual adaptation, adaptation to external change and adaptation for growth.

We are concerned here with evaluating the role complementarity of the marital partnership, the levels of conflict, benign and destructive, and the patterns of coping. Worthy of emphasis here are two special features of defense: (a) the use of the marital partnership to compensate anxiety and support one or both partners against the threat of breakdown; the use of external relationships to mitigate marital failure, to provide compensatory satisfaction. (b) The quality of integration of each partner into the marital role and the fit of marital and parental roles.

The performance of the parental pair can be similarly judged by: 1—the complementarity of parental roles; the mutuality of adaptation, adaptation to external change and adaptation for growth, 2—the levels of conflict, benign and destructive, 3—the integration of each partner into the parental role, 4—the effects of parental behavior on the child, 5—the effects of the child's behavior on the parents.

The final step in family diagnosis is the need to define the discrepancy between the actual performance of the family and an ideal standard of family functioning. One can assess: 1—the fulfillment of strivings and values, 2—the stability, maturity, and realism of the family, 3—the presence or absence of regressive and disintegrative trends, 4—the quality and degree of successful adaptation and growth.

The question here is, how far does the family fall short of what it might be, in the family's view of itself, in the community's view of family; and finally in terms of a professional standard of a mentally healthy family unit.

In the longitudinal perspective, similar evaluations may be made for each stage of the growth of the family, as previously indicated; 1—the stage of courtship, 2—early marriage, 3—the expansion of the family with the first child, 4—the family with multiple children, 5—the family in maturity, 6—the dissolution of the old family and the creation of new ones.

The child's adaptation to his family environment is viewed as a biosocial process. Hereditary factors influence such qualities as physical type, affectivity, motor reactivity, and intellectual potential, but the processes of socialization pattern the form of all behavior. The channels of expression of physiological need are organized by the social interaction of the child and parent, and by the typical interpersonal relationships within the family group. The individuality of the child is incomplete; he develops only a relative autonomy.

The stages of development of the child are viewed as advancing levels of biosocial integration with, and differentiation from his family environment. At each stage of maturation, his drive, defense, perception of self and others, conflict and anxiety are conceived as inter-related elements in a unit of adaptation. The body orifices, the skin, the activity of the internal organs and the muscle systems are regarded not only as sources of pleasure and means of avoiding pain, but also as somatic agencies for the interchange of energy between the inner and outer environment and as sub-verbal instruments of communication. As the child develops, he achieves different levels of emotional union with, and individuation from his parents. When a child acquires speech, independent mobility and increasing realistic mastery of his environment, his identity is further differentiated by his response to his two parents as a joined couple and by his relations with his siblings and grandparents. For purposes of definition, the child's emotional development is divided into stages. Each stage is conditioned by the previous stage, merges imperceptibly into and overlaps the next stage. With maturation from one stage to the next, the processes intrinsic to the previous stage do not cease but become less prominent and are differently integrated into the dominant patterns of the succeeding stage. These stages of development are best identified in terms of the characteristic trends of adaptation.

(1) The immediate post-birth stage reflects mainly a vegetative adaptation. The organism feeds, sleeps, cries when hungry. The integration of nervous system functions is incomplete; perceptual responses are crude, relatively unorganized and do not yet leave permanent psychic residues.

(2) The second stage is one of the primary biosocial union with mother. Though physically separated at birth, the infant is totally dependent for survival and development on symbiotic union with mother. It requires nourishment, tender warmth, touch contact and stimulation and protection from danger. At this stage the child's behavior alternates between the extremes of helplessness and defenselessness and a striving for omnipotent control. The urge for omnipotent mastery is conceived not as a function of the child as individual, but rather as a function of the child's biosocial union with mother. The child commands, the mother obeys; the mother commands, the child obeys. The child is not yet able to distinguish the mother's self from the own self. The mother functions not only as the source of love and security but also as the perceptive and executive agent of the child, communicating through her behavior her own affective interpretations of the prevailing realities and also her devices for dealing with them. At this stage the child is already capable of a tender, warm response to mother. Premature, excessive, shocking or sudden withdrawal of mother induces in the child feelings of panic, helplessness, fear of loss of life and outbreaks of aggression.

(3) The third stage is one of gradual separation of the infant's self from mother's self. As the child matures there is progressively less panic and less aggression on separation. The child begins to assert its separate self with increasing firmness. As he becomes ambulatory, he develops the power of speech and greater physical mastery over his environment. As the original biosocial unity with mother lessens, omnipotent behavior gives way to an increasing measure of real control and progressive testing of reality. Along with these trends social discipline of the child assumes increasing importance. The child comes to terms with parents and family. The mother's care and control of the child are influenced by the quality of her relations with father and family. As a child submits to parental discipline, he begins to internalize social standards, at first depending on the parent as an external source of control, but gradually incorporating these standards into his own personality.

(4) The fourth stage reflects the child's differentiation of the two parents according to sex, redirection of the child's love needs in accordance with the parents' masculine and feminine qualities and the relationship between them. In a parallel process, corresponding identifications emerge with each parent. There is deeper internalization of functions of conscience, now influenced by the distinction between male and female parent and the emerging sexual identity of the child. The further stages of submission to parental discipline are differentiated accordingly.

(5) The fifth stage is one of expansion of the emotional and social spheres of the child's interaction with his environment beyond the confines of his immediate family, testing of social reality and learning in the context of wider contact with peers and parent substitutes. This is a period of broadened social growth, education and preparation for adolescence.

(6) The sixth stage is one of pubescent growth, bringing in its wake the struggles of adolescent adaptation. Differentiated sex drives emerge and there are reorganization of the lines of identification, realignment of group allegiances and roles, and anticipation of and preparation for the tasks of adult life.

The role of family in the induction of child disorder rests on the emotional hurts inflicted upon the child, the timing of these assaults and their duration. The eventual outcome is determined by the maturational condition of the child as organism, the vulnerability of the child's personality, and the healing powers that can be mobilized by child and family together.

The more disturbed the family, the more are the relations of child and family bound to the theme of sacrifice, an emotional sacrifice imposed upon the individual as the price of membership. The child suffers this sacrifice as the victim of a form of prejudicial scapegoating that is characteristic of the given family. In malignantly disturbed families the prejudice is, in effect, *the child must not be;* in less disturbed families, *the child must not be different*. The scapegoating of the child may revolve around a range of prejudices which attaches to those qualities of the child that represent a threat to the parents. The prejudice may take the form of an antagonism to anything new, any expression of change or growth; it may be opposition to the assertion of difference, or to the expression of spontaneous feeling. The prejudice may revolve around issues of conflict between the younger and older generations. It may attach to the war of the sexes. It may become connected with brain versus brawn, smart vs. stupid, fat vs. thin, light vs. dark skin or to a variety of habits concerning food, clothing and cleanliness.

The emotional injury inflicted on the child may result in (1) a fundamental threat to the child's survival, in terms of body injury, neglect, starvation, physical or emotional, or both. (2) A pathogenic symbiosis of child and parent with a fixation of child's growth. (3) Susceptibility either to a major or minor mental illness.

The emotional sacrifice that family exacts of the child as the price of membership may be (1) relatively total, (2) partial and selective. In total sacrifice, *the child must not be*. He has no right to live, breathe, eat or move. The sacrifice imposed is extreme. The family maintains itself in a static equilibrium at the expense of the emotional life of the child. The growth potential of the child is impaired, warped or destroyed. It is this pattern of emotional injury that predisposes to psychotic development.

In the case of partial sacrifice, the relations of child and family are bound to the theme, *the child must not be different*. In order to assure security and approval, he must conform by surrendering a segment of his individual being. The family maintains its equilibrium by imposing upon the child this forced partial surrender. In this configuration of child and family, so long as conflict is contained and defenses are compensated, the disturbance results mainly in psychoneurotic development.

In a deviant pattern of partial sacrifice, where defense operations decompensate and there is a relative failure to contain conflict, the outcome becomes either exile or forced complicity in disordered family relationship patterns.

The result of this trend may be (1) alienation of the family members, each going his own way, (2) a pattern of sociopathic rebellion, indulgence in alcohol or drugs, etc. (3) a perversion of family relationships to the goal of power, degradation, and destruction, (4) psychosomatic disorder. Such disorders sometimes serve the purpose of offsetting a complete breakdown of defenses, and the outbreak of overt psychosis. By identifying patterns of prejudicial scapegoating and the characteristic forced sacrifice, it becomes possible to define those features of the family environment which act as "sensitizers," "pressurizers" and "precipitators" of disturbance in a child. At each stage of child development, the healing of conflict and anxiety may be either healthy or pathological. It is when healthy healing fails that deviant patterns in the child become fixed and persistent. As a child moves to the next stage, new deviations may be superimposed and added to the clinical picture. Thus, multiple types of pathogenic response and mixed symptoms may emerge, referable to different stages of development.

The child may react to threats in the family environment in one of the following ways: (1) he may attack his family and attempt thereby to coerce gratification of need. In this category fall the aggressive conduct disorders and the sociopathic forms of behavior disorder. (2) The child may withdraw from contact with his family. In this category fall the recessive personality developments and trends toward excessive preoccupation with self and body. (3) The child may react with excessive anxiety, internalization of conflict and with a production of one or another structured form of psychopathology: (a) excessive anxiety with internalization and encapsulation of specific conflicts as in the production of psycho-neurotic reaction, (b) excessive anxiety, defective emotional control, decompensation of defenses, paralysis or disorganization of adaptive functions which may induce sociopathic or psychosomatic tendencies, (c) excessive anxiety, disorganization of adaptive behavior, arrest of development and/or regression and reintegration at a primitive psychic level as in psychotic forms of reaction.

Psychiatric disorder in a child must be classified and correlated with the specific type of family environment. The classification of family types according to mental health functioning is a complex undertaking. With the limitations of present knowledge we can only suggest a crude tentative grouping of family types. From a genetic or developmental point of view:

(1) *The healthy or expansive growing family* (see below).
(2) *The accidental or unintended family*—one that is forced by external circumstances as, for example, in a marriage and family brought about by pregnancy or other accident of life.
(3) *The abortive or temporary family*—one that emerges out of a kind of life adventure, a trial marriage, a conversion of a sexual affair, unintended basically to endure or evolve into a normal family group.
(4) *The family of flight*—one that results mainly from the urge to escape from conflict with the family of origin or a kind of family that is brought about as a rebound from a prior disappointment in love.
(5) *The family of expediency*—one that derives from an arranged marriage, a pact of security or one that has the purpose of joining two larger families.

From a functional point of view:

(1) *The healthy family*—a theoretical ideal. Mother and father have a good fit both in the marital and parental partnership. They are able to share realistic goals and compatible values. They share awareness of these strivings and values, positive in emphasis rather than defensive. Compatibility is achieved in a reasonable measure in the emotional social, sexual, parental and economic areas. Conflict is not excessive, is under control and mainly has realistic content. When conflict arises, the parents are able to cooperate in the search for the solution or appropriate compromise. A transitory disturbance does not involve an excess or persistence of accusation, guilt feelings and scapegoating. There is empathic toleration of differences based on mutual understanding and respect and also tolerance of residual immaturities that might be present in one or another family member. There is sharing of pleasure, responsibility and authority. There is reasonable fulfillment of goals, both for the family as family and for the development of each member. There is appropriate concern for the welfare and development of other members of the family as well as for self. In the face of differences the mutual, unreserved acceptance of one family member by another makes these differences a stimulus for growth rather than a basis for conflict or alienation. The actual performance of the family reasonably approximates its goals. Relatively high emotional complementarity among the family members exists with no significant trends toward isolation, disintegration or regression.

(2) *The immature protective family*—the type of family which emerges out of an original need. One part needs to relate to the other in the role of parent. The relationships remain immature and protective.

(3) *The competitive family*—one in which relationships beginning with the parents are excessively influenced by motives of envy, jealousy and competitive admiration.

(4) *The family of neurotic complementarity*—a type of family in which the special neurotic needs of one parental partner are complemented by the other; one partner serves as a healer of the conflicts and anxieties of the other. The stronger partner in this arrangement is intended to provide immunity against emotional breakdown in the more vulnerable partner. In such families children are exposed to the imposition of a special kind of emotional sacrifice, one which requires them to surrender specific parts of their being as the price of belonging and protection.

(5) *The family of complementary acting out*—one in which the members join a shared pattern of acting out of conflicted urges. There is unconscious complicity in the acting-out pattern.

(6) *The detached or emotionally isolated family*—a family in which a tolerable balance is struck among the members conditional on maintaining a required degree of emotional distance and isolation.

(7) *The master-slave family*—a family with a characteristic role relationship: one partner seeks omnipotent control of the other. The master needs the slave; the slave needs the master. The one is aggrandized as the other is demeaned. The natural goals of love, sharing and identification are perverted to the goal of power to dominate, degrade, and ultimately destroy the partner. In essence, this is a symbiotic bond in which one partner expands at the expense of the other.

(8) *The regressive family*—a family dominated by a negative orientation to life. There is a shared fear of and prejudice against life and growth. There is a shared expectation of immi-

nent catastrophe. There is an implicit theme of total sacrifice. One member must surrender the right to live, breathe and move in order to assure the survival of other parts of the family. In its emotional orientation the family moves backward in life, rather than forward. Its relationships follow the master-slave pattern. This is the type of family that is most apt to produce psychotic disorder.

REFERENCES

Ackerman, N. W. *The Psychodynamics of Family Life*, Basic Books, 1958, N.Y.

Ackerman, N. W. A Dynamic Frame for the Clinical Approach to Family Conflict. In *Exploring the Base for Family Therapy*, Edited by Ackerman, Beatman and Sherman, Family Service Association of America, 1961.

Ackerman, N. W. Child and Family Psychiatry Today: A New Look at Some Old Problems, *Mental Hygiene* 47, Oct. 1963.

Ackerman, N. W. Prejudicial Scapegoating and Neutralizing Trends in the Family Group, *International Journal of Social Psychiatry*, Congress Issue, 1964.

Epstein, N. B. and Westley, W. A. Parental Interaction as Related to Emotional Health of Children, *Social Problems* 8, 87-92, 1960.

Rapoport, R. Normal Crises, Family Structure and Mental Health, *Family Process* 2, March 1963.

Meissner, W. W. Thinking About the Family, *Family Process* 3, March 1964.

Tyler, E. A. The Process of Humanizing Physiological Man, *Family Process* 3, Sept. 1964.

Vogel, E. F. The Marital Relationship of Parents of Emotionally Disturbed Children: Polarization and Isolation, *Psychiatry* 23, 1-12, 1960.

PART V

Family Therapy

Ackerman's notion of "failures of parenting" probably made conjoint treatment of the family group inevitable for him. This is particularly apparent in the early papers of this section (1952-59), fitting as they do with the later papers on child therapy. On the practical side, the culmination of the idea was his ambitious design of the Council Child Development Center, where family therapy was to be an integral part of the educational and therapeutic plan.

To judge from his papers, Ackerman's allegiance to traditional psychoanalytic practice further declined in the fifties. What we might call the "psychoanalytic" papers in this section (1959, 1962) seem to be his farewell to a mode of therapy that had long constrained him. (Note that the Family Institute was founded around the same time, 1961.)

Once past that point, Ackerman's published work no longer advances his earlier model of sequential interviewing of family, child, parents, etc. Rather, it is the conjoint family interview which is emphasized. Apart from noting this change in technique, the papers from the sixties do not need individual introductions. We are no longer presenting the gradual evolution of ideas, but now find the author in the fertile high plateau of his last decade. We can see reflected the clinical experience of nearly 40 years of clinical work and, at the same time, Ackerman's personal transition into the Grand Old Man of family therapy. (These papers, it should be remembered, were culled from the thicket of publications in which he over and over again presented family therapy to a curious but skeptical professional public.)

Reading these papers and the concluding group of clinical transcripts, however, we must also remember that family interviews were not Ackerman's exclusive format for therapy, nor were the published cases—most of whom had other therapists—only treated in this modality. But no matter who sat in front of him, Ackerman was always, in Murray Bowen's felicitous phrase, "thinking toward the family."

The three interview transcripts have been grouped together because of the bright spotlight they collectively throw upon Ackerman the therapist. Here his personality fairly leaps off the page. The open, challenging style, the ingenious use of metaphor (so curiously parallel to Milton Erickson), his refusal to shrink from "delicate" subjects—these are all hallmarks of Nathan Ackerman, clinician.

True, it is not always possible to connect Ackerman's clinical style with his theoretical ideas. For instance, the key concept of family homeostasis (or, to use his preferred term, homeodynamics) does not seem to influence his consulting room tactics. Rather, Ackerman regards the process of therapy as taking place *dyadically*, either between family members directly or else with the intermediate step of their relationships with the therapist. He seems to have grasped homeostasis better as a principle of symptom formation than as a principle of cure. This legacy of his psychoanalytic career does not, fortunately, diminish the vitality of the transcripts.

The first case, entitled "Non-verbal Cues and Re-enactment of Conflict in Family Therapy" (1965), was later recycled as a chapter of *Treating the Troubled Family*. In that later version, Ackerman interspersed the verbatim report with comments about his method and the family's responses. Our version is the original one in which a team of observing collaborators attempted to analyze the nonverbal elements of communication between family members and with the interviewer.

In the second transcript, "A Family Therapy Session" (1967), Ackerman introduced the format he would use extensively in *Treating the Troubled Family:* Reconstructing as parallel commentary what his thoughts and motives had been. It is doubtful whether these observations were consciously in his mind during the session. He once remarked to the Family Institute staff that an interviewer mostly flew by the seat of his pants and only after the fact could he describe (or invent) his reasons for this or that intervention.

The last interview, "To Catch A Thief" (1970), shows Ackerman's art in its highest form. This may be partly because it was a second, not initial, interview with the family. Ackerman always emphasized the importance of conducting family consultations in two sessions, or at least in two segments with an intermission. The family invariably returned to the second segment more accepting of the therapist and readier to reveal their inner selves. That this process could apply to therapist as well as to family is demonstrated in "To Catch A Thief," where the interview pivots on Ackerman's sudden, intuitive leap of thought connecting the boy's symptomatic behavior with the circumstances of his father's death. Any careful anamnesis might have led to the same *as a hypothesis*, but Ackerman jumps into more than a theoretical connection: He is able to see the unconscious fantasy directly.

To these transcripts, and to those of *Treating the Troubled Family*, therapists who knew Ackerman or who saw him demonstrate can easily supply the visual cues: the expressive cigarette, the twinkling eyes, the teasing yet challenging tone, the occasionally wagging finger. Fortunately, these memories also exist in a unique series of filmed interviews produced while Ackerman was with the Jewish Family Service of New York. These are another treasure, scarcely mined at present but at least preserved, in the Institute which bears his name.

CHAPTER 25

Family Diagnosis: An Approach to the Preschool Child

The motivation for this study is twofold: first, the traditional categories of psychiatric diagnosis for children prove of little avail in attempting a dynamic definition of child personalities in the era between birth and five years; secondly, the incomplete personality of the preschool child cannot be understood save in the context of a group dynamic definition of the family. Accordingly, we undertook to define such child personalities not as separate individuals, but rather as functional parts of the family group, more specifically, as an expression of the sociopsychological configuration of the family unit.

In order to define a young child in these terms, it is necessary to make both a dynamic and genetic study of the family group, going back to its original formation in the period of courtship between the two parents. Such a study needs to be pursued in several steps: 1) The development of the family group (aims, standards and values of the family) through conditioning effects of group influence, currently and in the past. 2) A definitive picture of the individual personalities of the parents and siblings. 3) The fusion and patterns of interaction of the parents at each stage in the history of their relationship, leading up to the point where the parental relationship and the individual personalities of each parent accommodate to the admission of the child into the family group.

Throughout such a study it is necessary to treat the persons and the environment as a continuum and to mark out the patterns of interaction between intrapsychic and extrapsychic factors. For this there is needed a systematic appreciation of the group psychological influences which condition the goals, values and defense reactions of each member of the family, as well as a knowledge of the intrapsychic determinants of behavior.

Briefly, our method consists of studying the families of preschool children presenting varied clinical pictures. The data on each family are the product of a professional team study, involving

Reprinted with permission from *The American Journal of Orthopsychiatry*, 1950, Vol. 20, 744-752.

This paper was co-authored with Raymond Sobel.

the collaboration of the child's nursery teachers, the psychologist, the respective therapists (psychiatrist or social worker) of mother, father and child, the group therapist of mother and father, the social worker and the pediatrician. Using such data, we try to group families according to their internal dynamics and social position, and to describe the child's present-day problems in terms of adjustive behavior required to maintain equilibrium within the disturbed family constellation.

We recognize that the disturbances of adult life are determined by the vicissitudes of the preschool years, and further recognize that the psychological functioning during the preschool years can be expressed only as a resultant of the multiple forces interacting within the family group. Therefore, our unit of definition is not the substantive child, but rather the interaction of the child and the significant persons in his environment.

Accordingly, we believe that the treatment of the young child should begin with the treatment of the family group. However, we find ourselves confronted with the fact that, up to the present time, no adequate criteria for family disturbances, as group disturbances, have been found. Until such criteria are formulated so that we may describe (and later classify) such family disturbances, we have no frame of reference for the treatment of families as groups, despite the claims of many child guidance clinics to the contrary. Although the trends in child guidance are toward family orientation, the child and the mother, *but not the family*, are treated.

We do not know whether it is possible to treat families as groups. Perhaps it is not possible. In the interest of further study of etiology and prevention of disturbances in young children, we must first have at hand reliable methods of describing their malfunctioning. This paper is an attempt to provide such a method in the light of the reciprocal psychosocial forces moving between the family group and the preschool child. Thereby, we hope to move one step closer to the goal of prevention.

The Council Child Development Center, an organization designed for the study and treatment of preschool children in a family context, has been the source of our case material. There are several different, yet integrated, levels of approach, including individual treatment by child analysts, a therapeutic nursery, group therapy of mothers and fathers, individual therapy of parents by psychiatrists and social workers, as well as educational talks by nursery teachers and pediatrician. The emphasis upon the child as part of a family group is maintained through "integration conferences," held at regular intervals, in which those of the staff in contact with the various members of the family group exchange observations and ideas and plan therapy.

We have taken several family studies from our files and, using our multiprofessional approach, have examined each family chronologically from its earliest beginnings at the time of the parents' first contact, through marriage, conception, birth of the child and, finally, the ensuing years. We have traced, as in the specimen study reported here, what we consider to be the main continuous thread, namely, the parents' interlocking needs of each other, of the child and, later, of the family. These needs, intrapersonal, physiologic, as well as culturally induced, explain the original impetus to courtship and marriage and later, though modified, become the conscious and unconscious frame of reference for the emotional life of the growing child. We have studied the determinants of these needs in each parent's background, and have attempted to trace the vicissitudes of the parental relationship according to the changes and modifications of such needs by the emergence of the family group. Inasmuch as the parent's needs may be conscious or unconscious, rational or irrational, the problem of tracing the family relationships through them is necessarily complicated. However, they do provide the key to the personality of the preschool child since they maintain the field of forces to which he must accommodate in his development. Our method of study is illustrated in the following case presentation.

George, five years and one month, was referred to us by a local hospital. His mother complained that he had been irritable and cranky since birth, which was full term and normal. He was breast fed for six weeks, during which time he cried constantly. The mother brought him to several doctors, finally being informed by one that she should wean him. She did this reluctantly, pumping her breasts for an extended period of time. When George was four months old, his mother again made the rounds of physicians, and was told that he needed an "extra dose of love" together with phenobarbital. He took his formula poorly, many changes of it being tried without result. The mother felt that at six months he was "snubbing her," and responded to his apparent lack of affection for her with anxious, frozen doubt and immobility. From the age of six to ten months, while the mother worked at night in a defense plant, George was cared for by his paternal grandmother, a domineering and overwhelming woman who was upset by his crying and objected to his mother's "spoiling him," but nevertheless picked him up to prevent his tears and noise.

George continued to be a tense and irritable baby, seemed to develop interminable colds, and was fed large amounts of candy and ice cream in the mother's anxious efforts to pacify him. At about eighteen months, he developed diarrhea and foamy stools, later diagnosed as celiac disease. He was placed on a starvation diet for a short period and lost considerable weight, and the mother became even more anxious about his food intake, at times resorting to forced feeding. At this time, he became fearful of taking his pants off as he had been receiving painful injections of iron in the buttocks. Finally, another diet was instituted and he regained weight, but still had symptoms for several months. The mother, feeling it would be too much of a burden for him, made no attempt at bowel training until George was three, when the diarrhea cleared.

At this time, she entered him in a nursery school but was upset by his disinclination to play with other children and his lack of vitality. She pushed him into activity whenever possible. He reacted by further withdrawal and retreat into solitary fantasy games of being a pussycat or gazelle. In other nursery schools at four and four and a half years, he was even more shy and withdrawn, avoiding any aggressive play. His mother felt self-conscious and inadequate because of this.

Our nursery teachers' description of George at the time of his entry in the Council Child Development Center confirmed the mother's fears that he was excessively withdrawn, showed ingratiating behavior, and made seductive efforts to gain adult attention. He did not form relationships with his peers, and remained at the periphery of the group as an onlooker. When introduced into other children's play, such as pirates, he would immediately become the pirate's pussycat. The over-all picture was of pathetic lack of emotional contact.

The mother, 30, is the product of an extremely disturbed home. She was unloved by her hysterical mother and browbeaten by her aggressive and hot-tempered father. At an early age, she despaired of the possibility of love and affection from her mother whose hysterical comas prevented any such ties. She found that her father could be pleased by intellectual achievement and from this managed to win some approval. She had always been solitary and lonely, but with great yearnings for intimacy and closeness, none of which ever seemed to be fulfilled. Her only sibling, a younger brother, was even more isolated than she, and since the significant people of her childhood were constantly involved in violent arguments and scenes, or in carrying grudges in cold and detached silence, no warm emotional contact with any member of her family was possible.

Her character structure developed toward extreme passive dependency, and her relationships became confined mainly to aggressive and overwhelming women. She had little feeling of self-esteem, viewed her outstanding intellectual successes at college as worthless, and, following her graduation with honors, worked as a clerk. At this time, a friendship with another girl developed into an active homosexual affair, which was to last two years and in which she ostensibly played a masochistic downtrodden role to fit in with her aggressive and sadistic partner's need for her submission. Her only sexual satisfaction was through making her partner achieve orgasm. After some time, her partner became unfaithful, finally abandoning her for another girl in a particularly cruel fashion. Because of the despair that followed, her father learned of the affair and threatened her with legal prosecution should she return to her partner. It was at this point that she met her husband.

The father, 34, also comes from a severely disturbed family. He is one of the several offspring of an irresponsible, alcoholic father and an aggressive, dominating mother. His past history is a continuous story of withdrawal from human relationships into intellectual pursuits and fantasy. He was lonely and unhappy for his entire life, and so withdrawn and shy that he could not get or hold jobs despite a doctorate in chemical engineering. Communication was almost impossible for him and he consistently shied away from any interpersonal contacts. Clinically, he is an ambulatory schizophrenic, lacking the major symptoms of this disorder. He is exquisitely sensitive to hostility and in almost an uncanny fashion senses rebuff or rebuke.

Mr. G met Mrs. G at a lecture on world affairs which each had attended to escape feelings of loneliness. He had just been rejected by the Army for neuropsychiatric reasons and, despite ample opportunities for jobs, was erratically employed in war work at a meager salary. He had few friends and had just lost his girl with whom he had as close a relationship as was possible for him. He had no other contacts with the world with the exception of his work and, at best, he had few there. He was lonely and felt acutely the need for companionship. Mrs. G met Mr. G while she was on the rebound and utterly desolate from her unhappy homosexual affair; she was seeking some emotional contact to assuage her desperate feelings of abandonment and isolation. She found some part of her unfilled need in the relationship with him, at the same time feeling that it was not what she really wanted. He felt that she was one of the few persons to whom he could relate safely and, in a hesitating and shy way, continued to see her. They would say scarcely a word to each other on their dates, at the time feeling the silence to be an indication of tacit understanding. However, she attempted several times to renew her old homosexual relationship, eventually being cruelly rebuffed by her former partner. Mr. G made an effort to break off the relationship with Mrs. G when this occurred, but changed his mind when she showed up in his apartment in a near panic.

The social situation at this time was as follows: She was living with a friend and he was living alone. Both were working below their capabilities. Eventually, she moved into his apartment for a few months during which time they seldom had any sexual contact. (The first time he kissed her she became angry, and it was not for some time that they ventured into sexual intercourse.) Although they were in financial difficulties, money was not important. The time they spent together was taken up by silent walks or museum visits. They shared little of their everyday experiences, had few friends, and were taciturn about their problems. They never discussed their former lovers with whom they were both still deeply involved.

Although she accidentally became pregnant shortly following their reconciliation, Mrs. G had fantasied having an illegitimate baby by Mr. G for some time previously. This fantasy child was to fulfill all her unrequited yearnings; and when she did find herself pregnant, she was intensely happy, having but few feelings of social disapproval. Despite her doubts about her husband-to-be, and his own difficulties in relating to women, she decided to have the baby. He agreed, and they were married two months after its conception. Each had always been acutely aware of the other's sensitivities and this feeling crystallized into a tacit agreement to keep distance and to avoid any expressions of hostility. Despite their factual living together, there was actually little contact between them, and neither made any attempt to break the long silences which prevailed at home. The fantasy of the loving child was always there to counteract Mrs. G's doubts and fears, and she was able to tolerate the actual lack of communication in the relationship. Mr. G, on the other hand, was satisfied with her physical presence alone. Despite economic privations and a housing shortage, they maintained a delicate balance between the dual threats of contact and isolation.

It was some time before Mrs. G became aware that the child could not fulfill her enormous needs for love, and within a few months she increasingly felt snubbed by him. It was not until she left her work in the war plant that she was fully aware of this feeling. She felt it to be a repetition of past experiences of perpetual disappointment—as one more episode in which the maternal loving which she had so constantly sought was not forthcoming. Neither lover nor husband had fulfilled her needs, and now the child had failed to fulfill them. Mr. G had been away for four months, completing his studies, and when he returned somewhat prior to this time, their relationship became further strained. Economic pressures increased and after the fiasco of his business venture with her brother, he became increasingly anxious, depressed and withdrawn. Rebuffed by the child, and unable to gain contact with her husband, the mother felt herself caught in the old pattern of her own family life and began to freeze up as she had in the past. The anxious detachment of both parents began to have its effect on the child not yet a year old, and George progressively refused to be fondled and loved. Irritability, crankiness and persistent crying further widened the gap between mother, father and child. Although Mrs. G repeatedly made efforts to play with George, her advances were either rebuffed or she misinterpreted his failure to respond quickly to her to mean rebuff. The father had but little to do with the child at this time, and the influence of the rigid and domineering grandmother during this period from six to ten months of age cannot be overestimated.

The social situation at this time has been alluded to above but, additionally, there were the following features: The trio, for they could scarcely be called a family at this point, were living in the grandmother's home. The mother was working in a war plant; the father was away from the house most of the time. The grandmother cared for the child in her characteristically domineering fashion. There were no social contacts on the part of the mother, whereas the father spent his evenings away from home at scientific meetings.

The family moved from the grandmother's house to another city when George was ten months old. The parental relationship was so strained at this point that the mother was secretly thinking of divorce, but the prospect so frightened her that she quickly repressed it. The tacit agreement of detachment (which heretofore had been comforting) became unbearable, but she preferred it to the separation, which she conceived of as complete ioslation. Her attempts at communication with her husband failed repeatedly, and their sexual life regressed to oral forms of intercourse, fellatio and cunnilingus. This one channel of contact became constricted, and after some time she responded with orgasm only upon being masturbated. Her attempts to communicate her dissatisfaction were infrequent, fraught with anxiety, and were met by superficial reassurance and denial of difficulties by her husband. Her reaction was to suppress all her feelings and to play the role of devoted wife and mother, at the same time being aware of the falsity of her position. Although she went through the motions of being a good mother, her activities were constantly underscored by hostility engendered by her frustrated needs.

The social situation had changed considerably for the worse. Throughout this time, they were living in a tiny, cramped apartment where George, although he had his own cubbyhole of a room, had ample opportunity to observe his parents' sexual activities. The mother was working and the unemployed father stayed at home doing most of the housework and taking care of George, who at the end of this time developed celiac disease. Money was extremely important for the family group and the nominal breadwinner found herself unable to work. Social contacts were very limited and the family was becoming progressively more isolated.

At this time (when George developed celiac disease) the parental relationship was beginning to change. Although the father retreated into himself as previously, the mother's similar defenses of suppression and withdrawal were insufficient to protect her from anxiety. She wished to be loved and cared for, but found herself involved in caring for a sick child, who required constant attention, and receiving no assistance from her husband. At this time Mr. G, who had been working, became unemployed (this was to continue for almost two years), and it was up to her to become the main support of the family, which she did by teaching. Mr. G cared for the child a great part of the time when he was two to four years old. He apparently handled him with some degree of ease as the child was not a threat to him. However, about the end of this period, when George's motility and language patterns were fully developed, this changed. Heretofore, George had shown what little hostility he was capable of in sly and devious ways, but now explosions of aggression against both parents became evident. The father reacted either with direct retaliatory violence or with complete withdrawal, at times even stalking out of the house. The mother assumed a pose of firmness and objectivity, which, in actuality, covered her rage as well as intense feelings of being hurt. Her reactive overcontrol broke down frequently and she would on occasion break out explosively with the same type of retaliatory violence shown by her husband. It became increasingly impossible for the parents to maintain their isolation and distance-producing defenses with each other in the face of George's behavior, and they were constantly drawn against their will into, among others, the problems of discipline and socialization. They could no longer ignore their interpersonal difficulties as previously, and a good deal of buck passing of their parental responsibility resulted. Mr. G finally sought psychiatric help but discontinued therapy after a few hours because of his inability to talk about himself and because he had been pressed into going by his wife. Mrs. G's explosive outbursts became more frequent and at the time of her application to the Council Child Development Center she had just begun psychotherapy with a private practitioner.

The family and its social situation at this time were chaotic. The mutual nonaggression pact had broken down; the parents' sex life was progressively deteriorating; stormy scenes alternated with days of silence. The father, as a result, found it harder to look for a job, let alone find one, and the mother was unable to support the family alone. The landlord made attempts to evict them, to which the entire family reacted with near panic. Because of his resemblance to her father, Mrs. G found herself completely helpless in his presence, reacting later with impotent rage and depressive anxiety attacks. She was unable to appeal for assistance to Mr. G who was even more frightened of the landlord than she. As a result, she covertly released her hostility by "accidentally" flooding the landlord's ceiling on several occasions, eventually bringing a lawsuit upon Mr. G.

George was becoming more and more withdrawn, and the efforts of both parents to show any real affection to him were met with sullen head shaking or, on occasion, by anal language, spitting and kicking. He uncannily found the weak spots of each parent and exploited them mercilessly when his frustrated needs for love were at a peak. At times, he became omnipotent in fact: he could put mother into a hysterical rage by sneaking behind her and pinching her buttocks; he could make father speechless or have him run out of the house in blind fury by taunting him with defiance; both could be made anxious by his stamping on the floor of their apartment, which was above that of the landlord. These manifestations were always followed by intense fright, fear of retaliation, and then by withdrawal into fantasy games and passive compliance. At the age of five years and two months, he entered our nursery.

George and his mother have received individual therapy for over a year now. During this time, Mrs. G has shown remarkable progress toward self-assertion and has lost a good part of her tendencies toward self-immolation. She has been able to face her own and her husband's unconscious role in the marriage and to talk about it with him rather than at him. Until recently, he has denied that there were any difficulties, but finally, with a year of successful and profitable work behind him, has decided of his own volition to resume therapy. As the mother has formulated her own difficulties, she has become increasingly aware of the fact that her needs were based in the past, that they were inordinate and unrealistic, and that neither George nor her husband could possibly fulfill them. She has been able to form and to recognize a deep dependency upon her therapist, which has given her considerable insight into the genesis of her rage which she has so greatly feared. The load of unreal expectation has been lifted from George to some extent. In his individual therapy, he has been able to work through successively his ingratiating compliance and intense hostility, finally getting to his basic problem, his need for love. It has become evident that his aggression was, in effect, a substitute for the anxiety brought about by the lack of contact with the family; after several months of therapy, he began to show some evidence of being able to accept and respond to love.

In summary, this paper is an attempt to evolve a methodology for the study of the preschool child in the context of the family group, by considering the psychosocial effects of the family members upon each other. We feel that this type of orientation is significant to the child guidance and mental hygiene field on the basis of our contention that the personality of the preschool child cannot be described as such but only in terms of his interpersonal and intrafamily relationships.

CHAPTER 26

The Home Visit as an Aid in Family Diagnosis and Therapy

The home visit has had a long and uneven history in social work and related fields. At different periods it has been used for different purposes, and has been focused on various aspects of the environment. At times it has been the only mode of contact with families in trouble; at others it has been criticized as constituting an infraction of privacy. This shifting attitude toward the home visit is primarily a result of dichotomizing the person and his environment. Originally the environment was stressed. When interest later shifted to the individual, his environment was all but forgotten. In the exploratory study of "family diagnosis,"[1] in which the central effort is to relate the behavior of the family as a group to the behavior of a family member, the authors have found the home visit to be a valuable tool. When it has been used as an adjunct to psychiatric interviews and psychological examinations of family members, we have been able to assess more accurately the actualities of the psychosocial functioning of the family.

Our particular use of the home visit reflects recent modifications in theory about the nature of emotional illness and the task of psychotherapy. We conceive of emotional illness as a phenomenon not confined to the behavior of a single individual but one that encompasses the individual's integration into a significant group. Rigid adherence to classical psychoanalytic theory and practice had resulted in emphasis being placed on the internal economy of the individual personality; hence the environment was accorded a relatively subordinate role. Often the eyes of the patient were the only ones through

Reprinted with permission from *Social Casework*, January 1956, Vol. 37. Copyright 1956 by the Family Service Association of America, New York.

This paper was co-authored with Marjorie L. Behrens.

[1]Nathan W. Ackerman, and Marjorie L. Behrens, "A Study of Family Diagnosis," in *American Journal of Orthopsychiatry*, January, 1956. Also, Ackerman and Behrens, "Child and Family Psychopathy: Problems of Correlation," in *Psychopathology of Childhood*, Paul H. Hoch, and Joseph Zubin (eds.), Grune & Stratton, New York, 1955, pp. 177-196.

which the therapist viewed the patient's world and life situation, a view frequently distorted by the patient's own sick perception.[2]

Several deficiencies persist in current practice. For example, insufficient consideration is given to relationships as two-way processes. A mother, for example, affects the child and the child affects the mother. Further, the behavior of the mother with her child is shaped not only by her individual make-up but by her interaction with the child's father, with other family members, and with the dominant culture patterns. In this context, mothering behavior is both a result and an expression of the character of the entire family life.[3]

Although the mother and even the father have come to be included more and more in the process of treating the child, an objective and comprehensive view of the family members as a group has not been an important consideration. The therapist must often depend for his understanding of the family on his ingenuity in piecing together the information the family members choose to give him and in observing their behavior in his office.

Theories concerning interpersonal communication[4] have increased our understanding of the processes of dynamic interaction between people. Knowledge of the effect of such interaction on the individual, and of the modifications he produces in others through the process of interacting, is gradually being incorporated into psychiatric theory and practice. Observation of the family in its own home is a means by which quicker and more accurate delineation of family environment and interpersonal relationships can be effected. One English psychiatrist goes into the child's home to carry on treatment. Erikson has developed a practice of never accepting a patient until he first joins the family at a meal in the home.[5] Thus it appears that the value of the home visit is becoming increasingly recognized.

CONCEPTS OF FAMILY DIAGNOSIS

Our study of family diagnosis[6] is concerned with the effort to develop concepts and methods for evaluating the psychosocial functioning of the family group and the relation of mental illness in the individual to the mental health of the group. This approach is briefly reviewed here to indicate the bases and structuring of the home visit.

Mental health is viewed as an expression of social process; the mental health of a family member bears a direct relationship to the mental health of the family group. The quality of emotional integration of the individual into his family may intensify or mitigate the negative expressions of his personality. Through a correct evaluation of this integration, a family member can be more accurately diagnosed and treated.

A child's adaptation and the gradual emergence of his personality are considered a biosocial process. His social experience is molded by the patterns of total family functioning and its typical interpersonal relationships, all of which tend to pattern his behavior. His social and psychic reactions are viewed as a functional expression of the social interaction processes characteristic of his family. The task with which we are confronted is one of determining the interrelationships between individual dynamics and the dynamics of the family group and between intrafamilial and extra-familial processes.

Our study starts with an examination of the patterns of interaction in the marital relationship. It then moves to a consideration of the internal interaction patterns of the family group and to patterns of family interaction with the outside community, including the impact of culture patterns. Internal family interaction patterns are viewed in terms of mutual interdependence and reciprocity of traditional family roles. We are concerned not only with the influence of the family on the child, but also with the effect of the child's disturbed behavior on the life of the family as a whole, on siblings, on parental functioning, and on the parental and

[2]Nathan W. Ackerman, "Interlocking Pathology in Family Relationships," in *Changing Concepts of Psychoanalytic Medicine*, Sandor Rado and George E. Daniels, (eds.), Grune & Stratton, New York, 1956.

[3]Nathan W. Ackerman, "Disturbances of Mothering and Criteria for Treatment," in *American Journal of Orthopsychiatry*, 26:252-263, 1956.

[4]Jurgen Ruesch and Gregory Bateson, *Communication: The Social Matrix of Psychiatry*, W. W. Norton & Co., New York, 1951.

[5]Erik H. Erikson, *Childhood and Society*, W. W. Norton & Co., New York, 1950, pp. 49-50.

[6]See Ackerman and Behrens, *op. cit.* for detailed exposition.

marital relationships. The family group and each individual member are therefore studied on several levels.

Special emphasis is placed on role adaptation and behavior in terms of the individual's integration into the group.[7] For example, we must determine the degree to which the mother's personality characteristics are integrated in relation to fulfilling the requirements of the maternal role, the specific manifestations of these characteristics in her actual behavior, the influence of her behavior on the role behavior of other family members, and the response of others to her. Observation in the home increases the understanding of group and individual functioning and can supply some of the necessary data, especially on a concrete behavior level.

PLAN OF HOME OBSERVATION

The visit itself is unstructured and informal and no notes are taken. The observations are focused primarily on family interactions and role behavior, and on the physical environment and atmosphere of the home. The scheme of observation parallels our over-all analysis of the family.

The home visit should be made at a time when all members of the family will be present at least part of the time. The best time to visit is around mealtime when normally the family is together. If the visit begins before the father comes home from work, the behavior of the family members before and after he arrives provides valuable clues to the group organization, attitudes, and feelings. A visit usually lasts three hours and is written up in detail the following day.

Objection may be raised that the method both of observation and of reporting involves the possibility of introducing bias. We have found, however, that the visit is most successful from the clinical point of view when the observer is a participant in the activities and interactions between family members, including total family interaction on an emotional level. Participation by the observer permits more spontaneity of family behavior and interferes least with the family's "normal" functioning. Such participant observation must, of necessity, be reported from memory since note taking would interfere not only with family spontaneity but with the observer's own interaction with the family. Omissions in reporting or the possibility of the observer's being selective as to events and impressions are far outweighed by the gains.

The kinds of insight gained by the observer are derived from the level of communication between him and the family members. The type of understanding of family relations achieved will vary according to the level of the observer's emotional participation. If the observer is integrated as a person into the usual family activities where verbal exchange is of secondary importance, the insights achieved will be different from those gained in a directed or non-directed interview, or in the genuine free-association interview typical of the analytic situation.

Observations made during the home visit are structured in the following way and include both qualitative and quantitative aspects of family functioning; equal emphasis is given to negative and positive aspects of functioning.

1. Physical aspects of the home and neighborhood (mainly as they conform or contradict other observations or add new insights with respect to emotional atmosphere)
   a. Furnishings and care of home as they reflect interest, pride in home, warmth, comfort, and family activities
   b. Opportunities for privacy, group activity, and the pursuit of special interests
   c. Appropriateness of the neighborhood to the socio-economic status of family; the potential for social interaction with neighbors, groups, and so on
2. Atmosphere of home (harmonious, tense, hectic, pleasant, warm, formal)
3. Interaction between husband and wife as marital partners
   a. Domination and passivity
   b. Warmth, affection, pleasure in each other
   c. Conflict and hostility (overt and covert)
   d. Mutual support and compatibility
   e. Co-operation and division of labor
   f. Communication
   g. Role behavior as husband and wife
4. Interaction between husband and wife as parents

[7] Nathan W. Ackerman, " 'Social Role' and Total Personality," *American Journal of Orthopsychiatry*, Vol. XXI, No. 1 (1951), pp. 1-17.

a. Division of labor in the care of children

b. Behavior in parent roles, compatibility of roles, pleasure in each other as parents

c. Behavior and attitude toward each other in relation to child, for example, exclusion, belittling, domination, mutual respect and support

5. Child-child interaction (where there is more than one child)

a. Behavior toward each other, for example, mutual respect, protection, warmth, common play; or neglect, rivalry, open conflict, isolated play

b. Behavior toward parents, for example, rivalry for parental attention

6. Child-parent interaction

a. Physical and verbal contact between parent and child, for example, dependence, warmth, pleasure, spontaneity, rejection, withdrawal, hostility

b. Demands made of each other — appropriateness of demands, manner of meeting them, preferences for certain family members

c. Parental attitudes on discipline, routines, habits; child's response

7. Interaction with other household members, such as grandmother or maid, reflected in isolation of these members from the group, integration into the group, and quality of behavior toward them

8. Interaction with visitor; acceptance or exclusion, comfort or discomfort, vying for visitor's attention, monopolizing visitor

9. Family group patterns

a. Unity and cohesiveness of family group, closeness as reflected in communication, empathy, pleasure, affection

b. Areas of conflict and dissatisfaction; areas of compatibility and satisfaction

c. Success and manner of enactment of family roles

d. Adaptation of members to each other

e. Distribution of power and authority; responsibility for decisions

f. Alignment of family members

g. Characteristic patterns in terms of economic, cultural, social, and religious identification and belongingness

10. Interactions with outside community (learned mostly through conversation)

a. Contacts with relatives, friends, neighbors, outside groups

b. Satisfaction with outside contacts and activities, as a group and as individuals

The written report of the home visit is divided into four parts: (1) the physical environment, (2) a summary of chronological events of the visit, (3) impressions of the interaction patterns and role behavior of the members of the family as a group, (4) a short description of each member of the household and additional impressions and material.

SOME SPECIAL CONSIDERATIONS

Although, in our family studies, a psychoanalytically oriented sociologist rather than a therapist or caseworker has made the home visits, this has been done as a matter of practicality rather than of conviction. It is our feeling that any trained, sensitive, and astute observer who can be at ease with strangers in a social setting and who is oriented toward the concepts and goals of the visit—whether therapist, caseworker, or other professional person, whether known or unknown to the family—can be equally effective.

If the visitor is the child's or parent's therapist, the visit need not interfere with the therapeutic relationship. The emotional tone of the visit is set by the visitor and by the mutual interaction of visitor and family. In any case the visit should not be placed on an interview or therapy level. One advantage of using someone other than the therapist is the possibility of checking impressions.

We have experimented with having the observer make visits both with and without knowledge of the problem or of background material. A certain emotional neutrality, lack of selectivity, and avoidance of bias are achieved when the clinical history is not known. However, there are advantages in his having prior knowledge. Such knowledge helps the visitor to feel less a stranger and assists the therapist since it ensures that central problems will be sufficiently noted. Having the observer meet the parents before the visit is not important, although it may ease the initial part of the visit.

In a previous experience at a mental health clinic, the authors discovered that the insecurity of the psychotherapists and the apprehension of the psychotherapists about invasion of their control of their patients were sources of resistance to home visiting. The visit was conceived as a threat to the family, an invasion of its privacy, and a complicating factor in transference behavior. On the basis of our experience with families, these objections seem to be invalid. If key family members are prepared for the visit by the therapist, who presents it to them as a clinical procedure necessary for understanding the child and related problems, any resultant anxiety of the parent can be handled before the visit. If the therapist does not convey anxiety on his own part, the parents usually will not be anxious. Frequently the visit is interpreted by the parents as proof of the therapist's attention and devotion, and the observer is perceived as part of a clinic team, a helping agent of the therapist who energizes expectations of more and better help. Actually, the idea of observing the child in the home can seem quite logical to the family. The social level of the visit puts the family at ease and its feelings of being "spied on" are reduced to a minimum. Absence of anxiety in both the therapist and the visitor is quickly reflected in family reactions.

The concern most frequently expressed about home visits is that the family members may not behave normally—that they may be on their "best behavior" and that the interjection of a stranger into the home creates an atypical situation. Such contentions are not pertinent to the basic purposes of the home visit. The home visit is only one means of evaluating the family and must be integrated with other findings. Discrepancies between observations made during a visit and clinical impressions are evaluated by therapist, visitor, and sometimes the parents. Such discrepancies may even provide additional insights. We believe, however, that family behavior during a visit deviates from its usual behavior only in degree and not in quality. We may not see the mother lose her temper with the child in either home or office but, whether her behavior is strictly typical or not, we can observe the quality of her relatedness to the child, her general attitudes and handling. We may not see open conflict between two parents but, to the astute observer, feelings and attitudes will be betrayed. More often than not, parents are anxious to show their own and their child's "worst side," as if they wished to prove the existence of their problems and thereby justify their need for help.

The fact that an outsider is brought into the home must of course be taken into consideration. The observer is a stranger, however, only in a special sense since he is identified with the helping therapist. Differing reactions of family members to the visitor can be quite significant. Sometimes the visitor is sought as an ally; his approval is desired and his attention vied for. At other times, he is noticeably excluded. In many families, the visitor becomes a catalyzer of family interactions and disclosures. Visits have been made to families with varying religious, socio-economic, and educational backgrounds, without significant differences arising in the matter of the visit itself. It may be of interest that with private patients a fee is charged for the home visit.

Usually a good deal of interest is shown by the parents in the observer's impressions. The therapist, of course, must use his judgment as to how much or little to reveal to the family and how to utilize the home observation therapeutically. The earlier the visit is made in the therapist's contact with the family, the more value it has both for diagnosis and for treatment planning. However, we have also used visits during the course of treatment to evaluate family functioning, to measure therapeutic progress, to check perceptions and reports of the family, or to assess special problem situations that arise. As a means of follow-up, they are indispensable.

ILLUSTRATION OF A HOME VISIT

Seven-year-old Bobby[8] was referred by his father because of his fears of physical injury and bleeding, anxiety when his parents went out, bedtime rituals, nightmares, and sibling rivalry. He was the oldest of three children in a wealthy upper-middle-class family. The father was a successful businessman who tended to be hypochondriacal and ritualistic. He was intelligent, had a poised and affable manner, but in discussing the boy he was anxious and tense. He worried because the boy was very much like

[8]For more detailed history and family background, see "Interlocking Pathology in Family Relationships," *op. cit.*

himself. The mother was ten years younger than her husband, attractive, tense, compulsive, and mildly euphoric. She said that her main concern was her children. She felt more relaxed with them when her husband was not present.

Each parent claimed to admire the other and maintained that their family life was ideal. However, in the early days of marriage there had been severe tension between the father's mother and his wife. The couple had always led an active social life.

Bobby was born during the first year of marriage. Both parents wanted a child as early as possible because the father was already in his thirties. During Bobby's early infancy, the parents were severely frightened by a medical report that Bobby had an enlarged heart. They became anxious, overprotective, and panicky at any signs of illness. Although they had been assured that Bobby was normal when he was a year old, their anxiety had continued and was carried over to the other children. They had always employed nurses and, currently, one nurse shared the care of the children with the mother.

Regular contacts with the parents and therapy for the child was initiated. A home visit was arranged for a Saturday morning when the father could be at home. The following is a condensed report of the visit.

Physical Environment

The T's live in an eight-room apartment in a good residential section. The home is ample in size, and is suitable and comfortable for family needs. It is decorated in a plain fashion without evidence of any particular concern for appearance or tasteful result. Bobby and his sister Alice, age 5, share a bedroom. Another room is used by the nurse and the baby, John, age 17 months. The parents' bedroom is adjacent to the baby's room. They are planning to move so that Bobby and Alice can have separate rooms. They employ a full-time maid in addition to the baby's nurse.

Chronological Events of Visit

I was greeted cordially by all family members. Mrs. T said that the children were terribly excited about my visit. She immediately asked if there was any particular situation in which I would like to see the family. I told her I was interested in whatever they normally did at this time.

We went into the children's bedroom. Mr. T asked if I wanted him and Mrs. T to stay in the room. He remained most of the time, but Mrs. T was in and out because she had to dress the baby. Bobby asked his father to help him sort some foreign coins and sat down at his typewriter to record their amounts and the countries of origin. Several times during the visit, Bobby went back to his coins, always asking for help from either me or his parents. Mr. T asked Alice if she would dance for me. She was eager to do so, and followed her father's suggestions. From time to time, Mr. T would unsuccessfully suggest to Bobby that he stop the coin play and do something else. Whenever Mrs. T came into the room, Bobby would ask her help and she would assist him.

Mr. T suggested we all go into the living room. He asked Bobby if he wanted to play the piano, which Bobby did immediately. Mr. T would look at me and beam with pride at everything his children did. Alice played patiently by herself, waiting for her father's attention. John was brought in by the nurse and Mrs. T followed. Alice took John over, watching over him, and so on. Bobby asked his mother to help with the music and she did. After Bobby exhausted the pieces he knew, he played with John's punching balloon. He then told Alice to lie on the floor so he could jump over her. She jumped over him also and they both jumped over John. After this, they jumped over the couch. When they got a little rough, Mrs. T told them to stop and they did. The two older children competed for John when they were all playing together, but it was Alice who gave in and let Bobby have his way. John went to both parents from time to time and each picked him up and hugged him. Mr. T left the room to telephone. When he returned, Mrs. T left. Alice then played the piano. Mrs. T has been teaching her, whereas Bobby takes lessons. Mr. T loudly praised Alice.

Mr. T told me that they exert control over the children with respect to watching television. They play with the children, suggest other amusements, and provide substitute entertainment. Whenever he told me anything in relation to the children, he always asked for my approval and advice. When the children heard "TV," they asked for it, but both parents said no. Mr. T suggested we all go back to the children's room so that they would have more room to play. Bobby immediately returned to his typewriter and coins. Both parents, particularly Mr. T, again tried to dissuade him. Bobby showed me his collection of pieces of coal and bottle caps. Alice then took out her bag of coal to show me. As soon as John came into the room, Alice went to him, but Bobby returned to typing.

The T's had planned a tugboat ride that afternoon. Several times, Mrs. T came in and told one or the other children that an invited friend could not come. She told Alice that she had asked another child; Alice did not respond. She asked Bobby if he wanted a certain friend, and he said he did. She returned to say that the friend was sick, but she had asked someone else. Later she told Bobby he was to go to this child's house for supper and would be walked home by his friend's brother. Bobby said he did not want to go for supper. When his father asked him why, he said they might have a hot meal there. Mrs. T said he knew he did not have to eat it. Then Bobby said he didn't like the dog, and his parents discussed this with him. Mr. T told Bobby he should chase the dog instead of letting the dog chase him. Finally, Bobby repeated he didn't want to go. Mrs. T said he would like it when he got there and tried to persuade him. Then Mr. T told his wife that it was all right if Bobby didn't want to go and she immediately agreed. Bobby replied that he did not tell them where to go and not to go and he did not want them to tell him either. The T's both agreed that this was right.

Mr. T pointed out to me that Bobby collects things and has a need to finish anything he is doing. Mrs. T said that difficulties arise because Bobby is very neat and Alice is disorderly. Also, Alice learns faster and with less effort. Both parents made it plain that they try to build up Bobby and help him to get attention, as with me. (It is easy to be diverted by Alice who is a very appealing child.) Mrs. T asked me if I needed to see John any more. Since I did not, John left for the park with the nurse. Repeatedly both parents again tried to dissuade Bobby from playing with the coins, but to no avail. Mr. T put on a victrola record and Alice played some drums. When I said good-bye Bobby left his coins to come to the door.

The Family as a Group

The T's appear to be an excessively, almost exaggeratedly, integrated group. Rapport between the parents seemed to be good. Neither appeared to dominate the other and no hostility was shown. They were overtly warm and affectionate when talking to each other, which was exclusively on the subject of the children. Neither one appeared to favor any one child, nor did the children show over preference. There seems to be more sharing of the care of the children than in most families, with Mr. T playing a prominent role. In speaking of themselves in relation to the children, both parents used "we" rather than "I." All members of the family were very close and intimately related to each other. Both parents seemed overanxious to do well with their children, were overinvolved with them, participated too much in the children's activities, gave too much direction, and overstimulated them. Mr. T constantly suggested changes in play activities, always being careful that each child had his share of attention. The result was both unnatural and unreal, the concern being more Mr. T's than the children's. Mrs. T is more relaxed than her husband, less directive, and apparently less anxious to see the children make a good showing. But she goes to exaggerated lengths to obtain companionship and arrange activities for them. Both parents lean over backward to build up Bobby because of Alice's charm and aptitudes. The older children constantly but independently ask for attention.

The children seemed to get along well with each other and occasionally played together. There was no fighting. Alice doted on the baby and was very maternal with him. There was some evidence of competitiveness between Alice and Bobby for the baby's attention.

Both parents were cordial and friendly to me, but Mr. T frequently sat very close, was confiding, anxiously sought my approval, and made some attempts to take me over for himself. He tried to impress me with the children's positive qualities. The mother maintained some distance. In both parents there was a hint of covering up in their marked resistance to conversation on any subject other than their children. Alice was friendly and accepting with me. Bobby related easily but only in terms of getting something he wanted.

Descriptions of Each Member of the Household

Mrs. T seemed warm, affectionate, interested, but overconscientious and manipulative with the children. She told me that, before taking Bobby to a psychiatrist, they had carefully weighed the idea for a year because they were fearful that his problems would be blown up too much. This seems typical of their attitudes in that careful thought and planning leave little room for spontaneity in their behavior.

Mr. T's behavior is similar to his wife's but is more pronounced in all respects. He seems to be much concerned about his children's behavior and less sure of himself as a parent. He appears to drive himself to be a good father, and is very anxious about each thing they do as parents. He asked repeatedly if I was getting what I wanted from the visit and seemed anxious to give me information about the children. Although Mr. T outwardly gave the impression of being relaxed, I felt he was really quite tense.

Bobby is detached and preoccupied. The contrast between Bobby and Alice is quite striking. He does not seem sufficiently aware of or related to what is going on around him and seeks refuge in compulsive activities. He can assert himself but is usually amenable to his parents' suggestions. He obviously resented his mother's planning for him, but made it known only in an indirect way.

Alice is not pretty but has a great deal of charm. She seems beyond her years in poise, physical ability, and ease of establishing relationships. She is affectionate, warm in her contacts, and related to the baby in a most understanding manner. It is easy for her to monopolize attention but she is tolerant in allowing Bobby to get his share. An outsider could easily allow her to shut Bobby out, since he easily withdraws.

John, the baby, walks well and speaks a few words with sufficient clearness to be understood. He reacts appropriately, is responsive and affectionate, and likes to play with the older children. He showed no preference for any one family member, including the nurse.

The nurse is a genial and pleasant woman in her thirties. She seemed equally interested in all three children and was flexible and warm in her behavior. She adapted easily to the parents' involvement with the children.

Evaluation of the Observations

The visit highlighted some of the family patterns. The intimate relatedness between children and parents indicated an exaggerated, strained, and unnatural cohesiveness, and a degree of child-centeredness that is atypical for a family of this socio-economic status. Although the parents appeared to be harmonious in their attitudes and behavior toward the children, there was an overemphasis on sharing between the parents both in decision making and in their care of and activities with their children. The father, especially, overinvolved himself in their play, wanted to show them off, and was concerned about dividing his attention equally among them. The mother, although more relaxed and distant, was overconscientious and manipulative. Although both parents seemed to be genuinely fond and proud of the children, they also seemed to need attention from them. Activities were carefully planned, overorganized, and involved excessive efforts at joint family activities and being together. Spontaneity was conspicuously absent in the parents and in Bobby.

The parents appeared to relate to each other only through their common concern with the children. Both parents were overtly warm, but controlled and somewhat formal with each other.

The children were competitive among themselves for parental attention. They also vied for attention from the visitor, strongly encouraged by the father. Bobby's ritualistic play, self-isolation, and preoccupation were in sharp contrast to the lively, outgoing behavior of his sister. At times both children competed for the attention of the youngest child.

The home was comfortable and appropriate to the family's socio-economic status, but the furnishings and decoration of the home did not reflect much concern or interest.

The home visit gave an immediate clue to the

atypical child-centeredness of the family group. (1) The parents exaggerated their parental solicitousness as a way of denying the emotional and marital barrier between them. (2) Exploitation of the children was highlighted in terms of the father's exhibitionistic needs. (3) The emotional immaturity of both parents could be seen in their need to live vicariously through the children. (4) There were hints of reversal of the usual sex roles in terms of the mother's allowing the father to assume a position of dominance in relation to the children.

The observations were evaluated in terms of the child patient and his clinical interviews. For example, the child sensed that the mother was really the supreme power. He resented her manipulation and thus empathized with his father. The social interaction patterns of the family had become absorbed into the child's pathology and internalized in his disturbance.

The mother was curious about the observations made during the home visit and the therapist acquainted her with the gist of the report. She admitted the validity of the observations and went on to reveal dissatisfaction with her husband and with the marriage from its inception. She was unable to respond sexually, found her husband's rituals and hypochondriasis unbearable, but felt that she had been successful in maintaining a facade of satisfaction. She said that this was the best solution and insisted that the children were her first concern.

When we added the observations made in the home to clinical data, we could verify some of our judgments and add to our understanding of the structure and functioning of this family. In addition, the visit performed the unlooked for function of removing the facade of happiness which originally had been presented. This made it possible to deal more directly with some of the main issues. The visit revealed the degree to which the parents were compensating for their own and their marital deficiencies by channeling through the children their quest for love, affection, and attention. Bobby's early "physical disability" and subsequent behavior played into this pattern. As long as the parents could evade the basic issues in their own relationship in a common concern for some "real" difficulties in Bobby and the other children, they could successfully escape facing up to their own dissatisfaction and disappointment in each other and the potential explosion that both feared.

We felt that if Bobby's behavior improved and if the parents could be guided to involve themselves less in the children's lives, sooner or later they would need to deal with each other on a more realistic level. This did occur several months later when Bobby began to show some real improvement. Subsequently, the marital relationship itself was treated and the mother undertook psychoanalytic treatment.

In the illustration given, the home visit brought into sharp relief the basic dynamics of this family. It added to our understanding of the child's reaction patterns and was an aid in planning treatment and evaluating expectations of success.

SUMMARY

We have described the use of the home visit as an aid in family diagnosis and therapy where the original patient is a child. The techniques of observation and the concepts involved were set forth in our article on the psychosocial structure of families, "A Study of Family Diagnosis." Home observations focus primarily on family interaction patterns, role behavior, and the physical environment and atmosphere of the home. The family is observed as nearly as possible in its usual daily functioning and interpersonal relationships. Through the home visit, the reactive behavior of the child can be more accurately evaluated and treatment plans for the child and his family can be made consonant with a knowledge of actual family functioning. When combined with other sources of information and clinical material, the home visit can contribute to the delineation of family functioning from the point of view of mental health.

CHAPTER 27

Toward an Integrative Therapy of the Family

Family diagnosis and therapy represent a new venture in mental health. Family therapy makes its entry because there is historical need for it. It comes into being especially through the need to encompass the phenomena of the relations of personality and social role adaptation.

As the knowledge of psychopathology expands, we can discern some of the limitations of individual psychotherapy. The main focus of traditional forms of individual psychotherapy has been on the internal economy of personality. Its techniques have been pointed to specific pathogenic conflicts and the resulting symptoms within the person, but it has not adequately conceptualized the problems of total personality organization and integration of personality into the tasks of group living. To whatever extent individual psychotherapy fails to confront the problems of personality and social role, it fails to be a true adaptational therapy.

My personal conviction as to the potential value of family diagnosis and therapy is strengthened by several relevant considerations:

1. In child psychiatry and child therapy certain problems continue to balk solution due to our inability up to now to formulate the psychodynamics of the family group, and thereby make possible reliable correlations of child and family behavior.
2. The role of the family in the stabilization of the mental health of the adult person has been largely neglected. Because of this, traditional standards of diagnosis, therapy and prognosis of emotional disturbances in adults remain deficient in certain respects. The interrelations of individual and family contribute to the determinants of mental health at every stage of maturation, infancy, childhood, adolescence, adulthood and old age. Such relations influence the precipitation of illness, its course, the likelihood of recovery and the risk of relapse. Receptivity or resistance to therapy is partly the product of emotional interaction with other family members. Prediction of changes in behavior is accurate only to the extent that family processes are taken into account.
3. Disorders of personality have undergone progressive transformation related to sociocultural change and corresponding shifts in family structure and function. Individual psychother-

---

Reprinted with permission from *The American Journal of Psychiatry*, February 1958, Vol. 114, No. 8, 727-733.

apy has not caught up with this challenge. The core of the problem is a shift in personality organization, particularly in defense operations, which favors externalization of conflict and "acting out."

4. For several decades, individual psychotherapy has had the center of the stage. The lure of absorption with the intricacies of individual therapeutic technique has been strong. In the meantime, the gap between psychotherapy and clinical diagnosis grew ever greater. The challenge to achieve better diagnosis, to understand more precisely what is wrong with the patient, to work toward the goal of psychological specificity in treatment method, was frequently bypassed. Surely, further progress in psychotherapy is in danger of bogging down unless we turn back once more to sharpen the standards of diagnosis. Therapy cannot be primary; it must always be secondary to the precise assessment of pathology.

5. At still another level, the absorption with individual psychotherapy has diverted attention from the confrontation of our relative failure in the field of prevention. In the long view, if we are to further the cause of mental health, it is self-evident that the goals of treatment, prevention, and education to healthy values in human relations must be drawn into closer alignment.

Health and illness are functions of the interrelation of organism and environment. The family is the basic unit of human experience; it is the primary group into which the functions of personality are integrated. The development of a social psychopathology of everyday family life is a responsibility of the first priority, if we are to meet the mental health challenge of our time. Requisite to this goal is an expansion of the dimensions of diagnostic thinking so as to make the unit of evaluation the individual within his family group, rather than the individual assessed in isolation.

Psychiatric illness is a process; it is neither static nor is it ever an exclusively endogenous disorder. The interrelations of individual and family are an integral part of such illness. Historically, psychiatry tended to equate symptoms with illness but symptoms are only a part of illness, not its entirety. So as soon as we expand the scope of our diagnostic concern to include total life performance and in particular the integration of personality into family roles, then the psychological life of the family as a whole must be encompassed in a broader conception of illness. In this scheme of things we are called upon to weigh, both in individual and family, the potentials for emotional health against the potentials for psychiatric distortion.

In the psychiatry of children, we are accustomed to evaluate the pathology of the family environment. In the psychiatry of adults, the study of family pathology has been neglected. It is true that the homeostasis of adult personality is relatively greater than that of the child. Nonetheless, the autonomy of the adult is partial and incomplete. We think of the behavior of the child as a kind of mirror of the psychological core of family. As we turn to the adult, however, we shift our view and perceive him as separate, autonomous and exclusively responsible for his life choices. This is a flattering view of the self-sufficiency of the adult person, but it far exceeds the known limits of human adaptation. Effective emotional integration into family roles is necessary for the stabilization of the mental health of the adult.

The goal of family diagnosis and therapy is to join person and environment rather than to dichotomize them. It signifies the assessment of adaptation and mental health, not exclusively in the frame of individual personality, but rather in the wider context of the person's organic involvement in his whole human community. It links person, family, community and culture. This constitutes a broader concept of the issues of mental health, requiring new hypotheses, new methods of research and validation, and different ways of applying the science of psychodynamics to the task of bettering the mental health of the community.

In previous publications (1-13), I have endeavored to develop basic concepts, dynamic principles and behavioral criteria which are relevant to the task of achieving family diagnosis. Foci of pathogenic disturbance are evaluated within the framework of the psychodynamics of the family entity *per se*, conflict between family and community, interpersonal conflict in family pairs, and finally, intrapsychic conflict and symptoms within individual family members.

In a recent paper (4, 12), I suggested a tentative scheme for establishing the lines of correlation between individual and family behavior. I repeat here only the bare outlines of this

TABLE 1

Individual	Family Pair	Family Group
1. Self-image or psychological identity.	Psychological identity of family pair.	Psychological identity of the family group.
2. Integrative capacity or homeostasis of individual personality.	Integrative pattern or homeostasis of family pair.	Integrative pattern or homeostasis of the family group.
3. Pathogenic conflict, anxiety, symptoms or other anxiety manifestations, and the corresponding mechanisms of restitution.	Pathogenic conflict in family pair, its manifestations, and the mechanisms of control and restitution.	Pathogenic conflicts in the family group, interplay of overlapping conflicts, their manifestations, and the mechanisms of control and restitution.
4. Adaptation to family roles, capacity to accommodate to new experience, reality testing, learning and new growth.	Adaptation to patterns of reciprocal role relations, capacity to accommodate to new experience, reality testing, learning and new growth.	Adaptation to the overlapping patterns of family role relations, to group identity, strivings and values, and the family's capacity to accommodate to new experience, to reality test, to learn and to achieve new growth.

scheme (Table 1).

The rationale for this scheme and definitions of terms are given in the above-mentioned paper.

I should like now to highlight certain common clinical observations which document the need for a social psychopathology of family life and a corresponding program of therapeutic intervention. In a particular family, the first person referred for psychiatric care may be the most sick or the least sick member of the group. Psychiatric patients come from disordered families. If the psychiatrist exerts himself to inspect the relations of the primary patient with other family members, he will be rewarded with some cogent information. The primary patient, whether child or adult, proves often to be an emissary in disguise of an emotionally warped family. A patient may enter therapy on his own to escape the unbearable tensions of an unhappy family; or, he is brought to a psychiatrist by his family. In the latter case, a variety of motivations in other family members may play a part in this first referral. Another member of the family may need to relieve his own guilt; he may seek to control and make over the primary patient's behavior; he may wish to punish the patient; he may use the primary patient as a scapegoat behind which other family members hide their own psychiatric warp. Occasionally, the tendency is to send first to the psychiatrist the weakest and most defenseless member of the family, a child or the more docile of the marital partners.

For example, a man of middle years, severely hypochondriacal, confused and unhappy in his family life refers first for consultation his niece, then his son, then his second wife, using such persons as a kind of scout to test the psychiatrist's benign intentions. After that, reassured against his fear of harm, this man requests psychiatric help for himself. Such an individual proves often to be the center of destructive force in family relations. To a varying extent the initial psychiatric referral reflects the unseen purpose of restoring a pre-existing emotional balance or power alignment in family relations. Thus, the first person referred to the psychiatrist may be viewed as a symptom of disturbed family homeostasis.

Psychiatric illness as a single or isolated instance in family life hardly occurs. Almost always other members of the family are also ill. The sick behaviors of these family members are often closely interwoven, and mutually reinforcing. A critical focus of conflict and anxiety may move from one member of the family to another or from one family pair to another. In this sense the family group serves as a carrier of emotional disturbance. Sometimes two members share the same illness or one illness is the complement of the other or they may clash. In the latter instance the continuity of the family may be thrown into jeopardy. It is by no means rare that the core of family life is dominated by these reciprocal patterns of psychiatric disturbance.

The clinical importance of this problem is reflected in still another way. More often than not, the incentive for referral of a patient for psychotherapy is the outbreak of a destructive family conflict rather than the recognition of the existence of specific neurotic symptoms in one family member. Sometimes the existence of neurotic symptoms is not even known until the psychiatrist identifies them as such. Surely there is a relation between psychoneurotic personality and the occurrence of conflict in family relations. But this relation is a circular one. Conflict in family relations precedes the emergence of psychoneurotic symptoms and at a later point in time further conflict in family relations influences the fate of these symptoms or plays a role in the induction of new ones. It is significant clinically that the main spur for psychiatric referral comes frequently from the suffering caused by family conflict rather than from the existence of mental symptoms *per se*. In many families there is no thought of psychiatric referral as long as the neurotic tendencies of the family members are tolerably well compensated within the pattern of reciprocal family role relations. The timing of the demand for professional help tends very much to coincide with acute decompensation of the balance of family relations, bringing in its wake a distressing family conflict. Critical upsets of the homeostasis of a family group thus become a significant mental health challenge.

Moving one step further, we may consider the same problem from still another standpoint. In the incipient phase of psychiatric illness, the breakdown in adaptation may at first be relatively localized. It may be restricted to the failure to fulfill the requirements of a single family role, as sexual partner, or parent, or household manager. It is only as the psychiatric illness unfolds and the decompensation of defenses against anxiety strikes deeper that the conflict and disordered social behavior spread to invade progressively all the family roles and the entire range of life activity. We are therefore compelled in each such situation to match the role functions where moderate health is preserved against those other roles where adaptation is disabled by conflict. At certain stages a given individual behaves in a sick way in some parts of his life and maintains a relatively adequate adaptation in others. Performance in some life roles is impaired less than in others. In psychotherapy we make optimal use of this struggle between the more sick and the less sick parts of a person. We mobilize the residually healthy aspects of personality in the battle against the psychiatrically twisted parts. Can we not do likewise in the psychiatric approach to conflict in family relationships and the dynamics of the family as a whole? Can we not weigh the areas of relatively healthy functioning against those other areas which reflect crippling of family functioning?

Due to the fundamental interdependency and reciprocity of behavior in family relations, frequently if one member is treated, others must be treated too. If a disturbed child is treated, so must the mother be. If the mother is treated, the father needs attention, too.

This concern with the maintenance of a certain desired emotional balance in family relations is nowhere so convincingly reflected as in the family lives of psychoanalysts themselves. Male analysts have their wives psychoanalyzed and vice versa. Often, their children undergo analysis, too. In a certain sense, this trend reflects a need for a kind of vaccination procedure, a quest for immunity against the toxic effects of neurosis, so that the unity of the family group may be preserved. Opinions differ as to the efficacy of this prophylactic measure but the underlying intent is nevertheless clear. In a particular instance an analyst's wife, unanalyzed herself, felt isolated from the main stream of her husband's busy life and blurted out: "What we analysts' wives need is to form a union."

In marital disorders, if one partner enters therapy, sooner or later the other demands help, too. Not infrequently a marital partner, though untreated, becomes deeply involved in the therapeutic experience of the treated one, sharing vicariously his emotional experience. Sometimes they engage in a kind of spontaneous therapy of one another. This may be judged good or bad by different psychiatrists, but the fact is that it occurs.

This is well illustrated in a remark of one patient who told me that she was getting two analyses for the price of one. She thanked me for the remarkable improvement in her husband's behavior while she was undergoing analysis. If one closely observes such marital pairs, one often finds that the therapist is a silent presence in the intimate exchanges between husband and wife as they face problems, share joys, and even as they engage in sexual relations. Thus, the therapist influences family life not only during the therapeutic session, but also from afar, as a living presence in the emotional life of the patient and in his relations with other family members.

From one angle, psychotherapy provides a tool for the restoration of an old balance in family relations following an upset or for bringing about a new and more desirable equilibrium. This is why the psychotherapy of an individual needs to be viewed within the frame of the total life of his family.

These are but a few relevant, empirical observations which affirm the importance of approaching issues of mental illness and health in the wider context of the individual joined to his family group, in addition to viewing the individual patient as a separate person. It is axiomatic that an integrated therapeutic approach to the family entity, if it is to aspire to psychological specificity, must rest on the foundation of comprehensive diagnosis of the family.

Family therapy implies solution of the question: what to treat, whom to treat, when to treat. It requires a formulation of intrapsychic conflict within the broader frame of salient patterns of family conflict, a correlation of disturbed homeostasis of individual personality with disturbed homeostasis of the family group. It also requires that the corrective approach to pathogenic foci be made within the context of an explicit judgment regarding a set of appropriate goals and values for a healthy family in our society.

Elsewhere (2) I have suggested that a therapeutic approach to the emotional disturbances of family life might be conceived in the following steps:

1. A psychosocial evaluation of the family as a whole.
2. The application of appropriate levels of social support and educational guidance.
3. A psychotherapeutic approach to conflicted family relationships.
4. Individual psychotherapy for selected family members oriented initially to the specific dynamic relations of personality and family role, and to the balance between intrapsychic conflict and family conflict.

Within this frame, individual psychotherapy is auxiliary to and dependent upon an integrated therapeutic program for the family as a social unit. Crucial to such a program is the consideration of appropriate levels of entry, and timing of such entry to affect in sequential stages specific components of the family disturbance. As an aid in the determination of such judgments, home visits by a trained person and careful recording of observations of family interaction in its natural setting are of the first importance. A check of insights gained in clinical office evaluations against intimate observations of family members made on a home visit reveals the special value of such aids to comprehensive family diagnosis. Interpretation of the relevant data according to a scheme already outlined in previous papers (14, 15, 16) is of material help in reaching judgments as to the need and suitable timing of intervention with social therapy, educational guidance, psychiatric first aid, psychotherapy for conflicted family pairs and individual psychotherapy for selected family members.

In acutely disturbed families, where loss of emotional control brings mounting signs of disorganized behavior, the assignment of a trained person to live temporarily with the family succeeds in restoring emotional balance in family relations. This has a preventive as well as therapeutic value. Occasionally, the use of such a device for first aid achieves a seemingly miraculous effect in calming a chaotic and violent family atmosphere, and thus reducing substantially the destructive effects on individual integration. This is especially pertinent to the protection of vulnerable children.

In further steps, family diagnosis and therapy moves ahead through a series of planned office interviews. Such interviews involve separate sessions with the primary patient interspersed with joint interviews of the patient with other family members. Since the primary patient is viewed both as an individual in distress and as a symptomatic expression of family pathology, the disturbance of this patient becomes the fulcrum or entering wedge for the appropriate levels of intervention into the disorder of the family relations. The sequence of office interviews is arranged with a view to further elucidation of the interrelations of the primary patient's affliction with the psychopathology of the family, and the corresponding interplay between his intrapsychic conflict and family conflict. The aim is to define the conflicts in which the patient is locked with other family members, to assay the disturbances in the bond of individual and family identity, and the interdependence of homeostasis of individual personality with the homeostatic balance of the role relations in family pairs and the family as a whole. It is possible, then, to mark out the patterns of family interaction which are potentially available for solution of conflict or for restitution.

It is important to appraise the extent to which family conflict is controlled, compensated or decompensated; how far family conflict induces progressive damage to salient relationships, impairs complementarity in role relations, and therefore predisposes to breakdown of individual adaptation. In this connection, complementarity in reciprocal family role relations is of special importance insofar as it assures mutual satisfaction of need, support for a needed self-image and crucial forms of defense against anxiety. Impairment of complementarity undermines the stability of emotional integration into family. It aggravates the internal stress of the primary patient, weakens his control of intrapsychic conflict, and intensifies his psychiatric disablement. Some forms of family conflict are temporary and benign; they may deepen and enrich family ties and spur further maturation of family members. Other forms which are prolonged, severe, inadequately neutralized, move toward alienation in family relations and progressive damage to individual adaptation. The support of constructive forms of complementarity in family role relations is of central importance, therefore, in family therapy.

The crucial question is this: can family integration be preserved despite conflict, or does conflict tend to destroy the link of individual and family identity and thus magnify the malignancy of individual pathology? Within the frame of family conflict, what are the vicissitudes of the individual's opportunities to resolve or at least mitigate the destructive effects of intrapsychic conflict? What chance is there to discover a new and improved level of family role complementarity and with this, a better level of individual adaptation?

In the final analysis, this is an issue of interpendence between the individual's defenses against anxiety and the patterns of control and stabilization operating in family relations.

The appropriate cues to the sequential involvement of other family members are derived from the above described orientation to the dynamic relations of internal and external conflict. Of necessity, the proper sequence of such interviews varies from case to case, family to family.

In the case of a child patient the interviews may, for example, take the following order: an interview with the child and mother together, an interview with the child alone, an interview with child and father and finally, an interview with the two parents without the child. Or it might entail at an appropriate point an interview of the child, and both parents, or the child and sibling together with one or both parents.

In the case of an adult patient this might entail a sequence of interviews in which one begins with the primary patient and after that, a joint interview of this patient with the marital partner and possibly after that an interview of the primary patient with his or her parent and/or sibling, depending upon the cues which derive from a continuing process of family diagnosis. An unfolding of exploratory therapeutic interviews of this kind has the desirable effect not only of mobilizing receptivity to therapeutic influence in the primary patient; it also promotes in family relationships a more favorable climate for the progress of therapy. It makes clear, too, the patterns of benign and malignant psychiatric distortion in the various individual members of the family and allows the psychiatrist an opportunity to draw discriminating judgments about the timing of involvement of other family members in a therapeutic undertaking. At certain stages it may be appropriate to work concentratedly with mother and child together, husband and wife together, or even mother, father and child together. In this setting, one is able to deal directly with certain distortions of perception of family members of one another. Working at this level through a process of reality testing, mediated by the participation of the therapist, one is able to dissolve away various irrational projections of one family member upon another. If at a certain stage certain malignant interpersonal conflicts among family members are ameliorated, it becomes possible to resume systematic individual therapy of one family member with the expectation of an attitude of receptivity to therapeutic influence and with a reduction of resistance. Again one may find at a still later stage that tension and conflict in family relations agitate the primary patient to a state of resistance and again one may choose to deal with this resistance through a therapeutic interview of this patient with the involved family pair.

Thus a pattern of procedure evolves which is a kind of flexible combination of individual and group psychotherapy involving salient family pairs, occasionally threesomes, in which there is distortion of reciprocal family role relations and damaging conflict. The planning of sessions with individuals, and sessions with two or more family members must be discriminatingly timed in accordance with indications which derive from the active and flexible application of the principles of family diagnosis. From one stage of therapy to the next, as the balance of reciprocity in family role relations shifts, and the focus of pathogenic disturbance moves from one part of the family to another, the therapist must be ready to institute corresponding shifts of the level of therapeutic intervention.

Family therapy is complex. It deals with multiple levels of conflict. It may require a division of labor, in which various phases of the therapy are carried out by members of a clinical team. But these therapists do not function in isolation with individual family members. To the contrary, periodically they meet together with the entire family group to deal with certain layers of shared conflict.

I have described here a tentative approach to illness as a function of family as well as a manifestation of individual behavior. This is only a bare beginning in a complicated but important clinical task.

BIBLIOGRAPHY

Articles by the author may be found in the following publications:

1. Am. J. Orthopsychiat., 20:4, October 1950.
2. Psychiatry, 17:4, Nov. 1954.
3. Social Casework, 35:p. 139, April 1954, and Feb. 1955.
4. Psychopathology of Childhood, New York: Grune & Stratton, 1955.
5. Changing Conceptions of Psychoanalytic Medicine. New York: Grune & Stratton, 1956.

16. Am. J. Orthopsychiat., 26:2, April 1956.

17. (With Marjorie L. Behrens, M.A.), Am. J. Orthopsychiat., 26:1, January 1956.

8. (With Marjorie L. Behrens, M.A.), Social Casework, January 1956.

9. Am. J. Psychoanal., April 1957.

110. Internat. J. Sociometry, January 1957.

11. Am. J. Orthopsych., 26:2, April 1956.

12. "Role of the Family in Diagnostic Process," American Orthopsychiatric Association, 1957, March—Paper.

13. "An Orientation to Psychiatric Research on the Family," Marr. and Fam. Living, 19:1, Feb. 1957.

CHAPTER 28

The Treatment of a Child and Family

INTRODUCTION

Principles of psychotherapy are secondary to a systematized understanding of human problems and defined forms of maladaptation and illness. The specific techniques of psychotherapy are derived, step by step, from an integrated theory of personality development, social interaction, and psychopathology. This theory provides us with a set of normative expectations with regard to the endo-psychic organization of personality, relations of individual, family, and wider society, and a corresponding set of standards for judging a range of deviations from the norm. The purpose of treatment is to correct what is deviant and wrong in a person's life adaptation and in his endo-psychic organization. The treatment process stands or falls according to the validity of this judgment as to what is wrong with a person at a given time and in a given social place.

Our purpose here is to describe the treatment of a disturbed child within the frame of a concomitant program of therapy for the child's family. The treatment of a disturbed child requires us to respect the child's individuality. But the concept of individuality in a child is often incorrectly understood. A child's "individuality" may be healthy or pathological. This distinction is an important one.

The concept of individuality in a child is frequently treated as if it meant everything in the child that is separate or different from his parents. Such an interpretation emphasizes the child's separateness, and even his opposition to parents, while seeming to ignore the principle that healthy separation in the child cannot go forward except in the matrix of healthy emotional union or identification with his parents. In other words, healthy individuality in a child represents a balance between two components: a component of togetherness with parents and family, and another component of autonomous development. Individuality in this sense absorbs within itself much of the social interactional content of family experience. It does not represent exclusively tendencies in the child which are

---

Reprinted with permission from *Case Studies in Counseling and Psychotherapy*, Arthur Burton (Ed.), 1959, 56-69.

This paper was co-authored with Marcille H. Lakos.

different from or opposite to those of parents and family.

The unfolding of a child's personality is, in great part, the product of social process. The family is the basic group within which the child is socialized. The child takes into himself something of the mother and something of the father, but also develops something unique and different. The child's uniqueness is influenced, beyond hereditary factors, by differences between the parents and the child's perception of the emotional relations between them. This interaction and merging of mother and father epitomizes the emotional essence of the family as a group; it is the core of the psychological identity of the family.

A child's personality is the end result of a certain fluid balance between tendencies toward psychic union with the parents and separation from them. The secure development of autonomy in the child's personality is thus contingent upon secure identity of the child with parents. Healthy identity with the parents means healthy separation; pathological identity means pathological separation. In circular fashion, whatever is deviant in the process of separation further distorts the pattern of emotional identification with parents and family.

The emotional disturbance of a child cannot be evaluated or treated in a social vacuum. Whatever is deviant in the child's behavior needs to be viewed as a symptom of the social psychopathology of the family group. In this sense, the traditionally demarcated professional field of child psychiatry might justifiably be called, instead, family psychiatry. If the pathological trends in a child's personality are to be successfully treated, the pathological trends within his family group must also be treated concurrently. If the child is to be restored to a path of healthy autonomous development, he must be restored to a position of healthy emotional union with parents and family. The unit of diagnosis and therapy is the child and family as an integral phenomenon rather than the child as an isolated being.

In the field of child psychotherapy, it is often claimed that family therapy is carried out at the same time as the therapy of the child. This usually means treatment of the child and mother, sometimes by separate therapists, sometimes by the same therapist. In a strict sense, however, this is not family therapy. This is an atomistic approach to child and mother as separate individuals, and it does not constitute a true therapy of the family group. Ordinarily, such treatment does not encompass a systematized conceptualization of the child-mother pair as a functional expression of the psychological configuration of the family as a whole. In the setting of traditional child guidance practices, the disturbances of parental attitudes are mainly related to the parents' individual personality, but not to the totality of role relations within the family group.

It is within the framework of viewing the child and family together as the basic phenomenological unit that we try to evaluate a disturbed child. It is within this conceptual orientation that we now describe the treatment of a particular case.

The primary patient is a ten-year-old boy referred with a series of complaints: failure in school work, chronic reading difficulty, depression and withdrawal, fear of father, jealousy of sister, and fears of illness and injury.

The early clinical interviews occurred in the following sequence: interview with both parents, with the child alone, with both parents again, each parent individually; then, interviews of child with both parents together and with each parent separately.

INITIAL INTERVIEWS WITH PARENTS

In the first interview with the parents, the father assumed the initiative. The mother sat by with a stony, impassive face but obviously listening very intently. The father placed himself instantly in the dominant position with a tacit assumption of superiority to his wife. He was clearly worried. There was a note of panic in his voice but his outward demeanor was controlled and reasoned. His wife sat stiff, constrained, frozen, offering only an occasional comment if her husband made a direct inquiry of her. At this time, and for some months thereafter, two significant pieces of information were lacking: the father was in personal analysis; and the school had recommended psychiatric consultation for the child two years back, but the parents delayed action on this recommendation right up to the point where the marriage was about to crumble. It was at the very peak of the family crisis that the parents became urgently motivated to request psychiatric help for the boy.

Sharply in evidence in the first interview was the father's wrath toward the child. He confessed it candidly. He stated that he never liked him, was critical of his intellectual failure, but also revealed his intense personal torment and guilt over the child's rejection. Ostensibly, his son was a severe disappointment to him because he seemed so stupid. The father leaned over backward to take the blame upon himself. He carefully sidestepped any temptation to be openly accusatory to his wife. We learned later, however, that in his own mind the father associated the boy with his mother and chalked them both up as stupid. He seemed to treat the boy exclusively as belonging to his mother. The mother was aware of this and said nothing. But the air between them was thick with unexpressed tension. Being an intellectual perfectionist, the father could not abide even the appearance of stupidity in any member of his family. Mother and son acted dumb, but weren't. It was merely that the father expected them to be so.

In the second interview with parents, the mother thawed out of her frozen state sufficiently to show some intense emotion. She choked up and cried. Only with support and encouragement from the clinician could she express even a small part of her tormented feelings. She felt an enormous guilt for the failure of both her and her son in the father's eyes.

FIRST INTERVIEW WITH THE CHILD PATIENT

Hubert was slightly undersized for his age, but, what is more important, he acted like a much younger child. He appeared blank and withdrawn. He was dull, sluggish, extremely walled-off. His attitude was removed, taciturn, depressed. He was unspontaneous and uncommunicative. He engaged in play in a self-absorbed way, ignoring everyone about him. Using building blocks he constructed a garage which he called a fortress. He admitted on questioning that it would be extremely difficult to get inside the walls of this building. When asked how long it would take, he muttered under his breath, "At least two years." He seemed to be intensely barricaded. His behavior suggested deep preoccupation with inner fantasies of power and destruction. Later, he alluded in a low voice to the toy building as the place where his father worked. His father was the director of an engineering school.

HISTORICAL BACKGROUND

The problems of this boy can hardly be understood except against the background of the disturbed relations of his parents and the twisted path of the development of his family. There was a religious difference between the parents; the father was Jewish, the mother Protestant. There was, beyond this, a further clash of cultural background which created a critical barrier between man and wife. This was especially complicated by the husband's extreme mistrust of the wife, a condition testified to by her husband's family.

Originally, this man and wife met at his place of work. She was a research assistant in the engineering school of which he was director. The courtship was a troubled one. It involved a long struggle with the man's parents to get them to accept the marriage. Throughout this struggle he was torn with conflict—trying, on the one hand, to placate his family, and, on the other, to win acceptance of the woman he wished to marry.

The opposition of his mother continued to be sharp and overt until a particular event occurred involving a bitter verbal battle between his older sister and mother. Out of her vindictiveness the sister declared vehemently that whether her mother liked it or not, her brother would be married. Promptly thereafter the mother collapsed, went to bed, but following this ceased to oppose the marriage.

The first phase of the marriage was tense and difficult. The new wife made an early but unsuccessful attempt to become pregnant. She felt she should have a child to please her husband. She was plagued with fears of sterility. Finally, she had a miscarriage which caused considerable anguish to her and her husband. Somewhat later she became pregnant with our patient, Hubert, but by this time her husband was inducted into the armed services. He left to go abroad with the military during her pregnancy. He arranged for his wife to live with his older sister. This arrangement was motivated strongly by his suspicion of his wife, his jealousy, and his fear that she might be unfaithful.

This jealousy is epitomized in one dramatic episode. On one occasion, the father, on returning home, secretly searched the mother's dresser drawer to be sure that her diaphragm was in its accustomed place. He was unable to find it, became infuriated, and charged his wife with infidelity. She was profoundly hurt and angry. All the time, the diaphragm was exactly where it should have been, but in his anxious haste the father had overlooked it. But the mother, as usual, and despite her humiliation, sided emotionally with her husband against herself. She felt, too, that a woman was not to be trusted. She shared with her husband an attitude of contempt and disparagement toward women. There were several critical episodes in her personal life in which she felt cruelly betrayed by women whom she had trusted as friends.

Hubert's birth took place while the father was abroad in military service. He was the first of four children. Prior to his birth, the mother dreamed idealistically of motherhood but was painfully disillusioned when the child finally arrived. She felt abandoned, utterly alone, and frightened and burdened by the responsibility of the child. She had little communication with the sister-in-law with whom she was then living. she felt tied to the baby but had virtually no other human contacts.

During the first phase of the child's life the mother was isolated and depressed. The child cried constantly. The mother used phenobarbital to quiet his crying and administered enemas to alleviate his cramps. He cried and screamed almost continuously up to the age of four months. She resented the baby's demands and felt estranged from him. She rarely held him in her arms or showed him any affection. His development was slow. It was two years before he spoke his first words. At 18 months he had difficulty with adenoids. He had distressed breathing and drooled at the mouth. Though depressed and deeply guilty, the mother kept her emotions to herself. This was the character of the mother's life situation until the father's return from the military.

Hubert was two years of age when the father returned. When the boy first saw his father, he screamed and refused to have anything to do with him. If he saw his father approaching his mother, he cried out in anguish. He seemed to go into acute panic when he saw his father in bed with his mother. Every member of the family was at this time severely troubled. The mother told the father little of how she felt. She was run down, exhausted, and did not look well. The father himself was morbidly unhappy. The parents felt estranged. The father showed little trust in the mother's affection for him. He escaped to his professional work. He came home late and saw little of his wife or the boy.

This situation continued until the mother became pregnant with the second child, a girl, toward whom Hubert later felt intense jealousy. During this period the boy continued his state of isolation; he did not play with other children. At the age of four or five Hubert became increasingly destructive. He showed no warmth to either parent, teased and struck his sister, and suffered criticism from both his parents. At five years he had a tonsillectomy, after which his mouth breathing and drooling diminished. The mother continued to be stern and cold toward him.

In kindergarten he was slow in learning and socially withdrawn. The teachers were puzzled because of his good intelligence. He daydreamed a good deal. The father, believing he was stupid, treated him harshly. During these years, Hubert had several minor accidents and developed an intense fear of bodily injury. The parents continually disagreed about the way to handle him.

The father tended to be indifferent to the child until his behavior became unbearable. He would then become abusive and insist, "That's enough." After an outburst of irritability, he would feel guilty and apologize to the boy. Otherwise, the father would simply ignore him. The mother resented this, and was critical of the father for not being more strict with the boy. The boy was consistently more difficult when the father was present. Later, two other children were born, making a total of four. The father enjoyed the younger children, and was especially fond of the second child, a girl. This tended, of course, to aggravate the patient's jealousy. These are the salient features of this boy's history.

At the time of referral a severe barrier existed between mother and child, also between father and mother, and father and child. The mother drew back sharply from the boy as if he were the worst part of herself. Both mother and boy felt they were to blame for the father's rejection of them; it was their own doing.

PROGRESS OF THERAPY

It seemed evident that if we were to make progress with this case we would have to confront the family problem as well as the boy's. We would have to move in the direction of dissolving the emotional barrier first between mother and child, after that between the parents, and finally, do something to restore the father's acceptance of the boy. Regardless of the father's involvement in personal analysis, our orientation was to commit both parents to participation in the therapy of the child. The father was involved in his family role as parent to this child and as husband to his wife. The mother was involved as parent to the child and as wife to her husband. The therapy was therefore conducted at several levels: individual sessions with the child, sessions with child and mother, individual sessions with mother, group therapy in a mother's group, and, later, sessions with the child and father. Therapy was mainly conducted by the female therapist, under the supervision of the male psychiatrist. Periodic family conferences were held, in which both male and female clinicians took part.

One event colored the entire course of treatment and should be related first. After about nine months of therapy, the mother terminated her individual sessions. Therapy of the child was continued, but the mother withdrew. The reasons were not immediately clear. The mother had an outburst of anger at the therapist when she discovered in group therapy sessions for mothers that women could enjoy sex and even experience orgasm. She felt bitter that her husband had withheld this information from her all these years. Until now she believed that men had a corner on sex and that women submitted purely out of a sense of duty. She was hurt and angry at her husband, but blew up at her female therapist. This was the precipitating situation.

But there were other reasons. Both she and her husband were suspicious of the therapist and fearful of injurious personal exposure. Her husband supported her decision to quit individual therapy, partly because of his belief that she was too stupid and too fragile, partly because of a submerged fear that she might get out of hand and turn toward another man. His jealousy of his own son was clearly a factor. Though interrupting individual therapy, the mother wished to continue in group therapy. It was judged wise, however, to remove her from group therapy as well, since we would have then no control over her emotional response to the group experience. This she resented. For a relatively short period, we continued the isolated treatment of the child, partly because of our uncertainty as to how this situation would unfold.

With the passing of the summer months, however, the mother returned, confessed that she was in error, expressed resentment regarding her exclusion from group therapy and asked to be reinstated both in the group and individual treatment. She did this on her own, with the father reluctantly assenting.

A quick preview of the sequence of changes in therapy is helpful for purposes of orientation. There occurred first a melting of the emotional barrier between mother and child. A new level of joining and emotional intimacy was established in this family pair. Following this there was improvement both in the boy and the mother. This left the way open for a beginning change in the relations between the two parents. It was the improvement in the parents' sexual relationship and the father's increased receptivity to both mother and boy which ultimately induced him to request a more active participating role in the boy's therapy. He also asked to have individual sessions to guide him in his paternal attitudes. Ultimately, there was substantial improvement in the intimacy of family relations at all levels.

The direct therapy of the boy began slowly. Initially, he appeared both oppressed and depressed. He bowed his shoulders; his movements were laboriously slow. He scuffed his feet as he walked across the room. He rarely looked at the therapist. His eyes were glazed and dull. His face was mask-like. His thought processes seemed to be split off from the movement of his hands. He was extremely reticent; he knelt quietly in a corner of the room and played with blocks in a feeble, detached, lifeless way. From time to time he interrupted his play to simply sit and indulge his fantasies. He seemed to resent any attempt at conversation. The therapist, therefore, sat quietly, saying extremely little.

This type of relationship persisted for four sessions with almost no verbal communication of any sort. There was only a slight show of interest when the therapist offered candy to the boy.

Beginning about the fourth session, his building activity became somewhat more organized and he showed increasing alertness to the therapist's presence. Now and then he cast sidelong glances at her and asked a few questions concerning the blocks. The therapist recognized his frightened and disguised appeal for her to take part in his game. She responded. He seemed pleased by this and proceeded then to test the therapist's reaction to his urge to destroy the building. When there was no sign of criticism, he proceeded to destroy the house, making a loud bang and relishing it.

In general his behavior continued to be cautious, fearful, suspicious, and walled-off. While believing himself to be stupid, he was nonetheless under compulsion to display his intellect to the therapist. This occurred mainly in the form of reciting to her fragmented pieces of information about current events. Gradually, as he felt safer in this relationship, safer both from criticism and from any compulsion to behave according to her dictates, he became more accessible. The therapist continued warm, friendly, but non-intrusive, waiting for cues from the boy as to the level at which he would accept her participation.

In the sixth session there came another change. He dropped his interest in blocks and proceeded to become interested in ball-playing. He confessed his total failure as an athlete. He said his fingers got in the way; he was awkward. But he seemed to appeal to the therapist to raise his confidence. She responded by joining him in a game of catch. At first his coordination was extremely poor. He was all hands and feet, but he was tenacious and the ball-playing continued. He improved rapidly. After a time, he jumped, and caught and threw the ball quite skillfully. His interest moved to other activities: finger painting, drawing (mostly of submarines), and depicting his own fantasies of outer space. He was ambitious to be the first man to visit Mars. He felt he might be happier there than on earth. The therapist was a full participant in all these activities. She talked only if the boy seemed to welcome it.

During this growing intimacy between boy and therapist, the boy slowly offered small confidences about his parents. This came without any pressure whatsoever. He was aware that his mother was coming to see the therapist once a week. He made clear how utterly alone he felt, how unable to communicate with anyone in the family. He felt incredibly inferior and dumb. He gradually became more assertive and complained of his parents' failure to understand him. He felt stripped of confidence as a result of the mother's alienation from him and also as the result of her guilty over-protection.

The mother, in response to her own conflict, tended to protect him from the father's criticism and tended to do the talking for him; in effect, she put words right into his mouth. She lived his life for him, treating him as a piece of herself rather than as a separate person. This was clearly the effect of her fright of the father's criticisms.

As the boy revealed himself increasingly to the therapist, he cautiously hinted that he would like his mother to join the session with him. He wanted to show her his drawings and display his new facility in ballplaying. But he was frightened. He wanted to ask her if she loved him, but he didn't dare. She would misunderstand and get bossy.

The mother was invited to be part of the boy's sessions. Initially, both boy and mother were extremely awkward with one another. Gradually, he drew her into games with him and hesitantly showed some of his feelings. The mother had previously felt completely rejected by the boy. She was shocked and elated to discover that she was so deeply important to him. When they sensed that each really needed the other, the relationship, at first wooden and blocked, warmed up. Finally, the boy, while caressing a toy animal, sat next to his mother, and took hold of her hand. The mother was touched to the core and could hardly hold back her tears. She seemed stilted, self-conscious, fumbling, and hardly knew what to do or say. Finally, in a labored, awkward manner she put her arm around her boy and they sat quietly together. They agreed later—it felt good! They walked out of the office arm in arm.

The patient responded to this reunion with his mother with an excited, buoyant mood. Their play together in therapeutic sessions became hectically animated. They reached a point where they experienced a climactic shared excitement in a playful fight with water guns. Ths boy doused the mother from head to foot; while at first self-conscious and scared, she came gradually to love it. Emotional communication became intense. They laughed and cried together.

Let us turn now to a consideration of what was happening in the meantime in individual sessions with the mother. Initially, she seemed frozen, guilt-ridden, defensive, and aloof. Her conversation was almost entirely on the surface. She surrounded herself with this protective wall as though to ward off expected attack. Nevertheless, she was earnest in her desire to help the child. She revealed quite unmistakably her feeling of lack of worth in her husband's eyes, and her tendency to agree with him that she was stupid. Yet, paradoxically, she rose to the challenge to try to prove her good intellect to the therapist, exactly as did the boy. She tried in every conceivable way to build up her sense of worth and importance, and to impress her husband and the surrounding community. Small successes meant nothing to her. The slightest disappointment confirmed her conviction of inferiority. Her whole demeanor seemed to radiate shame for herself and for her son. At first she showed little feeling. This gradually changed. She revealed her fear of admitting openly any closeness with the boy. She wanted to disconnect herself from the boy in her husband's mind.

At another level she discussed her husband's character, his severe suspiciousness, his jealousy, and his accusations of infidelity. Within the family there was no spontaneous joy. All issues were met with a heavy hand. There was little relaxation, no play, no humor. The emotional climate of the entire family group was heavy and depressive.

The therapist's role with the mother was one of sympathetic support and acceptance, providing abundant opportunity for the free expression of her conflicting emotions. The significant parts of her relations with the child and husband were discussed frankly with her. At times she was given direct advice concerning her conduct with the boy. She was encouraged to learn to listen to him as she herself was listened to.

A sharp change occurred when she learned in the mother's group that women had sexual orgasms. This was a real shock. She came to her individual session with anxious, pressured questions. Hitherto, she had carried out her obligation with her husband in a passive, frigid, immobile manner. This, to her, was the normal state of affairs in married life. As she talked, she became increasingly irate at the way she'd been cheated. She exploded at the therapist and quit. As has earlier been indicated, after a lapse of several months she began again where she had left off. The therapist responded earnestly to her urge to explore this sexual discovery. There was candid discussion of the sexual potentials of a woman. The mother was encouraged in the expectation of personal pleasure. Following a particularly tense session in which the mother discussed at length her experiences of treachery at the hands of women and confessed her fear of betrayal by the therapist, she began to show increasing interest in her sex life. She overcame her vindictive feeling toward her husband and participated more freely in sexual love with her husband. Her husband in turn reacted with considerable surprise, but also genuine appreciation. For the first time she had succeeded in winning from him overt, enthusiastic expressions of approval. This was a turning point in the relations between man and wife.

It also marked a change in her attitude toward the therapist. Following this improvement she became much more trusting. She confessed much more frankly her previous suspicions of the therapist, her fear of betrayal, her contempt for women, and her need to cut off her feeling in her dealings with them. About this time, she began to show intense feelings in the therapeutic sessions. She dropped her defensive barricade and literally poured out emotion.

Gradually, the mother's rigidity mellowed. She responded with increasing warmth to the boy; he, in turn, moved closer to her. The melting of the mutual mistrust between mother and son opened the way to a new level of emotional identity. Of particular importance in this newly discovered intimacy were the water fights in which Hubert directed a steady stream against his mother. It was quite striking to note in this connection the boy's increasing freedom in emotional communication with his mother. He dropped his mask. He no longer acted dumb. In place of his previous dull apathy, he now displayed some spark and real intelligence. He showed his most acute fear in connection with an open show of tears. He was convinced that it was weak and foolish of him to cry; but when mother and son cried together, this fear was eased.

As the intimacy between the mother and son unfolded, the boy talked increasingly about what was wrong with his relations with his father. He became guilty concerning this, however, and showed strong reluctance to belittling his father in his mother's eyes. The recognition of the boy's guilt over the temptation to use one parent against another induced the therapist to suggest sessions for the boy and the father. While considering this plan, the boy entered a plateau. He seemed for a time to freeze and he was unable to make further progress.

The anticipation of joined sessions with his father induced again a compulsive urge to prove his worth through a display of superior factual knowledge about the world. It was as if the father could tolerate the boy only at this level of intellectual superiority. Ordinarily, conversation between father and son was sparse and impersonal. When it did occur, it took the form of a detached, intellectual discussion, which tended quickly to deteriorate into an irritable argument about who was right or who knew better.

By this time the boy had a clear picture of his father's rejection of him, his suspiciousness, and criticism of his stupidity. With increasing awareness of his father's preference of the other children, the boy's hate and fear of his father emerged quite sharply.

In the therapy sessions with the boy and father, the father was at first reserved and defensive. His intelligence, essential honesty, and desire to really understand came to the fore, however. He listened both to the boy and the therapist with some respect. Gradually, the boy overcame his fear sufficiently to express directly to his father for the first time his conflicting feelings. The father was deeply impressed. He tended partly to justify his attitudes and partly to confess his guilt for failing to understand the boy. He admitted to the boy that he lacked confidence in him, that he preferred the other children, that at times he was disdainful and indifferent. While making these confessions, the father seemed depressed.

For this reason the therapist had several sessions with the father alone. She gave emotional support to the father for his intellectual understanding and his earnest desire to help his son. At the same time, a number of the father's misconceptions of the boy were challenged and discussed freely. When issues arose that had to do with the relations between mother and father, the father showed much more animation. He was at first more interested in his wife than his son. His motivation to improve his marital relations was stronger than his urge to help the boy. In short, he was more preoccupied with his own needs than with his son's needs.

Discouraged in the beginning, he talked of the complete stalemate in his relations with his wife; he did not know which way to turn. After a time, however, he gave recognition to a distinct change for the better in the behavior of both boy and mother. He was impressed with the improvement in his wife's sexual response.

At about this time, a joint conference was arranged which included the man and wife, the male psychiatrist, and female therapist. The purpose of this was to survey progress and decide further steps in therapy. The father admitted a lessening of his hostile feelings toward the mother. They were now finding more satisfactions together, which gave him real hope. Both man and wife agreed that things had been rough but they now expressed a desire to make the marriage a lasting one. The wife remarked, "I've learned something. I feel now that you don't have to know exactly what is going on but if things work out it is satisfying enough." She meant by this that she had dropped her effort to prove her intellectual adequacy, had ceased to cut off the flow of her feeling, and felt more alive. Of particular importance in this interview was the more candid discussion of the difficulties that resulted from the husband's jealousy. The wife was able to "tell her husband off." She expressed more openly her resentment of the father's jealousy and his refusal to allow her to leave the house unattended.

A month later, there was a very distinct change in the attitude of the father. He was more positive, no longer depressed, and spoke enthusiastically of the change in his relations with his wife. She was warmer, he was less suspicious; they found real pleasure in one another's company. This enabled him now to show a genuine interest in the boy.

In the meantime, Hubert responded well to the therapeutic sessions with the father. He regarded the achievement of a new contact with his father as something outstanding. Following this, he showed substantial improvement in his work at school. He was a more spirited, interested student. He continued to be a slow learner but his achievement was distinctly on the upgrade. At the same time he was less hostile toward his sister.

When the mutual hostility and suspiciousness between father and son eased, there were further individual sessions with Hubert. He began now to talk increasingly of his sexual feelings. He confessed his masturbation but was troubled because he got little feeling from it. During one such session Hubert showed considerable agitation and anxiety; he fidgeted and wrung his hands. With encouragement he related his worries. He confessed to several episodes of exploratory sex play with his sister. He was given every opportunity to talk himself out in these matters and much relieved to discover that his sex urges were by no means unique. They did not make him a bad, perverted person.

This encouraged him to talk more and more of his body experiences. He began to value his body more. His appearance changed; he became neater, and paid more attention to his looks. He began also to learn more of the skills which were required of him in social relations, ball-playing, and dancing. Through dancing lessons, he acquired a girl friend.

One day he came to therapy quite depressed and far away. He seemed lonely, and said little. after a considerable period of tortured reticence, he admitted finally that he continued to be worried about his masturbation. He hated to "jerk off," felt very guilty about it, and was sure that it hurt his penis. He complained that it was actually painful. He imagined that the liquid would run dry if his glands were overworked, and that they would cease to function. He had the thought that the semen was infected with germs and was a real danger if allowed to stay on his pajamas.

Discussion of these conflicts and fears led to the realization that he wanted to hear the male psychiatrist's view of these problems. This was arranged for. The problem of his masturbation and associated fears was discussed with female therapist and male psychiatrist together. The discussion was lengthy. The core of this conflict emerged finally: the boy was intensely disappointed because the pleasure of seminal discharge was somehow impaired. In fact, at times, he did not realize that he was having an orgasm unless he looked directly at his penis. He rubbed it harshly, angrily. Through various hints, it seemed probably that he was unconsciously equating his penis with his father. In the act of beating his penis, he was attacking his father—a symbolic act of vengeance. He seemed to disconnect himself from his penis, disowning it and treating it as if it belonged to his father. This disguised rage against the penis, the guilt, and fear of retaliation, took the pleasure out of the act. Interpretation of this conflict and further discussion of his anger and competitive battle with his father eased the patient's depression and worry.

This boy and family have been in therapy three years. It continues to the present time. The unity of the family has been preserved and enhanced. There is now no danger of a breakup of the marriage. The parents have a new bond. They enjoy one another. The relations of mother and son are vastly improved. The relations of father and son, though better, are still an area of tension. The boy himself is much happier and no longer withdrawn and depressed. He feels he has made great strides. He now feels accepted at school; he does better both academically and athletically.

(In its original publication, this paper concluded with Ackerman's answers to a series of questions posed to all contributors to the volume, Case Studies in Counseling and Psychotherapy. *They have been omitted here because they were clearly rooted in individual therapy concepts and practices, e.g.* Do you feel that this case developed significant insight? *and* Do you attempt to persuade the patient or significant relative to change his environment? *Although Ackerman did his best with these posers, the procrustean bed in which he found himself made for answers that were general and abstract in the extreme.)*

CHAPTER 29

The Psychoanalytic Approach to the Family

At the present stage of development of behavior theory a critical re-examination of the psychoanalytic approach to the dynamics of the family entity is a timely undertaking. The impetus for such an effort derives from several pertinent considerations. Although the family is assigned an important place in psychoanalytic ideology as the shaper and maker of personality, psychoanalytic theory has thus far, in fact, dealt mainly with isolated parts of the family phenomenon, rather than with the family as a whole. In the sixty years of psychoanalytic history, the understanding of the psychodynamics of the family as a unit has grown substantially. In Freud's early publications at the turn of the century, the family is envisaged in relatively static terms. Today, in contrast, we are impressed with the critical instability of family patterns, and the sensitive way in which these echo the impact of the contemporary socio-cultural revolution. The recognition of this impact raises a whole new set of problems with regard to the role of the family in personality development and social adaptation. The more recent conceptual trends in ego psychology, in the adaptational view of personality, in social science and in the theory of communication demand a rethinking of the basic question of the relations of individual and family behavior.

Psychoanalysis as a body of theory contains within it a profound riddle concerning the relations of individual development and family belongingness as they evolve in time. This riddle is dramatically reflected in the perpetuation of a fundamental dilemma in conceptualization. How far is personality individual and how far is it familial or social? How far does personality unfold autonomously from within, and how far is it influenced from without? How far does it tend to move outward and forward, and how far does it move inward and backward? In essence, this is the riddle of the inner and outer face of personality, the mystery of the relations of subject and object. How far are they joined, and how far are they separate?

A clear and valid solution to this problem still escapes us. We must search further in the reciprocal processes of integration and individuation in the natural history of family life. To facilitate this search, it is useful to view the fam-

Reprinted with permission from *Individual and Familial Dynamics*, Vol. II, J.H. Masserman (Ed.), 1959, 105-121.

ily as an integrated behavior system, and formulate the dynamics of individual development and family development within a unitary conceptual scheme.

In Freudian theory the salient points of reference are the unconscious, the instincts, the three-pronged structure of personality, id, ego and super-ego, the genetic development of personality and its basic conditioning in early life, and finally, the influence of family. Of all these, least clear and most equivocal is the role of family and social environment. A reasssessment of the family phenomenon requires us to give explicit recognition to the historical inadequacies of the psychoanalytic conceptualization of family.

Freudian theory endeavors to explain the behavior of the adult on the basis of the child who preceded the adult. The child is father to the man. But this hypothesis is by itself an insufficient framework for tracing the path of transition from the experiences of the family of childhood to the experiences of the family of adulthood. Freud disclosed with uncanny clarity how man falsifies his perceptual image of family, but he did not elucidate with parallel accuracy how man assimilates and uses the correctly perceived experiences, the realities of family interaction. His primary focus was, understandably, on the pathologic twists, not on the health of family relationships. His image of love as a positive, healthy force in family life was incomplete. So, too, was his view of the interaction and merging of old and new experiences. To this extent the Freudian theoretic system is deficient in its illumination of the forward moving, creative phase of personality development.

Close study of the evolution of Freudian thought reveals an interesting feature: On the one hand, the tentative, groping, partialized quality of its exploration of the mechanisms of mind encouraged a rich, fertile growth of hypotheses; on the other hand, it created a chronic dilemma in conceptualization, a kind of ambiguity and indecision, a form of splitting within the theory itself. While emphasizing the role of the family in the molding of the child's personality, Freud gave priority to inborn instincts. He dwelt heavily on the permanent patterning of personality in the first years of life, but reduced the importance of the later levels of social participation. He dramatized the biologic core of man, while diminishing the role of society. He gave primacy to irrational, unconscious mental processes, while underrating man's powers of reason. He pointed to parents as the epitome of all social influence, yet paradoxically played down the social factor in the causation of states of illness and health. The salient emphasis was on the projection of irrational, anxiety-ridden phantasy; the interpersonal reality of the contemporary group environment was largely bypassed.

Freud's writings show preference for man's inner mind. While not by any means ignoring the environment, he subordinated his concern for reality and postponed systematic investigation of the relations of individual and group. This trend is clearly reflected in the exposition of the relations of child and parent. The parent is the object of the child's inner mental life, but the parent as a dynamic element in family and community process is not explored. Freud described the child as a polymorphous perverse little animal. The parent personified reality and the restraints of society. The child was conceived as a pleasure-bent anarchist, the parent as antipleasure. This picture lends to the ethos of family life something of a puritanical tinge, a sacrificial, duty-bound conception of the role of parent, a view of the child as a pleasure-driven animal, subhuman, antisocial. In terms of basic life values, it is as if parent and child were locked in battle. They are enemies, each exacting sacrifice of the other, or at best achieving an uneasy truce. How valid is this perspective? Must we not raise here some critical doubts? Is it really so that what satisfies the child hurts the parent and vice-versa? Is sacrifice the core of parent-child relations?

Freud visualized brilliantly how it is that man becomes emotionally blind and repeats over and over the same human errors, how he re-enacts in adulthood the irrationalities of his childhood, and thus becomes impervious to new experience. But, I repeat, how is it at the other pole that he learns and grows? What is healthy development?

Freud conceptually opposed parent and child somewhat in the same way that he opposed reality and pleasure and culture and personal freedom. He saw vividly the oppositional aspect of these relations, but not the joining. This he seems to have understood less well. It is surely not inevitable that parent and child, reality and pleasure, culture and personal freedom are unalterably opposed. Nor is it that old and new experience need always be incompatible. Under conditions of health each may be the true complement of the other.

In Freud's conceptual picture there is a measure of obscuration of one phase of the problem, love as a positive force in family relations, a mutually enhancing experience which provides the impetus to social learning. It is the joining of man and wife, and parent and child in the fulfillment of love within the realities of family life that spurs learning. According to Ian Suttie, Freud had a "grudge against mothers and a mind blindness for love. He concentrated on father and sex to the exclusion of mother and love."

The Freudian ideology highlights trends to fixation and regression; it emphasizes the inertia of emotional development. But it does not disclose the secrets of the forward movement of personality, the capacity to learn, the element of creativity in human development. Freud, creative giant that he was, confessed his sense of failure and futility in trying to find an explanation for creativity. By his own admission, he could not understand the creative gift of the artist. Was this perhaps Freud's blind spot?

Freud's perspective suggests an ambivalent view of society. It appears as if he were for the individual and against culture. Culture and personal freedom were incompatible. Man pays a severe penalty, he believed, for whatever benefits he derived from civilization. With inevitable irony he expressed his wonder as to whether civilization was worth the price. Might we imagine that he meant family, too? If so, was he not raising the most impossible of all questions. Is life itself worth living? Freud's pessimism was active, not passive. He imaged the realities of life mainly as a source of danger and pain, but unavoidable. At best, we might resign ourselves to the disillusioning sadness of it.

Freud's concepts were tinged in some part by his grey mood, and his distaste for external reality. His theory disassociated the internal mental processes from the social environment. It gave priority to the individual, while neglecting the group. It viewed social force and reality as a contamination. It interpreted culture as a projection of man's biologic drives. It dichotomized biologic and social, conscious and unconscious, pleasure and pain, reality and fantasy. The chemistry of learning, however, compounds these elements. This historically determined one-sided emphasis on the individual and the inside of the mind, remarkably fruitful though it was, complicated the task of conceptualizing the interrelations of the individual and family process. In this respect, psychoanalytic theory is incomplete. It is lacking in a positive healthy image of family relations; it does not elucidate learning and creative development.

It is a strange paradox that despite the psychoanalytic axiom that the emotional fate of the individual rests on his family experience, there have been thus far so few direct studies of the family group as an integrated psychologic unit. Parts of the family have been intensely illuminated, but even these parts only in certain directions. And the elusive mystery of still other parts persists. In designing the Oedipal theory, Freud tended to isolate parent-child relations from the totality of the family phenomenon; the Oedipal myth is the story of a broken family. He depicted the parent's influence on the child, but not the child's influence on the parent, nor the parents' influence on one another. The vector of his thinking moved mainly from the inside of the mind to the outside. He did not visualize a two directional influence, from outside inward as well as from inside outward. Unsupported by present day knowledge of the role of culture in molding family constellations, he tended to stereotype the roles of father, mother and child. He arbitrarily assigned to the man the dominant role, subordinated the woman, and imaged her as an inferior version of the man. He made the long conceptual leap from family of childhood to the family of adulthood, while omitting systematic study of the crucial transitional phase of the family of adolescence. He overlooked the stabilizing influence of family on the emotional life of the adult.

The one early psychoanalytic text which attempts to deal with the family as a whole is Flügel's *Psychoanalysis of the Family*. It is hardly surprising to find here a deep imprint of Freud's own bias toward the entity of family—a large emphasis on the unconscious, irrational aspects of family relations, ambivalence, hate, guilt, incest, castration, etc. Perhaps even more revealing is the echo of Freud's pessimism toward the civilizing processes of family life. "The competition that exists between members of the same family is almost bound to engender some hostility.". . . "Oedipal jealousy is impossible to prevent altogether.". . . "All that can be reasonably hoped for is that the degree of jealousy may be held in check by feelings of affection.". . . "Still less perhaps can parents expect to avoid altogether the arousal of hatred due to causes other than jealousy.". . . "The desires of the child conflict too much with the comfort of the parents and with the established usages of society to be allowed free play.". . . "The individual inevitably sacrifices himself in becoming a parent." Flügel quotes George Bernard Shaw to the effect that children are necessarily and unavoidably a nuisance to grown-up persons. They are an ever present menace to the comfort and tranquility of adult life.

Here we see prominently displayed the theme of sacrifice in parent-child relations. The parent fears being exploited and enslaved by his child. But this is only one side of the equation. There is surely the twin danger of the parent exploiting the child. In highlighting the exploitive aspect of parent-child relations, Flügel fails to distinguish between healthy and unhealthy family patterns. He does not deal with the family as a psychic whole; nor does he interrelate unconscious mental processes to the realities of family life.

This historically influenced point of view, separating the unreal from the real, unconscious from conscious, and past from present left its mark on psychoanalytic therapeutic technique. Child-parent patterns are the core of transference phenomena. But in therapy transference processes are often not matched against the realities of contemporary family processes. Classical analysts pursue Freud's dictum that phantasies and dreams are the royal road to the unconscious. They often express the conviction that it is unessential to know the realities of the social environment. To the contrary, I believe that an accurate understanding of the unconscious and of transference is possible only as these dynamics are matched not only to the realities of the analyst's person but also to the conscious organization of the patient's experience, the total integrative patterns of personality and the prevailing interpersonal realities of contemporary family life.

The usual approach of the psychoanalyst to the phenomena of family life has been indirect rather than direct. It is still common practice for analysts to refuse to interview other family members on the premise that this would interfere with the conduct of the patient's analysis. This means that the analyst is solely dependent for information concerning family experience on the emotionally biased views of his individual patient. Traditionally the analyst detects the distorted perceptions of the patient in the processes of transference, but his evaluation of disparity between real and unreal is unaided by objective knowledge of family interaction. Thus, the reality testing powers of the analyst are handicapped. The traditional custom of the psychoanalyst, to avoid interviewing other family members lest this complicate his relations with his patient, needs to be re-examined for its dynamic implications.

Several relevant considerations must be carefully weighed: Is it correct to regard the day by day emotional interactions of a patient with his family as complications in the task of analytic therapy, or are they of the essence? Insofar as these processes are regarded as complications, they surely cannot be excluded from the private relation of analyst with his patient. They are carried with the patient into his analytic experience, and asserted most rigorously. They are not magically erased by the analyst's determined isolation of himself from the patient's family. Complications they may be, but they are clearly of the essence as well. The analyst who rigidly disregards other family members courts trouble. He may throw the continuity of the course of therapy into jeopardy. If he treats a wife and refuses to interview her husband, he should not be surprised if his bill remains unpaid. If he appears to strengthen the aggression of one partner against the other, he will sometimes be accused of being a homebreaker, causing divorce, or inducing a breakdown in the untreated partner. There is no safety in ritual avoidance of other family members. In the relations of individual and family, there is a mutuality of misperception that parallels the patient's transference misperceptions of the analyst. If the analyst interviews his patient together with other family members, he achieves a tremendous gain in his reality-testing capacity. Contact with family need not complicate the therapy of the primary patient. The issue is rather how contact is made and how appropriately it is used.

In classical technique the analyst has available to him the patient's image of self, his image of his family members, his image of the analyst; the analyst also has available his image of self and his image of the patient. But he has no dependable, accurate image of the patient's family members or of their image of the patient. Were he to observe the two-way emotional interchange of patient and family, he would then be in a position to match his perception of the patient and his family relationships, not only against the patient's perceptions, but also against the family member's perception of the patient.

Psychoanalysis is believed to be the only specific therapy for neuroses. And it is generally agreed that the main determinants of neuroses are social, that is, essentially familial in origin. In the psychoanalytic therapy of neuroses there have been notable successes and also dramatic failures. It is of some value to focus special attention on the failures insofar as they may shed light on relevant processes in the patient's contemporary family life.

It is assumed that psychoanalytic therapy corrects the patient's twisted perceptions of the family of his childhood and that, as these are modified toward reality, he will catch up with an accurate picture of the family relationships of his adult life. In classical analytic processes, the role of present realities is temporarily subordinated. This is the matrix for the unfolding of transference neurosis. For a period, the unreality of transference achieves not merely a position of prominence but one of dominance. Ultimately and by successive stages, the irrational content of transference is worked through the matched against the realities of the analytic relationship. The real qualities of the analyst's person are not revealed until the later stages. Thus, the check with reality is delayed. This theoretic framework implies that the realities of present family relationships will wait until the patient catches up with himself and achieves a realistic definition of his contemporary family problems. This theory provides the rationale for the principle of postponement of crucial life decisions during analysis.

But decision-making is of the essence of life. It means action. Action is the core of aliveness. Without decision, there is no action, no movement; there can be no life. Is there not a magic delusion involved in the idea that time and life can be stopped in their tracks while the patient prepares himself emotionally to deal realistically with his contemporary problems?

Perhaps, ideally, classical psychoanalytic technique works best in a group environment that is stable, fixed, definable and predictable. But where do we find this is in our present day community? We don't; we find the opposite. What happens in analytic therapy when the group envcironment and the relations of individual and group are unstable, discontinuous, difficult to define and predict? Since the structure of society and family is undergoing revolutionary change and is profoundly different today from what it was at the turn of the century, perhaps it is in order to rethink the role of transference in psychotherapy. Under conditions of radical social change and imminent external danger like those in Nazi Germany, it proved virtually impossible to do psychoanalytic therapy (Robert Fleiss, 1939). Perhaps in the turbulence of present day society we are approaching a similar condition.

The agitation in the patterns of human relations in our day is echoed in the character disorders that are now so universally the psychoanalyst's problem. Intrinsic to the dynamics of character disorder are the contagion and sharing of the experience of pathogenic conflict. Character disorders do not exist alone; they function in pairs and threesomes. For every person suffering from a character disorder there are one or more partners who share in the problem. In such persons, the defenses that come into prominence are projection, substitution of aggression for anxiety, magic thinking, isolation and acting out. The implementation of such defenses, particularly "acting out," calls for the complicity of a partner. Character disorders are a social as well as an individual phenomenon. Mutual and complementary "acting out" is a frequent pattern in contemporary family patterns.

The analyst's ability to help a patient move toward recovery through interpretation of transference and resistance and his ability to define the clash of real and unreal may fail if neither patient nor analyst possesses an accurate picture of the relevant interpersonal realities. In the analytic situation, the analyst is presumed to embody these realities within his own person.

The patient is expected to get well as he gradually perceives, stage by stage, the contradictions between his transference image of the analyst and what the analyst really represents. But the analyst personifies not only the reality of his own person; he must epitomize the realities of the patient's current interpersonal environment as well. It is obligatory, therefore, that the analyst have an accurate picture of the patient's family life and other significant group involvements. Otherwise, the analytic therapy will flounder. The challenge is not only to interpret the inappropriate transference expectations but also to enable the patient to accept, understand and use something that is new and different, *i.e.*, to learn from experience.

We know that the neuroses of various family members reinforce one another through family contagion. The traditional procedure of referring neurotically involved members of the patient's family to other analysts for therapy is a relatively feeble device for improving the emotional health of family relationships, for empirical experience reveals that the technique of individual analytic treatment for each neurotic family member by separate analysts often fails to ameliorate the pathologic interactions of the family.

Still another unsolved problem in psychoanalytic therapy is that which derives from certain forms of resistance to change in the patient, this resistance being continually fortified by his emotional position in his family. Sometimes the individual, emotionally speaking, is the virtual prisoner of an unhealthy extrafamilial role, for example, in a submissive relationship with a tyrannical employer. If so, generally, he is also bound to a similarly unhealthy family role. It is the family pattern that imprisons him to the job role. Subjectively the patient may feel protected in this role and yet be harmed by it. Although the security in the role is illusory, the patient clings to it because it symbolizes parental protection. In order to change, he must gamble; he must trade something he already knows for a way of life he does not yet know. The patient holds tenaciously to what seems familiar and safe, and the analyst is unable to wrench him loose.

When we view this problem in the context of current family relationships it becomes clear that, at least in some instances, it is not possible to achieve the cure of one person without simultaneously altering his family system. The emotional inertia of the individual partly expresses the inertia of the family group within which he functions. We recognize this principle very well in the case of child patients in whom, to effect cure, we undertake to treat family as well as child. But we are less prone to give recognition to analogous processes in the group life of the adult patient.

It is easy to recognize in this picture a familiar phenomenon, to which the psychoanalyst gives the name "secondary emotional gain." This term implies a kind of compromise formation in which a patient consoles himself for the suffering and impediment of his neurosis with situational advantages. He exploits his neurotic disability for purposes of winning attention, protection, or special favors, avoiding responsibility, or wreaking vengeance on parent figures. The patient attempts in this way to ease the stress and pain of his present position in the group. In effect, he demands a special bribe from those around him as compensation for his submission to a special role in which he feels cheated of a full reward. This bribe is supposed to assuage his anger. The phenomenon of secondary gain is thus linked to a patient's neurotic willingness to be tied to a failing role; while his family supports and compensates him in this role, it does not permit him to escape it.

This problem poses a special difficulty in psychoanalytic therapy. The obstacles in the way of separating the patient from a neurotically sick, failing family role and the associated secondary emotional gain often prove formidable. The psychoanalyst's position is weak if he cannot lessen the family's support of these patterns of secondary gain, as well as treat the individual patient. In the historical development of psychoanalytic theory, the processes of secondary gain have been conceived as relatively peripheral and not significantly tied to the fate of central conflicts. Because the phenomena of secondary gain are a vital link between individual and group, perhaps secondary gain should be reassessed as to its significance for ego integration and social role adaptation.

The lesson to be drawn is clear. The autonomy of the individual is relative, not absolute. The characteristics of an individual are predictable only within a concrete situation. The individual is personally responsible for his conduct only within certain limits. It is a sheer impossibility, at times, for an individual to buck his group all by himself. To accept change or be motivated toward it, he requires the group to change along with him. This makes it necessary to consider the family as a subject for therapy, as well as the individual member. Surely, there are individuals with an irrepressible urge to change and grow, regardless of the inertia of the surrounding group, but these are the exceptional persons. Most people change only as they can induce the group to change with them.

Still another unsolved problem in analytic therapy is the influence that the changed behavior in the patient produces on those family members who share his everyday life. As the patient changes, he affects the behavior of other members of this family; similarly as they change, the nature of their change further affects the patient. The process is circular. It is incumbent on the analyst, therefore, to know accurately the patient's contemporary family environment.

These considerations are of direct relevance to clinical judgments as to which cases are treatable and which untreatable. Some cases are deemed to be untreatable precisely because the individual is appraised in isolation from his involvement in the family group. The resistance to the acceptance of therapy or the fixity of the neurotic patterns of motivation are not adequately examined within the frame of the patient's family role involvement and the pathology of the family group itself. If these questions are examined more thoroughly, it is likely that different judgments may be reached as to whether psychoanalytic therapy will be hopeful or hopeless.

In many instances, the emotional preparation for the initiation of psychotherapy proves to be inadequate because the efforts are directed exclusively to a single individual in isolation. In actuality, something often needs to be done to modify the emotional climate of the entire family group. At the very least, certain warped family relationships, in which the patient's conflicts are locked, need to be altered before such a patient can be properly receptive to the influence of psychoanalytic therapy.

The same problems reveal themselves another way in the psychoanalysis of children. By tradition, child psychoanalysts work mainly or exclusively with their individual child patient. The inappropriate attitudes of the mother toward these patients are judged to be the product of the mother's personal neurosis. The child analyst undertakes therapy of the child patient, and where necessary, the mother is referred for therapy of her neurosis to another analyst. More rarely, the same child analyst may choose also to treat the mother. In the main, however, child analysts have no contact with the family as a group. They make no direct observations of the disturbed patterns of interaction that characterize the family as a unit. In other words, child analysts have little direct information concerning the realities of family life. A short time ago, I asked such an analyst if she treated the mothers of her child patients. Her reply was: "Oh, heavens, no!"

In general, the classical method of child analysis is less frequently employed, but the practice of child psychotherapy, combining treatment of child and parent and oriented pointedly to the realities of family, has increased by leaps and bounds. It is of great interest to ask why child analysis is in danger of turning fossil, and why there is more and more child psychotherapy. I believe the single most important reason is not the alleged inconveniences of child analytic practice, as many have said, but rather that the classical technique often fails to produce a cure. To whatever extent child analysis cuts itself away from the realities of group interaction in family life, it is doomed to die. Any form of child therapy, if it is to be successful, must surely avoid isolation from a parallel program for dealing with the mental health problems of the family group. In the future of child analysis systematic study of family process must surely grow in importance.

I have become increasingly skeptical of traditional clichés and stereotyped formulations regarding the psychodynamic relations of child and family. Such conceptions as Oedipus conflict, seduction, inconsistent discipline, overprotection, overindulgence, and narcissistic exploitation of the child can in no way be adequately understood unless the interaction processes of the family, as well as the personalities of each member, are subjected to systematic study. It has become crystal clear, for example, that such a trend as parental seduction of the child is an empty phrase unless it is explored fully in terms of the sexual maladjustment between the parents with the associated patterns of conflict and emotional alienation. Rejection has become a hackneyed term. It is often used to cover a real ignorance of the history of the child's sense of betrayal by the parent. Where there is rejection, it needs to be qualified in terms of its intensity, its form of expression, its relative specificity for the given child, the role of the rejecting motive in the economy of the mother's personality and the role of the rejecting behavior in the total psychosocial economy of the family life.

At present, it is extremely difficult to implement the conceptual structure of child analysis in an integrated theory of child development and adaptation. Freud's formulation of the psychosexual stages of the child's development, valuable as it is in its own right, fails to provide a satisfactory scheme. A serious difficulty emerges from the tendency of this theory to dissociate the biologic and social components of behavior. When a psychoanalyst characterizes a person according to his psychosexual make-up, oral, anal or genital, his term generally carries a dual connotation: (1) a specific level of instinctual organization, (2) an implied level of ego maturation or total personality organization related to the dominant patterns of instinctual drive. This twofold meaning is ambiguous and confusing. The reference to a presumed level of personality integration is vague and ill defined, and the dynamic relations of biologic drive to personality organization and to the dominant modes of social adaptation are not clearly communicated. To say this is by no means to discount the value of the psychosexual concept but merely to point to some of its present day limitations.

The validity of current theories regarding the emotional relations of child and family rests to a large extent on empiric wisdom deriving largely from psychotherapeutic experience. Such formulations depend mainly on the acuity and skill of the individual clinician. Truly amazing sometimes is the astuteness of the psychiatric clinician in drawing cogent, useful and, within limits, reliable dynamic interpretations. But, the fact remains that such conclusions are usually fragmentary and selective. Beyond the sphere of a few central correlations, the interpretations of the emotional interaction of child and family become progressively vague and eventually reach the point of mere conjecture. In the end, such a situation becomes critical and makes it impossible to judge which dynamic interpretations are right and which wrong.

In relation to the child patient, the main emphasis in such formulations has been on the correlation of specific types of child reaction with specific parental attitudes: rejection, inconsistency of discipline, overindulgence, overprotection, and the relation of specific body behavior in the child, oral, anal, genital, etc., to specific anxieties in the parent. This is a presumed correspondence between unconscious wishes in the parents and overt actions in the child, or between particular parental attitudes and conflicted unconscious needs in the child. Some correlations are made to the child's striving for the exclusive possession of the mother's love and fear of the punishing, rivalrous parent. Finally, conflict in the child is related to conflict between the parents. Clearly, such correlations are partial. They hypothesize a relation between a piece of the child and a piece of the parent. This piece of the child (usually a set of conflicted unconscious needs) is not defined in its proper relation to the whole child, or to the full breadth of the parental relationship or to the psychosocial configuration of the family as a whole. The determinants of parental role functioning are multiple. They derive partly from individual personality, but are otherwise influenced by the parent's interaction with the child, the other parent, the family group and the community. In addition, parental behavior, in accordance with these multiple influences, may undergo significant shifts at different stages of the development of the child and family. In this sense, the traditional correlations of child and parental behavior are inadequate.

In a lecture here in 1954, Anna Freud* emphasized the inevitable role of frustration and conflict in the emotional development of the child. She pointed out that the child must always experience some "delay and rationing" in the satisfaction of its needs; this is the background for the continuing struggle between pleasure and pain. Of historical importance was her pointed assertion that in the search for the causes of neurotic development in the child, the early emphasis on the father as the authority

*ANNA FREUD: Psychoanalysis and education, N.Y. Academy of Medicine, May 5, 1954.

figure and as the source of the castration threat gave way to increasing recognition of the importance of the mother as the parent who disciplines through the power of deprivation. There was a strong backward push in time from a first emphasis on Oedipal conflict as the core of neurosis to a more recent and sharper emphasis on pre-Oedipal conflict, from the father who denies sexual pleasure to the child to the mother who denies the child oral satisfaction. Whatever the level of conflict, it is the ego that mediates the struggle between pleasure and renunciation. According to Anna Freud, the ego takes its cue from the environment.

But here, curiously enough, she stops. Although she states that there are some mothers who are continuously rejecting, some intermittently rejecting, some who reject the child for accidental reasons and some whose very devotion is interpreted by the child as rejection, she goes no further in interrelating the emerging ego functions of the child with the social patterns of the family as a whole. She makes the point, however, that the child reacts with anxiety both to the parent who is punitive and to the parent who is permissive. In other words, a child requires parental control to feel protected; without it, he feels abandoned and insecure. Obviously, then, optimal child-rearing involves a modicum of satisfaction of basic needs, some inevitable frustrations, and an appropriate quality of social control exercised through the authority of the parent.

But, under what conditions does control mean protection to the child, and under what conditions does it become a threat? This is the very heart of the matter, and it hinges on the connotations of Anna Freud's statement that the child's ego takes its cue from the environment. It is generally recognized that control is experienced by the child as protection if the child's basic needs are understood and reasonably satisfied by the parents. Problems of discipline can be understood only as they are joined to the basic experience of security and family relations. If this is not the case, the child perceives control as a hostile assault and, by stages, becomes impervious to parental discipline. The central issue is how and by what processes the growing child internalizes the significant psychic content of his family environment. What is the dynamic correlation of ego, super-ego, and the social interaction patterns of the family?

In a quizzical though facetious mood, a South American analyst of some repute once raised this question. "Is psychoanalytic theory regressing? It seems always to go backward. First, it was the Oedipus conflict and castration fear; then came the theory of aggression, anal sadism and the death instinct, now we revert to oral insecurity, oral deprivation. Which is right?" Clearly, no one of these ideas provides a full answer. They are each of them partial theories. They are either all of them right or all of them wrong, depending on how we put them together into a unified view of the human being.

Psychoanalytic concepts ushered in a revolution in personality theory. But these concepts evolved piecemeal. It is time to integrate them and design a broader frame of reference within which it is possible more effectively to conceptualize and treat a person's disturbance within the matrix of his position in his primary group, the family.

As I have suggested earlier, it is useful to view the family as an integrated behavior system and place the dynamics of individual development and family development within a unitary conceptual scheme. In my book, *The Psychodynamics of Family Life,** I offer a tentative theoretic framework for this purpose. This is represented in the following diagram, a six pointed star in which one set of triangular variables is superimposed on another.

These are core concepts which attempt to answer for the dynamics of family process, the who and what of family life, and the resulting functional patterns of family relationships. They are an effort to provide a theoretic framework within which it is possible to establish more reliable correlations of individual and family behavior.

The concept of identity subsumes strivings, expectation and values. The concept of stability involves (1) the continuity of identity in time, (2) the control of conflict and (3) the capacity to change, learn and achieve further development, as paralleled by adaptability and complementarity in new role relationships.

---

*ACKERMAN, N.W.: *The Psychodynamics of Family Life; Diagnosis and Treatment of Family Relationships*. New York, Basic Books, Inc., 1958.

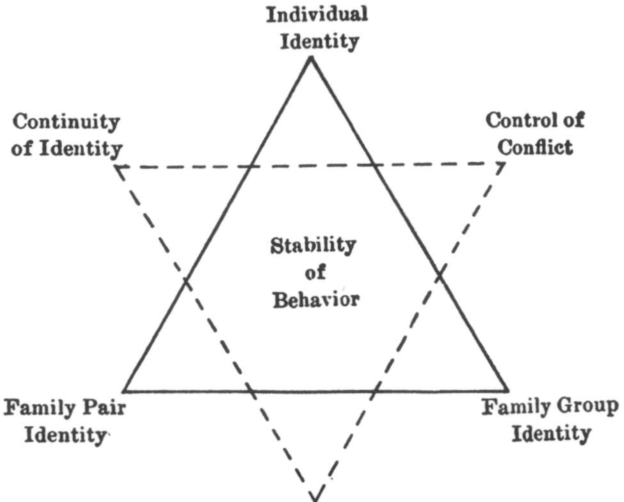

Fig. 1.—Scheme for family diagnosis.

The concept of identity refers to direction and content of striving, while stability refers to organization and expression of behavior in action. The full clarification of these concepts and their dynamic interrelations cannot be undertaken here. The present purpose is merely to indicate the urgency of the need for the development of a broader theoretic system within which one can encompass both the dynamics of individual and family group behavior.

CHAPTER 30

Family Psychotherapy and Psychoanalysis: The Implications of Difference

In our time we are witness to a spreading contagion of interest in the family approach to mental illness. There is a rising inquiry as to the possibility of understanding and treating psychiatric illness in a family way. Historically speaking, it was psychoanalysis that gave pointed emphasis to the role of family conflict in mental illness. It is of no small interest today, therefore, to observe how members of the psychoanalytic profession respond to the concept of the family as the unit of mental health and the unit of diagnosis and therapy. Here, as elsewhere, in matters pertaining to theory and practice, psychoanalysts are divided. Once again we discover the familiar split in the psychoanalytic family as between the conservatives and the liberals. In the evolution of ideas, here as elsewhere, there is value in both points of view. Toward the principles of family diagnosis and treatment, some analysts are critical and antipathetic from the start. They sense in it a threat to the established position of the psychoanalytic technique. One such analyst said to me: "The psychotherapy of the whole family makes me uneasy. It threatens my sense of mastery in the exclusive one-to-one relationship." Other psychoanalysts, skeptical to be sure, are otherwise open-minded and willing for the concept of the family as the unit of mental health to face the test of time.

Regardless of the dilemma of the psychoanalysts, present evidence suggests that this new dimension is here to stay. The family approach offers a new level of entry, a new quality of participant observation in the struggles of human adaptation. It holds the promise of shedding new light on the processes of illness and health, and offers new ways of assessing and influencing these conditions. It may open up, perhaps for the first time, some effective paths for the prevention of illness and the promotion of health.

In the perspective of the history of mental science, the emergence of the principles of family diagnosis and treatment is an inevitable de-

Reprinted with permission from *Family Process*, May 1962, Vol. 1, No. 1, 30-43.

velopment. It is the natural product of the coalescence of new conceptual trends in a number of fields: cultural anthropology, group dynamics, communication, the link of psychoanalysis with social science, ego psychology, and child development. The family phenomenon bridges the gap between individual personality and society. On this background, it is hardly a coincidence that some psychoanalytic associations now devote whole meetings to the themes of psychoanalysis and values, and psychoanalysis and family. It seems likely, therefore, that the evolution of family diagnosis and family treatment holds far-reaching implications for the future relations of culture change, behavior theory, and the evolving ideology of psychoanalysis and psychotherapy.

I shall present first a brief, impressionistic view of the techniques of family psychotherapy, and then attempt a comparison with psychoanalytic therapy within the frame of two contrasting theoretical models of psychotherapeutic process. In advance of this, however, I must mention two basic considerations. Just so long as we lack a unitary theory of human behavior and cannot accurately formulate the relations of emotion, body, and social process, we shall be unready to build a comprehensive theory of psychotherapy. We have no psychotherapeutic method that is total. We have no known treatment technique that can affect with equal potency all components of the illness process. The various psychotherapeutic methods presently available are, each of them, specialized, and exert partial, selective effects on certain components of the illness process, but not on all. It is the social structuring of a particular interview method which determines both the potentials of participant observation and the selective effects of a given therapy. In this sense, the psychoanalytic method provides one kind of participant experience, group psychotherapy another, and family psychotherapy still another. It is the specific point of entry of each of these methods which affects the kind of information obtained, the view of the illness process which is communicated to the therapist, and the quality of influence toward health that he may exert. Family interview and family psychotherapy hold the potential of shedding a different and added light on the illness phenomenon and provide still another level of intervention on the area of pathogenic disturbance.

RELEVANT CONCEPTS

Family psychotherapy and psychoanalytic therapy are different methods. For purposes of clarity, hereafter, the term "psychoanalytic therapy" will be reserved for the technique as originally formulated by Freud and his early disciples. The issue as to the essential differences between family therapy and psychoanalysis would be somewhat obscured if we were here to extend the term, "psychoanalytic therapy," to embrace the numerous neo-Freudian modifications of technique.

Psychoanalytic treatment focuses on the internal manifestations of disorder of the individual personality. Family treatment focuses on the behavior disorders of a system of interacting personalities, the family group. But in no sense need they be viewed as competitive or mutually exclusive; they may be complementary. The psychotherapy of the whole family may, in some instances, be the only method of intervention, or it may be the method of choice. In other instances, however, the psychotherapy of the whole family may constitute a required emotional preparation for intervention with individual psychotherapy, or, the two types of therapy may be employed in a parallel way. The relations between the two approaches will become more clear as we succeed in achieving a better understanding of the relations between the inner and outer aspects of human experience, between what goes on inside one mind, and what goes on between minds.

The basis of family treatment is the therapeutic interview with a living unit, the functional family group, all those who live together as family under a single roof and any additional relatives who fulfill a significant family role, even if they reside in a separate place. In this context, the unit of illness and health and the unit of treatment influence is then the family group; not the single parent in isolation, but father, mother, children, and sometimes grandparents as well. In family therapy one views the psychic functioning of the one person in the wider context of reciprocal family role adaptations, and the psychosocial organization of the family as a whole, both in the here and now, and across three generations. In this special setting, amelioration of emotional illness requires step-by-step correlation of intrapsychic and interpersonal processes. Within this context, it is essential to view the balance of forces at three levels of integration:

1) A condition of overt illness with the emergence of organized symptoms.
2) A condition of vulnerability to mental breakdown.
3) A condition of effective health.

By contrast with this, in classical psychoanalysis, one focuses in a selective way on the intrapsychic distortions of one individual. The expectation is that as one modifies the internal balance of the components of the personality, emotional health in the individual's relations with the family group will be spontaneously restored. Sometimes this expectation is realized; sometimes it fails. Clearly, a shift toward health in family relationships is not the inevitable product of psychoanalytic treatment. In fact, it is by no means rare that following psychoanalytic treatment of one family member, there occurs a paradoxical worsening of family relationships.

In the psychotherapy of the family group, several main principles must be borne in mind. The breakdown of one member of the family, the nature of his disablement and the associated symptoms, may be viewed as a reflection of the emotional warp of the entire family. One can frequently delineate a specific correlation between the emotional pathology of the family group and the breakdown of a particular member. The individual who is first referred for psychiatric help is either the scapegoat for the pathology of the family or a stand-in for a more critically disturbed member of the family. Often, a core of pathogenic conflict and associated defense patterns is contagiously passed down from one generation to the next. One must therefore be alert to the movement of a pathogenic disorder across three generations. As one observes a family at a given point in time, the elements of pathogenic conflict that originally contributed to the causation of a psychiatric disorder can still be traced in the contemporary conflicts of the family group, even though now they may be expressed in a modified way.

In disturbed families as a rule, there are multiple instances of psychiatric disorder. It is rarely the case that only one member of the family is emotionally disabled. The issue then arises as to the vicissitudes of interaction among the several disturbed members, and their further influence on the family as a whole, as well as their effect on the more vulnerable individuals. It is also clear that as one intervenes on the family, here and now, the focus of the most intense conflict and disturbance may shift from one part of the family to another. In this setting, it is possible to identify characteristic constellations of family conflict and characteristic patterns of family control. We shall return to this later.

THERAPEUTIC FAMILY INTERVIEW

In a typical therapeutic family interview, the family arrives in a state of distress. It is confused; it is in pain. Family as family has failed. The members know something is deeply wrong, but they cannot say what it is nor what to do about it. The therapist moves immediately into the life space of the family's current struggles. He joins in these struggles. He is taken into the fold as an older relative, perhaps as a grandparent endowed with some special wisdom concerning the problems of family living. He is observer, participant, supporter, activator, challenger, and reintegrator of family processes.

At the outset, the therapist observes the order of entry into the meeting room, and the spontaneous way in which the family members arrange their seats. Who sits next to whom? Who sits away from whom? Do they look at one another? Do they see, hear, and talk? What is the dominant emotion and mood—fear, hate, indifference, or apathy and resignation?

The therapist observes the characteristic reactions. Do the members lash out at or shrink from one another; are they alienated? He evaluates the quality of reaching out: Who wants what from whom and how? Is the assertion of these urges insatiable, or violent? Or is it overcontrolled, denied, disguised? Or do the members now cease to ask and expect satisfaction from one another?

The first responsibility of the therapist is to arouse the dormant hope of these troubled people. He endeavors to make of the interview a touching experience. He seeks to touch and be touched, in effect, to make it a feeling experience for all. He tries to enhance the quality of interchange among the family members and with himself, to make it more live, more meaningful. Toward this end he makes pointed use of the subverbal aspects of communication: mood, facial expression, posture, gesture and movement. Words may be used to reveal or conceal valid emotion. The therapist neutralizes the common tendency to strip emotion from words. Watchful of each cue, he undercuts mouthings of trivia, in order to get access to the more significant emotional and bodily aspects of communication.

Parts of the family, individuals or alliances of twosomes or threesomes, combine with and separate from elements of the therapist's identity in accordance with need and the means of coping with conflict. The processes of joining with and individuating from the therapist involve elements both of transference and realism.

Currents of mistrust, hostility, defensiveness, and the associated trends toward alienation are noted by the therapist. He observes the configuration of emotional splits within the family, the warring factions and the protective alliances. Who is against whom? Who is allied with whom? He evokes explicit admission of hurts and barriers. He spurs an expanding awareness of fears, avoidances, and the resulting fragmentation in the relationship patterns. He pays particular attention to defensive trends toward displacement of certain conflicts, substitution of one conflict for another, or the prejudicial assault and scapegoating of one part of the family by another. He evaluates the relations between such scapegoating and the unconscious selection of one member of the family as a victim, pushing that member toward a form of breakdown. In a parallel sense, he observes the compensatory healing functions of the family, the way in which one member is unconsciously selected to play the role of healer of family conflict and thus reduce the destructive effects of scapegoating. As he does this, the conflicts between and within family members come into cleared perspective.

Often the sense of tension and danger mounts in family interview process. The therapist must steer a path between Scylla and Charybdis. He must move between the extremes of rigid avoidance of the dangers of closeness, and the uncontrolled explosion of hostile conflict that tends toward panic and disorganization. Often, members of the family fear a loss of control. Through his own calm presence, the therapist offers the needed assurance against this danger. He marks out the interplay between individual defense against anxiety and family group defense of essential family functions. He engages in a process that I call "tickling the defenses," so as to undermine the pathogenic defense formations and encourage the substitution of healthier kinds of coping. He is alert particularly to the layers of insincerity in family relations, and attacks the hypocritical, righteous, self-justifying forms of defense. As the family conflicts become increasingly defined and more realistic solutions are sought, the intrapsychic symptom-producing conflicts of individual members tend toward external expression, that is, they are projected into the arena of family interaction.

A special challenge is the delineation of the core conflicts of the family and the family defenses. The therapist's aims in dealing with conflict are:

1) To help the family achieve a clearer, more correct perception of family conflict.
2) To energize dormant interpersonal conflict so as to bring them into the live processes of family interaction, where they are more accessible for solution.
3) To lift intrapsychic conflict to the level of interpersonal process, where again it may be coped with more effectively.
4) To neutralize irrational prejudice and scapegoating of one part of the family by another. The aim here is to remove an excessive load of anxiety from the victimized member by counteracting inappropriate displacements of hostility and conflict. Where possible the conflict is put back to its original source in the family group, often the parental pair. In this connection, the therapist often joins forces *pro tem* with the "family healer."
5) To activate an improved level of complementarity in family role relationships.

Family group defense against conflict, and the related impairment of family functions is distinct from individual defense against anxiety. Family defense may be specific or non-specific in varying degree. The end result of coping with conflict is the outcome of complex interplay between family defense and individual defense. The dominant forms of family defense play a potent part in the selection and in the operational efficiency of individual defenses against anxiety. A tentative group of family defenses is the following:

1) A shared search for a specific and suitable solution to conflict.
2) A shared avoidance or denial of a specific conflict.
3) Compromise formation: rational and irrational. This is exemplified in—
   a) emotional splitting of the family; fragmentation of the group
   b) riddance or isolation of conflict
      1) quarrels, alienation and reconciliation
      2) a shift in the zone and content of conflict by substitution, displacement, protection, etc.
      3) scapegoating and compensatory healing
4) Compensation: escape, diversion, drugs, alcohol, vacation and sexual escapades.
5) Shared acting out.
6) Reorganization of complementarity of family roles by means of:
   a) reversal of parental and sexual roles, reversal of parent-child roles
   b) "repeopling" of the family: removing or adding persons to the family unit
   c) tightening of the family organization: rigidification of authority, sharper division of labor, constriction and compartmentalization of roles
   d) loosening of the family organization:
      1) dilution of the family bond, distancing, alienation, reduced communication and role segregation
      2) thinning of the border between family and community, displacement of need and conflict from inside the family to outside

When these family defenses fail, the essential family functions become disabled, selectively and progressively. The family moves toward breakdown.

The responsibilities of the fmaily therapist are multiple and complex. They require the most flexible, open, undefensive use of self. The therapist must be active, spontaneous, and make free use of his own emotions, though in a selective and suitable manner. His prime function is to foster the family's use of his own emotional participation in the direction of achieving a favorable shift in the homeostasis of family relationships. He loosens and shakes up preexisting pathogenic equilibria and makes way for a healthier realignment of these family relationships. In this role, his influence may be likened to that of a catalyst, a chemical reagent, a resynthesizer. He seeks constantly to understand the relations between inner and outer, intrapsychic and interpersonal experience. He matches conscious against unconscious, reality against fantasy. He mobilizes those forms of interaction that maximize the opportunity for undoing distorted percepts of self and others, for dissolving confusion, and clarifying the view of the salient conflict.

The therapist provides, where needed, acceptance, affirmation of worth, understanding, and support. By his own attitudes, he validates genuine expressions of emotion, whether a frustrated need or justified anger. He offers a selective support for the weaker members against the stronger; he gives recognition to thwarted personal needs, crystallizes unreal fears of injury and punishment, opens up new avenues of satisfaction, and provides an expanded interactional matrix for reality testing. He injects into the family something new, the right emotions and the right perceptions in place of the wrong ones. Crucial to the entire effort is the breaking down of anxiety-ridden taboos against the sharing of vital family problems.

The therapist facilitates the efforts of the family to balance sameness and difference, joining and individuation in the ongoing processes of family life. He affirms the positive foundations for shared experience and identification. He awakens respect for differences. In this way, new levels of sharing, support, intimacy, identity, and a greater degree of mutual need satisfaction become possible. The therapist activates the need for a critical examination of family goals and values, especially those which pertain to the basic functions of husband and wife, father and mother, parent and child, child and sibling, parent and grandparent. As the members rearrange their lines of joining and separation, the therapist spurs recognition of the potentials of new growth and creative experience in family living.

Now, let us sum up the nature of this approach to the family as the unit of health. It offers the challenge of evaluating and treating a system of interacting personalities. It requires continuous correlation of the inside of the mind and the outside, the ongoing interconnections of intrapsychic and interpersonal experience. It necessitates a continuous juxtaposing of conscious and unconscious, real and unreal, inner and outer experience, individual and group. It presents the problem of integrating within a single theoretical system all elements of causation, specific and nonspecific, inner and outer, generic and contemporary. The field of observation and the field of influence in family diagnosis and therapy is an expanded one. It involves the internal organization of personality, the dynamics of family role adaptation, and the behavior of the family as a social system. Family therapy deals explicitly with the forces of both illness and health. It intervenes on contemporary conflicts with the assumption that the past sources of pathogenesis are contained in the present conflicts, though now differently organized. It defines the disorders of individual personality within the broader frame of the social psychological distortions of the family system. It assumes that the forces of the individual and the forces of the family are interdependent and interpenetrating, that these relations are relevant to causation, course and outcome of illness and response to therapy.

By contrast, psychoanalysis deals with the one isolated personality. It intervenes on pathogenic foci within the person, expecting that as the intrapsychic distortions are removed, the potentials for healthy readaptation will be spontaneously realized. As earlier indicated, however, this does not always occur. Psychoanalysis moves mainly from inside-outward, whereas family therapy approaches the relevant processes partly from outside-inward. In its orientation, psychoanalysis is biologistic, mechanistic, genetic. It tends somewhat to isolate the patient from family, and family from analyst. It focuses in a specialized way on older, entrenched forms of conflict with organized symptom formation. To some degree, it emphasizes the schism between fantasy and reality, pleasure and pain, individual and group, thus separating inner and outer experience. In order to minimize acting-out, it aspires to a halting of time and life, while the internal imbalance of the components of the personality are therapeutically realigned. It deals less with emotional health in a positive sense; it does not give us a picture of learning and creative expansive development. It does not give us a healthy image of family relations. To some extent, it obscures the core problem of homeostasis in family relationships.

This is not to raise the question of the one method of treatment being superior to the other. It is rather that they are differently oriented; each does something else. Of the two methods, psychoanalysis is more specialized; it achieves a unique access to disturbances which have their source in the unconscious mental life. By contrast, family therapy approaches conflict experience in a broader matrix of human relations and at multiple interpenetrating levels.

It is easy to exemplify the contrast in orientation of the two methods. Freud judged relatives and family mainly in terms of their nuisance value. In his view, they posed for psychoanalysis the threat of invasion and contamination. He said: "The interference of relatives in psychoanalytic therapy is a very great danger, a danger one does not know how to meet. . . . One cannot influence them to hold aloof from the whole affair."

Perhaps nowhere in the whole sphere of evolution of psychoanalytic thought is the question of the relations of the individual to his family group more crisply posed than in the field of child analysis.

Anna Freud pointedly indicated that the child's ego takes its cue from the social interaction processes of the family, but there she stopped, since she was not in a position to investigate these relationships. Interestingly enough, it was Anna Freud who first offered the candid assertion that both child analysis and the analysis of students of psychoanalysis violate the rules of analytic technique. Both in the relations of the child patient with his analyst, and in the relations of an analysand with his training analyst, there are face-to-face relations. The patient and analyst know one another as real persons. Direct gratification of need, support, control, even explicit guidance and advice, are a part of the analytic experience. To my mind, Anna Freud's significant disclosure that both child analysis and student analysis violate the classical rules of analytic technique raises some crucial questions concerning the theory of psychotherapy, as this affects the relations of real and unreal, individual and group.

At the extreme of the procedures of child analysis, Melanie Klein went so far as to prohibit the mother of a patient from sitting in the waiting room during the child's analytic session, lest this disturb the unfolding of the child's transference fantasies. The psychoanalytic philosophy concerning child-mother relationships epitomizes in a way the whole problem of the relations of the individual with his family group. In the more conservative forms of child analysis, when the mother is categorically excluded from the private sphere of the child's analytic experience, we have a representation of the tendency of psychoanalysis to isolate the one patient from mother and family. On one occasion, when I asked a well-known child analyst if she ever undertook the analysis of mothers of her child patients, her instantaneous exclamation was, "Oh, heavens no!"

In retrospect, one cannot help but wonder how far this historically-patterned isolation of the analytic patient from family is related to the limitations of therapeutic potency of psychoanalytic treatment. Concerning the therapeutic value of psychoanalysis, there is some persistent and lingering doubt. Weingarten's statistical survey of therapeutic results with psychoanalysis is not encouraging. Karl Menninger echoed a similar skepticism. He said: "True, Freud warned us against the emphasis on the therapeutic effect it does have, but in my opinion, were this its chief value, psychoanalysis would be doomed." Menninger emphasized not so much the therapeutic potency of psychoanalysis as its educational and research value.

Perhaps the problems of difference between family psychotherapy and psychoanalysis may be illuminated if we compare two theoretical models of psychotherapy:

1) The psychotherapeutic process conceptualized as a one-person phenomenon, non-social, though influenced by an external agent, the psychoanalyst.
2) The psychotherapeutic process viewed as a two-or-more person, true social phenomenon.

In the first model, with a non-social matrix of psychotherapy, the analyst is not a real person; he is anonymous; he hides his face; he is a mirror reflecting only what is shown to him; he gives no direct emotional satisfaction; he withholds the usual social cues; the social representations of reality are excluded.

In the classical model of psychoanalytic process, conflict with the analyst is reinterpreted in terms of conflict with older parts of the self. It is referred back to childhood conflicts with family. Transference is dominant over the existing realities. The analyst personifies objective reality, but the testing of such reality is postponed, both as epitomized in the real person of the analyst and in the objective world of human relations. Insofar as the analyst has no face, no identity, shows no emotions, this cannot be a true social experience.

Classical analytic technique favors the reliving of the symbiotic, autistic, magic core of the psyche—the egocentric, entrenched conflicts which contain the distorted percepts of the original, joined infant-parent relation and corresponding fragments of body image. The patient projects irrational conflict-ridden emotions, fantasies, and magic expectations; that is, primary process comes into a position of dominance. The analyst injects the modifying, organizing, and disciplining effects of secondary process. The patient subordinates his ego and external reality. He expands his unconscious, while the analyst contributes insight, reason, reality, and conscious control. Between the two persons, we have the functions of one mind.

The moment we shift to the second conceptual model, a two or more person interaction model, we have a true social experience; an interaction between two or more minds, as compared with patient and analyst recreating the symbiosis of one mind in the infant-parent union. In the second model, we have an expanded foundation for the dynamics of personality, a biopsychosocial model. In this therapeutic setting, we must match:

1) Intrapsychic and interpersonal events.
2) Unconscious and conscious organization of experience.
3) Unreal and real; transference and reality.
4) Past and present.
5) Individual and group.

Transference in this setting may be conceived as a failure of social learning. Transference, resistance, working through, interpretation, reality testing, all become interrelated parts of a unified process. Patient and therapist influence one another in a circular fashion.

In Freud's psychoanalytic frame, symptom, defense, transference, change, and cure have one kind of meaning. In family psychotherapy, with face to face relations and true social interchange, symptom, defense, change, growth and cure hold a broader significance. Conflict, symptom, defense in this setting are more than a walled-off intrapsychic distortion, a phobic, a hysterical conversion or an obsession. In family therapeutic process, they acquire the broader definition of certain recurring, predictable, interactional patterns inappropriate to the prevailing realities of the group. While intended to assure stasis for the individual, they actually impair homeostasis. They produce progressive distortion in the balance of family role relationships. In family psychotherapeutic process, a symptom becomes a unit of interpersonal behavior reflected in a constellation of shared conflict, anxiety and defense which is irrational, inappropriate, automatized, rigid, repetitive, and has the effect of constricting and distorting the range of new growth. The resulting impairments in family role adaptation move in one of two alternative directions: either toward rigidification, narrowing and stereotyping of roles, or toward an excessively rapid, fluid and unstable shift of multiple roles, which entails a threat of loss of self. Healthy family role adaptation reflects a quality of behavior intermediate between these extremes. It involves an optimal balance between the need to cling to elements of the old way and the ability to try a new way. The degree of success in coping with conflict molds this balance. An excess of anxiety impels a sticky clinging to the old way, narrows the receptivity to new experience, and reduces ability to discover new and better levels of family role adaptation. A lessened anxiety shifts the balance in the opposite direction.

In family therapeutic process, the realities of the group situation are an ever-present force. The therapist functions as a real person, as well as the target of projection. Though the realities of the group are fluid and changing over the course of time, the emotional impact on the family members is an immediate one. The family therapeutic experience offers a selective gratification of emotional needs. It favors motor release of emotion. It provides a matrix for the resolution of conflict at the level of action and reaction, in a continuous impact between the image of self and other. Conflict is lived out in interpersonal relations; it is externalized, experienced in action. Thus, therapy provides satisfaction of valid emotional needs, avenues for the solution of conflict, support of self-esteem, buttressing of healthy defenses against anxiety and an expanding interpersonal matrix for growth. In such a setting, the therapist injects something of himself that is new for the family members, the right emotions and perceptions to neutralize the wrong ones.

True change toward health comes with a progressive testing of new ways of thinking, feeling and doing. Gradually, a new synthesis of percept, affect, bodily expression and social action may be achieved.

CHAPTER 31

Family Psychotherapy—Theory and Practice

(The following excerpt constitutes perhaps half of this paper. The omitted section is an overview of family therapy's development out of child and group therapy, a topic already familiar to the reader of this section. In the final portion of the paper, note the paean to family therapy as offering "a new and different image of mental illness," "a profoundly honest way of intervening in human problems," and so on. These statements may be true, but for what audience was the rhetoric intended? We have the impression that is was the psychoanalytic community to whom Ackerman addressed this challenge. We come to this impression again in his sketch of the practicing family therapist. The unspoken point of comparison clearly is the practicing psychoanalyst.)

It is the therapist's responsibility to stir interaction among members; to catalyze and enhance a live and meaningful emotional interchange. He must establish a useful atmosphere of rapport, a touching quality of contact. As the family members come in touch with the therapist, they come into better touch with themselves.

The clinician integrates his knowledge and use of self in a special way. He is participant-observer. He is active, open, fluid, forthright. He moves directly into the stream of family conflict to energize and influence the interactional processes; he withdraws to objectify his experience, to survey and assess significant events, and then moves back in again. Weighing and balancing the sick and healthy emotional forces, he supports health and counteracts sickness by shifting his function at various stages of the family process.

His responsibilities are multiple and complex. They require a flexible, open, and undefensive use of self. Depending on the shifting foci of conflict and anxiety, one or another member joins with and separates from particular elements of the therapist's identity. These partial joinings and separations reflect elements of both transference fantasy and realism. The processes of transference, countertransference, and reality must be differently conceptualized in the matrix of family interaction. They may be interpreted as a fluid, changing balance between clinging to the old, and receptivity to the new in family

Reprinted with permission from *American Journal of Psychotherapy*, July 1966, Vol. XX, No. 3, 409-414.

experience. The potentials of effective reality testing in this special setting are much enhanced.

In the over-all picture, the therapist feels his way toward the idiosyncratic language of the family—how the members talk, what they choose to talk about, most importantly what they tacitly avoid. He makes rapid note of what is felt and communicated below the level of words in body stance, facial expressions, inarticulate gestures, and postural avoidances. He evaluates the outer face of the family, its protective mask. He perceives and assesses the deeper currents of emotion that parents fear and inhibit; the fright, the suspicion, the despair, the urge for vengeance. He identifies these sources of anxiety which freeze the reaching out of the members, the asking for closeness and understanding, one with the other, and with the therapist. He defines for himself the level of coping struggle that characterizes the particular family. He assays the interplay between preferred defense operations of the family group and individual defenses against anxiety.

In a continual process of communion with self, he brings to his awareness the emotions stirred in him by the deep streams of feeling moving among the family members and toward himself. He uses his disciplined insights into his personal emotions as a diagnostic yardstick for what is being experienced by the family. In so doing, he develops a series of clinical hunches which he progressively tests as he builds his diagnostic image of the family group. This embraces the balance of family functioning, the patterns of complementarity, conflict, and coping, the interplay of the family and individual defense and, finally, the struggle with conflicting representations of family identity, values, and patterns of action. In a selective manner, sequence by sequence, the therapist penetrates the family façade, the patterns of complicity, denials, and disguise of deeper currents of feelings of conflict and fear.

Acting as catalyst, the therapist provokes increasingly candid disclosures of dormant interpersonal conflicts; he lifts intrapersonal conflict to the level of interpersonal process. In due course, he can trace significant connections between family disorder and the intrapsychic anxiety of individual members. Often one part of the family armors itself, prejudicially attacks and sacrifices another part. When needed, the therapist intervenes to neutralize these sick patterns of attack. By counteracting scapegoating as a specific defense against anxiety, the therapist retransposes the underlying conflict to its place of origin in the family group; that is, the conflict may be moved back to its primary source. In this phase of therapy, it has become possible to identify a cluster of interrelated roles, that of persecutor, victim, peacemaker, or healer of family conflict.

In intervening on the interplay between family group defense and individual defenses, the therapist makes free use of the device of confrontation. By a variety of interventions, he penetrates and undermines the pathogenic patterns of coping and defense. He calls attention to the inefficiency, inappropriateness, and harmfulness of certain sickness-inducing defenses, and fosters the substitution of healthier ones. This has special relevance for the task of cutting into the vicious cycle of blame and punishment which represents nothing less than an unconscious collusion to prevent change.

To stir movement, the therapist pierces pathogenic operations by a device I call "tickling the defenses." This is a tactic of catching the family members by surprise, exposing dramatic discrepancies between their self-justifying rationalizations and their subverbal attitudes. He challenges empty clichés and static or pat formulae for the problems of family living. He halts fruitless bickering over routine, superficial, or unimportant matters.

Watchful for each clue, he reaches out for more honest and meaningful means of communication. In the service of this effort, he may make effective use of "body talk." He confronts the members forthrightly with the meaning of certain nonverbal forms of communication as revealed in mood, expression, posture, gesture, and movement. To counteract the tendency to substitute empty verbalisms for genuine emotional interchange, he catalyzes in the members the urge to explore the dramatic contradictions between these verbal utterances and body expressions.

Through his calm, firm presence, he functions as a controller of interpersonal danger, steering between the extremes of intolerable closeness and the risk of eruptions of explosive rage, which might lead to panic and disorganization. He executes other functions: he offers security, emotional support, acceptance, understanding, affirmation of worth, and direct satisfaction of valid emotional needs. He catalyzes the interchange among family members toward cooperation in the quest for solutions to conflict or toward finding more appropriate compromises. Along this path, he activates a shift in the allegiances of family members toward improved complementarity of needs.

As a real parent figure, the therapist offers emotional support on a selective basis, now to one part of the family, now to another; so he may, in all honesty, and with considerable effectiveness, support a weaker member of a group against the attack of a stronger. In the long view, the genuineness of the therapist's concern, his fairness, and the manner in which he continually shifts from one part of the family to another, minimizes any destructive rivalry.

At still another level, the family therapist provides support through a kind of substitute gratification, that is, by supplying the family with elements of emotional imagery of self and others in which the family has before been lacking. In this sense, reality testing, fortified by the therapist's activity, begins at the outset. In the spontaneous give and take among the family members, each has an opportunity to experience the self and other with a lessened sense of danger. Each takes a second look at every other, and at the therapist, and readapts toward a more realistic image of family relationships.

Then there is the question of the clash of competing identities and values. This is expressed in an ongoing contest of needs, identity, and value representations between parental partners which, in turn, can be traced to the links of identity and values of each parent with his family of origin. In this clash, the offspring are forced to take sides and thus the family is split into contesting factions. In such family warfare, each faction competes with every other to push change toward what they want the family to be and do for its members. In this struggle, the family therapist serves as educator to the problems of family living. He epitomizes in his own being a range of models of family health. He shakes up pre-existing alignments and splits and opens ways to new designs of family living. He stirs the family members to find constructive solutions or compromises of conflict, to discover new ways of intimacy, sharing, and identification, to support difference as well as union. Crucial to this, he energizes and enriches the processes of critical reassessment of family identity, goals, and values, especially those that pertain to the maintenance of indispensable family functions.

By the merging of these many functions, as activator or common challenger, common supporter, interpreter, reintegrator, the therapist shakes up pre-existing pathogenic relationship alignments and equilibria, and opens the way to discovery of healthier family bonds.

SUMMARY

The therapist's functions may be itemized as follows:

1. The therapist establishes a useful rapport, empathy, and communication among the family members and between them and himself.
2. He uses this rapport to catalyze the expression of major conflicts and ways of coping. He clarifies conflict by dissolving barriers, defensive disguises, confusions, and misunderstandings. By stages, he attempts to bring to the members a clearer and more accurate understanding as to what is really wrong.
3. He counteracts inappropriate denials, displacements and rationalizations of conflict.
4. He transforms dormant, concealed interpersonal conflicts into open, interactional expression.
5. He lifts intrapersonal conflict to the level of interpersonal exchange.
6. He neutralizes processes of prejudicial scapegoating that fortify one part of the family while victimizing another part.
7. He fulfills, in part, the role of a real parent figure, a controller of danger, a source of emotional support, and a supplier of elements which the family needs but lacks. His emotional nurturing of the family is a kind of substitutive therapy.
8. He penetrates and undermines resistances, and reduces the intensity of shared conflict,

guilt, and fear, using both confrontation and interpretation, but relying mainly on the former.

9. He serves as a personal instrument of reality testing for the family.
10. He serves as the educator and personifier of useful models of family health.

The future of family psychotherapy is hinted at in its unique potentials and revolutionary implications. It has a fascination uniquely its own. The therapist hits home, both literally and figuratively. Family therapy may not only unfold as a method in its own right, but may also serve to correct and improve some of the older methods. That this is so is borne out by the conviction of many psychotherapists who have had training in family therapy. "Once a therapist engages in family therapy, he ain't never the same again." Not only does he discover the value of family therapy; he also becomes a more effective psychoanalytic therapist.

Family therapy is a therapy in vivo not in vitro. It is a natural, not an artificial level of entry into human distress. It encompasses the interdependent, interpenetrating relations of individual and group. It does not pit individual against family or family against individual. It does not heal one part of the family at the expense of another; it supports both. It offers a new and different image of mental illness. It is a profoundly honest way of intervening in human problems. It highlights the importance of contagion of anxiety in family interchange. It provides a natural setting channel for the living-out of the pain and disillusionment deriving from this clash. It deals with disparities of depth and surface; inner and outer being; the interplay of intra- and interpersonal conflict, and the relations, mutually supporting or oppositional, between family group defense and individual defense. It confronts the interplay of multiple disturbances among family members. It offers an effective means for penetrating the vicious cycle of blame and punishment for things past. It provides an emotional matrix for enhancing mutual understanding, respect, and esteem.

Contrary to Freud's view of therapy, it does not merely take something away, a pathogenic feeling or idea; it adds something new and better to take the place of sick experience. It illuminates the homeodynamic principle of adaptation to change, the matrix for learning and growth in the family. It fosters healthy rather than pathologic healing of family disorders. It does not merely patch-up a damaged individual; it makes room for improved relationship patterns, a new way of life. It relates a valid ethic to the goals of family living.

For the interested therapist, family psychotherapy, however unstandardized it is in its presently evolving form, nevertheless, is full of challenge, full of surprises, and highly rewarding. A science of family behavior, a system of family diagnosis and psychotherapy, hold the promise of becoming a useful and significant addition to our armamentarium of mental health practices.

CHAPTER 32

The Family Approach and Levels of Intervention

The development of the family approach to psychotherapy impels us to take a fresh look at old problems, to re-examine and redefine issues pertinent to principles of diagnosis and treatment in the entire mental health field. It spurs a search for sharper answers to questions of appropriateness, specificity, and effectiveness of the older, more established therapies as well as of the family method. From the vantage point of our studies, diagnostic assessment of behavior within the context of family life is essential to the understanding of all psychopathologic states. We believe, further, that the family approach emerges not simply as the basis for an alternative treatment method, but as a necessary foundation for the choice and uses of other types of therapy.

Our experience leads us to take a stand against the implied bias of the assigned theme: family therapy *versus* individual therapy. It is not, in our view, an either/or problem. The two methods are not competitive or oppositional, but are essentially complementary. A confusion seems to have arisen between the changing conceptual approach to mental illness and the various means of treating it. The family approach is distinct. It is a basic view which provides a conceptualization for all levels of intervention. The key note is flexibility of treatment. The required orientation is to the specific needs of family and family members at different stages of the life cycle, at different levels of relations of family and individual, and in connection with particular crises in the life situation. In accordance with these factors, the indicated level of intervention may be the family method, therapy of a pair or of an individual, or any combination of these.

The history of science repeatedly reveals that a new method of observation alters our view of the problem. In this instance, the dynamically oriented interview of the whole family leads to a different perspective of the phenomenon of emotional and mental disorders, and, in turn, to different ways of modifying it. Behavior, both in health and in illness, is organized in two interrelated ways: one at the level of family experience, and another at the level of individual experience. Family therapy and individual therapy aim at different levels of human organization and hold different potentials of influence on selected components of disordered functioning.

Reprinted with permission from *American Journal of Psychotherapy*, January 1968, Vol. XXII, No. 1, 5-14.

This paper was co-authored with Majorie L. Behrens.

This altered and broader view of behavior disorders is fundamental to any ordered attempt to review the question of differential indications for one or another type of intervention.

RATIONALE

The rationale for the family approach and appropriate therapeutic intervention rests on certain empirically documented truths. Mental illness begins and is best conceptualized within the network of family relationships. The family is viewed not just as an external influencing agent, but as the essence of the illness phenomenon. The concept of illness is further expanded beyond the disorder of one family member to the dynamic interplay of a constellation of interrelated vulnerability patterns among family members. It is an attempt to correlate a way of life with susceptibility to emotional breakdown. It makes sense, therefore, to study, treat, and prevent illness in the family setting.

Family therapy, specifically, intervenes in a natural group, a primary social group, the members of which share identity, a way of life, and the struggle with emotion. It joins the individual to his family environment. It is oriented to the matrix of a sequential series of interdependent, interpenetrating disturbances across time and across the generations. It intervenes in central family relationship processes directly and specifically, rather than indirectly and peripherally as in more traditional procedures. A crucial consideration is the possibility of more accurate assessment of the effects of intervention on family relationships, and, therefore, of exerting greater control.

The family approach, by illuminating multiple levels of disturbed functioning, offers the therapeutic potential of multiple levels of entry. By the same token, however, it also imposes the crucial responsibility of determining the priorities of using family and other methods of intervention.

The complexity and variability of family networks and the range of possible types of integration of individuals within the family unit preclude any simple rules of thumb for the uses of family therapy and for the selection of priorities of intervention in one or another component of disturbance. At the present stage, there is no clear consensus on standards for using varying combinations of family and individual treatment. There are as yet no hard and fast rules which define exactly when to treat the whole family and when to focus on family pairs or individual members. From our point of view, however, the treatment of the whole family is the focal orientation.

The clinician may, at his own discretion, begin with the whole family or begin with the marital pair, or an individual, and then reach out to involve all members of the living unit, including grandparents. He must define for himself the nature of the family's internal war, the pattern of alignments and splits. Responding to the most destructive area of conflict, and with appropriate timing, he may intervene in the marital pair, parent-child pair, or parent-grandparent pair relationship. The purpose is to reduce tension and anxiety sufficiently in one or another part of the family to restore that part once more to the capacity for effective participation in the treatment of the whole family.

CHANGING DEFINITION OF MENTAL ILLNESS

Historically, the family approach has been influenced by changes in the image and definition of mental illness. At one time, mental illness represented something gone wrong inside the brain, then inside the mind. Now it has come to include what goes on between minds, between persons and includes the environment as well. Originally, psychoanalysis was mainly oriented to "primary process," to childhood experience, intrapsychic conflict, and related symptoms. It was basically a nonsocial form of treatment. The orientation later shifted to character structure, to the whole person, to relationships, role adaptation, to the here and now definitions of experience, and to the dynamics of the group itself. Currently, therapy turns increasingly in the direction of a true social experience. It deals with the interplay of intrapersonal and interpersonal experience, conscious and unconscious forces, and situational factors as well. Concern with family life is direct, rather than indirect; intervention points not to the individual away and apart from the family, but rather to persons within the family and to the family as a living whole. Conceptually, psychotherapy was, at one time, oriented inside outward. Now it has acquired a circular orientation moving from outside inward, as well as from inside outward. With this shift, the issue of differential indications for therapy can no longer rest so pointedly on a framework of symptom structure and related psychiatric classification. Nor can it be based exclusively on issues of mildness or severity of illness, though such features influence the implementation of the family method.

The family approach emphasizes an increased understanding of the relations between inner and outer experience. A central principle is the role of contagion of emotion in family process and the transmission of pathogenic conflict and coping from person to person and from one generation to the next. It is thus possible to correlate family and individual development at each stage of the life cycle and to conceptualize the relations of family defense of its identity, continuity, and functions on the one hand, and the expression of individual need and defense against anxiety on the other. Within this framework, the significance of acting out, of multiple and interpenetrating disturbances, and of the secondary gains of illness are illuminated. It is the constellation of interacting and interpenetrating disorders within the family unit that reflects and defines the balance of health. Within this same perspective, also, the learning and growth processes and the healing potentials, both of family and individual members, can be more clearly understood.

The family approach also involves reconceptualization of the concept of the individual. There is no individuality except in the family. Anything else labeled individuality is essentially pathogenic isolation. The individual is part of the family and the family is part of the individual. Neither is complete without the other. The individual takes from the family what he needs for growth and development. The family, in turn, takes what it needs from the individual to maintain its continuity and functions. Each projects wanted and unwanted qualities onto the other. The exchange of emotion and influence is a circular one from family to individual, and from individual to family. Any change in the behavior of the family brings a change in the behavior of the individual and vice versa. The correlation of individual and family behavior is differently determined for each stage of the evolution of the family group and for each stage of emergence of individual personality. The phenomenon of illness in this context becomes a cluster of interrelated tendencies toward morbidity among the family members. The challenge is to make emotional breakdown intelligible in terms of family processes and practices rather than solely in relation to the isolated individual.

A central goal of the family approach is to find the locus of the most destructive conflict and fear, to reduce this within the matrix of interpersonal relationships, and heighten the level of complementation of emotional needs. One must reinforce the immunity of the family against critical upsets by enhancing the harmony and balance of family functions, by strengthening the individual member against destructive forces within him and surrounding him in the family environment, and finally, by influencing the orientation of family identity and values toward health and growth.

APPLICABILITY OF FAMILY THERAPY

In principle, family therapy has a wide range of applicability to all classifications of psychiatric disorder, to all degrees of mildness or severity of such disorder, but it must be flexibly modified to accommodate to different conditions. It can be helpful in psychiatric disorders in which the interpersonal and social determinants loom large, in such conditions as acting-out types of disturbance, sociopathic behavior, neurosis, psychosomatic crisis, and functional psychosis. In marital disorders and in disturbances of parent-child relationships it is especially effective. It may even be indispensable as a procedure for the involvement of a sick but resistant member in a therapeutic experience. It can be of value at selective points in time of one member's involvement in individual psychotherapy, by braking the impact of resistance or bogging down, thus freeing the individual to resume progress. In a similar sense, it can be helpful in the emotional reintegration of a patient into his family in the final phase of his personal therapy, or in dissolving reinforcements of secondary gains of illness. The precise combinations of family and individual therapy selected must, in the last analysis, always be oriented to the emotional vicissitudes of the relations of family and its elements.

Within the framework of the family approach, it makes sense to deemphasize the principle of contraindications for family treatment and be more specific about those human situations in which the implementation of this method may be handicapped. In theory, there are no contraindications, but in practice, there may be conditions which sometimes make it inexpedient or impossible to carry through a total program of family treatment.

First and most obvious is availability of family members. If children are away at school, if grandparents live at some distance, or a parent or grandparent is disabled or is dead, individual or limited family treatment is the only possibility. Family therapy may be inexpedient if a crucially important member has a fixed organic or personal disorder which prevents his participation in family treatment. Still, a concerted effort to bring other members in, whenever possible, permits the therapist to build a comprehensive diagnosis, and to initiate therapeutic inroads on the family problems.

Most clear cut are situations which include an adolescent. By definition, the adolescent divides himself between two worlds, the peer world and the adult, family world. On principle, therefore, the therapist must make room to see the adolescent with his family and also separately.

In the area of more severe pathology, one cannot devise rigid and specific rules. The quality and severity of the particular brand of family disorder and personal pathology must be put to the therapeutic test. Sometimes family intervention is effective in reducing individual panic and the destructive response to panic in the labeled patient and in other family members. The confusion and turmoil one often sees in such families is a reflection of the fact that no one in the family really knows where the killing force lies. But, one can be sure it is between family members as well as in them. Family intervention, in these cases, can restore a sense of safety against feelings of imminent catastrophe and lessen the family propensity for damaging the individual and individual damaging the family.

In some families, the focus may be on the marital couple when it embodies the core pathology of the family unit. Incorporated in the marital identity is the residual pathology from the families of origin, plus the tension derived from the ongoing relations with the outside community and the couple's offspring. In such cases, the grandparents and children can be excused from the family interview. The priority here is to treat the pathology internalized in the marriage itself.

The therapist's submission to parents' or family members' refusal to attend a family interview is usually unwise. When one member balks, he is not acting alone. This is usually a symptom of a split family, a war between opposing factions. One must reach out for all sides. Sometimes parents obsessed with one child's disturbance are resistant to bringing in the whole family. They express fear of contaminating the other children. It is the therapist's responsibility to test the genuineness and validity of such protests. Are the other children uninvolved and unaffected? Do they really require special protection or are the parents hiding behind their children? Often this is a defensive façade concealing a pseudo-secret in the family which the therapist must then penetrate.

Sometimes it is necessary to accommodate to the stage of the family life cycle and the associated conflicts. For example, a young couple with a baby is seen at a time of acute tension between them and the husband's parents. The in-laws are invited to come in and the conflicts between the young couple and the older generation are worked out, without involving other family members.

One circumstance contraindicating family therapy is the existence of an irreversible and progressive trend toward family breakup. For some families, realistically speaking, it may be just too late to reverse the forces of fragmentation. Another such condition, in which family treatment might be critically burdened, is the dominance within the group of a concentrated focus of malignant, destructive motivation. For example, one member of a parental pair may suffer from an organized, progressive paranoid state, or a form of incorrigible destructiveness, criminality, or malignant sexual perversion. Or sometimes the rigid defenses of one parent exert an overwhelming and destructive effect on the emotional health of all members. In particular instances, the rigidity of defense behavior and the excessive walling off of one member of the family may suggest that, if this defense structure is penetrated in family treatment, the particular family member may be precipitated into an acute depression, psychosis, or psychosomatic crisis. In other circumstances, rigid patterns of alienation, distancing, and the associated barriers to contact and communication may render intervention by family therapy ineffective.

A special problem may also arise in families where there is danger of an outbreak of physical assaultiveness which can be neither effectively controlled nor compensated. Finally, organic disease or disablement of a progressive nature may preclude the effective participation of the involved individual in a family treatment interview. It is important to emphasize again that as a matter of principle these exceptional conditions represent not so much contraindications in a traditional sense, but family characteristics or circumstances of life which may excessively handicap the potential effectiveness of family intervention.

To clarify the issue of differential indication of types of therapy, we must aspire to greater specificity in terms of three questions:

1. What components or levels of disturbance are selected for therapeutic influence and in what order?
2. By what means?
3. With what potential for therapeutic change?

In actual practice, what happens? Regardless of which family member is labeled the "sick one," the whole family is invited to come in and talk it over. Most times families respond favorably to such an invitation. They are easily made aware that they all have a part in the existing emotional condition of the family and that they are all affected by one another's behavior, without regard to the particular member who is the patient. On the other hand, it often happens that for the first visit the parents may prefer to come without the children, or one parent, feeling assailed, misused, and martyred asks to come in first because of the urge to win the therapist's special protection against other members of the family. Nonetheless, in one way or the other, sooner or later, it is generally possible to bring in the nuclear family group, and often subsequently to bring in the surviving older generation, the grandparents. The preliminary series of exploratory interviews serves not only to highlight the central problems of the whole family, but also offers an opportunity in a selective way to unburden a scapegoated family member, to retranspose the load of conflict from that one member to its original source within the family group, where it can be coped with in a more direct way. The disturbance becomes recognized as a contagion of emotional pain within the whole family rather than the exclusive affliction of one member who is exploited to preserve a pathogenic family equilibrium. In the long view, there is no safety in the emotional integrity of other family members in a tenuous pathogenic equilibrium. When the therapist counteracts the scapegoating, he paves the way for a new and healthier alignment of family relationships.

The following case exemplifies the family approach by deliberately upsetting the family equilibrium and shifting the burden from the labeled patient, the child, to the parents and relations with grandparents.

Mr. Jones called about his son John, age nine, the oldest of three children. Although intelligent, the boy was doing poorly in school, and had alienated his friends. He wet his bed occasionally, had temper tantrums, and was unresponsive to discipline. His mother would scream at him, but then call the father to punish him.

In the family interview, the mother acted as spokesman. She was rigid, compulsive and controlling. The father sat silent. His expression was deadly serious as if he sat on the edge of a catastrophe. The mother began with complaints about John but then slid into complaints about her husband. The whole burden of disciplining was hers. Her husband was uninvolved and disinterested except when she broke into an explosive tantrum. Then he became oversevere with John, followed again by withdrawing from the boy.

The therapist excused the children and shifted emphasis to the parental relationship, thereby shelving their obsessive concern with John. The wife complained about their deteriorated sexual life. She had repeatedly threatened divorce. It was easily apparent that Mrs. Jones was taking out on John what she could not release on her husband. Mr. Jones resented the intrusion of his wife's parents into their home, especially of her father. Mrs. Jones had brought her parents to this country, and her husband, well established professionally, felt his wife exploited him now to provide security for her parents. She, in turn, accused him of being jealous and paranoid. It was soon learned that the husband was profoundly bound to a psychotic mother, and until he met his wife, had never dated.

Clearly the family disorder involved the older generation on both sides. The boy's disturbance was an expression of parental conflict which was, in turn, bound up with conflict with their own parents. In such cases, exploratory interviews move by stages to the involvement of three generations of family. Beginning with the failures of complementarity and functioning in marital and parental adaptation, we move back to the relationships of each parent to the families of origin. In this way we can correlate the link of identity and anxiety of each parent to the older generation. We then move forward from the parents to their offspring to conceptualize the division of the elements of identity and the disturbances of the parents as a couple among the brood of children.

Working first with the nuclear family, then moving back to the grandparent generation, then forward from parents to children is the usual sequence. Sometimes, however, the labeled patient is a grandparent. It is then necessary to bring in the married children and even the grandchildren at appropriate times.

Another case illustrates a different application of the family approach. In this instance, the patient was seen first, then the family, then the marital pair, followed by each parent individually. Finally the whole family became involved, excepting the original patient who had to be referred to a therapist in the city where he attended graduate school.

The identified patient was a young man of twenty-four, handsome, in a soft, effeminate way. He had been expelled from a series of schools and was ready to fail in graduate school. He was distressed about recurrent panics, about excessive drinking, and impotency. He had a girl in another city to whom he clung in desperation, though he was not faithful to her. In the interview, he was outwardly aggressive, but his contentiousness had a hollow ring. He had a background of teenage homosexual experiences in which he had involved his brother. Several trials at psychoanalytic treatment had been broken off because he felt the doctors had no respect for him, were contemptuous, provocative, and ridiculing.

He asked to come in with his parents and younger brother. His parents came, but without his brother. In this instance, the father took the role of spokesman. The mother, relatively quiet at first, later indicated her view of the boy's problem differed from that of her husband. She felt her husband's approach to the boy was alternately viciously attacking and contemptuously withdrawn. The father expressed resentment toward his wife for siding with the boy against him, thus undermining his paternal authority. He also expressed an earnest lament that he could never get a clear picture from the previous psychiatrists as to what was wrong with his son.

During the interview, by stages, the hostility between the parents became progressively sharper. At first, there was a formal, polite but distant interaction. When the therapist pricked the façade, the battle between the parents became increasingly hot. Two things stood out prominently: the son's belligerency toward his father which became more and more bitter as his father tried to maintain his composure and good manners; and the hint of family secrets. At this point the son was excused from the interview.

With the parents alone, the talk veered to conflict between them. They admitted deliberately keeping the younger son from the interview. Allegedly, he was "normal" and uninvolved. They claimed he knew nothing about his brother's troubles and should be protected against contamination. This was opposite to the actual truth. In fact, he had been embroiled by his older brother in the latter's fears, stresses, failures, and particularly had been drawn into his brother's homosexual preoccupations.

Toward the end of the interview, despite the therapist's explicit description of the core of the boy's illness, his tendency to panic, his depression, his withdrawal and poor contact with people, his proneness to argumentation, inner emptiness, loneliness, and sexual confusion, the father reiterated that he could not get a clear idea of what was wrong with his son. He did not seem to comprehend until told quite directly that his son was on the verge of a breakdown. At this point, he asked for an interview alone. He then revealed an affair of five years' duration which he felt his wife suspected but chose to ignore. His older son knew of the affair as a result of catching his father telephoning to the woman. The father wanted guidance. Should he get a divorce and marry the other woman?

At his request, his wife was also interviewed alone. She was torn between pacifying her husband, meeting his demands, and looking after her boy. She described her husband as restless and agitated. He wanted people around him all the time and insatiably caused his family to move, never satisfied. She wanted to keep her marriage going and, in a vague, indirect way, hinted she could tolerate his having other women as long as he did right by her and the boys. Subsequently, the father gave up the other woman and family treatment is continuing.

Such interviews are not mere explorations but an attempt to bring together the various elements of illness. In this way, the goals of the family approach are attained. It is possible then to delineate the most destructive locus of conflict and anxiety, to establish priorities for intervention and to mobilize the healing resources of the family for an effective struggle with conflict.

SUMMARY

Treatment must be problem oriented, not technique oriented. The integration of the various partial procedures derived from the family approach must be determined by the needs both of the family group and its individual members at any given point in time. It is the concept of the family as a unit of experience and growth that provides the framework for flexible patterns of therapeutic intervention on multiple, interpenetrating levels of disturbance. Rather than follow any preordained stereotyped treatment procedure, one may in an open-ended, elastic fashion shift from one level of intervention to another, depending on one's perception at any one moment of the areas of most malignant and menacing conflict. While making room for these clinically determined shifts of focus, one strives in progressive stages toward the ideal of treating the whole family.

CHAPTER 33

Child Participation in Family Therapy

A strange paradox marks the question of the participation of children in the family therapeutic interview. The central importance of the question is self-evident; without engaging the children in a meaningful interchange across the generations, there can be no family therapy. And yet, in the daily practice of this form of treatment, difficulties in mobilizing the participation of children are a common experience. It is all the more surprising, to realize, therefore, that there is not a single publication devoted to this special theme. Having come myself to the problems of family diagnosis and treatment through the psychiatry of children, I feel a certain responsibility to confront the question and hope that others will do likewise.

To illuminate some of the problems, let us, for example, consider the Hillcrest moving pictures produced by Van Flack, Birdwhistell, and Scheflen. This is an intriguing experiment in which four family therapists were filmed while interviewing the same family at different appointed times across a two day period. This was so arranged that none of the therapists knew what had transpired in the interviews conducted by the other therapists.

The family group consisted of a pair of young parents, each previously divorced and now joined in the care of four children ranging from 10 years down to 1½ years. One set of children, a boy and a girl, 10 and 8 years respectively, were by the father's first marriage; a girl of 5 by the mother's first marriage, and a baby girl, 1½ years, a product of the new marriage.

A review of the filmed interviews by these four therapists revealed remarkable differences among them in stance and accommodation to the parents, on one hand, and to the four children, on the other hand. The major impression among a group of twenty professionals studying these films was that two of the therapists focused on the parents and related to the children hardly at all. A third interviewer showed some responsivity to the children as little people, but involved them minimally. Only one of the four interviewers exhibited a strong rapport with the kiddies and actively engaged them in the treatment of the family as family.

We need to place this observation in the context of a wider appreciation of the response to this challenge of psychotherapists generally. It

Reprinted with permission from *Family Process*, December 1970, Vol. 9, No. 4, 403-410.

is commonly known that psychotherapists as a group are candid in confessing their preferred patient ages. Many like to work only with adult persons; they frankly admit discomfort with children and feel alien to the child's world. They are often at a loss as to how to handle themselves; close dealings with children demand too great an exertion. At the opposite pole, there are the child psychiatrists who relate easily to children, enjoy them, but are uncomfortable with adult persons. Still another group of therapists show a preferential leaning toward adolescent patients. Finally, there is that minor but distinct category of therapists who discover in themselves a particular talent for dealing with senior citizens.

With these considerations in mind, we must be reminded that in face-to-face transactions with a three generation group a special affinity often emerges between children and grandparents. Insofar as grandparents are in their second childhood, they exhibit a strong empathy for their kiddies, one generation removed. Frequently, they join in an alliance that tends to exclude the parents. Clearly, trends such as these must affect the therapist's task of engaging children in the interview process.

It is easy to understand the tendency of therapists to favor their own developmental stage in a preferential empathy and identification with family members of one or another generation. In the one-to-one psychotherapeutic engagement, the selective way of relating to children, teenagers, adults, or the aged may seem to pose no problem. On the other hand, if we interpret one-to-one psychotherapy as a treatment of family relationships in absentia, we must draw a different conclusion. Viewed within this framework, the bias of the therapist for one generation against another may, in fact, create real complications. In the face-to-face encounter with a whole family, the question cannot be avoided. The problem instantly leaps into the foreground; it brings a challenge of considerable magnitude.

In observing interviews one has an opportunity to compare and contrast therapists in regard to the quality of their empathic response to, and engagement of, parents, children, and grandparents. One quickly recognizes how these differences affect the order of involvement of family members. Some therapists first engage the parents, and then move on to involve the children and grandparents. Others proceed in the reverse fashion. Some therapists begin with the grandparents. The order of involvement of one or another part of the family has important consequences with respect to the theme, sequence and pacing of therapeutic transactions. These processes selectively predetermine the focus on one or another set of family problems and conflicts. The involvement of adolescent members is ordinarily not so difficult. For many therapists, however, the mobilization of the effective participation of pre-adolescent children is clearly the greater problem.

Clinical experience with a range of family types provides some useful guidelines. At the outset a therapist tries to glean some impression of the children's perception of the family encounter. What do they imagine? What do they expect? What are their anticipatory images, their needs, desires, suspicions, fears and resentments? A therapist must assay the child's fear of parents, also the parent's fear of a child.

Initially a therapist has no immediate bridge of communication with a child member of the family. Contact is, at first, indirect, i.e., mediated through the parents and influenced by the parents' perception of their children as extensions of themselves. The therapist must be aware at this stage that he is an utter stranger to the child. It is inappropriate and self-defeating to come too close physically or emotionally to the child until the therapist gets some clue that the child is ready. There is yet no basis for trust or intimacy. The respective roles are not yet delineated; what is offered and what is threatened is not clear. A feeling of trust and intimacy with a therapist takes time. In the meanwhile, the child's autonomy and initiative call for respect. He has the choice of accepting or rejecting the therapist. It is better for the therapist simply to offer a warm "hello," and yet stand off at a safe distance to give the child opportunity to accommodate his emotions. If the child is allowed this safe space, he may sidle up to the therapist, as he feels the therapist's empathy, his interest, and above all, respect.

A therapist does well not to deal in abstractions but rather with the specific behaviors of a child. He ought not to talk for example of helping the child; this is an abstraction he cannot comprehend. An early clue is derived from the seating arrangement. Does the child want in now? Does the child prefer a seat at the far end, or in a corner, or do the parents sandwich the child between them?

Children do not just come to the interview, they are brought. Their attitudes and expectations in the beginning are influenced by the parents' feelings, and what they have told the children about the interview. Sometimes they are told nothing in advance. Sometimes they are manipulated, coerced and lied to. Often, parents are ashamed and afraid of a visit with a psychiatrist and adopt a hypocritical posture. They do not inform the children that they will be talking with a "shrink." The parents say, for example, they are going to a man who will advise them about a school or a camp. Or they say they are going to visit with a "friend" of the family. Thus, anxious parents engage too frequently in deceit, manipulation; they mislead the child. But children are mighty quick to discover the truth. In the interview a child darts a fleeting glance at mother or father, or the parents send a threatening stare toward the child. The child wonders, is he allowed to open his mouth? If he does, will he say or do the wrong thing and get punished? The child may feel he is just brought along for convenience, but he's not supposed to stick his nose into the proceedings. The parents do the talking and the child simply sits there, folds his hands, and poses as a good boy. In a variety of ways the therapist must convey to the child that he is wanted and needed for himself, that he is an important member of the family in his own right; that his feelings carry a certain weight.

But parents also wonder: Will the child expose them? How can they avoid disclosure of certain shameful secrets before the child?

If the labeled patient happens to be a child, the parents' demand, in effect, is, do something to *this* child, and in some way to fortify the parents' failing authority. In this role, a parent often adopts an insincere posture as the therapist's assistant. Sometimes, when asked to bring all the children, parents come only with the one child that stands accused as the troublemaker. They offer a transparent alibi for absenting the siblings. They intimate they are shielding the other children from contamination. The scapegoating in such a family is all too obvious; the parents hide their problems behind the one "black sheep"; they shove this child out front, using him to run interference for themselves.

In many ways parents send double messages to the child that stir confusion. Sometimes at the very moment a child begins to talk, one or another parent cuts in with what looks like support. "It's all right, don't be afraid to talk, be honest." But the real message is the reverse; it is a disguised way of stopping the child in his tracks. It is, in fact, a hidden warning to watch his step. If he says the wrong thing, he'll catch it at home.

It is important for the therapist to relate to both levels, to parents as persons, to the children also as persons. The quality of rapport is necessarily different and so is the language. As the interview proceeds, a child may make a spontaneous gesture of getting into the act. The parent may show a burst of irritability and put pressure on the child to conform. If a child is ignored, minimized or put down, he ceases to listen. He will show signs of agitation or enter into some kind of disruptive behavior, or move into sulky retreat.

At such a moment the child may blurt out, "Momma, I'm hungry," or "Momma, I've got to go make." This is a clear hint of mounting tension. The parents rejoinder may be "You can eat later," "You don't have to go to the toilet at all," or "Be quiet and sit up straight." Frequently, the parents make a surface display of constraining their irritability. They do not want the therapist to think of them as mean and punishing and so hush themselves up as well as the child.

The surge of tension is a hint for the therapist to do something to involve the child with him. The therapist does so by pointedly according the child some respect and a sense of importance. He listens receptively, with a show of empathy and interest. If the child wants food, a therapist may say, "Johnny, would you like a lifesaver or a stick of gum?" or "We have some cookies and soda downstairs." That works wonders; one can engage the child's interest after that in more meaningful emotional interchange with the parents and with oneself.

In another variation, some parents push the children forward not so much to scapegoat them and punish them, but rather to show the children off, to win a vicarious acceptance and approval for themselves. This is an attempt at ingratiation with the therapist, and it often conceals the parents' feelings of guilt, weakness, and inadequacy.

Parents who are on the defensive tell the therapist only what they think is good for him to know. They slant the story so as to favor their own position. In assuming this posture, they tend to put the child member down, they do not give him a sense of importance in his own right. In this setting, if the parents present a twisted, false picture of what really goes on at home, the child makes a sour face, squirms in his seat, or kicks the foot of the table. This is often a useful clue that the parents are being hypocritical, or that they are handing out lies. The child resents this and responds with some kind of non-verbal protest. At this moment, if the therapist turns pointedly to these non-verbal communications and offers support and encouragement, the child may reward him with meaningful disclosures. It is a case of the old cliché, "out of the mouths of babes." If a child makes faces, the therapist may say, "I can tell you don't believe your parents." If the child kicks the table, the therapist may ask, "Are you mad? Kick harder, so I can see. Whom do you really want to kick?" The therapist must indicate it is safe to speak out. He must show he has the confidence and power to counteract the threat of punishment, that he can disarm the parents of their power to terrorize the child. The parents may resent the therapist's intervention, but out of deference to the doctor they allow this action, even though they do not like it. They are obedient that way, they rationalize and say, "Well, the doctor must have his reason," and so they comply.

The therapist's objective in the interview is to develop an interchange that reveals both the parent's image of the children and the children's image of the parents. There are a great range of non-verbal clues that suggest how the parents try to "snow" the therapist. If he gives the child support and encouragement, the child will blurt out in a simple, direct way what really goes on in the family. The therapist's purpose is to strike an appropriate balance between the communicative role of the parents, on the one hand, and the communicative role of the children, on the other hand. The disclosures of the children are an important level of checking, a kind of reality testing and consensual validation of the parent's descriptions of their troubles.

If a child is frightened and intimidated by parental constraint, he isolates himself. His eyelids droop, he seems to become drowsy, he mumbles under his breath. Or, he acts bored; he wants out; he wants to take flight altogether. If, affectively speaking, the child dies away, this is a clue for the therapist to move in. On other occasions, a child will take flight another way; he buries his head in a book; the book is provided by the parent, an intentional shut-out.

Sometimes an uptight child who can't honestly say what goes on, becomes a saboteur, a kind of wrecker of the proceedings. If so, this is again an important message to the therapist. By aligning himself with the child the therapist can tease out the background from which the child assumes the role of a wrecker.

We have referred to the child's fear of the parents, but we must also examine the other side of the equation, namely the parents' fear of the child. In some cases the parents' fear seems to be the greater. They are confused, anxious, and helpless. They can only deal with the child in desperate terms. When a child is in some measure a child of love, there is usually no great problem with discipline. To put it simply, it works if a child is valued. If not, there is trouble! The parents report that they have tried every conceivable form of discipline at home and nothing has worked. They have tried to reason with the child, they have tried deprivation. They have denied the child his "goodies." They have perhaps deprived the child of his supper and sent him to his room. Or, they have beaten the hell out of him. But all of this seems like water off a duck's back. The discipline does not take. When the discipline utterly fails, it is proof of a critical disturbance in the child's affective union with the parents. When a child does not have a basic sense of acceptance, security, and warmth from the parents, no amount of discipline will do a damn thing. It is desperate and futile. When the parents feel their impotence to control the child, they get panicky and go into wild rages. Then again, they are tossed back on their helplessness and once more a burst of rage. They look upon the child not as a human being, a person, but rather as a monster, as some kind of fiend who is about to explode and shatter the entire family.

Where the parents have lost control, the therapist needs to turn about to support the parents against the wrecking activities of the child. He must show that he has the strength to control the child, if need be, by physical constraint. The child may at first panic and cry bloody murder, "you're killing me," but a show of quiet strength of the appropriate quality, without vindictive feeling and without hurting, soon quiets the child; he gradually recognizes that he is only being held, not assaulted. In fact, he begins to like it. It makes him feel safe.

In this setting a therapist must know how tall he is; he must have an idea of how strong his biceps are and he must act accordingly. If in a quiet but firm way a therapist controls the child with passive-physical restraint, the parents' panic and fury also recede. The achievement of a balance in the war of the generations is of the essence. Having reestablished some kind of order and peace the therapist may continue his work.

If one is dealing with a scapegoated, terrorized child, the therapist must side with the child to equalize the relationship with the parents. If, at the other extreme, the child turns into a destructive monster and terrifies the parents, the therapist must again equalize the relationships. He must make an alliance with the parents, control the child, and ease the fright, both of the parents and of the child. It must be borne in mind, certainly, that the child monster is one that the parents have themselves created. It is their own hidden violence that erupts in the child.

Assuming progress in establishing a desired balance, things really begin to move. The children are involved. They take part actively, animatedly. This is an exciting phase in which the true story of the family emerges. The participation of the children can be optimally exploited to reality-test the pathogenic distortions of both sides of the family. The therapist balances the children's disclosures against the parents' account of what's wrong. This is all part of the work of family diagnosis.

In conclusion, I would underscore the importance in the initial contact of establishing empathy and rapport by showing interest and responsivity but keeping a respectful distance until the child makes a spontaneous move toward the therapist. The mobilization of effective participation of child members is essential to the elucidation, stage by stage, of the family war, the alignment and splits in the family group, the hidden conflict of the parents, the scapegoating, etc. Once the children catch on, they like it because, more often than not, they do not have the same chance to speak out at home. If they feel protected here and fairly dealt with, their sense of personal importance is gratifying. The experience expands their egos. Fundamentally, the child's drive for self-expression is a constructive and healing influence for the parents as well. It opens a path for a new way of relating, not only between parents and children, but also between the parents. What is involved is a movement toward a deeper and more appropriate kind of emotional honesty among the members.

CHAPTER 34

The Art of Family Therapy

Family therapy has produced striking innovations. We watch one another's work; we sit with other therapists as observers or as co-therapists; we view treatment sessions through a one-way window; we study records of treatment process on film, videotape, and sound tape. We have opened the door wide to new kinds of debates and to new conceptualizations of therapeutic process. Controversy assumes a new character. It is more open and honest, intensely skeptical and challenging. It gives a tremendous catalytic thrust to the evolution and theory of family therapy. The ethos of open sharing of the unsolved problems of therapeutic process finds increasingly warm acceptance. This ethos stands in dramatic contrast to the tradition of the secret, ivory-tower style of individual psychotherapy and to the tendency to lean on outmoded methods of training and supervision. The differences between individual therapy and family therapy have revolutionary implications. Watching one another's work not only brings to the clear light of day the controversies of the family method of treatment; more than that, it dramatizes some issues which are crucial in all forms of psychotherapy.

Since the practice of family therapy and its development are a highly personal matter, I offer myself as an illustrative case and take the liberty of reporting my own experience.

In the 1950s, prior to the popularization of audiovisual techniques, I was already giving clinical demonstrations of family psychotherapy in medical schools, mental hospitals, child guidance clinics, and social agencies. Somewhat later, in 1958, I began to use motion-picture records of family treatment process as well as conducting interviews. These procedures, especially the clinical demonstration of therapy with a family openly seated before a professional audience, represented a radical break with tradition. The impact of these experiences on professional viewers was electric. Initially, the response was one of startled shock and surprise. When the first shock wore off, there was a delayed response, a longer-lasting bout of agitation. The professional viewers buzzed excitedly among themselves. They were caught up in the emotional swell of a living involvement in the struggle with a distressed family. Their reactions

Reprinted from *Family Therapy in Transition* (International Psychiatry Clinics, Vol. 7, No. 4), 1970, 21-26. Copyright 1970 by Little, Brown and Co., Boston.

were not intellectualizations, not the judgments of detached, professional observers. Instead, they found themselves fully enagaged as feeling, sentient beings. Initially they were blind to the meaning of their emotional immersion. By degrees, however, they came to explicit awareness of this. More pointedly, they began to recognize the significance of excluding relatives, the therapeutic weakness it produced in coping with their patient's family experience. Also, they began to realize that their own personal entanglements in family life were a potent factor in shaping their responses. In any demonstration of family therapeutic process, the mood, the climate of the interview, the therapist's open use of his personality, his image of family, his value attitudes, his unique therapeutic style, all colored their individual interpretations. The imagery of their judgments reflected the depth and intensity of their involvement. It is important to bear in mind the profoundly subjective nature of these judgments.

Mainly, the viewers liked or disliked the clinical demonstration. There was a sharp polarization of feeling to two extremes. They said of me, for example: "brilliant," a "master clinician," an "unbelievable genius." Or they backed away, were revolted, frightened, or sometimes too upset even to formulate an opinion. Or they indicted me for being "exhibitionistic," "omnipotent," "overaggressive," "too involved"; or they said that I blatantly "took over" and "brainwashed" the family, that I cued the members to give me the answers I was looking for, that I toyed manipulatively with the family, that I injected a note of humor at the family's expense. This is but a small sampling of the range of responses. But whatever the nature of the judgments, there was one universal feature: all the viewers seemed roused and excited by the experience.

Through the years I examined my use of self in family therapy to try to discover the essence of what I did to stir these reactions. For years I reviewed over and over filmed records of my treatment sessions and, more important, listened "with the third ear" to those who observed my family interviews, to the evaluative comments of my close associates at The Family Mental Health Clinic, The Family Institute, and the Departments of Psychiatry at Columbia University and at Albert Einstein Medical College. But this was not enough. Putting the understandings of my colleagues and myself together, we still ended up with an explanation that was fragmentary and incomplete. Certainly a personal style was involved, but within this was a core of solid, verifiable, teachable principles. Our understanding was correct as far as it went, but it just did not go far enough. Some part of the essence of family therapy still eluded us.

Turning the problem over in my head again and again, I asked myself why I was so touchy about the intense reactions to my personal therapeutic style. By degrees I succeeded in loosening up my personal defensiveness. I began to see the problem in a different light. Maybe I should temporarily shelve the question of teachable principles and take a second look at my "art."

In so doing, I made a discovery that at first glance seemed trivial and yet on closer inspection turned out to be an important clue. I found, for example, that I regularly did several things in my therapeutic use of self which were almost never talked about: my use of first names in a family interview, my use of a personal brand of humor, and my promotion of mutual pleasure in the encounter. When I looked back on the contents of my book, *Treating the Troubled Family* (Basic Books, 1966), I woke up to a curious omission. In all the clinical illustrations I freely addressed family members by their first names; in every interview, barring none, I made ample use of a touch of humor; I sought to enjoy the interview and have the family enjoy it with me. And yet, strangely enough, in my chapter, "Functions of a Family Therapist," I made no explicit mention whatever of these approaches. When I turned back to previously published articles, I found again the same strange omissions. Why? I could come to only one conclusion. My long conditioning as a psychoanalyst, like that of my colleagues, involved a stricture against certain qualities of informality and intimacy with patients. Closeness of this kind was taboo. The psychoanalytic prohibition had the effect of closing off free and open discussion of this qestion. As a family therapist, I did some things that threw off the shackles of formal, constrained conduct and fostered an unusual depth of "intouchness," intimacy, openness, and honesty. And yet none of us talked about it. Are we as trained psychoanalysts ashamed and made anxious by exposure of "personality," by our countertransference? Is it this quality above all else that is so provocative of the response of shock among the viewers?

With this as a clue, I examined therapeutic process under a new light. If there are indeed teachable principles, they may in fact be inextricably intertwined with the personal performance of a given therapist. If we are to succeed in winnowing out the essence of family therapeutic process, the challenge is to glimpse and capture that essence through an appreciation of personal art and style.

For this effort, I got an added spur from the sociologist Norman Bell. He tossed out a challenge that was especially meaningful to me: "After seeing a number of your movies on family therapy, I came out of the experience feeling cheated. I feel the need for the therapist to explain himself, what he did, how, when and why, with a particular family." Again and again I try to do this but I am never sure that I succeed.

The art of family therapy is, in fact, a unique, spontaneous expression of self in the therapeutic role. It is the orchestration through the therapist's personality of all the partial themes of intervention: induction of rapport, channeling of communication, catalyzing of emotional expression, nourishment of intimacy, honest sharing, support, confrontation, reduction of conflict and anxiety, interpretation and realignment of the image of self and others in family interaction. All of these are seen as part of a symphonic theme led and integrated by the therapist's baton. It is the special combination and fit between the sounds of family members and the talent of therapist as conductor that shapes the outcome. The personal equation is a prepotent factor. Each therapist is his own conductor, different from every other. There is no imitiating the unique manner in which a given conductor wields his baton. It is within the art and skill of each therapist's performance that we may discern the expression and integration of the basic principles of family therapy.

By way of illustration, let us take a closer look at several aspects of my personal style of family therapy. I refer here specifically to the use of first names, the injection of humor, the pleasure of the experience, and the tossing into the hopper of issues of ethical choice and value orientation.

The tactic of moving into the interview addressing people by their first names is approached in various ways. Depending on the moods and receptivity of the members of the family, I may do this at the outset or I may edge up on it through preliminary channels of contact and communication, such as the manner of shaking hands and closing up the sitting arrangements, and through other subtle expressions of "intouchness." Addressing family members, including the parents, by their given names is an invitation to intimacy—"I'd like to come closer." Depending on my sense of the emotional temperature, sometimes I ask, "May I?" or, "Is it all right?" or I may move ahead to call them by their given names without asking. In so doing, I communicate below the level of words my own urge for their closeness, my own desire that they call me by my given name, if and when they become ready for this degree of intimacy. Occasionally family members may feel this as an insincere gesture, an intrusion, a ploy, or a way of talking down. However, with a quick series of soundings out of my feeling and attitude, the naturalness and warmth of this form of intimacy strike home. Very soon members of the family indicate that they prefer it that way. It relieves the air of anything formal, stiff, and excessively separate.

But this approach to intimacy must be understood in a wider context. It is part of a more general mood and setting influenced by the therapist's example, his own open, easy, spontaneous self-disclosure. In the last analysis, the quality of emotional interchange and the evolving relationships are determined by a delicate shifting balance between the desire for closeness and the fear and suspicion of possible injury in an unguarded exposure. The goal is to catalyze a shift away from fear and suspicion and toward trust and increasing warmth and intimacy.

The felt danger of personal exposure is softened by the sparking of hope and expectation of new satisfactions in family interchange. The sense of threat is diluted by a gentle sprinkling of humor. Nothing releases like a hearty laugh. It eases the jangled nerves of everyone, including the therapist. It releases tension, gives pleasure, enhances rapport, rewards openness and honesty, facilitates the uncovering of relevant emotions, and heightens the efficacy of the coping. The family is reaching me and I am reaching the family; I feel a deep zest in the closeness of the connection. It does my heart good.

CHAPTER 35

Non-verbal Cues and Reenactment of Conflict in Family Therapy

When an entire family is seen together in therapy, there is the opportunity to observe a reenactment of the specific conflict which has brought the family to treatment (1). This enactment of conflict is attributable to many factors, among which is the family's need to demonstrate their emotional turmoil to the therapist in order to gain his help in resolving the family neurosis. However, the family conflict also has a static, perseverative quality which leads to its continuance in all sorts of situations and and out of treatment. One of the major advantages of family therapy is the opportunity afforded the therapist to observe and intervene in these perseverative enactments *in situ,* on the very scene of battle.

Within any given session it is often difficult to detect the specific origins of a particular conflict enactment at the very moment it is occurring. These origins are doubtless of a multidimensional sort, but among them the significance of non-verbal cues has been noted with increasing frequency (5, 9). As a matter of fact, the significance of such subtleties of non-verbal communication as tonal inflections and fleeting facial expressions has long been noted as characteristic of the psychoanalytic situation (8, 10, 11), but only now are these data being explored in a systematic, scientific fashion. The development of such scientific recording devices as the tape recorder and motion picture camera has undoubtedly been a major factor in the study of fleeting aspects of non-verbal expressions. The scientific description of the startle pattern (6) and its diagnostic significance was made possible by examination of individual frames of motion picture recording.

The traditional role of the psychotherapist has tended to include relatively less attention to these non-verbal behaviors than to the verbal content that is communicated. Moreover, the specific relationships between non-verbal cues and the psychodynamics of family conflict have not yet been demonstrated in detail with illus-

Reprinted with permission from *Family Process,* March 1965, Vol. 4, No. 1, 133-162.

This paper was co-authored with Murray H. Sherman, Sanford N. Sherman, and Celia Mitchell.

trative case material. The problems of this type of study have been explored from the standpoints of kinesics (4) and of paralinguistic analysis (7), but our intent here is to deal with more molar cues that could be detected in ordinary therapeutic interaction, were the therapist to pay particular heed to these minute behavioral expressions.

The basic therapeutic data are exceedingly hard come by. It is only too well known that a therapist's own report of his sessions will often omit much of the most vital interaction, even where there is a sincere effort to communicate this material. Tape recordings lose much of the subtle interaction and communication of therapy, and non-verbal cues are often totally missed in taped transcriptions. Sound films are undoubtedly the most satisfactory form of recording of both verbal and non-verbal behavior, despite the almost prohibitive expense involved. Even these sound films require transcription if they are to be scientifically analyzed, and the transcription, if conscientiously done, is a most time-consuming task.

One gets the impression that something is transpiring in the therapeutic process which has almost its own resistance to deeper understanding. There seems to be an exceedingly subtle intercommunication that transpires at a very basic and even primitive level, and this process somehow eludes us when we try to translate it into verbal form. An almost transcendent, secretive quality becomes attached to the subtleties of a therapeutic relationship, which defies even the most searching and strenuous efforts at explicit description. It seems likely that non-verbal cues do play a most significant role in this tenuous process and a detailed investigation of their functions in the reenactment of family conflict may cast some light upon the more general problem of therapeutic communication.

THE B. FAMILY

It was decided to investigate a filmed sample of non-verbal behavior as this emerged within the context of family therapy. We were interested both in the therapeutic use that could be made of non-verbal behavior and also in the specific forms in which this behavior reflected the total family conflict.

The B. family was chosen for this investigation because a preliminary viewing of a sound film of one of their family therapy sessions indicated a plentitude of non-verbal behavior.

The B. family consisted of Mr. Jack B., aged 52, whose occupation was that of half-owner of a hardware business;[1] Mrs. Joan B., aged 43 and a school teacher; Sam, aged 16; and Ann, aged 10. The incident precipitating this family's coming to the clinic occurred about two months prior to the filmed session. Ann had become very angry and excited and had gone into a temper tantrum in which she had taken a large knife and threatened Sam with it. Sam was overcome by a fit of fear, ran into his parents' bedroom to tell them what was happening and had then apparently collapsed on the bed in a cold, perspiring faint.

This incident was the culmination of a long series of conflicts in which Ann had continually intimidated and manipulated the entire family. Mrs. B. was almost totally unable to discipline Ann and would resort to various manipulative strategems to make her eat or behave as she should; these strategems were admittedly ineffective. Mrs. B. would then make periodic efforts to draw up lists of preemptory rules of family behavior, which were soon ignored. Mrs. B. attributed her inability to discipline Ann to her relationship with her own mother, whom she described as overbearing, overprotective and highly demanding. Mrs. B.'s own father was described as passive and ineffectual; she called him a "horror," a term which she also applied to Sam as a difficult infant.

Sam's relation with his mother was a highly ambivalent and inconsistent one. Mrs. B. was overly solicitous about Sam's health and he would resent this and withdraw from it. On the other hand, when Mrs. B. got angry with Sam, he would become very disturbed, would reassure his mother that he loved her very much and plead that she not be angry with him.

Mr. B.'s parents had been divorced when he was seven, and he had lived with his mother who tried to encourage him to be "independent." In his own marriage Mr. B.'s work often kept him away overnight, and he generally took a passive and unassertive role. A particular in-

[1]Names and other identifying data have been disguised.

cident well illustrates the lines of control and interaction in this family. Ann had become angry with Sam and wanted to poke him in retaliation for something he had done. She asked her parents each to hold one of Sam's arms so she could poke him. Mr. B. refused to do this but stood by as Mrs. B. held both of Sam's arms, and Ann obtained her revenge.

For several years prior to coming to therapy at the agency, Mrs. B. had had a severe case of torticollis and had consulted a number of psychiatrists and other medical specialists. She had finally been cured by massive injections (nature undetermined) and used this as evidence that there had been no psychological meaning to the symptom. Sam's symptomatic picture included a bizarre masturbatory ritual in which he would telephone hospitals and ask them for information on how to feed a resistant infant. Sam would provoke his informant into telling him to use force if necessary, and this was highly exciting to him.

There is an interesting confluence of symptoms among the three generations. Mrs. B.'s own mother had had the habit of continually passing wind. Mrs. B.'s belching, as will be evident in the session below, was a highly significant aspect of her relationship to her husband. Sam, when emotionally disturbed, was prone to vomit. All three individuals apparently converted their aggression into an involuntary eruption through a bodily orifice.

The B. family was seen in family therapy by a caseworker over a period of one year and there were also periodic interviews (eight) by Dr. A. Ann's behavior became much improved. She was more controlled and the temper tantrums receded. Mrs. B.'s preoccupation with Ann's eating habits also receded but was replaced by an obsession with her school work. On one occasion Mrs. B. so annoyed Ann by inquiring whether she had done her homework that Ann deliberately tore it to shreds before her mother's eyes.

There was some active inquiry and handling of the sexual relationship between Mr. and Mrs. B. Mr. B. complained that his wife was not active enough in sex and said that he felt certain wives could learn a good deal from some prostitutes, whom he had known before marriage. Mrs. B. complained that her husband was an inadequate lover and did not satisfy her. She said that his demands, if she acceded to them, would make sex much too mechanical for her. During the course of therapy Mr. B. became more active in sex, but there was not a great deal of improvement.

Family therapy was hindered by a number of resistances which developed. When anger was expressed by the children during the sessions, Mrs. B. felt that this was very bad because it was just what she was coming to therapy to prevent. Mr. B. objected to the explicitness of sexual discussion. Various family members would become ill, which prevented the family's being seen together. There were also fee difficulties; the parents felt the fee was too high and they were frequently behind in payments. Nevertheless, despite all these difficulties, it was felt that therapy had made certain significant gains and that much had been accomplished in family understanding and improved relationships.

A FAMILY THERAPY SESSION

In order to develop the accompanying transcript of a sound film of family therapy, a tape recording was made from which the dialogue was taken. Then the film itself was watched approximately one dozen times to fill in the visual and other contexts. Many minute aspects of family communication, such as subtle facial expressions and small bodily movements, have nevertheless been lost, despite considerable effort to include some of the most essential and noticeable ones. One wonders whether the return from such effort merely to transcribe and communicate yields a commensurate reward. On the other hand, the very difficulty of this task leads one to believe that a special secret must somehow be buried in these mountains of words and gestures.

TRANSCRIPT OF SOUND FILM

1. Dr.: Jack, you heaved a sigh as you sat down.
2. Mr. B.: Just physical, not mental.
3. Dr.: Whom are you kidding?
4. Mr. B.: Kidding no one.
5. Dr.: (warningly) Jack!
6. Mr. B.: I'm tired because I put in a full day.
7. Dr.: Well, I'm tired every day. When I

sigh, it's never purely physical.

8. MR. B.: Really?
9. DR.: Yes. What's the matter?
10. MR. B.: Nothing. Really.
11. SAM: (laughs)
12. DR.: Your own son doesn't believe that.
13. MR. B.: Well, I mean nothing, nothing caused me to sigh specially today, or tonight.
14. DR.: Well, maybe it isn't so special, but—uh—How about it, Sam?
15. SAM: (shakes head no)
16. DR.: You wouldn't know? All of a sudden you put on a poker face. You do it very knowingly.
17. MR. B.: (laughs)
18. SAM: I really don't know.
19. DR.: Well, do you know anything about your Pop?
20. SAM: Yeah.
21. DR.: What do you know about him?
22. SAM: Well, I don't know except that I know something about him.
23. DR.: Well, let's hear.
24. SAM: Well, I (laughs nervously)—he's a man.
25. DR.: He's a man?
26. MR. B.: (makes beckoning gesture with his hand to Sam) Come on, come on, come on. Dr. A. wants some information from you.
27. SAM: All right, I'll tell you, Dr. A.
28. DR.: Your father uses his hand (referring to beckoning gesture), you know. Not like mother. She has another gesture. Give, give, give (demonstrates). Mother's gesture is this (shows). Pop's gesture is give. (Father laughing loudly all this while.)
29. SAM: I don't have much to say about Dad. He's just a normal man. He's my father. He's a good guy, that's all.
30. MRS. B.: May I make a suggestion?
31. DR.: What's your suggestion?
32. MRS. B.: Well, I have been keeping an anecdotal record of the time that has elapsed since we were here. Not every minute of the time, but anything that I think is important enough to relate. Now, I think this is good for many reasons. When you read, you sort of get a better view of things, and if you'd like me to read it, I will. If you feel you'd rather ask questions, you can. But—uh—that's my suggestion.
33. DR.: Well, I'm glad you called my attention to that notebook that's in your lap. You come armed with a notebook, a record.
34. MRS. B.: I've been doing this in school, as a matter of fact.
35. DR.: I see.
36. MRS. B.: And I've been keeping this record since last week, because I think it's very important. You forget very quickly what people say and how they say it, unless you write it down right away. Now, this is something that I do for children in the class that I have to have their case histories. And I think it's a wonderful idea.
37. DR.: Well now, what have you there? A case history on your whole family?
38. MRS. B.: Yes.
39. DR.: Marvelous! How long is it?
40. MRS. B.: It's not that long. I just started it. (Jack starts to read over Joan's shoulder.) There's something here that you didn't see last night.
41. MR. B.: Oh, you cheated!
42. MRS. B.: I didn't cheat. I just didn't tell you there was more to it, that's all. You read the front of the book, but—
43. MR. B.: That's cheating.
44. MRS. B.: No, it isn't. So, if you would like me to read it. It's sort of a little resume of my thinking in the last week. I was quite disturbed last week in the middle of the week, very disturbed. So much so that on the last day of school, a little girl in my class gave me a pin, a four leaf clover pin. Now I never told this little girl anything. She said, "Maybe this will change your luck." So I was very disturbed and that's what made me do this. I felt it's better to come with exact words and phrases rather than remembering things.
45. DR.: Now—uh—is this a four leaf clover? Is that what you've got?
46. MRS. B.: Yes.
47. DR.: That change your luck?
48. MRS. B.: No, not yet it hasn't, but—
49. DR.: Have you got it on you?
50. MRS. B.: No. I didn't wear it tonight but it was very sweet and I, I cried for a little while after she left, because I was so—
51. (Mr. B. picks at his finger and Dr. notices.)
52. DR.: Your finger hurting?
53. MR. B.: No, I was—had a little hangnail.
54. MRS. B.: That's a nervous ailment of his. He picks at his feet, at a rash there and he

picks at his fingers. That's a nervous ailment of *his*.

55. SAM: Pretty disgusting (laughs amusedly).
56. DR.: Pretty disgusting, is it?
57. SAM: (to mother) What about your nervous habits?
58. MRS. B.: I have quite a few.
59. SAM: Like sitting and—never mind. Quite a few.
60. MRS. B.: I said I have a few.
61. SAM: Yeah, and they're pretty bad, because when I—
62. DR.: Are you sore at mother because she's picking pieces out of Papa's uh—
63. SAM: Yeah.
64. DR.: Fingers?
65. SAM: Yeah; so what? So he has nervous habits. So don't we all?
66. DR.: What kind of a piece would you pick, like to pick out of Mama?
67. SAM: Huh? She has some pretty disgusting habits.
68. DR.: Well, what are they?
69. MRS. B.: I'll tell you what they are.
70. DR.: Now wait a minute. Sam is talking.
71. SAM: Uh—(laughs nervously).
72. MRS. B.: Well, Sam, you don't have to be bashful. This is to give information. You don't have to be—
73. DR.: He's not bashful.
74. MRS. B.: —embarrassed, in my mind.
75. DR.: Hold it, hold it, hold it. Now, Sam.
76. SAM: I don't know how to put it, if you want the truth.
77. MRS. B.: That's why I was going to put it for you.
78. SAM: Yeah, well I, maybe she has some better words for the thing.
79. DR.: No, no, no, no, now. This is, is that same old give, Sam, here to me (repeat father's gesture as above), the same old insincere ritual, you first Alphonse. Let's not be scared around these here parts. You started something. Finish it.
80. SAM: Mom—uh—she belches.
81. DR.: She belches.
82. SAM: Consistently, repeatedly, and disgustingly.
83. MRS. B.: That's right. I swallow air. I went to a doctor many years ago about it. It's a nervous habit, and when I'm very upset, evidently I swallow—
84. SAM: Why were you so upset tonight?
85. MRS. B.: Tonight was not for that, Sam.
86. DR.: Sam, when Mama belches, whom does she, whose face does she belch into?
87. MR. B.: Mine mostly.
88. SAM: His! (laughing and pointing vigorously to father)
89. DR.: His. (all laugh)
90. MR. B.: Mine, if you like, or anybody else who happens to be around.
91. SAM: Only with her choice friends she refrains (sic) herself. Somehow she doesn't swallow air when her good friends are around, her high class friends (sarcastically).
92. MRS. B.: That's right. It's not high class, Sam.
93. SAM.: Yes, it is.
94. MRS. B.: No, I wouldn't call it high class.
95. SAM: But you manage not to swallow air—
96. MRS. B.: Well, let me read what's in here (picks up notebook). Maybe this will give you a better idea—
97. DR.: Well, one moment now. Is that the only—
98. SAM: That's about the worst habit she has.
99. DR.: —habit, in your eyes?
100. SAM: Yeah, that's about the worst of it.
101. DR.: That's the worst? No others?
102. SAM: (giggles) No, I haven't got the nerve.
103. DR.: Come on, come on.
104. SAM: No, no, really. That's about all.
105. MRS. B.: Now I don't know what else he has reference to.
106. DR.: You know you're only playing a game now. That isn't fair.
107. SAM: I'm sorry. I'm not going to say anything else.
108. DR.: Now he's tensing up because he knows all about Mama's habits.
109. SAM: Then ask him (points to father, laughing embarrassedly).
110. DR.: No, I want to ask you first. You started this.
111. SAM: I'm sorry. I'm not going to tell you.
112. DR.: (perceiving Ann smiling broadly) Ann, Ann's got a trick up her sleeve, too.
113. SAM: I can't tell you that, Dr.
114. DR.: Oh, come on.
115. SAM: I'm sorry, I can't.
116. MR. B.: He doesn't want to embarrass his mother.
117. MRS. B.: I don't know what he has refer-

ence to so I don't—

118. DR.: You're a teaser, Sam—

119. SAM: I'm sorry, I—

120. DR.: — a teaser.

121. SAM: I can't.

122. DR.: You start to begin to commence to say something about your Ma. You make a big promise and all of a sudden you fade out. That's not cricket.

123. SAM: No, well, that's about the worst thing.

124. DR.: I know your Ma is impatient. She's looking at her—

125. MRS. B.: No, I was just—

126. DR.: —at her record.

127. MRS. B.: No, that's not impatience. I was just—looking at it (the notebook). But he's not saying anything so I've nothing to listen to.

128. SAM: No, I'll tell you the truth. I really don't have anything—I'm not going to say.

129. MR. B.: Might as well ask somebody else.

130. DR.: If you don't say, it's going to come out in the wash anyway.

131. SAM: So let it come out.

132. DR.: It might as well come out where it started.

133. SAM: I'm sorry. I will not do it (emphatically)!

134. DR.: (again noticing Ann) Ann, do you want to speak up ahead of Pop?

135. MR. B.: Come on, Ann.

136. (Ann hides head in her arms. Sam puts his arm around Ann in a friendly way and whispers to her.)

137. MRS. B.: Oh, Look now, you're wasting—

138. SAM: Come on, Ann.

139. ANN: I'm finished. Mommy's a nut. Daddy's a nut.

140. SAM: I'll say they are!

141. DR.: Always belching in pop's face.

142. (Mrs. B. and Ann laugh.)

143. DR.: Oh, Mom likes that! look at her giggle!

144. MRS. B.: You know why I'm giggling?

145. DR.: Why?

146. MRS. B.: I asked Jack as a favor to me, when I realized that I was going to do this, that he should keep some kind of a record of our relationship. I feel there's lots to be desired in it. Maybe if we can get it down on paper, you can help us with it. So—he—did do it for several days. Last night, I said, "*Please* write that thing for me. Because I want to know." I knew I had written it down. So he did write it down. And there were several things he wrote that were mostly about things that I don't care to discuss in front of the children. However, one of the things was about the belching. And I giggled because I refuse to take it seriously. I know it's nothing terrible. It's, it's a nervousness. And so I, I giggle. Now as a result of that giggling, evidently, it put him in a different frame of mind. And after he said he wouldn't let me see his paper until after I let him read what I had written. Well, some of this stuff is pretty — rugged. I mean, it's, it's what I think and it's not complimentary in some respects. But he read it and for the first time since we're married, which is twenty years, he *didn't* get—

147. MR. B.: More, dear.

148. MRS. B.: All right, it's a little more than twenty. He didn't get angry. And I can honestly say that's the first time that he ever acted like the kind of man I hoped he was. (Father sighs deeply.) He didn't get angry with, with it—at this notebook. Well, of course he didn't—

149. DR.: Oh, my, my. That's quite a bit of progress. Last week, you said he wasn't no man at all.

150. MRS. B.: Most of the time he, he does not react the way I would like him to. I can honestly say this is the first time he acted the way I would like him to and the way I would expect him to, the first time since we're married. It was a pleasure to see him *not* get angry at something that was the truth, and he, and it was, there was a sense of humor in it, and it was just lovely. And I, I would appreciate so much—

151. DR.: You mean Jack has a temper with you?

152. MRS. B.: Yes; he's either too good or too bad.

153. DR.: Too good or too bad. (Notices Jack protruding his tongue.) Look at his tongue.

154. MRS. B.: He can be a son of a bee or he can be an angel. And he doesn't always follow the middle course. Either he's too easy to get along with or for nothing he'll—

155. DR.: I asked you to look at his tongue.

156. MRS. B.: Well, I didn't see his tongue.

157. DR.: Why don't you look?
158. MRS. B.: Well, I was talking to you so I was looking at you.
159. DR.: Why do you have eyes for me only? What about Jack?
160. MRS. B.: Well, I think that when you talk to somebody, you should look at him, which is something he doesn't do. Which I have criticized—
161. MR. B.: (noting Mrs. B.'s pointing finger) Did you see that finger go? (laughs loudly)
162. MRS. B.: Which is something I have criticized him for many times. I think—
163. DR.: Well, what did you want to talk about that he had his tongue in a very special position?
164. ANN: (gestures) Like this.
165. MRS. B.: Well, I don't know why. I don't know why at all. He was laughing to himself. I don't know why.
166. DR.: (to Jack) Did you see what happened?
167. MR. B.: No, no. I would really appreciate it if you'd tell me.
168. DR.: (to Ann) How do you feel about that tongue of his?
169. ANN: I though it was funny.
170. DR.: (to Jack) What were you about to do with your tongue?
171. SAM: What a family!
172. MR. B.: It happens that my putting my tongue out is a habit (all laugh). It's a habit of maybe forty or forty-five years. Whenever I write, I can just sign my name, my tongue will be out.
173. DR.: You mean you stick your tongue out whenever you concentrate?
174. MR. B.: Whenever I do anything—
175. ANN: I know something I could say, but Sam would kill me and so would my father, so I can't.
176. MRS. B.: Nobody is going to kill you, Ann.
177. MR. B.: Nobody will kill you.
178. ANN: Sam will, Sam will.
179. MRS. B.: Sam won't kill you either. Nobody kills around here.
180. DR.: All right, spit it out, Ann. Let's hear.
181. MRS. B.: Come on, Ann.
182. ANN: Sam, Sam—
183. DR.: What were you going to say?
184. MRS. B.: Go ahead.
185. (Sam turns completely away from group, so that his back is turned to the camera and to the group members. He maintains this position for most of the remainder of this session, until the interaction noted in items 334 through 340.)
186. ANN: Today, he had a date with a girl and he locked the door, and when I was at the door, he said, "You're going to be in so much trouble!" And I think he likes the girl more than he does me, because whenever I have a date, he, I never lock the door. When I, I had to get something in the kitchen—and he, and it was locked when I—knocked. And he said, "I have to tell her that I don't like her." And then I found out that he was lying about that. And I don't think it's right to lock the door—because—Renee and Helen, we had to go around the back way and he wouldn't let us in.
187. DR.: Shows what your brother, Sam, did to you.
188. MRS. B.: That's another thing about Sam. He, he's like his father in that respect. He's either too good or too bad. Either he's an angel and, and a *doll;* or, for no reason at all, he'll blow his top and simply not be fit to live with.
189. DR.: (notices Ann grinning, making faces, and bidding for attention) See, as you were concentrating, you didn't see what Ann was doing with *her* top.
190. ANN: (giggles)
191. MRS. B.: Now, I hope Sam isn't angry after this session.
192. MR. B.: I was going to say that in my opinion, this is the case with most people, although Joan seems to think that this is a problem that we have a corner of the market on. I think that most people tend to go to either of two extremes. I think it's the unusual person who steers a steady, middle-of-the-road course constantly. I haven't yet met that person.
193. MRS. B.: Well, I think that's true, "constantly." But to get unduly upset over *nothing*, and, raise the roof, and get really nasty and mean—
194. DR.: How does he do that?
195. MRS. B.: Well, if I read these notes, you'll know how he does it. Otherwise, I can't really describe it to you, my inner feelings. That's the only way—
196. DR.: Before you read your notes now, I'd

just like to ask Jack one question. When you belch in Jack's face—

197. MRS. B.: (interrupting) Well, I don't deliberately do that.

198. DR.: Excuse me.

199. MRS. B.: I don't deliberately do that.

200. DR.: How does, how does it feel?

201. MR. B.: Well, her belching does something to me that, that I just can't explain, with as good a command of English that I think I do have. It is just like waving a red flag in front of my face. And has for years to the point where we went to doctors in Woodmere and with no satisfaction.

202. ANN: (interrupting) Sam—

203. MR. B.: And the thing that aggravates me more than anything is that with certain company, although she pleads that this is uncontrollable, and that she has no control over it, with certain company in the house, she can control it beautifully.

204. DR.: Well, now, when was the last time she belched in your face?

205. MR. B.: Last night.

206. MRS. B.: No, no, no.

207. MR. B.: Please don't say "no," because you belched—

208. MRS. B.: (interrupting) Most of the time—

209. MR. B.: —when I—The minute she gets into bed, she starts belching like mad.

210. DR.: In bed?

211. MR. B.: Yes.

212. MRS. B.: Yes, I think it's psychological.

213. MR. B.: Yes, the minute she gets into bed. Yes.

214. MRS. B.: I really think there is something psychological. I'm not feeling now. When I lie down, I begin to swallow air. I don't know why. And there are some times I don't do it, but on the whole, when I—

215. (Sam turns to Ann while his mother is talking. He smiles with Ann, puts his arm around her, whispers something, and then again turns away from group.)

216. ANN: (interrupting) Excuse me, but just now he—

217. MRS. B.: All right (trying to resume).

218. ANN: He said, "If you tell about that lipstick mark, I'll kill you!"

219. MR. B.: Oh, stop it now!

220. MRS. B.: Sam, you're being as silly as, as I would expect you to be now.

221. ANN: I'm going to bring it out.

222. DR.: As soon as I begin concentrating on the love life between Ma and Pa, you two kids start cutting up.

223. SAM: I'm sorry, but I don't like it one bit. (still turned away from group)

224. ANN: (raises hand) He—

225. DR.: (to Sam) Would you rather talk about your love life?

226. SAM: No. I'd rather talk about nobody's love life.

227. ANN: I'd like to say something.

228. DR.: Yes, Ann.

229. ANN: Well, he has a mark on his neck. And I was teasing him and saying it was lipstick from his girlfriend. And he said, "If you say that in front of Dr. A., I'll murder you." And I didn't like that—what he said.

230. MRS. B.: Sam has not got a sense of humor when it comes to things he's touchy about. He doesn't want to discuss his report card, which I said I would discuss tonight. And he said, "You'd better not, or else." And I think it's a very important thing to discuss.

231. DR.: Sam—

232. MRS. B.: (interrupting) Would you mind turning around and acting like a man?

233. MR. B.: Sam—

234. DR.: He's angry. It's—

235. MRS. B.: (interrupting) I can see he's angry at me, too, now.

236. (Ann whispers with her mother and changes places with her.)

237. MRS. B.: Now, please turn around. (Sam continues facing away.)

238. DR.: Now, we were—

239. MRS. B.: Yes.

240. DR.: —talking about his special date with his girlfriend and Ann felt *so alone*. Because, after all, Sam's your boyfriend, isn't he?

241. ANN: No.

242. DR.: No?

243. ANN: No. Never had one.

244. DR.: Is it bad? But Sam is also sore at me because he doesn't like it when—

245. ANN: (interrupting) He doesn't like it because—

246. DR.: —when we talk about, talk to Ma and Pa here about their love life. He doesn't like that at all. He wants to pretend like he knows nothing at all about their love life.

247. (Mother puts arm on Sam's shoulder and

tries to turn him back to group.)

248. MRS. B.: Will you—?

249. SAM: Stop touching me!

250. MRS. B.: Well, will you turn around and act like—

251. SAM: I don't feel like it.

252. MRS. B.: I know you don't feel like it, but turn around anyway.

253. SAM: (makes barely audible, objecting sound)

254. DR.: Sam, you're angry at me, not Ma.

255. SAM: No, I'm not angry at you. I'm angry at my sister and my mother.

256. ANN: Just because I told the truth.

257. SAM: Why don't you learn to shut up for a change?

258. ANN: Why don't you shut up?

259. DR.: Ann, when you changed seats, you wanted to get away from you brother. Are you angry at him?

260. ANN: Yes.

261. MRS. B.: You see—

262. DR.: (interrupting) You didn't like it when he had that girl in the apartment?

263. ANN: No.

264. DR.: What were you so sore about?

265. ANN: Because I had nothing to do. And I wanted to get something out of the kitchen, and he told me to go out.

266. DR.: Well, he wanted a little privacy with his girlfriend.

267. ANN: In a smooch.

268. DR.: Smooch. Well, what's wrong with a smooch?

269. MR. B.: What's wrong with that?

270. ANN: Because he had marks on his neck.

271. SAM: Will you shut up!

272. MRS. B.: Sam, you're acting so babyish.

273. SAM: Will you, will you, please, too.

274. DR.: Don't you think a guy like Sam can smooch a little bit with a girl, and get some lipstick on his neck.

275. ANN: (whispers) It's wrong.

276. DR.: What? It's wrong? It's bad?

277. ANN: (whisper) Yes.

278. DR.: The only thing I know that's bad about it is that he got the lipstick on his *neck*.

279. ANN: Yeah, so it's evidence.

280. DR.: Oh, you want to hang the man on evidence.

281. ANN: When we leave, he's going to murder me.

282. DR.: You're not going to smooch?

283. ANN: No.

284. DR.: What are you going to do?

285. ANN: Nothing.

286. MR. B.: What was that game you were playing at your dance, with a bottle in the middle of the room spinning around? Huh?

287. DR.: Anyhow, anyhow you two kids just—

288. ANN: I didn't get lipstick.

289. DR.: You two kids just pulled us right out of your parents' bed. We were in there in the double bed. Mom was belching in Pop's face and that's where you interrupted the story. Now, Joan, you say it's psychological.

290. MRS. B.: I felt—

291. DR.: The moment you go to bed with Jack—

292. MRS. B.: Not the moment. I wouldn't put it quite so—uh, like that. But I do—uh—begin to swallow air and I don't know why. I really don't. Now, maybe what I have written here will have some bearing on the subject.

293. DR.: Well, you can read that in just a moment. Seems you hurt Jack's feelings, torment him no end. He can't stand it when you belch in his face. Is that right?

294. MR. B.: Did you ever try, or think that you wanted to kiss a woman, and just when you're about to do it, have her belch in your face?

295. ANN: (giggles loudly)

296. DR.: I'm terribly sympathetic with you.

297. ANN.: (giggles again)

298. MR. B.: I mean—

299. DR.: It's really not what I would call kissing.

300. MR. B.: I mean—this is something!—Unless you wear a gask mask!

301. (Mrs. B. and Ann giggle together almost uncontrollably.)

302. DR.: Smells bad?

303. MR. B.: Blows your head to one side and it's really very unhealthy. And I just hope you never have, have the—

304. DR.: Exposure to gas?

305. (Mrs. B. and Ann continue to giggle, even louder now.)

306. MR. B.: Yes, specifically.

307. DR.: At the very moment you wanted to kiss her.

308. MR. B.: Well, you're afraid. I'm serious. I—

309. MRS. B.: Well, I think this is just part of an excuse on his part, really. Because I don't do it that often, or every night.
310. ANN: Just now!
311. MR. B.: You do it that often and you do it—
312. MRS. B.: Believe me when I tell you I don't. I, I cannot—it does not happen every night or anything like that. There are nights—
313. MR. B.: I didn't say it happened every night.
314. MRS. B.: All right.
315. MR. B.: There are nights when you will blame it on what you've eaten. There will be nights when you'll blame it on what you've drank. There'll be nights when you'll blame it on being upset. And other nights, you'll blame it on not sleeping enough the day before. (Joan and Ann are giggling.) And you will not always have an excuse, but the belching is there.
316. DR.: Ann, she just loves this. (Ann giggles.) Oh, boy, does she love it!
317. MR. B.: I'm not saying it was done deliberately, but—
318. DR.: (to Ann) You raised your hand. What did you want to say?
319. ANN: I want you to see the marks on Sam's neck.
320. SAM: Oh, never mind!
321. ANN: You want to stop it, I know. But I want to get him as mad as he got me today.
322. DR.: Now, just a minute. We're in your parents' bed. Can we stay there a few minutes? Or won't you let us? (brief silence) Now, (to Ann) suppose you move over again next to Sam, because we've got a problem between Ma and Pa here. We got to know what to do with this gas.
323. ANN: I don't want to go near him. (But she moves back, next to Sam.)
324. MRS. B.: Well, I'll leave out anything that has to do with bed. Because if it's going to disturb them, then I think it should be left out.
325. SAM: (angrily) It disturbs me.
326. DR.: I notice—
327. SAM: It's disturbed me for the last ten minutes.
328. DR.: I know that. You're mad at me. Because last week you said you didn't want to be here and we had to stop. Would you rather leave the room? (no answer) Sam?
329. SAM: I wouldn't like to answer that.
330. DR.: It isn't really that you don't know about this stuff. You just want to make out you don't know about this stuff.
331. (Mrs. B. whispers to Ann.)
332. SAM: (still turned aside from group) I don't want you to talk about it in my presence. I'm willing to talk about anything you want, which I think is wrong, if anyone else is present, but I don't want to be present.
333. MRS. B.: Well, why don't you leave?
334. SAM: All right, I'll leave. (Gets up and moves toward door.)
335. MRS. B.: It's perfectly all right. You can wait outside.
336. (All talk at once. Dr. restrains Sam as he is leaving.)
337. MR. B.: Wait a minute. Wait a minute. Let Dr. A. decide whether Sam is to leave or not.
338. MRS. B.: Well, I'm sorry. I thought—
339. DR.: Okay. Sit down.
340. (Sam then takes his chair and now faces group.)
341. DR.: If we come to a point, Sam, where it seems really sensible for both children to leave, I'll ask both of you to leave. If we want to deal with the *very* private part in the relations between Ma and Pa. But I want to know what bothers you so much.
342. SAM: It bothers me.
343. DR.: I know it bothers you.
344. SAM: I don't know why; it just bothers me.
345. ANN: I don't want to go out of here even at the private part because, because he's going to kill me if I go out.
346. DR.: (to Sam) Why so much?
347. SAM: I don't know; it just bothers me.
348. DR.: Yeah, but it would be very interesting to, to try to understand—
349. SAM: I really, I really wouldn't mind—
350. DR.: —why you act so terribly—
351. SAM: Well, I don't know. It just, it just bothers me.
352. DR.: You know that every Ma and Pa kiss.
353. SAM: I certainly do, but that—
354. DR.: So what's the trouble?
355. SAM.: It bothers me. I don't know what the trouble is. It bothers me.
356. DR.: Do you think, since we're all here together—

357. SAM: No, I'll tell you why it bothers me, if you want to know—

358. DR.: —that you make an attempt with us and see—

359. SAM: No, I'll tell you exactly why it bothers me. Because just like it bothers me that Ann is citing my private business, which I entrusted to her to just mind her own business. I didn't even ask her to, to bother me, when she, she insisted on bothering me. I told her something about, you know I wanted to tell the girl that I didn't like her, so she should please leave me alone. But what I do is my business and I think that what my parents do is their business. I may be very wrong. I—maybe it's everyone else's business. But I don't like it and I, I would rather not be present if you, or whoever wants it, wants to discuss it.

360. DR.: Now, Sam—

361. ANN: Just now—

362. DR.:—you don't want to be in on a thing that we talked about, the private love life between Ma and Pa, because if you are, you're afraid that Ma and Pa, and I, too, might invade your private love life.

363. SAM: No, that, that isn't possible, because I do not feel that way. Because *nobody* knows about my private love life except me. And—

364. ANN: And me.

365. SAM: —and that's the way it's going to stay as far as I'm concerned.

366. DR.: You insist on your privacy.

367. SAM: That's right.

368. DR.: Well, all right. Look, I can't keep you here. The door is wide open, but I would prefer, if you can tolerate it, that you stay with us, because I'm interested in helping the whole family. Even if it bothers you—

369. SAM: As long as you don't let Ann know, that's all I care about. As long as you know it annoys me.

370. DR.: —just to hear something.

371. SAM: Well, all right. Whatever you say, doctor.

372. DR.: Now, that's very good. Now, you let me know if it's too much for you because—

373. SAM: Well, as far as I'm concerned, the second it began was too much for me, because I don't like it. But if, as far as if you want me to stay—

374. DR.: I'd prefer it.

375. SAM: Okay. Whatever you say.

376. DR.: Good. (Ann raises her hand.) Ann.

377. ANN: Well, I, I don't want to go home tonight because he's gonna—

378. SAM: (in great exasperation) I, I—did I ever hit you or harm you?

379. ANN: Oh, today.

380. SAM: Well, I never did. So just be quiet.

381. DR.: Well, do you think he ought to kill you because of what you did, talking about his smooching?

382. ANN: Well, I—

383. DR.: do you think he ought to kill you?

384. ANN: Well, I saw those marks on his neck all right. Look if they're not lipstick.

385. DR.: Well, I already saw them. So what? What's terrible about that?

386. ANN: And telling me that story that he doesn't do anything. And—and—and he—and Sam was so mean to me. He, he, he, he was mad at me. He wanted me to call up my friend when he heard that she was coming, so that we wouldn't peek in on him, and so that he would have privacy with his girlfriend. And, and—

387. DR.: Well, now, don't you think when, when you're Sam's age, you'll want a little bit of privacy with your boyfriend?

388. ANN: Yeah, but if, if I had a little brother that had a date, and I wouldn't tell him to break the date.

389. MR. B.: Because he can't be sure you wouldn't invade his privacy. That's why.

390. DR.: Well, we'll, we'll settle this later, but he didn't do anything terrible.

391. ANN: And he locked the door. And when I knocked, he, he came out stamping his feet and yelling at me.

392. DR.: I think you're just jealous of that girl he had in there. That's all.

393. (Sam laughs)

394. ANN: I'm not jealous of that ugly girl.

395. DR.: Oh! She was ugly, was she?

396. ANN: Yes.

397. DR.: You mean you're better looking?

398. SAM: I'm going to smack her right in the face if she doesn't shut her mouth. Look (to father), do you mind if I leave?

399. MR. B.: No, I don't mind.

400. SAM: (gets up and starts to leave)

401. DR.: Wait a minute. (Sam leaves room.)

402. MRS. B.: You see, what Sam is doing now

is what he does at home, which I think is inexcusable. I feel that this child should have a great deal more control over himself than he has.

403. DR.: Well, you're a good preacher. I agree he ought to, but he doesn't. There are—
404. MRS. B.: That's right.
405. DR.: —reasons for that—
406. MRS. B.: I'm disturbed about what he just did.
407. DR.: —It's about Ann. (to Ann) You say his girl was ugly. Are you much prettier than she?
408. ANN: I think so.
409. DR.: Oh, you're pretty jealous of her.
410. ANN: I am *not* jealous of her.
411. DR.: Oh, you're teasing now.
412. ANN: I'm not.
413. DR.: You're a pretty good romancer yourself. Like to tease a lot, you and Sam both. Well, anyhow, let's be back to Ma and Pa. Is that all right with you, Ann? Hm? Well now, what did you do last night when she belched in your face? You wanted to kiss her and she belched.
414. MR. B.: No, I didn't want to kiss her. I merely said that that is my reaction. You asked what my reaction is and why I resent it, or why it upsets me, and I merely said it is very unhappy to kiss a woman and have her belch in your face.
415. DR.: Hmm.
416. MR. B.: Now, that doesn't mean that every time I attempt to kiss my wife she does it. But—it can happen more often than not.
417. DR.: Well, you know, you, you sound so reasonable right now that I don't believe a word that's coming out of your mouth. You're not that reasonable when you get belched at. Are you?
418. MR. B.: Well, it annoys me to the point where I have—
419. DR.: It does.
420. MR. B.: Yes. I have turned around and I have at times left the bed and gone inside and read the newspaper, and read a magazine or done other things. I've criticized her for it.
421. ANN: Can I please go out now?
422. DR.: Well we're going to bring Sam back in here in a little bit.
423. ANN: I'll come back if he starts to hit me.
424. DR.: You want to be with him?
425. ANN: No, I want to go out. (leaves room)
426. DR.: All right, folks, here's your chance to talk plain English. (From here the session continues without either of the children present.)

THE INTERACTION OF VERBAL AND NON-VERBAL BEHAVIOR AND ITS THERAPEUTIC SIGNIFICANCE

Within the context of our script there are certain relationships between verbal and non-verbal expressions which are evident. Perhaps the most obvious relationship is that of the inverse relationship between overt speech and non-verbal expression.

The verbal productivity of the group members is given in Table I. Three separate indices are used. The total number of words used gives a general indication of total verbal output. The number of items may indicate the proneness to intervene verbally or to respond to the therapeutic intervention. The number of items with twenty-five or more words may reveal the member's ability to hold the floor, so to speak, and the number of words in these twenty-five or more word items could indicate the member's tenacity in floor-holding.

Table I demonstrates that Mrs. B. is more

TABLE I

Verbal Productivity of Group Members

	Total Number of Words	Total Number of Items	No. of Items with 25 or More Words	No. of Words in 25 + Items
Dr. A.	1593	153	13	511
Mr. B.	679	52	7	370
Mrs. B.	1480	78	17	933
Sam	720	79	4	229
Ann	559	58	3	234

productive verbally than any other family member. Dr. A. does produce more words and also more items. His productivity, however, consists to a large extent of brief therapeutic interventions. Mrs. B. is the most determined "floor-holder" and produces the largest quantity of words in this capacity. These data do thus support the inverse relationship posited between verbal productivity and non-verbal expressiveness. Mrs. B., who makes the fewest gestures (see below), does most of the talking. Since we are mainly concerned with the specific non-verbal expressions in their clinical context, the data of Table I will not be analyzed in more detail.

Let us focus now upon the interaction between verbal and non-verbal behavior for each individual in the family, especially as this is responded to by the therapist. Look, for example, at Item 28, where Dr. A. reacts to the father's gesture rather than to Sam's remarks of the moment. Mr. B. responds to Dr. A.'s interpretation with a loud laugh, which in itself contains both release and defiance.

At Item 51 Mr. B. picks at his finger and the therapist immediately uses this gesture to open up an entire channel of inquiry. The whole subject of "disgusting habits" stems from this single observation, although the object of attention shifts from Mr. B. to Mrs. B. Mr. B. seems quite expert at averting inquiry, while Mrs. B. apparently takes on a scapegoat role (2) most readily at this point. Mrs. B.'s belching, another non-verbal expression, becomes the fulcrum about which the remainder of the session revolves.

Sam's attitude of provocative reticence is the channel through which the therapist is able to approach the parents' sexual conflict. It is of interest to note that the subject of belching and sex is again opened by a gesture interpretation (see Item 79). Sam exhibits two basic behavioral gestures in this session. The first is that of pointing vigorously to his father (Items 88 and 109). This gesture has both accusation and warmth, a kind of laughingly pointing to the perpetrator of the deed. It is as if Sam wants to turn the spotlight on the masked hero (or villain) and induce him to remove his disguise.

Sam's second gesture is that of turning entirely away from the group. He actually spends the major part of this session with his back turned to his family (Items 185 to 340) and soon after he does turn back to the group, Sam gets up and leaves the room. It is clear that Sam wants to remove his name entirely from the cast of players. And yet there is a kind of pretense to Sam's withdrawal. Despite his apparent wish to leave he both attracts attention and provokes anger by turning his back. Sam's very efforts to flee make him conspicuous and a topic of family concern.

In addition, Sam's apparent withdrawal has a hidden face. Although his verbal expressions to his sister are angry accusations, his behavioral gestures are warm and affectionate. He smiles warmly at Ann and puts his arm around her in a friendly fashion (Item 215). This behavior is quite contradictory to overt verbalization and would probably not be detected without motion picture recording.

Mr. B. has a number of small gestures. He sighs (Item 1), beckons with his hand (Item 28), picks at his finger (Item 51) and sticks out his tongue (Item 153). None of these escape the attention of his therapist. It is as if Mr. B. is trying to remain unnoticed, but is betrayed by involuntary cues, which demonstrate his instigatory role in the family circle.

Ann's gestures are not yet so definitively developed. She demonstrates with her whole body and by facial grimaces. Ann makes faces (Item 112), raises her hand (Item 134), hides her head (Item 136) or merely interrupts (Item 175). She cannot fully express herself in words and must take her part by actions and facial masks; this is primitive drama.

It is of interest that Mrs. B., who during this session reveals almost no behavioral gestures but sits rather stiffly and with frozen facial expression, speaks far more than any other family member. It is as if words take the place of actions that cannot come forth. Nevertheless, such suppressed activity has come out in the secret family life. Mrs. B. belches and is unable to control this involuntary betrayal of hostility. When the subject of belching is discussed, Mrs. B. and Ann go into uncontrollable giggles (Items 301, 305 and 315), which may demonstrate a conspiratorial alliance between the women of the family. In one sense Mrs. B.'s frozen face is itself a form of non-verbal expression, as is the entire gamut of facial expressions and mannerisms. Mrs. B. is the only family member who does not laugh on her own, and she communicates a sense of emotional isolation which may be related to her lack of non-verbal expressiveness.

There are numerous interpretations that can be made of the individual gestures and in fact the major therapeutic movement in this session arises from Dr. A.'s reflecting of gestures (Items 28 and 79) and calling attention to them. Thus Sam's frequent laughing may be a clue to his repressed aggression and inability to assert himself. Mr. B.'s sighs and movements with his tongue reveal his frustrated oral cravings.

Perhaps the most significant behavioral gestures are those of Sam putting his arm around Ann in a friendly way and whispering to her. His affectionate attitude in this behavior is quite at odds with the overt verbal communication, since the friendliness between the siblings is contradicted by their bitter quarreling. By analyzing the total behavioral sequence one can see that Sam provokes his sister into instigating his own aggression. He seems to provoke Ann's first contribution to the session (Items 136, 139: "Mommy's a nut; Daddy's a nut!") and then feels free to corroborate her comment (Item 140).

Later (Item 215) he smiles broadly at Ann, while threatening to kill her if she gives away his secret. Of course Ann complies with Sam's wish to interrupt the proceedings and, as Dr. A. notes, the children succeed in steering the conversation away from the topic of parental sex.

The most significant non-verbal behavior is that occurring outside this session: (1) Mrs. B.'s belching, (2) Mrs. B.'s notebook, and (3) Sam's lipstick mark. Therapeutic progress has already brought all of this behavior into treatment process.

NON-VERBAL CUES AND REENACTMENT OF CONFLICT

Let us turn from interpretations of gestures and behavior to some structural relationships within these data. It is our impression that the verbal communications among family members are *cued* by certain key gestures. On a relatively overt level we have seen how Sam cued Ann to interrupt an unwelcome topic of conversation. However, what about the gesture where Mrs. B. puts her hand on Sam's shoulder to persuade him to turn back to the family circle (Item 247)? This gesture, as seen on the film, seems more studied and artificial than spontaneous. Sam's immediate reaction is one of intense annoyance, but his only expression is a grunt. Dr. A. tries to clarify Sam's anger but then Ann again lends herself as a target of displaced hostility. In this sequence we can perceive (1) inadequate mothering, (2) reactive anger from Sam, and (3) Ann's provocative drawing of the anger from Mrs. B. to herself. The sequence thus illustrates the crucial traumatic interaction of this family in encapsulated miniature.

Let us examine Mr. B.'s tongue gesture (Item 153) and the behavior in which it is embedded. Mrs. B. and the therapist are engaged in an analysis of her husband's behavior, and she is expressing her pleasure at "the first time he ever acted like the kind of man I hoped he was." Mr. B. sighed deeply at this comment, and Mrs. B. went on to say that her pleasure arose mainly from her husband's lack of anger at reading what she had written about him. Dr. A. interprets Mr. B.'s manhood and his temper and then the tongue emerged.

It is clear that Mrs. B.'s concept of masculintiy is a significantly inverted one. Acceptable masculinity to her means compliance to her own wishes and a lack of aggression, but in twenty years of marriage she has been unable to get Mr. B. to accede completely to the passive role she would like to assign. Now Mrs. B. feels that therapy has succeeded in getting her husband to see the light. This was "the first time that he ever acted like the kind of man I hoped he was. He didn't get angry. . . ."

Mr. B.'s tongue gesture is soon mimicked by Ann, who also sticks her tongue out. When Dr. A. tries to clarify this interaction, Ann again evades him. She says merely that she thought her father was being funny, and then changes the subject back to Sam (Item 175). It is at this point that Sam turns his back on the family group.

Here we see a series of role inductions that starts with a conflict of role definition (masculine assertiveness) expressed by the mother, is transmuted into a gestural displacement by the father, which in turn is mimicked and sidetracked by the daughter, which then leads to the withdrawal from the family by the son. Again we have the total family conflict triggered and illustrated in miniature by a brief family exchange of non-verbal gestures.

Mr. B. is unable to take the appropriate role of assertive paternal responsibility. His wife expresses her dissatisfaction in terms of the fact that "he does not react the way I would like him to." Mr. B.'s inner conflict is unverbalized, but comes out in a gesture of his tongue. Ann mimics and makes fun of her father's plight, and then turns the spotlight on her brother. She verbalizes her father's latent rage and expresses it in terms of "Sam would kill me and so would my father." Sam is immediately provoked to leave the scene. *This sequence may well reproduce the conflict that originally brought the family to treatment*. That is, the daughter embodies the unexpressed but violent antagonisms of her parents. When she confronts her brother with this violence, he suddenly fades out of the scene. Does this not recall the incident in which Ann threatened Sam with a knife and he then fell in a dead faint in the parents' bedroom?

We could use these instances of *miniature reliving* of the family conflict as a way of conceptualizing one mode of effectiveness of family therapy. That is, family treatment offers the opportunity to mitigate the traumatic effects of conflict by re-inducing them in therapy and gaining insight into their origins and effects. In this process there is no doubt that the role of the family therapist is paramount and we turn now to an analysis of the therapist-family interactions.

It is clear that Dr. A. is the most active member of the group. He is continually trying to impart meaning to the behavior that takes place and he confronts each family member with the implications of the material that emerges. In addition, there is therapeutic effort to improve communication among the family and to permit each member to express opinions and feelings that have lain dormant. The subject of belching is a good example of behavior that has emerged for examination and discussion as a result of Dr. A.'s direct prompting and encouragement.

It is significant to note that Dr. A. is interested both in specific material that is being withheld and also in improving the overall efficiency of family communication. These two factors are interrelated, and it is a therapeutic challenge to attend simultaneously to both of them. The way in which this task is accomplished is well illustrated quite early in the session, at Item 28. Dr. A. had been prompting and encouraging Sam to express his feelings about his father. However, at the moment that Sam seems ready to reveal some material, the therapist interrupts to call attention to a gesture on Mr. B.'s part and he compares this to Mrs. B.'s gesture. This therapeutic maneuver brings Mrs B. into the session for the first time. She brings up the "anecdotal record" that she has been keeping, and this is the material that later in the session leads to her comments about the "kind of man" she wants her husband to be. Thus, by attending to both non-verbal cues and reluctance to be direct in expression, the therapist is able to uncover the subtle structure of family communication.

If we put all of this material together, we can see a unity to the family therapy session that emerges. There are various cues, verbal and non-verbal, that prompt each family member to reenact the traumas and conflicts that led the family to seek treatment. We see the family drama relived in miniature scenes, each of which reproduces the family conflict and the member's place in it. The therapist may then be seen as a kind of director or stage manager, who sets the scene and elicits the dialogue and stage action.

The factor that seems to lend most unity to the session is the total family interaction, which seems to have a quality of dramatic destiny. It is as though each family member is taking a role determined by an underlying plot design that has its own independence and intention. Thus, Mrs. B. comes into marriage and must then participate in a husband-wife team. She wants her husband to "act like a man," but her concept of this role has been conditioned by her father, who "was a horror." Soon there is a son, who also seems to Mrs. B. to be a "a horror," and later there is a daughter, who does not take the role her mother assigns to her and thus becomes a discipline problem.

Mr. B., who came from a divorced home, was raised to be "independent." Now, as a father, he tends to remain aloof from the battle. He assigns the role of disciplinarian to his wife, but at the same time mocks her (Item 161) in order to call attention away from his own role inadequacy (Item 153) and to undercut her authority, which he senses should belong to him.

Sam and Ann reproduce the provocative inconsistencies of their mother and father. Thus Sam incites Ann to antagonize him, and he in turn withdraws from the family in the same way his father abdicates his role. Ann similarly follows her mother in making fun of the masculine image of aggression ("Sam's going to kill me") but at the same time is overcome by her own aggressive impulses that she cannot control.

Non-verbal cues during this family session also illustrate a kind of hypocrisy on the part of the parents. Mr. and Mrs. B. have, on the surface of things, demanded certain forms of behavior from their children. Thus Mrs. B. asks Sam to act "like a man" and rejoin the family circle (Item 232), but her act of touching him has the actual effect of reinforcing his apparent rejection of the family (Items 247-253). Sam is quite "touchy" (Item 230) in his relationship with his mother, and here it is clear that her non-verbal behavior plays a direct role in instigating his touchiness. Mrs. B.'s words ask for one form of behavior but her actions elicit another. In some respects this contradiction resembles the "double-bind" situation, as described by Bateson and others (3, 12).

Mr. B., on the other hand, often makes perfunctory efforts to appear as the authority and disciplinarian of the family. Thus he insists that Sam respond to Dr. A.'s question (Item 26). However, at the same time that he makes this presumably authoritative demand, he simultaneously makes a hand gesture (Item 26) which betrays his own need to be given to rather than to direct the actions of others. When this need of Mr. B. is interpreted by the therapist (Item 28), Mr. B. laughs his acknowledgement and Sam merely continues his provocative withholding.

There is thus a power vacuum in this family, attributable to a mother with a distorted concept of masculinity and a father who partly fits the emasculated role assigned him and partly rebels from it. The vacuum plus the inconsistency of role prevent any true stability in the family structure. Perhaps, if Mr. B. were more totally accepting of the role his wife would assign him, the family would be more stable and perhaps also more distorted in their personality patterns. The nuclear problem might be resolved if Mr B. could assume the role of dominant and just father, but this does not seem within his present capability.

Before summarizing, some qualifying comments regarding the interpretative significance of non-verbal expressions should be mentioned. These non-verbal cues seem generally to derive from motivations which are less conscious than verbal expressions and they are therefore relatively less subject to deliberate control. Nevertheless, non-verbal cues may also to some extent be used in a defensive and perhaps deceptive sense. Sam responds to his mother's gesture of touching him on the shoulder (Item 247) as if it were a manipulative and controlling action, and this type of non-verbal behavior can be as contrived as any verbal expression. Non-verbal behavior may dramatize, deceive, disguise, express or betray; and each expression must be evaluated accordingly.

Also, the hypothesis positing an inverse relation between verbal and non-verbal expressions most likely obtains mainly in reference to verbalizations which are ineffective and fail to express true feeling. Non-verbal expressions must be judged in the context of the total family structure and alongside of verbal communications. They must not be judged solely in isolation but rather in the total context of which they are a part.

SUMMARY

(1) Non-verbal expressions tend to occur in inverse proportion to verbal expressions which are ineffective or fail to express true feeling. Family members who suppress their opinions tend to give vent to more non-verbal forms of expression than do family members who express themselves more fully in words.

(2) Non-verbal expressions may give clues to attitudes or traits which are directly contradictory to expressed verbal opinions. Thus, if the therapist is guided solely by verbalized responses, he may often miss the crux of what is occurring in therapy.

(3) The non-verbal expressions tend to act as hidden cues whereby the total family is prompted *continually to reenact miniature episodes of shared emotional conflict*. This reenactment of crucial role conflicts may have a cathartic effect and seem oriented toward discharge of accumulated tension. However, its perseverative quality reveals a helpless, repetitive aspect that requires therapeutic intervention.

(4) The therapist elicits suppressed opinions and attitudes of family members by direct chal-

lenge and confrontation of preconscious material. In addition, he may pay particular attention to non-verbal expressions, and by calling attention to them be able to reach and formulate some central aspects of the dramatic conflict of the family.

REFERENCES

1. ACKERMAN, N. W., *The Psychodynamics of Family Life*, New York, Basic Books, 1958.
2. ACKERMAN, N. W., "Prejudicial Scapegoating and Neutralizing Forces in the Family Group, with Special Reference to the Role of 'Family Healer'," *Internat. J. Soc. Psychiatry*, Congress Issue, 2:90, 1964.
3. BATESON, G., JACKSON, D. D., HALEY, J. and WEAKLAND, J., "Toward a Theory of Schizophrenia," *Behav. Sci., 1*, 251-264, 1956.
4. BIRDWHISTELL, R. L., "Kinesics Analysis in the Investigation of the Emotions," Address to the A.A.A.S., Dec. 1960, Mimeo.
5. EHRENWALD, J., *Neurosis in the Family and Patterns of Psychosocial Defense*, New York, Hoeber, 1963.
6. LANDIS, C. and HUNT, W. A., *The Startle Pattern*, New York, Farrar and Rinehart, 1939.
7. PITTENGER, R. E., HOCKETT, C. F. and DANEHY, J. J., *The First Five Minutes: A Sample of Microscopic Analysis*, Ithaca, New York, Paul Martineau, 1960.
8. REIK, T., *Listening with the Third Ear*, New York, Farrar, Straus & Co., 1948.
9. RUESCH, J., *Therapeutic Communication*, New York, Norton, 1961.
10. SCHROEDER, T., "Psycho-therapeutics: From Art to Science," *Psychoanal. Rev.*, 18, 37-56, 1931.
11. SHERMAN, M. H., "Peripheral Cues and the Invisible Countertransference," *Amer. J. Psychother.*, to be published.
12. WEAKLAND, J., "The 'Double-Bind' Hypothesis of Schizophrenia and Three-Party Interaction," in Jackson, D. D. (ed.) *The Etiology of Schizophrenia*, Basic Books, 1960, pp. 373-388.

CHAPTER 36

A Family Therapy Session

(An introduction by Sanford N. Sherman has been omitted. It explained the circumstances of the interview as a demonstration to a conference group at the New York Academy of Medicine.)

The family whose interview transcript follows is composed of mother, aged thirty-three; father, aged forty; Lora, aged ten; Alice, aged seven; and Martha, aged four. Neither the audience nor Dr. Ackerman was supplied with any history or summary of the four months of treatment the family had already undergone in the agency. Therapist and audience alike began with fresh, uninstructed minds, open to their own impressions and uninfluenced by the direction the therapy had already taken, the diagnosis or treatment aims of the family's caseworker. The parents had been asked to bring all their children. However, they brought only the two older daughters. More than circumstantial reasons probably lay behind this; as the interview develops there is a strong suggestion that Martha's omission from the interview was part of a defensive maneuver by the parents.

Verbatim Record	*Interpretive Comment*
ALICE. What's the microphone for? THERAPIST. Well, we have all kinds of microphones here, Alice. Oh, we have a little tussle about who is going to sit where. Do you want to sit in the middle, Mother? Or *(to daughters)* do you want to sit in the middle? FATHER. Well, not exactly. I felt perhaps that we two sit in the middle and let the two girls sit on the end.	The jostling for one or another seating arrangement is a common manifestation of family conflict—a power play indicating confusion with regard to authority.

Reprinted with permission from *Expanding Theory and Practice in Family Therapy*, Nathan W. Ackerman, Frances L. Beatman, and Sanford N. Sherman (Eds.), 1967, 136-177.

Verbatim Record	*Interpretive Comment*
ALICE. Well, can't us two girls sit together, because maybe we will have something to discuss? THERAPIST. Well, would you like to change the seats? LORA. All right. THERAPIST. How would you like to? Do you want to sit next to me? ALICE. Well, I'd like to trade seats with Daddy. THERAPIST. If we had a little music we would be able to play musical chairs. *(Father and daughter change seats.)*	
THERAPIST. So the girls had their way after all. MOTHER. It usually works out that way. THERAPIST. It does? Well, Pop showed a little resistance to Lora's feeling about where she wanted to sit. She wanted to sit right in the middle. I think she wanted to be right in the center of attention. LORA. No. THERAPIST. Is she that way? ALICE. I want to change seats with you. LORA. I don't care. Looks like we are playing musical chairs.	Therapist highlights the issue of the parents' guilty submission to their children.
THERAPIST. Pop, you lost out *(laughter)* in the seating arrangement for now, anyway, for the moment. Mom, you didn't have anything to say about this. No feelings about it?	Therapist underscores father's defeat and then invites a show of feeling from mother.
MOTHER. Well, I would prefer that they sit opposite because if they get started talking together, that would be the end of it. We have this at home, too. THERAPIST. You mean they raise the devil when they are together, these two kids. You got another one? MOTHER. Yes. THERAPIST. How old? MOTHER. She's four. THERAPIST. And her name is? MOTHER. Martha.	Mother is concerned with control: if the daughters join together, she loses control.
THERAPIST. So you've got Martha, four; Lora is ten; and Alice, you're seven and a half, going to be eight. MOTHER. I'm thirty-three and he *(indicating father)* is forty.	Therapist gets acquainted with the family, making a personal contact with each member.
THERAPIST. Yes. Well now, Alice, are you in a hurry to grow up? Do you want to be big quick? ALICE. Umm hmm, I have lots of things to do. THERAPIST. What have you got to do?	Therapist responds to and highlights the restless, competitive attitude of the younger daughter.
ALICE. Sometimes I want to be big and sometimes I want to be small, because I don't know what I want to do when I'm grown up, except I want to grow up because I want to do something when I grow up. THERAPIST. Well, that's a nice speech, but I still don't know what you want to do. ALICE. Well, sometimes I want to be a nurse and some-	Alice is ambivalent. She is unsure about whether she wants to stay a baby or be the big, dominant female in the group.

Verbatim Record	*Interpretive Comment*
times I want to be a singer and sometimes I want to be a movie star.	
THERAPIST. You talk so fast. Does she always talk that fast? MOTHER. Always	Therapist picks up on a nonverbal cue, Alice's rush of words.
THERAPIST. A nurse, in a doctor's office—— ALICE. A nurse in a doctor's office, a singer, or a movie star—I don't know which one to do.	Therapist refers specifically to Alice's fantasy of being father's number one girl (father is a doctor).
THERAPIST. Oh, boy, you lost me. You rattle away like a machine gun. Does she move as fast as she talks? MOTHER. Completely the opposite. THERAPIST. She moves slowly? MOTHER. Very. ALICE *(giggling)*. Very slow. It takes me about an hour to start my homework.	Mother is the watchdog for Alice, her critic and mentor.
THERAPIST. What did she say? A nurse in a doctor's office or—— ALICE. A movie star, a singer—— THERAPIST. A movie star or a singer. ALICE. Or a TV star. THERAPIST. A TV star. Well, you're a TV star right at this moment. *(Alice giggles.)* THERAPIST*(to Lora)*. You're on TV. What do you want to be? LORA. I don't know what I want to be, I have a lot of time anyway to decide. THERAPIST *(to parents)*. Has she got——*(He is interrupted by Alice.)*	Therapist is curious about the alternative competitive roles for Alice.
ALICE *(giggling)*. I know what Martha wants to be—she wants to be an athlete.	Alice uses her little sister as a shield; she is really expressing her own desire.
THERAPIST. Well, now, I'm having trouble with Ma and Pa because these two girls want to talk all the time. Is that what happens at home? Can you get a word in edgewise? FATHER. Not usually.	Again therapist highlights the daughters' tendency to seize the stage. The question is: Do the parents want to put the girls out in front so they can hide behind them?
MOTHER. We have to stop the conversation, tell them we are talking, and then they'll keep quiet, but they have to be reminded all the time. THERAPIST. Pop, you're a doctor? FATHER. Yes. THERAPIST *(questioningly)*. You have a quiet way of speaking? FATHER. It's normal.	Mother resents the competitive thrust of the girls.
THERAPIST. Oh, not like this little one *(referring to Alice)*. *(There is giggling in the background.)*	Therapist contrasts father's quiet way with Alice's noisy aggressiveness.

Verbatim Record	*Interpretive Comment*
THERAPIST. Mom, you look a little quiet too. Are you a little self-conscious? MOTHER. No, I don't think so. I don't feel it. I talk quietly except when I talk to the children.	Therapist teases both parents to draw them out. Are they in hiding?
THERAPIST. And then your mouth opens big? MOTHER. Yes. THERAPIST. Do you scream? MOTHER. I can, yes, very loudly.	Therapist's intuition is that at home there is a war of little and big mouths.
LORA. And how! THERAPIST. You agree. How do you feel when Mom screams at you? LORA. I feel like I was doing wrong, because I don't know when I'm doing wrong. Whenever she says, "Lora come up here," I know that I did something wrong already.	This is Lora's first uninvited entry into the conversation. She fears mother's "big mouth."
THERAPIST. You get ready to take a big punishment, do you? LORA. Well, my mother doesn't really give punishments, but she . . . she likes quarrels, like she scolds.	Now comes the theme of punishment. Lora feels she is mother's scapegoat.
ALICE *(intruding again)*. I know what Martha wants to be—she wants to be a tomboy. THERAPIST. She wants to be a tomboy. Well, what have we got—two girls and one boy in this family? Do you both want to be girls? ALICE. Yes.	The daughter who defies mother must be like a boy.
THERAPIST. You're sure about that? ALICE *(giggling)*. Yes.	Therapist feels Alice herself may be a tomboy.
LORA. She'd like to be Speedy Gonzales. THERAPIST. Who's that? FATHER. Speedy Gonzales is someone who is in "Dick Tracy." He's very, very fast.	Older sister supports therapist's hunch that the younger one is something of a tomboy.
THERAPIST. Does he shoot? Does he carry a gun? FATHER *(looking at Lora)*. Go ahead. ALICE. Goes like this, "phum phum," real fast.	In other words, does Alice need a weapon?
THERAPIST. Well, now, I thought I noticed a moment ago, Pop, that your elder daughter here— *(Lora shrinks away from therapist's cigarette as he gestures toward her.)* I won't burn you. Were you trying to get burnt? LORA. No. THERAPIST. You looked a little scared for the moment. All right, everything okay? LORA. Yes.	Therapist verbalizes Lora's fright (expectation of attack).
THERAPIST. Are you sure? *(Turns back to father.)* See, she deferred to you to tell me who Gonzales was, and then you said to Lora, "Go ahead." Do you make her the spokesman for the family? FATHER. No, but under these conditions I think that she might know a little bit more about Speedy Gonzales than I do. I just heard what he is. That's why I figured that she was best to tell you, to get the absolute——	Father shows a tendency to hide behind Lora.

Verbatim Record	*Interpretive Comment*
THERAPIST. And you know more about the body?	
FATHER. Yes.	
THERAPIST. Well, now, I'd like to try something. I think this is only fair, since you girls had your way. You were going to sit together, and I said to Pop it seemed that he lost out for the moment. You had your way and he didn't have his way; so let's give him his way for a moment.	Therapist takes the initiative in rearranging the seats so the parents can speak for themselves.
LORA. Yes.	
THERAPIST. All right. Do you want to sit over here again, Pop? Alice can take the other chair. Is that fair? Is that fair, Lora?	
LORA. Yes.	
THERAPIST. All right, now, let's see. . . . You got troubles here. What troubles?	
FATHER. Well——	
THERAPIST. I came in fresh. I purposely want to feel my way without any previous knowledge about what the difficulty is that you have with this family.	Therapist makes clear that he has no previous case history of the family.
FATHER. Yes, I was given to understand that. I feel that we have a normal family, well provided for. We have everything that actually anyone would really want, except that there is—I don't know if I ought to use the word *undercurrent*—but it's not normal in the respect that we can't get along with the children. The children can't get along with us. It's not constant, just a certain period of time, where you would ask your child to do something and it would have to be repeated over and over again many times. They simply disregard your requests.	Father's first emphasis is that he is a good provider. The children get out of control.
THERAPIST. The kids go wild?	
FATHER. I wouldn't say the kids go wild; I would say it was just more or less . . . like simply disregard our wishes.	
THERAPIST. Well, what happens? Can you draw me a picture of what it's like?	
FATHER. Well, now, let's say if we were talking seating arrangements at the dinner table. Well, I don't think—say in the last six, seven years—I don't think we've had a normal dinner at home. It always——	Chaos at the dinner table.
THERAPIST *(interrupting)*. That's very, very interesting. It interests me very much. You start out by saying you've got a normal family—you think you have a normal family—and then you say you haven't had a normal meal in seven years.	What is "normal"?
FATHER. Well, in this respect, as I said, we'll be sitting and having our dinner, then starts the action of the children, and in many instances the younger one will precipitate it, or else she *(nodding toward Alice)* will get the young one to precipitate this action, and then my	

Verbatim Record	*Interpretive Comment*
wife would get into the act and—— THERAPIST. These two stir each other up? FATHER. Well, I think that either one of them would stir the baby up, and then the action would start with these two with the baby and there'd be a three-way go, and just plain arguing. THERAPIST. And the baby, Martha, is four years old now? FATHER. Yes. THERAPIST. You still call her "baby"? FATHER *(contradicting himself)*. No. THERAPIST. You do; you just did. FATHER. Well, she is the baby of the family. THERAPIST. She is the baby of the family but she's four years old. So the baby of the family is the biggest hitter?	
MOTHER. Martha makes the most noise. THERAPIST. Martha makes the most noise?	Martha is the noisy rebel.
MOTHER *(softly)*. Yes, she does. *(Alice speaks inaudibly.)* THERAPIST. Could you talk a little louder? MOTHER. They're a little shy in front of a lot of people. THERAPIST *(to Alice)*. You're real shy now. It's funny; you know, you weren't shy in the beginning, Alice. You were hopping around here, talking a mile a minute, and all of a sudden you hush your voice and get shy *(Alice intrudes with a restless giggle)* and cover your eyes and giggle. Why was that? Because we started talking about Martha? I don't understand, maybe you, or Mother, or Father——	Mother has suppressed her voice, projecting her fear and constraint to her daughters.
ALICE. Well, they really shouldn't blame it on me because Martha makes me laugh with all kinds of funny faces. ALICE. Then Momma makes me go away from the dinner table, because she [Martha] makes me laugh and I can't stand it because I face her when I eat. THERAPIST. So you're a pickle-puss, huh?	Alice and Martha clown and provoke their parents.
ALICE. Yes, and ticklish. THERAPIST. You look very ticklish. Do you want me to tickle you? *(Alice giggles.)* You sure? Hmm? MOTHER. She can giggle her way through a meal. THERAPIST. Now, did you get quiet because you were afraid you were going to be blamed here instead of Martha, hmmm? ALICE *(giggling)*. Well——	Alice is teasing and seductive.
THERAPIST. Who was going to blame you? Mom? LORA *(intervening)*. I don't . . . I just think. . . . You're kind of embarrassing me. MOTHER. Just because we're here——	Therapist hints at mother's guilt and fear of blame.
LORA. No, not that. I don't care what we are, but you know when you do it, it feels like you tickle me inside. It feels like I have butterflies in my stomach.	Lora turns acutely anxious.

Verbatim Record | *Interpretive Comment*

THERAPIST. You mean, like when she——

LORA. No, when she says. . . . I think she's going to. . . . It gives me butterflies. I feel like something is going to happen.

Lora is suddenly apprehensive.

THERAPIST. What do you mean by that?

LORA. Well, I don't know. She [Alice] just does that and I'm afraid like she's going to get us blamed or something.

Lora fears blame and punishment for her sister's provocations.

THERAPIST. So you get scary; you get the jitters, hmmm?

LORA. Yes. You know, sometimes at home——

THERAPIST *(interrupting)*. Do you have the jitters right now?

LORA. No.

THERAPIST. Well, can you kind of give me a hint about what you imagine? What terrible things might happen?

LORA. Well, when she's going to blame me or something, I feel embarrassed, like my mother's going to start yelling and it embarrasses me if she yells in front of someone, so——

Lora's fear of mother's screaming mouth.

ALICE. Like, for instance, today we were going on our way and Lora said they will play with you, and then she said they're not going to play with you but I said, all right, I'll play with *you;* so then I said come on, and she just stands there and imitates everything I do.

THERAPIST. Who's that? Who's "she"?

ALICE. Lora.

LORA. In fact, there's one thing I can't pick up. You can't have any fun with her. I try and make fun with her but she always takes it hard; she always takes it hard.

Big sister's complaint against little one.

THERAPIST. You mean her feelings are easily hurt? Is that what you mean?

LORA. Yes.

ALICE. She gets mad at me if I don't do something right. I said to her, "Come on, Lora. Aren't you coming? Come on, we got to run." So she just walks very slow because she doesn't want to run, because what would happen if she fell and got this whole dress dirty? I'd get the blame.

The familiar theme of dirt and cleanliness, and the threat of punishment.

THERAPIST. Mom, are you a very clean housewife?

MOTHER. Yes.

THERAPIST. Do the kids know that about you, that you're fussy if they get themselves dirty?

MOTHER. No, they can get themselves dirty if they're playing. If I want to go someplace, they know to keep clean.

THERAPIST. Like today?

MOTHER. No, they didn't get dressed until late. They were riding their bikes—of course they had play clothes on—and they were on their bikes and when we were ready to leave they came and got dressed.

THERAPIST. Well, how come this one [Lora] is scared about being punished if she falls and dirties her dress?

Verbatim Record	*Interpretive Comment*
MOTHER. Yes, that always puzzles me because I have never restricted them while they were playing, as far as getting dirty. Lora never did get dirty.	
THERAPIST. When do you restrict them?	
MOTHER. Well, when they were dressed up, if I wanted them to go someplace—if they were ready to go—I felt then that they could wait until we got into the car, keep clean.	
THERAPIST. Alice, I was busy for a moment with Mom. Am I mistaken—your eyes look a little bit moist, like you're about to cry or something. Is that true? When we were talking about how easy you get your feelings hurt did you feel a little teary? *(Turns to mother.)* Does she cry?	Alice shows hurt feelings.
MOTHER. A lot.	
LORA. Yes, she cries, but what I mean in respect of feeling hurt, I didn't mean like I insulted or frustrated her or anything, but I just don't want to fall down and get my dress dirty.	
ALICE. Excuse me, but she can at least keep her promises.	
LORA. I *did*. I *did* walk fast.	
ALICE. But you don't run very fast. We were just, you know, running.	
LORA. I was afraid I'd trip on something.	
ALICE. Well, there weren't any rocks on the walk, and you don't have any laces.	
THERAPIST. She was worried about getting a lot of dirt on her dress.	
ALICE. Well when somebody says like, "All right I'll play with you, but I'll have to walk and tell my mother at least," and then doesn't play—"I did that on purpose," she says now to me, "I did that on purpose because I didn't want to play."	Alice voices her lament. Her big sister has broken her promise.
LORA. I didn't; I tried to play.	
MOTHER. At home this would never have been said in such a calm voice. She would have been crying.	
(Mother takes hold of Lora's hand.)	
THERAPIST. She started to cry. She's embarrassed. Is that why you took her hand, Mother?	
MOTHER. No, I felt I was trying to protect her.	
THERAPIST. Trying to stop this?	
MOTHER. Yes.	
THERAPIST. So that gesture with your right hand was to sort of interrupt the words, hmmmm?	Mother made a pretense of protecting Lora, but was really trying to shut her up.
MOTHER. Yes.	
THERAPIST. What did you want to stop her for?	
MOTHER. Because it would go on and on like this and she would——	
THERAPIST. Do you want to open your mouth?	Therapist challenges mother: Does she want to talk?

Verbatim Record	*Interpretive Comment*
MOTHER. No, I just wanted to calm her down.	
THERAPIST. Now, now, let's be honest. The truth, the simple truth—did you want to talk?	Therapist points up mother's insincerity.
MOTHER. No, what I had to say I said.	
THERAPIST. Oh, I was wondering. Listening to the two girls, you're so quiet here—the parents, Mom and Pop—so quiet. Pop, you started to grin when your smart daughter here, Lora, used that big word "frustrate." You liked that.	
MOTHER. Lora is like that.	Mother talks for father.
THERAPIST. Do you like the fact that she's a smart girl?	
FATHER. Well, yes, I do, but the problem is actually that she doesn't show that she is. I think she's intelligent, but she doesn't like to work at it.	
THERAPIST. Does she like to use big words like "frustrate"?	
FATHER. Not often.	
LORA. I don't use baby words.	
THERAPIST. Who uses baby words?	
ALICE. Martha.	
LORA. Yes, but I mean baby words like she gets all mixed up, so I take the baby words and I put them into a big word, see?	
ALICE. Excuse me, but sometimes when we're outside playing, like this morning, she does it on purpose. I told you [Lora] to get my bike out and bring it to me. I say please——	
LORA *(interrupting)*. Alice, wait——	A "normal" sisterly quarrel—the displaced hostility of both daughters to mother.
ALICE. —bring my bike, so she comes out and lets it drop on the floor so I have to pick it up, and I say, "Come on, Lora, you let it drop; *you* pick it up," and she says, "No. Why don't you do it?" and she threw it on the floor and she——	
LORA. No, but——	
THERAPIST. Mom, do you want to stop this again? This is going to go on forever.	
LORA. No, I'm not going to start anything, but could I just say something? I wanted to take my bike and she was all the way down the block. She said, "Please bring my bicycle," so I was trying to bring it along while I was trying to get *my* bicycle, so it fell on the floor.	
THERAPIST. Are you sure you're not going to start an argument?	
LORA. No.	
ALICE. She's lying.	
MOTHER. All right, that's enough. Come on.	Mother "superior" intervenes.
THERAPIST. You're getting mad, Mother.	
MOTHER. I'm getting very annoyed, yes.	
THERAPIST. Yes, you're getting angry. What do you want to do now that you're angry?	Therapist challenges mother's hostility.

Verbatim Record	*Interpretive Comment*
MOTHER. Well, if I were home I would have just said, "That's it. It's not necessary to go on like this and it's foolish," and it really is. *(To the girls.)* What are you going to accomplish by this? THERAPIST. Mother, is it true that—— ALICE. But there's a lot of—— THERAPIST. Hold it, hold it, hold it! MOTHER. Calm down now.	
THERAPIST. Don't you see I'm talking? Tell me, is it true Martha is the dirty one? This one [Lora] is the clean one, over here. MOTHER. No, the dirty one really is Alice.	Therapist reinforces respect for adult authority. He returns to the issue of dirt and cleanliness. The two sides of mother's ambivalent conflict are divided between the girls. Alice is the "dirty one," Lora the "clean one."
FATHER. It grows on her. She can be sitting quietly, just the way she is, and she can get dirty. THERAPIST. She's the real dirty one. Is this *(indicating Lora)* the clean one? MOTHER. Yes, she is. THERAPIST. Alice is the dirty one? FATHER. She has been, from the time that I can remember, from the time she was born. THERAPIST. Is that right? Does she hang on to her own dirt? Does she like to hang on to her own body dirt? MOTHER. No, no. THERAPIST. Does she take baths? MOTHER. Oh, yes, that's no problem. THERAPIST. Every night? LORA. Yes. THERAPIST *(to Alice)*. You too, every night a bath? ALICE. Every night. LORA. Not almost every night.	
THERAPIST. Wait a minute, now. Are we going to give Ma and Pa a chance? Don't you want to know which one is the clean one and which one is the dirty one between Ma and Pa? ALICE. Yes. THERAPIST. Do you know? LORA. No. ALICE. Yes. THERAPIST. Who's the clean one? ALICE. Daddy. LORA. No, Mommy. THERAPIST. Between Ma and Pa, who's the clean one and who's the dirty one?	Therapist transposes conflict back to the parents.
ALICE. Daddy should really be the clean one, because—— LORA. Well, if I——	Daughters quarrel about which parent is clean, which dirty.

Verbatim Record	*Interpretive Comment*
THERAPIST. I'm going to pin your lips in a minute, little one. *(The girls giggle.)* You don't let anybody else talk.	Therapist reasserts control.
LORA. They're both clean and they're both dirty. I mean, who can keep clean the rest of their lives and who can keep dirty?	Lora leans on "logic" as a defense.
THERAPIST. Now you're talking like a teacher and making a speech. *(Lora giggles.)* They're not the same, Ma and Pa, are they, about being clean? They're not the same, are they?	Therapist "tickles" this defense; then persists in his point.
LORA. I think no. I think—I don't want to like say anything—but I think Mommy's cleaner.	The truth will out: Mother is "cleaner."
THERAPIST. She looks cleaner. You look okay, Pop, but she looks cleaner.	
FATHER. It's true. It's true.	
THERAPIST. Mother's nicely primped up there, and you *(referring to father)* have a neat suit. You tried, but Mother is really dressed up for the occasion. Didn't you dress for the occasion?	
MOTHER. We're going to parties later with friends.	
THERAPIST. Well, this is a party, too, in one way, isn't it? A TV party.	
(The girls giggle.)	
FATHER. No, but it's true. It's true. She really is——	
THERAPIST. A little more fussy.	
FATHER. Oh, yes. oh, yes.	
ALICE. I——	
THERAPIST. Hold it, baby, just for a moment. See, I called you the baby.	
ALICE. That's okay.	
FATHER. Mother likes to be neat and trim and she will go out of her way to get that way, even say we get up on a Sunday, we want to go somewhere, and there isn't that much time on a Sunday——	
(Father has hands folded, as if holding himself together, or as in a gesture of prayer.)	
THERAPIST. May I interrupt for a second? I want to call your attention to something, maybe. . . . See how you feel about it, Pop. This is a gesture you started out with when you moved into the middle chair there, this kind of a gesture, and Mom has trouble with her hands; she's always picking her nails——	Therapist contrasts what the two parents do with their hands.
(The girls giggle.)	
MOTHER. I bite my nails. *(Turns to the girls, who are still giggling.)* Will you sit down and be quiet? Be quiet!	
(They continue giggling.)	
THERAPIST. Sit down. Her nails are real bitten down, huh? May I see?	
(Alice, giggling, mutters under her breath that mother bites her nails and spits them on the rug.)	

Verbatim Record	*Interpretive Comment*
THERAPIST. Ummm, all the way down, huh? There's nothing left to spit out. You sounded sad about that. Pop, how do you feel about the way Mom bites her nails? *(Mother makes silencing gesture.)* We're talking about you, Mom. You're not interested in how Pop feels about you and your nails?	Therapist evokes father's feeling about mother's nail-biting.
MOTHER. Yes, I was just making them be quiet.	
ALICE. May I interrupt?	
THERAPIST. Not yet.	
FATHER. She's neat, she's trim, she likes her clothes to be a certain way. Everything about her is——	Father affirms mother's compulsion to cleanliness.
THERAPIST. Except her nails. *(Turns to mother.)* You're A-1 except your fingernails.	
MOTHER. Practically.	
THERAPIST. Any other piece of your body? Any other place?	The question is: Is mother clean on the outside and dirty on the inside?
MOTHER. That what?	
FATHER. That she's not neat?	
THERAPIST. Yes.	
FATHER. No, I'd say not.	
THERAPIST. No other place on the body, only the nails.	
LORA. Please——	
MOTHER. Will you be quiet?	Mother's irritability rises.
THERAPIST. Well, now, you see——	
MOTHER. Yes, constantly interrupting.	
THERAPIST. Now, you feel at home. You feel at home now, right?	
MOTHER. Yes.	
THERAPIST. Okay. I want you to feel at home. If you get mad, let me hear you like that, okay? Now, back to the nails. What about that?	Back to nail-biting.
FATHER. I don't know.	
THERAPIST. What are you trying to hold together there?	Therapist refers again to father's hand posture.
FATHER. Maybe the world.	
(The girls giggle.)	
THERAPIST. This world, your little family.	Therapist's interpretation is that father is trying to hold his family "world" together.
FATHER. Well, if that's a symbol—perhaps, maybe, yes.	
THERAPIST. I wonder why, hmmm?	
FATHER. I don't feel right; I just feel kind of awkward.	
THERAPIST. You mean maybe it's the camera? All the time you've been conscious of the camera?	
FATHER. No, I don't think it's the camera, I think it's just——	
THERAPIST. Me?	
FATHER. No, I think it's the whole situation.	
THERAPIST. The family situation?	
FATHER. Yes.	
THERAPIST. You mean you have a sense of futility, as though you can't somehow keep holding your little world together, your little family world?	Again therapist's interpretation is that father fears failure with his family "world."

Verbatim Record	*Interpretive Comment*
FATHER. Well, I did feel that way, yes. I mean, that's why we came visiting the center.	And therefore sought family guidance.
THERAPIST. Ummmmmm. I promised Lora she could say something about her mother's nails. *(To Lora.)* What did you want to say?	
LORA. I think that is very insulting. I know if I was my mother. . . . But it wasn't very nice to say that because it's very insulting to say that like in front of a whole audience and for Alice to say she bites her nails and spits them out on the rug, it's very insulting. I know how *I'd* feel.	Lora comes to mother's defense; she acts out mother's anger toward Alice and therapist.
THERAPIST. Mama didn't like it.	
LORA. Well, I know how she feels, but I think it's very insulting. I know how *I'd* feel.	
THERAPIST. If you were Momma your feelings would be very hurt.	
LORA. Well, not as a mother, no, because I'd *ignore* my children, but if I now were my mother, I think I'd be very insulted.	
THERAPIST. But somehow Alice had a little image in her mind, a sort of picture of Mom at home right there biting her nails.	
LORA. But that's not true.	
THERAPIST. That means almost. . . . I don't know if it means that, Mom, but it sounds as though you're worried more about the rug than about your own nails?	Perhaps mother values the rug more than her own person. The rug must be kept clean; no matter what.
MOTHER. Yes, the rug——	
THERAPIST. You'll bite heck out of your nails, but heaven help anybody that drops dirt on the rug.	
MOTHER. Yes.	
THERAPIST. Do you care more about the rug than yourself?	
MOTHER. Well, there were times when I felt that way, yes.	
THERAPIST. Is it such a good rug?	
MOTHER. No, I think that's one of the reasons that—that was one of the reasons we had decided to come to family service, because the more I thought about trying to be different the worse I got.	Mother now admits need for psychological help.
THERAPIST. Explain that. I don't——	
MOTHER. Well, I didn't want to be so fussy. I wanted to relax more and I just couldn't, and that became more important than anything and I felt that I just had to be shown how to relax.	She recognized her rigidity and tension, her inability to have pleasure.
THERAPIST. So you feel your own rigidness about keeping everything just so in the house, clean, orderly, smooth, under control—but you lose control of the kids. Tell me, do you have full control of the "old man" here?	Therapist turns back to the parents. Does mother fear loss of control of father, as with the children?
MOTHER. Yes, I think I did.	
THERAPIST. Did?	

Verbatim Record	*Interpretive Comment*
MOTHER. Yes.	
THERAPIST. No more?	
MOTHER. Whatever I'm saying now is did and done. I think things have changed drastically.	Mother alleges that she no longer seeks to boss her husband. Is that really so?
THERAPIST. You don't boss him any more?	
MOTHER. No.	
THERAPIST. How did you stop bossing him?	
MOTHER. Well, it's just a little while, but I stopped bossing him when he started defending himself.	
THERAPIST. I see. Is this a change that has come about through therapy in family service?	
MOTHER. Yes.	
THERAPIST. How long have you been in therapy?	
MOTHER. Four months.	
THERAPIST. Once a week?	
FATHER. Yes.	
MOTHER. At the beginning it was twice a week.	
FATHER. The two of us together, and we went individually once.	
THERAPIST. Well, now, how do you stand up to Mom? You see, she says you have begun to stand up like a man.	
FATHER. Well, I'd yell right back at her, which I never did before.	
THERAPIST. You haven't raised your voice here yet. Mom has.	Therapist questions father's assertiveness with mother.
FATHER. I don't find it easy, I find it very difficult. I really have to——	
THERAPIST. How about raising a hand?	
FATHER. Oh, no!	This question shocks father. Does he fear physical violence?
THERAPIST *(noting Lora's gestures)*. What's the matter, Lora?	
LORA. Oy!	
THERAPIST. Oy what?	
LORA. He raises a hand and it can draw blood.	Lora chimes in. She feels a threat in father's violence.
THERAPIST. No kidding.	
LORA. He hit me this morning.	
THERAPIST. Is that right?	
LORA *(getting dramatic)*. I couldn't move my hand after that.	
THERAPIST. He broke your arm.	
LORA. Three times. Oh, I couldn't, it hurt me.	
THERAPIST. She's talking like she likes it.	
LORA. I don't like it, but ——	
(Mother murmurs something inaudible.)	
THERAPIST. Mom, I didn't hear you. What did you murmur?	
MOTHER. I see what you're accenting; that can wait.	
ALICE *(raising her hand)*. Well, you see——	
THERAPIST *(to Alice)*. I see your hand, just be patient, now. I'll call on you, like in class.	

Verbatim Record	*Interpretive Comment*
ALICE *(giggling)*. Well, you see, it doesn't really—— THERAPIST. Relax.	
LORA. I don't really like it. Who likes to get hit, I mean? But if I do something real bad I have to get hit; everybody has to get hit. THERAPIST. You deserved it? LORA. Yes. THERAPIST. It's good for you to get hit when you are a bad girl? LORA. Yes.	Lora justifies punishment.
THERAPIST. Well, now, what do you do that's really bad? What's the last bad thing you did? Were you bad this morning when he broke your arm? LORA. I'd rather not tell you. THERAPIST. Pop will tell, if you don't tell. LORA. All right, I'll tell. I'll tell. I told my mother to hold her horses. THERAPIST. Did you say it that politely, to hold her horses? LORA. No, I got so mad——	Therapist presses for disclosure of Lora's badness.
THERAPIST. Or did you tell her to shut up? LORA. Oh, I would never say "shut up." THERAPIST. You wouldn't dare. How did you tell her to shut her mouth? LORA. I was in my father's bathroom and my mother just cleaned it, so I was just combing my hair this little while and she heard me; so she said, "Get out of the bathroom. You know I just cleaned the bathroom." So I said, "All right, Mom, I'm coming," and I closed the medicine cabinet and the razor got stuck. So my father said, "Lora, get out of the bathroom," and I opened the cabinet and it was still stuck, and so I got so frustrated that I had to say, umm, that word, "hold your horses," you know; so my father comes in and hits me.	Therapist is purposely blunt to encourage a deeper emotional honesty.
THERAPIST. You didn't use any dirty words? LORA. I never use dirty words to my mother, but—— ALICE. She uses them. LORA. I do not. ALICE. She does so. LORA. That's your say. MOTHER. Will you stop! LORA. Mom never uses dirty words. THERAPIST. May I hear what Alice said?	Therapist links dirt and aggression.
ALICE. Well, she has a very bad habit. Sometimes when I'm watching TV, all of a sudden I do it, like suck my toe. THERAPIST. Suck your toe? Do you bite your toenails? ALICE *(giggling)*. Like this. No, I don't bite it.	Therapist's blunt, evocative attitude stirs Alice to a fantasy of the dirty habit of sucking her toe.
LORA. She's making that up. THERAPIST. She's making it up?	Lora protests that it is make-believe, not real.

Verbatim Record	*Interpretive Comment*
LORA. Yes. ALICE *(giggling and insistent)*. I did it this morning.	
THERAPIST. Is that with your bare feet? Show me, take your shoe and sock off if you like. Show me what you did. *(Alice, giggling, darts an anxious glance at mother.)* You're looking at Mommy. Are you scared to do that? Mom, will you give her permission? *(Alice only giggles in response.)* Mommy bites her nails; do you bite your toe? ALICE. No, I suck my toe. THERAPIST. The big one or the little one? ALICE. See. . . . I. . . . Some——	Therapist dares Alice to demonstrate.
MOTHER. You know, if you're going to talk, talk; if not, be quiet.	Mother is angry. She tries to shut Alice up.
ALICE. We just suck thumbs. THERAPIST. Who does? ALICE. Martha and me. THERAPIST. Both of you suck thumbs. Do you suck her thumb? ALICE. What? THERAPIST. Do you suck Martha's thumb? ALICE *(giggling)*. No, she sucks mine. THERAPIST. She sucks yours. ALICE. Sometimes. It's bigger than her mouth.	Alice acts out in a lively, defiant way the shared feeling of oral deprivation. She seeks therapist's attention.
LORA. She's making that up. She just wants to see how you react or something. ALICE. No, I'm not. MOTHER. Alice, Alice! THERAPIST. Well, we've got another difference in the family. Mom, you're a biter and she's a sucker. *(Laughter.)* MOTHER. They used to bite theirs. They all bit their nails, but I got them out of it.	Lora, like mother, seeks to shut Alice up.
THERAPIST. Oh, you cured them but not yourself. MOTHER. I cured them all right.	Therapist makes explicit mother's role as controller and preacher.
ALICE. Grandma cured me. THERAPIST. Well, tell me, when you put your toe in your mouth or Martha's thumb *(Girls giggle.)* how does it taste? When you suck your thumb there, does it taste clean or dirty? ALICE. Good. THERAPIST. Good? Sweet as sugar. Mother, what do you suck? MOTHER. I like to suck candy. THERAPIST. Candy?	This is the first mention of grandmother.
MOTHER. Yes, I like candy. *(The girls giggle.)* THERAPIST. What's so funny about that? LORA. Why would she suck her thumb? What would she	Mother likes sweets and yet is extremely thin.

Verbatim Record	*Interpretive Comment*
suck?	
ALICE. We have a habit in our family, I go like this. *(Giggling.)* Like I go kiss Mommy's nose or something.	Alice makes the transition from sucking to kissing.
THERAPIST. Do you do that to Mommy and Daddy?	
ALICE. Yes.	
THERAPIST. That's sweet and warm. Do you like that, Mother?	Therapist asks whether the mother gets some warmth from Alice this way.
MOTHER. Yes, terrific.	
THERAPIST. You like that. A kiss is a kind of suck, isn't it?	
LORA. Well, yes.	
(The girls make kissing noises.)	
THERAPIST. You're sighing, Pop. What's the matter?	
FATHER. Nothing, really.	
THERAPIST. Are you warm, Pop?	
FATHER. Just slightly. I'm kind of——	Father grows tense and warm. He feels on the spot.
THERAPIST. You're hot inside.	
FATHER. Warm.	
THERAPIST. Not yet hot.	
FATHER. No.	
THERAPIST. Can we make you hot?	
FATHER. Well, I may be embarrassed.	
THERAPIST. How might we embarrass you?	
FATHER. I may be slightly embarrassed with this chitter-chatter going on.	Father now feels the urge to shut Alice up. She exposes the family secrets.
THERAPIST. How does it bother you? What bothers you? You don't talk about your own feelings. What bothers you about this chatter back and forth?	
FATHER. Well, I know a lot that Alice is saying at this moment is a lot of figments of her imagination. I haven't ever seen her suck her toe.	
ALICE *(giggling)*. But I did it this morning.	
THERAPIST. You've got a very good imagination.	
(Alice giggles.)	
FATHER. I know that it's not true.	
ALICE. It is.	
FATHER. Excuse me, then it's a figment of your imagination, and well, maybe I feel that perhaps you or whoever is in on this conversation, that——	
THERAPIST. I've got to interrupt you again. Mother, you do something that bothers me very much. I've seen you do it a half dozen times already. When your husband is talking you don't pay any attention, you're looking at this little one *(gestures toward Alice)*.	Therapist now points up mother's nonverbal attitude of turning face away from father.
MOTHER. I'm not looking but I'm listening to what he is saying.	
THERAPIST. You're all the time ready to stop her from being naughty or getting dirty, misbehaving one way or another. You've got your eye on her, and you don't listen to your husband.	Mother is absorbed with controlling Alice, while she ignores father.

Verbatim Record	*Interpretive Comment*
MOTHER. I hear what he is saying.	
THERAPIST. What, with one ear? *(He notices that Lora is motioning for something to wipe her nose.)* I have a handkerchief here.	
LORA. No, I can use my father's handkerchief.	Lora tenses up and turns fearful. She refuses therapist's handkerchief.
THERAPIST *(to father)*. Does it bother you that Mother doesn't listen? That she looks at the little one?	
FATHER. This is only secondary.	
THERAPIST. What do you mean, "secondary"?	
FATHER. This *was* primary. It used to be primary and it has been transferred. Lora was the center of attention.	
THERAPIST. That started everything.	
FATHER. No, I'm talking as far as watching her to see that she does things properly.	
THERAPIST. You mean Mama mostly stands watch over this one *(indicating Lora)*?	
FATHER. She did.	
THERAPIST. "She did." It's different now?	
FATHER. Yes, yes, a great deal.	
THERAPIST. What's the shift?	
FATHER. The shift has been to Alice.	Mother was first obsessed with controlling Lora, now Alice.
THERAPIST. Oh, I see. First Mom was a police girl for Lora and now for Alice. Did you want her listening?	
FATHER. Yes, yes.	
THERAPIST. Well, I didn't want to interrupt your train of thought. You were telling me what upset you with this chatter here.	
FATHER. Well, as I said, you plus whoever else is in on this meeting—I know I shouldn't feel that way but I feel that, well, they're getting a wrong idea of actually what the situation is.	Father is fearful of personal exposure.
THERAPIST. Okay, I'm glad to hear that. Glad to hear that. Now, girls I'm going to ask you to excuse yourselves.	Therapist now asks the daughters to leave, in order to focus on the problems of the marital and parental pair.
LORA. Okay.	
THERAPIST. But one thing before you go. Come here, dear. You too *(to Lora)*, come over here. Did you want to sit on my knee?	
LORA. No.	
THERAPIST. You sort of looked at my knee as though you wanted to sit down. You're crying now.	As girls get ready to leave, therapist responds to Lora's show of tears. She wants comforting.
LORA. No, no.	
THERAPIST. No, why don't you tell me the truth? There are tears in your eyes.	
LORA. I always have tears in my eyes.	Lora attempts denial of sadness.
THERAPIST. Water just drips. Is that right?	
MOTHER. No.	
THERAPIST. She was crying a little.	
LORA. No.	
MOTHER. She has watery eyes.	

Verbatim Record	*Interpretive Comment*
THERAPIST. Well, I don't know. You know her.	
MOTHER. Her eyes are very watery.	
THERAPIST. Why were her eyes dripping?	
MOTHER. Well, she just yawned and she does have a lot of water in her eyes, but she can cry instantly.	
THERAPIST. Like the Niagara Falls?	
MOTHER. Yes.	
THERAPIST *(turning to Lora again)*. Were your feelings hurt at all at that moment, hmmm?	
LORA. No.	
THERAPIST. Were you scared of Mommy or angry at something?	
LORA. No, but like I feel this way, sometimes somebody does say a dirty word.	Now Lora reveals a family secret: "Somebody" uses a dirty word. She does not dare say it openly, but whispers to therapist.
THERAPIST. Oh, I agree that's important. Mommy does say a dirty word sometimes. Would you tell me one dirty word she says sometimes?	
LORA *(whispering)*. Son of a bitch.	
THERAPIST. To whom? All the children, when she's very angry?	
LORA. Um hmmmm.	
THERAPIST. Do you get scared when she uses that word?	
LORA. Yes.	Lora fears her mother.
THERAPIST. All right, you can go now. See you later.	
ALICE. Okay.	
THERAPIST. 'Bye Lora, Alice.	
GIRLS. 'Bye.	
THERAPIST *(to parents)*. Well, you can relax.	
MOTHER. Yes, I think we both feel tense in talking like that in front of the children. I guess mostly . . . well, I think in the beginning I tried to make them feel that there was no wrong that a parent could do.	"Mother can do no wrong."
THERAPIST. I'm silent for a moment today. I'm trying to digest that. You tried to make the children feel that parents are never wrong?	
MOTHER. Yes, I think—I don't think I was aware of it. I couldn't talk about certain things in front of the children. I don't know about what, but on an equal plane.	
THERAPIST. For instance, about what?	
MOTHER. Well, things like this. Just discussing things.	
THERAPIST. Well, you know Lora, when she whispered that little secret to me, she felt she couldn't say that bad word in front of her mother and father. Can we use it now?	
MOTHER. Yes, I heard it.	
THERAPIST. You heard. What did she say?	
MOTHER. Son of a bitch.	
THERAPIST. Well, you use a dirty word when you get really angry. You hurl these words at the children. You call them sons of bitches. Anything else?	The truth: Mother is clean on the outside, dirty on the inside.

Verbatim Record	*Interpretive Comment*
MOTHER. Well, I don't. . . . There was a time, a very short time that I did.	
THERAPIST. Like what? The children aren't here.	
MOTHER. Well, I'd say "lousy kid" but I don't think I've ever——	
THERAPIST. Uh huh. Well, now really, you sound very touchy about all that, because I guess it offends your own pride in yourself.	
MOTHER. Yes, I get very angry at myself.	Mother feels offended by her own dirty mouth.
THERAPIST. That's because you're such a trim, clean, orderly person otherwise, except for the fingernails. You hate to think of yourself spilling dirt out of your mouth.	
MOTHER. Yes.	
THERAPIST *(to father)*. How do you feel when she gets very angry and spills dirt out of her mouth?	Therapist turns to father. How does he "catch" dirt from mother's mouth?
FATHER. I feel like I have something that I must do, but what, I don't know.	
THERAPIST. That's the impression you give me watching you here, that you're lost and you have no power whatsoever to do anything about it at all.	Therapist interprets father's impotence, his choked-off rage.
FATHER. Well, I feel lost in this respect. I know that a family is supposed to be united.	
THERAPIST. Like this?	
FATHER *(laughing)*. I know that a family is supposed to be united and the mother and father are supposed to be united. If there is an argument between the mother and the child or the father and the child, the thing where I am lost is where does the other spouse stand? Does he go along with the mother, even though perhaps the mother is not completely correct? Does he go along with the child? Or does the parent stay neutral until this thing is over with and then discuss it with each one individually?	Father depicts his emotional paralysis: Must he be mother's stooge or dare he take a stand against her?
THERAPIST. Well, how do you feel about that? I don't want a thought in the blue sky about people in general, I mean this little world—your little family world that you can't get together.	Therapist again refers to father's failure to hold his family "world" together.
FATHER. I'm talking about myself.	
THERAPIST. Are you together with the lady?	Now therapist challenges father. He tells father that he really does not feel "joined" with mother.
FATHER. Yes.	
THERAPIST. Are you joined?	
FATHER. Yes.	
THERAPIST. I don't think so.	
FATHER. Joined?	
THERAPIST. Are you united?	
FATHER. I think we are.	
THERAPIST. No, you can't be.	
MOTHER. Well, we think differently about the children.	
THERAPIST. Can't be. I sit here and watch you two, and you start sharing your troubled feelings with me, and Mother looks the other way—that's not being united.	Therapist does not mince words. He speaks his mind, an example for father.

Verbatim Record	*Interpretive Comment*
She says she listens—I don't think she listens very well. Too busy controlling that bad kid over there, that little son of a bitch.	
FATHER. She really isn't that bad.	
THERAPIST. Did you hear that?	
MOTHER. Yes.	
THERAPIST. Well, now, there are differences between you. What are they? Put them on the table.	Therapist seeks a deeper honesty about marital and parental conflict.
MOTHER. The situations, I think, are completely out of hand. They shouldn't be. . . . There's no control. I'm beginning to feel that he's right.	Now mother is more open and direct than father.
THERAPIST. I'm beginning to get the hint that although you inwardly have a very different feeling than your wife, you anyhow felt you ought to back her up even though you felt she was wrong.	
FATHER. That's exactly where I was lost. I didn't know what to think, and it got to a point where I spoke to her and we decided we needed help. It can't be a one-way problem; it just can't be her problem. I must enter into this problem also. By not taking the problems on myself—in fact I tried to at one time, I would try to get her out of the picture altogether, and then I was the one who was starting to reprimand the children, yelling at the children, and well, it just——	Father assumed mother's guilt for himself.
THERAPIST. In other words, in your desperation you reached a feeling that she's doing such a lousy job with the children you're going to step in and take over.	
FATHER. I guess that would be the way to say it.	
THERAPIST. I know I'm putting it in strong words, but that's the way you felt.	
MOTHER. At my request.	
THERAPIST. You asked him to step in; you felt you were doing a lousy job. Do you feel you're a flop as a mother?	Therapist elicits mother's sense of failure.
MOTHER. Umm hmmm. I don't think so now. I think I'm learning control of myself, but I did think that then.	
THERAPIST. Do you fight, the two of you?	
FATHER. Do we fight?	
THERAPIST. Yes.	
FATHER. Not often, not often at all.	Father is again evasive.
THERAPIST. Really, why is that?	
FATHER. Maybe I didn't want to.	
THERAPIST. Why couldn't you permit a fight?	Therapist penetrates father's hiding of conflict.
FATHER. Inside me, I just felt——	
THERAPIST. The first thing I felt when you said that you didn't fight very often was that maybe you don't fight often enough.	
FATHER. Well, recently we have been——	
TERAPIST. You've been doing better recently?	
FATHER. Oh, yes.	

Verbatim Record	*Interpretive Comment*
THERAPIST. Much better? FATHER. Sparring more. THERAPIST. But you haven't hit her yet? FATHER. No, I don't think I ever could. THERAPIST. You could never raise a hand to Mother, but she's been pretty bad at times. FATHER. I notice it all focuses on her. Where do I get this picture? There's a problem with me too; I know it. THERAPIST. What's the matter with you?	Again, therapist hints at father's fear of his own violence.
FATHER. Well, let's put it this way—like my father would say, "I'm sure it will straighten itself out," not taking a forceful stand and saying, "Well, this is the situation; this is the way it has to be." I will . . . usually I can't holler. THERAPIST. Were you mollycoddled by your own dad, your own father? FATHER. No. Well, let's put it, that's my general make-up if something is wrong.	Father confesses his fear and constraint and associates it with his own father's attitude toward him.
THERAPIST. Were you raised to be a very good boy? FATHER. No, no. THERAPIST. Why did your father consider you a mollycoddle? FATHER. Well, the word that my father used—he never called me a mollycoddle. THERAPIST. What did he call you? FATHER. Well, until I was about fourteen he called me by my Jewish name. THERAPIST. Did you talk Yiddish in your own home? FATHER. Not too much. I can't speak it. THERAPIST. What did your father do? FATHER. My father, he was a businessman.	Therapist teases out father's strict early training.
THERAPIST. Are you a religious person? FATHER. Thank God! THERAPIST. Do you go to temple? FATHER. Yes, but not as often as we should. But my interest is in the temple. I find that I get a great deal of pleasure working there. THERAPIST. Are you active in the temple? FATHER. Well, I was. THERAPIST *(to mother)*. Were you raised in a religious home? MOTHER. Yes.	The issue of religious upbringing.
THERAPIST. An orthodox home? MOTHER. No. THERAPIST *(to father)*. Were your parents orthodox? FATHER. Mine were. My father was very orthodox. My father has a kosher home; he went from one extreme to the other and back again.	There is a difference of religious training between the parents.
THERAPIST. Did you feel, Pop, that you shouldn't disagree with your wife in front of the children? I get the impression that for a long while, even though you felt	Therapist points up father's fear of conflict with mother.

Verbatim Record	*Interpretive Comment*
very strongly the other way, you felt you had to support her. FATHER. Yes, that's exactly my feeling. I felt that I had to support her, that if she was making a stand with the children that it was my duty to stand behind her.	
THERAPIST. You talk very softly now. FATHER. I felt it was my duty to stand behind her.	Therapist reinforces awareness of father's fear, as manifested by his low voice.
THERAPIST. Do you feel now that somehow you've magnified the wrong things she was doing to the kiddies by backing her up in those circumstances?	Therapist underscores father's secret criticism of and anger toward mother.
FATHER. To this day—and I know that it is wrong—to this day I still can't jump in and pull her away. I will do it quietly with my hand or make a face, but I can't reprimand her in front of the children.	Father feels he must not show his anger toward mother in front of the children.
THERAPIST. You're a very respectful person. She's the boss; she's been the boss now for all these years—you're married fifteen years. FATHER. Yes. THERAPIST. Tell me, are you married to your wife? FATHER. I think so.	
THERAPIST. You think. You're not sure of anything. FATHER. No, I'm married to her. THERAPIST. You don't say you think. You're not united as parents and you haven't been; so I wonder whether you are united as man and wife. Are you? FATHER. Yes. THERAPIST. How well joined are you as man and wife? Is it very good now? FATHER. Yes.	Therapist emphasizes father's unsureness.
THERAPIST. Do you love her? FATHER. Yes. THERAPIST (*to mother*). Do you love your husband? MOTHER. Yes. THERAPIST. And so the loving between you now is better than it was? FATHER. Yes. THERAPIST. Well, what did it used to be?	Therapist moves into the area of their love life.
FATHER. Well, up to a certain time it wasn't a normal situation in the respect that you'd call normal.	Father hints vaguely at the existence of sexual problems.
THERAPIST (*sarcastically*). Well, now, I understand perfectly exactly what he means. Speak English. FATHER. I find it difficult to discuss. THERAPIST. In these circumstances? FATHER. In any circumstances. THERAPIST. Like your sexual life together? FATHER. I'm not talking about only under these circumstances; I'm talking about any circumstances. THERAPIST. Do you feel very sensitive about sexual matters?	Therapist challenges father's vagueness.

Verbatim Record	*Interpretive Comment*
FATHER. I think we both are. THERAPIST. Are you, Mother? You too? FATHER. When we hear people talk about their sexual life—I'm talking about friends and so forth—well, we tell them it's none of their business.	Both parents hide their sexual feelings.
THERAPIST. Are you telling me now it's none of my business? FATHER. No, no, because if there is an answer in that then we have to bring it out. THERAPIST. Well, I think there might be. I'd like to know what trouble you've had in your sexual life together. FATHER. Well, while we kept company, while we were going together—we went together about a year, over a year—I think we were very much in love. We had no premarital relations. We liked to go out with each other; we enjoyed each other's company. The night that we got married, it was like a shade was drawn, and sexual life was very poor. THERAPIST. Can you be a little more specific? I might understand.	Another instance of therapist's directness.
FATHER. Well, I just couldn't get to my wife. THERAPIST. She closed the gates on you completely on your honeymoon night. Pulled down the curtain, wouldn't let you in? FATHER. On the altar they pulled the shade. THERAPIST. How did you do that, Mother? MOTHER. I just couldn't—— THERAPIST. Tell me, how did you close him out? You married him and then——	Now comes the truth: The wife rejected her husband sexually.
MOTHER. I know, something snapped in me and I just couldn't—— THERAPIST. I'd like to understand that. MOTHER. I would have liked to, too. THERAPIST. What did it feel like? MOTHER. Well, I felt very jumpy. THERAPIST. You got panicky. MOTHER. Yes. THERAPIST. Were you afraid of sex? MOTHER. I never thought I was until that time.	Mother was frightened of sex.
THERAPIST. Now, you went together and kept company about two years. MOTHER. I got married at eighteen. THERAPIST. You got married at eighteen; so you met him at sixteen. How did you meet him? MOTHER. Through a friend. THERAPIST. On purpose or just . . . ? FATHER. I was going with her friend, and she went out with a friend of mine. MOTHER. We went to a party together.	Therapist elicits background and courtship phase.

Verbatim Record | *Interpretive Comment*

THERAPIST. What did you do, make a trade?
FATHER. No, no.
THERAPIST *(to mother)*. You were dating the other fellow and——
FATHER *(answering for mother)*. No, no, not dating; you know, one date. I was seeing this girl. I saw her every once in a while, and I had some friends that we double-dated with, and the girl I was going with asked my wife if she'd like to go out with this fellow just for that night.
THERAPIST. How did you feel when you laid eyes on her for the first time?
FATHER. I don't remember.
THERAPIST. All of a sudden your mind goes blank.

Again therapist points up father's evasiveness.

FATHER. To tell you the truth, I don't remember how I actually felt.
THERAPIST. All right, the second date—how did you actually feel about her, looking at her?
FATHER. Well, when I took her out herself, I think that I fell in love the first time I took her out.
THERAPIST. Love at first sight.
FATHER. No, I——
THERAPIST. Second sight.
FATHER. Maybe fourth, I don't know.
THERAPIST. What did you fall in love with? Tell me.
FATHER. Well, I think she was a very good companion, a very gentle girl.

This is interesting. Father was looking for a "gentle girl" and selectively saw only that side—façade—of mother.

THERAPIST. That's very important. You never met a girl and considered that before?
FATHER. No.
THERAPIST. You thought she was a very gentle girl?
FATHER. Yes.
THERAPIST. She didn't turn out to be so gentle.

This is blunt confrontation, therapeutically useful.

FATHER. Well I found that out after.
THERAPIST. She's got vicious teeth, sharp teeth; she bites. She never bit your head off?
FATHER. No, no. She'd yell at me, and——
THERAPIST. What did she call you in those days?

Therapist elicits father's feeling about mother's "dirty" mouth.

FATHER. You mean profane?
THERAPIST. Yes, yes.
FATHER. No, she didn't.
THERAPIST. What did she yell at you?
FATHER. Well, it started originally when I was going to school to really learn my Spanish. I never had Spanish in high school, and so I had my first year of Spanish in college and she started to tutor me, and she couldn't understand why I couldn't grasp it as fast as she wanted to teach it.

She humiliated him.

THERAPIST. You mean this gentle little girl treated you as if you were a dummy?
FATHER. Yes.

Verbatim Record	*Interpretive Comment*
THERAPIST. Are you a dummy? FATHER. No, I don't think so. THERAPIST. Is she smarter than you? FATHER. I think she has a little more intelligence. THERAPIST. Really? MOTHER. In what? THERAPIST. Pop just said he thinks you're smarter than he is. You've got a better head, have you? MOTHER. Not at all.	Father is too submissive. Does he really believe mother is smarter?
THERAPIST. A thin little head like that. . . . Were you always so skinny? FATHER. She was skinnier. THERAPIST. She was skinnier? What did he marry, a toothpick? *(Laughter.)* FATHER. Yes, yes. THERAPIST. How much did you weigh? MOTHER. Right now? THERAPIST. When you were dating him, how much did you weigh? MOTHER. Oh, at that time I was, I guess, under ninety pounds.	Therapist turns to mother's thin body, a sign of a long-standing feeding problem.
THERAPIST. Oh, I see, you got real trouble with your mouth; you're a poor eater, hmmm? MOTHER. Terrible. THERAPIST. You still are a poor eater? MOTHER. I'm an erratic eater, but I like my food now, and I can eat three meals. THERAPIST. Are you fussy about what you eat? MOTHER. No, not at all. I can eat anything. THERAPIST. Well, what did you do, just eat your nails, nothing else? MOTHER. Practically.	Mother is a "poor eater." Instead of trusting food, she bit her nails.
FATHER. She let them grow for the wedding; that's what I can't understand. They were nice and long, and after the wedding, there they went again. THERAPIST. Just for show, hmmm, to look good at the wedding you let them grow? MOTHER. I had tape on my nails for three months.	Now father begins to show a bit of his hostility.
THERAPIST. So it's more important to you how you look on the outside, not the way you really are on the inside?	Therapist again refers to mother's double nature; she wants to look good on the outside, while she is bad on the inside.
MOTHER. Well, I'm a different person in my home now. THERAPIST. How different? MOTHER. I'm calmer with the children. Things that normally would bother me, now I shut them up immediately.	Mother says she is better.

Verbatim Record	*Interpretive Comment*
THERAPIST. Well, you know one way of measuring how well a person is emotionally, you're in treatment and when you get better the inside and the outside of the person become the same. You're one person inside and another person outside.	Therapist's idea of a "cure" is when a person becomes the same inside and outside.
MOTHER. Well, it's pretty well equalized now.	
THERAPIST. Two people.	
MOTHER. I was, yes.	
THERAPIST. Your husband is very hurt about what you do with your nails—you let your nails grow only for show, but not for him.	
MOTHER. Two years ago they grew.	
THERAPIST. Wouldn't you like to have nice nails, attractive nails? Bitten nails don't look pretty.	Therapist offers encouragement.
MOTHER. No.	
THERAPIST. Do you want to be pretty?	
MOTHER. Very much.	
THERAPIST. Then you've got to do something else with your mouth. Anyway, comes the honeymoon night, you freeze. You pulled the curtain, locked the gate, no sex. That's an awful feeling for a man.	Therapist moves back into the sexual problem.
FATHER. Well, I felt that she was young and I had to treat her gently and I didn't actually force the issue. As I said before, it'll come in time.	Father again shows fear of violence and is overly gentle.
THERAPIST. So you're a very considerate fellow. You thought she was a very gentle girl; you're a very gentle fellow, hmmm?	
FATHER. Yes.	
THERAPIST. You are. You can't imagine yourself laying a hand on a woman, can you?	Therapist challenges the sincerity of father's compensatory gentleness.
FATHER. No.	
THERAPIST. So you waited.	
FATHER. Yes.	
THERAPIST. How long did you wait?	
FATHER. A short while.	
THERAPIST. And then?	
FATHER. I think that things started to calm down. She started to calm down, and I guess we got used to each other.	
THERAPIST. You panicked your wife?	
MOTHER. Well, when we came home from our honeymoon we moved in with my folks, and my folks were away on vacation, you see.	Parents feared the authority of the grandparents.
THERAPIST. Oh, I see, I see, and then when they came back. . . . When the cat's away, the mice begin to play. You had to get your Ma and Pa out of the house before you could come alive.	
MOTHER. We actually didn't have a happy married life until we moved into our own apartment.	
THERAPIST. So you took flight from your parents. Were	

Verbatin Record	*Interpretive Comment*
you brought up by them so you should never think of doing anything dirty like sex? MOTHER. Yes. THERAPIST. Sex is dirty. MOTHER. It was never spoken about. THERAPIST. Did you feel it was clean, Pop? FATHER. Yes, I was brought up that way. My father was very open. THERAPIST. About sexual matters. Was your mother too? FATHER. Yes, my mother never frowned upon it. We used to discuss certain things; it was never dirty. THERAPIST. Well, now, did you then really culminate your marriage? Did you have full intercourse after four or five weeks, or something? FATHER. Yes, then—— THERAPIST. She let you in. FATHER. Then it slackened down again after her parents came back, but when we moved to our own apartment—— THERAPIST. When Ma and Pa came in, you went out? MOTHER. Yes.	
THERAPIST. Let's say she shoved you out. She was married to her parents, not to you, is that right? FATHER. I think she was having relations with me while listening. THERAPIST. What kind of marriage was this with your parents? MOTHER. Well, their advice or their thoughts actually were more important to me then. It took me a long time to divorce myself from that. THERAPIST. I see, and as long as you were married to your parents you couldn't be married to your husband — either/or? They come home; you lock him out. How long did you live with your parents? MOTHER. Well, my mother died. She died nine months after we were married. THERAPIST. I see. So did you have to wait the nine months to get in again, Pop? FATHER. No, but as I was saying it was like . . . she was looking to her. . . . She was with me but listening to them. THERAPIST. That's very interesting, what you just said. Can you guess what I'm thinking? You can't—can you guess? MOTHER. Yes. THERAPIST. What?	Once again therapist is blunt.
MOTHER. I didn't want them to walk in on us or to be aware or——	The fear of being caught in the sex act. Have the parents substituted their children for the grandparents as the symbol of conscience?

Verbatin Record	*Interpretive Comment*
THERAPIST. Of course, she is smart. You didn't want your parents to catch you in the act, the dirty act. Now you treat your children like you treated your parents; you don't want them to walk in on you. What are the sleeping arrangements?	
FATHER. Now they have their own room.	
THERAPIST. Do you worry now, Mom, about the kids walking in on you while you're having intercourse, making love? You shook your head yes *(to father)*. Was she worried about that?	
FATHER. Was she? Oh, yes!	
THERAPIST. Worried about the kids walking into the bedroom?	
FATHER. Yes.	
THERAPIST. Did you ever walk in on your parents?	
MOTHER. No, not that I remember. No.	
THERAPIST. You never caught them in the act?	
MOTHER. No. I don't think I ever thought of them that way.	
THERAPIST. You mean in your mind your parents couldn't do such a thing; they're pure.	Therapist elicits mother's image of her parents' sexual purity.
MOTHER. Yes. Even after I learned all about it, I don't think it ever entered my mind.	
THERAPIST. Now, in the way you felt, your parents never did that. How many kids in your family?	
MOTHER. Two.	
THERAPIST. So they only did it twice.	
MOTHER. Ummm.	
THERAPIST. Twice in their lifetime—pretty clean people. *(Laughter.)* What are you laughing about, Pop?	A touch of the comic.
FATHER. Well, it's funny. I guess every child feels that way about his parents. I'm talking about a young child.	
THERAPIST. Not me. You say every child——	
FATHER. No, I say every *young* child feels, well, I mean when they actually don't know that. . . . You don't know that they have relations only for perpetuation of the race, and they feel, well, they just do it to have children and that's it, and the other way—well, it's just not done. That's the way children feel. Even with kissing, a child doesn't think that parents do it.	"A child doesn't think that parents do it."
THERAPIST. Well, that's very interesting. May I ask you, does your wife touch you?	
FATHER. Yes.	
THERAPIST. How?	
FATHER. In loving.	
THERAPIST. What kind of touch?	
FATHER. Oh, not too——	
THERAPIST. How do you feel about that, Mom? Is that all right?	
MOTHER. Yes.	

Verbatin Record	*Interpretive Comment*
THERAPIST. Are you a good kisser?	
MOTHER. Yes.	
THERAPIST *(to father)*. Is she a good kisser?	
FATHER. Yes.	
THERAPIST. So all the fighting is in public and the kissing and touching in private, right? As I said before, the outside and the inside, they're opposite. Mom keeps them separate—one way for the public, another way inside; two different people. Didn't we agree about that?	
FATHER. Well——	
THERAPIST. You don't agree?	
FATHER. No, I do agree; it has been brought to my attention when we are talking and by what she has to say—that sometimes she could feel that she's supposed to do it one way on the outside but yet something inside tells her, "No, you've got to hold back."	
THERAPIST. Just like that.	
FATHER. Yes, can't let herself go.	
THERAPIST. So that in her public side—in front of other people—she does a hell of a lot of screaming and saves the kissing for private.	
MOTHER. No.	
FATHER. No, she likes to kiss.	
MOTHER. I don't do it in front of other people; I don't scream when some other people are around.	Different behavior in public and private.
THERAPIST. Only in private? Sometimes you forget yourself; you started to right there.	
MOTHER. Oh, yes, I'm less reserved that way now.	
FATHER. She will yell in front of her father, but she wouldn't yell in front of anyone.	
THERAPIST. Tell me, did you have a troubled love life for many years? You're married fifteen years. It's better now?	
FATHER. Well, I'll tell you it went on for a number of years. I think since we moved away from her——	
THERAPIST. Ma and Pa.	
FATHER. Yes, it's gotten much better.	
THERAPIST. So you married a baby. What kind of a baby were you, Mom?	Therapist links fear of sex with mother's still being a "baby."
MOTHER. I still am.	
THERAPIST. Still are a baby. Did you put on any weight?	Another reference to her feeding problem.
MOTHER. I got to a certain point, I think——	
THERAPIST. What do you weigh?	
MOTHER. Hundred and five, four.	
THERAPIST. How tall are you?	
MOTHER. Five-one.	
FATHER. She weighed a lot more when we came back from our honeymoon.	
THERAPIST. You didn't have any sexual troubles of your own, any problems of any kind, Pop?	Therapist looks for impotence in father.

Verbatin Record	*Interpretive Comment*
FATHER. No. THERAPIST. We have to stop in a moment, but you started out, Pop, by saying about your family that they are very well provided for. You're a good provider; you're doing well in your profession? FATHER. Provided for, let's say, financially. I don't know about anything else. THERAPIST. Well, you were talking about the buck. You've always been a good earner and a good father that way, took care of your family materially very well. What do you earn now, about?	Father is proud of his potency as a provider.
FATHER. Oh, twenty-four, twenty-five. THERAPIST. Um hmm. You never had any troubles with your wife about the money you earned; she's not demanding that way? FATHER. No, not really. I think that I've earned enough. THERAPIST. So you should have gotten a better deal in marriage—good provider, good man like you, considerate man?	Therapist teases out the question: Does father feel cheated sexually?
FATHER. How do you mean a better deal: as far as our home life? THERAPIST. Your love life. FATHER. Well, I have no complaints about it now. You see, she provided for me when I went to school; she worked very hard while I went to school. THERAPIST. Oh, I see, I see. So now you're paying her back? FATHER. Well, I'm not paying her back. I've always been a hard worker.	Father feels obligated. He supports her now, because she supported him earlier.
THERAPIST. All right, but you're making good progress now in your treatment. FATHER. I feel we are, but I don't feel that it's complete. THERAPIST. I don't think so either, yet; we have a long way to go. All right, good luck to you both. FATHER. Thank you.	

CHAPTER 37

To Catch a Thief

This family psychotherapy interview is presented in verbatim transcript with an accompanying account (in italics) of the therapist's understanding of what was going on, and how he did his job. Important themes in the psychopathology of the family are mentioned as they first appear. They will recur.

The interview is preceded by a brief account of the family's background and a summary of the initial exploratory interview.

FAMILY BACKGROUND

Mr. and Mrs. M. were seen with son George, age 17, a child by her first marriage, and Mrs. M.'s parents. George was a medium-sized, round-faced boy with a blank, defensively frozen facial expression. He was cautious, afraid to give away what was on his mind. The mother is a substitute teacher and the stepfather a lawyer who has an administrative job as safety engineer. Both parents held a stiff posture. Their faces were tight, pinched, harassed, tormented, yet blank in unexpressiveness. They seemed compelled to do what they thought was expected of them. The maternal grandparents were anxious to give the impression that they were sincere and devoted, on the side of all that was good, but they were also aggressively invasive.

A few months prior to the interviews George cashed a $500 bond and took a jet to the west coast. Upon his return his stepfather refused to have him live with the family. At that point he went to live with his maternal grandparents, traveling across town to school. Before this he had been stealing small amounts of money from his mother and stepfather. George had been seeing a psychiatrist for a year but his parents saw no change, and this, combined with the recent episode, caused them to look for further help.

Four years ago, when George was 13, his father died suddenly at the age of 41. The mother's impression is that there had been difficulty before the father's death, such as George's doing poorly in school, being disobedient, and having "unrealistic ideas." There is a younger sister who is said not to be disturbed. Mrs. M remarried 2 years ago. Her present husband had been divorced and has a child younger than George in his custody from his first marriage. This child, too, is said to be free of problems. (Claims that the other children are undisturbed are more questionable.) George has a strong tie to his mother but she is conflicted about him. His stepfather charged her with overindulging

Reprinted with permission from *Family Therapy in Transition* (International Psychiatry Clinics, Vol. 7, No. 4), 1970, 173-221.

George. At the same time the stepfather feels that George is his wife's responsibility, even financially as far as therapy is concerned. Evidently, the mother recognizes that George is a threat to her present marriage and is depressed and ambivalent.

INITIAL EXPLORATORY INTERVIEW

The following persons were present: George, age 17, mother, stepfather, and maternal grandparents. In this summary, core themes will be noted parenthetically when they appear.

There was some interchange between Dr. A. and grandmother, who said she loved George, she loved all her grandchildren *(hypocrisy)*. Stepfather took over, giving an orderly, detailed chronology of George's stealing sums of money, keeping weapons and ammunition in the house, leaving the home *(compulsive aggression)*. George interrupted frequently, correcting stepfather on minor details *(contentious disruptiveness)*. Dr. A. commented on the battle between them. Stepfather stressed his responsibility for a safety program in his city and Dr. A. said he had the same problem in his family; they all needed a safety program *(impending disaster)*.

Dr. A. noted that George was biting his fingers and asked if he bit other people. When George said he bit only himself *(denial of involvement)*, Dr. A. designated him as a specialist in nonsafety. George addressed his stepfather by his first name; he said he did not consider him as father *(rejection of the stepfather)*. Stepfather said that this had been arranged in agreement with the mother. George's sister, on the other hand, calls him "father." George claimed indifference about whether or not he had a father. Mother said they had attempted not to make Mr. M. the father in order to help George, but it had not helped. George does not consider grandfather a father; he has no father. Grandfather agreed.

There followed more details of George's delinquencies *(criminality)*, with George contradicting grandfather, mother adding details, and stepfather filling in. Dr. A. commented that George saw these episodes differently, but George denied this. Mother mentioned summer school for George to make up lost time and Dr. A. said George had a different career. He asked George what he wanted to be. George said the family thought of him as the garbage man. He then said he wanted to be a lawyer, but denied that he wanted to be like his stepfather.

He wants to be a politician. Grandmother asked him to tell how he had worked hard for Barry Goldwater's election. George sees himself as working his way up in politics and becoming a senator. He is a conservative and would work for conservative principles. His family is not conservative, but he feels he has the right to differ from them. Stepfather is a Democrat "straight down the center." George quoted Benjamin Franklin, who said that he who gives up liberty for the sake of safety deserves neither. Dr. A. commented that stepfather played it safe and George was an extremist. George denied this and quoted Barry Goldwater. Grandmother claimed to be a liberal, and grandfather voted with no party. Dr. A. said that the family was split politically, as it was split in other ways. George denied that there was any conflict and when Dr. A. asserted the family was waging war, George said he did not know what he meant. He denied that he was in revolt against the grown-ups. He just wants to get away from them and from school, which he hates. He did not think that he needs to go to school in order to enter politics, as he can get the facts he needs outside of school, by reading books.

Dr. A. asked George what kind of a guy he is. George said he did not understand the question, then said he was a nonconformist. He said he had friends and in particular one close friend, Jack, who, however, supported Lyndon Johnson. He said also that he had many girl friends, but no steady. He is "playing the field." He thinks that he makes out "okay" with girls *(desire to appear a regular guy)*.

Dr. A. suggested that the family might leave, so that George and he could talk together, but George was not willing to do this. Dr. A. asked the grandparents how George was at their home. Apparently, there is bickering about what he wears, when he goes to bed, his messy habits, and so forth. Dr. A. commented that the grandfather, who runs a launderette, is neat and clean, and George is dirty, steals money, and so forth. Grandfather went into detail about the last stealing episode and the plane trip to California. In order to get a bank withdrawal slip, George had to climb through a window into his own home at night. Stepfather thought he might be a burglar and called the police. Dr. A. commented that George could have been shot but George minimized the risk. One always takes risks. One takes a risk in crossing the street. George forged a withdrawal slip by tracing over stepfather's signature and he got $850 from the bank. Dr. A. said that George had a *(criminal)* career carved out for himself.

Dr. A. asked if anyone had thought of having George locked up. He is getting away with murder. Everyone is supporting his career. Grandmother wanted to know if George was sick or a crook. Dr. A. said he was a crook for sure *("tickling the defenses" by asserting what is feared)*. Grandmother asked again about his being sick. Dr. A. asked George if he had a screw loose. George had no answer, but he had no use for a psychiatrist; he could take care of himself. Grandmother disagreed. George said that before the advent of psychiatry, people handled their problems alone. Dr. A. said that, without help, George could destroy himself and he wondered if it might not be better to lock him up *(a deliberate therapeutic provocation)*.

After the family left the room, grandmother remained and tried to give Dr. A. a sheaf of papers written by George, in which he expressed his political aspirations *(underhanded invasiveness)*. He wants to be president. Dr. A. said he would read them only if George knew about it. Since the grandmother had retrieved the papers from the wastebasket and George had not been told, Dr. A. refused to take them. His refusal is intended to communicate that he will take no part in this deceitful manipulation.

SETTING OF THE SECOND INTERVIEW

The family had accepted referral because of the pressure that they felt to get control of George. On a deeper level they feared disgrace and the breaking of their façade of respectability (as well as the breakup of the new marriage). The second interview occurred prior to case assignment, with the clinic staff observing behind a one-way mirror.

The major themes all appeared in the first interview: hypocrisy, compulsive aggression, contentious disruptiveness, impending disaster, denial of involvement, rejection of the stepfather, criminality, the desire to appear to conform to conventional standards, and underhanded invasiveness. All cover up. The therapist's job is to puncture the hypocrisy, to get at what is emotionally real.

SECOND INTERVIEW

Verbatim Record

DR. A.: Do you have exactly the same positions you had last week?

GRANDMOTHER: Except that the grandfather's here, and I was there.

DR. A.: Mmm. Well, in other words you're saying nothing, nothing changed since last week.

In this initial exchange, with the support of the stepfather, I challenge the mood of the family. I equate the seating arrangement with the "feeling situation." Same or different as compared to last week? The ambiguity of my question has several functions: it encourages reflection and awareness of alternatives, but more importantly it gets them a little off balance so that secrets are felt to be not so securely hidden and I am clearly in charge. They don't know if they should respond to my message or metamessage. I'm teasing. They don't know what I'm up to. I keep them guessing. When one family member moves into alliance with me, the collusive defense of the family is broken.

MOTHER: No.

DR. A.: They're all the same in this family? Exactly the same?

STEPFATHER: Yeah.

DR. A.: You agree, George?

GEORGE: Uh . . .

GRANDMOTHER: No, William [stepfather] was sitting here and mother was there.

STEPFATHER: Oh, the position. That's what you're talking about? I thought the, the *feeling* situation . . .

GRANDMOTHER: Oh, that.

STEPFATHER: . . You know . . .

GEORGE: Well, yeah.

GRANDMOTHER: I was just talking about the sitting arrangement, that's all, William.

DR. A.: And I'm talking about what's cooking in this family.

MOTHER: I think things are a little better.

Sounds like denial, an evasion.

MOTHER: I'm not quite as uneasy as I was before. I feel that we're working toward something that will help all of us and George.

Questions: Is the mother's hope real or pretended? Is she projecting a demand to the therapist to make things better? Asking for more intervention from me? Probably.

DR. A.: You have a little more hope this week, a little more . . .

MOTHER: Yes. Mmhm. [*She sounds not so sure.*]

DR. A.: Why, because I'm here?

MOTHER: Not only you here, because there's an interest being taken, and we're gonna find some direction that's right for all of us.

Whistling in the dark.

DR. A.: Mmm. Did you uh, almost feel like giving up before you came . . .

I appeal for a greater openness and honesty.

MOTHER: No.

DR. A.: . . . here?

MOTHER: No, I was impatient, let me put it that way . . .

DR. A.: Mmhm. [*skeptical*]

MOTHER: In fact, George came to visit us Sunday with my parents, which he hasn't done in quite a long time, really. That's different, too.

Mother offers "proof" that George is better.

STEPFATHER: Uhuh. [*equivocal*]

MOTHER: Right?

DR. A.: Did you want to, George? Make this visit to . . .

I turn to George to involve him, to invite consensual validation. He is evasive. Reality-testing isn't going to be easy.

GEORGE: Didn't matter.

He's not going to go along with his mother's story.

DR. A.: . . . with your mother and your stepfather? Hmm?

GEORGE: Didn't matter, really.

DR. A.: I don't know. That bothers me some. You could very well have refused to go. You've done it before . . .

Appealing for honesty, I challenge his stance that it doesn't matter. With my confrontation he is forced to be less evasive and brings out more of his truth. Parents and grandparents are coercive. He appeases them but is unchanged.

GEORGE: For convenience's sake.

DR. A.: How do you mean, just for convenience? Was it more convenient to go along with Grandma and Grandpa, than to stay by yourself?

GEORGE: No, I could have stayed home, I could have watched TV, read something, or done something. But if I don't go, they start, "Why aren't you going? You gotta see 'em," you know, all that.

A step toward honesty.

DR. A.: Who? Grandma and Grandpa?

GEORGE: Everybody.

DR. A.: Everybody.

GEORGE: . . . my mother also . . .

All the older generation are hypocritical.

DR. A.: So you went along just to shut their mouths?

I'm blunt, to foster honesty.

GEORGE: [sighs with resignation]

DR. A.: So you shouldn't be nagged? Is that what you did? To shut them up?

Pounding the point home.

GEORGE: It could be put that way.

He's reluctant.

DR. A.: Do you have trouble that way, can't shut their mouths?

GEORGE: Sometimes.

DR. A.: Who's the biggest nag in the family? You? [to grandmother] You've got a reputation now.

I'm acting on a clue: grandmother had started to take over early in the hour.

GRANDMOTHER: I don't think, really too bad, a little bit. Uh, I, I don't even think he's telling the truth. I think he did want to go to his mother's home, but . . .

She has all the answers.

MOTHER: Well, let him say it himself, I'm sure that's what the doctor wants.

My appeals for candor are rewarded: mother allies with son. Tension emerges between mother and grandmother.

DR. A.: Well, mother's trying to get you to be a little more honest about the way you feel, George.

I acknowledge my ally.

GEORGE: Well, I wouldn't say that.

DR. A.: No?

GEORGE: "Honest" is the wrong word.

A fog of obsessional resistance.

DR. A.: What's the right word?

GEORGE: Honest is saying that I'm not telling the truth now. But if I am . . .

DR. A.: Well, I used the word honest in a special sense. Maybe you're not aware of all your feelings.

I emphasize emotions.

GEORGE: How do you expect me to express them?

MOTHER: Because if you really didn't want to go, you wouldn't have come at all, George, if you really felt that way.

Mother gives me an assist, and I support her. We're allies in the search for honest feelings.

DR. A.: You know your own son.

MOTHER: That's right.

GEORGE: No, wrong, because if I . . .

MOTHER: Because if you really didn't want, you wouldn't have come.

GEORGE: . . . like last week she said I only came here. I didn't argue. Not that. I wanted to come, but to make everybody happy. You said that yourself last week.

Slippery George. He fails to confirm mother.

MOTHER: Well, that shows that you really want to help everyone, help them by coming.

Mother puts her son in a bind. On one level she says, "Do what I need; save me." On another, "You really want to help."

DR. A.: Well, how did George treat you?

MOTHER: Oh, fine.

DR. A.: Was he truly friendly?

MOTHER: Oh, yeah.

DR. A.: Was he friendly to you, William?

STEPFATHER: Same way he was before.

DR. A.: Not friendly.

STEPFATHER: Same way he was before.

DR. A.: You, you refused to have him live with you.

Stepfather lets out the truth. Stymied by a contagion of hypocrisy I shift gear to get help and to offset the scapegoating of George. Fakery is widespread in the family. Now, I confront stepfather with his real feeling toward George, rejection.

STEPFATHER: That's correct.

DR. A.: You pushed him out.

STEPFATHER: No, I didn't push him out.

DR. A.: What did you do?

STEPFATHER: He pushed himself out.

Stepfather denies responsibility, insists son forced his own rejection and exile.

DR. A.: I don't understand. A moment ago you agreed that you refused to have him live with you.

I play dumb.

STEPFATHER: Yes, for this reason, that things have occurred, each time it occurred, we said, look, it can't happen again. If it happens again, we have to take steps. You cannot be in a situation where he disturbed everyone, and he kept doing the same thing, so eventually he had to leave. I hope you . . .

DR. A.: Well, then, you, you pushed him out and he pushed himself out.

STEPFATHER: That's correct.

By stages we're reaching a more accurate image of what happened.

DR. A.: Both of you did the pushing, he and you!

STEPFATHER: Well, let's say this, I told my feelings to my wife and she picked the ball up from there. I didn't have any direct contact with George.

To avoid blame, stepfather passes the buck back to mother.

DR. A.: Helen [mother], what do you say?

MOTHER: Well, I had spoken to George many times. I'd said, this can't continue, George, we're trying our best. You have a good home, your own room, a nice neighborhood, schools, the temple, we made everything pleasant for George. He had to cooperate by trying to help us, and not repeatedly doing exactly the same things over and over again. . . .

Mother justifies self and blames George. She was everything a "good mother" should be.

DR. A.: Well, tell me, did it seem maybe, I'm using my imagination now, and I warn you I have a *wild imagination,* did it seem to you like George dropped out of the family like your former husband, his father?

Here I drop a catalytic bomb: I challenge mother with my wild imagination. In leaving mother's home, did George also "drop dead," like his father? This is an intuitive leap.

MOTHER: What do you mean, doctor?

She stalls, plays for time. There's panic in the air.

DR. A.: His father dropped dead of a heart attack?

MOTHER: That's right.

DR. A.: Very sudden?

MOTHER: Yes, no, I don't think, can't see the similarity. I'm sorry, what do you mean by that, doctor? Could you explain yourself?

Mother is caught off balance, is upset, stalls for time.

DR. A.: I don't know what I mean, I just . . .

I parry mother's stall by "playing dumb." Now it's my turn to hide in the fog and force them into the role of the "knowers." They can play my hunch if they will.

MOTHER: That's, uh, could you explain yourself?

DR. A.: I'm just imagining.

MOTHER: No, I'm certain, no, but he was always home, he, I mean, in certain ways he was always there.

Mother obfuscates, is unsure, confused, yet denies my implication that she might feel about George as if he were dead.

DR. A.: You're talking about his father, your former husband?

MOTHER: No, I'm . . .

She mixes up father and son, emotionally commingling the two images.

DR. A.: George?

MOTHER: I'm talking about George now.

DR. A.: Was it different when his father was alive?

MOTHER: Was it different when . . .

Stalls.

DR. A.: Ah, how was it then with George?

MOTHER: I didn't have these problems with George then. He was a normal youngster.

No need to scapegoat George then. George was "normal." A hunch: was father then delinquent?

DR. A.: Well, that's very interesting. George, when you had your own father, you were a normal youngster? Did you have a normal family then?

I play dumb and put him on the spot. Shift question of normalcy from George to the original family.

GEORGE: Well, you're using a term, normal, which doesn't mean anything, 'cause it's just a relative term. [Gestures with hands as he speaks contentiously.]

An obsessive defense. George parries.

DR. A.: Okay, I mean . . .

GRANDMOTHER: Put your hand down. [An order]

At this very point, Grandmother's aggressive thrust at George is interesting. She responds to the rising tension by cutting him down. Her message: don't get aggressive, don't stick it out.

GEORGE: . . . and, uh, . . .

DR. A.: . . . My language is very bad. I will, I'll let you choose the words.

GEORGE: No, no, but, uh, didn't mean it like that, but you're saying normal, what's normal?

Again, George is evasive. I press my challenge, but make a gesture of openmindedness. Now he must take some responsibility.

DR. A.: I don't know. Well, forget the word normal, what was right?

GEORGE: And, uh, it's, it's, that doesn't necessarily have anything to do with it at all.

DR. A.: You agree, my imagination is wild.

GEORGE: No.

He hedges, but senses my correctness.

DR. A.: You say your father's death had nothing to do with it at all?

GEORGE: Well, I said it doesn't necessarily have to.

Hedges and teases.

DR. A.: Well, I, I . . .

GEORGE: I'm, that's uh, what everybody says is, but uh, maybe it isn't.

Hedges and teases.

DR. A.: I don't know, this is only our second meeting. Give me an idea of what you were like then, what was the family like?

GEORGE: You mean, describe it? I don't know what you mean.

Hedges and teases.

DR. A.: Hmm?

GEORGE: I don't know how you want me to describe it.

George continues evasive.

MOTHER: Was the family, may I interject? Was the family situation a happy one?

Mother offers to talk for him, to cover up both for herself and him.

GEORGE: Yeah, yes.

DR. A.: Hmmm? [*skeptically*]

I register disbelief again.

GEORGE: Yes.

DR. A.: How'd you feel when your father dropped dead, that was quite a shock, was it?

Reaching for his feelings.

GEORGE: Yeah.

DR. A.: Happened very suddenly.

GEORGE: Mhmm. [*stalling*]

DR. A.: Do you remember, you were twelve at the time.

MOTHER: Thirteen.

GEORGE: Yeah, I remember.

Mother and George can't let my error pass.

DR. A.: Thirteen? What was it like, George?

GEORGE: What?

Stalling again.

DR. A.: How'd you feel?

GEORGE: Can't describe it.

DR. A.: You find no words for it?

GEORGE: No.

DR. A.: But I find the "wrong words." I stick my neck out and I use such meaningless words as "normal." I agree, very difficult word to be clear about. So when I use the wrong word to describe some part of your situation, you correct me, then you turn around and say you find no words of your own to describe how you felt. Were you numb?

I put up with a "one down" position to encourage him to take a risk himself. Then turn the responsibility back to him.

GEORGE: I don't know.

GRANDMOTHER: I think so. I really think so. [*insistent*]

Grandmother takes over. Really, she's very competitive; she will assert her power.

DR. A.: What was it like for all of you?

GRANDMOTHER: Complete disability. It was a very shocking experience. I know that George, when mother wasn't home right after the death, George was climbing into the different closets, looking for pictures that had been put away, snapshots of his father. I said, George where are you climbing, you'll fall off, you'll hurt yourself. He says, I'm looking for some pictures of my father. He couldn't say very much and neither did any of us.

Grandmother begins to expose what George and his mother were hiding. Now she's my ally.

DR. A.: George?

I again invite George to speak for himself. But he remains numb and dumb.

GEORGE: I don't remember any of that.

DR. A.: Do you feel bad, Grandma? George, you aren't looking at Grandma. She's crying her voice is quavering. Grandma, you're shaking with feeling now.

I make a point to focus on nonverbal expression. From the head to the belly button—the gut emotions. I confront George and his mother with grandmother's emotions.

GRANDMOTHER: George was numb. He didn't say anything, but he did put his arms around his mother and grandmother [father's mother] at the time of the funeral. And without talking, you could see that he was, it was just too much. And he was trying to be the brave one and take care of his mother and his grandmother who had come up from Florida. She was a very sick woman.

This is a big help. Still, there is a duplicity of motivation—she also shuts up mother and son.

DR. A.: Mmm. [*receptively*]

GRANDMOTHER: And this had been her only child who died. And George didn't say anything, and he isn't usually one to put his arms around. He just, uh, he wants to, but I don't think he can.

DR. A.: Mmm. Do you want my handkerchief? Do you have one?

I dramatize grandmother's show of grief.

GRANDMOTHER: Yes.

DR. A.: Do you feel all right now, Grandma?

GRANDMOTHER: Well . . . ?

DR. A.: What was your son-in-law's first name, George's father?

GRANDMOTHER: Henry.

DR. A.: You feel very much about Henry.

GRANDMOTHER: Yes, he was a very lovable person.

DR. A.: Mmm. [*skeptically*]

My "mmm" conveys a message: I'm unconvinced.

MOTHER: Yes. [whisper]

GRANDMOTHER: And just about a week or two before it happened, me and my husband were always welcome at the house. Henry made us feel very welcome, and, of course, my own daughter did too, but that I expected, but for a son-in-law to make you feel so welcome I knew was unusual, from many things that I heard. When I was there that night, for some reason or other in the next room, I saw Henry put his arms around George, and George was almost as big as he is now. I said to myself, it's really strange to see a man put his arms aroud a big boy. . . .

I doubt that Henry was all that noble. Is this reality or ritual talk? It's ritual; not genuine.

You know that a father loves his children, and he, he did a lot of loving with the little girl, but I didn't always see the love that he possessed; he was a very loving personality, Henry. His greatest love was being home with Helen and the children, having their friends there and the family. He didn't care about going out or doing anything else. He couldn't wait till he got away from the office to be home with his family.

Here Grandma really goes to town. Ritual protection of ritual sentiments.

DR. A.: Mmmm. George, I wonder if you feel what I feel that's going on right now. Grandma's voice is shaking, she's full of emotion as she recalls your father, Henry, who was so devoted and affectionate. But you're not showing any feeling, your mother isn't showing any feeling, William [stepfather] isn't showing any feeling. Grandma's showing the feeling for the whole family about your father, Henry. How about that, George?

Where's the real feeling? I turn from Grandma to George. I try here to give George his voice, to express his own feeling of loss. I point out sharply that everyone excepting Grandma is choking off emotion.

GEORGE: What do you mean, how about it?

DR. A.: How does it make you feel right now? Grandma's doing all the crying, all the mourning.

GEORGE: I don't particularly think that is, uh, helps a great deal if everybody just started crying when something bad or, uh, unfortunate happens. Have everybody walking around the streets crying, it doesn't solve anything.

George still persists in the suppression of his feelings.

DR. A.: Is that the way you felt when your father died? That you should control your feelings, suppress them, not break down into tears?

GEORGE: Well I, uh, yeah, I guess so.

DR. A.: Do you remember that, Helen?

MOTHER: He still does.

DR. A: He still comforts you.

MOTHER: Mhmm. [nods assent]

George conceals his grief as he comforts mother.

DR. A.: Tell me about it.

MOTHER: Well, he tries. You know, he's always been very warm with me. If anything should happen to me, if I don't feel well, he's always the one to try to take care of me, very affectionate and warm with me. Right, George?

Her "Right, George?" is a command to conform. He does. With father gone, mother leans on son. He fears he may lose her, too.

GEORGE: Yeah.

DR. A.: He's your man!

I dramatize mother's placing son in husband's position.

MOTHER: Mmmhm. [*stalling*]

DR. A.: So George took his father's place that way with you? Hmmm?

MOTHER: I suppose so. [*stalling*]

DR. A.: Did you break down . . .

MOTHER: No.

DR. A.: . . . when Henry died?

MOTHER.: No.

DR. A.: You and George, both of you, very . . .

MOTHER: Strong ones.

DR. A.: . . . very controlled, huh?

Mother and son identified in need to be overstrong, deny feeling, deny fright and vulnerability.

MOTHER: Supposed to be very strong in situations like this, I've been told.

DR. A.: Are you strong?

MOTHER: Outwardly, yes.

Contrast between inner feeling and outer mask.

DR. A.: Outwardly?

MOTHER: Mmhmm. But I've always been that way.

DR. A.: And inwardly?

MOTHER: I suffer inside.

DR. A.: When you said that, "I suffer inside," the expression in your eyes changed.

I pick up on the nonverbal sign that cannot lie. It is important to respond to signs of inner emotion.

MOTHER: Ummm. I suppose I feel all these emotions inwardly and I don't express them outwardly. I . . .

DR. A.: You're all choked up.

MOTHER: Mmhm.

DR. A.: What's going on inside you right now?

MOTHER: A lot of mixed emotions.

DR. A.: Tell me.

MOTHER. I can't express it that freely . . .

DR. A.: Mmmm. I don't know whether your son takes after you, or you take after your son, but you don't find the words, either.

They're in the same boat.

MOTHER: Mm. Find it difficult. I've always been quiet and self-controlled, all my life . . .

DR. A.: Both you and your son have trouble with emotions.

MOTHER: Uh huh. [agreement]

DR. A.: Hmmm? [*a reinforcing response*]

MOTHER: And, well, I never want to make anyone feel badly or upset anyone.

She's anxious about doing or saying the wrong thing.

GRANDMOTHER: Takes after her father.

Grandma interprets for me.

MOTHER: [laughs] And so, I try to control my, myself.

DR. A.: Grandpa's that way?

MOTHER: Mmhm. [agrees]

GRANDMOTHER: He's very good, and he always wants to hold everything to himself that's not pleasant. And I'm the one that says everything.

Grandmother offers a diagnosis of the whole family. Is she taking over my job? She competes for control.

DR. A.: You pour it out.

GRANDMOTHER: I pour it out.

DR. A.: Anybody else in the family . . .

GRANDMOTHER: And I'm a nag.

DR. A.: . . . pour it out, or only you?

GRANDMOTHER: My other daughter.

DR. A.: Hmm?

GRANDMOTHER: I have another daughter.

DR. A.: Does she pour it out? She's like you?

With repetition the emotion is building up.

GRANDMOTHER: Just like me.

DR. A.: And Helen is like her father.

GRANDMOTHER: That's right. Basically very good, but always wanting to, not to trouble anybody else. So they have all the troubles within themselves.

DR. A.: Mm.

GRANDMOTHER: So that when people came to console Helen after the tragedy, she didn't want to make anybody else miserable. Everybody else was consoling her and she was strong. Uh, now I feel guilty that I let her go back to work right after the tragedy and of course there, when you're doing a job you can't go around crying, you have to do a job. And taking care of children, about thirty-five children in a classroom, was not easy. And then to come home and take care of her own children, and the phone ringing as soon as she'd walk in, people calling her and finding out how she is. She has many friends, lovely friends, whom I admire. The way she has chosen them, they think the world of her, and she put up a stoic front even at the price of herself.

A lot of hypocrisy here.

DR. A.: Mother's face is melting now, though.

Prompt pickup of nonverbal expression.

MOTHER: Well, we all have to readjust to certain situations, and . . .

DR. A.: You look like you're about to, to pour.

MOTHER: Mmmm, not so easily [*indecisive*]

DR. A.: But your face changes . . .

I dramatize discrepancy between inner feeling and outer mask.

MOTHER: Mmm. [*undecided*]

DR. A.: . . . back and forth, between that frozen smile . . .

MOTHER: Yeah.

DR. A.: . . . and, uh, something like a silent cry.

MOTHER: Mmhm. [*undecided*]

DR. A.: You cry inside. So you choked up everything, and went right back to your teaching job.

This is "tickling the defenses," naming what was defended against: grief. Her teaching reinforced her denial.

MOTHER: Mmhm.

DR. A.: Right back to the classroom . . .

MOTHER: Not right back, it was something brand new . . .

DR. A.: . . . to take care . . .

MOTHER: . . . something I had never done before . . .

Mother makes a bid for support.

DR. A.: . . . to take care of other women's children.

MOTHER: . . . something I had never really done before.

DR. A.: What's that?

MOTHER: Teaching, full time.

DR. A.: Mmm. You [stepfather] want to say something, we're talking about Henry . . .

I've been temporarily licked by mother. I now involve William, the new husband and stepfather. His mouth is open and I see pressure in his face to talk.

STEPFATHER: I could have the pleasure . . .

DR. A.: . . . .how do you feel, while we're all talking about Henry?

STEPFATHER: I think it's healthy to bring it out, not because I, I want to know what's gone on before, I never question Helen, but in this situation I feel that's doing something to maybe solve the situation. Maybe, uh, certain things that have to be brought out to show the situation as it is right now.

He offers to be my ally in cutting through denial.

DR. A.: You never met your predecessor?

STEPFATHER: Never had the pleasure.

His formal use of the word pleasure *shows his detachment from the atmosphere of the session.*

DR. A.: He held the job before you!

STEPFATHER: Evidently, yes.

DR. A.: You say *evidently* . . .

STEPFATHER: Well, yes. [*equivocating*]

The new husband makes a polite bow. I pick him up on one word, evidently. *Here I catch a whiff of his rivalry with the old husband. He seems to rub out the first husband.*

DR. A.: You're not sure?

STEPFATHER: Oh, yes, let's say yes. Yes. And I'm, anything I've heard is always good about him.

DR. A.: You're a lawyer, so I guess you, uh, express yourself with care.

STEPFATHER: I have a habit of doing that.

The care defensively covers his underlying rivalry with the first husband.

DR. A.: Qualifying your phrases?

STEPFATHER: Yes.

DR. A.: But, you remind me of a man I once knew who had some family troubles. He had a right to them. He was with his fourth wife now. He had three sets of children, fourth wife. For his fourth, he married a woman who was twenty-six years younger. She was a widow, and when I talked with him, like I'm talking with you, William, about his feelings toward the husband who was there before him, who had evidently died, evidently! He talked a little bit like you, like he wasn't exactly sure where that guy was. I said, how do you make sure? He answered: "I go to the grave to make sure he's six feet under."

I use an anecdote to make the point. Second husband wants the first husband to stay dead.

STEPFATHER: [laughs] Even then he's not sure.

DR. A.: That's the way you sound, like you're not sure where that guy is.

STEPFATHER: Well, then, in my business, I mean we can never make, we have to make statements, but we have to make sure any statement we make is backed up. There can be no qualification, so therefore, when we go out for facts, we search every facet . . .

Stepfather gets lost in speechifying; he obfuscates the issue. His message: "you won't get me, you bastard."

DR. A.: Mmmhm.

STEPFATHER: . . . just to make sure there isn't one possibility that this information we're giving . . .

DR. A.: Well, I'll tell you something, there is, there is a possibility, and I think you feel it in some way that Henry's still here. The ghost of Henry is still around.

This will illustrate the therapeutic usefulness of the concept of the "family ghost."

STEPFATHER: I never felt that.

DR. A.: You never felt that?

STEPFATHER: No. I could say, definitely, I never felt it.

DR. A.: Never felt it?

Stepfather now tells how mother prematurely pushed him into the position of George's father, to interrogate and discipline George.

STEPFATHER: No. Only on one occasion. The first time that George took that money, that $500. We weren't married at the time. Helen was very much upset. She explained what happened, and she was really riled up. She said, perhaps you can talk to George. I'm not sure I volunteered or she asked me. I said, George, could you tell me what happened? I'm an outsider, but can I help you in any way? He said, no, no, no! Helen was sitting there, and said to him, look, I'll leave the room, I'll go in the next room, if you, maybe you have something to say to William personally. I said, George, what'd you do with the money? He doesn't know. I said, why'd you do this? He said, well, *it's my money*. I said, well, why do you take this attitude? He said, well, he said, he mentioned his father's death, that's the only time he ever mentioned it. He says, I have nothing to live for and I feel like killing myself, remember that, George?

Here I catch a feeling of George's underlying

despair. He substitutes "my money" for his dead father, and imagines killing himself.

GEORGE: No.

STEPFATHER: Yeah, well, that's just what he said to me. That's the only time uh, I, I . . .

DR. A.: But you really felt the wound, the cut.

I give him permission to be hurt, to put aside his invulnerability.

STEPFATHER: Well, I was an outsider, I was, practically a stranger in the family. I mean I only met Helen a few times before.

DR. A.: Well, you started out, William, by saying you never felt like Henry's ghost was around, except . . .

STEPFATHER: Well, since we're married . . .

DR. A.: . . . that one time . . .

STEPFATHER: . . . that time . . .

DR. A.: . . . you felt it plenty.

STEPFATHER: Yes, but I wasn't a member of the family then.

DR. A.: Right. You weren't yet married to Helen.

STEPFATHER: At that time, I wasn't.

DR. A.: Right. You [to George] don't remember that.

GEORGE: Remember that, I don't.

DR. A.: When you said you have . . .

GEORGE: No.

DR. A.: . . . nothing to live for, you might as well kill yourself.

GEORGE: No. That I don't.

DR. A.: That's very curious, isn't it? Are you curious that you can't remember that?

I confront George, test his denial of preoccupation with death.

GEORGE: No, not particularly.

DR. A.: It's only a few years ago.

GEORGE: A few years ago, you know, it's . . . it doesn't mean very much, if I asked you where were you September 10th, 1962, would you know? It's just a few years ago.

DR. A.: If my father had dropped dead, I'd remember, believe you me!

An example of my blunt use of my own feelings. This is a further step in confrontation.

GEORGE: Oh, I remember, but I don't remember the stages. Do you remember everything you say?

DR. A.: Well, all right. Do you remember any of these feelings of despair? We've learned this morning that you and mom are alike, you freeze up your feelings about Henry. Grandma cried her heart out, but neither you nor mother allowed feelings to come out.

GRANDMOTHER: Could I say something, Doctor? That $500 was in bonds that had been accumulated as a gift by Henry's aunt. Every time that George had a birthday, she would write that she had bought a bond and put it away for George. When Henry died, she mailed the accumulation of $500 worth of bonds to Helen for George and I believe those bonds were in George's name. So he may have had the feeling, well, they are mine.

At this point Grandma makes trouble in the family. She offers an alibi for George's "stealing" $500 in bonds. Was it stealing? Apparently not.

DR. A.: Uh huh.

GRANDMOTHER: I'm only telling you this because the thought has come to my mind many times.

DR. A.: Did the aunt do this because Henry had died, because George lost his father?

Was the money intended to console George for the loss of his father?

MOTHER: No, mother, that's wrong. [*sharply*]

Sharp conflict between mother and grandmother. The ghost of the dead husband actuates the original war between the two women.

GEORGE: No, she, she . . .

GRANDMOTHER: But I knew she had sent . . .

MOTHER: No, that . . .

GEORGE: You're completely wrong.

MOTHER: . . . wasn't from aunt.

In the war between the two women, the son gets rubbed out. Perhaps his father was too.

GRANDMOTHER: Well, that was my understanding.

MOTHER: No. They were bonds made out in his name. Who they came from . . .

DR. A.: George, you just sit back and wait, wait, and wait. [*a mild reproach and definite challenge to take a stand*]

Sensing this rubbing out, I challenge George to reenter the fray.

GEORGE: Some were Bar Mitzvah presents, some of them.

MOTHER: That's right.

DR. A.: You sit back, George, and wait for other people in the family to put their foot in their mouth, to make mistakes, and then you turn around and say they're wrong.

I confront George with his need to trap and undercut people in authority; the effort to smoke him out continues.

MOTHER: He's right. But he was right. That was . . .

GRANDMOTHER: I thought they were . . .

DR. A.: You've done that with me, George, you wait until I stick my neck out and then you chop it off.

GEORGE: Right.

The women renew their war and again erase the son (by ignoring him and his qualities, individuality). I insist on attending to the son. His gesture of agreement ("Right") is only a ploy to shut me up.

DR. A.: How is Grandma wrong about your aunt?

GEORGE: No, that, uh, that, that wasn't how the bonds got there. It was for my Bar Mitzvah.

DR. A.: Oh, I see. For your Bar Mitzvah.

GRANDMOTHER: I didn't know that. I thought they were from the aunt.

GEORGE: A couple of them were from there.

DR. A.: I see.

GRANDMOTHER: Oh, well, I didn't know.

DR. A.: Did you feel that was your money?

I again support George's assertiveness.

GEORGE: Uh, yes.

DR. A.: Bonds were in your name?

I legitimize the boy's action.

GEORGE: Yes.

DR. A.: I see. The couple of bonds from your aunt, did she give you those bonds after Pop died?

I tease out the context of George's "stealing" of his own money.

GRANDMOTHER: That's when you received them, Helen.

MOTHER: After that?

DR. A.: Well . . .

GRANDMOTHER: After Henry died.

MOTHER: I don't remember.

GRANDMOTHER: Not before.

Again, the war of the women crowds out the man.

GEORGE: I don't . . .

GRANDMOTHER: After.

GEORGE: . . . remember that. But uh, she had bought one every uh . . . birthday of mine, every year she bought one.

DR. A.: Mmmm.

GEORGE: And, uh, I don't remember when we got them.

GRANDMOTHER: George doesn't even know this, this aunt. Neither does Helen because she's lived far away.

DR. A.: I see. But, going back to a moment ago, George. You agreed with me. Every time I stick my neck out, you chop it off.

Again I challenge George as to his headchopping. In a nonverbal way I give him strong support, too. The pattern is for George first to comply with the women by erasing his male assertiveness, and then to launch a sly, vengeful counterattack.

GEORGE: Yeah.

DR. A.: You agree with that?

GEORGE: Mmhmm. No, that I'm trying to or want to.

DR. A.: You just do it by nature. Second nature?

GEORGE: Well, no.

DR. A.: It's your second nature to chop my head off whenever I stick my neck out.

I reach for his underlying anger, tickling the defenses, hoping to make him honest and emerge as a man. By posture and voice I continue to signal my warmth and support.

GEORGE: No.

DR. A.: What . . .

GEORGE: But, uh, by arguing with you, I can't convince you of anything. I, uh, by arguing with someone, you can't convince 'em. It's only by his own statements, can you convince somebody.

DR. A.: You hang a man on the evidence. You hear that, lawyer [stepfather]?

At the moment, my purpose is partly thwarted. George hides behind hostile legalisms similar to stepfather's (likely also father's). My shift to William takes George off the hook. It's an indirect message to the boy that he borrowed his sly, hypocritical hostilities from parents.

GEORGE: No, no.

DR. A.: "Lawyer" William?

GEORGE: [mumblings]

DR. A.: What?

GEORGE: I mean, like we found this very true,

you know, in the campaign.

DR. A.: Mmhm.

GEORGE: That me arguing with another kid won't get us any place. But if I can question him about his statements, and he can find out that they aren't true, well, then, then I can change views. But not by arguing.

DR. A.: I see. All right. I'm willing for you to cross-examine me.

I offer myself as an open target. He "chickens out."

GEORGE: I am not here to cross-examine you.

DR. A.: I think you are. You really are.

GEORGE: Why do you say that?

DR. A.: You hide that feeling, but I believe you have that feeling.

GEORGE: I don't come here to question you.

DR. A.: But you are involved when I express a wrong view. You have an urge to do something about that.

By cutting behind his sly counterattack, I make him honest.

GEORGE: Uh, yeah. Well, because it's all relative here. It's all trying to get, you're trying to get the story, so let it be told the right way.

DR. A.: Mmm. Okay. I'm listening. Tell it the right way.

GEORGE: What do you want me to say?

Again George stalls.

DR. A.: Tell your story about your father.

GEORGE: So . . .

DR. A.: The right way.

GEORGE: What's the story, "your father's story?"

The theme of "stealing" has led back to the story of father's death.

DR. A.: Hmm?

GEORGE: I don't understand what you mean, tell the story.

GRANDMOTHER: Didn't you love your father, didn't you go with him, didn't you have the same interests?

DR. A.: Right or wrong?

GEORGE: Right. [*emphatically*]

Finally, George speaks out decisively.

DR. A.: Right. What else about you and Pop? Did you feel very close to him?

I probe to uncover George's bond with father.

GEORGE: I guess so.

DR. A.: You were his first son. You have what, a sister or a brother?

GEORGE: A sister.

DR. A.: How old is she?

GRANDMOTHER: Just thirteen.

GEORGE: Thirteen.

DR. A.: Were you closer to Pop than your sister?

GEORGE: I don't know. I can't, uh . . .

More stalling.

DR. A.: Hmm?

GEORGE: I can't say that.

DR.: Mm.

GEORGE: I would say, yes, I guess. Relatively, she would have been smaller at that time.

DR. A.: Are, are you going to make me drag the story of your feelings toward your father out of you. It's like pulling nails. You want to work me to death.

Again, I forthrightly offer myself as target.

MOTHER: [interrupts Dr. A.] Dr. A., maybe because we're all here, is that, would that be a reason that George finds it hard to . . .

Mother covers for George, tries to take him off the hook, but encourages further evasion.

GEORGE: No.

DR. A.: Well, I don't know, last week . . .

GEORGE: I don't . . .

DR. A.: . . . if you remember, last time I asked him, do you want to talk with me privately? He said, no.

GRANDMOTHER: I don't think he wants to talk at all.

STEPFATHER: No.

DR. A.: Like pulling nails!

GRANDMOTHER: Mmhm. Oh, sometimes he'll start a sentence and I'll, I'll, I'll ask him a question and he'll say oh, never mind. Forget it.

Now the family is split, mother and George against grandmother and stepfather. Is grandmother assisting or competing with me?

DR. A.: Right or wrong? [to George]

GEORGE: That is, uh, that . . .

GRANDMOTHER: Except with politics.

I am ignoring the women and focusing on George. Grandma intrudes.

GEORGE: . . . that, uh, it's not that. It's like, you know, I would, uh, like I'd say, turn a light off and I'd see it was off and then I'd stop. And then she wanted to know what I said, and it didn't make any difference because the light was off, so, that's that . . .

[interrupted by Grandmother]

George tries falteringly to speak for himself.

GRANDMOTHER: He didn't want to prolong conversation, it's just a nuisance to him.

Grandmother shuts George's mouth and speaks for him.

DR. A.: Well, he's in the business of chopping heads off and shutting mouths. [*annoyed*]

I'm getting annoyed at George for not coming through.

GRANDMOTHER: No, I . . .

DR. A.: Two big, big responsibilities you [George] have in this family. To shut people up and chop their heads off when they make a mistake.

GRANDMOTHER: Well, may I interrupt? Uh, he's made friends with a very nice boy in my building. And he went down one, one evening, and the mother of this boy said that Raymond is going to do homework, he doesn't have time to spend with you. He said, could I just see him for a minute? She said for a minute, yes. He stayed 15 minutes and he left voluntarily, and he had a lot to say. In other words, if he likes a person he's with, he finds conversation. But this must be, he wants to evade this whole thing.

Grandmother chimes in: George trusts his buddy, not his parents or me.

DR. A.: To a buddy.

GRANDMOTHER: To a buddy he will talk.

DR. A.: Not to family.

GEORGE: No, no.

GRANDMOTHER: That's right.

DR. A.: Uh, wrong again!

GRANDMOTHER: That's my impression.

GEORGE: This is the difference of subject matter.

MOTHER: He was discussing politics . . .

GEORGE: No, no . . .

MOTHER: . . . to Raymond, no.

GEORGE: . . . not necessarily, but the point is, it's something that interests us. Whereas I wouldn't go over to my friend, start questioning him, psychoanalyzing him, because it has nothing to do with it.

DR. A.: George, how come you never take the lead in the subject matter?

I offer George another invitation to come forth.

GEORGE: I don't understand what you mean, take the lead.

DR. A.: You say it's a question of subject matter. If we were talking about something that interested you, you'd talk more, be more spontaneous?

GEORGE: Right.

DR. A.: You'd pour out more freely.

GEORGE: Right.

DR. A.: I wouldn't need a claw hammer to pull nails out of you?

A teasing challenge to assert himself.

GEORGE: Mmhm . . .

DR. A.: So, how come you don't change the subject?

GEORGE: Because the other subjects have nothing to do with this.

DR. A.: Well, like what, for example.

GEORGE: The recent one had been politics.

DR. A.: Politics, yeah. Well, we started to talk politics last week, you and I, we started.

GEORGE: Mhmm.

DR. A.: Well, I can talk politics, too.

GEORGE: Fine, but what? This is not getting us anyplace here. We could talk politics for five hours and it may not help you at all.

More stalling.

DR. A.: Because that's more impersonal.

GEORGE: Mhmm. Yeah. It has nothing to do with it.

DR. A.: Now, you're willing to talk about things that are less personal.

GEORGE: No, not necessarily less personal, but it interests me.

DR. A.: Mhmm.

GEORGE: It isn't whether it's personal.

DR. A.: Now that's very strange. You mean to say you're not interested in your own feelings about your dead father? You're not interested in that?

I enter with a forceful confrontation.

GEORGE: No, not particularly. Because I can't really see what difference it's going to make.

More resistance.

GRANDMOTHER: You mean to tell me you don't love your father?

Again, is this an assist from grandmother or an attempt to take over? The moment that grandmother opens her mouth, mother pipes in, too. The competition is intense.

GEORGE: No, I didn't say that.

MOTHER: Mother, please just a moment, you're talking too much. [to grandmother]

GEORGE: That's not what I said.

MOTHER: . . . maybe the hurt is so deep that you can't discuss it . . . feel that way.

DR. A.: I see. You want to pitch in, William, you stuck your finger out.

I pick up stepfather's gesture and ask him in.

STEPFATHER: No, I think they're all interfering with him. I'm, I'm interested in knowing what he has to say about it, too.

Who is interfering? Does he mean me or the women?

DR. A.: Mmm.

STEPFATHER: I think it's, it's everyone's interfering, I don't understand it. Maybe it's part of . . .

DR. A.: Am I interfering?

STEPFATHER: Oh, no, no, I'm not saying that. You're asking questions, but no one's giving him a chance to answer himself.

DR. A.: Mmm. You mean Grandma?

STEPFATHER: Well, it's Grandma, yes.

A rapid shift in the focus of conflict. Now, stepfather wants to shut Grandma's mouth. I join him in this, so does George. Now three men against Grandma.

DR. A.: Grandma, why don't you shut your mouth.

I confront Grandma.

GEORGE: You can tell her. It won't do any good.

George maintains his sense of defeat.

GRANDMOTHER: Because, uh, well, I don't know, should I . . .

DR. A.: Did you hear what you said? Won't do any good.

GEORGE: Gotta get her out of the room. That's the only thing that'll help.

DR. A.: Okay, get her out.

GRANDMOTHER: I'll go out.

Now, he confronts her. I support George enthusiastically. She resigns before she's fired.

GEORGE: No, it isn't going to help. I was just saying if you want her to be quiet that's the only way you'll do it.

George again "lowers his head."

DR. A.: All right. You can move your ass, you can escort Grandma out.

GEORGE: Well, do you want her out? [addressing Dr. A.]

He runs scared and tries to pass the buck for exclusion of Grandma.

DR. A.: Do you want her out?

GEORGE: It doesn't make any difference to me.

DR. A.: No, I don't believe you. You brought up the idea, the only way to shut Grandma's mouth is to excuse her from the room.

I pin him down.

GEORGE: Right.

DR. A.: Otherwise she can't stop talking.

GEORGE: Right.

DR. A.: You agreed she was the biggest nag in the family.

GEORGE: Okay. So.

DR. A.: Now on politics you state, you take a stand.

GEORGE: Mmhm.

DR. A.: And how come right now, you take no stand?

The theme repeats.

GEORGE: Mother, this . . .

DR. A.: Do you want your grandma out?

GRANDMOTHER: I'll go out.

GEORGE: No, not particularly. It doesn't make much of a difference . . . because I guess it's much better that, if she is here. I don't know.

DR. A.: Well, do you want to experiment? Do you want to try it?

GEORGE: I'll try it. There's nothing to lose.

DR. A.: Okay.

GRANDMOTHER: And you can take me by the arm.

DR. A.: You wait outside, Grandma, we might need you again.

GRANDMOTHER: Okay. [out she goes, submitting to Dr. A.]

GEORGE: My chair's over there! [He protests moving closer to Dr. A.]

This is another example of "repeopling' the family. I assumed the initiative in moving George's chair closer to mine. The physical move, the shift in seating arrangement, strengthens the confrontation. I further tickle his defenses: "You take a deep breath."

DR. A.: You take a deep breath! Am I right, you are getting ready to talk?

GEORGE: No.

DR. A.: No. You took a deep breath.

GEORGE: It's healthy.

DR. A.: I think you and mom both have a sense of relief now that grandma's mouth is outside. Can't interfere. You have the same feelings, mother, as George.

MOTHER: Well, mother . . .

DR. A.: . . . really impossible to shut your mother up.

My ploy to win mother over to son's side against

grandmother. The family as a system then will not be as able to hide their secrets.

MOTHER: Uh, not quite, well, she is a very uh, vocal person . . .

DR. A.: You told her to shut up.

MOTHER: And she sometimes interjects too much instead of, I'm sure we're here for a purpose, not to hear just one person.

DR. A.: So there's no competing with your mother's mouth.

MOTHER: That's right. And unfortunately she, not unfortunately, fortunately, she is a good speaker, and she's a bright woman, and she takes over a conversation.

DR. A.: True.

MOTHER: And it's true, I have to admit it.

DR. A.: You and your son can't compete with her mouth.

MOTHER: Very few people can.

DR. A.: Mmm.

MOTHER: We're not as vocal, not as articulate maybe. Not as free to express our own selves and our emotions as she is.

DR. A.: You and George can't open your mouths as big as grandmother.

MOTHER: Yes.

DR. A.: And you and George are closed.

Grandma shuts mouths, not George.

MOTHER: That's right.

DR. A.: Well, you were certainly closed up when Henry died. Both you and George.

I proceed to open their mouths. Back to the story of father's death.

MOTHER: Well, I think the shock was really too much for us. We couldn't understand what happened. We weren't at all prepared for anything like this.

DR. A.: Mmm.

MOTHER: There was no indication before, no clue, no hint, and to have something . . .

DR. A.: He was in good health.

MOTHER: That's right. And then I had to worry about the children and their welfare and how to support them financially. And I just didn't have the time to mourn actually . . .

Security is mother's first concern.

DR. A.: You didn't have the time.

MOTHER: I just had to find a job, I had to work, I had to support and take care of two children financially, and I did it all on my own.

DR. A.: Mmm. That's what you mean by saying you had to be strong on the outside.

MOTHER: That's right.

Mother is inwardly weak.

DR. A.: How'd you feel on the inside?

MOTHER: I think just numb.

DR. A.: You're still numb.

I'm empathic with her fright of feelings, her magical denial of death.

MOTHER: I am numb. Because it just couldn't happen, and it didn't happen.

DR. A.: It's not real.

MOTHER: That's it.

DR. A.: Mmm.

MOTHER: And I suppose we want to block out anything that's unpleasant to us and I suppose this is my method of doing it.

DR. A.: Then in your heart Henry is still alive.

I bring back the ghost of the father.

MOTHER: Apparently.

DR. A.: Since the death . . .

MOTHER: Apparently.

DR. A.: . . . so sudden, so shocking, not to be believed . . .

MOTHER: That's it.

DR. A.: Never digested . . .

MOTHER: That's it.

DR. A.: The realness of it. So he's still alive.

MOTHER: Evidently.

Mother's use here of stepfather's word is fascinating.

DR. A.: Shaking your head, William!

I bring stepfather back in. He is confused and resentful that they have not yet buried the ghost.

MOTHER: Pardon?

DR. A.: You're shaking your head. [to stepfather]

STEPFATHER: On no, not me, no.

DR. A.: No?

STEPFATHER: Not me.

MOTHER: I tried, try to analyze it and I just suppose I, I don't want to believe that it could have happened to me. And I try to make life for the children as pleasant as possible.

Here, mother ignores her new husband, like he doesn't belong.

DR. A.: How could you, how could you? Did you talk with George?

MOTHER: Yes.

DR. A.: About the death?

MOTHER: Not too much. Unfortunately, uh, maybe everybody should be taught how to react to certain situations, we go to school to learn things, education, a trade, a profession, but we don't learn how to express our feelings.

DR A.: You went to school, got trained to be a teacher.

MOTHER: Yes.

DR. A.: You're a teacher now, but you don't know how to teach anything about how to respond to a father's death.

MOTHER: Life. That's right. We're not prepared for these things.

Mother's unwillingness to deal with anxieties about death is sharply illuminated.

DR. A.: So what'd you say to your children?

MOTHER: Well, we had to explain it as best as we could, one of these very unfortunate circumstances, there was nothing we could even do to help them at the time, it happened so suddenly, even the doctor was unprepared for what happened.

DR. A.: Did he drop dead in an instant?

MOTHER: He went to work, he went down to his office, uh, I had just got, we had just come home from the beach . . .

GEORGE: Ma!

MOTHER: . . . that day, and he complained at the beach that he didn't feel well, that he had pain in his arm.

DR. A.: Were you there, George?

I turn sharply to George. I want to open him up to his feelings about the loss of his father. Mother intrudes, but I go right back to George.

MOTHER: Yes, George was there.

GEORGE: Yeah.

DR. A.: What happened?

MOTHER: Ellen [George's sister] wasn't there.

DR. A.: [to mother] Excuse me a minute. [to George] You were there, what happened? Did he complain?

GEORGE: No, at the beach I don't remember him complaining, unless it was all to my mother, but we came home, he went down to the doctor's office, and he said he should go to the hospital for a checkup.

MOTHER: Well, he was there too long, I took George upstairs—let me, just, because he doesn't remember the entire story.

Again, Mother intrudes; tries to shut George's mouth. A sure sign that she's hiding something.

DR. A.: One minute. [to mother]

MOTHER: I'm sorry.

DR. A.: You just cut George and me off.

I put mother on the hot seat.

MOTHER: I'm sorry.

DR. A.: I mean to cut off Grandma, that's one thing.

MOTHER: That's right.

DR. A.: You cut off Grandma's tongue, but your son and me?

I take mother to task. She intrudes to stop her son from joining me.

MOTHER: I'm sorry.

DR. A.: We'll get back to that in a minute. [to George] Go ahead.

GEORGE: Well, from what I understand then, he went to the doctor's and came home, he had dinner and said he had to go to the hospital for a checkup. My mother drove him and she told me that when they got there, they opened up the door, he just dropped, and they performed an operation, but it was no good.

DR. A.: He dropped dead on you? You were taking him to the hospital?

MOTHER: Yes.

DR. A.: You turned your face away. Helen, you feel it now.

MOTHER: Mmhm.

DR. A.: What do you feel now?

MOTHER: Very sad, sadness, that . . .

DR. A.: Your voice shook. What happened after that, George? You weren't there, he just dropped dead out of the car.

I pick up on mother's tone of voice: sadness, loss, and guilt. Again I show interest in George.

GEORGE: Well I didn't know anything when they came home, but uh, I, I did wake up earlier that morning and I did hear them talking and they thought I was still asleep, and uh, I, I was just in the room for a while, I don't remember what I did or anything, but uh . . .

He evades.

DR. A.: What'd you hear?

GEORGE: No, I heard that, uh, he was dead, you know.

DR. A.: Oh, you heard . . .

GEORGE: They were going to tell me when they woke up . . .

GEORGE: And they thought I was still asleep.

DR. A.: I see.

DR. A.: How'd you feel?

GEORGE: I don't know.

DR. A.: Did you let yourself feel?

I point up the suppression, constriction, and denial of emotion in both mother and George.

GEORGE: I tried not to.

DR. A.: It cut your heart out.

I confront George sharply; I want to pin him down.

GEORGE: I wouldn't say that.

DR. A.: Well, that's what it amounts to. Emotions come from the heart.

GEORGE: Well, you can still feel your emotions.

DR. A.: Your own heart. Hmm?

GEORGE: No, you still feel your emotions, it's just whether you express it or not. There's a difference.

DR. A.: Uh huh. What did you feel? You say you didn't express it, what'd you feel?

GEORGE: I, I don't, I can't.

DR. A.: What do you feel right now?

GEORGE: I, just an, right now, just an uneasiness, that's . . .

Mother and George begin to thaw.

DR. A.: Mmm. Mom's crying now. She has a lot of tears to catch up with. [to mother] You're crying. [back to George] It's not only I that's waiting, Mom is waiting for something from you. She's been looking at you with tears in her eyes.

The first real sign of a breakthrough. I crack another dam. She begins to weep. To soften George, I make him look straight into Mother's tearful face.

GEORGE: I don't know what you want.

DR. A.: You're afraid to look at mom now.

GEORGE: I'll look.

DR. A.: Hmm?

GEORGE: I can look at her.

DR. A.: You're uneasy.

GEORGE: Well, I'm uneasy, yes.

DR. A.: How about that uneasy feeling?

George's anxiety swells. He resists crying with mother.

GEORGE: What do you mean, how about it?

DR. A.: What's it like?

GEORGE: It's just uneasy.

DR. A.: Mmm.

GEORGE: Like you're expecting me to cry, or something. That's the way I feel now.

The giveaway.

DR. A.: You got it in you.

GEORGE: Mm. Maybe.

DR. A.: Just like mom.

I'm trying here to join son and mother together in their common grief.

GEORGE: Mm.

DR. A.: You wouldn't feel much more uneasy if you cried? On the outside as well as on the inside, like mom?

GEORGE: That, that I don't know.

DR. A.: Mm. I think so. So they thought you were asleep and you overheard them. And you learned your father had dropped dead. And they were going to tell you later.

There is a hidden problem. Why did mother try to hide father's death from George?

GEORGE: Yeah.

DR. A.: What'd you do then?

GEORGE: Well, I was just in the room for a while. I don't . . .

DR. A.: Hmm?

GEORGE: I was in the room, I don't remember what I did.

I catch a vague hint that George took up mother's secret guilt.

DR. A.: Tell me what happened after that.

GEORGE: Well, I went in the kitchen and they told me. I, that I don't remember.

DR. A.: Mm. You got a case of loss of memory. Suffering from amnesia?

I tease George about his convenient "forgetting."

GEORGE: No.

DR. A.: You don't remember what happened in the kitchen, you don't remember telling William what the hell, it doesn't make any difference. You don't care anymore, it doesn't matter what happens to you. Since your father dropped dead, you might as well kill yourself.

GEORGE: I don't remember that.

DR. A.: You have, that's what I said, a loss of memory.

GEORGE: I disagree with you.

DR. A.: What is your feeling?

GEORGE: No, I, it's not a loss of memory.

DR. A.: What is it?

GEORGE: I disagree with you. Like I pointed out before, I mean I don't remember. Ask most people what they did a certain time, two days ago, they won't remember.

Again, I stick my neck out; George chops off my head.

DR. A.: I see. Okay. What do you remember? What do you remember?

GEORGE: About what?

More stalling.

DR. A.: Anything about your father.

GEORGE: No, I, I remember, you know, we lived in Florida and my father was in the construction of houses there. Went over there to look at them, you know. I don't, I don't know . . .

DR. A.: That was Pop's business?

GEORGE: Yeah.

DR. A.: Was he building houses? Was he good at it?

GEORGE: Well, that I don't know, I mean, you know, I can only . . .

DR. A.: Mm.

GEORGE: You know, I feel as though I don't know enough about the business.

DR. A.: He took you, took you along with him to, to the sites of these new houses.

GEORGE: Yeah. Well, they were pretty near by.

DR. A.: He thought you might be interested, what?

GEORGE: Well, to show it to us.

DR. A.: I see.

GEORGE: He named the model of the house after my sister.

DR. A.: He did. After sister. What did he . . .

GEORGE: Yeah, the Ellen.

DR. A.: What did he name after you?

GEORGE: Well, nothing.

Is there an implication here of father preferring daughter over son?

DR. A.: Nothing?

GEORGE: It was uh, uh, much more attractive as far as advertising goes. For her, the feminine name.

DR. A.: I see. The name, Ellen, for the model home is more attractive.

GEORGE: More feminine rather than masculine.

DR. A.: I see. Well, then Ellen had something named after her by Pop, and you? Nothing named after you.

GEORGE: This is, I think, very immaterial, because, you know, he may have given me a lollypop one time and nothing to her, so uh, you know, I say this is, you know, very immaterial.

More evasion and clouding.

DR. A.: You're right. You're quite right. What'd he give you, a lollypop?

GEORGE: No, I was just saying that, you know. He could have given it to me and not given something to her.

Did son want to suck on his father?

DR. A.: What did he give you? If you remember. What'd you get?

GEORGE: What do you mean, what did I get?

DR. A.: What'd you get from your old man?

GEORGE: Materialwise, or what?

DR. A.: Any which way you like.

GEORGE: I don't understand what . . .

DR. A.: Mom's still looking at you very intently.

MOTHER: Because I, I know the words to put in his mouth, but I won't do it for him, I want him to tell it to you.

DR. A.: You don't want to talk like Grandma.

MOTHER: That's right.

DR. A.: Mm. Mmhm. Grandma has already talked for George.

MOTHER: And I realize we're here for a purpose.

DR. A.: George, didn't Pop give you something for yourself?

MOTHER: That's it. I want him to make the statement on his own.

Mother speaks for George and at the same time disclaims it: a "double bind."

DR. A.: [to Mother] Mm. Are you a little more ready to speak for yourself? [rather than for George]

I put her on the spot.

MOTHER: Not completely.

DR. A.: No. Are you willing to say what you got from Henry?

MOTHER: Mmhm.

DR. A.: What'd you get from Henry?

MOTHER: Now, there are things, love, affection, devotion, he was a wonderful father, very good family man, crazy about his children, and we were always together. But we had problems, like there are problems in any marriage.

Baloney!

DR. A.: What were they?

MOTHER: Well, he was a dreamer, and he went from one enterprise to another . . .

DR. A.: I see.

MOTHER: . . . and they were usually unsuccessful . . . enterprises.

DR. A.: Okay. I see.

MOTHER: Let's be, we'll be very honest. And financially he was not successful, and this was a very horrible thing for him, as a man.

At last, at last! The truth will out! Father was an ineffective dreamer, a chronic failure. This made mother extremely angry.

DR. A.: He felt like a flop in life?

MOTHER: Well, he was always . . .

DR. A.: He was a failure?

MOTHER: . . . striving for something . . .

DR. A.: Yeah, yeah.

MOTHER: . . . and I don't know what it was.

DR. A.: Big dreamer.

MOTHER: That's it. He was always dreaming.

DR. A.: Mmm.

MOTHER: His dreams never materialized.

DR. A.: And how did you feel about it?

MOTHER: But it didn't discourage him.

DR. A.: How did you feel about it?

MOTHER: Well, for the longest time I was very, very much against all these new ideas, but after a while, if you love somebody, you have to learn to live with certain things.

Baloney, again.

DR. A.: You tried to knock down these dreams.

MOTHER: To discourage, that's right.

DR. A.: To put a pin in these dream bubbles.

MOTHER: Unfortunately.

DR. A.: You punctured his bubble.

MOTHER: Well, after a certain amount of time, you do. Somebody has to be realistic and down to earth.

Mother retaliated. She stuck a pin in him.

DR. A.: Hmm. How'd he take it when you stuck a pin in him?

MOTHER: Well, no one takes discouragement.

DR. A.: How'd he take it?

MOTHER: He didn't take it too well, I'm afraid.

DR. A.: Did you fight?

MOTHER: Certain amount of arguing. Not fighting. I'm not a fighter.

DR. A.: Just stick a pin in.

MOTHER: I don't get hysterical.

DR. A.: Mm.

MOTHER: But in any home situation, you can't agree on everything all the time. Each one is an individual. Right or wrong. But he went ahead with each and every dream of his, whatever he wanted to do, he did.

Baloney, once again.

DR. A.: Mmhm. When you stuck a pin in, you didn't succeed in stopping him?

MOTHER: No.

DR. A.: He went right on.

MOTHER: Mmhm.

DR. A.: Blowing bubbles in the air.

MOTHER: That's right. Mmhm.

DR. A.: Did he go into hock?

Back to the question of money.

MOTHER: Lot of times.

DR. A.: Where'd he get the money?

MOTHER: This is most amazing, he always . . .

DR. A.: How'd he get capital?

MOTHER: . . . found somebody who would back him. He was a very bright man, very personable.

DR. A.: Well, he had to find a backer, you would back him.

MOTHER: He could always find, he could always find somebody. And this was our only area of dissension.

DR. A.: I see. Well, did he, uh, lose your money? In these enterprises?

MOTHER: Yes.

DR. A.: He bankrupted you!

The story now emerges of the father's habitual failure in business and his "stealing" mother's savings.

MOTHER: Yeah.

DR. A.: Tsk, tsk, tsk, how'd you feel about it?

MOTHER: Not very happy, naturally.

Mother barely admits her hostility.

DR. A.: Mmm. So Henry was in hock to you.

MOTHER: Well, he couldn't be in hock to me. Actually it's his money, if he's working, it was his money.

DR. A.: When you saved some money, he took it away from you?

MOTHER: Yes.

DR. A.: How much did you save that he took away?

I pin mother down with a blunt demand for a specific answer.

MOTHER: There were various amounts through the years, I don't remember them.

DR. A.: Why don't you remember?

MOTHER: I don't remember them.

Mother and son alike!

DR. A.: You have convenient "forgettery," too.

MOTHER: We all forget what we don't want to remember.

DR. A.: Like George?

MOTHER: Right, Dr. A.

DR. A.: Yeah. Well, was it a million bucks?

MOTHER: Uh, no, because we were never in that position. Whether it was $500, or a $1000, or $50, it would be gone sooner or later.

DR. A.: So, in effect, uh, your own husband, Henry, rifled your purse.

This phrase "rifled your purse" is used with double meaning. Husband robbed her from secret (anal) vault rather than coming in front.

MOTHER: I could have told you the same thing, Dr. A.

DR. A.: But you didn't.

MOTHER: It's a peculiar situation. You don't like your son to know these things and you don't want your husband to know these things.

She admits to hypocrisy, to her secret shame.

DR. A.: Oh, I see, I see, I see. But a moment ago you said they may as well know the truth. The truth will out.

Mother now looks anxiously at George. Then at her second husband, William. The final indictment, the dead father was a "thief."

MOTHER: Yes, you . . .

DR. A.: You looked at George.

MOTHER: Well, I . . .

DR. A.: You looked at William.

MOTHER: . . . diagnosed it, I don't want to call him a thief.

DR. A.: Hmm.

MOTHER: I can't use those words.

DR. A.: You can't use those words. You hear that, George?

GEORGE: Yeah.

DR. A.: Did you feel anything when your mother said that? She doesn't want to call your father a thief.

GEORGE: I don't, I don't understand, give me another lead.

George stalls again.

DR. A.: It's your own father, Henry.

GEORGE: I don't understand what you want me to . . .

DR. A.: What'd you feel when mother said that?

I try pointedly to test his feelings about this indictment of father.

GEORGE: Well, uh, do you mean do I feel it was right what he did?

DR. A.: I, I don't know.

GEORGE: I, well, that's what I'm asking you. You're asking me, I'd like to know what you're asking me.

DR. A.: What'd you feel? You were listening.

GEORGE: Yes.

DR. A.: Did you feel something when mother said that?

GEORGE: I don't know.

DR. A.: Mother's always tried to protect herself and you from painful things in the family. Unpleasant things. Threatening things. This was a big threat. Terrible danger. The man who is supposed to provide for the family, your husband, the children's father, was throwing it away on a dream house. Your food. George's food, Ellen's food. And he took more money right out of your pocket. You tried to hide that from George?

When George evades the question, I sharpen the issue.

MOTHER: Mmhm.

DR. A.: You think you succeeded?

MOTHER: Apparently not.

DR. A.: He's here, you can ask him.

MOTHER: Did I succeed in, did you realize what was going on?

GEORGE: Yeah, well, I had remembered some instances . . .

DR. A.: Hmm?

GEORGE: . . . when I heard, uh . . .

DR. A.: What'd you hear?

GEORGE: No, you know, uh, arguing about money and so, that's uh . . .

DR. A.: What'd you hear?

GEORGE: What, it was a long time ago, so I don't remember. But uh, and I know, you know, it was not so hot, the business and stuff.

DR. A.: You threw a great big fog around these things, George. Like your mother you're not supposed to see those things. You're not supposed to know about them. That's right, your mother didn't want you to know about them. Did you overhear anything about mother's anger at Pop for taking her money?

The drama here is like that of a scene in a courtroom.

GEORGE: No, that . . .

DR. A.: To dissipate her savings? Did you know about that? Is this all news to you, William? You didn't know?

The case is being tried. Who committed the crime? Who was an accomplice to it? Why do they hide?

STEPFATHER: Yes. In all our married life we, we never discussed Henry in any vein. The only thing I knew, he was an engineer, period. I mean we've never discussed Henry in any vein, whatsoever.

DR. A.: So all these secrets were locked up in the trunk. Or I should say in the coffin.

STEPFATHER: I didn't know about it. It doesn't make any difference to me at this point.

DR. A.: Made no difference?

STEPFATHER: Only it's, it's . . .

DR. A.: A clue to George's behavior.

STEPFATHER: A clue to something, that's exactly what it is.

MOTHER: That's a good way to put it.

STEPFATHER: Now, I see things a little different.

DR. A.: What do you see now that's different?

STEPFATHER: Well, to me, possibly he's emulating his father or trying to emulate his father, maybe through deep love or something.

Here's the ghost in the family closet. George emulates father's "stealing."

DR. A.: You mean like father, like son? I mean his father's a thief, he's a thief? Is that what you mean?

STEPFATHER: If you use that term, thief . . .

DR. A.: I see.

STEPFATHER: Well, if you use that term thief, that's the term I'd use then, but the fact remains that there are many things, for instance now, when I got to know Helen and the family, anything around the house that had to be done, they said George is as good as his father, he's a good engineer, he's a good mechanic, and all that. And he did things. Well, I'm not a mechanic, but I've seen things he's done and the limited knowledge I have, he doesn't do a good job.

Stepfather discloses his feeling of emasculation by his wife. Always George can do it! He, the stepfather, can't!

MOTHER: But he's very young, too, he has to . . .

STEPFATHER: I know that, I'm not saying that, honey, I'm not saying that.

DR. A.: Don't make like Grandma, now, William.

STEPFATHER: I'm not saying that . . . I'm not criticizing, but I'm saying, this is what they've always said, oh George could do it, he can, knows how to fix it.

DR. A.: Yes.

STEPFATHER: I watched how he had wired the TV set in the apartment yet, and you know, I'm a safety engineer, I shudder when I saw the wires all over the place, and you get three plugs coming out of one outlet, or four plugs; and then when we went over to the house there, I said George, I, I'd like to put up the antenna. He put it up, I don't think, it's not a professional job, I know. But it was strictly an amateur job; it has to be done better than that.

DR. A.: Henry was a lousy builder and now George is a lousy builder?

STEPFATHER: I don't know, but I'm saying they, they always match George [against me], they say George can do it, his father was a good mechanic or engineer.

Stepfather hits back.

DR. A.: And you say his father was very unhandy.

STEPFATHER: I don't know, I can't say.

DR. A.: George is very unhandy.

STEPFATHER: Well, let's say he didn't put everything into a job, that I imagine he could have done it better than he did. It wasn't a polished job, it wasn't a finished job.

DR. A.: George, how do you feel when your stepfather says you're no good with your hands?

GEORGE: Well . . .

DR. A.: You're a sloppy builder.

STEPFATHER: That's right. I won't say he's not good with his hands, I'll say that his job isn't finished. It's a sloppiness there.

DR. A.: A sloppy builder. How do you feel?

GEORGE: Hm?

DR. A.: How do you feel when your stepfather says that about you?

Time is up, and this interview must be ended. The emotional field is now open, or at least more open, for the next interview.

PART VI

Marriage

Although Ackerman was always conscious of the marital pair in his work with children, he only began to address the topic of marriage itself in the mid-fifties, when his ideas about family dynamics were already clearly formulated. He held that marriage relationships were but a fragment of family life and was ambivalent about considering them as a separate entity, at least in print. His clearest statement on the subject came in 1965, in "The Family Approach to Marital Disorders." Here he combined his interest in marriage as a social institution, as an expression of two families-of-origin, and as a clinical entity and challenge in its own right. In this paper he also essayed a typology of marriage, an effort obviously related to his long quest for a rational typology of families.

CHAPTER 38

The Diagnosis of Neurotic Marital Interaction

This paper is concerned with the means for evaluating the mental health of marital relationships. Within this context special emphasis is placed on the search for appropriate criteria for the psychosocial diagnosis of neurotic marital relationships. The mental health of family relationships is, in the main, an expression of social process. Unhealthy marital relationships, widespread as they are, are significant not only for themselves, but as the epitome and the very core of disintegrative trends in family life as a whole, and as forerunners of emotional illness in the offspring of such unions.

The rate of divorce has now reached a point where there is one divorce for every three or four marriages. Even when marital conflict does not culminate in legal divorce, the disturbance often reaches such a critical point as to bring about an "emotional divorce" of the parents. The day-by-day experience of psychotherapists, educators, and spiritual advisers affirms this as a crucial mental health problem in regard to both therapy and prevention.

We live in an age of social crisis. We have reason to believe that the intrinsic value conflicts of our changing culture have a direct bearing on the fate of family life and family relationships. It requires no great stretch of the imagination to realize that the survival or destruction of our kind of civilization will depend in no small part on how these value conflicts are resolved and what happens concurrently to the mental health of the family. It is the clear and present threat to our cherished values in family living which challenges us. The threat is a large one and it hits home, literally. Our anxiety is for ourselves and this impels us to take a stand on the issues involved.

Naturally, it would be our wish to apply the dynamic insights of psychoanalysis to the mental health problems of marital relationships and family life. We must admit, however, that up to the present our scientific concepts are not yet adequate to the task, though we are making

Reprinted with permission from *Social Casework*, April 1954, Vol. 35, 139-143.

progress in this direction. We can readily discern some of the relevant developments in the behavior sciences: the emphasis on multidisciplinary research, the joining of hands of psychoanalysis and the social sciences, the increased influence of the anthropological principle of relativity of behavior, the effort to move beyond Freud in linking the phenomena of biological maturation with the processes of social participation, the effort to correlate ego-dynamics with social interaction, the rediscovery of the ancient principle that behavior is determined not only by a person's view of his past, but also by his view of the future, and so on. In a recent lecture, Dr. Frieda Fromm-Reichmann made the statement that we are on the eve of a revolution in the development of our understanding of the principles of human behavior and the principles of psychotherapy.

Of particular importance is the need to evaluate pathology of individual personality not in isolation, but within the frame of the psychosocial structure of the family, and to establish the specific dynamic relations of personality and family roles. Only as we can correctly merge the dynamics of individual and group behavior does it begin to be possible to deal effectively with the mental health problems of family and marital relationships.

For several years I have been engaged in the study of the problems of family diagnosis. Naturally, a central aspect of this study is the development of criteria for the diagnosis of marital interaction. In this research on family diagnosis, our particular interest has been the exploration of the relation of emerging emotional disturbance in a young child to the group dynamics of family life. Toward this end, the child, though a distinct unit in the biological sense, is viewed not as an intact, separate individual but rather as a functional expression of the social interaction processes that characterize the given family. At each stage of development we explore the child's interaction with mother, with father, with parents as a couple; we explore further the relation of personality to the marital and parental roles and, finally, the family as an integrated social unit. We attempt then to relate these data specifically to the patterns of child rearing and child pathology.

The nature of this research requires a conceptual frame within which it is possible to interrelate the dynamics of the individual with the dynamics of the group—that is, to correlate intrapsychic processes with interpersonal ones, the phenomena of individual personality with the phenomena of family role—and finally to relate these partial processes to the psychosocial dynamics of the family as a whole. In accordance with this scheme, we have investigated thus far forty families, in which child and parent have been or still are in therapy. In the course of this study, it has been necessary to evaluate systematically the marital relationship, its history, its path of motivation, and the past and current pattern of marital interaction. The long-term goal is to build a conceptual framework for psychosocial diagnosis of the family, and also of marital and parental role function. In this context it is self-evident that the issues of mental health must be considered both at the individual and group levels.

In approaching the problems of diagnosis of marital relationships, we are concerned with the concept of diagnosis not as a mere label, but as a definitive evaluation that absorbs within itself the dynamics and the etiology of the disorder. In the mental health field, diagnosis and therapy are two facets of an essentially unitary process: diagnosis has meaning only in the context of devising a plan of action. When we seek to define what has gone wrong we are already embarked on the path of applying appropriate corrective action, a therapeutic program. Precisely because of the affinity and interdependence of diagnosis and therapy, it is poor practice to apply therapy in the absence of rigorous standards of diagnostic formulation.

Of first importance is the clear-cut recognition of the general category into which this problem falls. In undertaking to diagnose marital relationships, we are not concerned in the first instance with the autonomous functions and pathology of individual personalities, but rather with the dynamics of the relationship, that is, with the reciprocal role functions that define the relations of husband and wife.

A relationship represents more than the sum of the personalities that make it up. The whole is greater than the sum of its parts. A marital relationship, like a chemical compound, has unique properties of its own over and above the characteristics of the elements that merge to form the compound. A new level of organization creates new qualities. A marital relationship is therefore an entity, new and different, but, again like a chemical compound, its properties, while unique, preserve a specific dynamic relation to the elements that have joined in its creation. This is another way of saying that the psychological principles that govern the behavior of an individual and those that govern the behavior of a relationship are not the same, that we cannot directly extrapolate from our knowledge of individual personality to behavior of a relationship or a group, that the psychological processes involved at the relationship or group level must be viewed in a different dimension because a different level of biosocial organization is implicated. The dynamics of the two situations, individual and group, are therefore not interchangeable, and the integrative processes appropriate to the one level of biosocial organization cannot be imposed upon the other.

By way of pointing more sharply to the nature of our problem, let us consider the mental health implications of some common empirical observations. The outcome in mental health terms of a particular marriage relationship is not contingent exclusively on the character of the neurosis of the individual partners. The ultimate effects on mental health are determined rather by the dynamic part that neurotic conflict plays in the complex process of integration of the personalities of the partners into the reciprocal roles of husband and wife. The factors that shape this process are multiple; we shall discuss them at a later point. In some instances neurotic conflict destroys the marriage; in others, it seems to save the marriage. It is common knowledge that the neurosis of one marital partner often complements that of the other. Sometimes the traits of one partner reinforce in the other healthy defenses against neurotic conflict, so that its destructive effects are highly mitigated. Sometimes this form of "complementarity" decompensates and the marital relationship progressively disintegrates. The bad marriages that neurotic persons often make are notorious but what enables some to make good ones? The wonder is not so much that one neurotic marries another one but rather that some neurotics marry partners who enable them to strengthen themselves against neurotic regression and also support them so that they can function as reasonably good parents.

The potentially hopeful aspect of this whole problem is that some neurotics, despite traumatic childhoods, make fine marriages and fine parents. Neurosis in individual personality, therefore, is not the sole factor that predetermines the fate of marriage, family life, and the new crop of children. Were it so, there would be little hope for the world. The saving grace is that character can and does change after the crucial childhood years. If we are motivated to rehabilitate the mental health of a disturbed marital relationship, we must take into account not only the neurotic core of behavior but also the malleable aspects of character in both partners, the factor of realistic strength in their personalities, the residually healthy ego tendencies, the positive qualities of the marital relationship and of the family life, and the motivation of both partners for change; all these are needed to counterbalance neurotic tendencies.

THE SALIENT FACTORS IN MARITAL DISTURBANCE

Disturbances of marital relationship are characterized by two salient elements: (1) failure of reciprocity of satisfactions and (2) conflict. The conflict usually bears a specific relation to the failure of reciprocity in the relationship. With our present inadequate knowledge, it is easier to spot the more obviously pathological marital relationships than it is to be definitive regarding the standards of "normal" or "healthy" marital interaction. Yet, the goal of progress in scientific understanding of such problems requires a continuing effort to achieve an explicit formulation of "healthy" marital interaction, elusive and changing as this may be in our culture. We hope that, from the criteria for evaluating the dynamics of marital interaction which are here considered, we can evolve a useful operational definition for a healthy marital relationship.

For clinicians, conflict in marital relationships presents a knotty problem. The relevant factors are multiple and of a complex nature; they overlap and interact to such an extent that a clear and communicable definition of the problem is difficult to achieve. Our task is to reduce the salient issues to a clear-cut formulation, but this is more easily said than done.

In marital disorders conflict may be overt or covert, real or unreal, conscious or unconscious, in varying mixtures. The conflict between the partners, moreover, bears a special relationship to the structure of intrapsychic conflict in each partner. The very first question to arise is: What part of the conflict is real, what part unreal and determined by neurotic perception and motivation? Further, how does the unreal part secondarily distort the relatively more real aspects of marital interaction? Regarding that level of the interaction which is relatively realistic, all that is needed is accurate awareness of it, and a plan of action appropriate to this awareness. One cannot psychoanalyze realistic components of experience. The unreal part, structured by neurotic interaction, calls for a different program—definitive diagnostic evaluation and suitable psychotherapeutic correction.

In the first instance, then, it is important to see the neurotic pattern of marital interaction in the context of total interaction. Although it is easy to detect the more pathological types of neurotic marital relationships, the task of evaluating the mental health significance of specific patterns of neurotic interaction in the context of the total relationship and the prevailing social realities is a complex one. The effects of neurotic motivation may be variably diffuse or localized both in individual personality and in a relationship. Just as, in the individual, some areas of adaptive functioning may be heavily disabled and other areas relatively conflict-free and less disabled, so, in a relationship, some levels of interaction may be critically impaired while others are relatively conflict-free and less impaired.

It is common observation, however, that neurotic disturbance of a marital relationship is rarely, if ever, the creation of just one of the partners. In marital pairs ambivalently bound in neurotic love and neurotic competition, when one partner exhibits pathological anxiety responses, the other usually does too. Being immature and unready for full heterosexual union, the partners tend to parentify each other. Seeking the love and protection of a parent figure in the marital partner, each pushes the relationship toward the needed form of child-parent relationship. In this context, the marital relationship is forced to assume a compensatory and curative function for the anxiety-provoking features of the original child-parent experience. Insofar as the marital relationship is coerced into satisfying conflicted and regressed childhood needs, or compensating for the lact of fulfilment, the relationship is burdened with an extra and an inappropriate psychic load. It should be remembered, however, that some marriage relationships are so patterned as to bear this extra load with a minimum of damage to mental health.

In any case, a clinician faced with such a relationship problem must make some ticklish decisions. Should one or both of the partners receive psychotherapy? If both, should the two therapies be initiated at the same time or staggered? Should the two partners be treated by the same or different therapists? If by different therapists, can the therapeutic efforts be co-ordinated? If only one partner is to be treated, which one? And by what kind of psychotherapist? By what criteria do clinicians currently draw such judgments? If we speak with candor, we cannot but admit that at present such judgments are arrived at either intuitively, or with a relatively crude assay of the relevant facts, rather than with an ordered diagnostic formulation both of the facts and of the dynamic relations between them. Clearly, the latter is an ideal toward which we must strive.

Once psychotherapy is initiated, whatever the criteria, there are further problems. It is hardly possible with present knowledge to predict with any real confidence the effects of psychotherapy of one or both partners on the marital relationship itself. As any practicing therapist knows, such predictions are hazardous and are apt to be wrong as often as they are right. This empirical observation in and of itself attests strongly to the inadequacy of present-day criteria for both the diagnosis and therapy of marital disorders. The actual results of psychotherapy from our standpoint are extremely variable. Sometimes the psychotherapy of individual partners ameliorates the disturbance in the marital relationship. Sometimes it has little or no effect; sometimes, and this is quite striking, as one partner gets better the other gets worse, and the relationship suffers further damage accordingly. In a seeming paradox, the increased health and strength of one partner become an added menace to the other. As one partner matures and becomes sexually more adequate, the other gets depressed and shows signs of regression. This unfortunate result is more likely to occur when the psychotherapy of one of the partners is oriented to an abstract goal of cure of individual neurosis without regard to the complex factors that control the emotional balance between the partners. It is unreal to treat neurotic tendencies in a marital partner as if he existed in a social vacuum. The interdependence and reciprocity of the roles of husband and wife should be remembered. Any effect on the one partner will always influence the behavior of the other.

The hopeful assumption that therapeutic resolution of neurotic anxiety in one or both partners will mitigate the marital disorder proves on occasion to be unwarranted. Some of the reasons for this are clear; neurotic anxiety, although a significant etiological factor, is but one among the many that determine the fate of such a relationship. The causal factors lie partly in the pathology of the individual personalities, partly in the special characteristics of the relationship itself; the relationship is multiply determined in a variety of ways—by the compatibility of temperament, goals, values, and interests, by the quality of empathy and communication, by lines of identification, by reciprocity of emotional and sexual need, by the contingencies of ancillary relationships and of social events, and so on.

Finally, there is a specific factor deriving from the vicissitudes of the psychotherapeutic experience itself which is difficult to appraise. It matters considerably whether the patient's presenting complaint is his neurotic disability or conflict in the marital relationship. What the patient asks to be cured of is of no small importance since this affects his motivation for change. The effects of therapy are in part the result of who practices it and how it is practiced. The primary focus of classical forms of psychotherapy, especially psychoanalytic therapy, has been the internal economy of the individual personality, even though the therapy uses relationship process as its medium. The inner orientation to self and to neurotically conflicted personal needs receives the primary emphasis, rather than the processes of social interaction. Although the orientation to self affects orientation to other persons, and vice versa, there is by no means a one-to-one correlation between the two. This involves the elusive problem of the dynamic interplay of individual and group experience, many facets of which are not yet clearly understood. It is apparent, then, that the extent to which disturbance in a marital relationship is alleviated by individual psychotherapy of one or both partners varies with many factors: the nature of the pathology of the relationship; the secondary effects of ancillary relationships; the psychosocial status of the family as a whole and each marital partner's corresponding adaptation; and, finally, the nature of the pathology and psychotherapy of each partner and whether the therapy of the one partner is effectively coordinated with the therapy of the other.

A corrective approach to marital disturbance cannot, therefore, be a simple undertaking. It is a question of the therapy of "husbanding and wifing," rather than straight therapy for an individual neurosis. I have stressed some of the complexities of the therapeutic challenge because, as already indicated, diagnosis has meaning only in the context of devising a plan of action.

(The second half of the paper has been omitted here. It contains an overview of diagnostic assessment of marriage and comments on the role of the therapist. These were restated in more refined form a decade later, in "The Family Approach to Marital Disorders," which follows.)

CHAPTER 39

The Family Approach to Marital Disorders

It is common knowledge today that the social institution of marriage is not working as we should like it to. To be sure, the institution of marriage is here to stay, but it is not the same any more. It is rickety; its joints creak. It threatens to crack wide open. Although marriage may be ordained in heaven, it is surely falling apart on earth, at least in our part of the world. Three generations survey the record with dismay. The older married folks look down with silent reproach on the younger ones. The younger married folks look at themselves in shock and perplexity and wonder how on earth they got this way. The children look at their parents, not with reverent respect, but with bitter accusation. They indict their parents: "You are wrecking our family. What are you doing to yourselves and to us? You are failing miserably. Why?"

In the present-day community, anxiety about the instability of marriage and family is widespread. The sources of worry are the "side-wise" marriage, the teenage marriage, infidelity, desertion, divorce, multiple marriages, the loosening of sex standards, the war between the sexes, "momism," the weakness of fathers, the reduction of parental authority, the broken home, emotionally injured children, the anarchy of youth, and the trend toward delinquency. With all these problems comes a growing disillusionment with the tradition and sentiment of marriage and family.

If today the marriage bond is unstable, it is because the entire constellation of the contemporary family is itself unstable. As our way of life at all levels—family, community, and culture—is in a state of flux, the style of marriage must also echo the profound currents of change and instability.

Healing forces do emerge, but the healing itself is often warped. It is analogous to what surgeons call "the pathological healing" of a wound. For a multiplicity of reasons, we are challenged to take a new look at this old problem and, if possible, to discover a fresh approach to the marital disorders of our time.

For me, a psychiatric clinician, the marital problem poses a tantalizing challenge, comparable to that of a complicated jigsaw puzzle. We find one part that fits; instantly we hope and

---

Reprinted with permission from *The Psychotherapies of Marital Disharmony*, Bernard Greene (Ed.), 1965, 153-167.

expect that all the others will fall quickly into place and reveal the hidden design; but it is not so easy.

Marriage is more than sex; it is a whole way of life. It is a joining together in the work, joys, and sadnesses of life. Disorders of the marital relationship cannot be understood in a social vacuum. The fit or lack of fit of the partners can be properly appraised only within the framework of the family viewed as an integrated behavior system with dominant values and a definable organizational pattern. The marital adaptation must be seen within that larger network of relationships that reflects the identity connections of each partner with his family of origin and with the larger community. Relevant beyond sexual union are the basic functions of family that have to do with security, child-rearing, social training, and the development of the marriage partners both as a couple and as individuals.

To illustrate: A social worker of twenty-four years, married six months, was considering divorce. In the initial psychiatric interview, try as I might, I could not find the slightest hint of her motive. Why divorce? Finally, in desperation, I asked, "Is it your sex life? What in the world is wrong?"

"Oh, no," she said, "my husband is an expert lover. Believe me, sexual intercourse is just great. The only trouble is that there is no verbal intercourse at all." Diagnosis: physical relations, good; emotional interchange, none. The complaint of "silent treatment" in married life is a frequent one these days.

Interviewing another couple, a kewpie doll of a wife and a big, burly police captain of a husband, I had a different experience. This couple had been married ten years and had three children. The wife threatened divorce. She was cute, childlike, but she breathed fire. She let loose a barrage of bitter accusations. For the better part of an hour her husband sat mute; he could not get a word in edgewise. What was her complaint? Her husband had cheated her out of her rights as a woman. When they married, she had been naive and innocent. For ten years, her husband had not given her the remotest hint that a woman is supposed to enjoy sex. Only recently, at the New School for Social Research, had she learned for the first time that a woman may have an orgasm. Through gnashing jaws, she spat out a furious ultimatum. It was her husband's duty to see to it that she had an orgasm or else!

An interesting phenomenon is the group of couples who swap partners for weekends. Many of these marriages deteriorate rapidly. In a few cases, however, there is a paradoxical response. The adventure of infidelity seems to have a remarkable healing effect on the marriage. It is a disturbing invasion of the lives of both partners, but strangely enough, if they pass through this crisis, each may emerge a stronger person. They experience mutual learning, and their companionship grows closer, their love life richer. They both grow as people. In one such case, the wife reacted to the shocking discovery of her husband's romance with an attractive Negro actress with the prompt disappearance of her sexual frigidity. This change delighted her husband and impelled him to characterize his Negro *amour* as the best psychotherapist he and his wife could have had.

This case is but one small example of the attitudes of the sex-seekers of our time. One way or another, they engage in a frantic search for new sexual kicks that they expect to be magic cure-alls.

In another case, a wife reacted with pathological jealousy. She was "bugged" on her husband's imagined sexual antics with other playmates; she plagued him incessantly. She was depressed, agitated, unable to sleep—nor did she let her husband sleep. She knew that her husband had erotic interests in women wrestlers and weight-lifters. When her husband asked her to lift him or hold him in her lap she refused. "It might break my back." She entered the role of detective in order "to get the goods" on her husband. She discovered in his desk a batch of pictures of female weight-lifters in scanty attire. Finding a stain on her husband's underclothing, she sent a piece of it to the chemical laboratory. The report came back: "positive; many spermatozoa were found together with large numbers of squamous epithelial cells. The finding of many squamous epithelial cells is indicative of the presence of vaginal secretion along with the spermatozoa." This evidence clinched the wife's case. She crucified her husband with this "proof." She demanded that he confess the truth. What new sexual tricks had he learned from "these other broads"?

Both partners had been previously married, so that in this household there were three sets of children, the wife's children by her former marriage, the husband's children by his former marriage, and a new baby. From the word "go" the partners failed completely to build a true marital union. The courtship phase was intense. Both parties moved fast to dissolve their previous marriages to make way for this one. But they were hardly married before the husband began to withdraw interest. When his wife became pregnant, he stopped making sexual advances altogether. Sensing his sexual rejection, she then began to develop jealous delusions.

In this case, husband and wife came from very different cultural and religious backgrounds, but they had in common the special experience of a philandering, unfaithful father. Each, however, reacted in a different way. The husband sided with his father. He felt convinced that his father had in fact been killed by his mother. Through her persistent nagging and accusations of infidelity, he believed she had caused his father's final heart collapse. The wife, on the other hand, entered in empathic alliance with her mother, in an attempt to protect the wounded pride of the females of the family against what she felt was her father's cold, ruthless, and indiscriminate indulgence in sexual escapades.

In therapy, the wife related four dreams in succession. In each, she depicted a threesome involved in a horrible tangle, reflecting the profound emotional connections between conflict in her marriage and older sources of conflict in her family of origin.

To illustrate, in one such dream, she found herself in an automobile, a convertible, accompanied by her husband and his secretary, who was the object of her paranoid sexual jealousy. The three drove to the home of the patient's former husband, where she found other people. First, she spotted her father hiding in the bedroom, as if he were up to some mischief. Although he offered a plausible excuse for his presence, she knew that it was a complete lie. Then she became aware of the presence of other people—children, her husband's parents, his office secretary's parents, and so forth.

In this dream, we see three networks of family relationships, the husband's family, the wife's family, and the family of the secretary. We see the patient in the roles of both child and wife. At the very least, this dream reflects the complexity of the origins of marital jealousy in a way that embraces an extensive web of conflicted family relationships stretching across three generations. Marital disorders are clearly anything but simple. They are one aspect, a focal one to be sure, but nonetheless one aspect of an ongoing family phenomenon.

In our studies at The Family Mental Health Clinic in New York City, we have been oriented mainly toward these problems in the wider context of the family. We have preferred, at least in the first phase, to interview distressed marital partners together with their children and sometimes with their parents. The procedure is first to conduct a series of exploratory interviews with the whole family and then at the appropriate time to shift to specialization on the marital part of the broader family problem.

We learn to diagnose marital disorders by treating them. The marital relationship neither exists nor evolves in isolation. It has family in back of it; it has family ahead of it. Where there is marital conflict, it often involves prior conflicts between the respective partners, and their families of origin. Marital conflict is often displaced and reprojected, in modified form, into the relations of each partner with the offspring. The original problems of each partner with the family of origin are thus projected across time into husband-wife and parent-child relations. The marital relationship does not and cannot stand still. It moves forward or backward. It grows, or it withers. It must be nourished, it must make way for change, it must respond to new experience—otherwise it dies. As the marital balance shifts from one stage of the family cycle to the next, the diagnostic judgment must change accordingly. The diagnosis of marital disorders is complicated. It is influenced by the ways in which the disorder is viewed from different places by different people with different interests and purposes: by the marital partners themselves; by other parts of the nuclear and extended families and community; by the professional worker. The range and diversity of marital disorders in our culture are enormous. Our interest is not only how the relationship works but also to what ends. Diagnosis can be approached at three levels: descriptive, genetic, and functional.

At the descriptive level, we can classify disorders of the marital partnership in terms of symptom clusters reflecting deviant patterns of interaction—for example, in sexual failure, economic or social failure, persistent quarreling, misunderstanding, alienation, and disturbances of communication, sharing, and identification.

At the dynamic level, diagnosis means the definition of the core conflicts, the ways of coping, the patterns of complementarity and failure of complementarity, the distortion and imbalance of the multiple functions of the marital interaction, and finally, the realism, maturity, stability, and growth potential of the relationship. From an estimate of these characteristics, we can delineate what is inappropriate and warped alongside what is appropriate and healthy in the quality of the marital adaptation.

At the genetic level, we trace the dynamic evolution of the relationship through the phases of courtship, early marriage, the arrival of the first child, and finally the expansion of the family with more children.

Diagnosis of marital interaction may be subdivided according to current performance, level of achievement, origin and development, and deviation measured against an ideal of a healthy marital relationship.

1. *Current Performance*
   a. capacity for love
   b. mutual adaptation, adaptation to external change, and adaptation for growth
   c. levels of benign conflict and destructive conflict; patterns of coping; interplay of shared defenses of the continuity of the marriage relationship with individual defenses against conflict and anxiety; and finally the characteristic patterns of complementarity (In clinical terms, two features of defense are of special importance: first, the use of the relationship and adaptation to the marital roles to compensate for anxiety in one or the other partner, to offer support against emotional breakdown, and second, the use of external relationships to mitigate failure in the marital relationship and to provide compensatory satisfactions of individual needs.)
   d. the quality of each partner's integration into his marital role and the fit of marital with other family roles
2. *Level of Achievement*
   a. the strivings, expectations, values, and needs of the relationship and of each partner
   b. the maturity, realism, and stability of the relationship
   c. the trends toward fixation, regression, disintegration, and so forth
   d. the discrepancy between actual performance and an ideal
3. *Origin and Development of the Relationship: From Courtship to the Time of Referral*
   a. influence of the evolving patterns of motivation, of the ideals and images of future marriage and family on the development of the marital partnership
   b. influence of the same factors (including children) on the development of the parental partnership
   c. areas of satisfaction, dissatisfaction, harmony and conflict, and healthy and unhealthy functioning
   d. past achievement in relation to values, expectations, and strivings
4. *Discrepancy Between the Actual Performance and an Ideal Model of Healthy Marital Functioning*

Disorders of the marital relationship are clinically expressed in two ways, as conflict over differences and failure of complementarity.

Conflict over differences becomes organized in a special way. Neither of the marital partners fights the battle alone. Each tends to form a protective alliance with other family members, children, grandparents, collateral relatives. In this way, the family splits into opposing factions. One partner engages in prejudicial scapegoating of the other. Each warring partner puts on blinders and attaches a menacing meaning to the difference. The inevitable result is a war of prejudice revolving around subjectively distorted representations of difference, rather than around actual ones. This war rests on the false belief that striving for one way of life automatically excludes another. Each faction then tries to impose its preferred set of aims and values on the relationship. The manifestations of this conflict appear as disturbances of empathy, union, and identification; as chronic destructive quarreling, often about wrong or trivial matters; as defects of communication; as the failure of devices for restoration of balance following upset; and finally, in progressive alienation of the partners.

The outcome of such conflict depends less on the nature of the conflict than on the ways of coping with it. Coping with marital conflict is a shared function. It is carried on at both interpersonal and intrapersonal levels. In this connection, it is essential to trace the interplay between specific patterns for group defense of the continuity of the marriage relationship and individual defenses against the destructive effects of conflict and anxiety. At the relationship level, we may specify these patterns of defense: enhancement of the bond of love, sharing, cooperation, and identification; shifts in the complementarity of marital role adaptation brought about by a shared quest for the solution of conflicts, improved mutual need satisfaction, mutual support of self-esteem, support for the needed defenses against anxiety, and support of the growth of the relationship and of each partner as an individual; rigidification or loosening of the martial roles; reduction of conflict intensity by means of manipulation, coercion, bribery, compromise, compensation, denial, or escape; shifting alignments and splits within the family and prejudicial scapegoating of one part of the family by another, repeopling of the group, that is, the elimination of one member or the addition of another or a significant change in environment.

Failure in these patterns of coping produces, in turn, progressive failure of the quality of complementarity. The manifestations of such failure can be identified as particular units of interaction that become rigidified, automatized, inappropriate, and useless for the shared tasks of marital living.

The marital partnership may be oriented mainly to different goals, as in these examples:

1. A marital relationship in which each partner egocentrically preserves his premarital individuality largely untouched by the requirements of the marital bond.
2. A relationship in which the individuality of each partner is subordinated to the requirements of his marital role.
3. A relationship in which the individuality of each partner is subordinated to the requirements of his parental role.
4. A relationship in which the individuality of each partner is subordinated to conformity with the demands of the surrounding community.

Genetic or developmental failures include

1. The accidental or unintended marriage like, for example, a marriage necessitated by pregnancy.
2. The abortive or temporary marriage, begun as a kind of adventure, a trial marriage, or a conversion of a sexual affair and not basically intended to endure or to evolve into a family group.
3. The marriage used as a means to escape from conflict to rebel against the family of origin or to rebound from a prior disappointment in love.
4. The arranged marriage, which is a matter of security, of expediency, or of joining two larger families.

From the functional point of view, there are

1. The immature or protective marriage, motivated mainly by the need of one partner to relate, in the role of child, to the other, in the role of parent.
2. The competitive marriage based on concealed envy, jealousy, and competitive admiration.
3. The marriage of neurotic complementarity, in which the special neurotic needs of one partner are complemented by those of the other, in which one partner serves as the healer of the conflicts and anxieties of the other. (The stronger partner in this arrangement is intended to serve as a provider of immunity against emotional breakdown in the more vulnerable partner.)
4. The marriage of complementary acting-out, in which the two partners share an unconscious complicity in patterns of acting out conflicted urges.
5. The marriage of mutual emotional detachment, in which a tolerable balance is struck between the partners on the basis of a degree of emotional distance and isolation.
6. The master-slave marriage, a role partnership in which one partner seeks omnipotent control of the other. (Neither partner is a

complete being. The master needs the slave; the slave needs the master. The one is aggrandized as the other is demeaned. The natural goals of love, sharing, and identification are perverted to the goal of power to dominate, degrade, and ultimately destroy the partner. In essence, this bond is a symbiotic one, in which one partner expands at the expense of the other. A pathological balance of this type can be maintained only by means of coercion and intimidation.)

7. The regressive marriage dominated by a negative orientation to life. (There is shared fear of and prejudice against life and growth, shared expectation of imminent catastrophe. Implicit in the emotional content of such a partnership is the theme of total sacrifice. One partner must surrender the right to live and breathe in order to ensure the continued life of the other. In emotional orientation, the persons involved move backward in life, rather than forward. This type of marital couple is the most likely to produce psychotic offspring.)
8. The healthy marriage. (In this theoretical model or "pure" type, the partners have a good "fit" in the marital roles. They are able to share realistic goals and compatible values. When conflict arises, there may be transitory upset, yet, in the main, they are able to cooperate in the search for solution or appropriate compromise. A temporary disturbance does not involve excessive or persistent accusation, guilt feelings, and scapegoating. Each partner has a genuine respect for and acceptance of the other as a person, a tolerance of differences, and, more than that, a willingness to use them for the creative growth of the relationship.)

To a large extent, diagnosis rests on the therapist's special interest—on what he is trying to do about the marital condition. In this context, diagnosis is no mere label but an integral aspect of a plan of action, a strategy for inducing change. Through the implementation of the principles and criteria described here, we seek a more precise definition of the functional pattern of the marital partnership, not only how it works but also to what ends. We want to know what it stands for, its goals and aspirations, what keeps the couple together, what pulls the partners apart. In essence, we seek to learn what is separate and what is shared in the relationship.

We turn now to the challenge of treatment. In keeping with the concepts we have outlined, the psychotherapy of marital disorders is viewed as the focused treatment of a component of family disorder. It is a phase of family therapy, adapted to and specialized for the specific features of a marital problem. Because family begins with marriage, the disorder of marital interaction is a focal point in family dynamics and development.

As I have discussed elsewhere my views of the method of family psychotherapy, I shall merely highlight here those special considerations pertaining to problems of marital interaction.

Professional contact begins with exploration of the salient problems, a function of any therapeutically oriented interview. In fact, we initiate the treatment process before we know what the problem is all about. Only as we become engaged in the adventure of therapy, do we achieve, step by step, a systematic diagnosis.

How is the marital trouble viewed? How do the partners see the problem, the family, and the community? What is the same and what is different in these several views? What alternatives loom up? What has the couple tried? What has it not tried? Or what has it tried in the wrong way? Do the partners feel discouraged, beaten down? Have they surrendered hope and given in to feelings of despair? Do they console themselves with mutual punishment? In any case, what do the partners now want? What does the family want of them? What does the community expect? What does each partner need of the other, of the family, and of the community? In turn, what is each partner willing to do for the other, for the family, and for the community? Finally, what is the orientation of the therapist? What does he, in his turn, propose to do?

These are the pertinent questions that confront the therapist at the outset. To make effective progress in clarifying the issues and exploring the alternatives, he must cultivate an optimal quality of contact, rapport, and communication between the marital partners and between them and himself. He uses this rapport to catalyze the main kinds of conflict and coping. He clarifies the real content of conflict by dissolving barriers, defensive disguises, confusions, and misunderstandings. By stages, he moves toward a more accurate mutual understanding with the marital partners of what is wrong. By stimulating empathy and communication, he seeks to arouse and enhance a live, honest and meaningful emotional interchange. Figuratively speaking, he strives to make the contact a touching experience, a spontaneous and deeply genuine kind of communion. As the partners feel in touch with the therapist, they come into better touch with each other. Through the therapist's use of himself, his open, earnest sharing of his own emotions, he sets an example for the desired quality of interaction between the marital partners.

In the therapy of marital disorders, the therapist must know what he stands for, what he is trying to do. He must also know what he can and cannot do. He must have explicit awareness of his own ideology of marriage and family life. He must clearly define, in his own mind, whatever discrepancy prevails between his personal family values and those of the marital couple.

So often a central feature of marital conflict is competitiveness. Both partners are dedicated to the game of one-upmanship. Each seeks to get the best of the other. It is as if the business ethic of profit and loss invades the inner life of the married couple. Neither can be convinced of a gain unless he imposes a loss upon the partner, a semblance of sacrifice. The game of one-upmanship is the pursuit of a delusion. It is misleading, for it can end only in futility. The essence of the delusion is that the well-being of the one partner comes only with a measure of sacrifice and surrender from the other. In the marital relationship it cannot be that what is good for one is bad for the other. In the long view, what is good or bad for one must also be good or bad for the other. The very survival, continuity, and growth of marriage and family hinge on the acceptance of the principles of love, sharing, and cooperation. Without such acceptance, marriage and family have no meaning.

The goals of therapy for marital disorders are to alleviate emotional distress and disability and to promote the levels of well-being of both together and of each partner as an individual. In a general way, the therapist moves toward these goals by strengthening the shared resources for problem-solving; encouraging the substitution of more adequate controls and defenses for pathogenic ones; enhancing immunity against the disintegrative effects of emotional upset; enhancing the complementarity of the relationship; and promoting the growth of the relationship and of each partner as an individual.

The therapist is a participant-observer. To achieve the goals of marital therapy, the clinician must integrate his trained knowledge and his use of himself in the therapeutic role in a unique way. He must be active, open, flexible, forthright, at times even blunt. He must make the most free and undefensive use of himself. He moves alternately in and out of the pool of marital conflict. He moves in to energize and influence the interactional process; he moves out to distance himself, to survey and assess significant events, to objectify his experience, and then he moves in again. The marital partners engage in a selective process of joining with and separating from specific elements of the therapist's identity. The marital partners absorb, interact with, and use the therapist's influence in a variety of ways. The partial emotional joinings and separations reflect elements of transference and realism. The therapist must be adroit and constantly alert to shift his influence from one aspect of the marital relationship to another, following the shifting core of the most destructive conflict. He engages the partners in a progressive process of working through these conflicts. In the process, he fulfills multiple functions. He is catalyst, supporter, regulator, interpreter, and resynthesizer. These functions cannot be conceived in isolation but rather as a harmony of influences expressed through the unity of the therapist's use of himself.

He undercuts the tendency of the marital partners to console themselves by engaging in mutual blame and punishment. He stirs hope of a new and better relationship. He pierces misunderstandings, confusions, and distortions to reach a consensus with the partners about what is really wrong. In working through the conflicts over differences, the frustrations, defeats, and failure of complementarity, he shakes up the old deviant patterns of alignment and makes way for new avenues of interaction. He weighs and balances the healthy and sick emotional forces in the relationship. He supports the tendencies toward health and counteracts those toward sickness by shifting his function in accordance with need at changing stages of the treatment.

To sum up in more specific terms, once having established the needed quality of rapport, empathy, and communication and having reached a consensus about what is wrong, he moves ahead, implementing the following special techniques:

- the counteraction of inappropriate denials, displacement, and rationalizations of conflict;
- the transformation of dormant and concealed interpersonal conflict into open, interactional expression;
- the lifting of hidden intrapersonal conflict to the level of interpersonal interaction;
- the neutralization of patterns of prejudicial scapegoating that fortify the position of one martial partner while victimizing the other;
- the penetration of resistances and the reduction of shared currents of conflict, guilt, and fear through the use of confrontation and interpretation;
- the use of the therapist's self in the role of a real parent as a controller of interpersonal danger, a source of emotional support and satisfaction, a provider of emotional elements the marital couple needs but lacks (The last function is a kind of substitutive therapy in which the therapist feeds into the emotional life of the parties certain more appropriate attitudes, emotions, and images of marital and family relationships, which the couple has not previously had. By these means, the therapist improves the level of complementarity of the relationship.);
- the therapist's use of himself as the instrument of reality testing;
- the therapist's use of himself as educator and as personifier of useful models of health in marital interaction.

Using these various techniques, he proceeds, together with the marital couple, to test a series of alternative solutions to the marital distress.

PART VII

Adolescence

From early in his career, Ackerman was interested not only in the individual's relationship with family, but also in the individual's and the family's mutual place in society. This is exemplified in his papers on adolescence, but it must be admitted that sociology was never his strongest suit. His clinician's tools were simply not the appropriate ones for dissecting large trends in American or Western civilization. His fascination with adolescents too easily blended into his anxiety about adolescents. No doubt he assumed that the young child would be effectively sheltered from the world by its parents and that, at the other extreme, adults would have mastered the world at least a little. It is the adolescent who is vulnerable, lacking both the protections of the child and the social skills of maturity.

In the first paper, dating from 1962, the author's upset is apparent. In this jeremiad one looks in vain for balancing scientific or historical objectivity. He seems to be all the middle-class fathers whose telephones ring at 3 A.M. with the news that their children have been hauled in in a drug bust. It is consistent that his view of the adolescent's family role is a harsh one: "the carrier of pathology." At least fitfully he does recognize the adolescent's right to challenge the adult world, but even these passages have a self-pitying tone, the chilly aftermath of a father's rage: Where did we go wrong?

In the next paper, published two years later, the emotionalism has cooled. Now Ackerman views the troubled adolescent as the family healer, the agent of parental harmony, since the older generation must forget their differences as they race to the police station at dawn. In this paper adolescent disorder is viewed consistently with Ackerman's theoretical notions of family homeostasis, but the point is not developed in detail.

It should be noted that these papers are not Ackerman's only reference to adolescents. Several of the cases in this book center around teenage patients, notably "To Catch A Thief" and "Family Dynamics and the Reversibility of Delusional Formation." The papers grouped in this chapter were selected because of their focus on adolescence as a familial and social process.

The final paper, published in 1969, develops further the notion of the adolescent as "family homeostat." Its tone is less excited than its predecessors, though Ackerman was still never one to shrink from being judgmental, viz., "The family looks respectable on the outside but is rotten on the inside." The stress between family and society is noted without the going-to-the-dogs quality of seven years earlier. Ackerman had set aside the social critic and contented himself with the narrower confines of clinical data.

CHAPTER 40

Adolescent Problems: A Symptom of Family Disorder

The adolescents of our time are hoisting distress signals. In many ways, both direct and indirect, they let the rest of us know that they are in trouble. Their disordered behavior today is an almost universal phenomenon. We have in the United States of America the teenage gangs and beatniks; in England, the "angry young men"; in Germany, the "Bear-Shirts"; in Russia, the "Hoodlums"; in Japan, the split of the teenagers into "wet" and "dry." These are but a few examples of semi-organized group expressions of widespread adolescent conflict. Conspicuously in evidence are signs of disorientation, confusion, panic, outbursts of destructiveness and moral deterioration. The disordered behavior of the adolescent needs to be understood not only as an expression of a particular stage of growth, but beyond that, as a symptom of parallel disorder in the patterns of family, society, and culture.

In a setting of world crisis the distress of the adolescent may be viewed as a functional manifestation of the broader pattern of imbalance and turbulence in human relations. The family, as a behavior system, stands intermediate between the individual and culture. It transmits through its adolescent members the disorders that characterize the social system. In our native community we confront the special challenge of the anarchy of youth. The recurrent bursts of bizarre teenage violence are emblazoned for us in the daily papers and other mass media. This is dramatic and frightening. But the problem embraces far more than juvenile delinquency. While some adolescents explode crudely in extremes of destructive antisocial action, others manifest their distress in a more subtle, indirect and concealed way, no less serious for its inconspicuousness. Fundamentally, what underlies the entire range of disorders is the adolescent's fierce, often failing struggle to find himself in this chaotic world. He is searching for a sense of identity, for a sense of wholeness and continuity, in a society that is itself anything but whole and anthing but steady in its movement

Reprinted with permission from *Family Process*, September 1962, Vol. 1, No. 2, 202-213.

through time.

But let us not imagine that it is the adolescent only or exclusively who experiences this painful struggle. It is all of us, at all stages of life, who echo in our personal lives the disorder of the social system. The agitation of the adolescent surely does not exist in isolation. It is matched and paralleled by the emotional insecurity of his parents, the imbalance of the relations between them, and the turbulence and instability of the family life as a whole. The family, as family, does not know clearly what it stands for; its resources for solving present-day problems and conflicts are deficient. Not only are families confused, disoriented, fragmented and alienated; whole communities sometimes exhibit these same trends.

Let us glance for a moment at the community response when there is an eruption of teenage destructiveness. Generally, there is an immediate outcry, a show of fright, shock, worry, righteous indignation; then talk and more talk. Soon the excitement simmers down, until the next shocking eruption, and the process repeats itself. The recurrent bursts of savage, inhuman violence among juveniles strike a note of alarm in the community. They stir a deep-rooted anxiety among parents, teachers and community leaders. The community turns desperate. There is a loud call for action, for a program; something must be done. But the demand for action arises not only out of a sense of desperation; it expresses also a profound helplessness, a feeling of sheer impotence to do anything about it. Why? Because the finger of accusation points responsibility not to the delinquent adolescent alone, but to the whole disordered character of the human relations pattern of present-day family and community as well. Yes, there is something deeply wrong, and it is not just with our adolescents; it is with our whole way of life. Our social health is failing; and the effects of the failure cast a long shadow on our mental health.

With each outbreak of juvenile destructiveness comes a spate of suggested remedies — vocational training, work camps, recreational facilities, group activity and guidance programs, and finally, freer use of the big stick, physical punishment at home and in the schools; ultimately, stricter policing and even penalization of the parents who are presumed to be negligent. At the peak of such community agitation, there is much talk and a strong resolve to act, but as is the case with New Year's resolutions, nothing much comes of it. The conviction grows that these measures are mere sops, a feeble attempt to plug the hole in the dam. Then comes widespread disillusionment and finally, perhaps, the grudging admission that the real problem is not the adolescent alone, but rather the sources of disintegrative influence in a sick or broken family. And exactly at this point the loud talk subsides because no one yet has a program to offer for what ails the family. It is this that explains the adults' sense of helpless resignation and their temptation, shamefacedly, to turn away from the problem. In effect, then, these waves of panic and agitation are a kind of shadow boxing. People rant and rave, they lash out at the shadow, but are impotent with the real thing—the disorder of family life itself.

TRENDS IN JUVENILE PROBLEMS

Let us examine now the range of adolescent symptoms. The outstanding features are: (a) a tendency to antisocial behavior, specifically expressed in acts of violence; in close association, a vulnerability toward mob action with a propensity toward organized prejudice, bullying and scapegoating of innocent victims; (b) a revolution in sexual mores, shown in a tendency to promiscuity; (c) a wave of contagion that makes an obsession of everything "hot"—hot jazz, hot dancing, hot-rods; closely associated with a compulsive quest for an ever new kind of kick, as in the use of such drugs as benzedrine, marijuana and even cocaine; (d) a leaning toward overconformity with the peer group; (e) a quest for a safe niche, a sinecure, a steady job with a pension in industry, a "couple of little mothers" as they say in teenage jargon; a split-level home with an electrified kitchen in suburbia; (f) a tendency to withdrawal; a closely associated tendency toward a loss of hope and faith, disillusionment and despair with a gradual destruction of ideals; a conspicuous product of this trend is the static-mindedness of many adolescents, the lack of adventuresomeness and loss of creative spark; (g) disorientation in the relations of the adolescent with family and community; an inability to harmonize his personal life with the goals of family and society; in consequence, a trend toward confusion or loss of personal identity; (h) as the outcome of this magnified social disorder, the intensified vulnerability of adolescents toward mental breakdown.

The anarchy of youth in contemporary society is a thorny problem. Since 1948 there has been an overall increase of juvenile delinquency of over 70%, although the child population has increased only 16%. Since 1950, this represents a rise four times as fast as the population. F.B.I. data show that a sizable percentage of the major aggressive felonies (murder, manslaughter, rape, assault, robbery, larceny and automobile theft) are committed by young people under the age of 18. In 1956, the youth in this age group accounted for 45% of all arrests for such crimes, and two-fifths of these offenders were under 15. According to the F.B.I., the number of killings committed by juveniles continues to rise. About half of these young killers are under 18, and one-third are children below 16. It is estimated that by 1965, more than a million children will appear before the courts. As J. Edgar Hoover puts it, "Gang-style ferocity, once the domain of hardened adult criminals, now centers chiefly on cliques of teenage brigands."

A psychiatrist, Dr. Wertham, expressed his alarm a different way: "This is the age of violence and it began with the dropping of the first atom bomb on Hiroshima . . . younger and younger children commit more and more serious and violent acts . . . the current spate of child murders is like the difference between a disease and an epidemic. One such killing would be a crime, but ten or a hundred or a thousand, that is a social phenomenon."

Three main features can be discerned in this trend: the gross numerical increase of these acts of violence, the deepening severity of these acts, and the universality of the trend, as many nations throughout the world affirm the findings of the F.B.I.

A few illustrations: Not long ago, the public was stunned by the strange tragedy of Cheryl Turner Crane, her actress mother, Lana Turner, and her broken family. The pathos of this story is still sharply etched in our memory. Shortly after this event, I saw in consultation a friend of Cheryl Turner's, a young girl of 13. She had just tried to poison her father's whiskey.

In *The New York Times* there appeared the following item: A young army man, assigned to security work, was found dead in the burned wreckage of his car. He had sprayed the interior of his car with gasoline, poured gasoline all over himself and then set fire. What possibly could have been this young man's state of mind to induce this fiendishly violent form of suicide?

Again, not long ago, we were struck with horror by the photographs of that fanatic Japanese boy who stabbed to death a leading political figure.

Another aspect of the anarchy of youth is the tendency to indiscriminate sexual behavior. Mostly the grown-ups in the community are loath to look squarely at this problem, not because it is sex, but rather because it is sex in such a shocking form. It is the subhuman or even inhuman quality of adolescent sexual conduct that compels us to turn our faces away. There are the recurrent reports of organized sex clubs for teenagers, group orgies that combine violence and indiscriminate sexual indulgence. Such behavior is not in any sense confined to members of any one social class, certainly not confined to the working class or the uneducated. It also appears in our institutions of higher learning, the universities. In occasional instances a single disturbed girl in a college dormitory can wreak havoc with the student population, not only by multiple seduction of college boys, but also by disrupting the sexual standards of the female students. In such situations, the college authorities are hard put to know what to do. The dean and faculty have no desire to inflict harsh punishment, but neither can they permit a contagion of disorganized, irresponsible sex orgies. The community demands action and somebody's head must roll. Frequently enough, the reputation of innocent persons is hurt.

Closely related, emotionally speaking, is the almost hypnotic trance into which adolescents fall as they become absorbed in hot music, hot dancing, hot-rods and the crazy craving for ever new kinds of thrill and excitation, even the use of narcotic drugs. Observers have been forcibly struck by the madness that seems to take hold of these young people. It is as if they are caught in a spell. At the very peak, they become transformed into elemental beings and are oblivious to all else but the excitement of their senses. They seem to be drawn off to another world. Most of them recover, to be sure; for some, however, there is a point of no return.

Of course, it is not one-sidedly implied here

that such behavior is purely regressive and emotionally sick. It is only to be expected that the adolescent should have hot blood and venture forth in the search for the rhythm of life. It is normal for them to try to capture the rhythm of life for themselves; in fact, to become one with it. In many instances, it is surely true that an active quest for Nature's rhythm brings an enormous relief of tension and actually offsets the danger of destructive outbursts. If adolescents can feel the rhythm of life down to their bone marrow, they can more easily reorient their bodily surgings to the existing world and do so in more constructive ways.

At the opposite extreme there is a tendency toward a rigid conformity with the standards and expectations of the peer group. Such behavior is mostly undramatic and inconspicuous. It is nevertheless important insofar as it reflects the severity of the pressure to conformity, even to the extent of the adolescent's experiencing a submergence or loss of his individual self. In the extreme, this is exemplified by the fashions of the zoot-suiters, the black stocking fad, the contests involving the swallowing of gold fish and the squeezing of college boys like sardines into a phone booth; also, the habit of going steady and getting pinned, just because everyone else is doing it. This leaning towards submission to the peer group constitutes a danger precisely because of its implied renunciation of qualities of individual uniqueness and difference.

A great segment of the adolescent population is turning painfully cautious and conservative. In a topsy-turvy world with a radical change proceeding at a galloping pace, adolescents paradoxically turn cautious. They want to hold the world still long enough to catch up with it. So we see them seeking routine, dependable, safe jobs in industry. They become scared of adventure, withdraw from the center of strife and turmoil, pull away from politics, move to the suburbs and raise babies. They become good organization men, but they lose their sense of adventure and surrender their creative dreams.

The adolescent experiences the greatest hardship in building a satisfying sense of personal identity. He is pained by his failing effort to harmonize his personal life goals with the goals of family and community. This induces in him a terrible dilemma. It is almost a commonplace that adolescents in our day cannot say who they are, where they belong, where they are going in life. They complain of a sense of emptiness, futility, and boredom—so why try!

Then there is a tendency of the adolescent to flee from conflict into a state of isolation and withdrawal. Often some depression is linked to this withdrawal. Both of these tendencies serve the purpose of self-preservation in the face of excessive conflict and anxiety. However, these efforts boomerang insofar as they can be indulged only up to a point and at the cost of progressive weakening of the personality. One manifestation of this withdrawal is the inability to face up to the urgent life questions such as boy-girl relations and choice of career. On the part of many adolescents, there is an urge to escape from these necessary decisions, or at least to stall them.

From still another angle, there is the frequent trend toward loss of faith or resignation to the defeats of life, a disintegration of ideals, and a shift of mood toward cynicism. This is especially evident in relation to the future rewards of work and family life. It is conspicuously manifested in attitudes of disillusionment toward authority figures—parents, community and political leaders. Sometimes there is a cynical rejection of interest in the larger affairs of community, nation and world.

From all this there are serious consequences; the social disorders of the adolescents tend ultimately to sexual deviation and mental breakdown. In our time there is a tendency not only toward a rising incidence of breakdown, but also toward an increasing severity of breakdown.

So far I have had to indulge in some sweeping generalizations, which inevitably carry with them unavoidable risks of misunderstanding. There is the whole question of establishing the distinction of normal and abnormal adolescent behavior. Let us therefore introduce a few needed qualifications. A healthy, vibrant, sparkling adolescent is a pleasure to behold. There are still enough of them, even in our troubled world. Adolescent behavior is characterized by enormous variability. Within this range, it is entirely possible for a healthy teenager for a time to exhibit some of the above trends and yet recover his emotional balance, relatively untouched and unharmed. This is simply a phase of growth. In most instances the tendency toward such disturbance is mild, transitory, benign and reversible. It is influenced by a multiplicity of factors—social, economic, cultural, geographic, familial and personal. Of central importance, of course, is the emotional conditioning of the adolescent within a particular type of family. Nonetheless, while we recognize explicitly that most youngsters survive, the fact remains that these trends represent a distinct vulnerability for the adolescent group as a whole.

What I have described cannot be viewed simply as a phase of the normal growth, the inherent instability of adolescent personality. It is much more than this. The significant source of such disturbance is something outer rather than inner. Basically these adolescent trends are a sign and symptom of a sick kind of family living and a sick community. Significant anthropological studies have demonstrated that adolescents can mature in certain cultures without undergoing critical emotional storms and without serious explosions of destructive conduct. The trend in our particular culture is a dangerous one. It is a disposition to a type of social and emotional disorder that can have profound consequences for mental health.

ILLUSTRATION OF DISTURBED FAMILY AND ADOLESCENT

Let us view the above adolescent disorders as symptoms of the social psychopathology of the adolescents of our time. We must then make the further step of relating this to the social psychopathology of the family of our time. The misbehavior of the adolescent may be regarded as a symptom of chronic pathology in the whole family. The adolescent acts as a kind of carrier of the germs of conflict in his family. In many instances, he seems to act out in an unrational manner among his extrafamilial relationships the conflicts and anxieties of his family, particularly disturbances existing in the relations of his two parents.

The following illustration is typical:

A man of middle years makes an appointment for psychiatric consultation for his 18-year old son. John has flunked out of three schools, cannot concentrate, steals money from his mother, gambles, and while playing truant, escapes to the low-class movie houses on 42nd Street. He is frightened of encounters with homosexual men, and yet paradoxically goes exactly to those places haunted by them. He has been accosted and propositioned by these characters many times.

The psychiatrist requests that the whole family come for an office interview. Instead, John appears only with his mother. When asked, "Where is your father and older brother?", John and his mother in a single voice instantly exclaim, "Oh, you'll never get Pop here. He's against psychiatrists; he doesn't believe in them."

John is a boy of medium height, with attractive, delicate, girlish features. He has almost a baby face. He is nattily dressed and his skin-tight trousers stand out conspicuously. Despite the obvious care invested in clothing, his posture is slouched over, his head is bowed; he observes the interview proceeding in a detached, blank way. Now and then, he bursts into a fit of child-like giggling. He is amused at the silly quarrels between his parents. He thinks his father is cute, puts on quite an act. He handles his body awkwardly. He is self-conscious about his body. He is ashamed of his well-developed breasts and his "big can." He admits his fear of looking like a girl. Therefore, he won't appear in a bathing suit. He is fearful of homosexuals, but also very curious. He is apathetic toward girls. He has only a single interest—gambling; he wants to play the Wall Street game as his father does. His father brags of his talent in gambling. He swears he can beat the Wall Street game. With a false, exhibitionistic modesty, he declares he is a "gambling degenerate."

In subsequent sessions, Pop did come and treatment was begun with the whole family on the assumption that John's disturbance echoed the family disturbance. Pop put on a show. He was a real ham. He insisted on talking for everyone else in the family. He barely gave the others a chance to open their mouths; he intruded on them time and time again. He is a bright, quick, but tense, agitated, overaggressive man. He is plagued by diffuse hypochondriacal fears, cancer, cardiac collapse, bleeding from the rectum, etc. From the word go, the father launched a critical, reproachful, intimidating tirade against his family. In the most dramatic manner, he depicted himself as a hero and a martyr to the family cause. He described vividly how he came up the hard way on the streets of the East Side. He is a devoted father who "gives and gives and gives" to his family out of his pocketbook. He talked of nothing but the dollar, how hard it is to "make a buck," and how his family robs him. They demand more and more; they're never satisfied. He has to make sacrifices to keep "doling out the dough."

Severely provocative, the father stirred his family to counterattack. Mother kept quiet, but her face was depressed, embittered, and a sly contemptuous grin played about the corners of her mouth. She was intensely hostile. It was the older son, Henry, who assumed for the mother the role of attacking the father. He did so viciously. On the other hand, the younger son, John, merely grinned. He felt unable really to talk with his father. He was frightened of him. The only way he could reach him was to love him up physically. Each evening, when his father comes home, John hugs him and kisses the top of his head, he caresses him; sometimes he playfully pokes him in the belly with his fist, or as he says lovingly, "I wring the neck my father hasn't got." Father has a very short neck.

Here is a bird's-eye glimpse of a disturbed family in action, containing one pre-delinquent adolescent boy; a family in which John's failure in school, his stealing, his tendency toward homosexuality, and his insatiable craving to gamble, are symptoms of the disturbance of his entire family group. This disturbance has its origin in certain basic unsolved problems in the relations between mother and father.

From the word go in this marriage, there was trouble. According to father, mother shunned his love, she rejected him sexually, she was cold, ungiving. Mother, on the other hand, declared that he was excessively demanding. For the first week, he did not leave her bedroom. By his own admission, father was afraid to let mother out of his sight because he was jealous of other men. He imagined that she might be unfaithful. On the other hand, mother was filled with bitter feelings against father. He left her alone night after night; he never stayed home, he went out with the boys, drinking and gambling, and looking at other women. He amused himself with dirty pictures and dirty stories. Throughout the entire twenty years of marriage, mother and father could not agree about anything. If mother said white, father said black. Father terrorized mother with his explosive tantrums. She in turn took vengeance in sly, covert ways. She emasculated him. She declared openly for years that he was undersexed. She allied both boys with her against father; she made it three against one. The father felt rejected and exiled. He then turned about to become seductive with his younger son, John. He carried on an open flirtation with him. John became the second woman for his father, substituting for mother. Mother in turn trained her older son, Henry, to be her fighting arm against father.

DISTURBANCES IN SOCIAL NORMS

Now, besides the familial conflicts, one must consider the wider disturbances in social norms that reverberate in the behavior of adolescents. Today, the goals of society and family life are unclear. Between the two there is little harmony. In general, human relations are agitated, turbulent, out of balance. Families as families are confused and disoriented; it is difficult to be clear as to aims, ideals and standards. People marry earlier, separate and divorce more frequently. The small nuclear family gets separated from the extended family representations. Grandparents and other relatives fade out of the picture. Mother has no built-in mother's helper, no dependable sustained support for her duties with the children. The family moves about from place to place; it fails to grow roots in the community; it is weakly buttressed by church, school, social services, etc. In effect, there is a long gap between the old and new way of life—a discontinuity from one generation to the next. The connection of the family with its past is severed; its horizontal supports in the wider community are thin and unpredictable. It cannot see what lies ahead.

The family of our day therefore does not succeed in planning ahead. It deals with its problems in hit-and-miss fashion; it improvises, it often reacts in extremes. It fails frequently to achieve a real unity; parents are confused as to the kind of a world for which they are training their children. The binding power of love and loyalty in family living is fickle and undependable. The contemporary family cannot somehow hold itself together very well. Instead, each member tends to go his own way.

The emotional climate of the family is often pervaded by mistrust, doubt and fear; there is less feeling of closeness, less sharing, less intimacy and affection. The symbols of authority, the patterns of cooperation, the division of labor, are confused. No one knows clearly what to expect of anyone else in the family. There is considerable fuzziness concerning appropriate behavior for father, mother, and child. Because of this, it is extremely difficult to maintain the needed balance and harmony of essential family functions and thus the stability of family life is thrown into jeopardy.

Since father and mother do not know what to expect of one another, neither is sure what to expect of the child. Emotional splits develop within the group; one part of the family sets itself against another. There is a battle between the generations, or a battle between the sexes. Under the stress and tension of daily living, the family sacrifices one essential family function in order to maintain another. Family life gets rigid, it gets stereotyped; it also grows sterile and static. No longer is the kitchen the place of cozy exchange of family feeling; instead, it is the shiny, cold, impersonal, machine-like kitchen. Family relations get cold and almost dehumanized.

The two parents compete; neither can take the allegiance of the other for granted. The father tries to be strong, but fails. Mom takes the dominant position; Pop recedes to the edge of the family. Out in the world, Pop is a somebody; he counts for something. At home, he is not sure he has any role to play. According to Loomis, the modern father is something of a cross between an absentee landlord, a vagrant and a sap. He pursues what is called the suicidal cult of masculinity. It is not enough to be man, he must be a superman. The sexual relation ceases to be love-making; it becomes a proving-ground for technique, the struggle for competitive dominance. It becomes impersonal, dull, a hollow ritual; it dies a slow withering death. Within the family, often it is unclear who is the man and who is the woman. In fact, all the family roles tend to be confused; sometimes the children act like parents, they usurp control. The parents lean on their children for a sense of guidance which they do not derive from other sources. In this way, the natural difference between the two generations becomes obscured.

Parents seem to be afraid to love their children. It is as if loving is losing something they need for themselves. They function with an image of profit and loss in family relations. They fear to sacrifice that which they may need to spend on themselves. They feel that the demands of their children are exorbitant, they project to their children their fears and hates and unwanted qualities of their inner selves; they intimidate and scapegoat their children, and in turn are scapegoated by them. They do not give their children an appropriate sense of responsibility; often they are overprotective. They become self-conscious, stilted professional parents. They compete with their own children and sometimes try to play the role of big brothers and sisters rather than parents. Out of a sense of weakness and guilt they take recourse to manipulation and coercion. Their efforts to discipline the children are feeble and ineffective, and they resort weakly and artificially to devices of deprivation, or so-called reasoning with the child, but have no confidence that the discipline will work.

So, in our adolescents we see anarchy and violence, sexual revolt, excessive conformity, a quest for a safe, secure, unadventurous, uncreative niche in industry, or we see withdrawal, a sense of defeat and cynicism and a loss of faith, hope, and idealism; certainly a profound and bitter disillusionment in the symbols of parental authority. In this setting, the adolescents live out unrationally the elements of conflict, imbalance and destructive competition in the relations of parents and grandparents and also the conflicts between family group and the wider community.

From these considerations, one learns one simple lesson: the disturbed behavior of adolescents is not only a reflection of a personality problem, but also a symptom of a disordered family. The two components must be correlated, the adolescent disturbance and the parallel imbalance in family relationships. One needs to trace the fluid, shifting processes of identity relations of adolescent with family and family with the wider community. More precise diagnosis of these multiple, interdependent, interpenetrating sets of influence would enable us to develop a more effective remedy, an appropriate merging of family life education, social service and psychotherapy.

CHAPTER 41

Adolescent Struggle as Protest

In every age, youth draws judgment on the elders, the elders draw judgment on youth. In a sense, each diagnoses the other.

Justice Douglas characterized the role of youth as "his majesty's loyal opposition"—"Youth, like the opposition party in a parliamentary system, has served a powerful role. It has cast doubts on our policies, challenged our inarticulate major premises, put the light on our prejudices, and exposed our inconsistencies. Youth has made each generation indulge in self-examination." Thus, it is the duty of the son to provide a loyal opposition to his father—to challenge his goals, judgments, decisions, and actions. This is the universal pattern of the son's allegiance to his father. The son rebels, but his very rebellion adds to his father's stature and deepens his wisdom.

For each generation, in turn, the adolescent and adult members of the community must come to terms; they must reach some mutually effective accommodation. Each needs the other. Each is responsible to the other. Each diagnoses the attitudes and actions of the other. The interchange of feeling and influence between the adolescent and his adult environment is a circular one. Something of the character, the dynamic quality, and also the distortions of the close human environment leave their mark on the adolescent. But the converse is also true. Something of the inner warp and woof of the adolescent leaves its mark on family and community.

When this delicate balance gets out of kilter, tension and conflict mount on all sides, within family and community, within the adolescent, and in the zones of interaction between them. Family and community point an accusing finger at the adolescent and say, in effect, "There is something wrong with you; do something about it." The adolescent, in turn, points an accusing finger at family and community. He, too, says, in effect, "There is something wrong with this generation of adults, with our kind of family and community life; do something about it." Thus is sparked a two-way process of recrimination and reproach. Each side blames the other, initiating a circular contagion of accusation and scapegoating. Three themes emerge, which be-

---

come organized and expressed as a cluster of interrelated, interdependent role patterns, that of the attacker, that of the intended victim of the attack, the scapegoat, and a third role, that of the healer of the conflict.

In the adolescent's struggle to come to terms with his image of self and his environment, he experiences the surrounding disorder of human relations patterns, stretching across a span of three generations, not only as threatening but also as twisted and sick. He strives frantically to serve as healer of his environment. He is driven to do so in order that he may not himself fall ill. In this healing mission, he may succeed or fail. To the extent that he succeeds, he effects a change for the better in family and community. He is thereby satisfied and strengthened. On the other hand, if he fails in the healing mission, the warped, sick forces of his environment persist or are worsened. He is weakened in the effort, rendered more vulnerable; he may then turn delinquent or suffer an emotional breakdown.

(The next section of the paper, omitted here, is lifted from "Adolescent Problems: A Symptom of Family Disorder," published two years previously. Again, it is a broad social statement. A "clinical vignette" follows.)

A boy, John, aged fifteen, is involved with several cronies in planning a holdup. This boy is the third of four children, the abscess of the family, the bad seed. The other three children fit well into the family. It is a poor one; its main concern is survival. Otherwise, the family as a whole is dedicated to intellectual and artistic achievement, hard work, renunciation of pleasure for future reward. The family, as family, represents solidarity and sacrifice. John stands out like a sore thumb. He is described as selfish, lazy, impulsive. He is dramatically the black sheep; he threatens the integrity, the values, the continuity of the entire family.

Within the family, John is viewed as the sole criminal. He is treated as if he were on trial. He is indicted as different, alarmingly different. The parents prize scholastic achievement, the importance of reading and knowledge as a way of getting ahead in life. John hates books. He prefers outdoor activities—hunting and fishing. He enjoys using his body, not his brain. "Different people have different ideas," says John. Living inside the family is like trying to stay alive in a strait jacket. He feels humiliated and enraged that his parents indict him as being stupid simply because he does not conform to their goals and values. In self-defense, he asserts that each person is smart in his own way. He declares that his father and brothers are stupid when it comes to life outdoors. He would not insult people simply because they don't know certain book facts. Within the family, he acts dumb. Being viewed as stupid, he isn't expected to see, hear, or listen. Within the family, he feels small, unimportant; he has no voice; he plays dead. He comes alive only outside the family. He says, "I have more fun alone and with other people."

Says John, "No one in this family knows how to have any real pleasure. They are all deadheads." He charges his parents with being hypocritical and self-righteous. There is no real unity between them. Father is against mother, mother against father. Mother has some lively spark, but she chokes it off out of conformity. Father in turn accuses her of associating with shady characters.

The parents are here joined in a tight security pact, but their emotional bond is a loose, unsteady one. The goal of family solidarity comes first. Loyalty to family means sacrifice of personal desires. Beneath their surface expression of unity, however, the parents are divided. Romantically, they are painfully disillusioned with one another. Each competes with the other for the affection and allegiance of the children. The father is bombastic, grandiose, and contentious in his assertion of authority. Behind his façade, he is a weak, frightened, hypochondriacal, martyred person. He is a poor provider. Mother defers superficially to the man of the house, but is secretly contemptuous of his weakness. Consciously, she joins with father in the professed family ideal. At a deeper level, however, she rebels against the rigid requirement of sacrifice as the price of acceptance. She shares with John a suppressed dream of adventure and romance, and subtly fosters his rebellion against father. Father usurps the maternal position with John. Mother displaces her urge to emasculate father onto John. Thus, both parents scapegoat John; they sentence him to exile. John is the sacrificial lamb, on whom is heaped the family's accumulated resentment over the forced surrender of their individual differences.

(The second case is that of a psychotic girl and her family, described at greater length in the paper "Family Dynamics and the Reversibility of Delusional Formation" (1965), reprinted in this volume as part of the section on Schizophrenia. This case was also the basis for the training film In and Out of Psychosis.)

In a stable society characterized by continuity of tradition over generations, the struggle to reconcile transitory conflict is a soft, muted one; in a society undergoing revolutionary transformation, the struggle is noisy and turbulent. In our time, there is a head-on collision between instability and change in the adolescent, and instability and change in the patterns of family and community. There is an unavoidable time lag in the capacity of each to accommodate to the accelerated change in the other. With the galloping pace of change in the goals and values of family and community, the social environment for the adolescent becomes severely fluid, in effect, almost chaotic. As the adults turn confused about who they are and where they are going, the adolescent loses his guidelines. He is continuously perplexed and unsure about where to conform and where to rebel. In our time, the resources of the individual, and the shared resources of family and community, for bringing about a restoration of an effective equilibrium seem to be deficient.

If we now attempt to translate the adolescent's implied diagnosis of the noxious features in the surrounding human relations patterns, we might make the following interpretation. Family and community today fail in some measure to provide a receptive climate for adolescent needs. In human relations, both inside and outside the family, there is little of genuine loving. There is no easy, spontaneous show of warmth and tenderness. There is no cherished touch. People fear and mistrust closeness. They fear and mistrust an open show of emotion, as if all emotion were bad, destructive, even violent. People move apart; they do not feel one another. In the human relations climate, there is a sense of danger, too much danger. The parents and adult authorities in the community are scared. This makes the adolescents doubly scared. The elders deal badly with their fright. They turn their faces away from the threat. They withdraw and seek safety in isolation. They talk out of both sides of their mouths. They do not practice what they preach. They talk ethics, but are themselves corrupt. They say to youth, "Don't do as I do, do as I say." In the face of their single, all-encompassing drive for success, all other human considerations fade away. Competitive strivings run rampant. Each man races with the next, ruthlessly. The world is felt to be a jungle; it is each man for himself. With such opportunism, people become alienated, mechanized, and lose their human quality. The murderous competitiveness of the business ethic invades the private life of the family. The gain of one member is reckoned as the loss of another. Family relations are measured by indices of profit and loss, as in the business world. The goals of power and mastery assume an overweaning importance; they submerge the family ideals of love, unity, loyalty, sharing, and cooperation. To admit the need of others or to show tenderness is a confession of weakness. In its place comes the illusory striving for omnipotent mastery and self-sufficiency. Money and position are God. People come to be treated as things. Human relations become, in effect, dehumanized. At another level, there is the tendency to substitute the appearance for the real thing. This is an "as-if" kind of interpersonal reality. It is not who you are, but rather how you look. Everything in human intercourse is reduced to dress and cosmetics. Contact is skin-deep. From still another point of view, the adults lose the art of play. They preserve little of the natural zest and joy of life. They lose the sense of adventure and become workhorses.

To make a fuller and fairer statement of the problem, we would have to turn about and glimpse the other side of the equation. We would have to ask, in turn, what is contained in the struggle of the parents, what is *their* protest, *their* critical judgment of the adolescents, also of the surrounding community? Once again, we are faced with the same question, who is responsible for what? How far do parents blame the adolescents, the community, or themselves? Limitations of space do not permit a detailed look at this other side of the equation, however pertinent this task may be for a comprehensive statement of the problem. We will confine ourselves, therefore, to some limited remarks.

The parents of troubled adolescents are plagued by elements of malignant immaturity in their own characters. Though they may now be in their thirties or forties, they remain in many respects "tween-agers" themselves. The child is father to the man. There is a hangover of pathogenic immaturity in the adults, long after the passing of the teenage years. We have, then, streaks of teenage immaturity in the adults, as well as in youth. The end result is a circular contagion of the noxious consequences of elements of pathological immaturity in members of both generations, and contamination of the relations between them. Youth moves into adulthood, marries, and makes children. Making children is an easy and sweet thing, but raising them and meeting their growth needs is quite another. The adults today fear being cheated of the good things of life. They have a horror of aging and death. They hang on by their teeth to the superficial signs of youthfulness. They move heaven and earth to preserve their outer appearance, to keep looking young and attractive. They are obsessed with clothes, dieting, cosmetics. They carry this obsession to an almost grotesque degree, as manifested, for example, in the woman's need to spend hours making up; in the dyeing of her hair, wearing wigs, face-lifting, etc. This accent on youthful appearance at all costs proceeds to such an extreme that in the relations of mother and daughter, the daughter cries out in vigorous protest, "I want my mother to look like my mother, not like my sister. . . . I want my mother to be a mother, not a companion or a girl friend or a confidante. . . . I don't like to call my mother by her first name; I want to call her just plain 'Mommy.' " Fathers are no less obsessed than mothers with keeping young; they merely express it in a different way. They, too, expend much energy in looking neat, trim, and youthful. In their middle years, they must impress their employers and business peers with their vigor, their strength, and their indefatigability. To prove their youthfulness, they knock themselves out in competitive sports, in tennis, on the squash court, on the ballfield; aging men chase the pretty young skirts.

In many families, one finds both parents showing the telltale signs of prolonged and skewed adolescent growth. The immature qualities of their struggle extend far into adulthood and even into middle age. One discerns unmistakably the residue of unfinished teenage conflict—the exorbitant emotional demands, the clinging to unreal, romantic yearnings, the evasion of responsibility, the extremes of dependency and explosive impulsivity, the frantic indulgence in diversion and escape, the divided self, the inordinate leaning on façade, the outer face of personality, the unreadiness for adult commitment to work, love, and loyalty to family.

Unable to move forward to maturity, they act either like frightened children or like all-powerful supermen. They fail to join as effective marital and parental partners. They compete with one another and with their children. Each parent is anxious, conflicted, driven, too busy with his or her own needs to understand and meet the needs of spouse and children. Each wants something different of the family. The family members clash in their image of what the family is and ought to be. The parents set the example and the children follow suit. The family splits into warring camps. Each parent allies with grandparent or child against the other parent. In the emotional interchange among family members, the pain of anxiety and threat stimulates the urge to attack. Offense feels like the best defense. Better to strike fear into the heart of the other person than to admit one's own fear. In a vicious cycle, anxiety evokes aggression, aggression evokes more anxiety. As the family breaks up, one side battles with the other. One member assumes the role of attacker or punisher, another becomes the victim of assault, the scapegoat, and a third member rises to stem the tide of violence; he enters the role of intended healer of the family war. In struggles of this kind, the aggressive member hangs onto his own sanity by menacing the sanity of another. In the long view, everyone suffers. They become, in fact, families without an effective parent. The failure of parents to harmonize and balance functions becomes critical. Ultimately, each member goes his own way; the family falls apart.

With regard to the wider reflections of human relations disorder, there are two points of view. First, there is the point of view that these are inevitable manifestations of a society in transition, the signs of a phase of crisis in historical transformation. From this point of view, it is assumed that in the course of the struggle, the forces of disintegration evoke forces of reintegration. In fact, Talcott Parsons speaks of this as the "disintegration of transition." The implicit assumption is that a new order will ultimately be restored.

The other point of view is different. It is epitomized in the oft-repeated comment, "Ours is a sick society." Society is the patient. The crucial question is not the semantic one: Do we prefer to label the human condition as a "society in crisis," or a "sick society"? The really important issue is the quality of healing. In nature, when distortion or sickness occurs, a parallel process of spontaneous healing always emerges. The really vital question is, will the healing succeed or fail? In nature, again, if spontaneous healing fails or a form of pathological healing emerges, there are critical consequences. It is my impression that the danger in the contemporary crisis lies exactly here, in the aggravated risk of either failure of spontaneous healing or in pathological healing. In both cases, the underlying pattern of distortion or "sickness" is critically worsened.

When we consider the implications of the term "sick," we cannot be clear as to what exactly we do mean. Up to the present time, we have tended to one of two extremes. We have examined society in the mass, making a global assessment of the distorted balance of forces in human relations, or, at the other extreme, we have evaluated distortion and sickness as a malignancy inside the single person. Limiting ourselves to the evidence at these two extreme poles, we achieve at best only a vague, foggy conception of the meaning of the phrase, "Ours is a sick society." It seems probable that we can add a useful dimension to the clarification of this problem through close study of the dynamic interchange between the individual and his close personal group environment. It is in this special sense that I discuss the question, what part of the adolescent protest spells valid criticism, a useful diagnostic interpretation of existing elements of disorder and sickness in contemporary patterns of family and community? Only as we become clear as to the diagnosis of this human condition can we turn to the crucial question, what do we want to do about it?

CHAPTER 42

Sexual Delinquency Among Middle-class Girls

The theme of this paper is the relation between family disorder and sexual acting-out in the teenage girl. How shall we understand the emotional disturbance of the girl and of her family? How shall we identify the special type of family equilibrium that evokes sexual delinquency in the female child?

Let us pinpoint the problem at the outset by presenting a few brief clinical vignettes. One such family, from a middle-class suburb, consists of the two parents, a son of fourteen, and a daughter of thirteen. The girl was caught with a boy in a parked car, virtually naked and engaging in sex play. This episode was merely the culmination of a whole series of such activities. She had been running off to teenage clubs and bars, and hobnobbing with questionable characters, some of whom had police records and were addicted to drugs.

The girl's father has a relatively small printing business, earning about twenty thousand dollars a year. He is intelligent, emotionally constricted, conformist, obsessed with the goal of success, but plagued with a gnawing sense of disappointment; his status as a businessman is mediocre. The mother stays at home but chafes at her confinement. She is bright and more spontaneous than her husband, but her expressiveness is choked off by the constraints of her marital bond. Privately she cherishes a romantic dream of a more exciting, fuller life—getting out on a job and cultivating a wider set of friends—but she has compromised for the reward of a "secure" home life.

Between husband and wife there is an undercurrent of chronic tension. Sexually, the husband is demanding, can never get enough; the wife resents this, and rations her sexual response. Occasionally, he presses her to submit to sex contact other than intercourse, but she mostly fights him off. Between them there is a continual power struggle, though they are collusive in muting the overt manifestations of this competitive war.

The fourteen-year-old boy outwardly plays the game, conforming superficially to the rules of his family, but he is evasive, wily, and hypocritical. The mother laments her inability to control her daughter. She feels she cannot reach her and retreats from the battle. In so doing,

Reprinted from *Family Dynamics and Female Sexual Delinquency*, O. Pollak and A. Friedman (Eds.), 1969, 45-50, Palo Alto: Science & Behavior Books.

she incites the father to step into the breach to enforce discipline. His approach to his daughter is detached, rigid, fault-finding, and overbearing. He rips her down for disrespect of her parents' authority, but seems blind to the child's emotional hunger and loneliness, blind also to her appealing, pretty face. In a covert, disguised way, the mother pushes her daughter toward the father and, at the same time, reproaches him for his coldness, lack of empathy, and unresponsiveness to the girl's charm and beauty.

In the meanwhile, the brother hides behind the cloak of his role as the "good" child, siding with his parents while they exploit his "goodness" as the basis for chastising his sister.

The parents make it plain that their daughter's conduct is a threat to their way of life. Their status in the community is thrown into jeopardy. They fear disgrace and react violently, virtually imprisoning the girl in her home.

In the family interview, the girl presents a picture of abject wretchedness. She sits pathetically alone, her head bowed. At first she darts poisonous glances at her parents. Feeling some acceptance and support from the therapist, she launches a caustic attack on her parents. She reproaches them bitterly for their utter lack of understanding, their unfair punishments. She exposes the empty, dull, joyless atmosphere of the home, the absence of any show of warm feeling between her parents. She vividly describes their trumped-up hypocrisy and false pretense of respectability. She shows utter contempt for the sniveling ingratiation and sneaky lying of her brother.

In another family, there are two daughters. The older one, seventeen, is involved in a liaison with a boy now in jail for car theft. She visits him in jail at irregular intervals. The boy comes from a broken family on "the other side of the tracks," is physically handicapped, and has a long history of clashes with the law. The girl had been intimate with him, became pregnant, and had an abortion arranged by her father. Prior to this involvement she had engaged in loose sexual contacts with many boys, but is now loyal to the "one and only."

The family resides in a comfortable home in a good neighborhood. The father, a business executive, married late after a period of free and easy sexual indulgence with women for whom he had no feeling whatsoever. His own mother had been a volatile, explosive woman whom he tried to avoid. When he decided finally to settle down, he consciously sought out a wife who was intelligent, reasonable, and calm, with a family background much like his own. He felt he had found just such a woman, extraordinarily steady and controlled. It turned out not to be so. To the age of twenty-six years, when she married, this woman had been a virgin. She had earlier broken an engagement with a man of a different religion, of whom her parents disapproved. Her husband initiated her into a sex life, but it meant little to her. She was merely doing her wifely duties. She conformed to her husband's pattern of life, had only rare outbursts with him, but indulged in bitter, screaming tirades with her daughter. She was rigid, unaffectionate, and carping. Mother and daughter were never close. Father and daughter were closer and more empathic. The father alleged he had a "liberal" attitude toward sex; the mother superficially copied this attitude. Despite this, the parents were intensely suspicious of their daughter and checked her every movement. They accused her of lying and concealing her sexual activities. The mother forced her to submit to a vaginal examination—and yet each day both parents reminded her to be careful and checked to be sure that she took her contraceptive pill. They were frightened of the girl, placatory, and at the same time accusatory.

The girl was herself open and direct. While feeling inwardly guilty and damaged, she assumed a posture of superiority to her parents. She took them to task for their contradictory attitudes. She was flagrantly contemptuous of their fumbling, righteous efforts at self-justification. She bluntly asserted her mistrust of her parents and her conviction that her boyfriend loved her for herself, not for sex. She appreciated his kindly devotion to her. She admitted she did not enjoy sex but wanted to keep her boyfriend happy. She was saving money to rescue him from jail and hoped to keep him "on the straight and narrow."

In a third family, the father had nearly beaten his daughter to death when he caught her "making out" with a Negro boy on a park bench. The family lives in an interracial neighborhood, and when the father looks out from their apartment window and sees a Negro boy and white girl walking arm in arm, he goes into a frenzy. He is a sick man who has been in the hospital twice for a bleeding ulcer. The girl's mother is a depressed, agitated woman who has been hospitalized for her mental condition. She lives in terror of her husband's proneness to violence, goes into panic, and sobs uncontrollably. The sexual relationship between the parents has deteriorated to nothing. Father feels totally deprived, frantic. He has occasional spontaneous emissions. The daughter is desperate; she wants to leave home.

The term "delinquency" is basically a sociological concept. It refers to certain actions that are viewed as deviant and dangerous, and therefore are proscribed by the community; persons engaging in such actions come into conflict with the law or other representations of authority. Delinquency is, therefore, in no sense a psychiatric diagnosis. In its broader ramifications it is relatively nonspecific; it has multiple forms and determinants. It may be psychological, sociological, or both. In some of its manifestations, it overlaps with psychopathological conditions, but these fall into a wide range of categories: neurosis, character disorder, and psychosis. This is a significant qualifying consideration in clinical assessment of the relations of individual "delinquency" and family psychopathology.

Sexual delinquency in teenage girls has a different significance in families of the lower, socially deprived classes than in families of the advantaged middle class. I am here concerned mainly with female sex delinquency in the middle class. In general, delinquent behavior occurs less commonly in girls than in boys. When it occurs, however, it is apt to be more extreme, less tractable, and rather more likely to have a malignant outcome. Sexual acting-out in girls is part of a deeper and broader pattern of revolt against authority. The sexual aspect becomes the vehicle for an explosive discharge of aggression. It is a common observation that a teenage girl of this type is not yet awakened sexually, that she carries a secret prejudice against sex, is frigid, and does not enjoy the experience. On the other hand, she has somehow discovered the lure of her female body and the power of its use as an instrument for manipulating boys. She leans on sex not as pleasure but as a way of holding onto a boy, a way of assuring interest and protection, a way of denying dependency on mother, and a way of destroying female rivals.

Hidden beneath all this is a hungry, lonely child with a deeply injured self-esteem. In paradoxical fashion, while seeking a balm for a damaged sense of self, the girl engages in sexual contact that only degrades her all the more. Often she attaches herself to a boy who, in social and familial terms, is "beneath her," one who is delinquent, emotionally deviant, and occasionally even physically deformed. It is in this setting that a white, middle-class girl sometimes gets involved with a Negro boy. The girl feels rejected, wounded, scapegoated by her family, and, in reaction to this, attaches herself to one who she feels has suffered in the same way. The boy thus selected epitomizes in his personal and social identity a violent clash with the values and standards of the girl's parents and family. Boy and girl "mother" one another; they cuddle to supply one another with compensatory warmth. They form a hostile alliance against family and society.

The core sentiment underlying frantic acting-out is despair and depression. The girl gives up a desperate, failing struggle to find an acceptable place for herself in her own family. Feeling scapegoated and humiliated by them, she flees the living space of family to enter a new life space with her boyfriend. Family hurts girl, girl retaliates by degrading family through her acting-out. But in the choice of a particular boy, the girl reflects her profoundly damaged sense of self and her urge to self-destruction.

The special middle-class family setting is interesting in a number of ways. At one level, one detects a factor of emotional complicity on the part of one or both parents. While the parents overtly react to the girl's sexual activity with shock, indignation, and anger, they stimulate and facilitate the acting-out. One or another parent makes a sly aside, a belittling slur, or expresses an attitude of "I knew it!"—"I told you so!"—"She acts like a little slut!"—etc. In effect, the parents brainwash the child; they project to the girl their suspicious expectation that she will be bad, and the girl fulfills the prophecy. Then they punish her for it. In this setting, the girl lives out in her sexual behavior something implicit, covered over and choked off in the life of her parents. In a basic sense, the parents are partners in the sexual drama. They are in collusion with the girl's delinquency. From another point of view, one is impressed again and again by the dramatic contrast between the defensive hypocrisy of the parental pair, on the one hand, and the deep emotional honesty of the acting-out girl, on the other. Often it is as if the girl in her very acting-out is hurling the lie to her parents, puncturing their loud and false pretensions to goodness and respectability. The denials of the parents become all too transparent. The directness, the simple human candor, of the girl is impressive. Her need to show up the falsity of the parents often follows an earlier, failing effort to make them more sincere, more the kind of parents she needs. The pain of disillusionment in her parents, and her failure to make them over, drive her to extreme actions.

Yet despite the destructiveness of the girl's acting-out, she often shows elements of emotional health, in which her parents are strikingly lacking. In family therapy interviews, one is struck again and again with the realization that the parents are in some respects sicker than the child. The delinquency of the girl is a signal that the unity, integrity, growth, and health of the family is in danger. The acting-out induces a crisis, which demands that the family take a deep look at itself; it must change or it will fall apart.

From still another point of view, acting-out of teenage girls is a transitional phenomena, serving as a defense against depression or an acute psychosis. The girl's flight, her desertion of family for the arms of a boyfriend, offsets the threats of a mental crisis. Were she thwarted in the attempt to leave the living space of the family, she would be at the mercy of a flood of anxiety-threatening disintegration of her personality.

There are several considerations that merit intensive study. As indicated above, the flight from the living space of the family is a defense of personal integrity. The acting-out pattern is a sequel to an earlier failure to heal the emotional warp of the parental relationship. The girl's actions are a diagnostic clue to the psychosocial pathology of the family unit. It is a form of extreme protest, which implicitly contains a valid diagnostic judgment of the distortions and emotional deficits of her family group. Reading between the lines, one can glean something of the following:

(1) The acting-out is a resistance to a spurious pattern of control and conformity in the family. There is a deep split betwen the external façade of the family, the mask that the family presents to the wider community, and its inner life. The family looks respectable on the outside but is rotten on the inside.

(2) The nuclear family poses as being integrated to the larger community, but is really alone. It is emotionally cut off from grandparents and extended family, yet has not replaced the continuity of family tradition with appropriate horizontal supports in the community. The parents crave acceptance and approval by the community, seek it by way of surface conformity, and yet remain relatively isolated. They do not achieve close friendships with their social peers.

(3) Each parent is caught in an unresolved conflict in the simultaneous roles of child and parent, continuing to need the satisfactions of dependency and protection, while being required to function as strong, self-sufficient parents, genuinely and sacrificially concerned for the welfare of their children.

(4) The essential functions of the family are out of balance. The parents give their allegiance to security, stability, and social approval. They are hitched to the goal of success, money, status, good social conditions. At the same time, in the inner life of the family, there is a critical neglect of support of the affectional bonds among family members. The vital spark of family life is sharply reduced. There is little love, little sharing, little joy. The inner energies of the family are dedicated to maintaining a superficially smooth operation, while the heart of the family dies.

(5) The complementarity of the parental partnership is defective. There are failures of complementarity at the sexual, emotional, and social levels. In a basic sense, the parents are alienated, and yet before the world they pretend to be together. Beneath the surface, one of the parents is in secret revolt, and in a covert way spurs the child to act out this rebellion.

(6) Complementarity of parent-child relations is damaged. The emphasis is on the child *looking* good rather than *being* good. The prime value is placed on appearances, on a ritual of conformity to conventional standards of achievement, while parent-child relations fail in the areas of need satisfaction, support of self-esteem, quest for solutions to conflict, and respect for individual difference and creativity.

(7) The frustration in the sexual partnership of the partners results in a trend toward parental seduction of the child. This seduction expresses in disguise a suppressed and hidden tendency to sexual delinquency in the parent.

(8) Complementarity in child-sibling relations is disturbed. Disturbances in the parental partnership and the excessive importance of approval instill exaggerated rivalry among the children. The compliant, conforming adaptation of a sibling is used as a shield for the parents' denial of the deeper currents of strife and alienation. The parents alienate the children by setting the "good" one against the "bad" one.

(9) At the surface level, the acting-out of the bad female child fortifies the defensive alliance of the parents. This is a highly precarious alliance, but the parents use it to exclude the "bad" child from the family.

(10) With these progressive failures of complementarity, family contact deteriorates to endless bickering, mutual blame and punishment, or to progressive distancing and alienation. Temporarily this may lend support to an unstable, tenuous equilibrium for the relations of parents and the "good" child, but it is a dead end for further family development.

These trends prevent constructive change and lead to incomplete pathological healing of family conflict. They induce recurrent family crises and magnify the danger of family disintegration. A critical gap develops between the family as it functions in real life and the ideal of family living, bringing in its wake a progressively bitter disillusionment and the urge for escape. The family must find a way out of this impasse; it must learn to grow or it withers. The emotional destiny of the sexually delinquent girl is inextricably linked to the family's capacity and incentive for healing its inner warp.

PART VIII

Schizophrenia

Ackerman published a scant five papers on schizophrenia, two of which are reprinted here. These are the last two and seem to us to stand in sharp contrast to those written earlier.

One may speculate as to why Ackerman dealt with this issue in such a lackluster fashion. Family therapy theory and practice had two quite different roots. Ackerman represented its origins in psychoanalysis and child psychiatry; the Mental Research Institute group, Bateson, Jackson, Haley and their colleagues focused their attention on schizophrenia from the perspectives of cybernetics and systems theory. Personal reasons may be adduced as well; the breakdown of Ackerman's brother was a continually painful concern.

The three earlier papers seem almost to not recognize the concept of family. Acknowledging that in all likelihood "heredity lay down a degree of susceptibility . . . ," he goes on to say that it is "the social and emotional influence of family life that translates a dormant weakness in a psychotic illness." In the main, though, in these earlier three papers, Ackerman concentrates almost entirely on an elaboration of the concept of the schizophrenogenic mother originally put forward by Frieda Fromm-Reichmann. Beyond this, family is only mentioned insofar as the failure of the father to provide an antidote to this poisonous mother-child relationship ("Family Therapy in Schizophrenia"); "conceivably, the needed reparative influence might be introduced by the father, although there is a peculiar schism between mother and father . . . the father might provide the needed antidote, but he generally fails in this role." There is no mention of siblings, the index patient seems almost always to be a male, the three-generation family appears not at all. Ackerman's treatment of the Bateson et al. double-bind hypothesis seems best described as perfunctory and shallow.

The two papers we have chosen to reprint are at a completely different level from those that preceded them. Ackerman's attention and enormous sensitivity to affective issues, as well as his quite capable descriptive powers, produce a vivid picture of the affective climate in the family. The second paper, co-authored with his longtime colleague Paul Franklin, includes an extensive verbatim record of an interview, glossed with comments on the interviewer's reasoning. Here Ackerman is at his best and it is possible to follow in fascinating detail the logic of his moves in the interview. The modern reader may wish to consider these interventions in terms of theories of therapy that are of current interest, for example, those of Minuchin or of Selvini Palazzoli. This interview, a supervisory consultation, took place in the twelfth month of conjoint family sessions. It was filmed and presented under the title "In and Out of Psychosis."

CHAPTER 43

The Affective Climate in Families with Psychosis

In this report I shall try to communicate a hypothetical composite picture of the affective climate of families that breed one or more psychotic members. My approach here is strictly that of the clinician, not that of the researcher. In drawing this sketch, I lean on an accumulation of clinical hunches derived over time from the observation of families with psychotic trends. I watched a few of these across long periods of 10 to 30 or more years, many others for shorter periods. In a fraction of these families, I had opportunity to evaluate relationships across three generations. In previous publications (Ackerman, 1960, 1961, 1964, 1966; Ackerman and Franklin, 1965) I presented in condensed form a point of view toward the problem of family and schizophrenia; I shall endeavor here to elaborate on this view, with particular emphasis on the affective climate of such families.

In reassessing earlier case studies, I came to the inescapable conclusion that the traditional psychiatric study, focusing first on evaluation of the schizophrenic as an individual and then, in a separate procedure, adding a family history, is critically inadequate for our present purposes. Such a piecemeal history, put together from individual interviews conducted at separate times with one or more relatives, does not give us reliable insight into the significance of ongoing relationship processes. In the traditional procedure the conceptual orientation moves from the individual patient to the family group. This is one-sided, incomplete, and results in a selective and biased picture. It needs to be checked against a conceptual orientation moving in the opposite direction, from the family group to the patient. The one clinical procedure which compensates this deficiency is the therapeutically oriented, exploratory face-to-face interview with patient and family. With this new method of participant observation, we evolve a different conception of the relations of family disorder and psychotic illness.

The problem of correlating family life and schizophrenia has been investigated with many different approaches. Each of these studies contributes a special light on particular aspects of this correlation. We learn something of value from the experimental approaches (Cheek, 1964;

Reprinted with permission from *Problems of Psychosis* (Excerpta Medica International Congress Series, No. 194), 1969, 129-139.

Farina, 1960; Haley, 1962, 1964; Lennard and Bernstein, 1969; Lerner, 1968), from studies of communication processes (Bateson, 1960, 1961; Bateson et al., 1956; Haley, 1959; Weakland, 1960), from research into the cognitive and perceptual aspects (Singer and Wynne, 1963; Wynne and Singer, 1963) and also from investigations of the patterning of family role relationships (Ackerman, 1961, 1964; Bowen, 1960; Fleck et al., 1959; Jackson, 1957; Lidz and Fleck, 1960; Lidz et al., 1965; Wynne, 1961; Wynne et al., 1958).

It is my impression, however, that the raw quality of affective interchange among family members has thus far not received sufficient attention. Family role relationships and verbal communication are secondary, I believe, to the emotional interchange across three generations. I choose, therefore, to highlight the affective climate, the interactive emotional trends and related pathogenic phantasy formation.

The impact on the clinician's emotions and percepts of a live, face-to-face encounter with the whole family is profound; for me, this holds a special fascination. As I said in *Treating the Troubled Family* (Ackerman, 1966), the therapist, "In a continuous process of communion with self, brings to his awareness the emotions stirred in him by the deeper streams of feeling moving among the family members and toward himself. He uses his disciplined insights into his personal emotions as a diagnostic yardstick for what is being experienced by the family." The validity of this process is qualified by the clinician's capacity to reliably select which of the emotions stirred in him belong to his own family experience and which others are specific for the problems of the presenting family. This type of investigation is a root source of the clinical hunch concerning relevant familial processes. Step by step, the clinician develops a series of speculations which he progressively tests in a process of consensual validation. In this way, he gradually evolves his diagnostic image of the family group.

Taking into account the diversity of family types and recognizing also that many aspects of family experience are irrelevant, we are seeking here a core pattern of affectivity that may have a specific relation to the schizophrenic phenomenon.

In these families, the climate and emotional interchange at the surface represent a sharp contrast with what goes on emotionally in depth. The surface phenomena are the obverse of what is experienced among the family members in depth. The discrepancy between the façade and the emotional core of the family is dramatic. On the level of the family façade one gets the impression of stability, but what looks like stability may actually be stasis. Much of the time the atmosphere looks quiet and controlled. Superficially viewed, everything stays the same; nothing ever changes. A quality of affective deadness pervades the family. The interpersonal climate seems lacking in vitality. Relationships are robot-like and ritualized. In general, the atmosphere is tight and frozen; there is a minimum of spontaneity and free movement. When such an urge appears, it is more in the nature of a thrust that is quickly aborted. Intermittently, however, the deadly routine is interrupted by a volcanic eruption of anxiety and violence. Suddenly one part of the family comes to life. Another part responds with a sense of threat. A wave of agitation spreads through the entire family. A contagion of panic and rage takes over. Just as quickly, the surge of agitation dies down, and the family reverts to its usual routine.

In these families the joining and sharing are spurious; they are stereotyped and disembodied. With this denial of life, what remains is an empty shell of presumed human relations (Ackerman, 1961, 1964). There is a pervasive trend of make-believe—make believe there is a genuine emotional bond—make believe there is loyalty and caring. However, the family relationships are, in fact, shadowy and ghost-like. Contact is static and hollow. The members mouth the right words and ideas, but without feeling. They look at one another and yet they do not see. This not seeing is of the essence; the other person is an apparition. Thus, family relations are dehumanized. The capacities to adapt to new experience, to learn, to grow, are critically reduced. The family atmosphere contains a disguised, shared prejudice against new life. Life is movement, emotion, body experience; it is action. The emotional atmosphere permits a minimum of such vital movement; it is too dangerous. Only a single alternative remains: flight into a magic world of phantasy.

On the surface, there is a conspicuous ritualization of togetherness, an obsessive assertion of selfless devotion, solicitude and sacrifice; at the core, something very different! In depth, one is impressed with the enormous titer of anxiety. Despite a struggle to cope, the anxiety is not contained. The contagion of emotion is powerfully intense, especially the contagion of anxiety and rage. It is as if members of this family have a raw skin that is easily made to bleed. The anxiety has a special character; it is a foreboding of disaster. The anxiety about imminent catastrophic destruction is misty, ill-defined; it takes varied forms. It pervades every aspect of the emotional life of the family group. It would seem as if the only things that are real in such families are death and destruction, not life, growth and spontaneous pleasure.

However denied, cloaked over, or otherwise defended against, the contagion of anxiety recurrently breaks through. When it does, it runs wild and has a shattering effect. It is as if there is a dying in the family air. A life is being snuffed out; one part of the family must die, so that another may survive. At another level, the dread of destruction is that someone's mind is cracking open. The dread of dying and a loss of mind run parallel.

The undercurrent of terror stirs rage. Mostly the rage is choked off, yet the threat of a violent eruption is in the air. The basic concern is to maintain control and assure survival; all energies are bent to this one purpose.

The contagion of anxiety, the brooding about an imminent disaster, the strain of containing the violence require constant mental exertion; the drive for control is urgent; it is rigid and obsessive; it is, in fact, an unremitting pressure toward total magic control. The craving for omniscient knowledge, omnipotent power and absolute certainty of prediction is ever-present. The demand for magic reassurance is insatiable. If anyone withholds this reassurance, it is felt as a murderous offense. No matter what the cost, the dreaded disaster must be put off. It is in this setting that one can appreciate the imperious quality of the demand for certainty, the characteristic rigidity of the mechanism of denial. This mechanism, brittle as it is, works and does not work. It serves its purpose transiently, breaks down, and is once again reasserted.

A related trend is the contagion of guilt, a pervasive guilt for the destructiveness that is in the family air. The fear of being accused, condemned and punished is profound. From the contagion of guilt comes a powerful wave of blame and scapegoating. The urge to condemn and prosecute the other serves as defense against the threat of being impaled on the cross as the guilty party. Within this family mood emerges a pervasive current of harassment and persecution. Beneath the thin obsessive overlay of false solicitude and protection, there is no mistaking the viciousness of the persecutory force.

Notwithstanding the fierce efforts to deny and cloak the danger, the feeling persists that someone is being destroyed, that someone's mind is being wracked and tortured (Ackerman, 1964). Who did it? Who is to blame? Surrounding this plaguing question, there is a cloud of doubt and perplexity, an aura of ambiguousness and mystery. The smell of death hangs in the family atmosphere, yet no one can be sure as to the source of the killing. The mother asserts her selfless devotion, her martyrdom and innocence. She cues the father to act out her hostility; she can then blame him. But the sins of the parent are visited upon the child: it is the pre-schizophrenic child, perplexed as he is, who takes on the guilt for the killing. The air of mystery persists; the question never quite finds an answer.

In some families, the brooding over destruction and violence is projected onto the male members. The male is perceived as the symbol, the root source of brute violence. Sex and violence are thus linked, and both are constricted. Sex is not permitted a free, natural expression. It is feared, as is violence. Sex is relegated to a position of peripheral importance. It is tolerated as an inescapable form of body relief, something like the necessity for bowel movement. Often the fright of violence leads to a tacit, collusive suspicion and taboo, so that, in effect, within the family, "no males are allowed," or at the most, they are suffered as a peripheral presence. They may stay on condition they make no loud noise. Thus, both violence and sex are straitjacketed.

Three interrelated trends become crystallized: within the family there is an omnipotent persecutor and killer, a sacrificial victim, also an omnipotent rescuer, a lifesaver. Who in the family does what is never finally defined. The play goes on and yet it is never finished. In the meantime, the offspring selected as the sacrificial lamb is scapegoated and destined for schizophrenic destruction.

The morbid obsession with death and destruction makes survival the sole priority. Nothing else counts, nothing else is tolerated. Life is not lived; it is suffered. The emotional life of the family is mechanized and stultified.

The effects of contagion of panic and rage and the associated exertions toward magic control need to be understood within the matrix of two related conditions: 1) psychotic breakdown as a family phenomenon across three or more generations; 2) the closed quality of the family entity. The emotional climate herein described is transmitted from generation to generation. Characteristically, the pathogenic symbiosis is passed down from the relationship of grandmother and mother to mother and child. Occasionally, it seems focused on grandfather, father and child. Basically, the family is tightly knit, and fenced off from the wider world outside. There is a dominant value attitude which insists that the members hang together or they will hang separately. The outer community is looked upon with suspicion. It is felt to be harsh, dangerous and unfriendly, if not actually persecutory. The members of the family must conform to the principle of mutual loyalty and mutual dependency. They must feed off one another. Without the protection and nurture of family, they will perish. I am suggesting here the hypothesis that these emotional currents in depth and the associated pathogenic fantasy formation are a prime force in the patterning of family role relationships.

In the relations of the mother with the potential schizophrenic offspring, the quality of joining is a form of caricature, rather than a true joining. In this sick symbiosis, there is a massive, all-engulfing identification of mother and child. They live inside one another's bellies. The child is allowed to exist only as a part of mother; in turn the mother exists only as a part of the child. The mother commands; the child obeys. The child commands; the mother obeys. The roles of mother and child are often inverted. No separation is permitted. Any effort to initiate free movement becomes an instantaneous signal for the abortion or crippling of the vital urge. The mother is the soul of martyrdom; she is infinitely skillful in using self-pity as a weapon to induce guilt. She loudly protests her devotion, her loving sacrifice for the offspring; and yet wheels about to wipe out his existence. In one way she smothers and invades. In another she obliterates. In a dramatic posture, she offers food, physical care and slave-like services, but she offers these in place of herself. She puts the catering between herself and the child. As a whole person, she fades away. The child can relate only to the services, not to the mother as a person.

Despite denial and compensatory solicitousness, it is as if only one of the two is destined to survive. The one stays alive only at the expense of the other. A deep-rooted mutual perception of forced sacrifice pervades the bond. It is all or nothing; if the offspring comes to life, is expressive, the mother seems to lie down and die emotionally. If the mother is strong and vocal, the child seems to fade out, a kind of teeter-totter arrangement. If the mother keeps her sanity, the child loses it, or vice versa. As one patient expressed it, "Mother, between you and me, it is everything or nothing." The "everything" (mother) demands everything; the "nothing" (child) asks for nothing. How can nothing ask for something? Across time it is as though the child integrates into a compliant role of suffocating the self in order to assure the mother's continued existence.

The mother projects the fantasy of catastrophic danger hanging over the head of the child. She assigns the source of this destructive force to some demonic agent outside. Being over-solicitous, she designs imagined threats to the child's body and health. With this as rationalization, she invaded the child's psychic being and body. Often, this rape occurs as forced feeding, rectal insertion, handling of the sexual parts, and other body manipulations. Hidden beneath the self-delegated role of lifesaver lies the mother's annihilation anxiety and her need to govern every aspect of the child's being. Behind all the obsessive disguises, she acts to prevent any effective initiative or free movement. The child is allowed no life of his own; she erases it. The vital urge to separate is felt as a threat to her own survival. Should she permit movement in the child, she would lose control, lose her mind; in effect, she would be destined to die. Inherent in this behavior is the unspoken feeling, "If I drown, I take you with me." To assure her own survival the mother chokes off the breath of life and the movement of the child. He in turn plays her game. He obediently echoes the mother's image of self as omnipotent lifesaver and collusively denies the mother's covert assaultive invasion of his being. In such mother-child interaction, there is a critical failure of homeodynamic balance.

Conceivably, the needed antidote might be provided by the father. Yet, in these families, the mother is the doer; the father waits for things to happen. Generally, he fails to move in to repair the pathogenic imbalance in the mother-child relation. He is himself detached. He hangs back, waiting for the mother to make the first move. If she does, it is often a camouflaged attack, but the father's primary concern is to protect himself. To assure his own survival, he must not jeopardize his dependency on his wife. On occasion, the father reveals a clear jealousy of the child. He seems willing for the mother to consume the child. If he makes a ritual gesture, as if to defend the child, he is really barricading his own position. In any case, he fails to rescue the child from the symbiotic trap.

The "well sibling," so-called, "wants out." He senses the danger of the trap and avoids it, like father. The sibling may feel that mother prefers the first child. He may even feel some measure of neglect, yet the greater urgency is to stay away from mother's death trap. Should the first child be hospitalized or otherwise removed, the mother may turn her engulfing clutch onto the sibling.

The relevance of the theory of double bind, as advocated by Bateson et al. (1956), presents problems. It is highly suggestive, yet it may, in fact, act as a cover for complex emotional events. According to this theory there are five necessary elements: 1) two or more persons; 2) repeated experience; 3) a primary negative injunction; 4) a secondary injunction conflicting with the first at a more abstract level, and like the first, enforced by punishments or signals which threaten survival; 5) a negative injunction prohibiting the victim from escaping the field.

In my view the fifth element ought to be the first. The power of the other injunctions rests precisely on the prohibition against escaping the field. It is, first, a constraint on escaping the strangulation of the mother-child symbiosis, and beyond that, a constraint on escaping the field of family to outer living space. It is this mortal threat, I would guess, that compels the schizophrenic to strip away the metacommunication.

Is the double bind the real thing or the shadow? In my view, it seems more like a mechanism that disguises the core anxiety, the mother's annihilation fright and her need at all costs to maintain the suffocating symbiosis. The motive behind the mechanism is to freeze the child, to disconfirm rather than to confirm the vital force of the child, to stop the child from free movement away from mother to father or other persons. Should the child succeed in this move, the mother would be destroyed. She channelizes her hostility through father. She makes him the devil, herself the angel. She sets the child against father while she noisily asserts that she is the sole protector and lifesaver. In this interpersonal setting, the child is left with only one path, a retreat into psychotic fantasy.

In "schizogenic" families, one may hypothesize several pathogenic trends:

1. A family mood governed by a contagion of anxiety concerning total destruction.
2. The counteraction of the threat of catastrophe requires magic powers of control. The prime concern is sheer survival.
3. Family roles are integrated on an all-or-none scale; as magic persecutor, as sacrificial victim, as magic protector.
4. The child's vital urge to breathe, move, feel and act on his own initiative, while potentially healing and live-giving, is felt instead as a malevolent destructive threat.
5. The profound fright of his potential violence implies the danger of usurpation of control, driving the parent crazy, robbing the parent of the right of life.
6. Omnipotent powers are mobilized to counteract the perceived threat. The child is frozen and immobilized in an engulfing symbiosis, mediated by the mechanisms of double bind and scapegoating.

A brief comment is in order regarding the contrast between families with psychotic trends, families with neurotic trends, and families with acting-out delinquent trends. In the several types of families, the unconscious prohibition placed on the offspring is distinct. As I have suggested elsewhere, in neurotic families, the child *must not be different;* in psychotic families, the child *must not be!* In all three types there is double binding and scapegoating, though in a different form and with different consequences. In neurotic families there is more give and take. The felt danger is partial, not total. The neurotic surrenders a limb for a life. In conforming to the authority of parents and community, he gives up a part of his being, not the whole. At the very least, he experiences some true relatedness and loving, not the ritualized make-believe of psychotic families. In the acting-out, delinquent type, the offspring may not revolt against the parents. He is subtly encouraged to leave the living space of his family to vent his parents' destructiveness against authority symbols in the community. In essence, to glimpse the contrast of the three family types, we are required to trace the different patterns of injunction concerning departure from the living space of the family, the different organization of the forces of double binding and scapegoating, and also the mobilization of different patterns of rescue and healing.

CLINICAL VIGNETTES

1. In a family that I have watched for 35 years, now producing its fourth generation of offspring, four out of five of the children of the second generation suffered psychotic disorders. These breakdowns emerged in series, one at a time, and occurred at different stages of the family life cycle. They were: (1) a catatonic psychosis in a son, 35 years ago; (2) a postpartum psychosis in a daughter, 30 years ago, followed by a cyclic mood disorder; (3) a postpartum depression in the second daughter, 24 years ago; (4) a sociopathic disorder in another son with periodic eruptions of paranoid reactivity associated with bouts of alcoholism, beginning 12 years ago.

In the third generation, the son of the first daughter suffered an acute schizophrenic reaction, affectively tinged, beginning 10 years ago.

In other family members there was a diffuse assortment of personality disturbances, anxiety hysteria, hypochondriasis, washing compulsion, neurotic depression, etc.

It is interesting to note that while this family was literally pitted with mental and emotional disturbance, it was in other respects a tightly knit three-generation group, hardworking, ambitious, striving and self-sufficient. All members were strongly bound to the goal of survival and accomplishment.

The familiar manifestations of pathogenic symbiosis were observed in the grandmother-mother pair, and in the mother-child pair. The character, values and attitudes of grandmother and mother were strikingly similar. They catered to and aggrandized one another. They often reversed mother-child roles. Each brooded over the well-being of the other; each demanded inordinate attention and services from the other. Conspicuously present in the façade of the two women were attitudes of righteousness, martyrdom, over-solicitation, self-sacrifice and self-pity. Whenever anything went wrong, the blame was magically projected to outside influences. This assignment of responsibility to some demonic outside agent gave them an instantaneous excuse to moan and groan, to wallow in self-pity. They revealed a finely cultivated talent for using self-pity as a weapon to induce guilt in other persons.

Both women exhibited a false pride, a haughty self-justification, a kind of arrogance born out of martyrdom. They were extremely pushy, intrusive, and yet habitually justified this in terms of their selfless devotion. Beneath this pushiness they were basically detached. They engaged in coercive intrusions in the lives of their offspring: forced feeding, manipulation of the body, invasion of privacy, etc. The solicitousness was all-consuming and had an emotionally crippling effect on the child. The catering and being catered to were of a kind that fostered relatedness to the services rather than to the person. To the child, the message was unmistakable: without my protection and devotion you will not survive; other people are out to hurt you. A characteristic trend is the repetitive tormenting pressure of questions such as: "Are you sure you're all right? Aren't you tired? You sound like you have a cold, you need a rest." The over-concern with health and body is habitual. Eating is not for pleasure; it is to survive. It neutralizes a death anxiety. Food is not offered to the child; it is shoved into him. If refused, the mother pushes again and again, she cannot take no for an answer; she will not stop pushing till the child bursts with fury and sometimes not even then. If violently rejected, she will justify herself and project the blame to other members of the family. She then returns to the attack. If cornered, she secretly assigns her intrusive urge to a surrogate: "He'll be angry if I go into his bedroom, you go see if he's all right, but don't tell him I told you. He'll kill me; he'll refuse to talk with me." If being served dinner by a grown daughter, she may make a sacrificial gesture: "You feed me too well. Why do you feed me first? Do you have enough for yourself?"

On one occasion, when a grown son was spending the night with a girl friend, the mother telephoned the home of the girl friend at 6 A.M. The excuse was: "I was worried because you didn't answer your phone at home."

When not visited regularly by her adult children, the mother goes into a raging fit of martyrdom and self-pity, "Better I should die! Why do you torture me so? Do I demand anything from you? What do you want from me? Take everything—my money, my life—it's a miracle I'm still here. I wish I could take poison."

In general, the attitudes inculcated in the child towards the outer world were such as induced both terror and over-aggressiveness. The usual message was: The only person you can rely on is your mother, don't you dare trust or reveal yourself to people in the outside world. They will take advantage of you; they will hurt or destroy you. Stay with me!

The mother seems able to relate only to a helpless infant. The attitudes of the father are interesting in several respects. He is deeply dependent on the mother's care and servicing of him. In contrast with the mother he does not relate at all to an infant. He says, in effect, he can relate only when the child becomes a social being, when the child is old enough to walk and talk. Before that time the infant belongs entirely to the mother. The father is a kind of work drudge. Beyond his commitment to work, he seeks out avenues of relief for his hypochondriacal fears; for example, he engages in a long Sunday morning ritual, an enema followed by a hot bath; otherwise he escapes into reading or collecting newspaper clippings. In his relations with mother his attitude is: peace at any price. He placates her as far as he can. However, when his threshold of irritability is violated through the mother's nagging, he has a brief explosive rage which is the only way to stop mother's provocations. She then exploits this to stir the child to fear the father's explosive rage and thus binds the child to herself all the more.

The "well sibling" is detached; he tends to keep his own counsel. He avoids entrapment by the mother and cultivates a separate fantasy life.

2. In another family, middle class and strictly conformist, composed of parents and three children, the only daughter developed schizophrenia in her adolescence. Following a seemingly uneventful childhood as a "perfect child," a "little princess," her whole personality changed. She dropped out of college, turned to marijuana and LSD, became pregnant and had an abortion.

In this family, again we see a three generation grandmother-mother-daughter symbiosis. To quote mother, "We had the closest and happiest family. The children were great. Now I just can't live without my daughter. She can't take care of herself. She's like a two year old, she's easy prey for any boy." The mother is typically disaster-minded, tending always to imagine the worst. In her brooding worry and tendency toward panic, she nurses fantasies of the daughter being assulted sexually, being whisked off by a criminal. With this unceasing worry she is unable to sleep. Although violence is anathema in this family, mother exclaimed with fury that she could kill the young man who introduced her daughter to sex and LSD. "He's a demon, a pervert. He should be behind prison bars." She could murder her daughter's previous psychiatrist, "He should have known better. He could have stopped the whole illness. I could cut him up into shreds." Of the two brothers, one is a self-defeating obsessional personality; the other is a sociopathic gambler.

The father is deeply dependent on mother. He treats her as a cute child-wife. He flatters and placates her. He also teases her with half-jocular sarcastic comments. He clowns with his wife and children. His response to his wife's disaster complex is typically to try to laugh her out of it. When this does not work, he begins to fail physically; he develops heart pains. Basically, he is emotionally detached and has only a peripheral relationship with his children.

3. In another family, Italian Catholic, the pattern of sick symbiosis seemed to move from grandfather to father to sons. The first son broke down in his mid-thirties with a schizo-affective psychosis complicated by alcoholism. The sec-

ond son was afflicted with a cyclic mood disorder, a hypomanic reaction cloaking an underlying depression.

The family history is a long saga of repeated trauma and violence. Grandfather, a miner, was a tyrant who ruled his family with an iron fist. When the father was 16 years of age, the grandfather developed tuberculosis, suffered repeated hemorrhages, was ill and cared for at home for 14 years before he died. In this circumstance the father went to work in the mines at 16 and supported the whole family. For 14 years he lived in continuous terror, returning home from work each night, "waiting for the shoe to fall." While the father provided economic support for the family, the grandfather persisted as the ruler of the family. On one occasion when the father was about 10 years old, grandfather caught him attempting sexual contact with a domestic animal. The grandfather brought the wrath of God down on his son's head. He cursed him, calling him a sexual beast. He said: "You will never get a good woman as wife, you'd be better off dead."

Years later, the father's brother made repeated attempts to kill himself; he finally succeeded when the father was 30 years of age. For the five preceding years the father had a brooding, panicky worry concerning imminent disaster. He sought omnipotent power to forestall the brother's suicide and failed. Shortly thereafter, the father developed an acute phobic psychosis. He was not hospitalized, but required his wife's constant attendance. The father's one way of holding himself together was to dedicate himself to his job. Despite panic and fears of catastrophe, he worked seven days a week, never took a vacation and achieved outstanding business success. His wife was moralistic, self-righteous, rigid, compulsive and explosively irritable. She carried out her duty to her husband, but did it grudgingly. In the meantime she neglected her sons. Basically, she was a detached person; to father and sons she offered services rather than a warm relationship.

The relations between father and mother were severely strained. For all the years of their marriage there was a contagion of panic and explosive anger between them; this became so severe that they hardly dared to talk. They lived in the same apartment, but were virtually incommunicado. There was a deadly silence between them, a severe emotional distancing as a defense against the threat of violence.

The father treated the older son as strong, the younger one as weak. With the older son he was severe and dictatorial. With the younger one he was over-indulgent. The first son entered his business; the second son escaped to become an actor. The older son showed remarkable similarity with his father; he, too, was straitjacketed to the responsibilities of his job. This was the one area where he performed well. At home, however, there was again a contagion of panic and violence between him and his wife. His extreme fright of abandonment made him vulnerable to her control. She in turn had an obsession with horse breeding and put this preoccupation between herself and her husband. She neglected husband, children and home. There was also a shared pattern of sexual jealousy between them which led periodically to outbursts of violence. Over and over the son declared: His mother demanded that he be a saint; his father forced him into the role of superman. Over a period of years the son developed increasing depression and withdrawal and resorted to alcohol to control his panic. He was finally hospitalized.

SUMMARY

I have sketched here a tentative composite picture of the affective climate, interactive trends and pathogenic fantasy formation in families that breed psychosis. In such families, the discrepancy between the façade and the core emotion is dramatic. The façade is controlled, ritualized, emotionally frozen and dead. Beneath this, there is a brooding worry, a foreboding of disaster. Periodically, there are explosions of anxiety and rage, which act as a tidal wave surging through the entire family. Fright of the impending catastrophe impels the mobilization of total magic control. The prime concern is then survival.

Family roles are integrated on an all-or-none scale, as magic persecutor, as sacrificial victim, as magic protector. Who does what to whom is surrounded with an aura of mystery. The schizogenic parent is the soul of martyrdom. She loudly protests her loving sacrifice and yet wheels about to smother and invade the child. Parent and child are engulfed in a sick symbiosis. A deep-rooted mutual perception of forced sacrifice pervades the bond, as if only one of the two is destined to survive. Across time the child incorporates the parent's guilt, integrates into a compliant role of suffocating the self to assure the parent's continued existence. The second parent, absorbed with protecting his own dependent safety, fails to rescue the child from the symbiotic trap.

REFERENCES

ACKERMAN, N. W. (1960): Family focused therapy of schizophrenia. In: *The Out-Patient Treatment of Schizophrenia*. Editor: Milton Rosenblatt. Grune and Stratton, New York, N.Y.

ACKERMAN, N. W. (1961): The schizophrenic patient and his family relationships. In: *Mental Patients in Transition*. Editors: Greenblatt, Levenson and Klerman. Charles C. Thomas, Springfield, Ill.

ACKERMAN, N. W. (1964): Family therapy and schizophrenia—theory and practice. In: *International Psychiatry Clinics*, Oct. 1964, Vol. 1/4, Little, Brown and Co., Boston, Mass.

ACKERMAN, N. W. (1966): *Treating the Troubled Family*, pp. 237-288. Basic Books, New York, N.Y.

ACKERMAN, N. W. and FRANKLIN, P. (1965): Family dynamics and the reversibility of delusional formation. In: *Intensive Family Therapy*. Editors: I. Boszormenyi-Nagy and J. L. Framo. Harper Row, New York, N.Y.

BATESON, G. (1960): The group dynamics in schizophrenia. In: *Chronic Schizophrenia*, p. 90. Editor: Appelby. Free Press.

BATESON, G. (1961): The bio-social integration of behavior in the schizophrenic family. In: *Exploring the Base for Family Therapy*, p. 116. Editors: Ackerman, Beatman and Sherman. Family Service Association of America, New York, N.Y.

BATESON, G., JACKSON, D. D., HALEY, J. and WEAKLAND, J. (1956): Toward a theory of schizophrenia. *Behav. Sci.*, *1*, 251.

BOWEN, M. (1960): A family concept of schizophrenia. In: *The Etiology of Schizophrenia*. Editor: D. D. Jackson. Basic Books, New York, N.Y.

CHEEK, F. E. (1964): The schizophrenogenic mother in word and deed. *Family Process, 3/1*.

FARINA, A. (1960): Patterns of role dominance and conflict in parents of schizophrenic patients. *J. Abnorm. Soc. Psychol.*, *61*, 31.

FLECK, S., LIDZ, T., CORNELISON, A., SCHAFER, S. and TERRY, D. (1959): The intrafamilial environment of the schizophrenic patient. In: *Individual and Familial Dynamics*. Editor: Masserman. Grune and Stratton, New York, N.Y.

HALEY, J. (1959): The family of the schizophrenic. *J. Nerv. Ment. Dis.*, *129*, 357.

HALEY, J. (1962): Family experiments. *Family Process, 1/2*, 265.

HALEY, J. (1964): Research on family patterns. *Family Process, 3/1*, 41.

HESS, R. D. and HANDEL, G. (1959): *Family Worlds*. University of Chicago Press, Chicago, Ill.

JACKSON, D. D. (1957): The question of family homeostasis, Part 1. *Psychiat. Quart.*, *31/Suppl.*, 79.

LENNARD, H. L. and BERNSTEIN, A. (1969): *Patterns in Human Interaction*. Jossey-Bass, Inc., San Francisco, Calif.

LERNER, P. H. (1968): Resolution of intrafamilial role conflict in families of schizophrenic patients. In: *Family Processes and Schizophrenia*. Editors: Mishler and Waxler. Science House, New York, N.Y.

LIDZ, T. and FLECK, S. (1960): Schizophrenia, human interaction and the role of the family. In: *The Etiology of Schizophrenia*. Editor: D. D. Jackson. Basic Books, New York, N.Y.

LIDZ, T., FLECK, S. and CORNELISON, A. (eds.) (1965): *Schizophrenia and the Family*. International Universities Press, Inc., New York, N.Y.

RYCKOFF, I. M., DAY, J. and WYNNE, L. C. (1959): Maintenance of stereotyped roles in schizophrenia. *Arch. Gen. Psychiat.*, *1*, 109.

SEARLES, H. (1959): The effort to drive the other person crazy. *Brit. J. Med. Psychol.*, *Part 1/32*, 1.

SINGER, M. and WYNNE, L. C. (1963): Differentiating characteristics of parents of childhood schizophrenics, childhood neurotics and young adult schizophrenics. *Amer. J. Psychiat.*, *120*, 234.

STRODTBECK, F. L. (1954): The family as a three person group. *Amer. Sociol. Rev.*, *19*, 23.

WEAKLAND, J. H. (1960): The "double-bind" hypothesis in schizophrenia and three person interaction. In: *The Etiology of Schizophrenia*. Editor: D. D. Jackson. Basic Books, New York, N.Y.

WYNNE, L. C. (1961): The study of intrafamilial alignments. In: *Exploring the Base for Family Therapy*. Editors: Ackerman, Beatman and Sherman. Family Service Association of America, New York, N.Y.

WYNNE, L. C., RYCKOFF, I. M., DAY, J. and HIRSCH, S. I. (1958): Pseudo-mutuality in the family relations of schizophrenics. *Psychiatry*, *21*, 205.

WYNNE, L. C. and SINGER, M. (1963): Thought disorder and the family relations of schizophrenics. *Arch. Gen. Psychiat.*, *9*, 191.

CHAPTER 44

Family Dynamics and the Reversibility of Delusional Formation: A Case Study in Family Therapy

A family approach to investigation of the schizophrenic phenomenon requires commitment to a point of view. In previous publications (Ackerman, 1960, 1961), we committed ourselves to a theory concerning the schizophrenic illness and also to a theory of family therapy appropriate to this condition. The conceptual frame outlined in these publications assumes a correlation between the schizophrenic process and the homeostatic disorder of the organism. A further assumption is made regarding a basic interdependence between the homeostatic disorder of the schizophrenic individual and the homeostatic imbalance of the family group. The goal of family study is the elucidation of this relationship. In taking this theoretical position, we do not assert an exclusive or an exact one-to-one relation between family and individual homeostasis but only suggest that there may be a significant correlation. We draw this inference from a small but convincing series of empirical experiences in the treatment of the schizophrenic patient within the matrix of the emotional life of his whole family. With this type of intervention, we have been able, to our satisfaction, to alter the homeostatic equilibrium within the family unit and, in parallel fashion, to modify the course of the schizophrenic disorder. In essence, we have been able to bring about a shift in the integrative pattern of family relationships and a concurrent shift in the integrative functioning of the schizophrenic patient in the direction of health.

Let us go one step further in our thinking. In family study and treatment of schizophrenia, we observe circular effects: the influence of family on patient and the influence of patient on family. If, in selected cases, we succeed in reversing some of the central features of psychotic expe-

Reprinted with permission from *Intensive Family Therapy*, I. Boszormenyi-Nagy and J.L. Framo (Eds.), 1965, 245-287. Copyright 1965 by Harper & Row, Hagerstown, MD. This paper was co-authored with Paul F. Franklin.

rience by means of family intervention, we are adducing, thereby, evidence of the significant association between family and individual homeostasis. When, by this method, we are able to retard the pathogenic trend and draw the patient back into the real life space of his family group, we infer that the family method of therapy holds the potential power, not only to influence the secondary elaborations, but also to influence the primary manifestations of this disorder. In taking this stand, we do not assert that the social factor is the exclusive etiologic agent; we do not claim a cure. Nor do we say that such improvement can be achieved uniformly with all types of schizophrenia, at any and all stages of the illness, and with every type of family. We contend only that if such a result can be brought about in a few instances, this, by itself, is a significant reflection on the nature of the illness and on the crucial role of family interaction. In present-day controversy, this is an important consideration, since it is often asserted by organically minded investigators that psychotherapy influences the secondary manifestations exclusively, not touching the primary schizophrenic process. We do not agree with this point of view. For us, it is a striking observation that family psychotherapy, under favorable environmental and organismic conditions, seems to affect both the primary and secondary manifestations.

The therapy of the case here described was carried out in the Family Mental Health Clinic of the Jewish Family Service of New York City. This is a research-oriented clinic devoted to the study of the relations of family dynamics and mental health. As is the usual procedure, the family under discussion was first studied in a series of exploratory interviews conducted by the research psychiatrist and observed by the clinic staff. The family was then assigned to a staff psychiatrist for continued study and therapy. Interviews were conducted with the whole family, and also, when indicated, with the patient alone, and the parents alone.

In this family there were individual interviews in the early months with the daughter, and joint interviews with the parents. Later on, the daughter joined in regular family interviews but continued to have some individual contact with the therapist. After a year of therapy, the research psychiatrist had several follow-up interviews with the family, which were filmed for study purposes.

Our purpose in this chapter is to report a study of patient and family in which treatment of the whole family seemed to move toward reversal of the patient's psychotic experience. We present the relevant material in five main sections: (1) the illness situation; (2) the family background and diagnosis; (3) the course of family therapy; (4) verbatim record of a family interview; (5) an interpretive discussion based on the evidence of family study.

THE ILLNESS SITUATION

The patient was a 16-year-old girl brought by her parents for a psychiatric consultation because her mental condition seemed to be deteriorating and the parents were alarmed. For three years the patient had been undergoing psychotherapy in another clinic, with the assumption that she was suffering from a psychoneurosis. Neither this, nor any other diagnosis, had been shared with the parents; they were befogged as to the true nature of the patient's illness and falteringly tried to deny its seriousness. They preferred to view the patient as a child with a "vivid imagination."

The patient was withdrawn, had no associations with her peers, and refused to attend school. At home, she alternated between periods of barricading herself in her room and engaging in belligerent quarrels with her parents and, more particularly, with her grandmother. She made recurrent threats of suicide and exhibited an odd array of mannerisms: a bizarre cough, twirling her hair, averting her gaze, and wormy gestures of her hands and body. At times she used awkward, pretentious phrases that verged on neologism.

Overt signs of illness had appeared at the age of eleven against a background of lifelong shyness and withdrawal. The patient was born while her father was in military service. He met her for the first time when she was three years of age, having been overseas prior to this time. On his return home from the war, he was in poor condition, physically and mentally. He suffered from long debilitating infection and was malnourished, depressed, and irritable. At home, he was accused by his wife and mother-in-law of being overdemanding and of monopolizing his wife's attention, while, at the same time, being critical and irritably rejecting toward the child. When, in the later years, mother and grandmother joined in blaming him for causing the child's mental breakdown, he took sides with the women against himself. He assumed the total burden of guilt and hung his head in shame; he fully believed that he had inflicted severe damage on the child.

But this was not the whole story. The women had made a scapegoat of the father. Clinical study revealed that the child had suffered serious emotional trauma even before the father's return from the war. In these first three years while the father was away, the grandmother governed the family. The mother and grandmother were tightly bound in a dependent, ambivalent relationship. The grandmother was sharply critical of the mother's care of the baby. While resenting the grandmother's carping attack, the mother was unable to fight back. The grandmother accused the mother of neglecting the child, of total ineptness in failing to control the baby's crying, which might waken the grandfather. The grandfather was a shadowy, peripheral figure; he had been a working man and had died six months prior to the first consultation with the family. The grandmother nagged the mother to take the child out into the fresh air and sunshine, on the score that the air in the home was close and foul. In a rationalized, obsessional way, the grandmother pushed the baby out of the home. Though resentful, the mother complied with this coercive pressure. She was split between the need to care for the baby and the need to appease the grandmother. Nonetheless, the tight alliance between the two women continued, and they joined in isolating and scapegoating the father. They set father against daughter, daughter against father. They fortified in the child a barrier of suspicion and fright against the father as a male.

Examination of the patient revealed active hallucinatory experiences. She maintained regular communication with a planet in space called Queendom; she did this by sending and receiving something akin to radar waves. She exchanged messages with the reigning lady in Queendom, "Zena," by means of a "Zenascope." More of this later.

The presenting situation was critical. A prompt decision had to be reached as to the necessity of hospital care because of the danger of violence and/or suicide. Following close study, by means of filmed family interviews, a tentative decision was made to assume a calculated risk in keeping the patient within her own home and undertaking psychotherapy of the whole family.

The Family Background and Diagnosis

The living unit consisted of the two parents, the maternal grandmother, and the patient, an only child. The grandmother was in her mid-sixties. The father was 47 years old; the mother 45 years old. The parents had been married for 20 years. The father earned a better than average income and the grandmother contributed to the household. Both parents were college graduates, native-born, Jewish.

The parents had been drawn to one another out of their mutual dependent need and their shared ideals of family closeness, security, loyalty, and intellectual striving. In their respective families of origin, they had had certain anxieties in common. The father came from a broken family; the paternal grandfather died in the father's early childhood; the paternal grandmother, domineering and long-suffering, was oversolicitous and intrusive. The mother identifies closely with her own domineering mother, while she viewed her father as temperamental, ineffectual, and yet someone to be feared.

The father is a tall, handsome, distinguished-looking man. He is a rigid, obsessive, perfectionistic individual, with profound feelings of inferiority. He gives the impression of a frightened, guilty, self-doubting boy, rather than a man. He is inclined to be ingratiating and self-apologetic. He is almost womanly in demeanor. He talks in quick spurts or does not talk at all. He is fearful of his emotions and dresses up his thoughts in pretentious, intellectual phrases. He withdraws into scholastic pursuits. All this notwithstanding, he projects a certain childlike appeal and reaches out frantically for approval and support. His main defenses are obsessive obedience, repression of aggression, and emotional detachment. The mother is an attractive woman, but has a bland, vapid, expressionless face. It is difficult to find in her any trace of animation. In a shallow sense, she is an obsessively good person, self-righteous, judgmental, and full of clichés as to what is right and wrong. She shows little spontaneity. She is given to periodic hysterical outbursts and also suffers from migraine. Now and then she bursts into high-pitched, eerie laughter.

The grandmother is a rigid type, a severely dogmatic and aggressive person. She is never wrong and has an immediate answer for every problem. Beneath her hypocritical, self-righteous protests, she is contemptuous of everyone. If she does not get her way, she sulks and makes intimidating threats. She intrudes herself as mother's mouthpiece, harassing father and driving him into an isolated position. Both grandmother and mother have the urge to talk for the father, and also for the daughter. A fragment of symbiosis characterizes the relationship of mother and grandmother. Trying in a futile way to appease the women's fear of masculine aggression, father shrinks from the expression of his male powers.

The patient is an appealing teenager who looks pathetically disorganized and lost. She alternates between panic and explosive, defiant aggression. Her native intelligence, imagination, and perceptiveness show clearly through the curtain of her disturbance. At times her expressions are exquisitely sensitive and seem almost poetic. Mainly, she is in despair; now and again she lashes out in desperation but then withdraws.

On the surface these parents give lip-service to their close partnership, but they have not achieved a satisfying marital union; it is, instead, a parent-child relationship. The father fears the invasive powers of a woman; the mother is suspicious and fearful of male aggression. An undercurrent of competitiveness and hostility aborts the establishment of a firm emotional bond. The parents seem tacitly to collaborate in minimizing the importance of the sexual aspect of their union. When the child was born, it seemed to shatter the tenuous balance of family relationships. She was an intruder and had to be expelled. When she tried frantically to prove that she existed, that she should be given a place, the result was further disruption of the family group. The only alternatives were withdrawal into a psychotic world or suicide. It is on this background that the grandmother insisted that the patient must go to boarding school. This presumably would force her to make friends among her peers.

Casually viewed, this family might appear to be well-integrated, except for the one severely disturbed girl, but this was a deceiving appearance. On deeper examination, it was apparent that this was a profoundly disorganized and split group. In emotional terms, it was a paralyzed family, ridden with guilt and anxiety. The members were severely alienated; they lived in constant dread of the uncontrolled eruption of violence and destruction. In their inner life there was severe prejudice and scapegoating. The one male member of the family was viewed either as a monster or a helpless boy; the one daughter was treated as a disruptive intruder. Both were sentenced by the older women to punishment and exile. On the part of the daughter and father, there was a barely discernible yearning to get together in protective alliance against the older women, but this hardly got off the ground. All three adults united in scapegoating the sick child. They perceived her as a dangerous force and acted as if she must be either controlled or eliminated in order for the family to survive. While in a sly, covert way the patient showed an interest in her father, she mainly avoided him, as he avoided her. Mutually, they shunned direct gaze; they feared to touch one another. Father sensed an erotic element in his daughter's interest, shrank from it as taboo, and feared violence.

A deep rift had grown up between the patient and both parents. When the patient now and then made an abortive thrust to reach out to them, she was rebuffed. She argued with her mother, but her rage was directed mainly against her grandmother. She resisted parental authority, isolated herself in her room, and threatened violence if they invaded her privacy.

Between father and grandmother, there was a smouldering conflict. When originally he failed to oust the grandmother from the family he gave up. But his grudging resentment persisted. Behind his back, the grandmother engaged in a sneaky campaign to tear down his character. At present, the relationship between the father and grandmother is civil, but they hardly communicate. It is a cold war.

The mother, a bland, self-righteous person, slid out from between father and grandmother, as if unconsciously waiting for them to destroy one another. In daily relations with the patient, the adult members of the group were confused, disorganized, defeated, and yet tried to control her by means of threats and bribes.

At the conscious level, mother and father aspired to join in the ideal of a warm, close, loyal family unit. This was a complete fiction, however. In actuality, there was constant fear of the outbreak of open warfare. But the fiction persisted, since the adult members saw themselves as harmonious, peace-loving people. There was, therefore, this sharp, glaring contradiction between the ideal of family closeness and the actual condition, which was one of profound alienation in family relationships. Except for episodic explosions, the emotional climate in the home was static, half-dead; the mood was that of resigned apathy. The members of the group felt trapped. The functions of the family were carried out in a routine, constricted way. The family had little contact with the wider community.

As a family, they were an economic unit, but did not hold together either emotionally or socially. The sexual adjustment of the parents was at a low ebb; child care was disorganized. The family, as family, seemed to move backward, rather than forward; the relationships were severely constricted and lacking in vitality. The emotional atmosphere was pervaded by an attitude of fear and avoidance of life; the growth potential of the family group was almost nil.

THE COURSE OF FAMILY THERAPY

At the outset, the effort to treat patient and family together proved extremely difficult. The family was confused and fragmented. The grandmother campaigned forcefully for her plan to place the patient in a boarding school. The patient herself requested individual therapy, in complete isolation from her family. For the first four months, the planned procedure of family interviews was obstructed by the split condition of the group. Feeling thwarted, the grandmother aggressively sabotaged the entire proceeding. She competed with the therapist's influence, and she opposed his goal of treating all of them together. This conflict moved rapidly to a climax, after which the grandmother left the home and the therapy sessions.

In this first phase the patient and her family were seen separately. Generally, the patient was interviewed first, and after that her family, including, in the beginning, the grandmother. The early interviews with the parents were monotonous. They showed their bewilderment, fright, and guilt, as well as their deep resentment of the child's behavior. Because of their persistent panic, they continued to deny the severity of the patient's illness. They credited her hallucinatory experiences to her "vivid imagination," and the father minimized her illness by claiming that, like himself, his daughter was interested in science fiction. The therapist challenged this; he categorically asserted the position that the patient was mentally ill.

When they were finally forced to admit the girl's psychosis, the parents came into open conflict with one another. The father displayed a more genuine concern for the child's welfare, while being accused again and again by the older women of rejecting the child. According to both the mother and grandmother, the father rigidly maintained high standards and expectations, especially along intellectual lines. The father was berated for failing to relate to the child, except in terms of scholastic interests, and he submitted to this mortification. He became depressed. But as the therapist gave him increased support by firmly disagreeing that the father was the sole cause of the patient's illness, he felt greatly relieved and his depression lifted. He thanked the therapist volubly.

In the ensuing sessions, the father took a stronger stand against the grandmother's noisy criticisms of the patient. It is noteworthy here, however, that the father, now more openly opposed to the grandmother's aggressiveness, was not directly assertive with his wife. It was self-evident that he was trying to divide mother and grandmother, to free his wife from the grandmother's domination, and to get her for himself once again. In essence, he was reviving his original unsuccessful attempt to join with his wife and eliminate the grandmother from the home.

The conflict between the grandmother and the therapist came to a boil. Talking to her was like conversing with a stone wall, and the therapist expressed his anger to her. The parents were now driven into a corner and forced to choose between grandmother and daughter. It was either one or the other. The therapist pointed out how the grandmother monopolized relations with the mother and competed with the patient. In effect, the grandmother was denying a mother to the sick child. In the choice between grandmother and daughter, the father sided with the therapist. He became outspoken in his desire to separate his family from the grandmother. In contrast, the mother showed conflict and indecision. But, increasingly, she began to ventilate her anger against the grandmother. Finally, the therapist reached an agreement with both parents to "place the grandmother in boarding school," so to speak, rather than the patient. The grandmother was moved to the home of a relative, and after that family therapy moved forward.

In the office, the patient paced up and down agitatedly. She had made several suicidal attempts by swallowing small metallic objects, and she explained that her recurrent cough was an attempt to expel these objects. It was observed, however, that she coughed regularly whenever she darted a glance at her father or at the male therapist. At moments of high tension, when she was in acute conflict over the danger of closeness with her father or with the male therapist, she declared that if she only had the guts, she would jump out of the window.

Bit by bit she revealed the nature of her psychotic experiences. She spoke of hearing voices from another planet, Queendom. The inhabitants of this planet lured her to join them. There, the beings were of another species. They were not human; they were like machines. On this planet no males were allowed; they were all feminine, "not female, but feminine." These creatures were gorgeous beings, with the most exotic coloring of skin and hair. They had hormones, not for sex, but to make them attractive. On this planet there was no reproduction by sexual union, only by fission. The beings in Queendom lived in solar time, not Earthian time. There was no night or day. The inhabitants lived perhaps one hundred and fifty years. They were capable of sleeping for long periods. They were completely self-sufficient and experienced no fatigue. They had the power of clairvoyance. Everything on this planet was factory-made by chemical means. Nutrition was neither personal nor human. The source of food was not Mother Earth, but the factory, where all foodstuffs were chemically produced. In this planet, in outer space, there was no hate, no war, no killing, but also no love. The inhabitants devoted themselves to the cultivation of the arts: music, literature and painting. It was a culture of mind over body. Finally, in this universe there was magic control. There was none of the hate and danger of the Earthian way of life. Yet, some beings in this planet were afflicted with a mysterious disease, which progressively rotted the body while the spirit remained immortal.

Several times the daughter appeared for her session wearing a rubber mask depicting a horribly deformed, diseased person. She stared into a medical book in which there was a photograph of a patient afflicted with ugly, festering, mutilating sores. By implication, this was her fantasy image of her own deteriorating illness. She explained her urge to be rid of her body: the physical part of her being was an intolerable burden, for it continually had to be fed, nursed, cared for; she wanted only to preserve and enhance her spirit. She sought to eliminate her body and glorify her mind. She was in profound conflict with her bodily needs, especially with her sexual urges. She confided a disturbing encounter with a young man, a waiter at a summer hotel. As she described the incident, in a strange way she had suddenly found herself alone with him, and he took her in his lap and kissed her. She described this young man as a "wolf." He was "not even Caucasian"; he was like "a Formosan monster." When he kissed her, it was as if she felt abruptly transformed from a little girl into a woman. It was a shocking experience. She became panicky and escaped as quickly as she could.

In a peculiar, paradoxical way, despite her fears of sex and men, she showed flurries of intense interest in both her father and the male therapist. In one family session, she dramatized the conflict of allegiance between her psychotic community in Queendom and her real family. She remarked with high animation how perhaps she had made a mistake. She had allowed Zena and the beings in Queendom to talk her into their way of life, where no males were allowed. Maybe she was too obedient. She should have resisted more strongly. She felt tempted to conspire to take a male or two up to Queendom, "just to show them what the male species is like." The male or two were, of course, the father and the male therapist. Since no males were permitted in Queendom, she would have to smuggle them in. But then, "they could only stay a few minutes." She would "keep a sharp eye on them." They would have to behave or right back to Earth they would go.

In the second phase of treatment, when regular family interviews were begun, the patient at first sat as far as possible from her parents. She was hesitant, unsure, frightened. Frequently as her sense of threat mounted, especially in relation to her apprehension of open hostility, she made a gesture of leaving the room. Each time she did this, the therapist persuaded her to stay. In her mind, he had become her "defender."

Within several weeks, the patient began to touch and even gently to kiss the therapist on the cheek in her parents' presence. The therapist verbalized his wonder that she exhibited this kind of affection toward him but not toward her parents. The father remarked that when he tried to approach her, he was generally met with a belligerent, hostile attitude. When he tried to enter her room, she shut the door in his face and threatened him with a stick. The mother regularly intruded with comments that reinforced the patient's fear of her father, alluding repeatedly to the father's rigid, exacting standards and his rejection of his daughter. It gradually became clear that the main source of hostility toward the patient was the mother, not the father. When the father was critical, he seemed to be acting on cue from the mother. It was the mother who tended to reinforce the barrier between daughter and father.

One incident, in particular, stands out sharply as an example of this trend. The patient brought home from school a failing mark in one of her subjects. The mother warned her against revealing this to the father. When in family interview, however, the therapist, with the patient's permission, brought this failing mark to the father's attention, he reacted not with disappointment and criticism but, rather, with an expression of genuine concern for the way in which the patient felt about this failure.

As these sessions proceeded, one could observe a shift in the alignment of family relationships. The patient's hostility toward the father gradually diminished, and she became perceptively sharper in her attacks on the mother. She alternated these attacks, however, with some recognition, half-apologetic, that perhaps her mother could not really be blamed because she was so dominated by the grandmother. By stages, the patient expressed her anger toward the grandmother with increasing directness and force. On those occasions when the grandmother visited the family, the patient would say to her, "What do you want here? Go home. We don't want you again." But she did more than this; she appealed to the mother to wean herself from the grandmother: "Grandma has had her chance at motherhood. It's your opportunity now." When the therapist called attention to the father's basic sympathy with the patient's resentment of the grandmother, the father expressed the feeling that after all, "my daughter is fighting my own battle." He referred here, once again, to his original futile struggle to separate mother from grandmother.

After about a year of therapy, a further shift was observed. The patient reached out more actively toward her father. She mussed his hair and kissed his hand. The therapist called attention to the exaggerated and overintense way in which the patient expressed her urge to be close to her father. He asked her if she was devouring father, rather than kissing him. At the same time, he referred to father's fear of these aggressive approaches, his fear of any open dealing with sex, and his consequent shrinking away from contact. The father voiced his fright by telling his daughter to go find a boy of her own. The therapist dealt with this by interpreting that a daughter might also touch her father, that this was a different touch and need not be the same as the sexual touch of a wife. Inevitably, this led to an extended discussion of the father's lifelong fear of women, his relations with his own overpossessive mother, and his submissiveness to his wife and mother-in-law.

Returning to the incident with the "Formosan" waiter, it is noteworthy that the patient talked freely of this incident with the therapist but told her parents nothing. In her family, she felt that sex was not allowed, absolutely taboo. In her earlier years, when she directed any question about sex to her parents, she was given the "brush-off." The parents seemed embarrassed and evaded the issue. Instead, she was told to return to her studies or practice her piano. For example, she once asked her father how it felt to go on a date. Her father bypassed the question with a wisecrack; he quipped that a date, like a piece of fruit, gets squashed. The patient ceased to ask about sex.

Another aspect of this same problem was reflected in the patient's feeling about being an only child. Whenever she inquired about sisters and brothers, her parents evaded the question. Being an only child meant to her not only a lonely life, without companionship, but a proof that her parents disapproved of sexual activity. In fact, they rarely indulged. Whenever the therapist alluded to the patient's urgent curiosity regarding sex, she showed agitation and abruptly tried to cut off the conversation. On one occasion, she came to the session armed with a hammer. She towered over the therapist with the hammer, threatening to strike him if he persisted in talking of this taboo subject. The therapist countered her denial of sex with the remark that he was male, sexy. He could not help it. God made him that way. Gradually she relaxed and became less belligerent. She diluted her tension in this area by intellectualizing the whole subject. For example, one time, she delivered an oration on the role of genes in the human species.

Later, she came with a dream. In her dream, there was a considerable variety of nude pictures on the office wall, and a wild orgy was in progress. As the patient entered, the male therapist threw empty beer cans at her. While talking of this dream, the patient produced a deck of cards decorated with nude women. She pleaded with the therapist not to mention these cards to her parents; they would be horrified. Still later, she shared with the therapist a story she was writing in which a student nurse fell in love with a young intern. She spoke of planning a holiday, a real celebration. She would one day bring a bottle of champagne and she and the therapist would "have a ball."

Consistently, however, her admission of sexual interest was coupled with the threat of aggression. In one such instance, the patient took the therapist's hand and dug her fingers into his palm. The therapist said to her that he wasn't sure whether her desire was to touch him or to scratch him. He pointed out that, while she wanted to come closer to him, she was frightened of impulses emanating from her and him. The patient admitted that while she was terrified, she also felt increasingly safer with him because he was in no way critical of her. The therapist indicated that they might talk freely of these urges but need not act upon them. Each time she enacted one of these scenes with the therapist, she referred back to her difficulties with her father. She expressed her conviction that her father was as frightened of sex as she was. She reacted vituperatively "against this man." The therapist countered the patient's denial of wanting to have anything to do with the father by calling her attention to their common interests and their resemblance to one another: she imitated his use of big words, his interest in biology, and his use of medical terms. Gradually, her denials weakened and she admitted her desire to reach out to her father.

In the family sessions, typical patterns of family interaction prevailed. They were reenacted over and over and thus were entirely predictable. As the family members took their places in the interviewing room, the daughter sat at one end, the father at the opposite end. Between them sat the mother and grandmother. Later, when the grandmother no longer attended, it was the mother who kept daughter and father apart. As the sequence of interaction clearly revealed, the mother and grandmother not only intruded their physical beings between daughter and father but also their thoughts and words. Whenever it seemed that daughter and father might dissolve the wall between them through more direct interchange of feeling, the mother and/or grandmother intervened to block this. Each time they reinforced the barrier by reminding the daughter of her fear of men and the father of his rejection of his daughter. For example, when the father showed interest in joining his daughter in Queendom by way of a "special passport," the mother promptly reinforced the taboo against men. She instantly suggested that it might upset the daughter, that Queendom would no longer be as she preferred it: "No men allowed."

The therapist took an active role in counteracting the alliance of the two older women in barring every semblance of personal communication between the daughter and father. He undertook to put to the test of reality the daughter's and father's shared sense of catastrophic danger in any closeness between them. In this situation, the daughter displayed a characteristic ambivalence. She alternated between two extremes: a sudden spurt of reaching out to her father, followed by an anxious retreat, often reinforced by a gesture of walking out of the room. Father, in turn, showed a reciprocal quality of ambivalent conflict. He, too, revealed a flicker of interest, followed by anxious withdrawal. In his fright, he was all too willing for the therapist to take the lead for him in making contact with the daughter.

The therapist intervened in a special way. At an opportune moment, he suggested a rearrangement of places, so that daughter and father sat next to one another. He invited them to look squarely into one another's faces and express their feelings. He particularly challenged the father to come out of hiding, to show himself as a man and express directly his warmth for his daughter. The daughter and father stole furtive glances at one another, testing the dangers of contact. As they did this, the mother and grandmother persistently interfered. Finally, provoked by these repeated invasions, the therapist told them to shut up so that the daughter and father might get acquainted. Despite the shyness and fright of both daughter and father, some progress was made. By degrees, the mother and father joined in a mutual concern for the daughter, and father supported mother in emphasizing her difference from grandmother and her good intentions with daughter.

With this shift came an opportunity for the therapist to support the daughter in reality-testing her fantasy equation of sex and violence. He encouraged her to ask her parents more directly whether sex was allowed in this family. To this blunt question, both mother and father reacted evasively, "I hope so." Later, the father was more firm and answered, "Definitely, yes." At this point, the daughter projected a deep emotional appeal to the father to admit that he was human, real flesh and blood. She challenged his remoteness, his tendency to act like an impersonal robot with her. She craved from him a show of warm, personal interest.

The role of the therapist was active throughout. Into the emotional climate of the family he introduced those ingredients that were lacking: warmth and affection, an open and natural acceptance of sex, a linking of sex and affection, and more appropriate images of the family roles of man, woman, and child. The first step was to induce the parents to admit the malignancy of their daughter's illness. The next step was to offset the grandmother's persecutory intrusions and to neutralize her regressive, monopolistic possession of the mother. This required a melting away of the mother's fright and awe of the grandmother as an omnipotent and omniscient, dangerous person and the substitution of the therapist for the grandmother as a better parent figure. To bring this about, the therapist had to compete with the grandmother as being an omniscient, omnipotent, but also a wise, benign, and well-intended, grandparent.

By these means, the mother was gradually liberated from the symbiotic, engulfing union with the grandmother. In a further step, the therapist moved in the direction of counteracting the mother's fear of the lethal powers of the aggressive "male monster" and supported her in a more adequate marital and parental joining with the father. The value of sexual gratification was supported. The father's male prerogatives were reaffirmed.

After a year and a half of continued treatment, the patient lost interest in her relations with Zena and Queendom. There was progressively less mention of hallucinatory communications with the inhabitants of this planet, and finally she ceased altogether to refer to these experiences. Gradually she seemed to resume her place in the real life space of her family on Earth. It became clear that she was progressively withdrawing her interest from her psychotic world and investing more and more of her feeling in her struggle to find a new place in her Earthian family.

At the same time, she began again to attend school. Her ability to concentrate on her studies was restored and there were no further failures in class. She worked better and, in fact, achieved an average of 85%. This was a striking change, remarked upon with amazement by her teachers. At the end of the year, she expects to graduate from high school.

At another level, she improved her relations with her peers. She began to talk with the young people in her class and developed a friendship with a girl friend. She was able to attend a school dance and have contact with boys as well as with girls. In the overall picture, the patient showed marked improvement at home, in school, and in the larger community.

The following verbatim interview, which occurred in the twelfth month of conjoint family sessions and after sixteen months of combined individual and family treatment, was a follow-up interview conducted by the supervising and research psychiatrist.

FILMED INTERVIEW

Verbatim Record	*Evaluative Comment*
DR. A.: Well, Helen, how are you getting along with the old man these days? HELEN: (much faltering of speech) I . . . uh . . . I . . . well, the less talk the better agreement. DR. A.: You mean that if you and Daddy were to talk freely, you'd get into trouble. HELEN: (hesitates to answer; starts and stops) DR. A.: More disagreement? More conflicts? More fighting? HELEN: Well, yeah. DR. A.: Is that right? HELEN: (to father) You know that's right.	Therapist continues to test danger of daughter's closeness with father.
FATHER: Well, we still don't see eye to eye—let's put it that way. We still don't see eye to eye. HELEN: Well, he came back from Chicago. Everything was goody-goody for a while, but after he got through telling us about Chicago, then it was back to the same old routine again. DR. A.: What's the routine? HELEN: The same old grind.	Father uses the existence of differences to fortify the emotional barrier.
DR. A.: The same old gripe, did you say? HELEN: Same old routine, same old grind. DR. A.: Grind, what is that? HELEN: Well, you know what a grind is. You get up in the morning, you go to work, you come home, you eat, you watch television, you go to sleep—you know what I mean. DR. A.: You mean he's like a machine?	The therapist's use of the term "gripe" is not a slip on his part. His reinforcement of daughter's complaint against father is purposeful.
HELEN: Aren't we all in this modern, chaotic . . . it's all documentary. DR. A.: You mean in this modern, chaotic world we live in, people are no longer human beings? We all turn into machines? HELEN: In a way we are. DR. A.: Well, you have machines up in Queendom, but down on earth, well, I'm no machine. Am I a machine? HELEN: No.	Patient gets lost in diffusing the dehumanized quality of her father to all of society.
DR. A.: You've got a little allergy to somebody in the family. HELEN: Yeah, something doesn't agree with me. I don't know. DR. A.: Are you talking English (word not clear)?	Therapist applies the emotional force of the term "allergy" to sharpen everyone's awareness of daughter's inability to tolerate the loss of human quality in her parents.
HELEN: I guess I'm coughing the whole thing up. DR. A.: Well, as soon as I got you off the high level of generalization, as soon as I take you out of the atmosphere away from Queendom, when I bring you	Helen's coughing tic is triggered by tension and signifies her unconscious effort to expel an object (male) that threatens dangerous invasion.

Verbatim Record	*Evaluative Comment*
right down to earth in this family, you start coughing up.	
HELEN: I can't think of anything to say.	
DR. A.: I'm asking you a simple question: are you three together now? Is it all three for one and one for all, or are you apart?	Therapist shifts from an exclusive emphasis on joining with father to joining with the whole family.
HELEN: Well, I would say we're still pretty much . . . well, I guess there's more unity than there was the last time you saw us, but we're still not quite (unclear from here on).	
DR. A.: You mean the pieces in the jigsaw puzzle don't quite fit together in the right way to make the design.	The family members don't fit in a way that meets the patient's needs.
HELEN: Yeah, but there's a little more harmonization than there was the last time I saw you.	
DR. A.: Well, that's something.	
HELEN: (interrupting) But it's not a hundred percent, not a hundred percent.	
DR. A.: I'm not a perfectionist. I'll settle for a little improvement. Will you accept something better?	
HELEN: Yes.	
DR. A.: So there's a little more unity, a little more harmony, since we put Grandma out to pasture.	Therapist indentifies the family member (grandmother) who epitomizes the obstruction to emotional integration of the next generation of the family.
HELEN: Yes.	
DR. A.: You said a little while ago that you wanted to marry her off. Want to get rid of her?	
HELEN: Well, no . . . well, I don't know. Well, I guess the little we see of her now is enough, because after all, she does need a family now that she's widowed and she's alone . . . you know, well, you know, she'll call Phyllis (mother) up. Well, she's making more friends now and that's more than I can say for myself.	Patient hints at emotions of ambivalence and guilt concerning exclusion of grandmother.
DR. A.: Well, you've gotten Grandma out of the family and into a separate apartment, but she's still in the family.	
HELEN: Yeah, she goes into the department stores where she lives, she's a little happier. She goes into the stores where she lives, it's a little livelier.	
DR. A.: It seems to me that you won't feel really safe until you get Grandma married off.	Patient wants grandmother far away.
HELEN: To someone who lives in California maybe.	
DR. A.: Well, you remember we talked about that. Grandma said you were getting her a boyfriend. You were acting the part of a "shadchen" (marriage maker). (Father laughs at this point.) You were going to fix her up with a guy. Still working on that little enterprise?	Father joins daughter in the half-jocular, hostile satisfaction of exiling grandmother.
MOTHER: Well, to tell you the truth, I still don't see where Grandma plays such a big part in this thing. I honestly mean that. We get off on Grandma, but this relationship (father and daughter) is still the same,	This is mother's first entry into conversation. She overtly defends grandmother (covertly defends self) against the

Verbatim Record	*Evaluative Comment*
whether she (grandmother) is in the house or out of the house. Their reaction to each other is the same, completely. When we were in Albany, it was the same and there was no Grandma there. When we were in many places where Grandma was far away, it was the same situation. I won't say that Grandma isn't a meddler, or anything like that.	accusation of meddling in the relationship of daughter and father. Mother admits her ambivalence to grandmother.
DR. A.: Well, yes. MOTHER: But not to the point . . . . DR. A.: I exaggerate. MOTHER: Yes. DR. A.: I exaggerate on purpose. You've got a little bit of your mother in you? MOTHER: (beginning of her remarks unclear) I know my habits are very different from my mother's. HELEN: They are.	Therapist invites release of mother's hostility. Therapist makes explicit and overt mother's intrusive role. Mother again defends self, this time by asserting her difference from grandmother.
MOTHER: There are things that I resent about my mother and I certainly hope that I don't have the same . . . . FATHER: The same qualities. MOTHER: . . . qualities. DR. A.: What are those qualities? MOTHER: Well, as Dr. F. knows, she's a very domineering person. HELEN: She's very intrepid, very intrepid. DR. A.: Intrepid? HELEN: Yeah, intrepid, audacious, a virago. It's one of my fancy words. DR. A.: Is that a Spanish word? HELEN: No. It's an English word. A virago means a woman who's more or less of a battle-ax, you know. DR. A.: Well, if you say battle-ax, I know what you're talking about. HELEN: Yeah. They call it a virago. DR. A.: (to mother) Well, you hope you're not aggressive, the same virago, the same old battle-ax as your mother (grandmother). MOTHER: I hope so, because those are the very things that I resent so much. DR. A.: Um-hmmm. MOTHER: . . . her domination.	
DR. A.: (beginning not clear) But you do meddle a little bit. Just a little bit. MOTHER: Oh . . . no, no. You mean the joke? DR. A.: Yes. You cut in between daughter and father (when daughter was retelling father's dirty joke). MOTHER: In what way? DR. A.: You didn't let her tell the story. MOTHER: (laughs) Well, it wasn't between the two of them. HELEN: It was a very humorous story.	Therapist challenges mother's denial of being intrusive, like grandmother.

Verbatim Record	*Evaluative Comment*
Mother: It was a joke among us. It wasn't between the two of them. Nothing gives me greater pleasure than when I can see there is some repartee there, really. That I can sincerely mean (between father and daughter).	Again mother makes a typical display of righteous denial.
Dr. A.: Well, I was quite impressed when you came in. There was more coziness and more contact, feeling contact, now between Helen and her father than a year ago. Still, you did cut in on it a little bit.	
Father: Let me ask this question, Dr. A. Do you think she (mother) is cutting in to meddle, or is she cutting in to shield one of us from the other or each from the other?	Father comes to mother's support; he needs her to protect him from danger of violence.
Dr. A.: I don't know. I can't find out.	
Father: For fear of our coming to blows. In other words, I don't think her motivation is one of wanting to meddle per se, as much as it is wanting to shield one from the other. You know, the buffer.	
Dr. A.: Why? Are you going to hurt Helen?	Therapist challenges father as to his submerged violence.
Father: She knows I won't hurt her physically.	
Mother: He'd never do that.	Mother leaps to protect father from therapist.
Helen: Physically, well, what do you mean—mentally, morally?	
Father: The point I'm trying to make now is that I think what you would feel is mother's meddling, and my mother-in-law's, I think it's based on different motivation. In my mother-in-law's case, it would probably be the desire to dominate the situation. I think in her (mother's) case, it's as I said, to act as a buffer.	
Dr. A.: She's protecting Helen from your violence?	
Father: Or vice versa. I don't know which it is.	
Mother: (breaking in) I really, I don't, don't think that you understood.	
Dr. A.: Well . . .	
Mother: That I mean it when I say it really meant nothing to me when she told the joke in front of him. Will you believe that? I hope you do, because you've mentioned it several times, because I felt, you know, it was a little off-color. (Some over-talking here between Helen and her mother, and it isn't clear.) Well, I didn't know, all these people . . . there's a time and place.	Mother still defending self against therapist.
Dr. A.: These people have heard dirtier stories.	
Mother: I know, but they don't come here to listen to that particular story. It's putting a little too much stress on it. But I know what it is you're trying to get at.	
Dr. A.: Phyllis (mother), let me make a confession. I misunderstand all the time. (General laughter.)	
Mother: Don't give me that! Don't be sarcastic now!	

Verbatim Record	*Evaluative Comment*
DR. A.: Feel free to correct me.	
MOTHER: You're being sarcastic!	
DR. A.: I don't know too much about your actual feeling . . .	
MOTHER: (breaking in) You know a great deal! I'm pretty sure of that!	
DR. A.: I don't know about how you act with Helen and Daddy.	
MOTHER: You're just wondering if someone doesn't come in between these two that causes them to act that way. It's as simple as all that.	
DR. A.: It was simple. He was the male monster and Helen had a terrible fear of men and boys. Men were all monsters.	
HELEN: You mean they were all another species.	
DR. A.: That's right.	
MOTHER: I know that Grandma wasn't in Albany for eight years. She came to visit us perhaps twice in all that time, but she couldn't have played too much of a part in it.	
DR. A.: Well, I don't know about that. How did you feel when you and Grandma were separated? You and your mother, how did you feel about that?	
MOTHER: Very happy. (She laughs.)	Mother turns about. With a release of sarcastic laughter, she admits her own need to be free of grandmother's domination.
DR. A.: When you were here and Grandma lived someplace else?	
MOTHER: (hesitatingly) Well, I was . . . of course, and when I . . . well, let's put it this way, I didn't miss her too much. I have my own interests. Believe me, I have enough interests. And I'm kept quite busy. If you think I'm hanging onto her . . .?	
DR. A.: When you said, "Let's put it this way," there's more than meets the eye in that phrase.	Mother reveals her ambivalent dependence.
MOTHER: (breaking in) Do you think I'm holding onto her apron strings?	
DR. A.: I don't know. I don't know enough about you and your mother. How do you feel about it? You don't miss her at all? She calls you up.	
MOTHER: Yes, she does, now that we're living close by, she does call me up. She wants to be noticed. She wants attention.	
DR. A.: She doesn't want to be forgotten.	
MOTHER: She wants attention. She doesn't want to be forgotten. She hasn't any interest, very few interests, she hasn't many friends in her new apartment, so she'll call me up whenever she gets an opportunity, whenever she feels she wants to talk to somebody.	Mother again shifts to her indentification with grandmother.
DR. A.: Did she feel that she was sort of pushed out of the family?	

Verbatim Record	*Evaluative Comment*
MOTHER: No, I think she wanted to, she wanted to go out.	
DR. A.: Well, she wanted to shove Helen out, off to boarding school, didn't she? (Mother laughs.) Isn't that true, she (grandmother) wanted to shove her (Helen) out?	
HELEN: I'm glad that I don't have a mother like that. She could dominate a person's life actually. Now she's going to pay for me to go to art school. I don't know.	
MOTHER: That's why she thinks she wants to get rid of her.	
HELEN: I don't know what's taking place in that crooked mind of hers.	Patient is suspicious of grandmother's motivation.
DR. A.: Your feeling about Grandma is that she brainwashed you.	Therapist picks up cue, underscores patient's fear of grandmother's manipulation.
HELEN: I don't know. She just goes off on little binges here and there.	
MOTHER: Well, it isn't that. As far as the art class is concerned, she just feels it would be an interest and she (Helen) is good in drawing.	
DR. A.: But, Mother. . . .	
MOTHER: (cutting in) She (grandmother) doesn't have too much to say.	
HELEN: But, mother, she's had her chance at motherhood. It's your opportunity now. She's been a mother already. I mean, doesn't she feel that she can loosen her apron strings a little bit, at least enough to breathe with?	Patient makes pathetic appeal for the right to breathe.
DR. A.: Did you catch Helen's message?	
MOTHER: Well, no, she still holds on tightly to her children. I know these things. Helen wants me to be completely free. Grandma should get completely lost. Why? Because when Grandma talks to me, Grandma's taking some of my attention away, and she (Helen) doesn't like that. She doesn't want anyone to take any of my attention away. Not only Grandma. (Helen is talking in the background, but it isn't clear.)	Mother again comes to grandmother's defense. Mother accuses daughter of jealousy of grandmother.
DR. A.: Helen sent you a message on the Zenascope. This is your chance, perhaps for the first time, to be a fulltime momma for Helen. A fulltime momma!	Again, patient appeals to mother—this is mother's chance to care for her own child.
MOTHER: Shall I tell my mother completely to get lost? So what should I do when she calls me up? Hang the receiver up? (Helen is constantly talking in the background, but it can't be understood.)	Mother evades daughter's appeal. She's too busy with self-justification.
HELEN: I told you when you passed an hour (on telephone with grandmother).	
MOTHER: Well, that's true.	
DR. A.: What kind of a momma is Phyllis to you now?	
HELEN: Well, she's getting a bit more patient. I like her. At times she exaggerates, she gets so high-strung at	

Verbatim Record	*Evaluative Comment*
times, and we have our little differences, but I think we get along fairly well now.	
DR. A.: Are you closer to Momma now since Grandma's been out of the home?	
HELEN: Yes, I am. (Turning to mother) You know I am.	
DR. A.: Do you feel, looking back on it now, that somehow Momma was divided between you and Grandma, sort of torn between you and Grandma? (Helen's response is not clear.) You coughed again. That always means you're getting tense.	
HELEN: Getting tense?	
DR. A.: Every time I say something you don't like, you cough. Tenser, I should say. You're always tense. What's the matter?	Patient's cough seems now to be related to anxiety concerning closeness to mother.
HELEN: (faltering) . . . Uh . . . nothing.	
DR. A.: You had a thought. What was your thought?	
HELEN: Well, I think we're a little closer now that Grandma is a bit of a distance away, a little distance away, even if she's only five blocks away, we're a little closer.	
DR. A.: I saw you reach out to Momma. Did you want to hold her arm? (Mother laughs nervously.) Do you want to pat her? Do you want to do something?	Therapist challenges daughter and mother both to admit need for closeness and affection.
HELEN: I meant in reply to her, you know.	
DR. A.: (to mother) She sent you a little love message.	
MOTHER: I know. We have our moments of affection.	
DR. A.: (to Helen) Momma just reached out her hand to you. You didn't take it.	Mother and daughter join hands, but are extremely tense and uneasy.
MOTHER: (laughingly) Let's make him happy.	Mother is sarcastic, flip; she shows affection only to appease therapist.
DR. A.: For my sake? (Mother's laughter continues.)	
MOTHER: Every word is analyzed.	
HELEN: There comes a time when I have to be a little more independent. You know . . . a little more "iconoclastic." I like you, and all that, but I don't want to happen what happened with you (mother) and your mother (grandmother) previously. We can be close together. I still have to have some other diversion, you know.	Now daughter shows a rising anxiety as to the danger of closeness with mother, the same danger as exists in the symbiotic imprisoning bond of mother and grandmother.
MOTHER: And you know, the greatest thing for me is for Helen to be independent and not have to depend on me. I'm completely different from my mother. My mother would have liked me to be dependent. I want Helen to stand on her own. That's why I see no meeting of the minds at all between the two of us.	This is mother's disguised rejection of daughter. She moved to the extreme of detachment from daughter as a rebound from excessive, choking dependence on grandmother.
DR. A.: Well, Helen, Mommy says that she feels different towards you.	
HELEN: Well, I feel (turning to mother) . . . . Do you have enough confidence in me to feel that I could make the right decision at the right time, apropos?	Daughter again makes soft appeal to mother for acceptance.

Verbatim Record	*Evaluative Comment*
MOTHER: Well, Dr. A. would like to know, have I ever kept you from making your own decisions, if you felt they were right, if they would help you? Am I one of the icons? HELEN: Are you one of the icons? Well . . . (falteringly) . . . I don't get your opinion very often. DR. A.: Will you drop that, Helen. (Helen was handling the microphone and the sound wasn't clear.)	Mother feels on the spot with the therapist. She is too busy defending self against the male threat to receive her daughter's appeal. Instead, she wants to know if she, as one of the icons, should be destroyed.
HELEN: Well, I would say, you do have a certain amount of trust in me? Confidence? (to mother.)	Daughter renews her appeal to mother.
MOTHER: You know I have. If she weren't locked up like she is, I would have a great deal . . . I mean, I see her potentialities. DR. A.: Yes.	Mother talks defensively to the therapist, away from patient. She does not listen to her child.
MOTHER: But there is that locked little room there, you know. And if she could free herself. But I do see potentialities. Very much so. It isn't something I say now because there are people listening. I say that constantly to you. Am I wrong? HELEN: No.	Mother shows more of her ambivalent feelings. Continues defensively to plead for therapist's approval. Shows strong doubt of self.
DR. A.: So, somehow you and mother are a little better joined.	Despite mother's ambivalence, therapist supports better joining of daughter and mother.
HELEN: Uh-huh. I'm happy she (mother) has her interests now. She's going to art school. She sketches now. That made me a little more interested in drawing. DR. A.: Is there a better feeling that you share, the two of you now? HELEN: Yeah. DR. A.: Well, it's easier now, isn't it, since Grandma doesn't live with you? MOTHER: It's easier. HELEN: She (grandmother) had to have her say in everything, you know, like the U.N. General Assembly vote. She had to be the Speaker of the House, so to speak.	Daughter gives mother half-hearted praise, but is choked with fear of the danger of closeness.
DR. A.: It's very difficult to compete with Grandma's mouth. HELEN: She always had to put her two cents in.	Therapist supports defense against grandmother and, inferentially, against mother, too.
DR. A.: Uh-huh. So . . . what's doing with the male monster now?	With support for a better union of daughter and mother, therapist turns back to fear of father.
HELEN: Well . . . I don't know, I guess the male monster has his own problems. I don't know, I . . . (silence). What should I say about the male monster . . . he gets up, goes to work, comes home, sits down, and watches television . . . so I really don't know what's going on with him.	To patient, father is still a stranger.
FATHER: I think that what she wants to say is that there's still no togetherness there. MOTHER: They still have nothing to say to each other.	Father distances himself from relationship with daughter—"no togetherness *there*."

Verbatim Record	*Evaluative Comment*
Helen: As a matter of fact, once I made a little retort. I asked him sarcastically how many caps, how many gold inlays he put in today. He got very angry.	Daughter is caustic in a sad way about her father's remoteness.
Dr. A.: Why aren't you telling that to the male monster? Why are you telling that to mother?	Therapist invites daughter to point her feeling directly to father.
Helen: I don't know.	
Father: I guess she wants corroboration. (Both parents laugh.)	
Helen: I really don't know what to ask him. Shall I ask him how many . . . I don't know what to ask him when he comes home . . . how many incisors he capped or how many inlays he put in (mother laughs very hard) . . . or how many bridges he worked on . . . I don't know what to say.	In a forlorn way, patient gropes with the question, how to reach her father.
Dr. A.: Well, Helen, I recall when you and I were talking about a certain type of man long ago, you felt maybe one day you could get a man for yourself, get married, have children.	Therapist stirs patient's hope of a man of her own.
Helen: Well, I don't know.	
Dr. A.: And I asked you about Daddy . . . whether he knew anything about sex, and you said he must, because he's always putting his finger into people's mouths, getting hold of people's teeth, therefore, he must know something about sex.	Therapist brings patient's fear of sex into the open.
Helen: I don't know.	
Dr. A.: What you are really saying . . . when he comes home from the office and you want to know what should you ask him . . . you're really saying what kind of man is he? Aren't you?	Therapist makes explicit patient's urge to know her father as a man.
Helen: Yes. I can't ask him how he gets along with his assistants, how he gets along with his nurses, how he gets along with teeth.	
Dr. A.: Well, take a look at him. What do you really want to know about Daddy?	
Helen: (hesitantly) Well . . . I want to know what kind of a person he really is, outside of his dentistry, outside of any business matters.	
Dr. A.: You want to know if he's really a person, really a human being.	
Helen: Yeah.	
Dr. A.: . . . not just a work machine.	
Helen: Not just a drilling machine or a cavity filler.	
Dr. A.: Not just a mechanic.	
Father: A mechanical monster. (Mother laughs. Father joins in.)	Parents' laughter is a release of tension.
Helen: Whether you're flesh and blood.	
Dr. A.: So ask him. Are you alive, father?	
Father: Well, I don't know.	
Helen: I have to remind you (father) that you're flesh	

Verbatim Record	*Evaluative Comment*
and blood, that you breathe, that you eat, that you do other things, but you're flesh and blood, that you're not a robot, and that neither are we robots.	
DR. A.: Your daughter has to remind you that you have a throb in your veins, that you're not just a mechanical man.	
HELEN: A robot.	
FATHER: Especially now that spring is here.	
HELEN: What has spring got to do with it? You're the same way whether it's September or December, or whether it's May. (Mother breaks in laughing.)	
DR. A.: Well, what he's saying is that he's capable of a heart flutter in springtime.	
FATHER: That's right.	
DR. A.: Are you in love this spring?	
FATHER: (exaggeratedly) Oh, sure. (He and mother laugh.)	
HELEN: Are you in love?	
FATHER: Of course; all the sap starts flowing. (Mother continues to laugh. Father joins in.)	
DR. A.: Well, that's one thing robots can't do, have a heart throb.	Sap doesn't flow from robots.
FATHER: (Something, unclear, about spring not affecting robots.)	
HELEN: Well, that's something robots can't do. They have no heart throb, they are just made of metal.	
DR. A.: Well, as you look at this male monster, do you think he's capable of a heart throb?	
HELEN: I think he's capable of . . . well, other things, too.	Patient makes vague allusion to father's capacity for sexual love and making babies.
DR. A.: Like what?	
HELEN: I know he's flesh and blood; at times he may seem to be inanimate, inert.	Patient backs off from area of danger, to father's usual deadness and, once again, a moment later, he's alive, "scintillating."
DR. A.: Inanimate and inert?	
HELEN: Yeah.	
DR. A.: Like those mechanical beings up in Queendom you described to me.	
HELEN: Oh, not even like that. Like that lamp over there or that telephone or even that table. But I know that deep down he's a nice person; he's ingenuous, he's scintillating, he has a heart of gold, he's an all-round good fellow.	
MOTHER: She's looking for his personal attention. More attention.	
DR. A.: (to father) She wants to see your spark.	Therapist challenges father to show his "spark."
MOTHER: When he tells a story, she doesn't want him to tell the story to me. She wants him to tell the story to her.	Mother shows rivalry.
DR. A.: Father, she accuses you of hiding your manly talents.	

Verbatim Record	*Evaluative Comment*
FATHER: Well, you see, basically, and, of course, Dr. F. encourages this very definitely, she feels apart from the family. She doesn't feel included in the family circle.	Father talks to therapist, away from daughter, exactly as mother did earlier.
DR. A.: Father, you're starting to make a speech again. (Helen broke in here, but what she said wasn't clear.)	Therapist counteracts father's tendency to intellectualize.
MOTHER: Dr. A. knows that, but he wants to know why you feel that way.	
FATHER: Well, I'm sure you are aware of that phase of it.	
DR. A.: Helen looked at you and said that if she were to judge by surface impressions, you would seem to be an utterly inanimate, unfeeling, mechanical man, a robot. You say no. Comes springtime, you fall in love all over again.	
HELEN: And then every winter, he goes back. You know.	
DR. A.: Helen looks at you and says you hide from her. Your manliness . . . (Helen breaks in. It isn't clear.) (to Helen) Do you want to talk? (to father) She wants to see you.	
HELEN: I know. I know. He's a man. I know all these things. It's when he comes home.	
DR. A.: But you don't really know.	Similarly, he counteracts the patient's intellectualizing.
HELEN: But when he comes home, he is so tired he wants just to read his paper and eat. You know . . . he's too tired to talk. You know . . . I mean, he's pooped. You know.	
DR. A.: He's just nursing his body.	
HELEN: Yeah.	
DR. A.: Where's his spirit?	
HELEN: I don't know . . . but . . . (Long pause.)	
DR. A.: She wants to see your spark, Father.	
HELEN: It's like a vegetable. (Turns to therapist) When do you . . . I see you alone? (Mother laughs.)	Patient is discouraged, also fearful. She seeks escape in asking again to see therapist alone.
DR. A.: Well, at the moment you make me uneasy. At the very moment we talk about the question of what Poppa's hiding from you, his manly spark in springtime, he declares for all the world he is a man, he can be romantic, he can get excited about a girl, in the springtime especially, is that right?	
FATHER: Yes.	
DR. A.: At that moment, you (Helen) want to break it up. You want to talk to me privately. Do you want to send him (father) walking?	
HELEN: That was rather rude of me.	
DR. A.: I'll talk with you alone, but let's explore this a little bit, talk a bit further, can we?	Therapist neutralizes patient's fear and resistance.
HELEN: Well, I don't know. I think you're getting down a little too deep. Once you pass the clothesline . . . well . . . I don't know . . . I think you're get-	Patient refers directly to her fear of exposure, of self and of father.

Verbatim Record	*Evaluative Comment*
ting a little too deep . . . you know, like an oil well that's going down.	
DR. A.: You mean you're getting scared. You mean it sounds almost like I'm about to undress him before you?	
HELEN: Well, I don't know. (Pause.) Well, perhaps it happens elsewhere, but it never happens in this group.	
DR. A.: You mean there's no sex in this group?	Therapist continues to challenge resistance.
HELEN: I mean, let's be a little more conservative. (General laughter.)	
FATHER: May I impose upon you?	
DR. A.: Sure, what do you mean "impose" upon me? (Father requests a cigarette from doctor. Dr. A. also offers one to Helen.) Does Helen smoke?	
HELEN: I don't smoke. I don't drink, don't have sex. I'm just. . . .	
DR. A.: You don't smoke, don't drink, you don't have sex. Well, you can do without drinking and smoking, but I don't know about the other.	
HELEN: Well, I'm naughty in other ways. I tell lies.	
DR. A.: Is it naughty to have sex?	Therapist continues effort to bring sexual problem into the open.
HELEN: (Grunts and falters for an answer) I don't know.	
DR. A.: Well, you see, we're back at the point where we were earlier. It's a very important problem, because in this imaginary world you've created for yourself up in Queendom, no sex allowed, no males allowed	
HELEN: Everyone is self-sufficient.	
DR. A.: They're all mechanical beings up there, created in a factory? They reproduce only by binary fission?	
HELEN: (to father) By the way, how is Chicago this time of year?	Patient is mildly evasive, while making a joke of it.
FATHER: Beautiful.	
HELEN: Anything to change the subject. (Mother laughs.)	
FATHER: We're getting a little deep. We're probing and beginning to reach the nerve. This is the only way we'll reach. . . .	
DR. A.: I think we have to reach a decision as to whether sex is allowed in this family down on earth or not? Yes or no?	Therapist wants a commitment: Is sex allowed, yes or no?
HELEN: Well, I don't understand. I thought . . . what do you mean by sex? I just can't understand . . . I thought we were all meant to be together no matter what sex we are.	Patient evades.
DR. A.: Oh, I can't agree with you that it doesn't matter what sex one is. It matters to me very much that I wear pants, it matters to mother that I wear pants. (Father and mother laugh. Mother makes a comment that is inaudible over the laughter.) It matters very	

Verbatim Record	*Evaluative Comment*
much. You and Helen agree. No undressing. MOTHER: Well, it all depends. If I were in art class, I would be very happy. HELEN: Or nature . . . a nature club.	
DR. A.: Let's pretend that this is a nature club for a moment. Why don't you ask your parents if they allow sex in this family? HELEN: (to parents) Well, do you?	Therapist induces patient to face parents directly with the sex question.
MOTHER: Well, *I hope* we're normal in that way. DR. A.: Well, yes or no? (Mother and Helen both start to talk. Helen apologizes for interrupting.)	"I hope we're normal"—a typical ambiguity.
HELEN: I know your brother and sister-in-law sure enjoy sex. MOTHER: Helen's afraid we don't because there's only one child in our family. HELEN: They have five, you know. DR. A.: They keep pretty busy. (Mother laughs.)	Patient puts parents on the hot seat. Others enjoy sex, why don't they?
MOTHER: You see, she's always resented so much the fact that she's an only child. HELEN: Oh, well. DR. A.: Helen asked you a direct question. Is sex allowed or isn't it allowed in this family? Yes or no? FATHER: Yes, of course.	Mother intellectualizes.
HELEN: That's like saying is eating allowed in this family, is digestion allowed in this family or isn't it. Or is breathing allowed in this family. DR. A.: That's right. Do you want to know from your Pop? You can ask him. HELEN: (to father) Is sex allowed? FATHER: Definitely.	Patient affirms that sex is natural, like eating and breathing.
HELEN: Definitely? FATHER: Of course. HELEN: You mean no red tape? FATHER: Your mother and I are normal married people, *I hope*. DR. A.: Do you mean you have sex together? HELEN: Oh dear, I didn't think it would be anything like this. MOTHER: I just wonder about this, because it's never been taboo in our family, that we wouldn't tell an off-color joke. I mean, the way I answered at first wasn't because I was afraid for them. I know there are families like that, where it's completely taboo, where they never mention it, where they never tell a dirty joke.	Helen, turned to parents' unsureness and vacillation, disbelieves father's assurances. She is right; he is simply complying with therapist's wish that he be definite about sex. Almost immediately, the unsureness returns, in the standard, stereotyped form. Mother is again defensive, self-justifying in an obsessional, literal way.
HELEN: Your mother (grandmother) was pretty conservative, wasn't she. MOTHER: Yes, but she loved them (dirty jokes). DR. A.: Grandma likes jokes? MOTHER: Of course she does. And she likes all kinds of stories.	

Verbatim Record | *Evaluative Comment*

HELEN: You mean "Little Miss Conservative"?

DR. A.: Is that what you call Grandma?

HELEN: Conservative Rose.

DR. A.: You mean as far as sex is concerned, you think she was a reactionary? You mean she was agin it? (Helen hesitates to answer.) She was pretty bossy. Did she permit sex between your mother and father?

HELEN: Well, she says things . . . that . . . well, I wouldn't have the audacity to say. She comes out with remarks here and there that I wouldn't have the audacity to say.

DR. A.: Well, give me an example.

HELEN: Well, do you remember the time where she said when you and father were first married?

MOTHER: Oh, yes, I know what you're trying to say. Go ahead.

HELEN: Father was busy with his practice and you were busy helping him? And she was the instigator in the case, that, I mean . . . that . . . well . . . .

MOTHER: I know what you're trying to say.

DR. A.: Don't say it for her.

MOTHER: All right, I know what she wants to say. Go ahead.

DR. A.: Don't put words into her mouth.

A vague allusion that grandmother claimed credit for urging parents to have a child. Mother interrupts repeatedly; due to her anxiety, she shuts off daughter's flow. She has the urge to think and talk for her.

HELEN: . . . that you didn't care for a family . . . I mean . . . that you didn't care to have children . . . and she was the one . . . she was the inspirer, the instigator . . . I don't know.

MOTHER: She made a senseless statement.

HELEN: Well, that was a senseless statement. I'm surprised that she even had the audacity to say it.

MOTHER: I gave . . . .

HELEN: You gave her hell for it.

Mother again defensive. Do mother and daughter have an unconsicous confusion as to whose daughter Helen is (mother's or grandmother's)?

MOTHER: You know, she is so anxious to get Helen to care for her, that she makes these completely irrational statements. They're as far off . . . (mother breaks off).

DR. A.: So, there is some actual basis in fact.

HELEN: She said that you and father didn't want children, for the time being.

MOTHER: She (grandmother) said it was because of her we had Helen, because of her . . . her influence.

HELEN: I don't know . . . her something or other.

MOTHER: . . . influence. She said that to Helen once and I gave her holy hell. You're a witness. What did I say to Grandma?

HELEN: I don't know. You gave her a piece of your mind.

MOTHER: It was really so stupid! My husband and I never consulted my mother whether we should have a child or not, and my husband and I both wanted Helen

Mother shows usual righteousness.

Verbatim Record	*Evaluative Comment*
very much. I don't know where she came in the picture at all.	
DR. A.: Well, today, this morning, Helen, do you think you could get a straight answer about sex from your two parents?	Therapist returns to the question: Is sex allowed in this family?
HELEN: Could I get a straight answer from them on sex?	
DR. A.: Yes.	
HELEN: You mean if I asked them to explain the facts of life, would they do so without a blush of embarrassment? Would they tell it to me freely? Would they. . . .	
DR. A.: Would they give it to you straight?	
HELEN: Would they uncover any mysticism I might have had or would they . . . or would they keep it all a hush-hush, top military secret?	
MOTHER: It's not a question of misinformation. Helen knows more about it. She knows everything.	Again, mother shows her obsessional literalness. She has a "school-marm" attitude to sex.
HELEN: I read this in books, you know.	
FATHER: I'd like to explore this a little further (to Dr.).	
DR. A.: I know it isn't just a question of sheer facts, Momma. (Mother laughs.)	
MOTHER: Interfering again?	
DR. A.: Yes.	
FATHER: I'd like to explore this with you. Please continue (to therapist).	Father urges therapist on. He depends on therapist to take initiative for him.
DR. A.: I think it's very important that Helen has the feeling that she can talk with you honestly and undefensively, in a simple, direct way, about sex. That she can ask you questions. That your attitude would be that you would want to answer. It isn't just a question of the information. It's a question of the quality of the relationship, the feeling that counts, whether you make it a deep, dark, mysterious and dirty secret, or whether you discuss it openly.	
MOTHER: Well, we've discussed it hundreds of times . . . where babies come from, and so forth. It's not a taboo question. How many times have we talked about it?	
HELEN: I know. I know there are many people who are very conservative, prudish-like.	
DR. A.: Are you calling Momma a prude?	
HELEN: (to mother) Do you approve of S-E-X?	
MOTHER: (laughingly) Oh, very much so.	
HELEN: I mean . . . if you could change nature . . . you know . . . would you do so? Would you make it possible to reproduce like an amoeba, you know, without sex . . . an amoeba, you know, splits in two.	
DR. A.: Are you for it or agin it?	
MOTHER: I just hope I've never shown her that I've been agin it in any way.	Again a righteous protest.

Verbatim Record	*Evaluative Comment*

DR. A.: If you want to get a straight answer, ask them a straight question.

HELEN: Well, why about sex? I could . . . .

DR. A.: Well, do you want to know the way in which they feel about you as their daughter? Will they give you a straight answer, or will it be hush-hush? Or will Momma get embarrassed and act like a prude? Or will Daddy act shy, like he's afraid of losing his pants or something?

HELEN: I don't know about him. I certainly would! (Mother laughs.)

DR. A.: So, you'd be shy?

FATHER: So, you're the one that's conservative?

HELEN: Maybe I'm the one that's conservative . . . I don't know. (General laughter.)

DR. A.: Daddy's right, you're the prude.

HELEN: I don't know. I get the impression that he can talk about the stocks and bonds, he can talk about retirement, old age pensions . . . but, but, sex? . . . you know . . . I mean . . . men and women? . . . you know what I mean.

DR. A.: Well, ask him a question!

FATHER: When you ask me any questions, do I ever dodge them?

HELEN: Do you ever dodge them?

FATHER: Well, did I ever give you any misinformation?

DR. A.: You did.

FATHER: Did I?

DR. A.: I'll remind you, Helen. You told me a little story once, you came to Daddy, you asked him what is it like to have a date.

HELEN: Did I ever ask that question?

DR. A.: Yes. You told me that Daddy made a joke of it. He said a date is like fruit, you squash the date.

HELEN: He beat around the bush maybe? And ignored it maybe?

DR. A.: Yes. Would you like to ask him the same question again?

HELEN: I, well . . . I don't know, because . . . it's . . . it doesn't . . . oh, gee!

DR. A.: Well, would you go into the library, please (to the parents)?

MOTHER: I was just going to mention that he (father) gets embarrassed if she (daughter) touches him and I think that gives her a feeling of inadequacy and doubt as to how to act to other boys, because every time she touches him, in any way, he draws away, you know.

DR. A.: Do you, Father? Do you shrink everytime Helen touches you?

MOTHER: I think that's very important.

Verbatim Record	*Evaluative Comment*
HELEN: You know, he moves to another couch.	
MOTHER: Well, she probably thinks if he's going to be like that, what is it going to be like with another boy?	
DR. A.: How does he act when you (mother) touch him?	
MOTHER: Well, not like that at all. He feels at ease with me, but he feels that she should be at ease with boy friends, not with her own father.	
DR. A.: Well, when you touch father, he doesn't fade away.	
MOTHER: No, because he feels that's the proper relationship.	
DR. A.: That's proper, but when your daughter touches you, that's improper. Is that the way you feel, Father? Well, it's a different touch when Helen touches you.	

DISCUSSION

We have described an acute psychotic reaction in a 16-year-old girl, studied and treated within the matrix of her family group for a period of eighteen months. In this case, some of the primary features of psychotic experience were shown to be reversible. During the period of therapy, the patient moved in and out of her psychotic world. The dominant shift was a movement away from the psychotic world in space, back to her real life space in her Earthian family. In this connection, a number of significant questions must be considered.

The psychotic reaction of this young patient germinated in a set of disturbed family relationships. By what criteria do we define the disturbance of this family? What components of this disturbance are specifically pathogenic for the patient and bear a direct relation to the precipitation of an overt psychosis? What other pathogenic components in this family are relatively nonspecific for psychosis but have other consequences for the emotional health of the family as family and for the members as individuals?

Let us try first to discern those components of the pathogenic make-up of this family group that may bear a specific relation to psychotic development in the daughter. The emotional make-up of this family unit revealed a family pair, mother and grandmother, regressively joined as one and asserting an exaggerated, righteous goodness and sacrifice. The quality of this union was such as to require the expulsion of a dangerous and bad element. To begin with, this bad element was epitomized as the "male monster," the father, who was seen as alien and dangerous, invading the bond of the two older women with sex and aggression. Sex itself was equated with violence. Sex and body contact in general were sharply reduced. The all-powerful governing grandmother established a taboo on a true sexual union of father and mother. Sex was symbolized as a dirty and destructive contaminating force and dissociated from warmth and affection. To save his own life, father joined with the older women against the only child. He did not provide for this child the needed antidote to the destructive invasive force of the two older women.

The daughter came to symbolize the alien and dangerous element in this family. She became the "bad seed" and was expelled. She had only two choices: retreat into a psychotic world or commit suicide. In either instance the end-result would be self-destruction; she would comply with the overwhelming expulsive force in the family and wipe herself out.

In the interactional processes observed in the family interview, it was noteworthy that when mother and grandmother came to life, i.e., asserted their aggressive dominance of the situation, the patient tended to die off emotionally, to withdraw. When, by contrast, the therapist supported the patient against the invasive force of the older women, the patient came to life. In turn, whenever Helen expressed herself with animation, the older women seemed to die off.

In this setting, the father seemed paralyzed and lost. Passively, he followed the therapist's lead in an ingratiating, submissive way, or made a feeble, short-lived attempt to join with his daughter which he could not sustain except with the active support of the therapist. In effect, then, when one part of the family raised its voice aggressively, the other part lay down and died, and vice versa. In this connection, it is interesting to speculate as to a possible essential difference in the quality of emotional interaction in the family that breeds a psychotic member and, by contrast, the family that mainly breeds neurotic members: the neurotic family implicitly lays down the taboo, *the child must not be different;* whereas in the family that breeds a psychotic, the taboo is: *The child must not be*. This family has a covert fear of new life, a prejudice against birth, growth, movement, any newness in life. This child lost the right to breathe; she was choked off.

Of great interest in this case is the possible diagnostic significance of the human relations scheme which the patient designed for her psychotic universe in Queendom. The social pattern which the patient created for her psychotic community in outer space seems to cast a long shadow on the pathogenic distortions of her real family on Earth. It is fascinating to speculate on the meaning of the contrast between the way of life in Queendom and the way of life in her Earthian family. What may this contrast signify for the illness process itself? What may we usefully infer from the value clash which is dramatized in the contrast of the two worlds? What is the same and what is different in the two universes? In Queendom, the patient designed a way of life which merged elements of her Earthian family with other elements of change which she seemed to require as a defense against the disintegrative anxiety of her illness. In her psychotic world, she remade life in a special way, altering the whole value system of the community in Queendom. To recapitulate briefly, she removed whatever was dangerous and ugly in her Earthian family life and introduced magical forms of self-protection. Queendom represented an effort at magic repair, a compensatory design. It erased the Earthian threats, but, beyond that, did not point the way toward growth and health. It was, however, more bearable than the pattern of her Earthian family. Such considerations as these may be relevant to the correlation between the interactional distortions of the family group and the development of psychosis in an only child.

Another question emerges: What components of pathogenic disorder exist in this family group that are relatively nonspecific for psychotic development in an offspring and yet have extensive consequences for the remaining nonpsychotic personalities in the family? In this parental partnership, there is a conscious joining in an allegiance to the goals of security, harmony, loyalty, and intellectual pursuits. There is, however, a profound contradiction between the conscious value striving of this parental pair and their actual way of life. The conscious pretext of peace and harmony is thin. It is virtually a fiction. In actuality, the parental couple slides into a pattern that is routinized, mechanized, static, half dead. Their relationship is extraordinarily lacking in vitality and growth. In the joined obsessional effort to control the dangers of uncurbed aggression, sex and spontaneity of expression are reduced to a minimum. It is apparent that a basic shared anxiety concerning destruction pervades the whole family and rigidly constricts its range of development. The goals of sexual fulfillment and forward growth of the family, in terms of a child, are almost totally sacrificed to the interest of sheer survival. In this setting, all members suffer in their emotional health. Grandmother becomes fixed in the role of the martyred persecutor. Mother becomes anchored in an obsessionally vapid existence. Father, severely castrated, moves off into a detached. mechanized, static preoccupation with intellectual matters. The child is given no right to eat, breathe, or grow.

In a family of this type, there is a progressive patterning of pathogenic roles, the grandmother in the role of persecutor, the mother in the role of the chronically immature child-wife projecting toward her own child only a ritual concern, the father in the potential role of protector and rescuer of the child but too impotent and frightened to be effective. Therefore, in this family group, there is no effective integration of any member into a role as healer of family conflict and no effective integration of anyone in a creative or growing role. There is only progressive reinforcement of a sick pattern of prejudice, scapegoating, victimization of daughter and father, and a mounting force toward regression.

With these pathogenic trends in mind, the therapy moved toward the following objectives:

1) To break the regressive symbiotic alliance of mother and grandmother.
2) To counteract grandmother's role as omnipotent destroyer, to puncture her hypocritical pretense of always being "right" and of loving the granddaughter better than the parents did.
3) To wean mother from grandmother, eliminating the need for complicity with her, and to encourage mother to accept the "male monster," and, for the first time, to join him in marriage; to counteract the image of sex as violence.
4) To join with and fortify father in undertaking a role as "family healer" in order to provide the needed antidote to the destructive invasion of mother and grandmother.
5) To save daughter and father from their roles as scapegoats.
6) To induce mother and father to accept their daughter.
7) To overcome the fear of touch contact between mother and father.
8) To permit daughter to touch father in a different way, thus neutralizing the fear of incest and violence.
9) To induce the parents to admit the value of growth—open, free, emotional growth; to neutralize their perception of the child as the "bad seed"; to support the daughter in finding a healthy role as child in this family; to protect her right to be born, to grow, to assimilate a natural, rather than an omnipotently destructive, image of sexual union and childbirth.

REFERENCES

ACKERMAN, N. W. (1960). Family-focused therapy of schizophrenia. In S. C. Scher and H. R. Davis (Eds.) *The Out-patient Treatment of Schizophrenia*. New York: Grune & Stratton, pp. 156-173.

ACKERMAN, N. W. (1961). Schizophrenic patient and his family group. In M. Greenblatt, D. J. Levenson, and G. L. Klerman (Eds.) *Mental Patients in Transition*. Springfield, Ill.: Charles C. Thomas, pp. 273-282.

PART IX

Research

Two papers on research are reprinted here. Ackerman said of himself, "I am a psychiatric clinician first, an investigator and theorist after that," thus making clear that he was not a researcher and that he approached research issues as a clinician. His goal was to stimulate researchers and acquaint them with the perspective that came from clinical struggle with families. Thus his emphasis throughout is on the proper conceptualization of the phenomena being investigated, and with the purposes and goals of research, rather than with methodological issues, on which admittedly he was not an expert.

In both papers he is preoccupied with the necessity of developing adequate conceptualization of behavior in both psychological and social terms. Thus, in 1957, he writes, "Success or failure of adaptation rests on whether or not the environment lends support of a particular self-image and corresponding defenses against anxiety," and later, in 1961, "Can we safely presume to have a valid science of psychopathology in advance of developing a parallel science of social psychology and social psychopathology?"

The second paper seems to have been mistitled, giving an apparent emphasis to prevention which does not actually appear in the text itself, probably in an attempt to conform to the theme of the book in which it appeared. Both of these papers can be read for their clinical insight as well as for the research directions indicated.

CHAPTER 45

An Orientation to Psychiatric Research on the Family

The appropriate sphere of interest for psychiatric study of the family is the role of the family in mental illness and mental health. Is psychiatric research on the family needed? Is it timely? Is it feasible? My answer is an emphatic "yes" to these questions. The need to formulate the dynamics of the family group as a psychological entity in and of itself, to search out means for classifying family types according to their mode of adaptation and mental health, and to find criteria for correlating the mental health of the family to the mental health of its individual members represents an urgent priority. It becomes increasingly clear that the traditional psychiatric focus on the separateness and autonomy of the individual has brought us to something of an impasse with respect to improving our systems of diagnosis, therapy, prognosis, and prevention of mental illness. Perhaps for the first time systematic psychiatric research on the family becomes a feasible undertaking. Up to now, the necessary framework for interrelating the roots of individual and group behavior has simply been lacking. Today it begins to be a reasonable venture, thanks to recent accretions of useful information in the field of interpersonal relations, the interconnections of personality and role behavior, communications process, group dynamics, and, last but not least, to increasing facility in the implementation of the interdisciplinary method of study. In other words, only now do we begin to have the rudiments of a useful science of social psychology and social psychopathology. For his part, the psychiatrist can investigate the interpersonal disturbances of family relationships and reach out aspiringly toward a psychopathology of everyday family life. This would provide a sound foundation for a specific psychotherapy of the family. Though this is a considerable departure from the conventional core of psychiatric thought, it is one that may yet reap a rich reward.

The family may be likened to a semi-permeable membrane, a porous covering sac, which

Reprinted with permission from *Journal of Marriage and the Family*, February 1957, Vol. 19, No. 1, 68-74. Copyright 1957 by the National Council on Family Relations.

allows a selective interchange between the enclosed members and the outside world. "Reality" seeps through the pores of the sac selectively to affect the enclosed members in a way predetermined by the quality of the sac. The influence exerted by the family members on the outside world is also affected by the quality of the sac. Adverse conditions within the sac or in the surrounding environment may destroy it, in which case the members lose their protective envelope. Menacing external conditions may cause the pores of the sac to shrink, thereby contracting the sac and holding the members more tightly within it. A family sac thus contracted and isolated from the environment cannot carry out its functions normally nor long survive. Favorable external conditions expand the sac and promote a more fluid interaction within the outer environment. Excess tension within the sac arising from a distorted balance among the enclosed members may warp the sac and, unless balance is restored, the accumulated internal pressure will eventually burst it.

The traditional focus of psychiatric study has been the deviant behavior of the individual patient, not the family. The family was conceived as contributing to mental illness at three levels: (1) heredity, (2) the trauma of childhood conditioning in family experience, which produces the "pre-morbid personality," an individual whose emotional development has been injured and who is therefore vulnerable to mental illness, and (3) the trauma of adult family experience which acts as a precipitant of mental illness.

For our purposes here, it is best to leave the hereditary factor to the technical judgments of the psychiatrically oriented geneticist.

When we assume a normal biological substrate, the social molding of behavior becomes of paramount importance. At this point there comes into the picture the problem of the relative weighting of past and present social determinants of behavior. In our field, the central role of family in shaping the personality of the child is axiomatic. The concept of the role of family as a stabilizer of the mental health of the adult is less well understood.

By tradition, the psychiatrist has regarded mental illness as an internal disorder of personality. He concerned himself with the impact of environment on the morbid dispositions of personality. He took account of "the noxious stimuli of the family environment," but the phenomena of family were conceived in a peripheral, adventitious way. Individual personality was conceptualized as an entity, essentially separate and autonomous, but the family, while affecting mental states, was otherwise considered something external. It is understandable that psychiatry, having its roots embedded in medicine, tended historically to give preferential weight to the biological factor, to organic processes, to mind as the functional expression of the central nervous system.

With the work of Freud came the concept of the unfolding of personality from within. The main emphasis was placed on the biological core of personality, expressed in the emergence, stage by stage, of hereditarily patterned instinctual drives. Environment was given a role, to be sure; in accordance with the pleasure-pain principle, it curbed and molded the unfolding instincts. Nonetheless, the entity of mind was approached as having an essentially physical and endopsychic origin. Personality was analogized to a closed energy system, according to Freud's understanding of the thermodynamic laws. A closer scrutiny of these physical laws raises the critical question as to whether Freud has not actually misconstrued their meaning. If one takes into account the relatively minute dimensions of the individual behavior system, the influence of external forces is considerable, rather than negligible. Man is therefore to be regarded as an open rather than a closed energy system, as Freud's libido theory implied. The influence of Freud was paradoxical. He pointed to the importance of family environment and yet gave it a subordinate place in his theoretical framework. The needs of the individual and the forces of culture were regarded as irrevocably opposed. "Every individual is virtually an enemy of culture."—"Every culture must be built on coercion and instinctual renunciation." In Freud's view, culture and personality could never be on the same side.

In this whole conceptual trend, there is reflected a dichotomization of the biological and social determinants of behavior. The inner self is separated from the outer self and the environment. The prime concern is with endopsychic events, and these endopsychic mechanisms are dissociated from the corresponding interpersonal processes. The role of environment is played down or ignored. The main preoccupation is with partial mechanisms of personality, those specific psychopathological processes which cause symptoms, rather than with the total patterns of personality organization and the corresponding modes of social adaptation. But the mechanisms of symptom formation are not equivalent to the entity of mental illness. Symptoms are a part of illness, not its entirety. For a long time, this absorption with microscopic investigation of pathogenic foci within the personality postponed examination of the broader questions of mental illness and health. It is only now that we begin systematically to relate the finer details of internal symptom-producing processes to total personality and social behavior. In order to do this, a theory of role and of group behavior becomes indispensable. The need arises, then, to broaden the conception of mental illness and mental health so as to make the group environment an integral part of the behavior phenomenon rather than something external.

I have reviewed this background in order to demonstrate that the more traditional frames of reference for personality and for mental illness and health are no longer useful for certain kinds of research. They are too limiting and also incorrect. For family study, a new framework must be devised.

I should like now to document this thesis through concrete references to clinical experience. I shall allude to a series of observations which can in no way be fitted into the older conceptual frames. The known systems of diagnostic classification of psychiatric disorders in children proved to be seriously inadequate for clinical work with disturbed children. These diagnostic groupings were mainly descriptive, symptom-oriented, static, and left little room for the relevant dynamic considerations or the factors of causation. The criteria for these diagnostic groupings reflected too strongly the psychobiological principles underlying the diagnostic orientation to psychiatric disorders in adults. The specific processes of growth and development in children, and the crucial biosocial differences between the child's interaction with environment and the adult's were not adequately taken into account. Finally, the dynamic connotations of difference between normal and abnormal behavior in a child as constrasted with the adult were not clearly delineated. The prevailing criteria for psychiatric diagnosis of children were therefore virtually useless as a guide for the planning of child therapy and modifying parental attitudes. As a basis for research on the correlation of child and family behavior, they were utterly hopeless. The reason is now clear. The child's family environment is an integral part of the unit of behavior under examination. It cannot be treated as peripheral.

In child guidance, concern for the child's family environment was epitomized in the personality of the mother. The problem was approached as if, in effect, there were a one-to-one cause and effect relationship between the emotional disorder of the child and the specific deviation in the mother's personality. The mother personified the pathogenic features of the child's environment. In a sense she does, but insofar as this is so, her behavior is a projection of the total psychological content of the family group, not simply an expression of the woman's individual personality. Her child-rearing attitude represents the integration of her personality into the maternal role in a particular family. It is molded by the reciprocal behavior of the husband acting as father, and the psychosocial structure of the family as a whole.

In traditional child guidance practice, child and mother were studied and treated separately. Each was assigned to a separate therapist. Sometimes this procedure of separate treatment had the paradoxical effect of drawing mother and child apart rather than bringing them together. The suggestion that a form of psychotherapy be tried which deals with the child and mother together aroused anxiety and even consternation among some guidance personnel.

Increasing consciousness of these and related problems led inevitably to other pertinent observations concerning family interaction. If one member of a family group is treated and improves, another member may get worse. Sometimes if a child responds favorably to therapy, the mother's emotional state becomes aggravated. If the mother's anxieties are relieved in therapy, the father slides downhill. The reverse also happens. The improvement of one family member brings a remarkable change for the better in another member who lacked the benefit of therapy. The improvement occurs as if by a process of osmosis in family interaction. Often, it is the case that one person balks at therapy and we learn that he cannot perceive of himself as changing unless others in his family change at the same time. In other words, some individuals remain virtually imprisoned to a warped family role, unless the family member fulfilling the reciprocal role is simultaneously freed. The obstacle to effective therapy in some instances is a family configuration which permits some individual members to adapt only to a single family role. This explains why certain patients are clinically judged to be uncooperative or untreatable. It sheds light also on some components of the phenomenon of habitual "acting out." The impulsive living out of elements of irrational conflict is partly dependent on a corresponding pattern of "acting out" in the person occupying the paired family role. The appropriate stimulus from the other person is a necessary element. This is especially conspicuous in disordered marital relationships, where in effect the two partners share a single form of emotional illness.

Still other relevant observations may be mentioned. Contrary to usual expectations, certain neurotic parental pairs occasionally produce healthy children. Other parental pairs, consisting of seemingly healthy adult personalities, nevertheless produce emotionally disturbed children. Certain married couples achieve a workable mutual adaptation so long as they exclude offspring. With the arrival of a child, the previous good adjustment disintegrates. The reverse also occurs. Other couples experience intense conflict and are on the brink of divorce until they have children. With the enlargement of the family, the marital relationship shows striking improvement.

In the clinical study of family relationships, one can frequently discern a subtle shift in the location of the pathogenic focus of anxiety and conflict. At one point, the greatest weight of pathogenic disturbance will be contained within the personality of a particular member. It may then shift and become expressed predominantly as conflict in the zone between this person and another family member. Still later there may be a shift of the focus of tension, and a destructive conflict will emerge in another family pair. Individual members or family pairs may thus serve as carriers of pathological family disturbance. The link of family members acts as a conveyor belt for a variety of forms of emotional illness.

Observations such as these inevitably raise a serious question as to the validity of treating adult personality as separate and autonomous. Is this not something of an illusion? It is true that the personality of the adult is characterized by greater intactness and autonomy, but the difference between child and adult is one of degree. The operations of adult personality are also dependent on the social environment. The adult, though possessing more freedom of action, has limited control of his environment and has not the power to change it at will. Success or failure of adaptation rests on whether or not the environment lends support to a particular self-image, and corresponding defenses against anxiety. This principle is easily documented in those instances of critical transformation of adult personality which occur under special life conditions, for example, the military, concentration camp, the fascist state, confinement in prison, or long time deprivation of the companionship of women. I am impelled, therefore, for purposes of evaluation of adult adaptation, to use as a model the dynamics of the child's interaction with family environment. This leads in turn to a conception of mental illness as involving three factors: (1) the group; (2) individual integration into the group; (3) the personal history of the individual.

In 1941 we initiated an ongoing exploratory study of the mental health of family relationships in order to elucidate a series of interrelated problems; disturbances of mothering and fathering; the correlation of the behavior of child and family; the problems of integration of personality into family role; the disorders of marital and parental relationships; and the dynamics of the fit or lack of fit for the same person of the requirements of multiple roles, familial and extra-familial. We used as source material the comprehensive study of 50 families, in which two or more members were in psychotherapy. This is essentially a clinical study, empirically oriented, and useful mainly as a hypothesis-finding method. We felt it important to approach the phenomena of family life as an experiment in nature. By conceptualizing the totality of the family phenomenon, and preserving the relations of the parts to the whole, we might more clearly define the interrelations of individual and family group. An empirical investigation of this kind does not easily lend itself to statistical analysis, nor to the application of rigorous control groups. At most it is possible to set up rough approximations of contrast groups. We are convinced, nonetheless, that such empirical, exploratory studies have their own intrinsic value. The tentative hypotheses which emerge can later be subjected to the test of statistical method in more specialized kinds of research design. In an abbreviated way we speak of this work as a Study of Family Diagnosis.

The specific objectives of the Study of Family Diagnosis are the following:

1. The formulation of criteria for the differential classification of family types according to their psychosocial configuration and mental health functioning.
2. Within the definition of the family type, the formulation of criteria for evaluating emotional disturbances of family pairs and triads: mother and child; child and sibling; husband and wife; father, mother, and child, etc.
3. The formulation of criteria for evaluating the disturbances of emotional integration of individual members into family roles.
4. Delineation of the emotional mechanisms through which adaptation to one family role supports or clashes with the requirements of adaptation to another; also, the emotional mechanisms involved in the mutual reinforcement or clash of familial and extra-familial roles.
5. The formulation of criteria for the diagnosis of disturbances of individual personality which emphasize the dynamic interrelations of the mental health of individual and family. This encompasses the processes of union of individual identity and group identity; also, the processes by which the individual in maturing separates his image of self from his image of family.

As indicated, the source of data was the material of 50 families, in which two or more members were in psychotherapy. Of these, 36 families were studied at the Child Development Center in New York, a mental health clinic for the preschool child and his family. Six families, in which the primary patient was a child with learning retardation and emotional disorders, were studied at the Hunter College Educational Clinic; the remaining families were studied in the private practice of psychiatry. The families of the Child Development Center were urban, Jewish, lower middle class, second generation Americans. The families at Hunter College were of mixed ethnic background, working class or lower middle class. The families of private psychiatric practice were middle class.

Comprehensive data for family study consists of case history, psychiatric and psychological evaluation of family members, data from therapeutic interviews, nursery reports, and systematic observations of family interaction within the home.

The main categories of information sought may be itemized as follows:

1. Development of the central relationship of man and wife, past to present, the early interaction in the courtship phase, the marital phase, and finally, as a parental couple. Pertinent here are the value attitudes, emotional expectations, and actual achievement of the marital relationships; also, the specific patterns of integration, compatibility, conflict, the devices for restoring emotional balance, and the extent to which the marital relationship supports the emotional development of each partner.
2. The development of the family group since its inception, its internal organization in terms of unity, stability, satisfaction, potential for growth, and its external adaptation to the extended representations of family, friends, social organizations, and community-at-large.
3. The development of the individual in continual interaction with his family group at each stage of maturation.
4. The adaptation of individual personality patterns to the requirements of familial and extra-familial roles.
5. Specific child-rearing behavior and the child's reactions.

We have selected empirically certain criteria for the appraisal of the psychosocial functioning and mental health of the family group, family pairs, degrees of success and failure of integration of personality into family role, and the fit or lack of fit for the same person of the requirements of multiple roles. It becomes possible then to mark out the relatively healthy and unhealthy areas of family functioning, the balance between them, and the specific compensatory or restitutive trends in the family relationships. The mutuality or clash of the pathological dispositions of members of a family pair or triad can be delineated. And the dynamics of the individual can be defined as an integral part of family interaction. The data are organized according to a Guide for Family Study, and the relations of the mental health of individual and family, child or adult, are evaluated according to a special scheme.

The special problems of this method are considered in detail elsewhere. They are mainly the global nature of such investigation, and the difficulty of narrowing the field and limiting variables without distorting the phenomenon under investigation; there is the need to integrate all parts of the whole on whatever level they occur in the process of family and individual development. There is the special problem of selecting a minimum number of categories for analysis of the data that will be adequate for description and pertinent to mental health. The indices need to be of universal application to permit comparison of one family group with another and individuals of one group with those of another. There is the further problem of specification of bases for judgment in analysis of the data; that is, the evaluation of actual life performance against a psychiatric model of "ideal" family and individual mental health. Also, the question of the flexible modification of such evaluative judgments according to cultural milieu, value orientation, and expectations of the family. Also to be considered is the bias introduced by the cultural position of the observer and analyst of the data.

Finally, there is the problem of working out concrete, specific, usable definitions of terms, so that the method is communicable, and the results of family diagnosis can be applied to tasks of therapy, prevention, and also prediction of behavior.

Inevitably in psychiatric research on the family there is the problem of introducing system and exactness into a field where pertinent clinical observations are of the first importance, and yet by their very nature are subjective, evaluative, and inexact. This is the paradox which must be constantly borne in mind in the effort to investigate family phenomena. It often happens that in the search for measurable variables the real dynamic "meat" of the family is lost. The striving for exactness makes research procedure rigid in such a way as to take the very life out of the family picture. Though the precision of certain partial study procedures may be enhanced, in the end, the accuracy of evaluation of the total family picture is impaired. The ultimate overall objectives of family study must not be subordinated to the preoccupation with conventional standards of research. The appropriate methods must grow out of a better understanding of these very objectives. In family study, we must not lose sight of the woods for the trees. Nor can we afford the luxury of keeping very busy measuring the wrong things. The moment we get absorbed in rigid statistical study, we find ourselves counting the number of freckled mothers and fathers. This is an exaggeration, to be sure. Nonetheless, it points sharply to the importance of thorough investigation of each family as an individual case study. When we have obtained a clear and integrated picture of a family as a functioning unit, we can then compare it with others.

Beyond certain broad generalizations, we have found it exceedingly difficult to categorize or type the families we have studied. The network of complex emotional processes within the group, between group and community, and within each person belonging to the group create a uniqueness which we must learn to pin down. As already mentioned, part of the problem is the haziness of many descriptive terms and definitions, and the need both to broaden and spcify such terms so as to cover the variations from one family to the next. Another difficulty is the fact that families do not stay the same; they change. This raises the question for systematic inquiry as to when to study the family, at what point in time or over what span of time. Contact with the same family at different stages of its history gives us different data and new problems of interpretation. Part of the problem then is how to accommodate study procedure to the significant stages of evolution of family life. We need to learn something of the likely changes which take place in the various stages of family life, and in accordance with this, discriminate which are the strategic points in time for the study of various family processes.

This problem then becomes involved with another variable, the influence of the observer on the very phenomena which he is observing. In our form of investigation of the problems of family diagnosis, the observer is also therapist. He is therefore a participant observer. He intervenes, catalyzes, and modifies the very events he is recording. Furthermore, the path of his intervention is influenced by intuitive as well as more explicit knowledge of the family's problems. Because the clinician and therapist cannot pursue identical paths of intervention in any two families, his research cannot be experimental; it can only be exploratory. In one sense, this is far from being a detriment. Through this very kind of intervention, the dynamic processes of family life, healthy and unhealthy, come to life, and can be identified and carefully defined. What emerges as of central significance can be broadly and systematically studied. This is the path I have outlined, and the goal I pursue.

CHAPTER 46

Preventive Implications of Family Research

In 1954, Anna Freud (24) referred to the growing pessimism concerning the possibility of preventing childhood neuroses. She pinpointed a significant issue. In the early years of psychoanalysis, the expectation of applying dynamic insights into the mental life of the child to the tasks of child-rearing and education stirred a wave of optimism concerning the prospect of preventing childhood neuroses. With deeper study, however, it became plain that the sources of mental illness in childhood receded ever further into the past. In the historical unfolding of the causes of neurosis, there was a strong backward push in time from the father who denies the child sexual pleasure and threatens castration to the mother who denies the child oral pleasure and disciplines through the withholding of love. Need satisfaction, therefore, is never total; it is rationed. Thus, frustration, conflict, and anxiety are inevitable. With this recognition, the first wave of optimism about the possible prevention of childhood neuroses gave way to a mood of sheer pessimism.

It is the child's ego that mediates the struggle between pleasure and pain, and the ego takes its cue from the social interaction patterns of the family, said Anna Freud. But how is it, at the very point where the child's ego is joined to the family environment, that we feel so powerless? Why does the curtain suddenly drop, and the attitude toward prevention turn dark and bleak, as soon as we move from inside the child's mind to the life space between the minds of family members? Surely the recent pessimism concerning prevention is no more objective than the early optimism? There is no warrant for overestimating our capacity to cope with the distortions of the child's inner mind, while underestimating our power to deal with the pathogenic forces of his environment.

Prevention of mental disorders requires two things: (1) a specific body of knowledge concerning the forces that contribute to mental illness and the forces that promote positive mental health, (2) the organization of the community's values, incentives, and powers in a pattern that supports the application of this knowledge to an appropriate program of social action.

Were we able to build a program of prevention, what would it be? A maximum effort would

Reprinted with permission from *Prevention of Mental Disorders in Childhood,* G. Caplan (Ed.), 1961, 142-167.

entail a huge job in social engineering; it would produce nothing less than a social revolution, a fundamental transformation of the values and forms of family and community. A minimum program toward prevention would require family-life education, social therapy, and psychotherapy of parents and the family group. Whether the preventive effort is grand and sweeping or modest, it must move toward a remolding of the dynamic functions of family life in order to supply the needs of children for healthy development.

In relation to building the needed knowledge through research, I echo the sentiment expressed by F. Redl:* "Sometimes the search is taken out of research; what is important is not the convention of research, but rather invention and discovery." And with regard to the challenge of measurement, I quote Einstein on the relations of mathematics and reality: "Insofar as the laws of mathematics refer to reality, they are not certain; and insofar as they are certain, they do not refer to reality."

For some years I have pursued with special interest the interrelations of the mental health of the family group and the mental health of its individual members. The main effort is to explore those component family processes, both interactional and transactional, that may bear a specific relation to the production of psychosis, neurosis, and character disorder. This includes concern for the clinical, therapeutic, research, and value aspects of the problem, with particular emphasis on the correlations of child and family behavior. This work is variously reported in a series of papers and in a recent book (1-16, 18).

PERSPECTIVES ON PREVENTION

The immediate challenge is to define with the greatest possible specificity the forces of pathogenic contagion that cause mental illness in childhood on the one hand and those experiential factors that strengthen immunity and promote healthy development on the other. How can we search out and define those noxious components of family relations that a child sops up and incorporates into his evolving self in the early and vulnerable stages of his development? How can we identify the trigger mechanisms in the child's interaction with his personal environment that precipitate the acute phase of illness? What are the relevant influences that are handed down from the older to the new generation of family, and what are the relevant aspects of emotional interchange between the contemporary family and the surrounding peer groups? More specifically, what is the clash, interweaving, and meshing of child-rearing values within the frame of the total life of the family group, influenced by past experience, current problems of adaptation, and the view of the future? How can we pinpoint the experiential patterns in the inner life of the family and in the relations of family with wider society that are relevant to prevention?

From where we now exist in our culture, primary prevention of mental disorder is a most difficult idea to grasp. It is as though we are submerged in the depths; in order to see above where we are, we need a periscope. On the basis of past work in the field, we tend to make several assumptions. We believe that we know more about illness than about health; more about child development than family development; more about distorted development than healthy, expansive growth; more about what goes on inside the mind than about what goes on between minds. We know something about individual personality, something about culture. The family is the natural bridge between the larger forces of culture and the internal mechanisms of personality; and yet, concerning the dynamics of family life, we know little. Thus we assume that we know more about illness than health, but I wonder: Can we really? Or is this possibly a mirage, a self-perpetuating illusion? Can we safely presume to have a valid science of psychopathology in advance of developing a parallel science of social psychology and social psychopathology?

Fundamental to all else is our operational conception of the terms *mental health* and *mental illness*. In human functioning, we are confronted with a labile balance of tendencies toward health and tendencies toward illness. Actual performance in life is the outcome of an unceasing struggle to maintain the dominance of health.

Mental illness and mental health are not, however, opposites. Mental health is not merely the absence of mental illness, nor is illness the ab-

*Personal Communication, November, 1959.

sence of health. People achieve adaptive efficiency or fail to achieve it. Health and adaptive efficiency are interrelated. The failure to achieve effective adaptation leads to impaired productivity, to unhappiness, and to illness. Illness, therefore, is a significant though not the sole consequence of adaptive failure.

Often, people as we see them are neither purely healthy nor purely sick. Elements of both kinds of behavior coexist in many persons. Often there are people who are not sick in the clinical sense, and yet neither can they be said to be healthy; they function somewhere in the border area.

The prime difference between healthy and sick behavior is the plasticity and variability of adaptive behavior in health, the preservation of the potentials of growth, as compared with the rigid, constricted, automatized, stereotyped, and repetitive quality of behavior in sickness. In the sick state, the potentials of growth and new social learning are impaired or lost. The road to illness is a narrow one. The paths to health are many and broad.

Positive mental health is a process, not a static quality in the possession of anyone. It is not self-sustained. It can be maintained only by continuous striving, and the emotional support of others is needed to keep it. Mental health has to do not only with the achievement of inner emotional harmony and of selfhood but also with an optimal relatedness of person, family, and society. Fundamentally, the unit for judging conditions of health and illness must be the person within a defined environment, not the person in a social vacuum.

In the interest of prevention, it is self-evident that we must study healthy families. But how to find them—that is the question! They are strangely elusive. In many families at one time or another there are disturbances of varying kinds and intensity. At best, we can only identify families as being more or less healthy, and recognize that the degree of health varies at different stages of family development. We can try to define the healthy components of family behavior alongside the components of disturbance in a range of family types. We can attempt to specify the family forces that keep the emotional relations of the members in balance, or at least lessen the tendency to breakdown and illness.

DISTURBANCES IN CONTEMPORARY HUMAN RELATIONS PATTERNS

In our time we must give pointed attention to the sociocultural factor in states of illness and health. Contemporary society is experiencing a critical integrative disturbance that is echoed in parallel disturbances of individual and family. The cultural continuity of values in successive generations of family groups is disrupted. The turmoil and unsteadiness of social patterns invade the inner life of the family. The balance of power between individual and group is altered; and this influences the social-character development of the child.

The family of today stands in special jeopardy as a result of the extraordinary rapidity of social change. The homeostatic powers of the family group are threatened. It often fails in its functions as psychic stabilizer for child, adolescent, and adult. Many families left to their own resources fail utterly to achieve and maintain a balance of essential functions. Intervention from the outside is indispensable to the restoration of family control. Often the balance of family role relations is disturbed: man to wife, parent to grandparent, parent to child, and child to sibling. As tension and anxiety mount, there is greater imbalance in the paired tendencies to conform and to rebel. The trend toward alienation in family relations becomes magnified; it impairs the processes of identification and aggravates the pressures toward pathogenic dismemberment of the family group.

More and more in our time, the individual tends to identify with the group with only a fragment of his personal identity, rather than with the whole of himself. Frequently, this identification is defensive in nature rather than a positive expression of the integration of personal identity with the life of the group.

Such disruptive trends assume great importance when we take into account the familial pattern of our culture, which rests the fate of the child almost exclusively on the emotional health of a single set of parents. The supportive influence of auxiliary parents in our culture is sharply reduced. Thus, there is little opportunity for an auxiliary parent to serve as antidote to the pathogenic influence of a disturbed mother. Most baby-sitters are among our worst-paid workers, and little trained for child care.

Under such conditions, children develop their characters in a disordered way. They experience a distressing struggle in synthesizing a personal identity that is congruent with the requirements of the modern family and the modern social community. They have difficulty in pulling themselves together into one piece. They tend to experience themselves in parts, rather than as intact, whole beings. With the instability and unpredictability of social norms, it is difficult for children to know what is real and not real, appropriate and inappropriate. They cannot depend securely upon their parents's standards because the parents themselves are chronically unsure.

The parents are disoriented in their social position. They feel lost and alone. They are cut off from the past, cannot predict the future, and hang precariously in the present moment. In the effort to feel more complete and whole, they seek to join at least a piece of their identity with that of others. Problem-solving, decision-making, and action become less a function of the individual and more a function of shared though fragmented identity with others.

Conflict is no longer snugly contained within one person, but is externalized and lived out in the zone between person and environment. This brings into prominence such defenses as projection, magic thinking, substitution of aggression for anxiety, and "acting-out." "Acting-out" is not a function of the isolated individual; it requires the complicity of one or more partners. This phenomenon is immediately significant for the disturbances of the contemporary family and the manner in which they become echoed in the behavior of children. Especially noteworthy are the "anarchy of youth," the trend toward delinquency, and the "sexual revolution" among teenagers.

In our time the relative loss of horizontal supports in the wider community for the continuity of the family pattern is conspicuous. The resulting disturbances in the nuclear family unit may be referred to as the "normal psychopathology of contemporary family life."

FAMILY DEVELOPMENT AND CHILD HEALTH

The problem has three parts: the development of the family, the development of the child, and the value patterns of the community and culture that influence the balance between the two sets of processes. Because child development can be clearly conceptualized only within the broader matrix of family development, prevention must begin within this matrix. The optimal unit of study is the family group, moving, growing, changing through three generations, parents, children, and grandparents. Within a single unit of time there is a crossing of lives, and a significant reciprocity of influence toward change in the interrelations of the three generations. The identity of the family, its values and strivings, its typical configuration of role patterns, its continuity and discontinuity can be best understood in this way. In seeking the knowledge required for prevention, it would hardly be appropriate to confine the study process to one generation of offspring.

We need to know what tasks, emotional and otherwise, must be successfully completed at each stage of family development in order that the family group may advance to the next stage. Within this context, we can try to correlate family and child behavior, stage by stage. We need to know what goes wrong and also what goes right in family experience over the stretch of time. We need to know how one or another kind of family deviation harms the child's development. We also need to know how such deviations become differently structured in a variety of family types. In other words, what ingredients contribute to the health and strength of the emerging personality of the child? What elements fortify the child's immunity to illness?

We must be concerned, therefore, with the psychodynamics of the family group at every stage of its evolution. We must go the full circle: courtship, marriage, the family organization before the advent of children, the progressive shift in family organization after children are added, and finally the gradual transformation of family pattern through each stage of the child's development from infancy to adulthood, culminating once again in marriage and the creation of a new family.

To further the aims of prevention, it is essential to understand the vital processes of family life in much the same way that we try to understand a living person. A family as family has strivings, conflicts, patterns of emotional control, an inner face, and an outer face; it has, so to speak, a soul of its own. Much like a person, it has a natural life history, a beginning and an end. It passes through sequential stages of development. It has a certain growth potential. Just as one may hypothecate progressive stages of maturation in the individual, so too one may hypothecate for the family group analogous stages of maturation and related levels of functioning.

1. Primary bond of mother, father, and child (primary biosocial union).
2. Interdependency, affectional intimacy, and identification.
3. Individuation and progressive autonomy.
4. Mature, creative expansion of family functions.
5. Aging and gradual dissolution into newly created family units.

For the family group the impairment of homeostatic balance, the failure to harmonize family values and functions, and the loss of potentials of growth constitute potent forces for breakdown and mental illness. Health in family living, as in the individual, is correlated to the preservation of adaptive plasticity and powers of growth, to the way in which the multiple functions of family life are regulated and balanced. Family failure in this sense brings social disorder, ultimately mental disorder. Some families are mainly sick, others are predominantly well. Some are not sick, clinically speaking, and yet do not achieve positive health.

It is necessary for our purposes to design a conceptual model of an integrated healthy family group, which relates family health to the balancing of essential family functions. I have tentatively formulated these functions as follows:

1. The provision of food, shelter, and other material necessities to sustain life and provide protection from external danger, a function best fulfilled under conditions of social unity and cooperation.
2. The provision of social togetherness, which is the matrix for the affectional bond of family relationships.
3. The opportunity to evolve a personal identity, tied to family identity, this bond of identity providing the psychic integrity and strength for meeting new experience.
4. The patterning of sexual roles, which prepares the way for sexual maturation and fulfillment.
5. The training toward integration into social roles and acceptance of social responsibility.
6. The cultivation of learning and the support for individual creativity and initiative.

The family molds the kinds of persons it needs to carry out its functions. The members mold the family processes to suit their needs. The total configuration of family molds the forms of behavior that are required in the roles of husband and wife, father and mother, parent and child, child and sibling. Clearly this process is a continuously evolving one, for the psychologic identity of a family changes over time. Each member responds with a unique balance of tendencies to conform or rebel, to submit or actively to alter the family role expectations.

Family allegiance to one set of values or another structures the identity of the family, patterns its functions, its role adaptations, and the corresponding family alignments. A conflict of values and strivings brings a rift, a split in the family, which mobilizes one segment of the family against another. Such splits may be horizontal, vertical, or diagonal.

In the creation of a new family, the man and woman come with formed identities of their own, influenced by their families of origin. But the identity of the child must be created *de novo*. The infant is born into a set of ongoing relationships. His identity is shaped by the fit or lack of fit of parents with child and child with parents. Although physically the child is a separate and distinct organism, socially and psychologically he is an incomplete entity. His reactions can be evaluated as a response to his integration into the network of ongoing relationships that characterizes the given family group. This is a circular phenomenon: the family affects the child, the child the family. In order to illuminate these relationships, it is necessary to conceptualize the totality of the family entity and, within this frame, to see the proper position of its parts. Such a study requires examination of the relevant data both in cross section and longitudinally.

Of special relevance is the role of values in the psychosocial development of the family group and the temporally conditioned interplay of family values and wider cultural values. What is the effect of this upon the characters of the parents, their adaptation to marital and interparental relations, and to parent-child relations? We must pay particular attention to the interweaving of the values of child-rearing with other family values: sexual fulfillment, the strivings of the parents both as a joined couple and as individuals; the goals of security, economic and social success, prestige, and the creative aspirations of the family. Can we discern in a given family how far it is possible to bring into harmony the goals of marriage and sex, the personal aims of the adult partners, and a set of expectations with respect to child-rearing? How is it that certain marriages are foredoomed in the task of merging and balancing these multiple family values? How is it that certain marital partnerships from the very beginning provide no emotional room for a growing child? How is it that in certain families a child disrupts the marital partnership? How can we detect and define the stages of evolution of the network of family relationships as they affect health and illness in the child?

Present evidence suggests, for prevention of childhood disorders, the overwhelming importance of close scrutiny of the stage of courtship, adaptation of man and wife in the first marital phase, readaptation after the birth of the child, and evolving processes of change in the family pattern during the first years of the child's life.

In conceptualizing health and illness, therefore, we cannot dichotomize child and family. The health of a child must be assessed at three interrelated levels: (1) what goes on inside the child's mind, (2) what is emotionally interchanged between child and family that shapes the child's role within the family, (3) what are the evolving psychosocial processes of the whole family.

The challenge of establishing correlations between child and family behavior is a question of interrelating the growth curve of the child with the developmental processes of the child's integration into the family group. It is the interaction and merging of biologic and social factors, stage by stage, that molds the characteristics of personality. Parent-child interaction and parent role-functioning must be defined within the broader context of the dynamic pattern of the family as a whole.

Dynamic correlation of child and family behavior requires:

1. A system of diagnostic appraisal of child personality.
2. A system of evaluating specific pathologic units of experience in the child within the total integrative patterns of the child's personality and the dominant modes of social adaptation.
3. A theory of child personality, specifying the stages of development in terms of progressive levels of biosocial integration into the family group.
4. Definitive criteria for the development, psychosocial status, and mental health functioning of the family group.

Each stage in the development of child personality is conditioned by the previous stage, merges imperceptibly into and overlaps the next stage. This is best characterized in specific patterns of adaptation, which may be schematized as follows:

1. The immediate postbirth stage, mainly vegetative adaptation.
2. The stage of primary union with mother.
3. The stage of gradual separation of the infant's self from the mother's self.
4. The stage of the child's sexual differentiation paralleling the recognition of the sex differences of the parents, the relations between them, and a corresponding shift in expression of the child's love needs and identifications.
5. The stage of expansion of the emotional and social spheres of the child's interaction with his environment beyond the immediate family, testing of social reality, and new learning.
6. The stage of pubescent growth, with the emergence of differentiated sex drives and reorganization of lines of identification, realignment of group allegiances and roles, anticipation of and preparation for tasks of adult life.

The child's development and behavior may be influenced in varying degrees by the internal makeup of the mother's personality, by her adaptation to the mothering role in the given family, by the marital and parental relationship, and by the psychosocial structure of the family as a whole. Of particular significance is the interdependence and reciprocity of family roles and the effects of this emotional complementation on the child's adaptive response.

Analysis of data on the family may be organized in the following manner:

1. Man-wife relationship: motivation for marriage, goals, and actual achievement.
2. Parent-child relationship: character of parents, motives pertinent to child-caring, goals and values in child care, actual parental achievement.
3. Internal organization of family group: goals for family as a group and actual achievement.
4. External adaptation of family group: goals in relation to community; interaction with persons and groups outside family; actual achievement.
5. Child behavior: reactions and trends in relation to parents, parent surrogates, and family group.

In correlating child and family behavior, it is necessary to weigh healthy against unhealthy areas of functioning, those components of family interaction that are disabled by anxiety against those that are functionally effective and reciprocally satisfying.

DISTORTIONS OF FAMILY AND CHILD DEVELOPMENT

In the interest of prevention, it is important to delineate useful levels of entry into family life. Preventive influence may be exerted at each and every stage in the development of the family group, in the premarital courtship phase, and in each successive phase thereafter.

If the family group loses its power to solve problems, learn, and grow, it undergoes a process of attrition; it develops distortions (17, 19-36). A disordered family can be detected through the presence of a critical imbalance in the regulation and carrying-out of its essential functions. As the adaptive powers of a family group become constricted and disabled, the family gives preference to one or another function; it sacrifices one for the other. The breakdown of plasticity in family adaptation occurs not all at once but selectively and in serial fashion over a period of time. One family gives the priority to security strivings, another to conformity with the values of the older generation or the peer group, another to sex or other pleasure pursuits. In some families, the first breakdown occurs in the sexual adaptation, whereas parent-child relations are preserved; in other families, this may be reversed.

Families often disclose specific prejudices and scapegoating mechanisms. Such patterns bear a causal relation to the selection of a particular family pair or individual member as the object of assault and disparagement. The specific quality of scapegoating influences both the form and the timing of the emotional breakdown. In sick families, we are often confronted by multiple personality disorders in several members of the family group who interact in a special way, and this influences the course and outcome of these illnesses. If we can intervene early enough in such a situation, the implications for the mental health of as yet unaffected members of the family are obvious.

A disturbed child referred for professional help is only one link in the chain of family disturbance. He may be the most sick or the least sick member of the family. The warp of the family interaction invades the child's emotional life; the child's behavior in turn penetrates and modifies the processes of family interaction. The child absorbs and reprojects the pathogenic contagion of the family group. He must be viewed not only as a distressed individual, but also as the symptom of a psychopathically twisted family group. His behavior offers a specific clue to the distortion of homeostatic control of family functions.

A child may be emotionally scapegoated in a great variety of ways. As the focus of pathogenic disturbance shifts from one part of the family to another, the scapegoating pattern also changes, and the emotional development of the child is influenced accordingly.

Clinical study points up the need to explore specific kinds of distortion in family development, especially in the evolution of marital and parental relations. We must try to define the pathogenic potential of a whole range of marital partnerships. For example: the accidental or incidental marriage; the forced marriage; the marriage on the rebound; the marriage of puppy love, the union of two immature, unrealistic people, unready for the responsibilities of family life; the parentifying marital relation, in which one partner is required to serve as parent for the other; the marriage of neurotic persons, in which one partner is required to buttress the other's defense against anxiety; the marriage of sociopathic persons; the marriage of psychotic persons with corresponding disorganization of family relationships. In many instances, such marriages are never really culminated: psychologically viewed, they are aborted.

In a parallel sense, there is the large range of distortion of parental partnerships. There are the many patterns of competitive relationships between the parents, with one parent siding with the child against the other parent. There is the competition of parent with child. There is the exclusive mother-child pair, which virtually shuts out the father as a significant parent. The father becomes a fading figure. As Loomis expressed it, the father is viewed "as a bully, a sap, or an absentee landlord." In such a setting, in effect, the child is raised by a single parent, the mother. There is the associated phenomenon of "momism" with all its invidious connotations. What is the effect of "momism" on child development, especially on the male child, when a healthy model of masculine parent is lacking?

When a mother destructively invades the emotional life of the child, the father may offer significant protection. He may provide a specific antidote to the mother's exploitive invasion of the child. When a mother is detached, cold, and hostile, a father may offer tender warmth to the child. In this role, the father compensates the child for the deficiency of the mothering. (Interestingly enough, a generation ago it was exactly the opposite pattern that caused concern: the tyrannical, punishing father and the submissive and soft mother.)

In those families that reveal a pathologic symbiosis between mother and child, the father holds the power to neutralize or mitigate its effect. He or an equivalent parent figure may inject an antidote to the destructive effects of such symbiosis. Without such antidote, the child may suffer a schizoid development.

There is the special problem of the child-wife: the clinging of such an immature woman to her own mother, her failure of sexual adaptation and feminine fulfillment, her need for the husband to serve as a mother-surrogate, and her failure to fill the requirements of mothering for her own child. She presses her own child into the role of mother, thereby producing, in effect, a reversal of parent-child roles: The parent is the child, and the child is forced to act as parent. This obviously leads to a confusing and overlapping of the generations. Insofar as the woman fails to integrate into her appropriate family roles, the man must also fail; if the role relations of man and wife are out of balance, conflicted, and disordered, the child cannot himself fit into a healthy and satisfying family role. Sometimes by parental default the child usurps the power position and becomes the omnipotent ruler of the family group.

Confusion is also associated with the parent's need to seduce the child sexually. Such seduction provides a channel for displacement of aggression intended for the other parent; it is a disguised, hostile invasion of the child's body, with a resulting distortion in the unfolding of the child's body image.

In certain families, there is the tendency toward reversal of the sexual roles of man and wife. The woman loses femininity, the man loses masculinity; ultimately, the woman fulfills the masculine part and the man fulfills the femine part. In such situations, the father is often characterized as "passive male." This is an oversimplification and obscures the disguised, circuitous, and vengeful behavior of the man against the woman. Many of these "passive males" are not truly passive, and the expression often turns out to be a myth. In actuality, the man is busy protecting himself from the woman's aggressions by a placatory effort to keep the peace. In so doing, he misconstrues the woman's aggression as a superior strength. He fails to perceive her underlying fright. He cannot then balance his sexual position with the woman or play the needed part as male parent. But appearances are deceiving. He is not basically passive. With appropriate intervention, his incentive can be mobilized for the active role needed by both his wife and his child.

In terms of prevention, it is noteworthy that clinical study of the preschool child and his family demonstrates that therapeutic alteration of family role relations often brings striking improvement in the emotional health of the young child, even though that child has received no individual psychotherapy whatever.

If the pathology of the family group and the pathology of the child are parallel phenomena, it follows that treatment of family and child apart from one another is an incorrect procedure. The pathogenic conflicts within the family group continue to be operative at all stages of the child's illness and affect its course. Thus, once initiated, the pathogenic process within the child continues to be influenced by the family's way of coping with its interpersonal conflicts.

Techniques for intervention in the emotional life of parents and family are needed, as well as techniques for the direct individual psychotherapy of the child. It is a distortion of the true nature of the problem to place first importance on the child's disorder, while assigning to the disorders of parents and family a position of secondary or peripheral importance. It is unfitting, therefore, in the pattern of traditional guidance clinic practices to provide the child with the most skilled professional help (psychiatric or psychoanalytic therapy) while leaving "second best" to parents and family (case work therapy). It is clearly a twist of human ethics to view the child as being "good" while indicting the parents and family as "bad." If we provide intensive care for the child while allowing the family to go to seed, the child cannot stay well. Under such conditions, a disturbed child may improve while under therapy, but must inevitably again fall ill. Of what value is such treatment if prevention and positive mental health are our goals?

The finding of early cases of disturbed children does not by itself ensure the powers of prevention. It is one thing to know what a child needs; it is another to make over parents and family to meet these needs. Case-finding, while a desirable therapeutic goal in itself, must deliberately be exploited as the basis for early identification of sick families. In a parallel sense, the development of a method of therapy for the family group is of paramount importance.

A clinician who gains favorable access to the inner life of the family, regardless of which member is first referred for help, often has the power to prevent emotional illness in other family members, especially in the younger children. On repeated occasions, through the "here and now" therapeutic entry into the group life of the family, it has seemed possible to prevent the development of neurosis or stop a trend toward delinquency. Sometimes, extraordinary effects can be observed in a short series of therapeutic family interviews in which the focus of pathogenic conflict is lifted away from the child and put back where it belongs, into the parental relationship. In one case, the danger of a child's knifing the parents and, in another, the threat of child suicide were averted by this type of family intervention.

In contrast, however, there are the many situations in which the clinician can identify the pathogenic potentials of a particular family and yet feel utterly impotent in the task of prevention, precisely because he lacks the power to intervene at the appropriate levels.

In these remarks, I have barely skimmed the surface of the many complex problems to be faced in this broad field. I have merely outlined an orientation, a point of view toward the challenge of family research. In the studies previously mentioned, I pay particular attention to the issues of family diagnosis and therapy. Intervention at the family level offers a means of exerting a simultaneous influence toward health on both child and family. The family-interview procedure provides the possibility of direct correlation of intrapsychic and interpersonal processes. What is inside the child's mind can be immediately matched against what goes on between child and mother, mother and father, child and sibling.

METHODS OF STUDY

In family research, one can explore the relevant processes retrospectively or prospectively, or one can focus on the "here and now." None of these approaches in isolation can give a complete picture. Each offers a selective access to partial phenomena. As of now, I am more interested in combining the "here and now" with prospective observations of family life.

The "here-and-now" type of family interview inevitably evokes a considerable body of historical communication. As the members of the family struggle with their current conflicts, they spontaneously offer relevant historical material. The challenge is to find the optimal use of these background data to illuminate current family processes.

The goal of previous studies in the family approach to mental health, as I have said, is to establish a method of family diagnosis and therapy. The effort is to find means to identify the family as a psychological entity in and of itself, a way of assessing its psychosocial configuration and mental health functioning, a basis for classification and differential diagnosis of family types, and finally a means for establishing the specific dynamic interrelations of individual and family behavior. The ultimate goal is a social psychology and social psychopathology of family life, and a corresponding means for therapy, prevention of illness, and promotion of positive health.

I am endeavoring now to establish the differential features in the component family processes that have a specific relation to three main conditions: psychosis, neurosis, and character disorder. I pay special attention to the task of achieving a family diagnosis at one point in time and a similar diagnosis at a further point in time, while evolving criteria for the assessment of change in family interaction in the intervening period. I believe that family diagnosis at any one time represents essentially an evaluation of processes of change confined to a narrow time period; it is really a measurement of short-term change. I have been concerned with the need to distinguish short-term change and long-term change, to separate transitory effects from lasting patterns of change.

Close observation of family interaction in a therapeutic setting leads to psychodynamic formulations and clinical hunches. In constructing hypotheses, I am especially interested in translating psychodynamic formulations and clinical hunches into operational hypotheses based upon units of nonverbal communication. Systematic observation of nonverbal behavior is useful because it lends itself more readily to measurement.

For example, there is in one family group a persecutory undercurrent in the relations of an obsessional mother and schizoid son. In the interaction of mother and son, one can measure change by noting a quantitative shift in the mother's gesture of pointing a menacing forefinger at her son, by a more frequent occurrence of relaxed smiling, and in the son by a lessened occurrence of spitting or puking behavior, and by a greater willingness to listen or receive food from the mother.

In such studies, we depend on a range of procedures to obtain the relevant data: therapeutic family interview, moving picture studies of interview process, psychiatric and psychologic examination, and home visits. The data gathered by these various means are integrated and recorded through the use of systematic schedules, so as to obtain comparable data on a range of family types. We are making special use of moving picture recordings, using what is called the "hidden camera" technique, with the photographic equipment set up in a room adjoining the interviewing room. We are now in the process of evolving specific research designs for the evaluation of these moving picture records of family interaction process. We are devising multiple methods of evaluation: (1) psychodynamic evaluation by the clinician; (2) spontaneous evaluation of the interview events by the family group viewing its own film; (3) interactional analysis by the Bales method; (4) a special study of family identity and values; (5) a special study of agreement, disagreement, and coalitions in family relations; (6) a special study of the relations of prejudice and scapegoating to problems of family mental health.

THE SPECIAL PROBLEMS OF FAMILY RESEARCH

Family research may be approached by many pathways. It may take its point of departure from a wide range of theories and clinical hunches. Because the task is huge and comprehensive, it must be subdivided. One can pursue a series of interrelated studies, step by step, each such study concentrating on a part of the problem.

Although family research is still relatively crude and experimental, it seems possible to bring some order and system to the multiple variables and different levels of human functioning that are involved. In the traditional approaches to mental health problems, it has been usual to begin with the individual, moving from there to his environment. It would be equally logical to begin with the group structure, moving from there back to the individual. Recognizing the principle of the interdependent and reciprocal relations of individual and group, the influence of one on the other in the process of change, it would be appropriate to study these influences in either direction or both, moving from outside inward, or from inside outward. Since, in the past, more disciplined knowledge was available of the psychodynamics of the individual than of the dynamics of the group, the tendency was to move from the individual to the group environment. In this present study, there may be some strategic advantage in emphasizing the opposite direction of movement, that is, from family to the individual.

In any case, whatever the path of study, the component processes to be considered are the relative autonomy of the individual, the individual's emotional integration into the group, the interrelations of personality and role adaptation, the fit or lack of fit for the same individual of the significant familial and extrafamilial roles, and the dynamics of the family group itself, the interplay of the family's internal organization and external adaptation in the community. At these various levels, discrepancies of conscious and unconscious organization of experience must be taken into account.

A further step involves the need for establishing a psychiatric ideal of family and individual mental health in a given milieu and for measuring ill-health as a deviation of specific degree and kind from this ideal. This proposition takes into account the relativity of behavior in different social environments and uses adaptation to environment as one index of mental health. It implies also that judgments of mental health would be different in different societies in accordance with the dominant value orientation and the strivings of the family as a unit. The family is judged then in accordance with the prevailing value system and the consensually validated interpretations of social reality. In this frame, it is understood that the professional observer is influenced in his judgments by his own social-economic position and corresponding value orientation; the observer is participant as well as observer, and his conclusions are prone to be shaped by whether or not he occupies the same or a different social position as the families and individual he is appraising.

There is the special feature of the global nature of family process and the need to maintain the proper relations of parts to the whole. There is the responsibility for choosing for study the more important clinical problems. There is the difficulty of narrowing the field and limiting variables without distorting the phenomena under investigation. There is the special problem of selecting a minimum number of categories for analysis of the data that will be adequate for description and pertinent to mental health. Indexes need to be universal in application to permit comparison of one family group with another and of children of one group with those of another. There is the further problem of specifying the bases for judgment in analysis of the data; that is, the evaluation of actual life performance against a psychiatric model of ideal family and child mental health. There is the further question of flexible modifications of such evaluative judgments according to cultural setting, value orientation, and expectations of the family. Also to be considered are the biases introduced by the cultural position of the observer and the analyst of the data. There is the problem of designing appropriate controls and checking the sources of error—an alternative designed to test a limit. And it must not be forgotten that this observer is a clinician, a very definite influence on the phenomena he is observing.

Finally, there is the problem of working out concrete, specific, usable definitions of terms so that the method is communicable and the results of family study can be applied to the issues of prevention.

Inevitably in such study there is the problem of introducing system and exactness into a field where pertinent clinical observations are of the first importance, yet by their very nature are subjective, evaluative, and inexact. Often it happens that in the search for measurable variables the dynamic meat of the family is lost. The striving for exactness tends to make research procedure rigid in a way that takes the very life out of the family picture; we find that the ultimate objectives of family study cannot be subordinated to the preoccupation with conventional standards of research. Each family must be regarded as an individual case study; only when we have obtained a clear and integrated picture of the family as a functioning unit can we compare it with others.

Another difficulty is the fact that families do not stay the same; they change. This raises the question of systematic inquiry into the right time for family study: At what point in time? Over what span in time? Contact with the same family at different stages of its history gives us different data and new problems of interpretation. Part of the problem is how to accommodate the study procedure to the significant stages of evolution in family life.

DISCUSSION AND CONCLUSIONS

The study of the psychodynamics of family life and, more specifically, the correlation of processes of family and child development, opens up some new avenues of possible prevention of mental disorders in childhood. The goal of primary prevention poses a gigantic challenge. Can we remake family and culture, from the bottom up? Surely it would be unreal to conjure up the vision of building an ideally healthy family in a social vacuum; the process is one of historic evolution. Realistically, we must start from where we are now. We must find the way to move from existing family types, whether sick, fragmented, or merely agitated and unstable, toward the ideal of robust family health.

To foster evolutionary change from where we are in family life and child care to where we would like to be requires an appropriate merging of the goals of primary and secondary prevention. We need to be oriented to twin purposes; to neutralize pathogenic potentials and promote positive mental health in family living.

By its very nature the goal of prevention cannot be pointed to a single child, or to any individual viewed in isolation. A preventive program must deal with the essential continuity of the relations of individual, family, and community. It must be oriented to clusters of persons whose lives interweave, cross, and join. It must point to those networks of human relationships that represent a sharing of emotion and identity. The family is the natural bridge between the forces of culture and the forces of the individual personality. For purposes of prevention, therefore, the family is the nodal group; it is the basic unit of illness and health.

The optimal unit of intervention is the family constellation moving across three generations. The relevant emotional processes of this family entity must be evaluated both in cross section and longitudinally. The residual resources for the maintenance of health must be weighed against the pathogenic potentials. It may be assumed that component processes involving conflict, pathogenic influence, and associated devices of control are contagiously passed down through the three generations. In this sense the past is contained within the present. The original "pathogens" are still operative in the contemporary family pattern, although they now express themselves in an altered way. Both the old and the new are woven into the present adaptational pattern of the family group.

In the here-and-now adaptational pattern, the paired tendencies toward joining of identity and individuation manifested in the role adaptations of the individual to salient family pairs and to the family as a whole can be checked by means of three main variables: (1) the continuity of identity in time; (2) the adaptation to new experience, the ability to learn and grow, and the related capacity to achieve further maturation through the discovery of new levels of complementation in family role relationships; (3) the control of conflict. The dynamic balance between the first two variables is influenced by the third. The tendency to cling to the old and familiar in family experience and the receptivity to the new are two aspects of a single phenomenon; the relative prominence of the one or the other is a function of the control of conflict. If the control of conflict and anxiety decompensates, there is a greater clinging to the old, greater sameness and rigidity; if the control of conflict is effective and healthy, there is greater receptivity to the new, increasing plasticity of adaptation, and a higher potential for new learning. Within this scheme, the identification processes and the complementation of role relationships can be assessed. Complementarity in family role patterns may be measured by the following: (1) the level of need satisfaction; (2) the avenues provided for the solution of conflict; (3) the degree of support offered for a needed or favored self-image; (4) the buttressing of healthy rather than pathogenic defenses; (5) the promotion of further emotional maturation both of the relationship and of each partner as individual.

Within this conceptual frame one can examine the conflict patterns of the family. Conflict exists at multiple levels: (1) conflict between the family and surrounding community; (2) interpersonal conflict between individual family members; and (3) intrapsychic conflict between individual family members. At each of these levels the conflicts may be defined in terms of disturbances in role adaptation. The aim is to delineate the central conflicts of the family group at these various levels, to define their intensity, their lability, and their location within the life space of the family. Within the patterns of contemporary conflict one traces the pathogenic influence that has come up out of the past. One must also appraise the family's resources for the solution, containment, and compensation of conflict, so as to maintain health. In this connection it is important to discern the dynamic relations between individual defense against anxiety and family group defense against threat to its continuity of function.

The aims of prevention with respect to family conflict would be:

1. To help the family to achieve a clearer and sharper definition of the real content of conflict. This is done by dissolving the disguises of conflict and resulting confusions in family relationships. A greater accuracy of perception of family conflict is the goal.
2. To counteract inappropriate displacements of conflict.
3. To neutralize the unrational prejudices and scapegoating involved in the displacement of conflict. The purpose here is to put the conflict back where it came from in family role relations, that is, to reattach it to its original source, and attempt to work it out there, so as to counteract the trend toward prejudicial assault and disparagement of any one member.
4. To relieve one victimized part of the family, either an individual or a family pair, of an excessive load of conflict.
5. To energize dormant interpersonal conflicts, bringing them overtly into the live processes of family interaction, thus making them accessible to solution.
6. To lift concealed intrapsychic conflict to the level of interpersonal relations, where it may be coped with more effectively.
7. To activate an improved level of complementarity in family role relations.

The task of neutralizing the pathogenic potential in the family group is of special importance in regard to what I consider the "normal psychopathology of contemporary family life." It is my impression that the relative isolation of the middle-class nuclear family unit and the relative loss of significant horizontal supports in the relations of the nuclear family group with members of the extended family and with representations of the wider community intensify the tendency to breakdown and illness. Therefore, in the interest of prevention, it is of importance to try to find substitute lines of emotional support for the nuclear family unit.

For the promotion of positive health, we need a theoretical model of an ideally healthy family, with special reference to child-rearing. In family care oriented to prevention of illness and promotion of positive health, it is important to strive toward an integration of the goals of psychotherapy, social treatment, and family life education.

It is reasonable to assume that qualified professionals can be trained in the techniques of psychotherapy of the family group, social treatment, and family life education. The special role of family therapists needs to be more carefully defined. Toward this end a training program needs to be developed for general practitioners of medicine, pediatricians, nurses, and social workers.

REFERENCES

1. ACKERMAN, N. W. "Behavioral Trends and Disturbances of the Contemporary Family." In GALDSTON, I. (ed.), *The Family in Contemporary Society*. New York: International Universities Press, 1958.
2. ACKERMAN, N. W. The diagnosis of neurotic marital interaction. *Soc. Casework, 31* (4): 139, 1954.
3. ACKERMAN, N. W. "The Emotional Impact of In-laws and Relatives." In LIEBMAN. S. (ed.), *Emotional Forces in the Family*. Philadelphia: Lippincott, 1959.
4. ACKERMAN, N. W. "Interlocking Pathology in Family Relationships." In RADO, S., and DANIELS, G. (eds.), *Changing Concepts of Psychoanalytic Medicine*. New York: Grune & Stratton, 1958.
5. ACKERMAN, N. W. Mental health and the family in the current world crisis. *J. Jew. Com. Serv., 34* (1): 58, 1957.
6. ACKERMAN, N. W. Mental hygiene and social work, today and tomorrow. *Soc. Casework, 36* (2): 63, 1955.
7. ACKERMAN, N. W. An orientation to psychiatric research on the family. *Marriage and Family Living, 19* (1): 68, 1957.
8. ACKERMAN, N. W. The principle of shared responsibility for child-rearing. *Internat. J. Soc. Psychiat., 11* (4): 281, 1957.
9. ACKERMAN, N. W. "The Psychoanalytic Approach to the Family." In MASSERMAN, J. (ed.), *Science and Psychoanalysis*. New York: Grune & Stratton, 1959, Vol. II.
10. ACKERMAN, N. W. *The Psychodynamics of Family Life*. New York: Basic Books, 1958.
11. ACKERMAN, N. W. Theory of family dynamics. *Psy-*

choanal. & Psychoanalyt. Rev., *46* (4): 33, 1960.
12. ACKERMAN, N. W. Toward an integrative therapy of the family. *Am. J. Psychiat.*, *114:* 8, 1958.
13. ACKERMAN, N. W. and BEHRENS, MARJORIE L. "The Family Group and Family Therapy." In MASSERMAN, J., and MORENO, J. L. (eds), *Progress in Psychotherapy*. New York: Grune & Stratton, 1958, Vol. III.
14. ACKERMAN, N. W., and BEHRENS, M. L. A study of family diagnosis. *Am. J. Orthopsychiat.*, *26* (1): 65, 1956.
15. ACKERMAN, N. W., and LAKOS, M. H. "Treatment of a Child and Family." In BURTON, A. (ed.), *Case Studies in Counseling and Psychotherapy*. Englewood Cliffs: Prentice-Hall, 1959.
16. ACKERMAN, N. W., and SOBEL, R. Family diagnosis. *Am. J. Orthopsychiat.*, *20:* 744, 1950.
17. BATESON, G., and JACKSON, D. Toward a theory of schizophrenia. *Behavioral Sci.*, *1:* 251, 1956.
18. BEHRENS, M. L., and ACKERMAN, N. W. The home visit as an aid in family diagnosis and therapy. *Soc. Casework*, *37* (1): 11, 1956.
19. BOTT, E. *Family and Social Network*. London: Tavistock, 1957.
20. BURGESS, E. W. The family in a changing society. *Am. J. Sociol.*, *53:* 417, 1948.
21. CAPLAN, G. "Some Comments on Family Functioning in Its Relationship to Mental Health." Paper presented at American Orthopsychiatry Association, 1956.
22. ERIKSON, E. The problem of ego identity. *J. Am. Psychol. A.*, *4:* 56, 1956.
23. FISHER, S., and MENDELL, F. The communication of neurotic patterns over two or three generations. *Psychiatry*, *19:* 41, 1956.
24. FREUD, A. "Psychoanalysis and Education." Lecture delivered at New York Academy of Medicine, June 1954.
25. GALDSTON, I. "The American Family in Crisis." Paper delivered to Pennsylvania Mental Health, Inc., May, 1957.
26. HANDEL, G., and HESSE, R. D. *Family Worlds*. Chicago: University of Chicago Press, 1959.
27. JACKSON, D. The question of family homeostasis. *Psychiatric Quart. Supp.*, *31* (1): 79, 1957.
28. JOHNSON, A. M., and SZUREK, S. A. The genesis of antisocial acting out in children and adults. *Psychoanalyt. Quart.*, *21:* 323, 1952.
29. LIDZ, T., PARKER, B., and CORNELISON, A. R. The role of the father in the family environment of the schizophrenic patient. *Am. J. Psychiat.*, *113* (2): 126, 1956.
30. LIDZ, R. W., and LIDZ, T. The family environment of schizophrenic patients. *Am. J. Psychiat.*, *106:* 332, 1949.
31. LIDZ, T., CORNELISON, A. R., FLECK, S., and TERRY, D. The intrafamilial environment of the schizophrenic patient: marital schism and marital skew. *Am. J. Psychiat.*, *114:* 241, 1957.
32. LIDZ, T., *et al.* The intrafamilial environment of the schizophrenic patient: 1. The father. *Psychiatry*, *20:* 329, 1957.
33. MITTELMANN, B. Complementary neurotic reactions in intimate relationships. *Psychoanalyt. Quart.*, *13* (4): 479, 1944.
34. MITTELMANN, B. Concurrent analyses of married couples. *Psychoanalyt. Quart.*, *17:* 182, 1948.
35. SPIEGEL, J. New perspectives in the study of family. *Marriage-Family Ser.*, *16:* 4, 1954.
36. SPIEGEL, J., and KLUCKHOHN, F. *Integration and Conflict in Family Behavior*. Report 27, Committee on the Family, Group for Advancement of Psychiatry. 1954.

Nathan W. Ackerman Bibliography

BOOKS

Anti-Semitism and Emotional Disorder (with M. Jahoda). New York: Harper & Brothers, 1950.

The Psychodynamics of Family Life. New York: Basic Books, 1958.

Exploring the Base for Family Therapy (edited with F. Beatman, and S. Sherman). New York: Family Association of America, 1961.

Treating the Troubled Family. New York: Basic Books, 1966.

Expanding Theory and Practice in Family Therapy (edited with F. Beatman, and S. Sherman). New York: Family Service Association of America, 1967.

Family Process (edited). New York: Basic Books, 1970.

ARTICLES

Juvenile psychosis with favorable response to treatment. *Bulletin of the Menninger Clinic*, 1:44-52, 1936.

*Accidental self-injury in children. *Archives of Pediatrics*, 53:711-721, 1936.

Treatment techniques in a school for retarded children (with C. F. Menninger). *American Journal of Orthopsychiatry*, 6:294-312, 1936.

*The family as a social and emotional unit. *Bulletin of the Kansas Mental Hygiene Society*, 12:2, 1937.

A plan for maladjusted children. *Bulletin of the Menninger Clinic*, 1:67-69, 1937.

*Reciprocal antagonism in siblings. *Bulletin of the Menninger Clinic*, 2:14-20, 1938.

The unity of the family. *Archives of Pediatrics*, 55:51-62, 1938.

Newer methods in schizophrenia (with E. Friedman). *Clinical Medicine and Surgery*, 45:361-364, 1938.

Constructive and destructive tendencies in children: An experimental study. *American Journal of Orthopsychiatry*, 8:265-285, 1938.

Paranoid state with delusions of injury by "black magic." *Bulletin of the Menninger Clinic*, 2:118-126, 1938.

Personality factors in neurodermite. *Psychosomatic Medicine*, 1:3, 1939.

The reactions and behavior of schizophrenic patients treated with metrazol and camphor. *Journal of Nervous and Mental Disease*, 90:310-332, 1939.

Techniques of therapy. *American Journal of Orthopsychiatry*, 10:665-680, 1940.

Group psychotherapy from the point of view of a psychiatrist. *American Journal of Orthopsychiatry*, 13:678-687, 1943.

*Psychotherapy and "giving love." *Psychiatry*, 7:129-137, 1944.

Dynamic patterns in group psychotherapy. *Psychiatry*, 7:341-348, 1944.

Neuropsychiatric aspects of rehabilitation: Proceedings of the citywide conference on the veteran and the community. *Jewish Social Service Quarterly*, 21:3, 1945.

Psychiatric disorders in servicemen and veterans. *American Journal of Orthopsychiatry*, 15:352-360, 1945.

*Some theoretical aspects of group psychotherapy. In J. Moreno (Ed.), *Group Psychotherapy: A Symposium*. New York: Beacon House, 1945.

What constitutes intensive psychotherapy in a child guidance clinic. *American Journal of Orthopsychiatry*, 15:711-720, 1945.

Group psychotherapy with veterans. *Mental Hygiene*, 30:559-570, 1946.

Some general principles in the use of group psychotherapy. In B. Glueck (Ed.), *The Current Psychiatric Treatment of Personality Disorders*. New York: Grune & Stratton, 1946.

---

*Denotes articles reprinted in this volume.

*Interview group psychotherapy with psychoneurotic adults. In S. R. Slavson (Ed.), *The Practice of Group Therapy*. New York: International Universities Press, 1947.

*Antisemitic motivation in a psychopathic personality: A case study. *Psychoanalytic Reivew*, 34:76-101, 1947.

*The dynamic basis of anti-Semitic attitudes (with M. Jahoda). *Psychoanalytic Quarterly*, 17:240-260, 1948.

*Failures in the psychotherapy of children (with P. Neubauer). In P. Hoch (Ed.), *Failures in Psychiatric Treatment*. New York: Grune & Stratton, 1948.

Toward a dynamic interpretation of anti-Semitic attitudes (with M. Jahoda). *American Journal of Orthopsychiatry*, 18:163-173, 1948.

The training of case workers in psychotherapy. *American Journal of Orthopsychiatry*, 19:14-24, 1949.

The adaptive problems of the adolescent personality. In *The Family in a Democratic Society — Anniversary Papers of the Community Service Society*, New York: Columbia University Press, 1949.

Cultural factors in psychoanalytic therapy. *Bulletin of the American Psychoanalytic Association*, 7:4, 1950.

Character structure in hypertensive persons. In *Life Stress and Bodily Disease*, Vol. 29. 1949 Proceedings of the Association for Research in Nervous and Mental Disease. New York: Association for Research in Nervous and Mental Disease, 1950.

Reflections on the program of the Council Child Development Center. *Quarterly Journal of Child Behavior*, 2:390-403, 1950.

*Psychoanalysis and group psychotherapy. *Group Therapy: Journal of Sociopsychopathology and Sociatry*, 3:204-215, 1950.

*Family diagnosis: An approach to the preschool child (with R. Sobel). *American Journal of Orthopsychiatry*, 20:744-753, 1950.

*Group dynamics: I. "Social role" and total personality. *American Journal of Orthopsychiatry*, 21:1-7, 1951.

*Selected problems in supervised analysis. *Psychiatry*, 16:283-290, 1953.

Psychiatric disorders in children—diagnosis and etiology in our time. In P. Hoch and I. Lubin (Eds.), *Current Problems in Psychiatric Diagnosis*. New York: Grune & Stratton, 1953.

*The diagnosis of neurotic marital interaction. *Social Casework*, 35:139-143, 1954.

*Interpersonal disturbances in the family: Some unresolved problems in psychotherapy. *Psychiatry*, 17:359-368, 1954.

Some structural problems in the relations of psychoanalysis and group psychotherapy. *International Journal of Group Psychotherapy*, 4:131-145, 1954.

Child and family psychopathy: Problems of correlation (with M. L. Behrens). In P. Hoch, and I. Lubin (Eds.), *Psychopathology of Childhood*. New York: Grune & Stratton, 1965.

*Group psychotherapy with a mixed group of adolescents. *International Journal of Group Psychotherapy*, 5:249-260, 1955.

Interaction processes in a group and the role of the leader. In *Psychoanalysis and Social Science*, Volume 4. New York: International Universities Press, 1955.

*Mental hygiene and social work, today and tomorrow. *Social Casework*, 63-70 February 1955.

*Trends in the terminal phase of student analysis. *American Journal of Psychoanalysis*, 15:107-114, 1955.

A study of family diagnosis (with M. L. Behrens). *American Journal of Orthopsychiatry*, 26:66-78, 1956.

*Interlocking pathology in family relationships. In S. Redo and G. Daniels (Eds.), *Changing Conceptions of Psychoanalytic Medicine*. New York: Grune & Stratton, 1956.

*Psychoanalytic principles in a mental health clinic for the preschool child and his family. *Psychiatry*, 19:63-76, 1956.

Disturbances of mothering and criteria for treatment. *American Journal of Orthopsychiatry*, 26:252-263, 1956.

*Goals in therapy: A symposium. *American Journal of Psychoanalysis*, 16:9-14, 1956.

*The home visit as an aid in family diagnosis and therapy (with M. L. Behrens). *Social Casework*, 37, 1956.

The family group and family therapy. *International Journal of Sociometry*, 1:52-54, 82-95, 1956-1957.

A changing conception of personality. *American Journal of Psychoanalysis*, 17:78-86, 1957.

Five issues in group psychotherapy. *Review of Diagnostic Psychology and Personality Exploration*, 5:167-176, 1957.

Mental health and the family in the current world crisis. *Journal of Jewish Communal Service*, 34:58-72, 1957.

*An orientation to psychiatric research on the family. *Marriage and Family Living*, 19:68-74, 1957.

The principles of shared responsibility for child rearing. *International Journal of Social Psychiatry*, 2:1957.

Psychological dynamics of the "familial organism." In I. Gerson (Ed.), *The Family—A Focal Point in Health Education*. New York: The New York Academy of Medicine, 1957.

Behavioral disturbances in contemporary society. In I. Galdston (Ed.), *The Family in Contemporary Society*. New York: International Universities Press, 1958.

Concepts of family striving and family distress: The contributions of M. Robert Gomberg (with F. L. Beatman and S. N. Sherman). *Social Casework*, July 1958.

Discussion of masochism. In J. Masserman (Ed.), *Science and Psychoanalysis*, Vol. 1. New York: Grune & Stratton, 1958.

The family group and family therapy. *Progress in Psychotherapy*, 3, part 3, 1958.

*Toward an integrative therapy of the family. *American Journal of Psychiatry*, 114:727-733, 1958.

The adolescent. In E. Rabb and G. Selznick (Eds.), *Major Social Problems*, Evanston, IL: Row & Peterson, 1959.

The emotional impact of in-laws and relatives. In S. Leibman (Ed.), *Emotional Forces in the Family*. New York: Lippincott, 1959.

The family group and family therapy: The practical application of family diagnosis (with M. L. Behrens). In J. H. Masserman and J. L. Moreno (Eds.), *Progress in Psychotherapy*, Vol. 3. New York: Grune & Stratton, 1959.

*The psychoanalytic approach to family. In J. Masserman (Ed.), *Individual and Familial Dynamics*, Vol II. New York: Grune & Stratton, 1959.

Selection of schizophrenic patients for office practice. In A. N. Rifkin (Ed.), *Schizophrenia in Psychoanalytic Practice*. New York: Grune and Stratton, 1959.

*Transference and counter-transference. *Psychoanalysis and Psychoanalytic Review*, 46: 17-28, 1959.

*The treatment of a child and family (with M. H. Lakos). In A. Burton (Ed.), *Case Studies in Counseling and Psychotherapy*, New York: Prentice-Hall, 1959.

Family focused therapy of schizophrenia. In S. C. Scher and H. R. Davis (Eds.), *The Out-Patient Treatment of Schizophrenia*. New York: Grune & Stratton, 1960.

Psychotherapy with the family group. In J. Masserman (Ed.), *Science and Psychoanalysis*, Vol. 4. New York: Grune & Stratton, 1960.

*Theory of family dynamics. *Psychoanalysis and Psychoanalytic Review*, 46:33-49, 1960.

A dynamic frame for the clinical approach to family conflict. In N. Ackerman, F. Beatman and S. Sherman (Eds.), *Exploring the Base for Family Therapy*. New York: Family Service Association of America, 1961.

The emergence of family psychotherapy on the present scene. In M. I. Stein (Ed.), *Contemporary Psychotherapies*. New York: The Free Press, 1961.

Family diagnosis and therapy. *International Mental Health Newsletter*, 1961.

Family study and treatment. *Children*, July-August 1961.

Prejudice, mental health, and family life. New York: American Jewish Committee, Institute of Human Relations, 1961.

*Preventive implications of family research. In G. Caplan (Ed.), *Prevention of Mental Disorders in Childhood*. New York: Basic Books, 1961.

The schizophrenic patient and his family relationships—A conceptual basis for family-focused therapy of schizophrenia. In D. Greenblatt, D. Levenson, and G. Klerman (Eds.), *Mental Patients in Transition*. Springfield, IL: Charles C Thomas, 1961.

*Symptom, defense and growth in group process. *Journal of American Group Therapy Association*, 11:131-142, 1961.

*Family psychotherapy and psychoanalysis: The implications of difference. *Family Process*, 1:30-43, 1962.

*Adolescent problems: A symptom of family disorder. *Family Process*, 1:202-213, 1962.

Child and family psychiatry today: A new look at some old problems. *Mental Hygiene*, 47:540-545, 1963.

The family as a unit in mental health. *Proceedings of the Third World Congress of Psychiatry*. Toronto: University of Toronto Press and McGill University Press, 1963.

Family diagnosis and therapy. In J. Masserman (Ed.), *Current Psychiatric Therapies*, Vol. 3. New York: Grune & Stratton, 1963.

Family psychotherapy. In A. Deutsch and H. Fishman (Eds.), *Encyclopedia of Mental Health*, Vol. 2. New York: Franklin Watts, 1963.

Family therapy: An ideal for the future (with H. B. Richardson). In H. Lief, V. Lief, and N. Lief (Eds.), *Psychological Basis of Medical Practice*. New York: Harper & Row, 1963.

Mental illness—1963. *Journal of the Kansas Medical Society*, 65:6-11, 1964.

*Adolescent struggle as protest. In S. M. Farber (Ed.), *Man and Civilization: The Family's Struggle for Survival*. New York: McGraw-Hill, 1964.

The family in crisis. *Bulletin of The New York Academy of Medicine*, 40:3, 1964.

Family therapy and schizophrenia: Theory and practice. In L. Kolb (Ed.), *International Psychiatry Clinics*, Vol. 1, No. 4. New York: Little Brown & Co., 1964.

*Prejudicial scapegoating and neutralizing forces in the family group, with special reference to the role of "family healer." *International Journal of Social Psychiatry*, Congress Issue, 2:90, 1964.

The uneasy family. *This Week*, April 6, 1964.

Family diagnosis and therapy. In J. Masserman (Ed.), *Current Psychiatric Therapies*, Vol. 3. New York: Grune & Stratton, 1963.

*The family approach to marital disorders. In B. Greene (Ed.), *The Psychotherapies of Marital Disharmony*. New York: The Free Press, 1965.

*Family dynamics and the reversibility of delusional formation: A case study in family therapy (with Paul Franklin). In I. Boszormenyi-Nagy and J. Framo (Eds.), *Intensive Family Therapy*, Hagerstown, Maryland: Harper & Row, 1965.

*Non-verbal cues and reenactment of conflict in family therapy (with M. Sherman, S. Sherman and C. Mitchell). *Family Process*, 4:133-162, 1965.

The social psychology of prejudice. *Mental Hygiene*, 49:27-35, 1965.

*Family psychotherapy—theory and practice. *American Journal of Psychotherapy*, 20:405-414, 1966.

Family psychotherapy today: Some areas of controversy. *Comprehensive Psychiatry*, 7:375-388, 1966.

Family therapy. In S. Arieti (Ed.), *American Handbook of Psychiatry*, Vol. 3. New York: Basic Books, 1966.

Classification of family types: A discussion. In N. Ackerman, F. Beatman and S. Sherman (Eds.), *Expanding Theory and Practice in Family Therapy*, New York: Family Service Association of America, 1967.

The future of family psychotherapy. *Ibid.*

*A family therapy session. *Ibid.*

The emergence of family diagnosis and treatment: A personal view. *Psychotherapy: Theory, Research and Practice*, 4:125-129, 1967.

Pathogeny in the family system. In I. Boszormenyi-Nagy and G. Zuk (Eds.), *Family Therapy and Disturbed Families*, Palo Alto: Science and Behavior Books, 1967.

Prejudice and scapegoating in the family. *Ibid.*

Developments in family psychotherapy. In J. Masserman (Ed.), *Current Psychiatric Therapies*, Vol. 8. New York: Grune & Stratton, 1968.

Divorce and alienation in modern society. In J. Fried (Ed.), *Jews and Divorce*. New York: Ktar Publishing House, 1968.

The emergence of family psychotherapy: A personal account. In J. Peterson (Ed.), *Marriage and Family Counseling*. New York: Association Press, 1968.

*The family approach and levels of intervention (with M. Behrens), *American Journal of Psychotherapy*, 22:5-14, 1968.

*The role of the family in the emergence of child disorders. In E. Miller (Ed.), *Foundations of Child Psychiatry*. Oxford: Pergamon Press Ltd., 1968.

To save or not to save a marriage. In N.C. Kohut (Ed.), *Therapeutic Family Law*. Chicago: Adams Press, 1968.

*The affective climate in families with psychosis. Excerpta Medica International Congress Series No. 194: *Problems of Psychosis*. Elsevier North-Holland: Amsterdam, 1969.

Ethical issues in psychotherapy. *Conservative Judaism*, 23: 231-254, 1969.

*Sexual delinquency among middle-class girls. In O. Pollak and A. Friedman (Eds.), *Family Dynamics and Female Sexual Delinquency*. Palo Alto: Science and Behavior Books, 1969.

*Child participation in family therapy. *Family Process*, 9: 403-410, 1970.

Childhood disorders in interlocking pathology in family relationships (with P. Papp, and P. Prosky). In C. Koupernik and J. Anthony (Eds.), *The Child in His Family*, International Yearbook for Child Psychiatry, Vol. 1. New York: John Wiley & Sons, 1970.

Family psychotherapy today. *Family Process*, 9: 123-126, 1970.

Family interviewing: The study process. In N. Ackerman (Ed.), *Family Therapy in Transition*. Boston: Little, Brown & Co., 1970.

*The art of family therapy. *Ibid.*

*To catch a thief. *Ibid.*

A house divided. In C. Sager, T. Brayboy, and B. Waxenberg (Eds.), *Black Ghetto Family in Therapy*, New York: Grove Press, 1970.

Summerhill: Heart or head. In A. Neill (Ed.), *Summerhill: For and Against*. New York: Hart Publishing Co., 1970.

What happened to the family? *Mental Hygiene*, 54: 459-463, 1970.

Family healing in a troubled world. *Social Casework*, 200-205, April 1971.

The growing edge of family therapy. *Family Process*, 10: 143-156, 1971.

Some considerations for training in family therapy. *Career Directions*, 2: 2-13, Sandoz Pharmaceuticals, 1972.